Better Homes and Gardens®

Heritage
Cook Book

© Meredith Corporation, 1975. All Rights Reserved.
Printed in the United States of America. First Edition. Fourth Printing, 1976.
Library of Congress Catalog Card Number: 74-80392
SBN: 696-00760-6

The food history of America dates back to the days when cooking was done on an open hearth. Many of the recipes had a hearty, satisfying quality that survived the test of time. The early cooks drew the best from America's great bounty and gave us a rich food heritage including—*Steamed Clams, Cod Cakes,* hot cider with stick cinnamon stirrers, *New England Boiled Dinner,* roast turkey with *Corn Bread Dressing,* and *Yankee Red-Flannel Hash.* (See index for recipe pages.)

Contents

BETTER HOMES AND GARDENS BOOKS

Editorial Director: Don Dooley
Managing Editor: Malcolm E. Robinson   Art Director: John Berg
Asst. Managing Editor: Lawrence D. Clayton   Asst. Art Director: Randall Yontz
Food Editor: Nancy Morton
Senior Food Editor: Joyce Trollope
Associate Editors: Sharyl Heiken, Rosemary Hutchinson,
Elizabeth Strait, Sandra Granseth
Assistant Editors: Diane Nelson, Catherine Penney
Designers: Harijs Priekulis, Faith Berven, Candy Carleton
Test Kitchen Director: Marion Viall   Asst. Test Kitchen Director: Kay Cargill
Test Kitchen Home Economists: Sharon Golbert, Marilyn Cornelius,
Maryellyn Reese, Carolyn Lewis
Contributing Editor: Mary Cable
Recipe Researcher: Helen Duprey Bullock   Picture Researcher: Shirley Green
Technical Consultant: Dr. Terry Sharrer, Smithsonian Institution
Consultants: Irwin Glusker, Wendy Murphy

Our seal assures you that all recipes in the *Heritage Cook Book* (except 35 in italics for reading interest only) are endorsed by the Better Homes and Gardens Test Kitchen. Each recipe was tested and updated to preserve the original goodness for enjoyment today.

Discovering America's Food History

When people move, they take their favorite recipes with them. Some are written—some are not, but the recipes are an important memory of home. History books say a great deal about clearing land, building cities, or fighting battles, but very little about what was on the dinner table while these events occurred. This is a different kind of history book— it is a working cook book with the emphasis on the people who settled this country and what they ate. Historical details help you keep track of what was happening.

Every family, whether colonist, pioneer, or immigrant, hoped to cook in the new home just as they always had. Things seldom worked out that way. Food was either more scarce, more abundant, or just different from what they were used to. Coping meant trying new foods, changing recipes, and generally adjusting to a new way of life. They liked the results; we believe you will too.

The recipes come from old manuscripts, travelers' accounts, ethnic celebrations, early cook books, and family hand-me-downs. They have been tested with today's ingredients and equipment keeping as close to the original as possible. To add to your enjoyment, the margins contain bits of information about how or when the food was used, why a particular ingredient was important, or an anecdote about the recipe.

And this book is more than just a collection of seven hundred recipes; for we have included five small chapters that trace the history of the American kitchen from colonial times right up to the present. You'll find out how food was preserved in the early days and follow the development of cook books in America.

For all those who like to cook or have an interest in knowing where their favorite dishes came from, we dedicate this book.

The Editors

Corn—America's most important native food—plays a recurring role in history. First cultivated by the Indians, it sustained waves of colonists, pioneers, and nation builders. Now it feeds the world.

The Indians:
Corn, Beans, and Squash

Chapter 1

The Indians: Corn, Beans, and Squash

When you sit down to a table laden with a golden roast turkey stuffed with peanuts and wild rice, dishes of roast or boiled potatoes, Boston baked beans or sliced squash and tomatoes, cranberry sauce, a platter heaped with yellow corn on the cob or tender corn bread, and spicy pumpkin pie, you can attest to the succulence of American food. But will you recognize the Indian origin of these delicious foods?

When Christopher Columbus first sighted the small island of San Salvador nestled in the Bahamas, most of the Indians of what today is America included corn, beans, and squash as staples of their diet. The desert area of the Great Basin (Nevada, Colorado, and lower Wyoming) where the Digger Indians scrounged out a living, along the California coast where it was not rainy enough for the cultivation of corn, and in the Northwest where fish was abundant were the only areas where the everyday diet was not mainly corn, beans, and squash.

The Indians who flash across the movie screen or flicker into our living rooms via the television tube are as unlike the Indians in 1492 as the *Queen Elizabeth* is unlike the *Pinta*. The almost 1 million Indians who lived in the land named for Amerigo Vespucci were settled in tribes that spoke languages other tribes could not understand, practiced religions as diverse as the winds that blew across the untillable prairie, engaged in crafts of a richness and color associated only with settled peoples, and were banded together in tribal leagues or lived in democratic societies. To provide food to eat, most of these tribes farmed. (Some of the Indians raised a few domesticated animals—the Spanish introduced sheep to the Pueblo Indians of New Mexico, but they were few in number.) Those Indians who did not farm extensively lived by hunting, fishing, or gathering seeds; but all the Indians engaged in commerce with surrounding tribes to obtain whatever they lacked. The hunters exchanged game for corn or fish; fishermen traded cod or salmon for plant foods and meat; and the seed gatherers of California worked with the Washington Chinooks who acted as traders between the Indians of the lower Pacific coast and the Indians of the Plateau, east of the Rockies.

American Indians were excellent farmers and were the first to cultivate what today comprises almost 50 percent of the world's plant foods—maize (Indian corn), beans, peanuts, potatoes, manioc (also known as cassava), tapioca, squashes, pumpkins, papayas, guavas, avocados, pineapples, tomatoes, chili peppers, cacao (for chocolate), chicle (for chewing gum), and many other vegetables and fruits. The most important of these is corn, for it will grow in areas that are too dry for rice or too wet for wheat, and its yield per acre is double that of wheat. Long before the Jamestown gentlemen had erected their wicker wigwams and the Pilgrim settlers had excavated their dugouts, corn was already being grown in Europe.

The Pilgrims at Plymouth happened on corn by accident. After leaving the *Mayflower* they trekked inland for several miles and came across:

> A heap of sand...newly done, we might see how
> they (the Indians) had paddled it with their hands—
> which we digged up,...and found a fine great

Corn is rice to the Asian, wheat to the English, oats or barley to the European, and corn or maize to the Americans. Actually, the term "corn" refers to the principal grain of any country. The Indian maize that Columbus found cultivated in the New World had been harvested for more than 2,000 years. Had the Italian explorer ventured inland he would have been surprised at the wide variety of corn hybrids the sophisticated North American Indian farmers had developed.

Ironically, the second most important crop the American Indians gave the world—the potato—was at first rejected by the colonists. Early Spanish explorers took the potato to Europe, and it did not reappear in this country until brought here by the Irish in 1719.

basket full of fair Indian corn; and digged further,
and found a fine great basket full of very fair
corn of this year, and with some six and thirty
goodly ears of corn....[1]

Governor Bradford, the leader of this group, further describes this find in this way, "It was a great mercy to this poor people, that here they got seed to plant them corn the next year, or else they might have starved, for they had none, nor any likelihood to get any until the [planting] season had been past."[2]

This corn (actually stolen from the Indians) enabled the Pilgrims to survive the first winter and later to plant a crop so plentiful that they celebrated their first Thanksgiving the next autumn with a feast of geese, ducks, turkey, lobsters, oysters, clams, venison, corn (roasted, parched, or soaked in maple syrup), cornmeal, johnnycakes, beans, and squash.

The most varied of the North or South American foods that Columbus introduced to the Old World in his quest for a spice route to the Indies was beans. Lima, sieva, curry, kidney, navy, haricot, snap, string, common, butter, pole, and frijole beans all issued out of this continent, as did such exotically named beans as Madagascar, Burma, French, and Rangoon. With such a wide variety, it is no wonder that beans figure as a favorite item in most diets in the world. Virtually all but soybeans came from America and were being farmed and cooked by North American Indians when the colonists made their epic voyage across the Atlantic.

Because of the high nutritional value of corn, beans, and squash, especially when supplemented with wild game and the abundant fruits found in this land of plenty, the Indians who sat down to council with the Jamestown tobacco farmers or traded with the Plymouth settlers were generally more healthy than the average sixteenth-century European.

To best understand how North American Indians lived, it is well to divide them according to how they obtained their food: the farming woodsmen of the eastern forests, extending from the Northeast down into the southern tip of Florida; the Pueblo farmers of the Southwestern states; the desert dwellers of the Great Basin; the seed gatherers of California; the Northwest fishermen of Washington and Oregon; the Plateau fishermen who lived east of the Rockies, and the hunters of the Plains.

Woodsmen of the Eastern Forests: In the heavily wooded area bounded by the Atlantic Ocean and stretching inland as far as Minnesota and down through southeast Texas, the Indians whom the early colonists met were for the most part hunters, fishermen, and farmers.

To the north in the area touching the Gulf of St. Lawrence, the Indians of the Malecite tribe existed on a subarctic diet of fishing and a little hunting. Farther inland, around the western Great Lakes, the Ojibwas hunted and fished and gathered wild rice instead of planting corn. But in all other areas of the eastern forests, farming was the basis for food sources.

The settled farming tribes of the Northeast, principally those tribes who made up the Iroquois — Seneca, Cayuga, Onondaga, Oneida — lived in bark- and skin-covered longhouses. Usually, the longest house — some of which were as long as hundred yards — was the central meeting place. These were tribes in which the women did all the farming, and because of their importance as the principal food gatherers it was they who chose which men were to sit on the ruling council. The men fished and hunted for the animals which provided clothing, as well as meat.

Wild rice was harvested from a small boat poled through the marshy areas. The heavy heads on the stalks hung over the boat edge where they were beaten with a club until the seeds dropped.

After the rice was dried the Indians stamped on the grain to loosen the hulls. Then, using birch bark trays or a blanket, they tossed the rice in the air so the hulls would blow away. It was stored in a hole lined with animal skins.

It was a motley collection that sat down to the first Thanksgiving dinner. Forty pilgrims in cut-cloth clothing and 89 Indians dressed in animal skins and gaily colored turkey feathers gathered before groaning tables. Most honored of the Indians was the legendary Squanto who had met the Pilgrims one year earlier and had taught them how to make use of the corn they had found, how to find wild greens in spring, and how to fish for eels and other seafood. But the early Pilgrims were not good students, and needed to learn the necessity of planting and cultivating foods that would sustain them year round. So once again the Indian farmers warded off starvation for the Pilgrims through the winter.

How the Indians Obtained Their Food

The Indians whom the early explorers encountered subsisted chiefly on corn, beans, and squash. But the ways they rounded out this diet was as varied as the climates in which they lived.

In the Northeast and Southeast where the woods were thick and often lush, Indian farmers cleared the land to grow crops. Other northern Indians tapped the maple trees for syrup, while in the Midwest they searched the Great Lakes region for wild rice. On either side of the continent, abundant fish and shellfish supplemented the daily diet. Only on the Plains did the Indians rely on the hazardous business of killing buffalo for food. But wild or cultivated, from the land or from the waters—the foods of the Indians were the first contribution to the American cuisine.

Seed gathering tribes lived in the Great Basin area.

After the Spanish brought horses to America, the hunter tribes of the Plains used them to hunt buffalo.

Indians of the Great Lakes region harvested wild rice by beating the grass and catching the rice in their canoes.

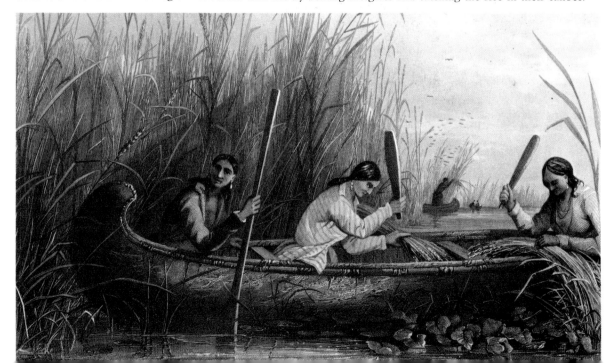

Wherever maple trees grew, the Indians collected the sap and made it into syrup.

The Indians of the Northwest were experts at catching all types of fish.

The Indian farmers of the East scared the birds away from their crops of corn, beans, and squash by banging on wooden bowls.

*The Green Corn Ceremony was one
of the corn rituals during which
some Southeastern tribes gave thanks
for the harvest bounty. It
was held each year when the roasting
corn was mature. The women
began with a ritualistic cleaning of
their homes — burning old
clothes and destroying pottery and
making new ones. Just before
the corn festival, the fire on the
hearth was extinguished.
The ceremony began with building
on the communal altar a new
fire from which individual fires
were then started. After
the ceremony the feasting began with
roasted corn, game, and
baked sweet potatoes as the main fare.*

*Parched corn provided a portable
meal for the Indians. The
corn, first dried slightly over hot
coals, was pounded very
fine. Sometimes dried berries, chopped
meat, or maple sugar were
pounded with the corn for flavoring.
Out on the trail, water was
added to the mixture making the
parched corn an
instant mush — no cooking needed.
Hunters and warriors
preferred their parched corn without
maple sugar, because they
had watched the branches of maple
trees swaying in the
wind. Sugar from such a tree, they
concluded, would surely
make them dizzy and spoil their aim.*

Although the women did all the farming, the men cleared the land for tilling. As the three-crop plantings tended to exhaust the land, the Indians sought new farmland every few years, generally moving the entire tribal village to the new location. In autumn the men cut away strips of bark from around the soft pine trees on the new field site. The following year they felled the dead trees, cleared the area, and set the field afire. Left for almost six months, the ash helped fertilize the soil. The women planted the following spring, humping hillocks two or three feet apart and dropping the "magic" four corn seeds, together with several small herring into each hillock.

Between the corn rows beans and squash were planted. The bean plants used the cornstalks for support and the squash spread out over the ground, shading it, thus keeping the ground moist, and choking out many weeds. When the corn was mature the tribes made preparations for the Green Corn Festival. The women harvested the corn and selected the finest ears for the next year's planting.

According to Samuel de Champlain, a French explorer:

> They make trenches in the sand on the slope of
> the hills, some five or six feet deep, more or
> less. Putting their corn and other grains into
> large grass sacks, they throw them into these
> trenches, and cover them with sand three or four
> feet above the surface of the earth... In this
> way, it is preserved as well as it would be
> possible to do in our graineries.[3]

During the winter months the Indian women were kept busy baking corn bread either on hot, flat stones or wrapped in leaves in the ashes, or they cooked cornmeal mush mixed with beans, vegetables, and nuts. For a special treat they cooked cornmeal bread or pudding mixed with berries or maple sugar. Wild game and birds were plentiful during the winter and spring months, and the Indian women roasted or boiled the meat over open fires or made stews with cornmeal and vegetables. It was in the Northeast area that the Indians first barbecued. Later, Mexican seasonings in the Southwest Pueblo area added the pungent spices that flavor the barbecue sauces we enjoy today.

The women of the Northeast also raised sunflowers, the seeds of which they pounded and mixed with cornmeal to make bread. They gathered milkweed, marsh marigold, yellow dock, pigweed, mustard greens, dandelions, wild onions, garlic, watercress, mushrooms, roots, and several tubers — including groundnuts — and harvested nearly thirty-six wild fruits which they dried for use in the winter.

Farther to the south, the Indians of the Southeast — the Cherokee, Catawba, Muskogee (Creek), Chickasaw, Caddo, Atakapa — tilled the land for corn, beans, and squash, as well as picked wild roots, nuts, and fruits. Long, hot summers enabled them to plant two crops: a fast-growing corn which grew to four feet and was cut down in May, and a slower-growing type which grew to ten feet and was harvested late in the autumn.

These Indians divided work differently: the men hunted and fished but also did the farming. The women took care of the children and fed the men.

In many towns or villages, a headman was selected each year to gather the daily work crew together by blowing on a conch. The men marched in file with a bone or shell hoe or ax on their shoulders to work the fields.

Anyone who was lazy had to pay a fine. When the crops were ready, each family harvested a part of the field.

Unlike the Northeast Indians, they did not clear the land of dead trees. Planting took place between the fallen limbs. If this sounds inefficient, remember that one acre of Indian corn, beans, and squash yielded five times as much nutrition as one acre of English wheat.

In those areas where it was not possible to store food underground, cemented storehouses kept vegetables, fruits, and grain safe from freezing in the winter months, and cool and free from vermin in the summer.

The Southeast Indians generally had a varied diet. Besides the basic corn, beans, and squash, they had luscious fruits and nuts, including the acorn, and a form of milk made from walnuts or hickory nuts. Fish from coastal waters or freshwater fish were plentiful, as was game, including bear, deer, turkey and wildfowl. Among their special dishes were bear ribs, root jelly, hominy, corn cakes and corn soup, baked yams, a bread of cassava, delicious-tasting sweet grapes, fragrant stews, and soups of oysters, shrimp, blue crab, flounder, whitefish, and drum.

Pueblo Farmers of the Southwest: The Pueblo Indians lived in adobe huts set in clusters along the banks of the Rio Grande, and farmed their dry land. Weathering out dust storms, drought, and occasional famine, they planted their crops along the riverbed; or, for those Pueblo Indians living west in Arizona, they located their garden plots at the mouth of river washes to use the runoffs from the precious rain when it fell.

The last of the corn-beans-and-squash-growing Indians lived a quiet life. Fighting was forbidden, and even excessive individualism was frowned upon. There were no social classes, and everyone in the Pueblo (village) shared in the work and whatever wealth these hardworking people possessed. Using wooden digging sticks and hoes to till the hard earth, the men planted corn, beans, squash, tobacco, and gourds. Special teams of men chased deer and antelope into pitfalls and stockades while both men and women engaged in rabbit hunts. Rabbits were chased across the dried earth until caught and clubbed to death, or the Indians sometimes used a curved stick and hurled it at the prey. Besides farming and hunting, the Indians gathered pinon nuts, berries, and fruits of the cacti and yucca.

After the coming of the Spanish and after Francisco Vasquez de Coronado plundered the Pueblos, many of the Indians fled their ancient dwellings. Those who survived the era of the conquistadors turned to growing other crops such as Mexican chilies, European wheat, onions, melons, apples, and peaches. To supplement this diet and provide food and clothing, the Indians raised sheep which had been introduced by the Spanish. The Pueblo Indians also acquired horses from the Spanish. Later, the Apache and other Plains Indians stole horses from the Pueblo Indians and used the horses for raiding parties such as those most often associated in popular literature with the North American Indian.

Indians of the Great Basin: Farther north in Colorado, Utah, Nevada, and lower Wyoming, the Indians of the Great Basin eked out a living as best they could, digging the desert for roots and scavenging for plants, seeds, berries, and nuts. These Digger Indians sometimes were fortunate enough to catch deer, antelope, and mountain sheep, which they downed with bow and arrow on the high grounds.

But, in general, they were always on the edge of starvation. Often their diet included roasted grasshoppers, prairie dog, lizard, mice, birds, and

Maple trees were tapped by making a V-shaped gash in the trunk. A birch bark pail sealed with pine pitch was hung at the base of the gash to catch the sap. The sap was collected and boiled slowly until the syrup was thick. It was then poured into molds or a trough so the syrup could harden into sugar.

In the Northeast it was maple sugar or syrup, but in the Southwest, "sugar" was obtained by having young girls chew on corn kernels. The combination of cornstarch and mouth saliva produced the "sugar."

rabbits trapped with nets. Typical of these Indians were the Shoshone, who lived in small units consisting of one or two families during the spring and summer and banded with as many as fifteen families during the winter.

Contrary to what many snow cone devotees might think, these icy treats are not a twentieth-century concoction. Rather, the Indian women scooped up balls of ice and smothered them with maple syrup for a delicious winter treat long before the Pilgrims' ship battled the Atlantic.

Seed Gatherers of California: Along the Pacific West coast, extending up to the Washington border (of today), the California Indians were fortunate to have plenty of fruits and plants on hand. These Indians did not farm but hunted for wild game and gathered fruits and nuts.

As the almost 300,000 Indians who lived in this area west of the Rockies did not have sufficient rainfall to grow corn, they gathered and ground acorns to use as bread meal (after removing the poisonous tannic acid). Often they are referred to as the Acorn Indians.

They gathered many wild plants in the mild climate area of California, and picked such plants as yucca and sage. Fish from the freshwater streams and shellfish from the coastal waters supplemented the diet—as did elk, deer, small game, birds, reptiles, rodents, and certain kinds of insects which they hunted or gathered.

For any of the tribes that hunted, the progression of a boy to manhood was firmly tied to his skill in hunting. At first an Indian boy was given toy weapons until he was old enough to handle real ones safely. He was then instructed by the older men in his family on all aspects of hunting—on the habits of the animals, how to make and use weapons and traps, and the deep religious significance of hunting. The novice hunter began with birds and small game, gradually working up to the larger animals such as deer, bear, or buffalo. Each time a boy killed his first of a particular type of game, he gave it to his family to eat. He was not permitted to taste the food. With each new kill, he gained added status in the tribe. A young man was not allowed to marry until he had killed a major game animal.

Fishermen of the Northwest: Tribes of the Northwest were different from all other North American Indians. Acquisitive with a culture based on status, they had slaves and showed off their wealth with elaborate ceremonies known as the potlatch during which the Indians gave away much of their possessions. So important was status that the receivers of the gifts were compelled to save face by giving even more lavish and extravagant potlatches. Before each tent stood an elaborate totem pole.

These Indians could devote much time displaying their wealth because they had such an abundant source of food and hunting, fishing, farming, or gathering required only a minimum of time and effort.

Whale, halibut, flounder, herring, sole, sturgeon, smelt, cod, culachon or candlefish, seal, and otter, were easily fished from the ocean. Wild game, too, was in abundance. Waterfowl—ducks, geese, and gulls—swooped along the shore for fish and made themselves an easy target to the bone or shell throws of the Indians. Inland deer, elk, bear, and wild goats provided meat. This was more than supplemented by plover and lark in the forests, and camas roots, wild carrots, potatoes, beans, acorns, hazelnuts, wild salad greens, sweet huckleberries, blackberries, wild strawberries, blackcaps, and salmonberries from the fields.

The first run of salmon was the Indians' important spring festival. Great care was taken with the first salmon caught. The fish was cleansed with ferns, cut lengthwise, and cooked on a stick before an open fire. Clams, mussels, and barnacles, which accompanied the fish, were steamed upon heated rocks. Much of the fish later caught was smoked in this same manner, dried, and saved for use during the winter months. Fruits, too were dried for winter. Vegetables were cooked in tightly woven water-filled baskets that were heated by plunging hot stones into the water. Sometimes greens were wilted in hot fat or fish oil.

Fishermen of the Plateau: In settlements along rivers and streams just east of the Rockies, dwelt the Plateau Indians. They had no agriculture, but fished for salmon, sturgeon, and eels. These were caught in large quantities during the season, split, and dried for food in the winter. Camas, kouse, and some roots and often berries and grasses were either dug or gathered and used in a variety of food dishes. Deer and other game supplemented the diet. But when the rivers and streams froze during the

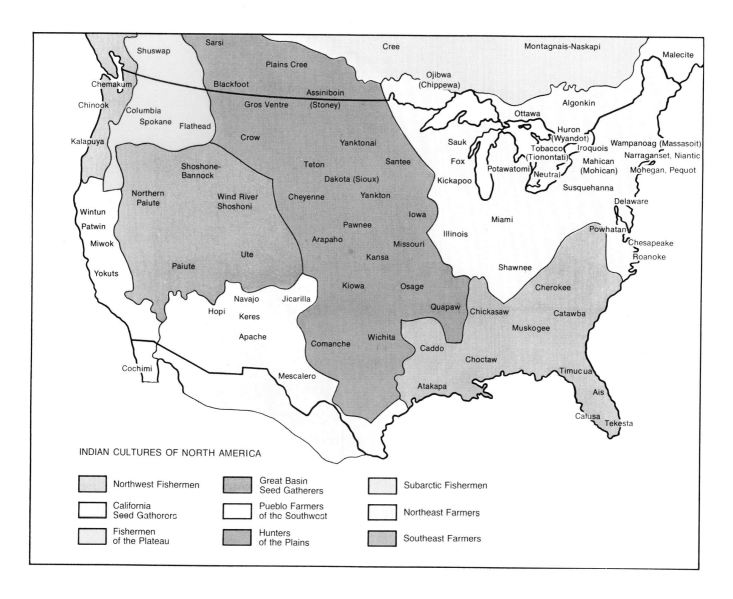

INDIAN CULTURES OF NORTH AMERICA

▨ Northwest Fishermen	
▨ Great Basin Seed Gatherers	
▨ Subarctic Fishermen	
▢ California Seed Gatherers	
▢ Pueblo Farmers of the Southwest	
▢ Northeast Farmers	
▨ Fishermen of the Plateau	
▨ Hunters of the Plains	
▨ Southeast Farmers	

winter, the food supply often was reduced to such an extent that the Indians were forced to resort to a gruel of moss and the inner bark of certain trees.

Hunters of the Plains: Corn was the staff of life to the majority of North American Indians, as was buffalo to the Plains Indians. It fed them, clothed them, and the skin covered their shelters. The women made stews from the shanks and briskets, and roasted large haunches over the campfire. The ribs and joints were slowly simmered in savory soups. To this simple fare venison, rabbit, and buffalo berries would be added.

The nomadic Plains Indians spent much of their time traveling with all their possessions loaded on a dog-pulled travois behind the herds of buffalo. Only later did they begin using horses to develop war parties for defending their lands from the invading pioneers.

On the other hand, the river basin Prairie Indians — the Siouan-speaking Osages, Missouris, Kansas, Otos, Omahas, Iowas, and Poncas — lived in villages, practiced agriculture, gathered food, and hunted for game and birds.

The Indians of North America were remarkably sophisticated when Columbus made his journey. Most of them had an elaborate social system, were not warlike, engaged in stunning craftswork, and nearly all raised corn, beans, and squash. Without the Indians, food patterns of modern America would be significantly different.

The tepee of the Plains Indians had a symbolic significance as well as a practical use as a home. Its floor symbolized the earth that gave the Indians a living, the walls the sky, and its poles the sacred paths to the spiritual world. The Sioux followed a strict tepee etiquette. If the flap was open, all visitors were welcome. If closed, the visitor announced his presence by rattling the flap and waited to be invited into the tepee. If two crossed sticks appeared over the door, the owners were either away or not receiving visitors.

The Colonists:
Famine and Feast

Chapter 2

The Colonists: Famine and Feast

The settlers at Jamestown built wigwams using the materials at hand—bark, thatch, and mud.

Writers in the 1600s, even some who had never been to America, wrote many grand words about the virtues of the New World. It was descriptions such as this one of Virginia that lured Europeans to America!

"Virginia, Earth's onely Paradise. Where Nature hath in store Fowle, Venison, and Fish And the Fruitfull'st Soyle Without your Toyle, Three Haruests more, All greater than you Wish.... To whose, the golden Age Still Nature's laws doth give No other Cares that tend, But them to defend From Winter's Rage That long there doth not live...."[1]

The Pilgrims at Plymouth colony excavated dugouts similar to the ones pictured here.

In the beginning America's shores seemed to be the shining solution to all problems. Colonists flocked to the New World for a host of reasons—both philosophic and economic. At first America was a land in which they could find material wealth; later, others came to escape the old feudal order, and a number wanted a country where they could practice their own form of religion.

The problems the early American colonists faced were many. Landing on the shores of Virginia, they found themselves in the paradoxical situation of struggling for survival in the midst of unprecedented plenty. Each little band had to cope with certain urgent and basic needs. They had to learn how to provide themselves with shelter and food, how to ward off sickness, and how to deal with the Indians. For the earliest arrivals, it was often nip and tuck, but for all of them it was a chance not to be passed up—a longshot at happiness.

Some of those who came later were more prepared for success. Voyages were scheduled so the colonists would arrive early in the spring when crops could be planted. They also learned to bring ample provisions: wheat, oatmeal, dried peas, vinegar, salt, oil, and brandy were regarded as absolute essentials, and sugar, dried fruit, root vegetables, and spices were strongly recommended. Supplies also included seeds, graftings, poultry, and, if possible, all types of farm animals. One could improvise beds, tables, chairs, and most other household gear, but such essentials as knives, tools, and iron cooking pots had to be brought from home, at least until ironworks were established in America.

Despite grueling hardships, within a few years houses had been built, fields cleared, orchards and gardens planted. Among English vegetables, carrots, parsnips, turnips, cabbages, and radishes were the easiest to grow, but these were soon supplemented with asparagus, peas, "hartychoaks" (globe artichokes), green beans, spinach, and eventually all the crops that the colonists had been used to in their old homes. America, as one colonist wrote, was "nature's nurse to all vegetables."[2]

But everyone had to become accustomed to the new foods available in this new land. Corn and cornmeal came first, followed by squash and pumpkins. Shellfish, though an item of diet in England, was new to those colonists who had never lived near the sea, and they approached with caution the succulent lobsters, clams, oysters, and scallops of American waters.

The settlers enjoyed shellfish with "sallet" greens and olive oil and vinegar. This simple dish might be found on menus today, but other recipes for fish seem bizarre. For instance, in one recipe brought from England, lobster was stuffed with eel, gooseberries, grapes, almond paste, anchovies, and garlic. Perhaps lobster was such an ordinary food that it needed dressing up in order to tempt appetites. In 1630 a colonist in Massachusetts writing home to England remarked, apropos of lobsters, "The least boy in the Plantation may both catch and eat what he will of them."[3]

Wild turkey was not hard to get used to, nor was maple sugar, which, after 1675, the colonists were producing in surplus quantities to sell to England. Cider vinegar was a colonial invention, used widely for sousing and pickling. (Wine never lasted long enough to turn into vinegar.)

All the colonists were dumbfounded by the abundance of game. Most of them had had little opportunity to hunt in England, where that activity was a privilege reserved for the upper classes. They had to learn from the Indians ways of finding and killing certain kinds. When the wild fowl were migrating, the skies were darkened by flights of thousands of ducks, geese, passenger pigeons, and other game birds. A visitor to New York harbor in the autumn of 1695 wrote that there were so many wild swans that "the bays and shores...appear as if they were dressed in white drapery."[4]

Anyone shooting into such flocks of game could hardly fail to bring down several birds for his dinner. Some birds could even be captured by the hundreds. Passenger pigeons, once the most abundant of birds, were hunted in such numbers that now they are extinct. Wild turkeys, as numerous in the woods then as rabbits are today, were already becoming scarce by 1700. John Josselyn, in his **New England's Rarities,** wrote, "I can assure you that I have eaten my share of a Turkie Cock, that when he was pull'd and garbidg'd weighed thirty pound."[5] Josselyn also mentioned a flightless bird called a wobble that looked something like a penguin. He said it was very good to eat and, indeed, he must have been right, for not a wobble remains in existence today. Some large wild birds, however, did not exactly melt in the mouth. Josselyn mentions an attempt to eat a goose "that was a very old one and so tuff that we gladly gave her over although exceedingly well roasted."[6]

Tough meat was a challenge that every colony met by making one-pot meals, involving long, slow cooking. In New England, it was boiled dinner; in New Amsterdam, *hutspot;* among the Pennsylvania Dutch, sauerbraten and other forms of marinated dishes; and in the south, Brunswick stew or burgoo.

During the colonial period several important new foods became popular. Though all of them originated in this hemisphere, the colonies didn't use them until they had been to Europe and back. Most important was the white potato which Pizarro had sent back to Spain along with Inca gold when he conquered Peru. It did not make much of a hit, perhaps because some people thought they were supposed to eat the flower and fruit of the plant — which happen to be poisonous. Spanish soldiers cultivated it in Florida; the English found it during one of many small skirmishes with the Spanish and took it back home as a curiosity. The potato did not come into its own until someone introduced it into Ireland, where it was an immediate success as a cheap, nourishing, and easily raised vegetable, much preferred to the turnips that had been the Irish people's mainstay until then. It was probably brought to America by Irish settlers. Colonial cooks were apt to mix potatoes with sugar, spices, and raisins.

Cocoa was used to make a drink much relished by the Aztecs, but the conquering Spaniards were not impressed, finding it too bitter. Later, in the royal kitchens of Spain, a recipe using sugar was developed and the resultant hot chocolate became a favorite drink at court. When the Infanta Maria Theresa went to France in 1660 to marry Louis XIV, she took along a cook who knew how to prepare chocolate. He let the secret out, and soon this drink was all the rage — but only among the rich, however, because the cocoa beans from Mexico were very expensive. In the colonies it was obtainable at coffeehouses in the big port towns, but the average American was unfamiliar with it until Revolutionary times.

Coffee, which was often served Turkish fashion — very thick and sweet — was known only to the sophisticated, but tea, first introduced among Dutch families in New York, quickly became popular. As it was expensive, house-

Never had the world known such a rich bounty of foods as colonial cooks worked with. Yet a modern homemaker would be dismayed by the lack of some ingredients considered staples in today's kitchens. Colonial women managed to prepare family meals without using baking powder, granulated sugar, unflavored gelatin, compressed or active dry yeast, cooking oil, and commercial shortening. In addition, such flavorings as vanilla extract, prepared mustard, tomato catsup, Worcestershire sauce, and prepared horseradish were still in the future. To make matters even more difficult, citrus fruits were real luxuries and only on very special occasions were lemon and orange juices used. Nevertheless, colonial American cooking was among the best of its time.

Contrary to popular belief, alcohol and spirits played an important part in the life of the colonists — and this was true for every region. A man might begin the day with a drink of rum, whiskey, or peach brandy before breakfast. Even temperate drinkers like John Adams were likely to start the day with a glass of hard cider. To counteract any ill effects from water, beer or cider was mixed with it and the mixture served at meals. Everyone partook, even women, children, and yes, the stern clergymen. The belief that spirits prevented malaria added to their popularity.

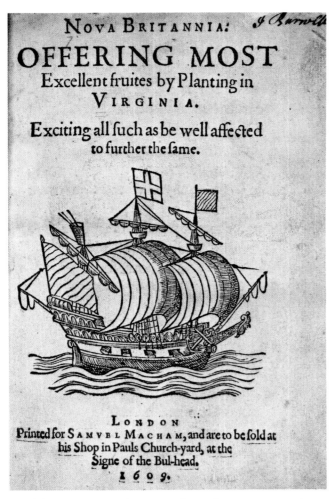

Why they came

The first colonists looked to the New World as the place where all the ills of life in Europe could be overcome. The Spanish came in search of legendary wealth hidden away in kingdoms such as *Quivira*. The backers of the settlement at Jamestown thought the bounty of America would easily fill their pockets. And the Separatists who landed at Plymouth wanted to be free to practice their own religion without interference. For the most part the colonists failed in their original aims. The Spanish never found *Quivira*, the Jamestown settlement failed dismally, and the Pilgrims, although free to practice their religion, had to struggle to survive. In spite of their troubles and failure, the colonists succeeded in achieving something far greater. Out of the New World's lonely, hazardous wilderness, they chiseled a great new nation.

Pamphleteers promoted the wonders of the New World. *Nova Britannia* was written by Robert Johnson in 1609.

The Separatists (later called Pilgrims) board the ships that will take them from Holland to the New World.

Sir Walter Raleigh supervises the planting of the flag formally claiming Virginia for England.

The Spanish explorer, Coronado, led by the Indian scout *El Turco*, searches through what is today Kansas for the legendary kingdom of *Quivira*.

The early settlers welcome a long-awaited shipload of wives arriving in Jamestown.

24 *colonists*

During the Stamp Act controversy an anonymous letter writer declared in a newspaper that "the Americans, should they resolve to drink no more tea, can by no means keep that Resolution, their Indian corn not affording an aggreable or easy digestible breakfast."[7]

To this Benjamin Franklin promptly replied, "Pray let me, an American, inform the gentleman, who seems ignorant of the matter, that Indian corn, take it all in all, is one of the most agreeable and wholesome grains in the world; that its green leaves roasted are a delicacy beyond expression; that samp, hominy, succotash, and nokehock, made of it, are so many pleasing varieties; and that Johnny cake or hoecake, hot from the fire, is better than a Yorkshire muffin. But if Indian corn were so disagreeable and indigestible as the Stamp Act, does he imagine we can get nothing else for breakfast; did he never hear that we have oatmeal in plenty; for water gruel or burgoo; as good wheat, rye and barley as the world affords, to make frumenty; or toast and ale; that there is every where plenty of milk, butter and cheese; that rice is one of our staple commodities; that for tea, we have sage and balm in our gardens, the young leaves of the sweet hickory or walnut, and above all the buds of our pine, infinitely preferable to any tea from the Indies; while the islands yield us plenty of coffee and chocolate? Let the gentleman do us the honour of a visit in America, and I will engage to breakfast him every day in the month with a fresh variety, without offering him either tea or Indian corn."[8]

wives often mixed it with peach leaves or herbs. Sugar to accompany tea was offered in a "bite-and-stir" box of silver or pewter.

As everyone knows, tea was intricately involved in the events that led to the American Revolution; so were molasses, fish, and rum.

One source of colonial prosperity was a commercial arrangement known in history as the triangular trade. There were other triangles, rectangles, and straight lines of trade, but the most famous—or infamous—was this one: New England distilled large quantities of rum for which she needed a great deal of molasses. Her ships carried the rum to West Africa where it was traded for slaves. The ships then made the run to the West Indies, where the slaves were traded for molasses. Completing the triangle, the molasses was transported to New England where most of it was distilled into rum and the rest was sold as "poor man's sugar."

This triangle began when the French decided to forbid their West Indian colonies to send molasses to France (lest the manufacture of rum in France ruin the French brandy industry). The West Indian sugar planters, anxious to find a new market for their molasses, were willing to sell it at cut-rate prices to the American colonies. In response to loud complaints from the sugar growers in the British West Indies, the English parliament passed the Molasses Act of 1733, placing a high duty on molasses imported by the colonies from the French West Indies. The result was a wholesale flouting of this law. Although the duty on molasses was eventually reduced in 1764, duties on sugar imports were raised. The Americans continued to evade the new "taxation without representation"—a high priority on the colonies' list of grievances against the mother country.

The British attempt to prevent trade with the French West Indies also interfered with the New England fishing industry, for New Englanders sold large amounts of "refuse" fish to the French plantation owners for use as fertilizer and slave rations. Onions, potatoes, and apples, as well as cattle and horses, also went to the French Caribbean islands in the Yankee ships that returned home laden with molasses. As John Adams later wrote, "I know not why we should blush to confess that molasses was an essential ingredient in American independence."[9]

The duty on tea, a later imposition, was a kind of last straw. Patriotic Americans gave up tea drinking, relying on herb teas made of mint, camomile, rose hips, and such, which the people called Liberty Tea. A tutor, working for a Virginia plantation family wrote in his diary, "Drank Coffee at four, they are now too patriotic to use tea."[10] When citizens of Boston dumped 45 tons (342 chests) of tea into the harbor on the night of December 16, 1773, the English punished Boston by closing the port. But all the other colonies came to her aid with supplies.

For all the diversity in people who came and in their reasons for coming, there was an amazing similarity in what they ate after they arrived. Corn, beans, and squash or pumpkin were quickly adopted as staples by Spaniard, Englishman, Dutchman, German, or Swede. Diets in every colony expanded to include a wide variety of fish and game. And, when wheat was either shipped in or raised here, bread baking began in earnest.

Battles have specific dates and locations. Recipes do not. In fact, they appear and reappear throughout a long time period. Favorites from the old country supplement native bounty. So it is with the recipes that follow in this chapter. They begin with what everybody ate, then take you to individual colonies to sample the food that combines the old world and new.

NEW ENGLAND

WEST INDIES

WEST AFRICA

The colonists' need for molasses to distill rum was met by a triangular trade arrangement with West Africa and the West Indies. Ships full of rum were traded for African slaves which in turn were traded with West Indian plantation owners for molasses. When the English parliament imposed a tax on molasses imported by the colonies from the French West Indies, colonists claimed taxation without representation.

For the early colonists pumpkin was often the difference between survival and starvation. It was fit only for peasants, said Europe. But the colonists soon overcame this prejudice, and pumpkin became an almost daily staple in the New World. Listen to writer **Peter Kalm in Travels in North America** *describe how many ways the colonists fixed pumpkin: "The French and English also slice them and put the slices before the fire to roast; when they are done they generally put sugar on the pulp. Another way of roasting them is to cut them through the middle, take out all the seeds, put the halves together again and roast them in an oven. When they are quite done some butter is put in, which being imbibed into the pulp renders it very palatable. The settlers often boil pumpkins in water and afterwards eat them alone or with meat. Some make a thin pottage of them by boiling them in water and afterwards macerating the pulp. This is again boiled with a little of the water, and a good deal of milk and stirred about while it is boiling. Sometimes the pulp is kneaded into a dough with maize and other flour; of this they make pancakes. Some make puddings and tarts of pumpkins."*[11]

Colonial Pumpkin Pie

2 cups mashed cooked
    pumpkin *or* 1 16-ounce
    can pumpkin
¾ cup sugar
2 teaspoons ground cinnamon
¾ teaspoon ground nutmeg
¼ teaspoon ground cloves

3 slightly beaten eggs
½ cup whipping cream*
½ cup milk*
1 unbaked 9-inch pastry
    shell (see recipe,
    page 351)

Combine pumpkin, sugar, spices, and ½ teaspoon salt. Blend in eggs, cream, and milk. Pour into pastry shell. Bake at 400° till knife inserted off-center comes out clean, 40 to 45 minutes. Cool (filling may crack).

*1 cup light cream may be substituted for whipping cream and milk.

Steamed Pumpkin Pudding

6 tablespoons butter
¾ cup packed brown sugar
¼ cup granulated sugar
2 eggs
1½ cups all-purpose flour
½ teaspoon salt
½ teaspoon baking soda

½ teaspoon ground cinnamon
½ teaspoon ground ginger
¼ teaspoon ground nutmeg
¾ cup mashed cooked pumpkin
    or canned pumpkin
½ cup buttermilk
½ cup chopped walnuts

Cream butter and sugars together till light. Beat in eggs. Stir together flour, salt, soda, cinnamon, ginger, and nutmeg. Mix pumpkin and buttermilk; add to creamed mixture alternately with dry ingredients, mixing well after each addition. Fold in nuts. Spoon into greased and floured 6½-cup ring mold; cover tightly with foil. Bake at 350° for 1 hour. Let stand 10 minutes. Unmold. Serve with whipped cream, if desired. Serves 12 to 16.

Molasses-Pumpkin Pie

In mixing bowl combine 2 cups mashed cooked pumpkin *or* one 16-ounce can pumpkin, 2 cups milk, 3 eggs, ½ cup packed brown sugar, ½ cup molasses, 2 teaspoons ground cinnamon, ½ teaspoon ground ginger, and ½ teaspoon salt. Beat mixture till well blended. Pour into unbaked 10-inch pastry shell with edges crimped high (see recipe, page 351). Bake at 400° till knife inserted off-center comes out clean, 50 to 55 minutes. Cool.

Buttermilk Pancakes with Pumpkin Sauce

4 cups coarsely cubed
    unpeeled pumpkin *or* 1½
    cups canned pumpkin
¾ cup sugar
¾ teaspoon ground cinnamon
⅛ teaspoon ground nutmeg
⅛ teaspoon ground cloves
⅓ cup raisins

¼ cup milk*
1¼ cups all-purpose flour
1 tablespoon sugar
1½ teaspoons baking soda
½ teaspoon salt
1 beaten egg
1⅓ cups buttermilk
2 tablespoons lard, melted

Cook pumpkin, covered, in boiling salted water till tender, 15 to 20 minutes. Drain. Remove rind. Mash pulp; press through sieve. Measure 1½ cups pumpkin. (Or use canned pumpkin.) Mix pumpkin, ¾ cup sugar, spices, and ½ teaspoon salt. Stir in raisins and milk. Heat through; keep warm. (Sauce will be thick.)

For pancakes, mix flour, 1 tablespoon sugar, soda, and salt. Mix egg, buttermilk, and lard; add to dry ingredients; stir till moistened. Using ¼ cup batter for each pancake, bake on hot, greased griddle till golden; turn once. Serve with sauce. Makes 8 to 10.

*If using canned pumpkin, increase the amount of milk to ½ cup.

Baked Glazed Squash *(see photo, page 64)*

2½ pounds butternut squash
⅓ cup packed brown sugar

2 tablespoons butter
¼ teaspoon paprika

Slice squash in 1-inch thick slices; remove seeds. Arrange squash rings in a 13x9x2-inch baking pan. Cover with foil. Bake at 350° till almost tender, 45 to 60 minutes. Meanwhile, in saucepan combine brown sugar, butter, paprika, ½ teaspoon salt, and dash pepper; cook and stir till bubbly. Spoon mixture over squash. Continue baking, uncovered, till squash is tender, about 15 minutes more, spooning mixture over squash occasionally. Serves 8.

Stuffed Patty Pan Squash

6 patty pan squash
4 slices bacon
⅓ cup finely chopped onion

¾ cup seasoned fine dry
    bread crumbs
½ cup milk

Cook squash in boiling salted water till tender, 15 to 20 minutes. Drain; cool. To make squash cups, cut small slice from stem end. Scoop out the center of each squash, leaving ½-inch rim at edge. Finely chop squash from center; set aside. Sprinkle squash cups with salt. Cook bacon till crisp. Drain; reserve 2 tablespoons drippings. Crumble bacon; set aside. Cook onion in reserved drippings till tender. Stir in crumbs, milk, and chopped squash. Fill squash cups; sprinkle bacon atop. Place in 12x7½x2-inch baking dish; cover. Bake at 350° for 30 to 35 minutes. Makes 6 servings.

Green Corn Pudding *(see photo, page 29)*

4 ears corn
3 egg yolks
2 tablespoons butter,
    melted

2 tablespoons sugar
1 teaspoon salt
2 cups milk
3 stiffly beaten egg whites

With sharp knife, make cuts down center of kernels on each row. Scrape cob. Measure 1¾ cups corn. Beat egg yolks till thick and lemon-colored. Stir in corn, butter, sugar, and salt. Slowly beat in milk. Fold in egg whites. Bake in 8x8x2-inch baking dish at 350° for 45 to 50 minutes. Serves 6 to 8.

Hasty Pudding *(see photo, page 29)*

1 cup yellow cornmeal
Butter

Maple syrup, brown sugar,
molasses, *or* light cream

In a bowl combine the cornmeal and 1 cup cold water. In heavy saucepan bring 3 cups water and ½ teaspoon salt to boiling. Carefully stir in the cornmeal mixture, making sure it does not lump. Cook over low heat, stirring occasionally, for 10 to 15 minutes. Serve pudding with a pat of butter and maple syrup, brown sugar, molasses, or cream. Makes 6 or 7 servings.

Indian Corn Sticks

1 cup cornmeal
½ cup all-purpose flour
¾ teaspoon salt

1 cup milk
1 egg
2 tablespoons lard, melted

Mix cornmeal, flour, and salt. Add milk, egg, and lard. Beat till smooth. Fill well-greased corn stick pans almost to top. (Or, pour into greased 8x8x2-inch baking pan.) Bake at 425° for 12 to 15 minutes. Serve hot corn sticks with molasses or maple syrup, if desired. Makes 10 to 12.

From the Indians the colonists learned to plant squash to counteract the debilitating effect on the soil of growing corn year after year in the same field.

The words pumpkin and squash were used interchangeably. Although winter squash—acorn and Hubbard—are the ones we hear about most, summer squash like patty pan squash (cymlings) were also popular. This small, fluted, light green squash was native to America and provided a welcomed addition to the colonial diet. Unlike winter squash it could not be stored for long periods, but its yield was so abundant it was used as feed for cattle and other livestock.

Green Corn Pudding was a perennial favorite in many homes. The secret in this recipe is cutting down through the center of the kernels (not between kernels) before scraping the corn off the cob so that the "milk" goes into the pudding.

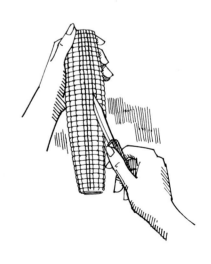

Pictured opposite: Corn appeared in many forms on the colonists' table. Clockwise from lower right: *Green Corn Pudding, Indian Pudding* (see recipes, page 27), *Succotash,* corn bread, corncob jelly, and *Hasty Pudding* (see recipe, page 27).

Colonists quickly came to depend on corn as a vital staple.
When times were hard, it was not uncommon for them to eat some form of corn three times a day — fresh, dried, or ground into corn-meal. Lacking most fruits and vege-tables during the winter months, the resourceful women brought variety to meals by using cornmeal to make a wide selection of porridges, breads, puddings, pancakes, and pies. Leftover cornmeal porridge was sliced and fried for breakfast.
Later the colonists used an old Indian method to create an Indian Pudding *that featured molasses, butter, and spices. Here are two versions. One includes the colonial luxuries — eggs and white sugar.*

Indian Pudding

3 cups milk
1/2 cup molasses
1/3 cup yellow cornmeal
1/2 teaspoon ground ginger

1/2 teaspoon ground cinnamon
1/4 teaspoon salt
1 tablespoon butter

In saucepan mix milk and molasses; stir in cornmeal, ginger, cinnamon, and salt. Cook and stir till thick, about 10 minutes. Stir in butter. Turn into a 1-quart casserole. Bake, uncovered, at 300° about 1 hour. Serves 6.

Sweet Indian Pudding

3 cups milk
1/3 cup molasses
1/3 cup yellow cornmeal
1 beaten egg
1/4 cup sugar

2 tablespoons butter
1/2 teaspoon ground ginger
1/2 teaspoon ground cinnamon
1/4 teaspoon salt

In saucepan combine milk and molas-ses; stir in cornmeal. Cook and stir till thick, about 10 minutes. Remove from heat. Combine egg, sugar, butter, gin-ger, cinnamon, and salt. Gradually stir in hot cornmeal mixture. Bake, uncovered, in a 1-quart casserole at 300° about 1½ hours. Serves 6.

Johnnycakes

2 beaten eggs
1 cup water
3/4 cup milk
2 tablespoons lard, melted

1 teaspoon salt
2 cups yellow cornmeal
Butter
Maple syrup

In bowl mix eggs, water, milk, lard, and salt. Stir in cornmeal. Stir well before making each johnnycake. For each cake, place a scant 1/4 cup batter on a hot, well-greased griddle, spread-ing to 1/4 inch thick. Cook till golden, 2 to 3 minutes per side. Serve warm with butter and syrup. Makes 12 to 14.

Baked Johnnycakes

2 cups water
1 cup yellow cornmeal
1 tablespoon butter

1/2 teaspoon salt
Butter

Mix water, cornmeal, 1 tablespoon butter, and salt. Cook and stir till thickened. Cover with waxed paper. Cool. Shape into four 3-inch squares. Place on greased baking sheet; make indentations in top of each cake with the edge of a spoon. Bake at 400° for 25 minutes. Serve with butter. Serves 4.

Succotash

2 cups fresh *or* frozen baby
    lima beans
2 ounces salt pork
1/2 cup water
1/2 teaspoon salt
1/2 teaspoon sugar

Dash pepper
2 cups fresh *or* frozen
    whole kernel corn
1/3 cup light cream
1 tablespoon all-purpose
    flour

In saucepan combine beans, pork, wa-ter, salt, sugar, and pepper. Cover; sim-mer till beans are almost tender. Stir in corn. Cover and simmer till vegetables are tender. Remove salt pork. Blend cream slowly into flour. Stir into veg-etable mixture. Cook and stir till thickened and bubbly. Serves 6.

One of the hearty main dishes was Boston Baked Beans. While Boston gets the credit for this dish, it was actually popular through-out all the colonies. Since Boston Baked Beans could be made a day ahead, this dish was a favorite with those whose religion restricted work on the Sabbath. Often it was served fresh for Saturday night supper, and either warm or cold for Sunday noon. Today's cooks are more likely to use leftover beans in Baked Bean Patties.

The Jerusalem artichoke was first seen by Samuel de Champlain in 1605 in the gardens of Indians on Cape Cod. To Champlain it tasted like the globe artichoke, and so he called it an artichoke, but there the similarity ends. Actually, the Jerusalem artichoke is a tuber-bearing type of sunflower. It is a knobby vegetable and ranges in color from purple to yellowish white; the flesh is white and crisp. It was cultivated extensively by all the colonies, not only for its flavor, but because it could be stored through the winter much like a turnip. The word "Jerusalem" is thought to be a corruption of, girasol, meaning "to turn to the sun."

Boston Baked Beans *(see photo, page 34)*

3 pounds dry pea beans *or* navy beans (6 cups)
1½ cups dark molasses
1 tablespoon dry mustard
½ pound salt pork, diced
1 large onion, chopped

Rinse beans; in a large kettle combine beans and 24 cups (6 quarts) cold water. Bring to boiling; simmer 2 minutes. Remove from heat. Cover; let stand 1 hour. (Or, add beans to water and soak overnight.) Bring to boiling; simmer till beans are tender, about 1 hour. Drain, reserving liquid. Combine molasses, mustard, 1 teaspoon salt, ½ teaspoon pepper, and 3 cups reserved cooking liquid. In 6-quart bean pot, mix beans, salt pork, and onion. Stir in molasses mixture. Cover; bake at 300° for 3½ to 4 hours, stirring occasionally. Add more reserved cooking liquid, if needed. Serves 15.

Baked Bean Patties

In a bowl mash 1 cup cold baked beans slightly. Add ½ cup fine dry bread crumbs, ½ cup grated carrot, and ⅓ cup finely chopped onion. Mix well. (Add water to moisten, if needed.) Using ⅓ cup each, shape mixture into 6 patties; coat with additional fine dry bread crumbs. Cook patties in 2 tablespoons butter till browned on both sides, 5 minutes per side. Serves 6.

Jerusalem Artichokes with Parslied Cream Sauce

1 pound Jerusalem artichokes
2 tablespoons butter
2 tablespoons all-purpose flour
½ teaspoon salt
Dash white pepper
1 cup light cream *or* milk
¼ cup finely snipped parsley

Wash and peel artichokes; slice. Cook, covered, in a small amount of boiling salted water till tender, 10 to 15 minutes. Drain well. Melt butter in a saucepan; blend in flour, salt, and white pepper. Add cream all at once. Cook and stir till mixture thickens and bubbles. Remove from heat. Stir in parsley till sauce is smooth. Serve over cooked artichokes. Serves 4 to 6.

Jerusalem Artichoke Relish

1 pound Jerusalem artichokes
1 cup sugar
1 cup white vinegar
8 whole cloves
¼ teaspoon salt

Wash and slice artichokes. Cook, covered, in a small amount of boiling salted water till tender, 10 to 15 minutes. Drain well. In a saucepan heat sugar, vinegar, cloves, salt, and 1 cup water till boiling. Pour over the artichokes; refrigerate overnight. Drain before serving. Makes 3 cups.

Fish Chowder

1 pound fresh *or* frozen fish fillets
2 cups cubed potatoes
3 slices bacon
½ cup chopped onion
2 cups milk
3 tablespoons all-purpose flour

Thaw frozen fish. Cut fish into 2-inch pieces. Cook potatoes in 2 cups water for 5 minutes. Add fish, 2 teaspoons salt, and ⅛ teaspoon pepper. Simmer, covered, 10 to 12 minutes. Cook bacon till crisp. Drain and crumble; reserve drippings. Cook onion in drippings. Add bacon and onion to fish mixture. Mix milk and flour; add to chowder. Cook and stir till thickened. Serves 6.

Pease Soup

8 cups water
1 pound dry green split
    peas (2¼ cups)
1 pound beef stew meat, cut
    in ½-inch cubes
½ pound salt pork
1 cup chopped onion
½ teaspoon salt
½ teaspoon dried basil,
    crushed

¼ teaspoon dried marjoram,
    crushed
⅛ teaspoon pepper
3 cups chopped fresh
    spinach *or* sorrel
2 cups sliced celery
¾ teaspoon dried mint
    leaves
    Croutons

In a large Dutch oven combine water, peas, beef cubes, salt pork, chopped onion, salt, basil, marjoram, and pepper. Bring mixture to boiling. Cover and reduce heat. Simmer till beef is barely tender, about 1½ hours. Remove and discard salt pork. Mash pea mixture slightly. Add spinach or sorrel, celery, and dried mint. Cover and cook till meat and celery are tender, about 30 minutes more. Garnish soup with croutons before serving. Serves 8.

Beef-Vegetable Soup

1 pound beef stew meat, cut
    in ½-inch cubes
3 tablespoons all-purpose
    flour
2 tablespoons lard
    • • •
¼ cup snipped parsley
¼ cup chopped celery leaves
2 bay leaves
1 clove garlic, crushed

½ teaspoon dried thyme,
    crushed
3 cups chopped cabbage
1 cup sliced carrots
1 cup sliced parsnips *or*
    diced turnips
½ cup chopped onion
2 teaspoons salt
¼ teaspoon paprika
⅛ teaspoon pepper

Thoroughly coat beef cubes with flour. In a large saucepan or Dutch oven melt lard. Brown beef cubes in lard. Stir in parsley, celery leaves, bay leaves, crushed garlic, and thyme. Cook and stir meat-vegetable mixture for 5 minutes. Stir in 5 cups water. Cover and simmer 30 minutes. Add cabbage, carrots, parsnips or turnips, onion, salt, paprika, and pepper. Cover and simmer till meat and vegetables are tender, about 1½ hours, skimming fat from surface and stirring occasionally. Remove bay leaves. Serves 6 to 8.

Salt Rising Bread *(see photo, page 34)*

1 medium potato, peeled and
    thinly sliced
2 cups boiling water
2 tablespoons cornmeal
1 tablespoon sugar
½ teaspoon salt

2 packages active dry yeast
7 cups all-purpose flour
1 cup warm milk (110°)
2 tablespoons cooking oil
1 teaspoon salt
¼ teaspoon baking soda

Place potato slices in a medium bowl. Pour boiling water over potato. Stir in cornmeal, sugar, and the ½ teaspoon salt. Set bowl in a warm place, uncovered, till mixture is foamy and has a yeasty odor, about 24 hours. Strain starter mixture, discard potato, and add water if needed to make 1¾ cups liquid. Add yeast; stir to dissolve. Stir in *3 cups* of the flour, the milk, oil, 1 teaspoon salt, and soda. Beat well. Cover; let rise in a warm place till very light (about 1 hour). Stir in enough of the remaining flour to make a moderately stiff dough. Turn out onto a lightly floured surface. Knead dough till smooth and elastic, 6 to 8 minutes. Divide in half. Cover and let rest 10 minutes. Shape dough into 2 loaves. Place in two greased 8½x4½x2½-inch loaf pans. Let rise in a warm place till nearly double (about 45 minutes). Bake at 375° for 30 to 35 minutes. Makes 2 loaves.

Soups were America's first convenience foods. Women often left soup simmering on the fire and added leftover vegetables and meat each day. No time to fix a meal? There was always soup to eat, hot and ready.

In colder areas soup was hung in an outdoor shed! A paddle with a hole in the handle was frozen upright in a huge batch of soup. The solid soup was removed from the kettle and hung up by the hole in the handle. Later, chunks of soup were chopped off and reheated with water.

This recipe for Beef-Vegetable Soup *is from the hand-written* Monroe Family Cook Book. *"Lay the meat in the bottom of the pan with a lump of butter. Cut the herbs and roots very small and lay them over the meat. Cover it close and set it over a slow fire. This will draw out the herbs and roots and give them a different flavor from putting water on at first. When the gravy produced by the meat is almost dried up, pour pan up with water in it. When your soup is done take it up and when cool enough, skim off the grease quite clear and put it on again to heat it and then dish it up. For the first 20 minutes after the soup begins to boil it should be skimmed incessantly. If this is not done not only will little dark looking particles stick to the meat but they float on the soup looking like little rags. Soup should boil very slowly. It ought to be 6 or 5 hours on the fire. The proper vegetables are carrots, turnips, and parsnips, a little cabbage, and a little onion."*[12]

*Baking bread from a natural starter
dates back to at least 4000 B.C.
and has been important in American
eating since colonial days.
The colonists perpetuated their
leavening by carefully saving
part of the dough from one baking
time to the next. Today we call
it sour dough, and this recipe has a
starter that can be kept active
by adding sugar and storing in the
refrigerator for several days.*

Starter Bread

1 cup Starter (room
  temperature)
1 package active dry yeast
1½ cups warm water (110°)

5½ to 6 cups all-purpose
  flour
2 teaspoons sugar
½ teaspoon baking soda

Prepare Starter. In mixing bowl soften yeast in warm water. Blend in 1 cup Starter, 2½ *cups* of the flour, sugar, and 2 teaspoons salt. Mix 2½ *cups* of the flour and the soda; stir into flour-yeast mixture. Stir in enough remaining flour to make a stiff dough. Knead on a floured surface till smooth, 5 to 7 minutes. Place in a greased bowl, turning once to grease surface. Cover; let rise till double (about 1½ hours). Punch down; divide in half. Cover; let rest 10 minutes. Shape dough into 2 round loaves. Place on greased baking sheets. With sharp knife, make parallel slashes in tops. Let rise till double (1 to 1½ hours). Bake at 400° for 35 to 40 minutes. Remove from baking sheets; cool. If desired, brush with butter. Makes 2 loaves.

Starter: Soften 1 package active dry yeast in ½ cup *warm* water (110°). Stir in 2 cups *warm* water, 2 cups all-purpose flour, and 1 tablespoon sugar. Beat mixture till smooth. Cover Starter with cheesecloth; let stand at room temperature till bubbly, 5 to 10 days; stir 2 or 3 times a day. (If room temperature is warm, fermentation time will be shorter than if room is cool.) Cover; refrigerate Starter till needed.

To keep Starter going: After using some Starter, add ¾ cup water, ¾ cup all-purpose flour, and 1 teaspoon sugar to remainder; stir well. Let stand at room temperature till bubbly, at least 1 day. Cover and refrigerate. If not used within 10 days, stir in 1 teaspoon more sugar. Repeat the addition of 1 teaspoon sugar every 10 days.

Brown Bread

2 cups buttermilk
¾ cup dark molasses
1 cup raisins
1 cup whole wheat flour
1 cup rye flour

1 cup yellow cornmeal
¾ teaspoon baking soda
½ teaspoon salt
  Boiling water

In a large mixing bowl blend together buttermilk and molasses. Stir in raisins. Thoroughly stir together whole wheat flour, rye flour, cornmeal, baking soda, and salt; stir into buttermilk mixture till blended. Divide batter among three greased 20-ounce clean food cans. (Or, fill four 16-ounce cans.)

Cover cans tightly with foil; place on a rack set in a large Dutch oven. Pour boiling water into Dutch oven to a depth of 1 inch. Cover and simmer over low heat, steaming bread till done, 2½ to 3 hours. Add more boiling water as needed. Remove bread from cans and cool on a rack. Makes 3 or 4 loaves.

*There are many stories about the
origin of Sally Lunn. According to one story it was a kind of
bun named for an English girl,
Sally Lunn, who sold baked goods at
Bath. Another says the words
"sun" and "moon" in French, soleil,
and lune, were used to describe
the brown tops and white bottoms of
the rolls. We may never know
the truth; but we do know it was
served in colonial America as
a tea bread. It is traditionally baked
in a Turk's head mold.*

Sally Lunn

1 package active dry yeast
¼ cup warm water (110°)
¾ cup warm milk (110°)
    • • •
6 tablespoons butter

3 tablespoons sugar
2 eggs
3 cups all-purpose flour
1¼ teaspoons salt

In a small bowl soften active dry yeast in warm water. Stir in warm milk and set aside. In a mixing bowl cream butter and sugar. Add eggs, one at a time, beating after each addition. Combine all-purpose flour and salt; add to creamed mixture alternately with yeast mixture. Beat well after each addition. Beat batter till smooth. Cover batter

and let rise in a warm place till almost double (about 1 hour). Beat down and pour batter into a well-greased Turk's head mold or a 9-inch tube pan. Let rise in a warm place till almost double (about 30 minutes). Bake at 350° for 40 to 45 minutes. Remove bread from mold or tube pan. Serve bread either warm or cool. Makes 1.

Turkey with Oyster Stuffing

½ cup chopped celery
½ cup chopped onion
1 bay leaf
¼ cup butter
6 cups dry bread crumbs
1 tablespoon snipped
 parsley
3 cups shucked oysters
 with liquid

2 beaten eggs
1 teaspoon poultry
 seasoning
1 teaspoon salt
 Dash pepper
1 10- to 12-pound ready-
 to-cook turkey
 Cooking oil

In a medium saucepan cook chopped celery, chopped onion, and bay leaf in butter till vegetables are tender, but not brown. Discard bay leaf. Stir in dry bread crumbs and snipped parsley. Drain oysters, reserving liquid. Add drained oysters, eggs, poultry seasoning, salt, and pepper to crumb mixture. Mix thoroughly. Stir in enough reserved oyster liquid to moisten. Spoon some of the oyster stuffing into the wishbone cavity of turkey. Pull neck skin to back and fasten with a skewer.

Spoon remaining stuffing into tail cavity. Tuck legs under band of skin or tie legs securely to tail. Twist wing tips under back of turkey. Place bird, breast side up, on rack in shallow roasting pan. Rub skin with cooking oil. Insert meat thermometer in center of inside thigh muscle without touching bone. Roast, uncovered, at 325° till meat thermometer registers 185° and drumstick moves easily in socket, 4 to 4½ hours. When about done, cut skin or string between legs. Serves 12 to 14.

In British America, hunting was a way of life. To survive, the colonist had to be an expert marksman and learn to prepare all types of game from venison to turkey.

Perhaps the most abundant of all early game, was the purplish passenger pigeon. Legend has it that the skies were darkened by their sheer numbers and trees would break under the weight of the numbers of birds roosting in them.

Often, instead of using valuable gun powder, the colonists used torches at night to confuse and blind the birds, and then clubbed them to death. Unfortunately, so great was the demand for these birds — which were related to the mourning dove — that they are now extinct.

Creamed Dried Beef

¼ cup butter
¼ cup all-purpose flour
 • • •
1¼ cups milk
1 cup light cream

1 3-ounce package dried
 beef, cut in thin
 strips
 Hot mashed potatoes *or*
 baked potatoes

In a heavy saucepan melt butter; stir in flour. Cook and stir over medium heat till mixture is golden brown, about 5 minutes. Add milk and light cream all at once. Cook and stir till

mixture is thickened and bubbly. Add dried beef; simmer till heated through, 3 to 5 minutes. Season to taste with salt and pepper. Serve over hot mashed or baked potatoes. Serves 4 or 5.

Beef Steak Pie

1½ pounds beef round steak,
 cut in 1-inch cubes
¼ cup all-purpose flour
1 large onion, cut into
 pieces
2 tablespoons lard
2 cups water
1 teaspoon salt

¼ teaspoon dried thyme,
 crushed
⅛ teaspoon pepper
2 cups diced potatoes
 Pastry Topper
 Salt
 Pepper
 Milk

Coat beef cubes with flour. In saucepan cook beef and onion in lard till beef is browned and onion is tender. Add water, 1 teaspoon salt, thyme, and pepper. Cover; simmer for 1½ hours. Add potatoes. Cover; simmer 20 minutes. Prepare Pastry Topper. Transfer meat mixture to 1½-quart casserole. Season to taste with salt and pepper. Cut slits in Pastry Topper. Place on hot mixture. Turn under edge and

flute. Brush with milk. Bake at 450° till golden, about 15 minutes. Serves 6.
Pastry Topper: Stir ¾ cup all-purpose flour and ¼ teaspoon salt together. Cut in ¼ cup lard till mixture resembles coarse crumbs. Sprinkle 2 to 3 tablespoons cold water, 1 tablespoon at a time, over mixture; gently toss with fork. Form into a ball. Roll on a lightly floured surface to a circle ½ to 1 inch larger than casserole.

Early homemakers baked their pies quite differently from the way we do today. The baking dish was set on a trivet in a large black Dutch oven over the fire. Because these pies were more steamed than baked, the crusts were often wet and soft. No matter the soggy crust and the difficult baking process — flavorful pies like Beef Steak Pie were a must on colonial tables.

Baked Chicken and Almond Pudding

1 4-pound ready-to-cook
    stewing chicken, cut up
1 cup sliced celery
1 medium onion, cut in
    wedges
¼ cup snipped parsley
½ cup chopped onion
2 tablespoons butter

3 cups firm-textured bread
    crumbs
¾ teaspoon poultry
    seasoning
¼ cup butter
¼ cup all-purpose flour
3 slightly beaten eggs
½ cup slivered almonds

In a Dutch oven combine chicken, celery, onion wedges, parsley, 6 cups water, and 1½ teaspoons salt. Cover; cook till chicken is tender, about 2 hours. Remove chicken from broth; strain broth. Skim off fat. Measure 3 cups broth; set aside. Cool chicken; skin and bone. Cube meat. Cook chopped onion in 2 tablespoons butter. Add bread crumbs and poultry seasoning; cook and stir till crumbs are browned; set aside. To make sauce, melt ¼ cup butter; stir in flour. Add reserved broth. Cook and stir till thickened and bubbly. Stir moderate amount of hot mixture into eggs. Return to remaining hot mixture. Cook and stir 2 minutes more; remove from heat. Place *one-third* of chicken in bottom of 12x 7½x2-inch baking dish. Sprinkle *one-third* of the crumb mixture over chicken. Top with a layer of chicken, another of crumbs, and remaining chicken. Pour sauce over. Sprinkle with remaining crumbs. Top with almonds. Bake at 325° for 25 to 30 minutes. Serves 8.

Chicken Pie

1 4-pound ready-to-cook
    stewing chicken, cut up
4 cups water
1 cup chopped onion
1 rutabaga, peeled and cut
    in chunks (3 cups)

½ cup sliced celery
½ teaspoon ground sage
    Lattice Crust
⅓ cup all-purpose flour
1 beaten egg

In Dutch oven combine chicken, water, onion, 1 tablespoon salt, and ¼ teaspoon pepper. Bring to boiling. Reduce heat and simmer, covered, till chicken is tender, about 1½ hours. Remove chicken; cool. Remove meat from bones; discard skin and bones. Cut up meat; set aside. Skim fat from broth. Remove ½ cup broth; set aside. Measure 3¼ cups of the remaining broth; return to Dutch oven; add rutabaga, celery, and sage. Bring to boiling. Reduce heat and simmer, covered, till vegetables are tender, about 20 minutes. Meanwhile, prepare Lattice Crust. Blend the reserved ½ cup broth slowly into flour; stir into vegetable mixture. Cook and stir till thickened. Add chicken; heat through. Transfer mixture to 2-quart casserole. Place 5 of the pastry strips atop hot mixture. Place 5 more strips atop at right angles. Trim to fit. (Or, weave a lattice on waxed paper; flip atop pie.) Place remaining 3 strips around edge of casserole; trim to fit. Seal; flute edges. Brush with egg. Place pie on baking sheet on oven rack. Bake at 375° till crust is browned, 35 to 40 minutes. Serves 6 to 8.

Lattice Crust: Mix 1¼ cups all-purpose flour and ¾ teaspoon salt; cut in ⅓ cup lard till pieces are size of small peas. Combine 1 beaten egg and 2 tablespoons cold water; sprinkle over flour mixture, 1 tablespoon at a time. Gently toss with fork. Repeat till all is moistened. Form into a ball. Roll on a lightly floured surface to a 10x9¾-inch rectangle. Cut into thirteen 10x¾-inch strips.

Baked Dressed Fish

Using one 3-pound fresh *or* frozen dressed fish, thaw frozen fish. Remove head, if desired. Rinse and dry fish. Place in a greased baking pan. Brush fish, inside and outside, with ¼ cup melted butter and sprinkle with 1½ teaspoons salt and ⅛ teaspoon pepper. Bake, covered, at 350° till fish flakes easily when tested with a fork, 45 to 60 minutes. Makes 6 servings.

Pictured opposite: Familiar recipes often have a number of variations as each cook makes her own adjustments. The lattice top on *Chicken Pie* is one variation. It may also be made with either regular gravy or sweetened gravy depending on the area. Some New Englanders flavor their *Boston Baked Beans* (see recipe, page 30) with brown sugar while others prefer to use molasses. One way to vary bread baking is by the leavening used. *Salt Rising Bread* (see recipe, page 31) is a popular alternative to yeast bread.

Like the goose that laid golden eggs, young, egg-producing chickens were far too valuable to slaughter, so old hens were used to prepare Baked Chicken and Almond Pudding. Over the years it became a specialty of the eastern seaboard colonies and Pennsylvania.

Fish such as herring, shad, and mackerel were among the first foods the colonists ate. Cod, however, was the most popular.

Stuffed Deviled Clams

1 pint shucked clams *or*
  2 7½-ounce cans minced
  clams
1 teaspoon ground mace

1 teaspoon ground nutmeg
2½ cups soft bread crumbs
¼ cup butter, melted

Drain and coarsely chop fresh clams (or drain canned clams); stir in mace and nutmeg. Spoon into 6 greased individual baking shells. Toss soft bread crumbs with melted butter. Sprinkle buttered crumbs over clams. Bake, uncovered, at 375° for 15 minutes. Serve clams hot. Makes 6 appetizer servings.

Glazed Pork Loin

Hogs generally were killed after the first frost since the cooler temperatures made it easier to process the pork. The thrifty colonists used every part of the hog and made a variety of products. Some of the meat was served fresh as in this recipe for Glazed Pork Loin. The biggest portion was salted, pickled, or smoked as hams, bacon, or salt pork. The rest was made into head cheese or sausage. Waste-not, want-not cooks served the pig's tail, feet, or ears to stretch the food supply. The fat was rendered into lard or served as chitterlings.

Place a 4- to 5-pound boneless pork loin roast on a rack in a shallow roasting pan. Insert meat thermometer. Roast at 325° for 2¼ hours. Meanwhile in 8-inch skillet, heat and stir ½ cup sugar till a deep golden brown. Slowly stir in ⅔ cup *boiling* water. Stir in ⅓ cup vinegar and 1 teaspoon hickory smoked salt. Boil gently till mixture is reduced to ½ cup, about 10 minutes. (Mixture thickens with cooling.) Brush pork with vinegar mixture. Continue roasting till thermometer registers 170°, 15 to 30 minutes more; brush often with vinegar mixture. Makes 10 to 12 servings.

Apple Butter

6 pounds tart apples
6 cups apple cider *or*
  apple juice

3 cups sugar
2 teaspoons ground cinnamon
½ teaspoon ground cloves

Core and quarter apples; cook with cider in large heavy saucepan till soft, about 30 minutes. Press through food mill. Boil gently 30 minutes; stir often. Stir in sugar and spices. Cook and stir over low heat till sugar dissolves. Boil gently, stirring often, till desired thickness, about 1 hour. Pour into hot ½-pint jars; adjust lids. Process in boiling water bath 10 minutes (start counting time after water returns to boil). Makes 8 half-pints.

Jumbles

One of the earliest "biscuits" or cookies was Jumbles. Also spelled Jumbals, these cookies were shaped in several ways depending on the stiffness of the dough. They could be dropped as in this recipe, or rolled out and cut with a fluted cutter, or shaped into a rope and tied into a knot.

1 cup butter
1 cup sugar
1 egg
2 tablespoons brandy *or*
  milk

½ teaspoon vanilla
2 cups all-purpose flour
1 teaspoon ground cinnamon
  Raisins *or* walnut halves
  (optional)

Cream butter and sugar. Add egg, brandy or milk, and vanilla; beat well. Stir flour and cinnamon together; add to creamed mixture. Mix well. Drop by teaspoonfuls onto ungreased cookie sheet. Place a raisin or nut in center of each. Bake at 375° about 10 minutes. Cool on rack. Makes 48.

Orange Fool

Fool, an old English dessert, was popular throughout the colonies. One version combined sieved gooseberries and a custard or cream. Another variation used orange juice in place of the berries. It made a refreshing summer dessert then and still does today.

3 beaten eggs
1 cup light cream
½ teaspoon grated orange
  peel

¾ cup orange juice
¼ cup sugar
  Dash ground nutmeg
1 teaspoon butter

In saucepan combine eggs, cream, orange peel, orange juice, sugar, and nutmeg; cook and stir over low heat till mixture thickens slightly and coats a metal spoon, about 7 minutes (do not overcook). Remove from heat; stir in butter till melted. Pour into dessert dishes. Chill. Makes 4 servings.

Colonial Sponge Cake

1½ cups all-purpose flour
¾ cup sugar
8 egg yolks
1 tablespoon lemon juice

1 teaspoon vanilla
8 egg whites
1 teaspoon cream of tartar
¾ cup sugar

Mix flour and ¾ cup sugar. Make well in center. Mix egg yolks, lemon juice, vanilla, and ¼ cup cold water; add to flour mixture. Beat batter till smooth, about 2 minutes at medium speed of electric mixer. Beat egg whites with cream of tartar and ¾ teaspoon salt till very soft peaks form; add ¾ cup sugar, *two tablespoons at a time*. Con-

tinue beating till stiff peaks form. Fold egg yolk batter gently into egg white mixture. Pour into an ungreased 10-inch tube pan. Carefully cut through batter, going around pan 5 or 6 times. Bake at 350° till top springs back when touched lightly, 50 to 55 minutes. Invert pan; cool. Remove from pan. Serve with fresh fruit, if desired.

Delicate wafers, rolled to form a cone, then filled with whipped cream and served with fresh berries were a special treat. The long-handled iron used in their preparation was a popular engagement present for a man to give his bride-to-be. Oftentimes, the initials of both the bride and groom as well as the date would be stamped on the iron.

Crisp Wafers

2 cups all-purpose flour
½ cup packed brown sugar
1 teaspoon ground cinnamon

6 tablespoons butter
1 beaten egg
¼ cup milk

Mix flour, sugar, and cinnamon. Cut in butter till mixture resembles fine crumbs. Add egg and milk; mix well. Form dough into balls using 2 tablespoons for each. Bake in preheated

krumkake *or* pizelle iron over medium heat till crisp and golden, about 1½ minutes per side with krumkake iron (about 2½ minutes per side with pizelle iron). Cool on racks. Makes 12.

Crisp Wafers, *adapted for a krumkake or pizelle iron, makes thicker cookies than the rolled wafers shown above, so serve these cookies flat.*

Queen of Puddings

4 egg yolks
4 cups milk
4 cups dry bread cubes
¾ cup sugar
2 tablespoons butter, melted
1 teaspoon grated lemon peel

1 teaspoon vanilla
½ cup strawberry, raspberry, *or* apricot preserves
4 egg whites
½ teaspoon vanilla
¼ teaspoon cream of tartar
½ cup sugar

In mixing bowl beat egg yolks slightly; stir in milk, bread cubes, ¾ cup sugar, butter, lemon peel, and 1 teaspoon vanilla. Beat with rotary beater till sugar is dissolved. Pour mixture into ungreased 12x7½x2-inch baking dish. Bake at 350° for 40 minutes. Remove from oven; spread preserves over hot pudding. Beat egg whites, ½ teaspoon vanilla, and cream of tartar till soft peaks form. Gradually add ½ cup sugar, beating till stiff peaks form. Spread egg white mixture over preserves, sealing to edges. Return to oven; bake till light brown, 10 to 12 minutes more. Makes 8 to 10 servings.

Custard Bread Pudding

3 slices white bread
½ cup raisins
Boiling water
3 beaten eggs
3 cups milk
¼ cup sugar

½ teaspoon vanilla *or* rosewater
Butter
2 tablespoons sugar
½ teaspoon ground nutmeg

Let bread stand uncovered overnight to dry. Cover raisins with boiling water; let stand 5 minutes. Drain. Mix eggs, milk, ¼ cup sugar, and vanilla or rosewater. Place raisins in ungreased 10x6x2-inch baking dish. Pour egg mixture over. Spread bread slices with butter; cut each slice diagonally into 4 triangles. Place atop egg mixture, buttered side up. Sprinkle with mixture of 2 tablespoons sugar and nutmeg. Set baking dish in pan on oven rack. Pour hot water into pan to depth of 1 inch. Bake at 350° till knife inserted halfway between center and edge comes out clean, about 45 minutes. Serves 6.

Currant Pound Cake

1 cup dried currants
¼ cup brandy
2 cups butter
8 eggs

2¼ cups sugar
• • •
4 cups all-purpose flour
½ teaspoon ground nutmeg

In jar mix currants and brandy. Cover tightly; soak at room temperature several hours or overnight. Drain. Have butter and eggs at room temperature. Cream butter; slowly add sugar, creaming till light. Add eggs, one at a time, *beating well after each*, about 10 minutes total. Stir in flour and nutmeg; blend well. Fold in currants. Grease *bottom only* of two 9x5x3-inch loaf pans. Turn batter into pans. Bake at 325° about 60 minutes. Makes 2.

Wassail Bowl

1 medium orange, halved
10 whole cloves
2 ⅘-quart bottles claret

½ cup sugar
4 inches stick cinnamon

Stud orange halves with cloves. In a saucepan mix orange halves, claret, sugar, and cinnamon. Cover; simmer about 15 minutes. Remove cinnamon and orange halves. Serve punch hot in small bowl. Makes 14 (4-ounce) servings.

Spanish: Beeswax, Wine, and Wheat

Spanish Possessions

Long before the English set up their colonies on the eastern seaboard, Spain was establishing a foothold in Florida and in the vast territory north of the Rio Grande. The first European cooks in North American recorded history were sixteenth-century Spanish soldiers and priests. The Spanish established the fort of Saint Augustine on the east coast of Florida in 1565, and founded a short-lived mission in the Chesapeake Bay area in 1570. Their influence was so strong that when English colonists first came ashore in 1607 at the future site of Jamestown, they were startled to be greeted by an Indian who spoke Spanish.

The early history of Florida is almost entirely concerned with Spanish forts and missions, and the frequent attacks upon them by Indians, English, and French. Another Spanish holding, California, had no European inhabitants until 1769 when Franciscan priests established their first mission at San Diego. A first concern of the missionaries was to obtain wine and wheat for holy communion and beeswax for altar candles. The bees they brought from Spain and, with the help of their Indian converts, they planted vineyards and wheat fields. Citrus fruit trees were also brought from Spain, as were dates and figs. Two other foods that grew well in these places were brought from Mexico: sweet potatoes and avocados.

The most flourishing Spanish outpost in North America was New Mexico. In 1598 a party of colonists led by Juan de Oñate traveled north from Mexico and on the banks of the Rio Grande established a settlement they called San Juan, near present-day Santa Fe. Oñate brought sheep to his new settlement and was thus responsible for introducing sheep to the Indians.

Later, in 1610 the Spanish founded Santa Fe. Also dating from the seventeenth century were several smaller southwestern towns.

The Spanish colonists brought with them favorite foods—among them, saffron, olive oil, and anise and combined these with foods of the local Indians and the Mexican Indians to make a New Mexican cuisine that still flourishes today. From Mexico and the Aztecs came green and red chili peppers that grew well in the climate of northern New Mexico.

Aside from cornmeal and beans the early Spanish foods differed considerably from the foods of the other colonists and from what is thought of today as Mexican food. From the Indians, Spanish women learned to serve young squash, lightly stewed, and fried squash blossoms in batter. They also served blue-corn tortillas piled like pancakes with a sauce of chilies, meat, onions, cheese, and perhaps a fried egg on top—a hearty one-dish meal known then as *enchiladas*. *Posole* (hominy) cooked with tripe made another filling dish, as did a mild version of Spanish rice. A rich chocolate drink was made with cocoa beans, nuts, cinnamon, sugar, and milk.

Sprouted wheat, called *panocha,* mixed with caramelized sugar and cooked a long time, made a delicious, nourishing dessert. For meat, goat and sheep were the most common domestic animals, and, of course, there was plenty of game. Early chronicles speak of birds "with great hanging chins" and "cows covered with frizzled hair that resembles wool."[13] Both these strange creatures, reported the chronicler, were delicious roasted.

The Aztecs had credited chili peppers with fine medicinal properties, and they were not far wrong. One large green chili contains as much vitamin C as an orange, and the red chilies are an excellent source of vitamin A.

Surrounded by mountains, Santa Fe was founded during the winter of 1609-1610 by Pedro de Peralta, the third Spanish governor of the Province of New Mexico. He named his new capital *La Villa Real de la Santa Fé de San Francisco de Asis*—the Royal City of the Holy Faith of St. Francis of Assisi. A pack train service called the Mission Supply brought supplies from Mexico City every three years.

Red Chili Sauce

4 medium tomatoes (1½
    pounds) *or* 1 15-ounce
    can tomato purée
¼ cup lard
¼ cup all-purpose flour

½ cup chili powder
1 cup water
1 clove garlic, minced
1 teaspoon salt

Peel and quarter the fresh tomatoes. Place in blender container; cover and blend till nearly smooth. Measure 2 cups tomato purée. In a skillet melt lard. Stir in flour. Add chili powder, stirring till the chili is completely moistened. Stir in tomato purée, water, garlic, and salt. Cook and stir till the mixture is thickened and bubbly. Makes about 3 cups sauce.

In the Southwest, Posole *is both the name of this dish as well as the type of hominy used to prepare it. Traditionally it was prepared with scraps of meat left after butchering the hogs.*

Posole *(see photo, page 43)*

1½ pounds boneless pork,
    diced
2 cups water
1 teaspoon salt
• • •
2 14½-ounce cans white *or*
    golden hominy
¼ cup chopped onion

1 clove garlic, minced
½ teaspoon ground cumin
¼ teaspoon dried oregano,
    crushed
¼ teaspoon salt
    Red Chili Sauce (see
    recipe above)

Trim fat from pork; cook trimmings in a heavy 4-quart Dutch oven till 2 tablespoons drippings accumulate. Remove trimmings; brown diced pork in hot drippings. Stir in the water and the 1 teaspoon salt. Cover and reduce heat. Simmer till meat is very tender, 1½ to 2 hours. Add the undrained hominy, onion, garlic, cumin, oregano, and the ¼ teaspoon salt. Cover and simmer 15 minutes. Serve with the Red Chili Sauce. Makes 6 servings.

Chili Meat Sauce, New Mexico-Style

1 pound ground beef *or* pork
1 cup chopped onion
1 clove garlic, minced
• • •
2 cups chicken broth
1 tablespoon crushed dried
    red chili pepper

1 teaspoon dried oregano,
    crushed
1 teaspoon ground cumin
¼ teaspoon salt
¼ cup cold water
2 tablespoons all-purpose
    flour

In saucepan cook beef or pork, onion, and garlic till meat is browned and onion is tender. (Break up meat as it cooks.) Stir in chicken broth, chili pepper, oregano, cumin, and salt.

Cook, covered, over low heat about 1 hour. Blend water slowly into flour; stir into meat mixture. Cook, stirring constantly, till thickened and bubbly. Makes 3½ cups sauce.

New Mexican chili sauce is hot, hot, hot! The abundant use of ground red chili pods makes this delicious sauce distinctive—and hot. Prepared with ground meat, garlic, and a variety of herbs, it is typically served as a topping for enchiladas, poached eggs, or main dishes.

Stacked Enchiladas *(see photo, page 43)*

½ cup finely chopped onion
2 tablespoons lard
1 tablespoon all-purpose
    flour
½ cup milk
1 4-ounce can green chili
    peppers, drained and
    chopped (⅓ cup)
½ teaspoon salt

2 cups diced cooked beef
2 medium tomatoes, peeled
    and chopped (1 cup)
8 Corn Tortillas (see
    recipe below) *or* frozen
    tortillas, thawed
¼ cup cooking oil
1 cup shredded Monterey
    Jack cheese (4 ounces)

In skillet cook onion in lard till tender but not brown. Blend in flour. Add milk, chili peppers, and salt. Cook, stirring constantly, till thick and bubbly. Stir in beef and tomatoes; heat through; keep warm. In small skillet heat tortillas, one at a time, in hot oil till limp, about 15 seconds per side.

Drain on paper toweling. Place a hot tortilla in 9x9x2-inch baking pan. Top with about ¼ cup beef mixture and a small amount of cheese. Repeat with remaining tortillas, beef mixture, and cheese to make a stack. Bake at 350° till hot, about 20 minutes. Unstack to serve. Serves 4.

Don't expect rolled enchiladas from New Mexico—authentic New Mexican enchiladas are flat tortillas spread with a meat filling and stacked one on top of another. When available, a green tomato variety known as tomatilla *is preferred in the sauce.*

Corn Tortillas

2 cups corn flour
    (masa harina)

1 cup water

Combine corn flour and water; mix with hands till dough is moist but holds its shape. Add more water, if needed. Divide dough into 12 balls. Dampen dough slightly with water; press between sheets of waxed paper to 6-inch diameter, using a tortilla press or flat baking dish. Carefully peel off top

sheet of paper. Place, paper side up, on hot ungreased skillet. Gently peel off top sheet of waxed paper. Cook till edges begin to dry, about 30 seconds. Turn; cook till puffs appear in tortilla. Repeat with remaining dough. Spread with butter, fold in quarters, and eat as bread, or fry in hot oil. Makes 12.

Spicy Hot Chocolate

4 cups milk
5 1-ounce squares semisweet
    chocolate

6 inches stick cinnamon
1 teaspoon vanilla

In saucepan combine milk, chocolate, and cinnamon sticks. Cook, stirring constantly, just till chocolate melts. Remove from heat and remove cinna-

mon. Stir in vanilla. Beat mixture with rotary beater till frothy. Serve in warmed mugs with cinnamon stick stirrers, if desired. Makes 4 cups.

When Cortez landed in Mexico in 1519 he was treated to a delicacy: chocólatl—*a cold, bitter, syrupy beverage. To adapt it to their taste, the Spanish added sugar and sometimes vanilla and cinnamon and served it as a hot beverage.*

Pictured opposite: Corn was as much a staple in New Mexico as in New England. The way the New Mexican settlers served it, however, reflected their Spanish influence, as does this kitchen in Casa de Adobe, Southwest Museum in Los Angeles. *Stacked Enchiladas* (see recipe, page 41) features corn tortillas layered with a tomato-chili-beef sauce. In *Spanish Vegetables* corn is combined with zucchini, tomatoes, onion, and spices. A form of corn known as hominy is the basis of *Posole* (see recipe, page 40). This meat stretcher is served with a chili sauce.

For the Spanish settlers, like their compatriots at home, rice was a favorite dish. It was usually prepared with fresh herbs. Unlike later versions of Spanish rice, few chilies were used.

The Spanish in California commonly cooked vegetables in "butter fat," which was not really butter at all. The large pieces of fat around the intestines of cattle were ground and rendered to produce the settlers' butter fat.

Settlers in California in the early 1700s were pioneers in more ways than one. They made the tomato a staple in their diet long before it was popular or even considered edible in other places.

Chilies Rellenos

6 fresh whole pimientos *or*
   2 4-ounce jars whole
   pimientos, drained
½ cup chopped peeled
   tomato
1 tablespoon butter
¼ cup regular rice
1 small clove garlic,
   minced
⅓ cup water

½ cup shredded Tilamook *or*
   Monterey Jack cheese
¼ cup all-purpose flour
6 egg yolks
3 tablespoons all-purpose
   flour
6 stiffly beaten egg whites
½ cup olive oil *or*
   cooking oil
Beef gravy (optional)

Place fresh pimientos on baking sheet. Bake at 450° till skins form dark blisters, about 15 minutes, giving a quarter turn once. Cool. Peel and remove stems and seeds. Place tomato in blender container; cover and blend till nearly smooth. Melt butter; add rice and garlic. Cook and stir till rice is browned. Stir in the blended tomato, water, ¼ teaspoon salt, and dash pepper. Cook, covered, till rice is done, about 15 minutes. Remove from heat; stir in cheese. Stuff pimientos with rice-cheese mixture; roll in the ¼ cup flour; set aside. Beat egg yolks, the 3 tablespoons flour, and dash salt together till thick and lemon-colored. Fold in egg whites. In 12-inch skillet spoon ⅓ cup batter for each relleno into hot oil; spread to a 3-inch circle. (Do three at once.) As batter sets, top each with a stuffed pimiento. Cover each with ⅓ cup more batter. Cook over medium heat about 5 minutes. Turn; cook till brown, 5 minutes more. Drain on paper toweling. Serve at once. (Or, if desired, place in a 15½x 10½x1-inch baking pan; top with beef gravy. Bake, uncovered, at 375° till hot, 20 to 25 minutes.) Serves 6.

Early Spanish Rice

In skillet cook ½ cup chopped green pepper; ¼ cup chopped onion; 1 clove garlic, minced; ½ teaspoon dried basil, crushed; and ½ teaspoon dried rosemary, crushed, in 2 tablespoons hot olive oil *or* cooking oil. Cook till vegetables are tender. Stir in 2 cups water, 1 cup regular rice, 1 cup chopped peeled tomato, 1 teaspoon salt, and ⅛ teaspoon pepper. Cook, covered, over low heat till rice is done, about 20 minutes. Makes 6 servings.

Spanish String Beans

1 pound green beans, cut
   in 1-inch pieces
   (3 cups)
½ cup chopped green pepper
¼ cup chopped onion
1 tablespoon olive oil *or*
   cooking oil

2 medium tomatoes, chopped
1 teaspoon salt
½ teaspoon dried basil,
   crushed
¼ teaspoon dried rosemary,
   crushed
⅛ teaspoon pepper

In saucepan cook beans, covered, in small amount boiling salted water till tender, 15 to 20 minutes; drain. Meanwhile, cook green pepper and onion in hot oil till tender but not brown. Stir in tomatoes, salt, basil, rosemary, pepper, and green beans; heat through. Season to taste with salt and pepper. Serves 8.

Spanish Vegetables

Cut kernels from 2 large ears corn (1 cup corn); do not scrape cob. In skillet cook ½ cup finely chopped onion and 1 clove garlic, minced in 1 tablespoon olive oil till onion is tender but not brown. Stir in corn; 1 pound zucchini, sliced; 2 cups chopped peeled tomatoes; 1 teaspoon dried oregano, crushed; 1 teaspoon salt; and ⅛ teaspoon pepper. Cook, covered, over low heat till tender, about 15 minutes. Serve in bowls. Serves 4 to 6.

Baked Onions with Meat Stuffing

4 medium onions (2 pounds)
2 beaten eggs
¾ cup soft bread crumbs
2 cups finely chopped
  cooked beef, lamb, *or*
  pork
¼ cup chopped canned
  pimiento

2 tablespoons snipped
  parsley
1 teaspoon salt
½ teaspoon dried oregano,
  crushed
Canned pimiento, cut
  in strips
½ cup boiling water

Peel onions. Cook, covered, in large amount of boiling salted water till nearly tender, about 20 minutes. Drain; cool. Remove tops; remove centers to form shells about ¼ inch thick. Chop centers; reserve 2 tablespoons chopped onion (use remaining onion elsewhere). Mix eggs and crumbs. Add meat, chopped pimiento, parsley, salt, oregano, ⅛ teaspoon pepper, and reserved chopped onion. Mix well. Sprinkle inside of onion shells with salt; stuff with meat mixture. Place in 8x8x2-inch baking dish. Garnish tops with pimiento strips. Pour boiling water into dish. Bake, covered, at 350° till onions are tender and stuffing is heated through, about 30 minutes. Serves 4.

Rice Pudding

Another rice dish popular with the Spaniards was Rice Pudding, *a favorite dessert spiced with cinnamon, enriched with cream, or sweetened with raisins — or all three.*

In heavy saucepan bring 3 cups milk to boiling; gradually stir in ½ cup regular rice, ⅓ cup raisins, and ¼ teaspoon salt. Cover; cook over low heat, stirring occasionally, till most of milk is absorbed and rice is creamy, 30 to 45 minutes. Spoon into dessert dishes. Dot with butter; sprinkle with a mixture of ¼ cup sugar and ¼ teaspoon ground cinnamon. Serves 6.

Anise Cookies

1 cup lard
¾ cup sugar
2 eggs

1 tablespoon aniseed
2½ cups all-purpose flour
½ teaspoon salt

Cream together lard and sugar till light and fluffy; beat in eggs and aniseed. Stir together flour and salt; stir into creamed mixture. Wrap dough in waxed paper; chill several hours. Using a slightly rounded teaspoonful of dough, roll with hands on lightly floured surface to a 4x¼-inch rope. Place on ungreased baking sheet, crossing ends to form a handwritten letter "l." (Or, shape dough in two rolls 8 inches long and 1½ inches in diameter; chill. Slice ¼ inch thick; place on ungreased baking sheet.) Bake at 375° till edges are golden, 10 to 12 minutes. Cool on racks. Makes about 60.

Zucchini Salad

Adapting to the New World meant adopting the food plants at hand. From the Indians, the Spanish learned how to prepare the prickly pear cactus for their salads. The cactus was singed to remove the spines then peeled and parboiled. When in season zucchini was also served in salads. An old Spanish saying claims: "To make a perfect salad there should be a spendthrift for oil, a miser for vinegar, a wiseman for salt and a madcap to stir the ingredients up and mix them well together."[14]

1 cup white wine vinegar
¾ cup olive oil
2 tablespoons sugar
1 teaspoon dried basil,
  crushed
1 clove garlic, minced

4 cups sliced zucchini
Leaf lettuce
¼ cup sliced green onion
  with tops
2 medium tomatoes, cut
  in thin wedges

In screw-top jar mix vinegar, oil, sugar, basil, garlic, 1 teaspoon salt, and few dashes pepper. Cover and shake well. Cook zucchini in small amount boiling salted water till crisp-tender, about 3 minutes; drain. Arrange *half* the zucchini in one layer in 10x6x2-inch dish. Shake dressing; pour *half* over zucchini. Top with remaining zucchini and dressing. Cover; chill overnight. To serve, drain zucchini; reserve ¼ cup dressing. Arrange on a lettuce-lined plate; top with onion. Arrange tomatoes around zucchini; drizzle with reserved dressing. Chill before serving, if desired. Serves 8.

Glazed Oranges

6 navel *or* Temple oranges
2 inches stick cinnamon,
    broken
10 whole cloves

1 cup dry white wine
¾ cup sugar
2 tablespoons vinegar

With a sharp knife remove peel from oranges. Reserve peel from *one* orange; discard remaining peel. Remove most of the white membrane from reserved peel; cut peel into very thin strips. Tie spices in a cheesecloth bag. Drop peel and spices into boiling water; cook about 5 minutes. Drain, reserving peel and spice bag. Carefully cut off all outside white membrane from all of the oranges. In a saucepan combine the spice bag, wine, sugar, and vinegar. Bring to a boil; stir till sugar dissolves. Add oranges and peel. Simmer, uncovered, about 15 minutes, turning oranges often. With a slotted spoon transfer oranges and peel to serving bowls. Discard spices. Top oranges with syrup; cool to room temperature. Cover; chill well. Serves 6.

Orange seeds were first planted near San Diego, California, in the 1780s, but it wasn't until the founding of the San Gabriel Mission around 1800 that orange groves were planted. The adaptability of the tree to the climate soon distributed the crop throughout the south of California. Today the citrus industry is California's most extensive agricultural enterprise.

Rabbit Fricassee

¼ cup all-purpose flour
½ teaspoon salt
⅛ teaspoon pepper
1 2- to 2½-pound ready-to-
    cook rabbit, cut up
1 tablespoon butter
1 cup water
2 parsley sprigs
¼ teaspoon dried marjoram,
    crushed

¼ teaspoon dried oregano,
    crushed
⅛ teaspoon ground allspice
⅛ teaspoon ground cloves
1 teaspoon lemon juice
2 tablespoons cold water
1 tablespoon all-purpose
    flour
Hot cooked rice

Mix ¼ cup flour, salt, and pepper. Coat rabbit pieces with flour mixture. In a skillet brown rabbit slowly in butter. Reduce heat; add 1 cup water, parsley, marjoram, oregano, allspice, and cloves. Cook, covered, till tender, about 1 hour. Remove rabbit to warm platter. Discard parsley. Measure pan juices; skim off fat. Add lemon juice and enough water to make 1 cup liquid; return to skillet. Blend the 2 tablespoons cold water into 1 tablespoon flour; stir into cooking liquid. Cook and stir till thick and bubbly; cook 2 minutes more. Season to taste. Serve gravy over rice. Serves 4.

The early Spanish fathers depended on the game that the first Indian converts brought with them to the missions. The Padres could choose from deer, quail, or rabbit. They often fried or boiled their game, but rabbit they preferred fricasseed.

Spiced Meatball and Bean Soup

1 pound dry garbanzo beans
    (2¼ cups)
8 cups beef broth
½ cup chopped onion
½ cup chopped green pepper
1 tablespoon snipped
    parsley
¼ teaspoon salt
¼ teaspoon ground coriander
2 beaten eggs

1 tablespoon milk
¾ cup soft bread crumbs
¼ cup finely chopped onion
1 tablespoon snipped
    parsley
1 teaspoon salt
    Dash ground cinnamon
    Dash ground nutmeg
1 pound ground beef

In Dutch oven mix beans, *4 cups broth*, and 4 cups water. Bring to boiling; simmer 2 minutes. Remove from heat; let stand, covered, 1 hour. Stir in remaining broth, ½ cup chopped onion, green pepper, 1 tablespoon parsley, ¼ teaspoon salt, coriander, and ⅛ teaspoon pepper. Simmer, covered, 1¾ hours. Meanwhile, combine eggs and milk; add crumbs, ¼ cup onion, 1 tablespoon parsley, 1 teaspoon salt, ⅛ teaspoon pepper, ground cinnamon, and ground nutmeg. Add ground beef; mix well. Shape meat mixture into about 40 meatballs using a tablespoonful meat mixture for each. Add meatballs to soup; cover and simmer 15 minutes. Makes 10 servings.

Lime Chicken

1 2½- to 3-pound ready-to-cook broiler-fryer chicken, cut up
½ teaspoon grated lime peel (set aside)

¼ cup lime juice
¼ cup butter, melted
¼ cup all-purpose flour
½ teaspoon salt
½ teaspoon chili powder

Brush chicken pieces all over with lime juice. Place in a 13x9x2-inch baking dish; cover and refrigerate 1 hour. Uncover; brush all over with the melted butter. In a paper bag or a plastic sack combine the flour, salt, chili powder, and lime peel; add the chicken pieces, a few at a time, and shake to coat with flour mixture. Return chicken pieces to baking dish. Bake, uncovered, at 375° till done, about 1 hour. Makes 4 servings.

Broiled Lamb Chops Mission-Style

½ cup dry white wine
¼ cup olive oil *or* cooking oil
¼ cup chopped onion
¼ cup snipped parsley

½ teaspoon salt
⅛ teaspoon pepper
1 clove garlic, minced
6 lamb chops, cut ¾ inch thick

In a small bowl combine the wine, olive oil, onion, parsley, salt, pepper, and garlic. Place the lamb chops in a shallow baking pan. Pour wine mixture over the lamb chops. Cover and let stand 2 hours at room temperature or place in the refrigerator about 5 hours, spooning the marinade over several times. Remove the lamb chops and reserve the marinade. Place the lamb chops on rack of a broiler pan; brush with the reserved marinade. Broil 3 inches from the heat for 6 to 8 minutes. Turn the chops; brush with additional reserved marinade. Broil 6 to 7 minutes longer. Makes 6 servings.

The *presidio* (a military garrison), the *pueblo* (a community for a colonizing population), and the mission laid the foundation for Spanish occupation of California. Twenty-one Franciscan missions were founded about a day's journey apart between San Diego and Sonoma. The mission, established to help convert the Indians, was also a cultural and agricultural center for the colonists.

Virginia and Maryland's Bountiful Table

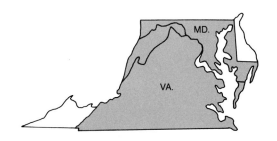

The first permanent English settlement in North America was established on the James River in Tidewater, Virginia in the spring of 1607 by a group seeking their wealth in the new land. The first season went badly. There were too many "members of the gentry" in the group who had no work experience and who were not accustomed to being told what to do. Expected supply ships didn't arrive, Indians were hostile, sickness swept away almost half the settlers, and the survivors quarreled incessantly. When one of them, Captain John Smith, managed to take charge and bring order, the second winter went much better. Smith wrote, "And now, the winter approaching, the rivers became so covered with swans, geese, ducks, and cranes that we daily feasted with good bread. Virginia pease, pumpion...and diverse sorts of wild beasts as fat as we could eat them."[15]

But then new colonists arrived, among whom "no man would acknowledge a superior," and chaos set in; so that a "starving time" was upon them and the colony was "constrained to eat dogs, cats, rats, snakes, toadstools ...and what not."[16] The tide turned when more shiploads of settlers and supplies arrived and laws were passed to insure that everyone worked hard and planted corn and gardens as well as the cash crop, tobacco.

For the colonists of both Virginia and her neighbor, Maryland (first settled in 1634), tobacco-planting was to be the source of their prosperity. Plantation owners discovered that it was economically sound to ship out tobacco and ship in supplies. The real problem of early tobacco planters was that supply ships often failed. Also because tobacco is a plant that soon exhausts the soil, planters had to use increasingly larger areas of virgin acreages for planting. Settlers in both colonies were entitled to headrights — fifty acres per settler and an additional fifty for each woman, child, or servant he might bring over from England. In Maryland, large "manors" were at first granted by King Charles I; and later Charles II gave large tracts of land to some of his favorites. But, in general, building up an estate was possible only by paying the passage of others.

Although African slaves were brought to America in 1619, slavery did not become an important economic factor until the very late seventeenth century; then great landowners owned many slaves.

Most plantations in colonial Virginia had their own dock where ships could anchor to deliver supplies and take on tobacco. This accessible transportation made it possible for plantation owners to import whatever they desired. Imported food plus native game provided a varied diet as illustrated by the diary of William Byrd II. Beaver, roast beef, veal, pigeon, seafoods, wild turkey, strawberries, nectarines, watermelon, and many wines are mentioned in his diary of Virginia life in the 1700s.

Maryland was equally renowned for good things to eat. Famous Maryland dishes were roasted oysters, stuffed crabs, and diamondback terrapin. The latter food was considered so common that slave owners fed it to their slaves as often as three times weekly.

If the first settlers could have seen what they'd eventually have, they would no doubt have felt better about those "dogs, cats...and what not."

The life of plantation owners, such as the Carters of Virginia who owned more than 333,000 acres, was one of great comfort and plenty. For example, according to Philip Fithian, a young tutor employed on the plantation of Robert Carter in 1774, "the Family" every year consumed "2700 Lb. of Pork; & twenty Beeves, 550 Bushels of Wheat, besides Corn — 4 Hogsheads of Rum, & 150 Gallons of Brandy."[17] These lavish provisions, of course, did not reach Carter's slaves. Their weekly rations, according to Fithian, were "a Peck of Corn & a Pound of Meat a Head! And Mr. Carter is allow'd by all, & from what I have already seen of others, I make no Doubt at all but he is, by far the most humane to his slaves of any in these parts! Good God! are these Christians?"[18]

Jamestown was founded in May of 1607 by the Virginia Company of London, on what was then a marshy peninsula of the James River. The original settlement at James Fort was a few huts within a triangular blockhouse.

Duckling with Sausage Stuffing

½ pound bulk pork sausage
4 cups dry bread cubes
1 cup chopped peeled apple
1 cup chopped celery
½ cup chopped onion
¼ cup snipped parsley
½ teaspoon dried thyme, crushed

½ teaspoon dried marjoram, crushed
½ teaspoon salt
Dash pepper
4 tablespoons water
1 4- to 5-pound ready-to-cook duckling
Salt

In a skillet cook sausage till lightly browned; drain well. In a large bowl stir together cooked sausage, bread cubes, apple, celery, onion, parsley, thyme, marjoram, ½ teaspoon salt, and pepper. Toss with *2 tablespoons* of the water. Sprinkle the cavity of the duckling with salt and stuff lightly with the sausage mixture. (Reserve any remaining stuffing.) Place the bird, breast side up, on a rack in a shallow roasting pan. Tie the legs together; tie legs to tail. Twist wing tips under the back. Prick skin all over with a fork. Roast, uncovered, at 375° till tender, 1½ to 2 hours. Drain off excess fat as necessary. Place any reserved stuffing in a 1-quart casserole; sprinkle with the remaining 2 tablespoons water. Cover; bake remaining stuffing during the last 30 minutes. Serve with duckling. Makes 4 servings.

Chicken Hash

In Virginia and Maryland the local name for creamed turkey or chicken in colonial times was turkey or chicken hash. This term is still used in many places in the South today.

¼ cup butter
¼ cup all-purpose flour
¾ teaspoon salt
Dash pepper
2 cups light cream *or* milk

2 cups cubed cooked chicken *or* turkey
2 hard-cooked eggs, chopped
¼ cup dry sherry
Toast triangles

In a saucepan melt butter; blend in the flour, salt, and pepper. Add light cream or milk all at once. Cook, stirring constantly, till the mixture is thickened and bubbly. Stir in chicken or turkey, eggs, and sherry. Heat through. Serve hot over toast triangles. Makes 4 to 6 servings.

Stuffed Heart

1 2½- to 3-pound beef heart
¼ cup chopped celery
2 tablespoons chopped onion
2 tablespoons butter
3½ cups dry bread cubes
1 tablespoon snipped
    parsley
¼ teaspoon dried thyme,
    crushed

⅛ teaspoon salt
¼ cup dry red wine
2 teaspoons instant beef
    bouillon granules
1¾ cups boiling water
3 whole black peppercorns
2 whole cloves
1 bay leaf
¼ cup all-purpose flour

Remove hard portions of heart. Close slit with short skewers. Lace string around skewers; tie ends. Cook celery and onion in butter till tender. Mix with bread, parsley, thyme, salt, and ⅛ teaspoon pepper. Toss with wine. Place heart, pocket end up, in a bowl. Fill pocket with stuffing. Cover opening with foil; tie securely. Place in Dutch oven. Dissolve bouillon in boiling water; add peppercorns, cloves, and bay leaf. Pour into Dutch oven. Cover; simmer till heart is tender, about 2½ hours. Remove skewers and string. Remove to hot platter. Skim fat from juices; add water to make 1½ cups. Blend ½ cup cold water into flour. Stir into juices; cook and stir till thick. Season to taste. Simmer 2 to 3 minutes. Serves 6 to 8.

Spiced Beef Pot Roast

4 teaspoons whole cloves
4 teaspoons whole allspice
¼ teaspoon whole black
    pepper
1 teaspoon salt
½ teaspoon ground nutmeg
½ teaspoon ground mace

1 3- to 4-pound beef pot
    roast, fat trimmed
2 tablespoons packed brown
    sugar
2 tablespoons vinegar
2 tablespoons lard
¼ cup all-purpose flour

Coarsely crack cloves, allspice, and pepper; mix with salt, nutmeg, and mace. Rub over meat; press in. Place meat in shallow dish. Combine sugar, vinegar, and ¼ cup water. Pour over meat; refrigerate overnight. Turn meat often. Remove meat; reserve marinade. In Dutch oven brown meat in hot lard. Add marinade and ½ cup water. Cover; cook till tender, about 2 hours. Add more water if needed. Remove meat to warm platter. Strain juices; skim off fat. Add water to juices to make 1½ cups. Slowly blend ½ cup cold water into flour. Stir into juices. Cook and stir till thick. Cook 1 minute more. Season to taste. Serve sauce with roast. Makes 6 to 8 servings.

Creamed Oysters and Sweetbreads

1 pound veal sweetbreads
¼ cup celery leaves
2 tablespoons vinegar
4 parsley sprigs
1 bay leaf
    Ice water
6 tablespoons butter

¼ cup all-purpose flour
½ teaspoon paprika
⅛ teaspoon white pepper
2 cups light cream *or* milk
1 pint shucked oysters
2 slightly beaten egg yolks
8 baked patty shells

In a saucepan cover sweetbreads with cold water. Add celery leaves, vinegar, parsley, bay leaf, 1 teaspoon salt, and ⅛ teaspoon pepper. Bring to a boil; reduce heat; simmer 15 minutes. Drain. Immediately cover sweetbreads with ice water; let stand 15 minutes. Remove and discard white membrane and tubes. Cube sweetbreads. Melt butter; stir in flour, paprika, white pepper, and 1 teaspoon salt. Add cream. Cook and stir till thick. Stir in sweetbreads and undrained oysters; cook just till edges of oysters curl. Blend moderate amount of sauce into egg yolks; return to hot mixture. Cook and stir for 1 minute. Serve in patty shells. Makes 6 to 8 servings.

This early tidewater Virginia and Maryland recipe was served over waffles made with an iron similar to a wafer iron (see page 37). It made Sunday breakfast worth rising for.

Pictured opposite: Plantation dinners were famous for elegant serving of delicious foods such as *Country-Style Ham, Maryland Rusks* (see recipe, page 53), and *Orange-Raisin Cake* (see recipe, page 54).

Good home-cured hams could be found in every colony, but those of Virginia and Maryland were special. There the hogs were fed on mast—a mixture of fruits from the oak, hickory, chestnut, beech, chinquapin, and persimmon trees.

Today, Smithfield hams are the most famous country-style hams. To earn the name Smithfield a ham must be cured, given a heavy smoke, and be aged as long as a year within the city limits of Smithfield, Virginia, and the hogs must be fed on peanuts. Unlike most hams available today, which are fully cooked, country-style hams must be cooked before eating.

Corn Bread Dressing

Southern Corn Bread
1 cup chopped celery with
  leaves
1 cup chopped onion
2 cups chicken broth

2 beaten eggs
1 teaspoon poultry
  seasoning
1/4 teaspoon salt

Prepare Southern Corn Bread; cool. Crumble enough corn bread to make 6 cups. Cook celery and onion in broth for 5 minutes; cool. Mix eggs, poultry seasoning, salt, vegetables with broth, and corn bread. Use to stuff an 8-pound turkey *or* bake in 1 1/2-quart casserole at 325° for 30 to 35 minutes. Makes 6 cups dressing.

Southern Corn Bread: In mixing bowl thoroughly stir together 1 1/2 cups yellow cornmeal, 1/2 cup all-purpose flour, 1 teaspoon baking soda, and 1/2 teaspoon salt. Stir in 1 1/2 cups buttermilk, 2 tablespoons melted lard, and 1 beaten egg; mix well. Pour batter into greased 9x9x2-inch baking pan. Bake at 400° about 20 minutes.

Country-Style Ham

Thoroughly scrub and rinse a country-style ham. Soak in water overnight; drain. Place in large kettle; cover with water. Bring to boil; reduce heat and simmer for *20 to 25 minutes per pound.*

When cool enough to handle, remove skin from ham and trim fat. Stud fat side with whole cloves; sprinkle with brown sugar. Bake, uncovered, at 350° for 20 minutes. Slice thinly.

Oysters Baked in Half Shells

18 oysters in shells
  Rock salt
2 tablespoons butter
2 tablespoons all-purpose
  flour
1/8 teaspoon ground nutmeg
3/4 cup milk
1 egg yolk

1/3 cup dry white wine
1 4 1/2-ounce can shrimp,
  drained and chopped
2 tablespoons snipped
  parsley
1/3 cup grated Parmesan
  cheese

Open oyster shells. With a knife, remove oysters. Wash shells. Place each oyster in deep half of shell. Arrange shells on a bed of rock salt in shallow baking pan; set aside. In small saucepan melt butter over low heat. Blend in flour and nutmeg. Add milk all at once. Cook, stirring constantly, over low heat till mixture is thickened and bubbly. Beat together the egg yolk and

wine. Add a moderate amount of hot mixture; return to hot mixture in saucepan. Cook and stir over low heat 1 to 2 minutes more. Stir in shrimp and parsley. Bake oysters at 400° for 5 minutes. Top each oyster with 1 tablespoon sauce mixture and about 1 teaspoon cheese. Bake at 400° till heated through, 10 to 12 minutes. Makes 3 main dish or 6 appetizer servings.

Oysters Fried in Batter

1 pint shucked oysters
1/2 cup all-purpose flour
1/4 teaspoon salt
  Dash pepper

2 beaten eggs
• • •
Cooking oil

Drain shucked oysters; dry thoroughly on paper toweling. In a bowl combine flour, salt, and pepper. Stir dry ingredients into beaten eggs; beat till smooth. Cover; let stand 10 to 15 minutes. Pour oil into deep skillet to

depth of 1 inch; heat to 375°. Dip oysters in batter a few at a time; fry oysters in hot oil till golden brown, about 2 minutes. Drain hot oysters well on paper toweling. Keep cooked oysters hot. Makes 3 or 4 servings.

When Sir Walter Raleigh tried to establish a colony in Virginia, one of his companions, Thomas Hariot, described the abundance of fish and seafood. He said: "For four months of the year, February, March, April, and May, there are plenty of sturgeon; and also in the same months of herrings, some of the ordinary bigness as ours in England, but the most part far greater, of eighteen, twenty inches, and some two feet in length and better; both these kinds of fish in these months are most plentiful and in best season which we found to be most delicate and pleasant meat.

There are also trouts, porpoises, rays, oldwives, mullets, plaice, and very many other sorts of excellent good fish, which we have taken and eaten, whose names I know not....

There are also in many places plenty of these kinds which follow...Also mussels, scallops, periwinkles, and crevises.

Seekanauk, a kind of crusty shellfish which is good meat about a foot in breadth, having a crusty tail, many legs like a crab and her eyes in back. They are found in shallows of salty waters; and sometimes on the shore.

There are many tortoises both of land and sea kind, their backs and bellies are shelled very thick; their head, feet and tail, which are in appearance, seem ugly as though they were members of a serpent or venomous; but notwithstanding they are very good meat, as also their eggs. Some have been found of a yard in breadth and better."[19]

Oyster Stew

2 tablespoons all-purpose
   flour
2 tablespoons cold water
1½ teaspoons salt
1 teaspoon Worcestershire
   sauce

Dash bottled hot pepper
   sauce
1 pint shucked oysters
¼ cup butter
4 cups milk, scalded

In saucepan blend flour, water, salt, Worcestershire, and hot pepper sauce. Stir in undrained oysters and butter. Simmer over very low heat, stirring gently, till edges of oysters curl, 3 to 4 minutes. Add hot milk; remove from heat and cover. Let stand 15 minutes. Reheat briefly. Float pats of butter and oyster crackers atop, if desired. Makes 4 or 5 servings.

Scalloped Oysters

Cook ¼ cup chopped celery and 2 tablespoons sliced green onion with tops in ¼ cup butter till tender. Blend in ¼ cup all-purpose flour, ¼ teaspoon salt, ¼ teaspoon paprika, and dash pepper. Cook and stir 3 minutes. Stir in 1 pint undrained shucked oysters, 1 teaspoon lemon juice, and ½ teaspoon Worcestershire sauce. Pour into 1-quart casserole. Combine ½ cup soft bread crumbs and 1 tablespoon melted butter. Sprinkle atop oyster mixture. Bake at 400° till heated through, about 30 minutes. Makes 8 to 10 servings.

Turtle Soup

1 pound boned turtle meat,
   cut in ½-inch cubes
Fat for frying
2 cups chopped cabbage
2 stalks celery with
   leaves, cut up
2 medium carrots, cut up
1 medium onion, cut in
   wedges

6 whole black peppercorns
3 sprigs parsley
2 cloves garlic
2 bay leaves
1½ teaspoons salt
1 cup thinly sliced fresh
   mushrooms
½ cup dry sherry
¼ teaspoon Kitchen Bouquet

Brown meat in small amount of hot fat. Stir in 1 cup water; simmer, covered, till tender, 1½ hours. Meanwhile, in large saucepan combine cabbage, celery, carrots, onion, peppercorns, parsley, garlic, bay leaves, salt, and 5 cups water. Simmer, covered, 1 hour. Strain broth; discard vegetables and spices. Return broth to saucepan; stir in *undrained* turtle meat, mushrooms, and sherry. Heat through. Stir in Kitchen Bouquet. Serves 4 to 6.

Fresh Corn Chowder

6 medium ears corn
¼ cup chopped onion
4 cups milk
2 tablespoons butter
¼ teaspoon white pepper

3 tablespoons all-purpose
   flour
1 beaten egg
Snipped chives (optional)
Paprika (optional)

With sharp knife make cuts *through center* of kernels. Cut corn off cobs; scrape cobs. In a saucepan combine corn, onion, ⅓ cup water, and ½ teaspoon salt. Bring to a boil. Reduce heat and simmer, covered, till corn is barely done, about 15 minutes, stirring occasionally. Stir in 3½ *cups* of the milk, butter, pepper, and 1 teaspoon salt. Blend together remaining ½ cup milk and flour; stir into corn mixture. Cook and stir till thick and bubbly. Gradually stir a moderate amount hot mixture into egg; return to hot mixture in saucepan. Cook, stirring constantly, over low heat for 2 minutes more. Garnish with chives and paprika, if desired. Makes 6 servings.

French Dressing

4 hard-cooked eggs
2 tablespoons cold water
¼ cup olive *or* salad oil
¼ cup tarragon vinegar
2 teaspoons prepared
  mustard

1 teaspoon sugar
8 cups torn mixed greens
  (lettuce, watercress,
  endive, and chicory)
¼ cup sliced green onion
  with tops

Separate egg yolks and whites; slice whites and set aside. Mash yolks with water. Stir in oil. Pour into screwtop jar. Add vinegar, mustard, sugar, and 1 teaspoon salt. Cover and shake vigorously. In salad bowl combine egg whites, greens, and onion. Pour dressing over; toss to coat. Serves 8.

Virginia Dressing

In top of double boiler (not over heat) place 4 egg yolks and 2 tablespoons cold water; beat slightly. Slowly stir in ¼ cup wine vinegar, 1 tablespoon sugar, 1 teaspoon dry mustard, and 1 teaspoon salt. Place over, but not touching, hot (not boiling) water. Cook and stir till thickened. Cool. Fold in 1 cup dairy sour cream. Serve over shredded cabbage. Makes 1½ cups.

Maids of Honor *(see photo, page 99)*

2 beaten eggs
3 tablespoons dry sherry
¾ cup sugar
4 teaspoons all-purpose
  flour

¼ teaspoon ground nutmeg
¾ cup almonds, ground
  Rich Pastry
  Strawberry, raspberry *or*
  plum jam

Mix eggs and sherry. Combine sugar, flour, and nutmeg; stir into egg mixture. Stir in almonds. Roll Rich Pastry ⅛ inch thick and cut twenty-four 2½-inch circles; fit into 1¾-inch muffin pans. Spoon dot of jam into each shell; pour egg mixture atop. Bake at 350° till wooden pick comes out clean, 23 to 25 minutes. Makes 24.

Rich Pastry: Stir together 1 cup all-purpose flour, 1 tablespoon sugar, and ¼ teaspoon salt. Cut in ¼ cup butter till mixture resembles small peas. Using ¼ cup milk, sprinkle 1 tablespoon milk at a time over part of mixture. Toss with fork; push to side of bowl. Repeat sprinkling and tossing till all is moistened. Form into ball.

Maryland Rusks *(see photo, page 51)*

4½ to 5 cups all-purpose
  flour
1 package active dry yeast
1¼ cups milk

3 tablespoons sugar
2 tablespoons butter
1½ teaspoons salt
3 eggs

In large mixing bowl combine *2 cups* flour and yeast. In saucepan combine milk, sugar, butter, and salt; heat just till warm (115-120°), stirring constantly. Add to dry ingredients in mixing bowl; add eggs. Beat at low speed of electric mixer ½ minute, scraping bowl. Beat 3 minutes at high speed. By hand, stir in enough remaining flour to make a moderately stiff dough. Turn out on lightly floured surface; knead till smooth (5 to 8 minutes). Shape into ball. Place in greased bowl; turn once. Cover; let rise in warm place till double (1 to 1½ hours). Punch down. Divide dough in 5 portions. Shape each into a ball; cover, let rest 10 minutes. Roll each portion into a 5-inch circle. Place circles on greased baking sheets. Cover; let rise in warm place till double (30 to 45 minutes). If desired, brush with milk; sprinkle with sugar. Bake at 375° till golden, 15 to 20 minutes. Cool completely. Slice bread ½ inch thick or halve. Place slices or halves on baking sheets. Toast in 275° oven 40 minutes; turn and toast till golden, about 20 minutes.

This French Dressing *comes from* The Virginia Housewife *written by Mrs. Mary Randolph, a relative of Thomas Jefferson. She also gives these directions for preparing salad greens. "To have this delicate dish in perfection, the lettuce, peppergrass, chervil, cress, etc. should be gathered early in the morning, nicely picked, washed, and laid in cold water... just before dinner is ready to be served, drain the water from your salad, cut into a bowl, giving the proper proportions of each plant... and lay around the edge of the bowl young scallions, they being the most delicate of the onion tribe.*"[20]

George Bagby in The Old Virginia Gentlemen *describes the plenty of Virginia. "I am tolerably certain that a few other things beside bacon and greens are required to make a true Virginian. He must, of course, begin on pot-liquor. He must have fried chicken, stewed chicken, broiled chicken, and chicken pie; old hare, butter-beans, new potatoes, squirrel, cymlings, snaps, barbecued shoat, roas'n ears, buttermilk, hoe cake, pancake, fritters, pot-pie...sweet-potatoes, June apples, waffles, sweet milk, parsnips, artichokes, carrots, cracklin' bread, hominy, bonny-clabber, scrambled eggs, gooba-peas, fried apples, popcorn, persimmon beer, applebread, milk and peaches, mutton stew, dewberries, buttercakes, mushmelons, hickory nuts, partridges, honey in the honeycomb, snappin'-turtle eggs, damson tarts, catfish, cider, hot lightbread, and cornfield peas all the time, but he must not intermit his bacon and greens.*"[21] The damson tarts Bagby mentions are known today as Maids of Honor.

Orange-Raisin Cake *(see photo, page 51)*

Orange-Raisin Cake was originally prepared by housewives using a salamander. This long-handled iron plate was heated in the fire and then held over pastry to brown it. To finish the Orange-Raisin Cake, the orange juice and sugar glaze was poured over the baked cake and then the hot salamander was waved over the surface until the glaze was melted and lightly browned.

1 cup raisins
½ cup chopped walnuts
   Peel of 1 medium orange, with white membrane removed
• • •
1 cup sugar
½ cup butter

2 eggs
1 teaspoon vanilla
2 cups sifted cake flour
1 teaspoon baking soda
½ teaspoon salt
1 cup buttermilk
1 cup sugar
⅓ cup orange juice

Combine the raisins, nuts, and orange peel. Put mixture through a food grinder; set aside. Cream together 1 cup sugar and the butter. Add eggs and vanilla, beating till fluffy. Stir in the ground orange peel-raisin mixture. Sift together the cake flour, baking soda, and salt. Add dry ingredients to creamed mixture alternately with buttermilk, beating well after each addition. Turn batter into a greased 9x9x2-inch baking pan. Bake at 350° till wooden pick comes out clean, about 45 minutes. In small saucepan heat together the 1 cup sugar and the orange juice till sugar dissolves. Prick top of cake all over with a fork. Spoon sugar-orange juice mixture over warm cake.

Regal Plum Pudding

The Tidewater area of Virginia and Maryland was settled for the most part by Englishmen and their descendants. The English influence on all aspects of life was considerable—food was no exception. Roast beef, Sally Lunn (see recipe, page 32), eggnog, and fruitcake were all Tidewater favorites. Of all English recipes, what is more English than plum pudding?

4 slices bread, torn in pieces
1 cup milk
6 ounces beef suet, ground
1 cup packed brown sugar
2 beaten eggs
¼ cup orange juice
1 teaspoon vanilla
2 cups raisins
1 cup snipped pitted dates

½ cup diced mixed candied fruits and peels
½ cup chopped walnuts
1 cup all-purpose flour
2 teaspoons ground cinnamon
1 teaspoon ground cloves
1 teaspoon ground mace
1 teaspoon baking soda
½ teaspoon salt
   Foamy Sauce (optional)

Soak bread in milk; beat to break up. Stir in ground suet, brown sugar, eggs, orange juice, and vanilla. In a large bowl combine raisins, dates, candied fruits and peels, and nuts. Stir together the flour, cinnamon, cloves, mace, soda, and salt; add to the fruit mixture and mix well. Stir in the bread-suet mixture; mix well. Pour into well-greased 2-quart mold (do not use ring mold or tube pan). Cover the mold with foil and tie foil on tightly with string. Place the mold on rack in deep kettle; add boiling water to the kettle to depth of 1 inch. Cover and steam the pudding 3½ hours; add more boiling water when needed. Cool the pudding about 10 minutes; remove from the mold. Serve the pudding with Foamy Sauce, if desired. Serves 16.
Foamy Sauce: In large bowl beat 2 egg whites to stiff peaks, gradually adding 1 cup sifted powdered sugar. Beat 2 egg yolks and ¼ teaspoon vanilla till thick; fold into egg whites. In small bowl whip ½ cup whipping cream till soft peaks form; fold whipped cream into egg mixture.

Baked Custard with Coconut

½ cup grated fresh coconut
4 eggs
½ cup sugar

1 teaspoon vanilla
3 cups milk, scalded and cooled

(To prepare grated coconut drain the liquid from coconut and crack off shell. Peel off brown skin and discard; grate coconut.) Beat eggs slightly with a fork. Stir together ½ cup grated coconut, beaten eggs, sugar, and vanilla; slowly stir in cooled milk. Pour into eight 6-ounce custard cups; set cups in shallow pan on oven rack. Pour hot water around custard cups in pan to a depth of 1 inch. Bake at 325° till a knife inserted just off-center comes out clean, 40 to 45 minutes. Serve warm. Makes 8 servings.

Baked Celery with Almonds

1 bunch celery
2 cups boiling water
3 tablespoons butter
3 tablespoons all-purpose
  flour

1⅓ cups milk
3 tablespoons toasted
  slivered almonds
1 tablespoon melted butter
¼ cup fine dry bread crumbs

Wash celery; cut into ½ inch slices (5 cups), reserving tops. Combine celery, tops, boiling water, and ½ teaspoon salt. Cook till celery is tender, 12 to 15 minutes. Discard tops; drain, reserving ½ cup cooking liquid. Melt the 3 tablespoons butter. Blend in flour, ½ teaspoon salt, and ¼ teaspoon pep- per. Add milk and reserved liquid. Cook and stir till thickened. Remove from heat. Stir in celery and *half* the nuts. Turn into 1-quart casserole. Top with remaining nuts. Combine melted butter and crumbs; sprinkle atop. Bake at 350° till heated through, 20 to 25 minutes. Serves 4.

Chef's Tarts

Prepare pastry for 2-crust 9-inch pie (see recipe, page 351); roll to ⅛-inch thickness. Cut eight 5- or 6-inch rounds; fit into 3-inch muffin tins. Flute edges. By hand beat together 3 eggs, 1½ cups sugar, 6 tablespoons melted butter, ¼ cup dry white wine, and 1 tablespoon lemon juice just till combined. Pour filling into un- baked shells. Bake at 350° till wooden pick comes out clean, 30 to 35 min- utes. Serve chilled. Makes 8.

Forever festive, *Regal Plum Pud- ding* is a spicy cakelike mixture of candied fruits, nuts, and plumped raisins. Spoon on the foamy sauce before serving for a "snowcapped" holiday treat.

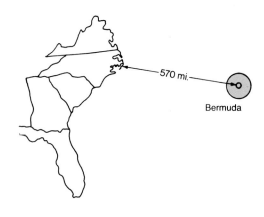

Five years after the founding of Jamestown, a colony was formed on Bermuda. It built a thriving commerce with the island's ambergris, which was used to make medicine and perfume. Eventually a lively trade developed with Virginia, as well as a hearty competition for monetary backing from England. The tall ships were soon carrying more than trade goods as cooks in both colonies began swapping recipes. Cucumber-Stuffed Red Snapper and Pumpkin-Corned-Beef Dinner are both part of our legacy from Bermuda.

Pumpkin-Corned Beef Dinner

In 7½-quart Dutch oven barely cover one 3- to 4-pound corned beef brisket with water. Add ½ cup chopped onion; 2 cloves garlic, minced; 2 bay leaves; ½ teaspoon dried thyme, crushed; and ½ teaspoon whole black pepper. Simmer, covered, till meat is almost tender, about 2½ hours. Skim off fat. Add 6 medium potatoes, peeled, and 2 pounds pumpkin *or* squash, cut into 6 portions. Cover; cook till vegetables are tender, 30 to 35 minutes. Remove meat and vegetables to platter; keep warm. Strain liquid, reserving 1½ cups. Blend ½ cup cold water slowly into ¼ cup all-purpose flour. Add to cooking liquid. Cook and stir till thick and bubbly. Serve over meat and vegetables. Serves 6.

Cucumber-Stuffed Red Snapper

1 1½-pound fresh *or* frozen dressed red snapper
2 tablespoons chopped onion
2 tablespoons butter
3 cups dry bread cubes
1 cucumber, peeled, seeded, and chopped (1 cup)
2 tablespoons chopped green pepper
1 tablespoon snipped parsley
¼ teaspoon grated lemon peel
¼ teaspoon dried thyme, crushed
¼ teaspoon ground sage
1 tablespoon butter, melted
1 tablespoon lemon juice

Thaw frozen fish. Cook onion in 2 tablespoons butter. In a large bowl combine cooked onion, bread cubes, cucumber, green pepper, parsley, lemon peel, thyme, sage, ¼ teaspoon salt, and dash pepper. Sprinkle cavity of fish with salt and pepper. Place in well-greased shallow baking pan. Stuff fish with bread mixture. Brush with melted butter; drizzle with lemon juice. Cover pan with foil. Bake at 350° till fish flakes easily when tested with a fork, 45 to 60 minutes. Transfer fish to serving platter. Makes 3 or 4 servings.

Note: Bake any extra stuffing in 1-quart casserole, covered, till heated through, about 30 minutes, stirring occasionally. Stir just before serving.

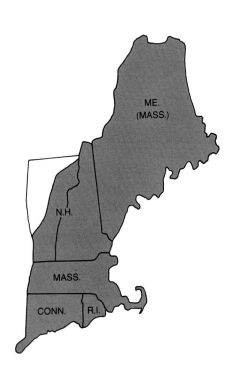

New England Colonies: Cod and Cranberries

After Jamestown, the next permanent settlement on the East Coast was that of the Pilgrims, in Plymouth, in 1620. A rhyme said to have been composed during the early years of the Plymouth Colony ran,

> *We have pumpkins at morning and pumpkins at noon.*
> *If it were not for pumpkins we should be undoon.*

If "undoon" means starving or dead, the rhymester was correct. Those who founded Plymouth arrived in December, and had it not been for food that they either received as gifts from the Indians or stole from them, they would all surely have died. Even so, more than half of them did die, probably as a result of scurvy and malnutrition.

Nevertheless other settlers followed, some to Plymouth and others to found new towns along the Massachusetts coast. In 1630 Boston was founded by a group of seven hundred, led by John Winthrop. Wisely,

they timed their arrival for the planting season. John Winthrop wrote in his journal "And there came a smell off the Shore like the Smell of a Garden."[22] New England, with its rocky soil and harsh winters, was not an easy garden to tend, and the colonists had to learn how to extract the plenty from the land, like the iron from the ore.

W heat was hard to grow in New England until farmers learned to understand the vagaries of soil and climate. Rye did well. A flour of rye and cornmeal was often used for bread. And if there were crusts left over, they went into a pudding rather uncompromisingly called must-go-down, in which the crusts were boiled with molasses and milk.

Throughout the colonial period, the New England frontier pushed north into Maine and New Hampshire and west through inland Massachusetts and Connecticut to the borders of New York. Where transportation was available, farmers were able to operate on a commercial basis. For example, farmers on the Connecticut River bred horses and raised apples and potatoes. These were shipped downriver to the coast and thence to the West Indies. The ever-growing seaport towns—Newport, Boston, Salem, and others—provided an eager market for outlying farms. However, the majority of New England farms were isolated and therefore largely self-subsisting.

Farming and housekeeping were not easy for families of "the first frontier." The long winters offered but one advantage: housewives could quick-freeze pies and keep them all winter. Also dried fruit would last for months and apples ripened beautifully in the fall air.

From the Indians, the settlers learned to slow-bake a pot of sweetened beans. The Indians buried their bean pots in the embers of a fire or in a preheated hole beneath it; the Puritan housewife placed hers in a brick oven either at home or at the town bakery on Saturday and left it overnight.

A New Englander, Samuel Adams, organized one of the earliest American protests, the Boston Tea Party. He was known as a rabble-rouser and spurred the political resentments of the colonists with words such as: "A colonist cannot make a button, a horseshoe, nor a hobnail but some sooty ironmonger or respectable buttonmaker of Britain shall bawl and squall that his honor's worship is most egregiously maltreated, injured, cheated and robbed by the rascally American republicans."[23] His plan for a raid on a ship with a cargo of tea in Boston harbor captured the imagination of 50 colonists. These men dressed in feathers and smeared with red ocher, dumped more than 300 chests of tea belonging to the East India Company into the water.

Beans, like seafood, seem synonymous with New England. The baked beans of the early colonists, were a type of lima bean they called a scarlet runner. The pea or navy bean, which we now regard as the real New England bean came from the Pacific shores at the time of the California Gold Rush. These could last the long journey around the South American continent in the holds of the clipper ships.

Thus, by not cooking on the Sabbath, she avoided breaking the second Commandment. Even after molasses became cheap and plentiful, some women preferred the Indian way of sweetening beans with maple sugar or syrup.

Cookery distinctive of New England usually meant ingenious adaptations of basic Indian foods: corn bread, cornmeal mush, johnnycakes, Indian pudding, hasty pudding, green-corn pudding, and other corn dishes; fish chowders, boiled lobster, steamed clams; and blueberry grunt or slump.

Few of the New England colonists had had experience in deep-sea, commercial fishing; but they were a practical people and when they saw the abundance of fish in their coastal waters they heard the Lord say, "Fish!" Their religion taught them that any decent occupation is a "calling"— meaning that is, God has called one to it — and therefore must be honorable and good. In the case of fishing, it was also very profitable. The Bay Colony government offered special tax benefits and exemption from civic duties to men who would help build a fishing industry, and before long New Englanders were growing rich by exporting salted cod and herring.

As New England seaports prospered, they began to import exotic foods. Ships from the West Indies brought pineapples, bananas, oranges, lemons, and live sea turtles. A well-to-do family in Boston might buy one of their three-hundred-pound turtles and invite friends for a "turtle frolic." On the whole, however, the Puritan ethic still prevailed and wasteful ostentation was frowned on. Abigail Adams is said to have served a plain cornmeal pudding as a first course for dinner. It toned down appetites and prevented the rest of the food from disappearing too quickly.

New England Boiled Dinner *(see photo, pages 2-3)*

A dinner of meat and vegetables boiled together became a tradition in New England because it "cooked itself." Colonial women would let the meat and vegetables simmer all day while performing other tasks.

1 3- to 4-pound corned beef brisket
4 ounces salt pork
6 small onions
4 medium potatoes, peeled and quartered
4 medium carrots, quartered

3 medium parsnips, peeled and cut in chunks
2 medium rutabagas, peeled and cubed
1 small cabbage, cored and cut into wedges

Place brisket in large Dutch oven; add water to cover. Add salt pork. Bring to boiling; reduce heat. Simmer till tender, 2½ hours. Remove meat and salt pork. Add all vegetables *except* cabbage. Cover and cook 15 minutes; add cabbage. Cover; cook till cabbage is tender, 15 to 20 minutes. Add corned beef; heat through. Season to taste. Makes 6 to 8 servings.

Chicken in Herb Sauce

The pilgrims sacrificed many comforts to come to the New World— but not their herbs. As soon as possible they planted herb gardens with seeds brought from home. Herbs made bland meals tasty and disguised meat that wasn't quite fresh. Sage, savory, dill, parsley, and thyme were used for seasoning, lavender, hyssop, and angelica were used for medicines and fragrances.

½ cup chopped celery
¼ cup butter
¼ cup all-purpose flour
1 teaspoon snipped chives
¾ teaspoon dried rosemary, crushed
¼ teaspoon dried chervil, crushed

¼ teaspoon dried tarragon, crushed
1 cup milk
1 cup chicken broth
2 cups cubed cooked chicken
• • •
Toast points *or* frozen patty shells, baked

Cook celery in butter till tender, about 10 minutes. Stir in flour, chives, rosemary, chervil, and tarragon. Add milk and chicken broth. Cook and stir till thickened and bubbly. Stir in chicken. Season to taste with salt and pepper. Heat through. Serve on toast or in patty shells. Serves 4.

New England Succotash

1 pound dry navy beans
1 3-pound ready-to-cook
    broiler-fryer chicken,
    cut up
1 2½-pound corned beef
    brisket
4 ounces salt pork
3 cups sliced potatoes
1 cup chopped turnip

1 cup chopped carrot
1 medium onion, sliced
½ teaspoon dried thyme,
    crushed
2 14½-ounce cans golden
    hominy, drained
Salt
Pepper

Rinse beans. Place in a large kettle with 4 cups water. Bring to boiling; boil 2 minutes. Cover and let stand 1 hour. (Or, mix beans and water and let stand overnight.) Meanwhile in a covered saucepan, cook chicken in 4 cups water over low heat till tender, 35 to 40 minutes. Drain chicken, reserving broth. Cool chicken; skin and bone, refrigerate. Add corned beef, salt pork, and reserved chicken broth to beans. Cover and simmer 1 hour. Add potatoes, turnip, carrot, onion, and thyme. Cover and simmer 1 hour more. Remove corned beef and salt pork. Discard salt pork. Mash beans slightly. Dice corned beef; return to bean mixture. Add chicken and hominy. Season with salt and pepper. Simmer about 15 minutes more. Makes 10 servings.

The New Englanders were quick to learn from the Indians and one dish they speedily adopted was New England Succotash. This recipe differs from the more conventional Succotash (see recipe, page 28) in that it combines corn, beans, chicken, beef, and salt pork into a hearty stew. Today, it is served to celebrate Forefathers Day on December 21 in Plymouth, Massachusetts.

Steamed Clams *(see photo, pages 2-3)*

24 soft-shelled clams, in
    the shells
3 gallons cold water

1 cup salt
1 cup hot water
Butter, melted

Thoroughly wash clams. In a large kettle combine *1 gallon* of the cold water and ⅓ *cup* of the salt. Place clams in salt-water mixture and let stand 15 minutes. Rinse well. Repeat salt-water soaking and rinsing twice more. Place clams on a rack in the kettle with the hot water. Cover tightly and steam just till shells open, about 5 minutes. Discard any clams that do not open. Loosen clams from shells; serve with butter. Makes 4 servings.

Cod Cakes *(see photo, pages 2-3)*

8 ounces salt cod
• • •
3 cups diced potatoes
1 beaten egg
2 tablespoons butter

⅛ teaspoon pepper
¾ cup finely crushed
    saltine crackers (21
    crackers)
Fat for frying

Soak salt cod in water to cover for 12 hours, changing water once. Drain well. Dice cod. Cook potatoes and cod, covered, in large amount of boiling water about 15 minutes; drain. Beat cod and potatoes with electric mixer till well mashed. Add egg, butter, and pepper; beat well. Using ¼ cup cod mixture for each, shape into 2½- to 3-inch cakes, about ½ inch thick. Coat with crackers. Fry, a few at a time, in deep hot fat (375°) for 2 minutes; turn and fry till golden, about 2 minutes more. Makes 12 cakes.

The sea and its food have always been a part of New Englanders' life-style. Who else could invent the social and culinary joys of the clambake? Colonists cooked theirs in a rock-lined pit on the beach. A roaring fire was built atop the rocks and allowed to burn till the rocks were red hot. Then the ashes were raked aside and a layer of wet rockweed was tossed atop the hot rocks. The food was added and another layer of rockweed. The colonists then used green branches to cover everything. A wide range of seafood was prepared this way including hard- and soft-shell clams, lobsters, oysters, and snails. The modern clambake is done much the same way except a canvas tarpaulin is used in place of green branches, and chicken, corn, potatoes, frankfurters, and fish have been added to the menu.

Boiled Lobster

Carefully select active, live lobsters. Plunge lobsters into enough boiling salted water to cover. Return to boiling; reduce heat and simmer 20 minutes. Remove lobsters at once. Place on their backs and with a sharp knife, cut each lobster in half lengthwise. Remove the black vein that runs to tip of tail. Discard all organs in body section near head except red coral roe (in females only) and brownish-green liver. Crack claws. Serve with cups of melted butter. Allow 1 to 1½ pounds lobster per serving.

New England lobsters are the Maine- or true lobster. Unlike the spiny or rock lobster, they have large front pincers. The colonists fished for the Maine lobster off the northern Atlantic coast.

New England Clam Chowder

1 pint shucked clams *or*
  2 7½-ounce cans minced
   clams
4 ounces salt pork, minced

• • •

4 cups diced potatoes
1½ cups water

½ cup chopped onion
2 cups milk
1 cup light cream
3 tablespoons all-purpose
  flour
1½ teaspoons salt
Dash pepper

Dice clams (except canned clams) and set aside. Strain clam liquid, reserving ½ cup. In large saucepan fry salt pork till crisp. Remove bits of pork; set aside. To drippings in pan add reserved clam liquid, potatoes, water, and onion. Cook, covered, till potatoes are tender, 15 to 20 minutes. Stir in clams, 1¾ *cups* of the milk, and the cream. Slowly blend remaining milk into flour; then stir into chowder. Cook and stir till boiling. Add the salt and pepper. Sprinkle reserved salt pork bits atop. Makes 6 servings.

New England Clam Chowder has been on New England tables since colonial times. This hearty soup mixes clams and a cream sauce. It wasn't until later that tomatoes and clams were combined for Manhattan Clam Chowder *(see recipe, page 156), and there has been a battle raging between advocates of both types ever since. Tradition has it that Rhode Island and Connecticut households prefer Manhattan chowder while the rest of New England is devoted to the creamy type.*

White Pease Soup *(see photo, page 64)*

1 pound dry navy beans
10 cups cold water
1 pound beef stew meat, cut
  in cubes
1 cup chopped onion *or*
  leeks
1 cup sliced carrot
1 large parsnip, peeled
  and sliced
1 large turnip, peeled
  and cubed

2 slices bacon, cut up
1 tablespoon salt
½ teaspoon dried savory,
  crushed
½ teaspoon pepper
¼ teaspoon ground allspice
2 cups shredded lettuce
3 slices bacon, crisp-
  cooked and crumbled
  (optional)
Croutons (optional)

Rinse beans. Add water; bring to boiling. Boil 2 minutes. Cover; let stand 1 hour. (*Or* mix beans and water; let stand overnight.) Do not drain. Add beef, onion, carrot, parsnip, turnip, raw bacon, salt, savory, pepper, and allspice. Bring to boil; reduce heat. Cover and simmer till meat and beans are tender, about 2½ hours. Remove meat and mash vegetables, if desired; return meat to soup. Season to taste with salt and pepper. Stir in lettuce; heat through. Serve soup with crumbled bacon or croutons. Serves 8.

Many of the early colonists kept diaries as faithfully as Mr. Pepys—and as detailed. The daybook, as it was called, recorded daily events as well as such information as tax records, lists of household furnishings, and treasured family recipes. White Pease Soup *is one of many recipes found in family daybooks.*

Pumpkin Bread

3¼ to 3½ cups all-purpose
  flour
2 packages active dry yeast
¼ teaspoon ground ginger
¼ teaspoon ground nutmeg
¼ teaspoon ground cloves
¾ cup milk

¼ cup packed brown sugar
2 tablespoons butter
1½ teaspoons salt
½ cup cooked mashed
  pumpkin
¾ cup raisins

In large mixing bowl thoroughly combine 1½ *cups* of the flour, yeast, and spices. In saucepan heat milk, brown sugar, butter, and salt just till warm (115-120°), stirring constantly. Add to dry mixture in mixing bowl; add pumpkin. Beat at low speed of electric mixer for ½ minute, scraping sides of bowl constantly. Beat 3 minutes at high speed. By hand stir in raisins and enough of the remaining flour to make a moderately stiff dough. Turn out onto lightly floured surface and knead till smooth and elastic (5 to 8 minutes). Shape into ball. Place in lightly greased bowl, turning once. Cover and let rise in warm place till double (about 1 hour). Punch down; cover and let rest 10 minutes. Shape into loaf; place in greased 8½x4½x 2½-inch loaf pan. Cover; let rise till double (about 30 minutes). Bake at 375° for 35 to 40 minutes. Remove from pan; cool. Makes 1.

Pumpkin has been described as the "fruit which the Lord fed his people with till corn and cattle increased." [24] *Pumpkin was indeed a staple to New Englanders as it was to people in all the colonies. The most common way to preserve pumpkins was drying. Pumpkins to be preserved were sliced and placed on racks in the sun or else hung from a string on beams or rafters till dry. When the fruit was to be used, it was usually rehydrated by boiling in water.*

New Englanders soon learned to make profits as well as dinners from the abundant fish in their coastal waters. Early commercial fishing was done from the deck of a schooner using "handliners" with two or three hooks. As the fish were caught, they were salted in barrels, then dried.

Yankee Red-Flannel Hash *(see photo, pages 2-3)*

⅓ cup finely chopped onion
¼ cup butter
3 cups diced cooked
    potatoes
1 16-ounce can diced
    beets, drained

1½ cups diced cooked
    corned beef
⅓ cup milk
½ teaspoon salt
1 or 2 drops bottled hot
    pepper sauce

In skillet cook onion in butter till tender. Toss with potatoes, beets, corned beef, milk, salt, and pepper sauce; spread evenly in skillet. Cover; cook over medium heat till brown and crusty. Makes 4 servings.

Savory Quail

8 4- to 6-ounce ready-to-
    cook quail
¼ cup all-purpose flour
1 teaspoon salt
¼ cup butter

½ cup dry white wine
2 tablespoons sliced green
    onion with tops
½ cup light cream
2 egg yolks

Tie legs of each quail together with string. In bag mix flour, salt, and ⅛ teaspoon pepper. Add quail 2 or 3 at a time; shake well to coat. In skillet brown quail in butter. Add wine and onion. Cover and simmer till birds are tender, 25 to 30 minutes. Remove quail to warm platter; keep warm. Reserve ½ cup pan juices in skillet. Beat cream with egg yolks, ¼ teaspoon salt, and dash pepper; slowly stir into pan juices. Cook and stir till thickened. *(Do not boil.)* Serve sauce over quail. Makes 4 servings.

Game of all kinds was plentiful in New England, even coot according to this recipe. "Place the bird in a kettle of water with a red building brick....Parboil the coot and brick together for 3 hours. Pour off water, fill the kettle and again parboil for 3 hours...throw off the water, refill the kettle and...let the coot and brick simmer together overnight...throw away the coot and eat the brick."[25]

Rye and Indian Bread *(see photo, page 64)*

(see photo, page 64)

Rye and Indian Bread *was often baked in colonial homes in a black Dutch oven with coals piled on the lid so that heat came from all directions. Its name comes from the fact that it features the unusual combination of rye flour and what used to be called Indian meal.*

2 cups all-purpose flour
¾ cup cornmeal
1 package active dry yeast

1 cup milk
¼ cup molasses
¾ cup rye flour

In mixing bowl mix *1½ cups* of the all-purpose flour, cornmeal, and yeast. In a saucepan heat milk, molasses, ½ cup water, and 1 teaspoon salt till just warm (115-120°); add to flour mixture in bowl. Beat at low speed of electric mixer for ½ minute, scraping sides of bowl constantly. Beat at high speed 3 minutes more. Stir in rye flour and remaining ½ cup all-purpose flour. Cover; let rise in warm place till almost double (about 1 hour). Punch down; place in a greased 1½-quart casserole. Cover; let rise till almost double (about 45 minutes). Bake, uncovered, at 325° for 30 minutes; cover top of bread with foil. Continue baking 20 minutes more. Makes 1 loaf.

Anadama Bread

A New England fisherman with a lazy wife is credited with having invented Anadama Bread. *As the story goes he had to do much of his own cooking because his wife would not. Thus, says the story, he named the bread he created "Anna, damn her."*

4½ to 4¾ cups all-purpose flour
2 packages active dry yeast
2 cups cold water
1 cup cornmeal
½ cup molasses

⅓ cup lard
1 tablespoon salt
2 eggs
2 tablespoons butter, melted

In large mixing bowl mix *1 cup* of the flour and yeast. In saucepan mix water and cornmeal. Cook and stir till thickened and bubbly. Remove from heat; stir in molasses, lard, and salt. Cool till just warm (115-120°). Add to flour mixture; add eggs. Beat at low speed of electric mixer for ½ minute, scraping sides of bowl. Beat 3 minutes at high speed. By hand, stir in enough remaining flour to make a moderately stiff dough. Turn out on lightly floured surface; knead till smooth (8 to 10 minutes). Place in greased bowl, turning once to grease surface. Cover and let rise till double (about 1 hour). Punch dough down; divide in half. Cover and let rest 10 minutes. Shape in two loaves and place in two greased 8½x4½x2½-inch loaf pans. Cover; let rise till almost double (about 45 minutes). Brush with butter. Bake at 375° for 20 minutes; cover with foil. Bake 20 minutes longer. Makes 2 loaves.

New England Whole Wheat Bread

3 cups all-purpose flour
2 packages active dry yeast
2 cups water
¼ cup butter
3 tablespoons packed brown sugar

3 tablespoons honey
2 teaspoons salt
• • •
2¾ to 3 cups whole wheat flour

In large mixing bowl combine the all-purpose flour and the active dry yeast. In saucepan heat water, butter, brown sugar, honey, and salt just till warm (115-120°), stirring constantly. Add to dry mixture in mixing bowl. Beat at low speed of electric mixer for ½ minute, scraping sides of bowl constantly. Beat 3 minutes at high speed. By hand, stir in enough of the whole wheat flour to make a moderately stiff dough. Turn out onto a lightly floured surface and knead till smooth and elastic (about 8 minutes). Shape into a ball. Place dough in a lightly greased bowl, turning once to grease surface. Cover and let rise in a warm place until double (about 1 hour). Punch dough down; turn out onto lightly floured surface. Divide in half; cover and let rest 10 minutes. Shape dough into two loaves and place in two greased 8½x4½x2½-inch loaf pans. Cover dough and let rise in a warm place till almost double (about 35 to 45 minutes). Bake at 375° for 20 minutes. Cover with foil and bake till bread tests done, 15 to 20 minutes more. Remove loaves from pans and cool on wire racks. Makes 2 loaves.

Maple Candied Sweet Potatoes

3 pounds sweet potatoes
½ cup maple syrup *or*
　maple-flavored syrup

½ cup packed brown sugar
2 tablespoons butter
½ teaspoon salt

Cook sweet potatoes in boiling salted water till tender, 30 to 40 minutes; drain and peel. Cut sweet potatoes into 1-inch slices. In a saucepan combine maple or maple-flavored syrup, brown sugar, butter, and salt. Bring to boiling; simmer 5 minutes. Place potatoes in 11x7½x1½-inch baking pan. Spoon syrup mixture over potato slices to coat. Bake, uncovered, at 350° for 30 minutes, basting potatoes frequently. Makes 8 to 10 servings.

Maple syrup is another of New England's natural products that the colonists learned to use extensively. In many areas, it was often the only type of sweetening available. Two common uses for maple syrup were to dress up sweet potatoes and to add flavor to beans.

Over the years quite a controversy has arisen in New England around whether baked beans are best made with brown sugar and maple syrup or with molasses (see recipe, page 30). To this day no one seems able or willing to settle the question.

Baked Beans with Maple Syrup

1½ pounds dry navy beans
　(3¾ cups)
4 ounces salt pork, cubed
½ cup chopped onion

½ cup packed brown sugar
½ cup maple syrup
1 teaspoon salt
1 teaspoon dry mustard

In kettle rinse beans; add 12 cups cold water. Bring to boiling; simmer 2 minutes. Remove from heat. Cover; let stand 1 hour. (*Or*, add beans to water and let stand overnight.) Bring beans and water to boiling; simmer till beans are tender, about 40 minutes. Drain, reserving liquid. In 3-quart casserole or bean pot, mix beans, pork, onion, sugar, maple syrup, salt, mustard, and 1½ cups reserved bean liquid. Cover; bake at 300° about 2½ hours. Stir occasionally. Add more reserved liquid, if needed. Makes 8 servings.

Creamed Onions

3 cups sliced onion
¼ cup butter, melted
2 tablespoons all-purpose
　flour

1 teaspoon salt
¼ teaspoon dried thyme,
　crushed
1 cup milk

Cook onion, covered, in a large amount of boiling salted water till tender, 20 to 25 minutes. Drain. In saucepan mix butter, flour, salt, thyme, and dash pepper. Blend in milk; cook, stirring constantly, till thickened and bubbly. Stir in onion slices. Heat through. Makes 6 to 8 servings.

Scootin'-'Long-the-Shore

4 cups sliced potatoes
1 cup sliced onion

3 tablespoons bacon
　drippings

Mix potatoes and onion; season with salt and pepper. In skillet fry, covered, in drippings for 10 minutes. Uncover; turn and cook potatoes on the other side 5 to 10 minutes, loosening occasionally. Makes 6 to 8 servings.

Cape Cod fishermen have long prepared this simple potato and onion dish while at work. As a result it is always eaten while "scootin'-'long-the-shore." In Maine a very similar dish is called "very poor man's dinner."

Glazed Carrots

2 pounds carrots
⅓ cup sugar
6 tablespoons butter

½ teaspoon ground cinnamon
　or ¾ teaspoon ground
　ginger

Peel carrots and cut in julienne strips. Cook, covered, in small amount of boiling salted water till just tender, 6 to 8 minutes. Drain well. Mix sugar, butter, and cinnamon or ginger in large skillet. Cook and stir till well blended. Add carrots; cook over low heat, stirring often, till carrots are shiny and well glazed. Garnish with parsley, if desired. Makes 8 servings.

Molasses Doughnuts

In large mixing bowl beat together ½ cup molasses, ¼ cup sugar, and ¼ cup lard. Add 1 egg; beat till blended. Stir together 3½ cups all-purpose flour, 1 teaspoon baking soda, 1 teaspoon salt, ½ teaspoon ground cinnamon, and ½ teaspoon ground nutmeg. Add flour mixture and ¾ cup buttermilk alternately to sugar mixture, beating till just blended after each addition. Cover and chill about 2 hours. Roll dough out on lightly floured surface to ⅜-inch thickness. Cut with floured doughnut cutter. Fry in deep hot fat (375°) till golden, turning once, about 1 minute per side. Drain on paper toweling. Roll in granulated sugar. Makes about 2 dozen.

Pictured opposite: Colonial cooking methods included baking in the beehive oven or coal-covered Dutch oven and cooking in the black pot or long-handled spider. Shown from oven in far back: Rye and Indian Bread, Muster Day Gingerbread, Baked Glazed Squash, Hoe Cakes, and White Pease Soup. (See index for pages.)

Muster Day Gingerbread

⅓ cup lard
½ cup packed brown sugar
½ cup molasses
1 egg
2 cups all-purpose flour

1 teaspoon baking soda
¾ teaspoon ground ginger
¾ teaspoon ground cinnamon
¼ teaspoon ground cloves
½ cup boiling water

Cream lard and sugar till light. Add molasses and egg; beat well. Stir together flour, soda, spices, and ½ teaspoon salt. Add to creamed mixture alternately with boiling water; beat after each addition. Pour into greased and floured 8½x4½x2½-inch loaf pan. Bake at 350° till done, about 50 minutes. Cool 10 minutes. Remove from pan; cool. Wrap; store overnight.

On muster days all the men came to town for militia training. The drills took only a short time and the rest of the day was spent celebrating. The day wasn't complete unless the men had lots of rum and molasses gingerbread. The holiday has vanished with many others, but, fortunately, Muster Day Gingerbread remains.

Hartford Election Cake

2¾ cups all-purpose flour
1 package active dry yeast
¼ teaspoon salt
¼ teaspoon ground nutmeg
1 cup milk

⅓ cup granulated sugar
¼ cup packed brown sugar
¼ cup butter
1 egg
1 cup raisins

In large mixing bowl combine *1 cup* of the flour, yeast, salt, and nutmeg. In a saucepan heat milk, granulated sugar, brown sugar, and butter just till warm (115-120°), stirring constantly. Add to dry mixture in bowl. Add egg; beat at low speed of electric mixer for ½ minute, scraping sides of bowl constantly. Beat 3 minutes at high speed. By hand stir in remaining flour and raisins. Cover; let rise in warm place till double (about 1½ hours). Stir dough down. Spoon into greased 9x5x3-inch loaf pan. Let rise till nearly double (about 1 hour). Bake at 350° for 40 minutes. Makes 1 loaf.

In New England, town meetings were held in March and often lasted all day. During the noon recess, the colonists would go to the village store to eat March Meetin' or 'Lection Cake. Later, in Hartford, Connecticut, these cakes were eaten to celebrate an election victory or while awaiting the returns.

Scripture Cake

½ cup butter
¾ cup molasses
2 cups all-purpose flour
½ teaspoon baking soda
½ teaspoon ground cinnamon
¼ teaspoon ground cloves
⅛ teaspoon ground ginger

3 beaten eggs
½ cup buttermilk
⅓ cup honey
1 cup raisins
1 cup chopped dried figs
½ cup chopped almonds
½ cup wine *or* orange juice

In large mixing bowl cream butter till light; blend in molasses. Stir together flour, baking soda, cinnamon, cloves, ginger, and dash salt. Combine eggs, buttermilk, and honey. Add egg mixture and dry ingredients alternately to creamed mixture. Mix well. Stir in raisins, figs, and almonds. Turn mixture into greased and floured 9x5x3-inch loaf pan. Bake at 325° for 40 minutes. Loosely cover with foil. Bake 50 minutes more. Let cool in pan 10 minutes, remove from pan. Cool on rack; brush all sides with wine or orange juice. Wrap in foil and store 1 to 2 days in refrigerator. Makes 1.

You had to "know your Scripture" to bake the colonists' Scripture Cake. The recipe makes baking like a treasure hunt: Cream ½ cup Judges 5:25 till light; blend in ¾ cup Jeremiah 6:20. Stir together 2 cups I Kings 4:22; ½ teaspoon Amos 4:5; dash Leviticus 2:13; and II Chronicles 9:9. Mix 3 Jeremiah 17:11; ½ cup Judges 4:19; and ⅓ cup I Samuel 14:25....Stir in 1 cup I Samuel 30:12; 1 cup Nahum 3:12 and ½ cup Numbers 17:8.... Bake at 325° for 40 minutes...brush all sides with Proverbs 31:6....

Pine Tree Shillings

½ cup light molasses
¼ cup packed brown sugar
¼ cup lard
1½ cups all-purpose flour

½ teaspoon ground cinnamon
¼ teaspoon baking soda
¼ teaspoon salt
¼ teaspoon ground ginger

Cream together molasses, brown sugar, and lard. Stir together flour, cinnamon, baking soda, salt, and ginger. Blend into creamed mixture. Divide into 6 portions. On lightly floured surface shape into six 10-inch long rolls. Wrap; chill several hours. Slice into pieces a little more than ¼-inch thick. Place on greased cookie sheet. Press each cookie with thumb till about ⅛ inch thick. Bake at 350° for 5 to 8 minutes. Makes 16 dozen.

Because the English government would not allow its colonies the right to mint coins, New Englanders took matters into their own hands and the Massachusetts Bay Colony illegally began minting operations. In 1652, a coin was struck one side of which bore the image of a tree. Often a pine, but sometimes an oak or a willow. These coins have become known as pine tree shillings. The cookies of that name are the size of a shilling. Was it defiance or a sense of humor that made colonists decorate the cookie by pressing the coin into the dough?

Snickerdoodles

2 cups sugar
1 cup butter, softened
2 eggs
¼ cup milk
1 teaspoon vanilla

3¾ cups all-purpose flour
½ teaspoon baking soda
½ teaspoon cream of
tartar
1 cup chopped nuts

In mixing bowl cream sugar and butter till light. Add eggs, one at a time, beating well after each. Blend in milk and vanilla. Stir together flour, baking soda, cream of tartar, and ½ teaspoon salt; stir into creamed mixture. Blend in chopped nuts. Form dough into 1-inch balls. Place balls 2 inches apart on greased cookie sheet. Lightly flatten balls with sugared bottom of tumbler. Bake at 375° till done, 10 to 12 minutes. Makes about 8 dozen.

Joe Froggers

4 cups all-purpose flour
1½ teaspoons ground ginger
½ teaspoon ground cloves
½ teaspoon ground nutmeg
¼ teaspoon ground allspice

2 tablespoons rum
1 cup dark molasses
1 teaspoon baking soda
1 cup sugar
½ cup butter

Stir together flour, ginger, cloves, nutmeg, allspice, and 1½ teaspoons salt. Mix rum and ⅓ cup water. Combine molasses and soda. Cream sugar and butter; add *half* the dry ingredients and *half* the water mixture, then *half* the molasses mixture, blending well after each addition. Repeat. Chill dough for several hours or overnight. On well-floured surface, roll dough ¼ inch thick; cut with a 4-inch cutter or 1-pound coffee can. Bake on greased cookie sheet at 375° for 10 to 12 minutes. (Watch carefully so cookies don't burn.) Let stand a few minutes; then remove from cookie sheet. Makes 18.

An old black, Uncle Joe, who lived on the edge of a frog pond in Marblehead, Massachusetts, made the best molasses cookies in town. They were called Joe Froggers *because they were as large as lily pads and as dark as the frogs in the pond. Fishermen found they would keep on long sea voyages and began trading rum for Uncle Joe's cookies. Today these big molasses cookies will keep as well in the cookie jar as they did in the fishermen's sea chests.*

Brandy Snaps

½ cup packed brown sugar
6 tablespoons butter,
melted
¼ cup molasses

1 tablespoon brandy
¾ cup all-purpose flour
½ teaspoon ground ginger
½ teaspoon ground nutmeg

Combine brown sugar, butter, molasses, and brandy; mix well. Stir together flour, ginger, nutmeg, and ⅛ teaspoon salt. Stir into butter mixture. Drop batter by level teaspoonfuls 4 inches apart onto an ungreased cookie sheet. Bake at 350° for 5 to 6 minutes. (Bake only 3 at a time.) Let cool *2 minutes* on cookie sheet; remove with wide spatula. *Immediately* roll each cookie to form a cone. (Reheat in oven for about 30 seconds if cookies harden before they are rolled.) Cool completely; store in airtight container. Fill with sweetened whipped cream, if desired before serving. Makes 60.

Homemade Mincemeat Pie

1 pound beef stew meat
4 pounds apples
4 ounces suet
1 15-ounce package raisins
2½ cups sugar
2½ cups water
2 cups dried currants
½ cup chopped mixed candied
    fruits and peels
1 teaspoon grated orange
    peel

1 cup orange juice
1 teaspoon grated lemon
    peel
¼ cup lemon juice
1 teaspoon salt
½ teaspoon ground nutmeg
¼ teaspoon ground mace
• • •
Pastry for 2-crust 9-inch
    pie (see recipe,
    page 351)

Cover beef with water; simmer, covered, till tender, about 2 hours. Drain; cool. Peel, core, and cut up apples. Put beef, apples, and suet through coarse blade of food grinder. In kettle combine all ingredients *except* pastry.

Cover; simmer 1 hour. Stir often. Line 9-inch pie plate with pastry; fill with *3 cups* mincemeat. Adjust top crust. Seal; cut slits. Bake at 400° for 35 to 40 minutes. Freeze remaining mincemeat in 3-cup portions. Makes 12 cups.

Homemade pies were a favorite in most colonial households. In the fall New England housewives often prepared great numbers of pies when fruit was plentiful and froze the pies in an outdoor shed. Before a pie was served, it was thawed in the warming cupboard above the fireplace.

Cranberry-Nut Pudding

1¼ cups fresh cranberries
¼ cup packed brown sugar
¼ cup chopped walnuts
1 egg

½ cup granulated sugar
½ cup all-purpose flour
⅓ cup butter, melted
    Vanilla ice cream

Spread cranberries in a buttered 9-inch pie plate. Sprinkle with brown sugar and nuts. Beat egg till thick; slowly add granulated sugar, beating till

blended. Add flour and butter; beat well. Pour over cranberries. Bake at 325° for 45 minutes. Cut in wedges. Serve warm with ice cream. Serves 6.

The legendary history of Cape Cod's cranberry bogs goes something like this. During an argument over who was the most powerful, an Indian medicine man cast a spell and mired the Reverend Richard Bourne in quicksand. In order to settle their differences, the two men then agreed to a 15-day marathon battle of wits. Unable to move, the Reverend Bourne was kept alive by a white dove which fed him a succulent berry from time to time. The medicine man could not cast a spell on the dove, and finally he fell to the ground, exhausted from his own lack of food and water. The spell on the Reverend Bourne was released. In the course of these events, one of those berries fell to the ground and took root—thus we have wild cranberry bogs.

Squash Pie

2 cups mashed cooked
    Hubbard squash
½ cup sugar
1 tablespoon butter,
    melted
½ teaspoon ground cinnamon
¼ teaspoon ground ginger

⅛ teaspoon ground nutmeg
2 slightly beaten eggs
1¾ cups milk
1 unbaked 9-inch pastry
    shell with edges
    crimped high (see
    recipe, page 351)

Combine squash, sugar, butter, spices, and ½ teaspoon salt. Stir in eggs and milk. Pour into pastry shell. Bake at

400° till knife inserted off-center comes out clean, about 50 minutes. (Filling may seem soft.) Cool.

Applejack Pie

Pastry for 2-crust 9-
    inch pie (see recipe,
    page 351)
• • •
½ cup packed brown sugar
¼ cup granulated sugar
1 tablespoon cornstarch

¼ teaspoon ground nutmeg
⅛ teaspoon salt
¼ cup applejack (apple
    brandy)
6 tart apples, peeled,
    cored, and sliced
3 tablespoons butter

Line 9-inch pie plate with pastry. Combine brown sugar, granulated sugar, cornstarch, nutmeg, and salt. Stir in applejack and apples. Turn into pastry-

lined pie plate. Dot with butter. Adjust top crust and cut slits for escape of steam; seal. Bake at 400° till golden, 45 to 50 minutes.

Applejack is a legacy of colonial times. Its potency has made it the subject of many tall tales, including this modern one: A farmer was carrying some applejack "…and was caught on a trestle with trains approaching from both directions. In his fright he dropped the jug, which exploded, blew up the bridge, wrecked both trains, and killed all the fish in the river…."[26]

Blueberry Slump

2 cups fresh *or* frozen
   blueberries
1 cup water
½ cup sugar
¾ cup all-purpose flour

¼ cup sugar
½ teaspoon baking soda
¼ teaspoon salt
½ cup butter
2 tablespoons buttermilk

In a 3-quart saucepan mix blueberries, water, and the ½ cup sugar. Bring to boiling. Cover, reduce heat and simmer 5 minutes. Combine flour, the ¼ cup sugar, soda, and salt. Cut butter into flour mixture till mixture resembles coarse crumbs. Stir in buttermilk just till flour is moistened. Drop batter by tablespoonfuls atop *bubbling* blueberry mixture, making six dumplings. Cover pan tightly; simmer 15 minutes (don't lift cover). Makes 6 servings.

The difference between the New England desserts slump and grunt is confusing to most people. Generally a slump is a sweet dumpling mixture dropped onto a boiling sugar and fruit mixture. On Cape Cod, slumps are also called grunts. In other parts of New England, however, a grunt is usually a steamed pudding with berries in it.

Apple Bread Pudding

3 cups dry bread cubes
   (4 slices)
1½ cups applesauce
⅛ teaspoon ground cinnamon
   Dash ground nutmeg
2 tablespoons butter

2 beaten eggs
2 cups milk
½ cup sugar
½ teaspoon vanilla
   Dash salt
   Ground cinnamon

In a buttered 8x8x2-inch baking pan layer *half* the dry bread cubes. Combine applesauce, ⅛ teaspoon cinnamon, and nutmeg. Spread applesauce mixture over bread cubes. Layer remaining bread cubes atop. Dot with butter. Combine eggs, milk, sugar, vanilla, and salt. Pour over bread mixture. Lightly sprinkle cinnamon over top. Bake at 350° till a knife inserted just off-center comes out clean, 55 to 60 minutes. Makes 6 servings.

The New World had no apple trees, so when the pilgrims arrived in New England, they lost no time in starting trees from seed. Apple orchards became so valuable that by 1648, Governor John Endicott traded 500 apple trees for 250 acres of land.

Stonewall

1 jigger applejack
   (apple brandy)
   (1½ ounces)

1 tablespoon dark rum
   (½ ounce)
   Crushed ice

Combine applejack and rum. Spoon crushed ice into cocktail glass. Pour applejack mixture over ice. Serve immediately. Makes 1 serving.

According to legend the Stonewall was the favorite drink of Ethan Allen and his Green Mountain Boys. In those days, they drank it at cellar temperature, but today we would add ice.

Haymaker's Switchel

8 cups water
1 cup sugar
½ cup cider vinegar

½ cup molasses
½ teaspoon ground ginger

In saucepan heat together water, sugar, vinegar, molasses, and ginger till sugar is dissolved. Chill before serving. Makes 18 (4-ounce) servings.

In haying season, farmers used switchel to quench their big thirsts. It was kept cool in a well and served in the field or with the noonday meal. Switchel was used as a substitute for water because it was believed that drinking water too fast made one more susceptible to sunstroke. Although switchel was usually served straight, some farmers were known to spike it with hard cider or brandy.

Rum Punch

6 cups water
1 cup sugar
1 ⅘-quart bottle rum
2 12-ounce cans beer
1 cup brandy

1 cup apple juice *or* apple
   cider
1 tablespoon grated lemon
   peel
1 cup lemon juice

In a large kettle combine water and sugar; bring to boiling, stirring to dissolve sugar. Add rum, beer, brandy, apple juice, lemon peel, and lemon juice. Heat through. Serve warm in mugs. Makes 32 (4-ounce) servings.

Our Dutch Inheritance

New Amsterdam

The Hudson River was explored in the early seventeenth century by the Dutchman whose name it bears, Hendrik Hudson. During the succeeding half century, a small Dutch colony took shape there, centering around a trading post at the tip of Manhattan Island and another at Fort Orange (Albany). In those days, England and Holland were struggling for supremacy in the colonial world; and as the result of hostilities between them in 1664, England acquired New Netherland, subsequently changing its name to New York. At the time of the English takeover, the largest city, New Amsterdam (now known as New York City) had a population of fifteen hundred people. The city grew and prospered and by the time of the Revolution, it was one of the New World's most cosmopolitan cities.

Because the Dutch colonists, however, retained their language, religion, and customs for another hundred years the colony was distinctly Dutch. The Dutch were excellent farmers and dairymen. As early as 1625, farm animals were sent over from Holland in special ships equipped with clean, sanded stalls, the best oats, hay, and straw, and plenty of water. Each animal had its own caretaker who had been promised a reward if his charge arrived in the New World in good condition. Dutch cattle and dairy products had long been regarded as the best in Europe, and the shores of the Hudson provided a good environment to continue this tradition. However, there was no large-scale commercial dairying until after 1800. New York farmers also raised grains including wheat, rye, and oats which they sold to the other colonies.

In the little port on Manhattan the houses were made of bricks with high gables, stoops, and Dutch doors. Each family had an herb and vegetable garden and perhaps an orchard. Pigs ran free in the streets (as in most colonial towns), and the cows were in the charge of a communal cowherd.

Each autumn the cellars were filled with bountiful provisions. There were barrels of red apples packed neatly in sawdust or straw and kegs of hard cider and homemade wines, along with sherry and port from Spain and Madeira. Live clams were kept in the cellars all winter in a mixture of cornmeal and sawdust, thoroughly doused twice a week with seawater.

The shad, a fish unknown in Europe, ran each spring in the Hudson and the colonists ate quantities of it; shad roe became a gourmet delicacy. Salmon and sturgeon also swam in the Hudson, and New York harbor offered a bonanza of giant crabs, twenty-five-pound lobsters, and clams so big that they were eaten roasted and sliced like meat. Venison could be bought at the door from traveling hunters for pennies or traded for cloth.

Dutch women were great bakers. From Dutch kitchens came *koekjes* (cookies) and *krullers* and *olykoeks* (fried cakes something like doughnuts, but without the hole); flat, crisp gingerbread figures made in cookie molds shaped as courtiers and ladies; and molasses cake.

On New Year's Day in well-to-do circles, a lavish spread of food and drink—especially drink—was prepared by the ladies of each household, while the gentlemen went from house to house, wishing everyone a Happy New Year and sampling the hospitality. This custom was taken over by the British, as was another cheerful Dutch custom, that of St. Nicholas bringing toys, sugarplums, and oranges for children at Christmastime.

When a well-to-do Dutch family celebrated, no expense was spared. For example, a wedding cake for a bride of the Schuyler family used 12 dozen eggs, 48 pounds of raisins, 24 pounds of currants, four quarts of brandy, and a quart of rum. It was mixed in a washtub and probably taken to the baker's big oven. Christenings and funerals were also occasions for lavish eating and drinking. Dutchmen were apt to provide in their wills for a pipe (126 gallons) of wine to be drunk at their funerals.

Finance and lower Manhattan grew up together. In its first year the tiny settlement of New Amsterdam on the tip of the island fully repaid the Dutch West India Company's original investment. In fact, the 4,000 beaver pelts and 700 otter skins shipped that year proved highly profitable.

The Dutch earned a reputation for prodigal use of their excellent dairy products. Wrote Peter Kalm in 1749, "In the evening they made a porridge of corn...in the center they poured fresh milk....As they ordinarily took more milk than porridge, the milk in the dish was soon consumed....After that they would eat some meat left over from the noonday meal, or bread and butter with cheese...."[27]

Roast Goose with Apple Stuffing

Chop the liver from one 10- to 12-pound ready-to-cook goose. Cook with 1 cup chopped onion and 2 tablespoons butter till onion is tender and liver is done. Mix with 5 cups dry bread cubes; 2 cups chopped peeled apple; 1/4 cup snipped parsley; 3/4 teaspoon dried sage, crushed; 1/2 teaspoon salt; and 1/8 teaspoon pepper. Mix 2 beaten eggs and 1/2 cup chicken broth; toss with bread mixture. Use to fill goose cavity. Tie legs together; tie to tail. Prick legs and wings with fork. Place on rack in shallow roasting pan. Insert meat thermometer in center of inside thigh muscle without touching bone. Roast at 350° till thermometer registers 185° for 2 3/4 to 3 hours; spoon off fat. Serves 10 to 12.

Cottage Cheese *(see photo, page 72)*

1/4 tablet rennet *or* 1 tablespoon dairy sour cream 2 tablespoons water	2 quarts milk 1/4 cup buttermilk 1/2 cup light cream

Dissolve rennet in water. Heat milk till just cool to touch (no more than 80°). Add rennet or sour cream and buttermilk. Cover and let stand at room temperature till milk solidifies to a smooth curd, 12 to 24 hours (longer in winter). Break curd into chunks. Heat all to 100°; hold at this temperature in a pan of hot water 20 to 30 minutes, stirring occasionally. Line a colander with several layers of cheesecloth; place in a large bowl. Pour curds into cheesecloth; drain off liquid, 4 to 6 hours. Turn out cheese; break into curds. Stir in light cream and 1/2 teaspoon salt. Makes 1 pound.

Coleslaw *(see photo, page 72)*

½ cup whipping cream
3 tablespoons cider vinegar

2 tablespoons sugar
4 cups shredded cabbage

Combine cream, vinegar, sugar, ¾ teaspoon salt, and ⅛ teaspoon pepper.

Toss with cabbage to coat thoroughly. Serve immediately. Makes 6 servings.

Dutch Spiced Flank Steak

Score 1 to 1½ pounds beef flank steak; coat with 1½ to 2 tablespoons all-purpose flour. Brown meat in 2 tablespoons butter. Season with salt and pepper. Add 1¼ cups hot water, ¼ cup vinegar, 4 whole cloves, 2 bay leaves, and ⅛ teaspoon cayenne. Cover; simmer till tender; 1¼ hours. Serves 4.

Sweet Waffles of Flatbush

½ cup butter
½ cup sugar
3 eggs

⅔ cup milk
1 cup all-purpose flour

Cream together the butter and sugar. Combine the eggs and milk. Add egg mixture alternately to creamed mixture with flour, beating till smooth. Bake on preheated greased waffle baker. Makes two 9-inch waffles.

Hutspot

2 pounds fresh beef brisket
4 cups water
2 teaspoons salt
3 pounds potatoes, peeled
    and cut in quarters
    (6 potatoes)

2 cups sliced carrots
1½ cups chopped onion
2 tablespoons butter
⅓ cup cold water
3 tablespoons all-purpose
    flour

In 4-quart Dutch oven combine beef brisket, 4 cups water, and salt; cover. Bring to boiling; reduce heat and simmer till meat is nearly tender, about 2½ hours. Add potatoes, carrots, and onion. Simmer, covered, till vegetables are tender, about 30 minutes. Remove meat. Drain vegetables; reserve 1⅔ cups liquid. Add butter to vegetables; mash. Season with salt and pepper. Blend cold water slowly into flour. Stir into reserved liquid. Cook and stir till thickened and bubbly. Season to taste. Makes 6 servings.

Buckwheat Griddle Cakes

2⅔ cups all-purpose flour
1⅓ cups buckwheat flour
1 package active dry yeast
2½ cups warm water (110°)

3 tablespoons packed brown
    sugar
2 tablespoons lard, melted
¾ teaspoon baking soda

Mix flours and 1 teaspoon salt. Soften yeast in water; stir in *1 tablespoon* brown sugar. Stir into flour mixture; mix well. Cover; let stand overnight at room temperature (bowl must not be over ½ full). The next morning, stir batter. Add remaining sugar, lard, and baking soda; mix well. Refrigerate *1 cup batter for starter* (keeps several weeks). Bake remaining on hot, lightly greased griddle. Makes 16 pancakes.

To use starter: Place starter in large mixing bowl. Stir in 2¼ cups all-purpose flour, 2¼ cups water, and 1¼ cups buckwheat flour. Stir till smooth. Cover; let stand overnight as before. Next morning, stir batter. Stir in 2 tablespoons packed brown sugar, 2 tablespoons melted lard, and ¾ teaspoon baking soda. Again reserve 1 cup batter for starter. Bake remaining batter on hot, lightly greased griddle.

Cabbage for Coleslaw *was only one of the many fruits and vegetables grown in New Amsterdam gardens. An attorney, Adrian Van Der Donck in* **A Description of the New Netherlands,** *1653, describes the wealth of these gardens. The kitchen gardens "...consist of various kinds of salads, cabbages, parsnips, carrots, dill, sorrel, radishes, cresses, leeks, and besides whatever else is commonly found in a kitchen garden. The herb garden is also tolerably well supplied with rosemary, lavender, holy onions, dragon's blood, together with laurel, artichokes and asparagus, and various other things on which I have bestowed no attention. We have also introduced morecotoons (a type of peach), almonds, figs, several sorts of currants, gooseberries, and thorn apples...."[28]*

The word Hutspot *or hodgepot was used to describe a beef dish popular among the Dutch. The dish was prepared by cooking beef, potato, carrot, and onion all together. Then, the vegetables were removed and made into a colorful mashed potato mixture that was served with the meat.*

In the early years starter breads were made when yeast was nonexistent or in short supply and breads had to be fermented by the natural bacteria in the air. Buckwheat Griddle Cakes, an updated version of a colonial favorite, is made with a yeast starter. Make them as often as you wish. Simply refrigerate a portion of the starter to reuse in the next batch.

Raisin-Almond Pound Cake

1 cup sugar
¾ cup butter
4 eggs
2 cups all-purpose flour
1 teaspoon ground nutmeg
½ teaspoon salt
¼ teaspoon baking soda

½ cup buttermilk
1 cup raisins
½ cup finely chopped
   candied orange peel
½ cup finely chopped
   almonds

In large bowl cream together the sugar and butter till light and fluffy. Add eggs, one at a time, beating well after each. Sift together flour, nutmeg, salt, and soda. Add dry ingredients to creamed mixture alternately with but-

termilk, mixing well after each addition. Fold in raisins, orange peel, and almonds. Pour the batter into greased 9x5x3-inch loaf pan. Bake at 350° for 70 minutes. Cool in pan. Wrap and store overnight, if desired.

Oliebollen

3¼ cups all-purpose flour
2 packages active dry yeast
1 cup milk
⅓ cup sugar
¼ cup butter
1 teaspoon salt
1 teaspoon vanilla
2 eggs

3 egg yolks
½ cup raisins
½ cup chopped mixed candied
   fruits and peels
   Fat for frying
½ cup sugar
1 teaspoon ground
   cinnamon

In a large bowl combine *2 cups* of the flour and yeast. In a saucepan heat milk, the ⅓ cup sugar, butter, and salt just till warm (115-120°), stirring constantly. Stir in vanilla. Add to dry ingredients; add eggs and egg yolks. Beat at low speed of electric mixer for ½ minute, scraping bowl. Beat 3 minutes at high speed. Stir in the re-

maining flour, raisins, and candied fruits and peels. Cover; let rise till double (about 30 minutes). Carefully drop batter by tablespoonfuls into deep hot fat (375°); fry about 3 minutes, turning to brown on all sides. Drain well on paper toweling. While warm, dust with a mixture of ½ cup sugar and ground cinnamon. Makes 36.

Molasses Cake

1 cup boiling water
½ cup packed brown sugar
½ cup molasses
¼ cup lard
1½ cups all-purpose flour
1 teaspoon baking soda

1 teaspoon ground cinnamon
½ teaspoon ground allspice
½ teaspoon ground cloves
¼ teaspoon salt
1 beaten egg
½ cup raisins

In mixing bowl pour boiling water over sugar, molasses, and lard. Stir together flour, baking soda, spices, and salt; stir into molasses mixture. Add

egg; beat till smooth. Stir in raisins. Pour into greased and floured 9x9x2-inch baking pan. Bake at 375° till done, 30 to 35 minutes.

Champagne-Rum Punch

1 ⅘-quart bottle rum
3 cups orange juice
2 cups water
1½ cups brandy

¾ cup lemon juice
¾ cup packed brown sugar
1 ⅘-quart bottle
   champagne

Combine rum, orange juice, water, brandy, lemon juice, and sugar. Chill.

Before serving, gently add champagne. Makes about 25 (4-ounce) servings.

Pictured opposite: The Dutch deserved their reputation for hearty meals featuring garden-grown vegetables and herbs plus home dairy products. Shredded cabbage tossed with whipped-cream-based dressing became "sla," better known to us as *Coleslaw* (see recipe, page 71). *Cottage Cheese* (see recipe, page 70) was served at least once a day, often topped with fresh dill or another herb. Deep fried balls of sweetened dough called *Oliebollen* were a notable treat.

That Dutch recipes often involved long preparation is shown by this 1740 recipe for Oliebollen. *"About twelve o'clock set a little yeast to rise, so as to be ready at five P.M. to mix with the following ingredients...flour... sugar...butter and lard... milk, 6 eggs...raised yeast....Place in a warm place to rise. If quite light by bedtime, work them down by pressing with the hand. At nine next morning make into small balls.... They are frequently ready to boil at two o'clock...boil each one five minutes. When cool roll in sifted sugar."*[29]

Washington Irving in the Legend of Sleepy Hollow *describes the bounty of the Dutch table. "Such heaped-up platters of cakes of various and almost indescribable kinds, known only to experienced Dutch housewives. There was the doughty doughnut, the tenderer oly koek, and the crisp and crumbling cruller; sweet cakes and short-cakes, ginger cakes, and honey cakes, and the whole family of cakes."*[30] *One of the cakes the author classifies as the "whole family of cakes" is the popular Dutch stroophoek or Molasses Cake.*

Tea Punch

In saucepan combine 4 cups strong tea, 1 cup brandy, ¾ cup sugar, ½ cup orange juice, and ½ cup rum. Heat through. Serve in mugs. Makes 5 cups.

Gingerbread Men

2 cups packed brown sugar
1½ cups butter, softened
1 egg
• • •
4 cups all-purpose flour
2 teaspoons ground cinnamon

1 teaspoon ground
   nutmeg
½ teaspoon ground cloves
¼ teaspoon baking soda
   Purchased decorator icing
   in tubes

Cream sugar and butter; add egg. Beat till light and fluffy. Stir flour with spices and soda; add to creamed mixture. Mix well. Cover; chill dough about 2 hours. On floured surface, roll dough to ⅛-inch thickness. Cut with a gingerbread man cutter. Place on ungreased cookie sheet. Bake at 350° till lightly browned, 8 to 10 minutes. Cool 1 to 2 minutes; remove to rack. If desired, decorate with purchased decorator icing. Makes about 72.

Raised Doughnuts

3 to 3½ cups all-purpose
   flour
2 packages active dry yeast
¾ cup milk
⅓ cup sugar

¼ cup lard
2 eggs
   Fat for frying
   Sugar (optional)
   Glaze (optional)

In large mixing bowl combine *1½ cups* flour and yeast. In saucepan heat together milk, sugar, lard, and 1 teaspoon salt just till warm (115-120°), stirring constantly. Add to dry mixture; add eggs. Beat at low speed of electric mixer ½ minute, scraping sides of bowl often. Beat 3 minutes at high speed. By hand, stir in enough remaining flour to make a moderately soft dough. Turn onto lightly floured surface; knead till smooth and elastic (5 to 8 minutes). Shape into a ball. Place in lightly greased bowl; turn once. Cover; let rise in warm place till double (45 to 60 minutes). Punch down; turn onto lightly floured surface. Divide in half. Roll dough to ½-inch thickness. Cut with floured doughnut cutter (has hole in center). Cover; let rise in warm place till very light (30 to 45 minutes). Fry in deep hot fat (375°) till golden, about 1 minute per side. Drain on paper toweling. If desired, roll warm doughnuts in sugar or frost with Glaze. Makes 18 to 20.

Glaze: Mix 2 cups sifted powdered sugar, ¼ cup milk, 1 teaspoon vanilla.

Crullers

⅓ cup granulated sugar
¼ cup butter
2 eggs
2 tablespoons milk
• • •
1¾ cups all-purpose flour

½ teaspoon salt
½ teaspoon ground
   nutmeg
¼ teaspoon ground mace
   Fat for frying
   Powdered sugar

Cream together granulated sugar and butter till light and fluffy. Add eggs, one at a time; beat well after each addition. Add milk (batter may appear slightly curdled). Stir together flour, salt, nutmeg, and mace. Stir into the creamed mixture. Chill at least 1 hour. On lightly floured surface roll *half* the dough *(rolling in one direction only)* to a 16x8-inch rectangle. Cut into 2-inch squares *(do not reroll).* (Use pastry wheel for pretty edges.) Repeat with remaining dough. Fry in deep hot fat (375°) till golden on both sides, about 1½ minutes total. Dust with powdered sugar. Makes 64.

One of the earliest groups to press for the equality of men and women were the Quakers or Society of Friends. Their teachings emphasized that the responsibility for worship and church organization was to be equally shared between men and women.

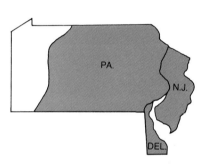

Middle Colonies: Garden Medley

The Middle Colonies of Pennsylvania, New Jersey, and Delaware shared a similar climate and landscape. As a result, the foods and cooking of this area have always been similar in many ways. The histories of these three colonies, however, are richly diverse.

Pennsylvania ("Penn's Woods") was granted in 1681 by King Charles II to Quaker William Penn — thus making Penn the largest landowner in the new world next to the king himself. In addition to being the largest colony, Pennsylvania was also the only English colony that from its very beginning received large numbers of non-English colonists. Within its first two years, fifty ships brought more than seven thousand settlers and among these were sizable contingents of Welsh, Irish, Dutch, and German. The first arrivals settled in or around Philadelphia or in the nearby Delaware Valley which, once cleared and planted, was a farmer's paradise.

"Here are peaches in abundance . . . I have seen them rot on the ground and the hogs eat them,"[31] wrote one astonished colonist. Throughout the colonial period, the Delaware Valley produced wheat and rye as cash crops, as well as corn for fodder for the wide variety of farm animals raised.

The area that is now Delaware and New Jersey was first settled by the Dutch and later by the Swedes. Delaware, for its part, became a semi-autonomous part of Pennsylvania, retaining a rich Swedish tradition of hard work and good husbandry.

The area which is now New Jersey, on the other hand, came under the control of the Duke of York. He granted the land to Sir John Berkeley and Sir George Carteret. The Colony was called Nova Caesarea (later New

In 1638 a group of Swedes settled the land near the Delaware River. They built Fort Christina (now Wilmington) and introduced the log cabin to America. Swedes were used to log cabins in their homeland and, besides, they required only wood and an ax for construction. The bark was left on the logs and the ends were notched so they would fit snugly and they could be stacked, layering side and end walls alternately. The cracks between layers were filled with wood chips, clay, and moss. The houses often lacked windows and were heated by a stone fireplace.

Jersey) after the island where Carteret had protected the Duke from Puritan forces in England. Over the years New Jersey became a rich agricultural area growing apples, peaches, cranberries, beans, wheat, and flax. As a result New Jersey's nickname today is the "Garden State," and the state seal shows three plows and the goddess of the earth holding a cornucopia.

The English tradition in cookery was generally dominant in the Middle Colonies, with a Dutch influence near the Hudson. But wherever there was a preponderance of Germans, there developed that wonderful brand of regional cooking that came to be called Pennsylvania Dutch. These "Dutch" (the German *Deutsch* sounded like "Dutch" to English ears) tended to keep to themselves and to be left to themselves, due to their different language and religion plus a reluctance on both sides to accept the unfamiliar. Many of them pioneered in remote woodland areas not previously claimed. Some of their religious sects, such as the Amish and the Mennonites, believed in staying aloof. This isolation, whether voluntary or involuntary, helped create and preserve their distinctive ways with cooking.

Some of their food was straight from the old country: sauerbraten, for instance, and a predilection for dumplings and noodles. Other dishes grew out of the wedding of American foods and abundance with the ingenuity of housewives. They invented new ways to cook corn, for example, their famous chicken corn soup. They made all manner of relishes and jams ("seven sweets and seven sours" were said to be on every table) using local ingredients.

Baking was especially important. When a young couple moved into a new house, the names of three housewives known for good baking were said over a bowl of yeast, as a sort of incantation. The dough trough was the first article to be carried into a new kitchen or bakehouse. Friday was baking day. Among the specialties of Pennsylvania Dutch ovens were crumb cakes, and many kinds of coffee cake; shoofly pie; apease, or apees, a kind of sandtart; pudding cake; cheesecake and cheese pie.

And, in short, so many other things that it's no wonder the Pennsylvania Dutch had a saying, "Kissing wears out; cooking don't."[32]

Hot Buttered Toddy

1 cup water	2 tablespoons butter
½ cup honey	Dash ground nutmeg
1⅓ cups dark rum, warmed	

In saucepan heat water and honey till boiling; stir in warm rum. Top with pats of butter; sprinkle with nutmeg. Makes 4 (6-ounce) servings.

According to tradition the first "cocktail" was served at Halls Corners in Elmsford, New York, in 1776. The bar used cocktail feathers to decorate the area behind the bar, and when a customer asked a barmaid for a glass of those "cocktails," she served him a mixed drink with a feather in it.

Pickled Oysters

1 pint shucked oysters	2 teaspoons whole black
⅔ cup vinegar	pepper
1 tablespoon sugar	1 teaspoon whole allspice
1 teaspoon salt	½ teaspoon whole cloves
1 small onion, sliced	1 bay leaf
2 teaspoons celery seed	

Drain oysters; reserve liquid. Add water to make 2 cups. In saucepan mix oyster liquid, vinegar, sugar, salt, and sliced onion. Tie celery seed, spices, and bay leaf in cheesecloth sack. Add to liquid; bring to a boil, add oysters. Simmer 10 minutes, skim off foam. Chill. Makes about 1½ cups.

Delaware Crab Cakes

1 beaten egg
½ cup finely crushed
   saltine crackers
⅓ cup milk
½ teaspoon dry mustard
⅛ teaspoon white pepper
⅛ teaspoon cayenne

1 7½-ounce can crab meat,
   drained, flaked, and
   cartilage removed
1 tablespoon snipped
   parsley
3 tablespoons lard
   Lemon wedges

In a bowl combine egg, crushed crackers, milk, mustard, white pepper, and cayenne. Stir in crab meat and parsley. Using ⅓ cup mixture for each, shape into patties. Cover and chill patties at least 30 minutes. Heat lard in skillet; add patties and cook over medium heat till golden brown on both sides, 6 to 8 minutes. Drain and serve immediately with lemon wedges. Makes 5 patties.

The cooking of Delaware and Maryland has historically been very similar. Both states have always had an abundance of seafood and both have become famous for their crab dishes. In this part of the country, crab cakes have ranked high in the hearts of seafood lovers since the 18th century. These cakes are heavily seasoned with pepper, just the way the people of Delaware like them.

Island Beach Clam Pie

2 7½-ounce cans minced
   clams
½ cup chopped onion
¼ cup chopped green pepper
2 tablespoons butter
3 tablespoons all-purpose
   flour
¼ teaspoon dried rosemary,
   crushed

Dash pepper
   Milk
1½ cups diced cooked
   potatoes
2 hard-cooked eggs, chopped
   Pastry for 2-crust
   9-inch pie (see recipe,
   page 351)

Drain clams, reserving liquid. In a 1½-quart saucepan cook onion and green pepper in butter till tender but not brown. Blend in the flour, rosemary, and pepper. Add enough milk to the reserved clam liquid to make 1 cup. Slowly stir liquid into the flour mixture. Cook and stir till thickened and bubbly. Stir in clams, potatoes, and eggs. Line a 9-inch pie plate with pastry. Fill with clam mixture. Adjust top crust, cutting slits for escape of steam; seal and flute. Bake at 375° for 35 to 40 minutes. Serves 6.

Candied Cranberries

1 16-ounce package
   cranberries (4 cups)

2½ cups sugar

Spread the cranberries in the bottom of a greased 13x9x2-inch baking pan. Sprinkle cranberries with sugar. Let stand at room temperature for 30 minutes. Stir. Cover with foil and bake at 350° for 45 to 50 minutes. Stir the cranberries occasionally by carefully lifting and turning cranberries with metal spatula. Chill till ready to use. Makes 3 cups.

The bouncing quality of cranberries was first noted by a New Jersey grower, John I. Webb. "Peg-Leg John," as he was called, stored his berries in the loft of his barn. Since he could not carry them down from the loft, he poured the cranberries down the steps. Only the firm fruit bounced to the bottom, the bruised fruit remained on the steps. His observation led to the development of the first cranberry separator.

Cheese Wafers

½ cup butter
½ cup shredded Cheddar
   cheese (2 ounces)
2 cups all-purpose flour

4 to 5 tablespoons water
2 tablespoons butter,
   melted
   Paprika

With a pastry cutter cut ½ cup butter and cheese into flour till mixture resembles fine crumbs. Sprinkle *1 tablespoon* water over part of flour mixture. Gently toss with a fork, push to side of bowl. Repeat with additional water till all is moistened. Form dough into a ball. Divide dough in half. Roll *each half* to a 12-inch circle. Cut into circles with 1-inch round cutter. Place on ungreased baking sheet. Brush with melted butter; sprinkle with paprika. Bake at 450° for 8 to 10 minutes. Makes 72 wafers.

Sack-Posset

3 beaten eggs
¼ cup sugar
¼ teaspoon ground nutmeg

1½ cups milk
½ cup dry white wine

In a heavy 1½-quart saucepan combine the eggs, sugar, and nutmeg. Gradually stir in the milk. Cook over low heat, stirring constantly, till the mixture coats a metal spoon. Remove from heat; cool pan at once in cold water. Stir a minute or two. Slowly stir in wine. Chill. Makes 2½ cups.

Whitesbog Blueberry Jam

4 cups finely chopped
    peeled apples
2 cups water

4 cups fresh *or* frozen
    blueberries
3¾ cups sugar

In a 4- to 6-quart kettle mix apples and water; simmer, uncovered, till apples are soft, 15 to 20 minutes. Mash, if necessary. Stir in berries. Simmer, uncovered, 5 minutes. Stir in sugar. Bring to a rolling boil; boil till jam sheets off a metal spoon, 5 to 6 minutes. Pour into hot clean jars, leaving ½ inch headspace. Wipe edge with damp cloth. Spoon on *thin* layer of melted paraffin. Cool. Spoon on second *thin* layer of paraffin. Makes 6 half-pints.

Potatoes Scalloped with Ham

2 cups cubed fully cooked
    ham
6 cups thinly sliced
    potatoes
¼ cup finely chopped onion
⅓ cup all-purpose flour

2 cups milk
3 tablespoons fine dry
    bread crumbs
1 tablespoon butter, melted
2 tablespoons finely
    snipped parsley

Place *half* the ham in a 2-quart casserole. Cover with *half* the potatoes and *half* the onion. Sift *half* the flour over; season with salt and pepper. Top with remaining ham, potatoes, and onion. Season with additional salt and pepper. Sift remaining flour atop. Pour milk over. Mix crumbs and butter; sprinkle atop. Top with parsley. Bake, covered, at 350° till potatoes are nearly tender, 1¼ to 1½ hours. Uncover; bake 15 minutes more. Serves 6 to 8.

Potato Dressing

In a skillet cook ¾ cup chopped onion and ¼ cup chopped celery in ¼ cup butter till tender but not brown. Thoroughly combine with 2 cups mashed cooked potatoes (2 medium potatoes); 1½ cups soft bread crumbs; 2 beaten eggs; 2 tablespoons snipped parsley; ¾ teaspoon salt; ½ teaspoon dried marjoram, crushed; and ⅛ teaspoon pepper. Use to stuff poultry or bake, covered, in a 1-quart casserole at 375° for 45 minutes. Makes 3 cups dressing.

Cranlilli

1 cup fresh cranberries
1 medium onion, quartered
1 medium green pepper,
    quartered

½ cup sugar
½ cup vinegar
¾ teaspoon salt

Put cranberries, onion, and green pepper through a food grinder, using coarse blade. In a saucepan combine cranberry mixture, sugar, vinegar, and salt. Simmer, covered, for 10 minutes. Uncover and simmer 10 minutes more. Chill. Serve as an accompaniment to meat or poultry. Makes 1⅓ cups.

Sauerbraten

2½ cups water
1½ cups red wine vinegar
2 medium onions, sliced
½ lemon, sliced
12 whole cloves
6 bay leaves
6 whole black peppercorns

1 tablespoon sugar
1 tablespoon salt
¼ teaspoon ground ginger
1 4-pound beef rump roast
2 tablespoons lard
Gingersnap Gravy

In large bowl or crock mix water, vinegar, onions, lemon, cloves, bay leaves, peppercorns, sugar, salt, and ginger. Add roast, turning to coat. Cover and refrigerate meat about 36 hours; turn meat at least twice daily. Remove meat from marinade; wipe dry. Strain and reserve marinade. In a Dutch oven brown meat in hot lard; add strained marinade. Cover; simmer till meat is tender, about 2 hours. Remove meat; reserve 1½ cups pan juices. Prepare Gingersnap Gravy. Serves 10.

Gingersnap Gravy: In a small saucepan combine the reserved pan juices and ½ cup water; add ⅔ cup broken gingersnaps. Cook, stirring constantly, till thick and bubbly.

Pork Pot Roast

1 4-pound pork shoulder
  roast
2 tablespoons lard
4 cups water
1 large onion, cut in
  thin wedges
2 teaspoons salt
½ teaspoon pepper
3 large carrots, cut in
  1-inch pieces

2 medium turnips, peeled
  and sliced (1 cup)
½ cup cold water
2 tablespoons all-purpose
  flour
Few drops Kitchen Bouquet
Salt
Pepper
2 tablespoons snipped
  parsley

In a large Dutch oven brown roast in hot lard. Add the 4 cups water, onion, 2 teaspoons salt, and ½ teaspoon pepper. Bring to a boil; reduce heat and simmer, covered, till meat is nearly tender, 1¼ to 1½ hours. Add carrot pieces and sliced turnips. Continue cooking till meat is fork tender and vegetables are done, about 30 minutes. Drain, reserving broth. Keep vegetables warm. In saucepan blend cold water slowly into flour; add *1 cup* of reserved broth and a few drops Kitchen Bouquet to color. Cook and stir till thickened and bubbly; season to taste with salt and pepper. Serve vegetables and gravy with meat. Sprinkle vegetables with parsley. (Use remaining reserved broth and 2 cups cubed cooked pork for Pork Pot Pie.) Serves 4.

Pork Pot Pie

3 cups pork *or* chicken
  broth
Chicken broth
2 medium potatoes, peeled
  and thinly sliced
1 cup chopped celery

1 large carrot, sliced
Salt
Pepper
2 cups cubed cooked pork
Noodle Squares

Mix the 3 cups pork or chicken broth and enough additional chicken broth to make 5 cups liquid. Mix broth, potatoes, celery, and carrot. Simmer, covered, 10 minutes. Season with salt and pepper. Add pork. Bring to boiling; stir Noodle Squares into broth. Cook till noodles are tender, 10 to 12 minutes. Serve in bowls. Serves 4.

Noodle Squares: In a mixing bowl combine 1 beaten egg; 3 tablespoons water; 1 tablespoon butter, melted; and ¼ teaspoon salt. Gradually stir in 1¼ cups all-purpose flour to make a stiff dough. Form into a ball; knead till smooth and elastic. Roll dough on a floured surface to a 12x9-inch rectangle. Cut dough into 1½-inch squares.

Beef cattle were rare in Pennsylvania Dutch country before the Revolution and most farmers considered them prized possessions. Many were the traditions and strange were the superstitions that developed about the proper way to care for the animals. For example, cattle could become homesick, so they should never be allowed to see where they were going when they were sold or they would return to their original owner. Hay for the cattle should be left out on Christmas Eve, so that dew of that holy night would touch it and bless it. Also, the first farmer to feed his cattle on New Year's Eve would have healthy cattle all year.

This is the traditional Mennonite version of pot pie. The absence of a top crust makes this pot pie quite unusual. The dough is simmered in the broth.

Chicken Stoltzfus

1 3- to 5-pound ready-to-
    cook stewing chicken,
    cut up
6 cups water
1 tablespoon salt
6 whole black peppercorns
    • • •
1½ cups all-purpose flour
½ teaspoon salt
⅓ cup lard

¼ cup ice water
    • • •
½ cup butter
⅔ cup all-purpose flour
⅛ teaspoon ground saffron
1 cup light cream
¼ cup snipped parsley
    Salt
    Pepper

Place chicken pieces and 6 cups water in large kettle. Bring to boil; skim off surface. Add 1 tablespoon salt and peppercorns. Simmer, covered, about 1½ hours. Remove chicken; cool and remove meat from bones; cut meat into bite-size pieces. Discard bones. Remove excess fat from broth; strain broth, reserving 4 cups.

Meanwhile, combine 1½ cups flour and ½ teaspoon salt. With a pastry cutter, cut in lard till mixture resembles coarse crumbs. Sprinkle ice water over flour mixture; toss with a fork. Press dough into a ball; place on lightly floured surface. Roll dough to ⅛-inch thickness. Cut with a sharp knife or pastry wheel into 1-inch squares. Bake at 450° till lightly browned, 12 to 15 minutes.

In 4-quart Dutch oven melt butter; blend in ⅔ cup flour and saffron. Stir in reserved broth and cream. Cook, stirring constantly, till mixture is thickened and bubbly. Reduce heat; add parsley and chicken pieces; heat through. Season with salt and pepper. To serve, place pastry squares on individual plates and spoon chicken mixture over squares. Serves 8.

Pictured opposite: The hardworking Pennsylvania Dutch appreciated good food—and an abundance of it. A typical meal might have included *Chicken Stoltzfus* featuring creamed chicken served over pastry squares. The main dish would be complemented with a variety of sweets and sours such as *Cucumbers in Sour Cream, Pepper Relish,* and *Dried Corn Salad* (see recipes, page 82). A favorite dessert was *Apple Pandowdy* (see recipe, page 84).

Hot Mummix

½ cup chopped onion
½ cup chopped green pepper
1 clove garlic, minced
2 tablespoons butter
1 teaspoon salt
¾ teaspoon dry mustard

½ teaspoon sugar
⅛ teaspoon cayenne
2 cups ground cooked beef*
2 cups cubed cooked
    potatoes (2 medium
    potatoes)

In a medium skillet cook chopped onion, chopped green pepper, and garlic in butter till tender but not brown. Stir in salt, dry mustard, sugar, and cayenne. Stir in the cooked beef and cubed cooked potatoes. Cook, covered, till the meat and potatoes are heated through, about 10 minutes. Serve immediately. Makes 4 servings.

Note: 1 pound ground beef may be substituted for cooked beef by the following method. Cook beef with onion, pepper, and garlic. Drain. Stir in seasonings and potatoes. Heat through.

Mummix and hexel are Pennsylvania Dutch words that stand for anything that is left over, scrambled, or made into a hash. This recipe for Hot Mummix *was designed to use up leftover cooked beef and leftover boiled potatoes. However, it works well with fresh ground beef, too.*

French Goose

2 pounds bulk pork sausage
2 pounds potatoes, peeled
    and diced (4 cups)
2 cups sliced celery
1½ cups sliced carrots
½ cup finely chopped onion

1 teaspoon dried thyme,
    crushed
1 teaspoon dried basil,
    crushed
½ teaspoon salt
⅛ teaspoon pepper

In a mixing bowl combine uncooked sausage, diced potatoes, sliced celery, sliced carrots, chopped onion, thyme, basil, salt, and pepper. Mix well. Stuff the sausage mixture into a 15x10-inch (or larger) clear roasting bag; tie the opening and punch holes in the bag on top and on bottom. Place the roasting bag on a rack in a roasting pan. Cover with lid or foil. Bake at 350° for 3 hours; remove fat occasionally. Let stand 10 minutes. Slit roasting bag; carefully remove mixture. Makes 6 servings.

The Pennsylvania Dutch were as frugal as any other colonists and found ways to use every part of a butchered animal. They even used the cleaned pig stomach. It was considered a special treat and was usually stuffed with sausage and vegetables, then baked. But the origin of its name, French Goose, *is a mystery.*

Stirabout

Stirabout is a thick chicken porridge featuring saffron. This most costly of spices, native to Southern Europe, was brought here by a group of Celesians called the Schwenkfelders. Since then, the Pennsylvania Dutch have mastered the art of using saffron—and it is an art—especially in chicken dishes.

5¼ cups chicken broth*
4 cups sliced potatoes
1 cup chopped celery
2 tablespoons snipped
  parsley

½ teaspoon salt
⅛ teaspoon pepper
⅛ teaspoon ground saffron
2 beaten eggs
½ cup all-purpose flour

In large saucepan bring the broth to a boil; add potatoes, celery, parsley, salt, pepper, and saffron. Simmer, covered, till potatoes are almost tender, 15 to 20 minutes. In a small bowl beat eggs and flour with a fork to make a thin paste. Drop by teaspoonfuls into boiling broth. Cover and boil gently for 7 minutes. Makes 6 servings.
Note: Use leftover chicken broth or if desired, use three 13¾-ounce cans chicken broth.

Buttered Sugar Peas

A sugar pea in one region is a Chinese pea pod or snow pea in another. Pennsylvania Dutch cooking, especially in Lancaster County, included this delicacy from early times. It has a thin tender pod that is eaten with the peas.

4 cups fresh sugar peas *or*
2 6-ounce packages
  frozen pea pods
½ cup water

1 teaspoon salt
½ teaspoon sugar
2 tablespoons butter

Wash fresh peas. In saucepan combine fresh or frozen pea pods, water, salt, and sugar. Cover and bring to boiling. Boil 2 minutes; drain well. Meanwhile, melt butter over medium heat. Cook, stirring occasionally, till butter is light golden brown. Add butter to the drained pea pods; toss to coat evenly. Season to taste with salt and pepper. Makes 6 to 8 servings.

Cucumbers in Sour Cream *(see photo, page 80)*

Legend has it that every meal had to include seven sweets and seven sours. Actually, the number and kind of pickles and relishes were chosen to complement each particular meal. Pennsylvania Dutch cooks are too wise to be rigid about legends.

2 medium cucumbers, thinly
  sliced
1 medium onion, very thinly
  sliced

½ cup dairy sour cream
1 tablespoon sugar
1 tablespoon vinegar
½ teaspoon salt

Combine the cucumbers and onion. Stir together the remaining ingredients; toss with vegetables. Cover and chill; stir occasionally. Makes 3 cups.

Pepper Relish *(see photo, page 80)*

6 sweet green peppers
6 sweet red peppers
6 medium onions

1 cup sugar
1 cup vinegar
1½ teaspoons dillseed

Finely grind green peppers, red peppers, and onions. Drain well. In a saucepan mix peppers and onions; cover with boiling water and let stand 5 minutes. Drain. Add sugar, vinegar, dillseed, ½ cup water, and 1½ teaspoons salt. Boil gently for 5 minutes. Fill hot clean half-pint canning jars to within ½ inch of top; adjust lids. Process in boiling water bath 5 minutes (start timing when water returns to boiling). Makes 10 half-pints.

Dried Corn Salad *(see photo, page 80)*

Dried corn was first made by the Pennsylvania Dutch by drying fresh kernels in the sun for five days and then in a slack oven for two more. To cook the corn, it had to be soaked in water, then salted and simmered.

½ cup dried corn
3 cups shredded cabbage
¾ cup chopped green pepper

½ cup vinegar
⅓ cup sugar
½ teaspoon dry mustard

In saucepan mix dried corn and 1½ cups boiling water. Let stand 1 hour; do not drain. Stir in cabbage, green pepper, vinegar, sugar, mustard, and ¼ teaspoon salt. Simmer, covered, 30 minutes. Serve warm or chilled. Serves 6.

Chicken-Corn Soup

    1 5- to 6-pound ready-to-
        cook stewing chicken,
        cut up
    6 cups water
    ⅓ cup chopped onion
    2 teaspoons salt
    ¼ teaspoon pepper

    1 bay leaf
    6 ears fresh corn*
    1½ cups uncooked Homemade
        Noodles (see below)
    1 cup chopped celery
    2 tablespoons snipped
        parsley

In a large kettle combine the chicken, water, onion, salt, pepper, and bay leaf. Bring to a boil; reduce heat and simmer, covered, till chicken is tender, about 2 hours. Meanwhile, with sharp knife make cuts down *center of corn kernels* in each row of the ears. Cut corn off and scrape the cob. (Should equal 2 cups corn.) Remove the chicken from broth; cool and remove meat from bones. Cut chicken into

bite-size pieces. Set aside. Skim excess fat from broth. Discard bay leaf. Bring the broth to a boil. Add corn, the Homemade Noodles, celery, and parsley. Simmer, covered, till corn and noodles are barely done, about 8 minutes. Add cooked chicken and heat through, about 5 minutes. Season with salt and pepper. Makes 8 servings.

Note: One 16-ounce can cream-style corn may be substituted.

Although churning butter was a strenuous task, it was done by the women and children. Early churns were of the plunger type while later models featured a hand crank on the side. After churning, carrot juice and salt were often added to improve the color and flavor. Next, the butter was scooped into a wooden bowl and pressed with a paddle to work the water out. The butter was then packed into buckets or molds.

Homemade Noodles

    1 beaten egg
    2 tablespoons milk
    ½ teaspoon salt

    All-purpose flour (about
        1 cup)

Mix egg, milk, and salt. Add enough of the flour to make a stiff dough. Roll very thin on floured surface; let rest 20 minutes. Roll up loosely; slice ¼ inch wide. Unroll. Cut into desired

lengths. Spread out; dry 2 hours. (Store in covered container till needed.) To cook, drop noodles into boiling liquid; cook, uncovered, 8 to 10 minutes. Makes 3 cups uncooked noodles.

Apple Pandowdy *(see photo, page 80)*

(see photo, page 80)

Apple Pandowdy *is a molasses or maple-flavored deep-dish apple dessert. Traditionally the dessert is dowdied before serving— that is, the crust is broken up with a spoon or knife and stirred into the apple filling. Oddly enough, over the years this type of "messed up" appearance has come more often to be applied to people than to desserts. It is common in our language for an individual to be referred to as dowdy in appearance.*

Pastry for 2-crust
  9-inch pie
  (see recipe, page 351)
¼ cup butter, melted
½ cup sugar
½ teaspoon ground cinnamon
¼ teaspoon ground nutmeg

Dash salt
10 cups thinly sliced peeled
  apples
½ cup light molasses
¼ cup water
3 tablespoons butter,
  melted

Roll out pastry to 15x11-inch rectangle; brush with some of the ¼ cup melted butter. Fold in half. Brush with more butter; fold again and seal edges. Repeat rolling again, brushing with butter, and folding. Chill pastry. Mix together the sugar, cinnamon, nutmeg, and salt; toss with apple slices. Place in 13x9x2-inch baking dish. Combine the molasses, water, and the 3 table- spoons melted butter; pour over apples. Roll pastry to 15x11-inch rectangle. Place over apples; turn edges under and flute. Bake at 400° for 10 minutes. Reduce heat to 325°; bake 30 minutes more. Remove from oven. "Dowdy" the crust by cutting through the crust and apples with a sharp knife. Return pandowdy to oven for 10 minutes more. Serve warm. Serves 6 to 8.

Shoofly Pie

Shoofly Pie *is perhaps the most famous of Pennsylvania Dutch recipes. While there are no firm theories on how the pie got its name, the explanation that the sweetness of the pie made flies a nuisance seems logical.*

1½ cups all-purpose flour
½ cup sugar
¼ teaspoon baking soda
¼ cup butter
½ cup light molasses

½ cup hot water
¼ teaspoon baking soda
1 unbaked 8-inch pastry
  shell (see recipe,
  page 351)

Thoroughly stir together the flour, sugar, and ¼ teaspoon baking soda. Cut in butter till mixture is crumbly. Stir together molasses, hot water, and ¼ teaspoon baking soda. Pour *one-* *third* of the molasses mixture into un- baked pastry shell; sprinkle with *one-* *third* of the flour mixture. Repeat layers, ending with flour mixture. Bake at 375° about 40 minutes. Cool.

Cracker Pudding

2 cups milk
2 beaten egg yolks
¼ cup sugar
1 cup coarsely crushed
  saltine crackers

½ cup shredded coconut
1 teaspoon vanilla
2 egg whites
¼ cup sugar

In saucepan gradually stir milk into egg yolks. Add ¼ cup sugar. Cook and stir over medium heat till thick and bubbly. Remove from heat. Stir in crackers, coconut, vanilla. Pour into 1-quart casserole. Beat egg whites till soft peaks form. Gradually add ¼ cup sugar; beat till stiff peaks form. Spread over hot pudding. Bake at 350° for 12 to 15 minutes. Serves 6 to 8.

Apees

Once *(says legend), a woman named Ann Page made such delicious cookies that she carved her initials into them like a sculptor signing her work. So was born* Apees *(APs) or, as it may be spelled now, apeas, epise, or epees.*

1 cup butter
1 cup sugar
1 egg

½ cup dairy sour cream
2 cups all-purpose flour

Cream together the butter and sugar till the mixture is light and fluffy. Beat in egg. Fold in the sour cream. Stir in the flour a little at a time, beating till the mixture is well blended. Wrap the dough and chill thoroughly. Roll dough on a lightly floured surface to ⅜-inch thickness. Cut with a 2-inch round cutter. Place rounds on an ungreased baking sheet. Bake at 350° till edges are golden, 8 to 10 minutes. Makes about 72.

Cottage Cheese Pie

1 cup all-purpose flour
1 tablespoon sugar
½ teaspoon salt
3 tablespoons butter
3 beaten egg yolks
1 tablespoon lemon juice
2 tablespoons cold water

1½ cups cream-style cottage
   cheese (12 ounces)
⅔ cup sugar
2 tablespoons butter,
   melted
½ cup milk
2 stiffly beaten egg whites

Stir together flour, the 1 tablespoon sugar, and salt. Cut in 3 tablespoons butter till pieces are the size of small peas. Stir in *1 egg yolk.* Sprinkle lemon juice over mixture. Gently toss with fork; push to side of bowl. Repeat procedure with the cold water till all is moistened. Roll out on floured surface to 11-inch circle. Fit into 9-inch pie plate; flute edges but do not prick.

Bake at 350° for 5 minutes. Meanwhile in mixing bowl, beat together the cottage cheese, ⅔ cup sugar, 2 egg yolks, and melted butter till nearly smooth. Gradually stir in milk. Fold in stiffly beaten egg whites. Pour into the partially baked pie shell. Bake at 350° till a knife inserted just off-center comes out clean, 25 to 30 minutes. Chill.

Early Southern Hospitality

Although the southern colonies of the Carolinas and Georgia were neighbors, each had its own very distinctive characteristics. Most of the colonists who chose North Carolina were small farmers who had to get away from the competition of enormous, slave-working plantations and do their own farming. An eighteenth-century writer called North Carolina "a valley of humility between two mountains of conceit."[34] Throughout the colonial period, it remained a sparsely populated land of sturdy farmers. A small but noteworthy group of settlers were the Moravians, a religious sect from Europe who settled in several areas of the United States. These hardworking and peace-loving people were also exceptionally good cooks.

In South Carolina there was a considerable difference between up-country people and those who lived in the lowlands near the sea. The inland areas attracted German, Swiss, and Scotch-Irish farmers, as well as many of English stock who migrated from Virginia. On the coast, the unique element was a population of Huguenots — refugees from Louis XIV's France — who had education, ability, and enough money to get started. Arriving at Charleston in 1680 shortly after that city had been founded, many of them took advantage of generous land terms to acquire huge plantations. Others went to work in the town as artisans and merchants. As soon as these artisans and merchants prospered they built elegant houses in Charleston. The city also became a summer resort for the wealthy planters from the lowlands.

Rice became a source of wealth in South Carolina by accident. In 1694 a ship carrying rice from Madagascar to England was forced off course and stopped at Charleston for repairs. The colonists were glad to see the ship and treated the captain and his crew very well. To express his appreciation

One of the legends that led to the founding of Georgia was the idea that mulberry trees grew wild and in great numbers there. Georgia's promoters had visions of raising silkworms in the colony and eventually England would monopolize the silk industry. Alas for such dreams! The silkworm has its own ideas about food and will eat only the leaves of the white mulberry tree, not those of the black mulberry tree — which was the only type that grew in Georgia.

The maze of waterways in South Carolina helped shape its history. In early days the colonists adapted the abundant rivers and streams into elaborate water systems needed to grow rice. All types of transportation and travel took advantage of the waterways. Slaves paddling boats called periaugers floated the rice crop to Charleston and exchanged it for supplies.

The rice industry of the South had its beginnings in 1680 when a sea captain forced to stop in Charleston repaid the town's kindnesses with a gift of some of his cargo of rice. It grew so well in the Carolina climate that slaves were imported to clear the swampy riverbanks for rice plantations. During the 1700s, rice was called Carolina gold and used as currency. Today, tobacco and cotton are more important.

the captain left the colony some of the only thing he had—rice. Within a short time rice was a staple on Charleston dinner tables. Rice pilafs, rice and seafood, and chicken curries with rice made Charleston famous for its cuisine in which French and African cooking were subtly blended.

In addition the rice fields attracted ducks and other game birds, as well as deer. Shrimp, crab, and succulent fish were at the doorstep. Charleston families kept turtle pens in their yards to insure a good supply of turtle soup and turtle eggs. Yams were used for pone, puddings, pies, and apple dishes. Charleston was famous for benne wafers and for that foamy treat, syllabub—a cool froth of cream, wine, and lemon.

Even the slaves were likely to eat better in Charleston than elsewhere. Typical rations were grits, black-eyed peas, yams, pork, molasses, salt fish, and occasional small amounts of beef.

Georgia was founded in 1733 by social planners General James Oglethorpe and Lord John Percival. Their motives for founding the colony were many, including philanthropic ones providing independence for Great Britain's poor, and economic ones providing freedom from Italian dominance of the silk market. Because of the shortsightedness of its founders the colony had a long hard struggle before becoming firmly established. But succeed it did. In the generation preceding the Revolution, Georgia attracted many German, Scotch-Irish, and Scottish settlers. This, plus the proximity of Spanish Florida, gave the colony a cosmopolitan touch.

Clam Scallop Shells

1 pint shucked clams *or* 2
   7½-ounce cans minced
   clams
½ cup chopped celery
¼ cup chopped onion
2 tablespoons butter
1 tablespoon all-purpose
   flour
¾ teaspoon salt

¼ teaspoon dried thyme,
   crushed
Dash bottled hot
   pepper sauce
1 beaten egg
1 cup soft bread crumbs
2 tablespoons snipped
   parsley
1 tablespoon butter, melted

Drain clams. Coarsely chop whole clams. Cook celery and onion in the 2 tablespoons butter till tender but not brown. Blend in flour, salt, thyme, hot pepper sauce, and dash pepper. Stir small amount of hot mixture into the egg; return to hot mixture. Add clams, *half* the bread crumbs, and parsley. Spoon mixture into 4 or 5 buttered individual baking shells (coquilles). Combine remaining crumbs and the 1 tablespoon melted butter; sprinkle over clam mixture. Bake at 400° till browned, 10 minutes. Serves 4 or 5.

Creamed seafood dishes were often served in scallop shells by colonists living along the ocean where the shells were plentiful. As the settlers moved westward, they brought these shells with them. Serving in shells was so popular that before long, both real and porcelain shells were being shipped up the Mississippi River to be sold at inland trading centers.

Seafood Ragout

½ pint shucked oysters,
   drained
3 tablespoons butter
½ cup sliced fresh
   mushrooms
¼ cup chopped onion
2 tablespoons all-purpose
   flour
½ teaspoon salt
⅛ teaspoon cayenne

⅛ teaspoon ground nutmeg
2 cups light cream
1 pound fresh *or* frozen
   shelled shrimp,
   cooked and drained
1 cup cubed cooked chicken
2 tablespoons snipped
   parsley
2 tablespoons dry sherry
Hot cooked rice

In a saucepan cook oysters in butter till edges curl. Remove oysters; set aside. In same pan cook mushrooms and onion till tender; blend in flour, salt, cayenne, and nutmeg. Add cream all at once. Cook, stirring constantly, till thickened and bubbly. Stir in shrimp, chicken, and oysters; heat through. Stir in parsley and sherry. Serve over hot cooked rice. Serves 6.

Pilaf with Pistachio and Pignolia Nuts

½ cup pignolia nuts (pine
   nuts) *or* toasted
   slivered almonds
¼ cup pistachio nuts

2 cups water
1 cup regular rice
¼ cup butter, melted
1 teaspoon ground mace

Remove shells from pignolia nuts and shells and skins from pistachio nuts. In 2-quart saucepan mix water, rice, and 1 teaspoon salt. Cover tightly; bring to a boil. Reduce heat; continue cooking 14 minutes (do not lift cover). Remove from heat; let stand, covered, 10 minutes. Mix melted butter and mace; pour over hot rice. Add whole nuts. Toss lightly to mix. Serves 6.

Pignolia nuts or what we commonly call pine nuts today were considered quite a delicacy in the colonial South. So much so, that wealthy families imported them from the Middle East for special dishes like Pilaf with Pistachio and Pignolia Nuts.

Hoe Cakes *(see photo, page 64)*

2 cups cornmeal
½ teaspoon salt

1 cup boiling water
Butter

Combine cornmeal and salt. Stir in water; cool. Divide mixture into 8 portions (about ⅓ cup each). Shape each portion into a 3-inch round patty. Fry over medium heat on well-greased griddle, turning to brown both sides, about 7 minutes per side. Serve with butter. Makes 8 hoe cakes.

Cornmeal and water baked into cakes was used throughout the colonies; corn was inexpensive and grown everywhere. In the South they were called Hoe Cakes because they were sometimes baked on the end of a hoe by slaves.

*Hominy, still enjoyed particularly
in the South, was introduced
to the colonists by the Indians. The
name is Indian for parched
corn. To make hominy, colonists
soaked corn in a lye solution
until the hulls dissolved and the
kernels puffed. Then the
hominy was washed and either
baked or boiled.*

Baked Hominy in Cream

2 tablespoons chopped onion
1 tablespoon butter
• • •
2 beaten eggs
1 cup light cream

½ teaspoon salt
⅛ teaspoon white pepper
2 14½-ounce cans golden
   hominy, drained

In small skillet cook onion in butter
till tender but not brown. In a bowl
mix the eggs, cream, salt, and pepper;
beat well. Stir in hominy and onion.

Turn hominy mixture into 10x6x2-
inch baking dish. Bake at 350° just till
set, 25 to 30 minutes. Let stand 5
minutes before serving. Serves 6 to 8.

*A group of Lutherans from Salzburg,
Austria, came to Georgia
in 1734. In 1736 they settled at a
site on the Savannah River
called Ebenezer. Fortunately for us,
Salzburgers brought their recipes
with them and their reputation as
fine cooks became widespread.
One of the recipes they used is Hot
Snapbean Salad.*

Hot Snapbean Salad

4 slices bacon
½ cup finely chopped onion
⅓ to ½ cup vinegar
2 tablespoons sugar
½ teaspoon salt

⅛ teaspoon pepper
3 cups cooked cut green
   beans, drained, *or*
2 16-ounce cans cut
   green beans, drained

In a skillet cook bacon till crisp. Remove bacon; crumble and set aside.
To drippings in skillet stir in onion,
vinegar, sugar, salt, and pepper; cook

2 minutes. Add green beans, stirring
to coat thoroughly with dressing. Heat
through. Turn into a serving bowl;
top with crumbled bacon. Serves 6.

*According to legend Hush Puppies
were so named because they
were used to quiet the hounds. This
poem illustrates just how:
"Hound puppies howls in Georgia
Hound puppies howls at home
I 'spect dey crises in Paris An' I
her'd dey squeks in Rome
But de hunters an' de hounds
Dey don't make a sound
After you all passes Dese here
pones around."* [35]

Hush Puppies

1 cup cornmeal
2 tablespoons all-purpose
   flour
¼ teaspoon baking soda
¼ teaspoon salt
1 beaten egg

¾ cup buttermilk
3 tablespoons finely
   chopped onion
• • •
Lard

In a large bowl stir together the cornmeal, flour, baking soda, and salt. In
a small bowl stir together the egg, buttermilk, and onion. Stir the liquid ingredients into the cornmeal mixture
just till the dry ingredients are moistened. In a 10-inch skillet melt enough

lard to give a depth of ½ inch. Drop
the batter by scant tablespoonfuls into
the hot fat, spreading the batter slightly
to make a patty. Fry till golden, 2 to 3
minutes, turning once. Drain thoroughly on paper toweling. Serve
warm. Makes 24 hush puppies.

*There are several stories about how
Hoppin' John got its name.
One says that children used to hop
once around the table before
eating. Another says that it was
named after the custom of
inviting a guest to eat by saying,
"Hop in, John." But we know
no story to explain why it brings
good luck if served on New
Year's Day—as Southerners still do.*

Hoppin' John *(see photo, page 91)*

1 cup dry black-eyed peas
   (6 ounces)
8 cups water
• • •
6 slices bacon
¾ cup chopped onion

1 clove garlic, minced
• • •
1 cup regular rice
2 teaspoons salt
¼ teaspoon pepper

Rinse the black-eyed peas. In a large
saucepan combine the peas and water;
bring to boiling, then boil for 2 minutes. Remove from heat and let stand
1 hour. Drain, reserving 6 *cups* of the
cooking liquid. In a heavy 3-quart
saucepan cook the bacon, onion, and
garlic till the bacon is crisp and the
onion is tender but not brown. Re-

move bacon; drain on paper toweling;
crumble and set aside. Stir the black-
eyed peas, rice, salt, pepper, and the
reserved cooking liquid into mixture
in saucepan. Bring to boiling; cover
and reduce heat. Simmer 1 hour, stirring occasionally. Stir in the crumbled
bacon. Turn into a serving bowl. Serve
immediately. Makes 8 servings.

Half and Half Bread

2¾ to 3 cups all-purpose
   flour
1 package active dry yeast
1 cup water
¼ cup packed brown sugar
2 tablespoons lard

½ teaspoon salt
• • •
½ cup mashed cooked sweet
   potato
¾ cup cornmeal

In large mixing bowl thoroughly combine *1½ cups* of the flour and the yeast. In saucepan heat water, brown sugar, lard, and salt just till warm (115-120°), stirring constantly. Add to dry mixture in mixing bowl; add potato. Beat at low speed of electric mixer for ½ minute, scraping sides of bowl constantly. Beat 3 minutes at high speed. By hand, stir in cornmeal. Add enough of the remaining all-purpose flour to make a moderately stiff dough. Turn out onto lightly floured surface and knead till

smooth and elastic (5 to 8 minutes). Shape dough into a ball. Place dough in lightly greased bowl; turn once to grease surface. Cover; let rise in a warm place till double (about 1 hour). Punch down; cover and let rest 10 minutes. Shape into a loaf; place in greased 8½x4½x2½-inch loaf pan. Cover; let rise till nearly double (30 to 45 minutes). Bake at 375° for 50 minutes. (Cover with foil after 30 minutes to prevent overbrowning.) Remove from pan; cool. Makes 1.

Sweet potatoes were considered a staple in many places in the colonial South. They were used in all sorts of recipes, including breads. One example is Half and Half Bread. *Originally this Salzburger recipe called for equal parts of flour and cornmeal—hence the name.*

Cracklin' Bread

4 ounces finely diced pork
   fat (1 cup)
1 cup cornmeal
1 cup all-purpose flour

1 teaspoon baking soda
¾ teaspoon salt
1 cup buttermilk
2 beaten eggs

To make cracklings, fry pork fat till crisp. Drain, reserving ⅓ cup drippings. In mixing bowl stir together cornmeal, flour, baking soda, and salt. Add buttermilk, eggs, and reserved

drippings; beat till smooth. Stir in cracklings. Turn into greased 10-inch oven-going skillet. Bake at 425° till done, 15 to 20 minutes. Cut in wedges. Serve warm. Makes 6 servings.

Dixie Pudding

1½ cups soft bread crumbs
   (2 slices)
¼ cup molasses
1 cup grated sweet potato
1 beaten egg
¼ cup packed brown sugar
3 tablespoons butter
½ cup all-purpose flour
1 teaspoon ground cinnamon

½ teaspoon baking soda
½ teaspoon grated orange
   peel
¼ teaspoon ground cloves
   Dash salt
1 cup raisins
½ cup coarsely chopped
   walnuts
   Orange-Brandy Sauce

In a bowl soak bread crumbs in molasses; stir in the grated sweet potato, egg, brown sugar, and butter. Stir till well combined. Stir together the flour, cinnamon, soda, orange peel, cloves, and salt. Stir in the raisins and coarsely chopped walnuts and mix well. Stir in the sweet potato mixture. Grease and lightly flour a 1-quart mold (not a ring mold). Spoon pudding mixture into the mold. Cover the mold with foil and tie with string. Place the mold on a rack in a deep kettle; pour boiling water into kettle to a depth of 1 inch.

Cover and steam till done, 1¾ to 2 hours, keeping the water boiling gently. (Add more boiling water as necessary.) Serve pudding warm with warm Orange-Brandy Sauce. Makes 6 servings.
Orange-Brandy Sauce: In a saucepan combine ¼ cup packed brown sugar, 2 teaspoons cornstarch, and dash salt. Stir in 1 cup orange juice and 3 tablespoons brandy. Cook, stirring constantly, over medium heat till mixture is thickened and bubbly. Stir in 1 tablespoon butter till melted.

Most colonial puddings were boiled in a pudding bag rather than steamed in a mold. Often these bags were made of muslin or cotton and looked like a stocking cap. To use a pudding bag, it had to be dipped in boiling water and floured. Next, the pudding was put in the bag until it was half full, leaving room for the pudding to swell. Then, the bag was dropped into a kettle of boiling water. After the pudding was served, careful homemakers washed out the pudding bag to use another time.

Pictured opposite: Many foods are linked with specific occasions and traditions. Most Southerners feel *Hoppin' John* (see recipe, page 88) must be served on New Year's Day to insure good luck in the coming year. *Fried Pies,* esteemed throughout the colonies, were sometimes called Crab Lanterns because of their shape, or Preaching Pies because they were given to children to keep them quiet during the long church services. In Moravian churches baskets of food, such as *Moravian Sugar Cake* were passed during the hymn singing. It was a love feast to symbolize the brotherly love of those who broke bread together.

An excerpt of the original recipe for this dessert reads:
"*Of the fruit with which Eve her husband did cozen*
Well pared and well chopped at least half a dozen.
Six ounces of bread, let Moll eat the crust....
Six ounces of sugar won't make it too sweet ...
Three hours let it boil without haste or flutter
But Adam won't eat it without wine and butter."[36]

The Moravians were members of the Church of the Brethren which started in Bohemia, Moravia, and Poland. They came to evangelize in Pennsylvania in 1734 and a year later they established their first settlement and mission in Savannah, Georgia. Another mission was later established at Salem, which is now part of Winston-Salem, North Carolina. In addition to the heritage of religious beliefs they left behind, they also left us this recipe for Moravian Sugar Cake.

Fried Pies

1 8-ounce package dried
   apples, cut up
3 cups water
1/4 cup granulated sugar
1 tablespoon lemon juice
1 1/2 teaspoons ground cinnamon
3/4 cup shredded sharp
   Cheddar cheese

3 cups all-purpose flour
1 1/2 teaspoons salt
1 cup lard
3/4 cup cold water
• • •
Fat for frying
Sifted powdered sugar
   (optional)

Rinse apples. In saucepan combine apples and 3 cups water. Cover; simmer 20 to 25 minutes. Drain. Combine apples, sugar, lemon juice, and cinnamon. Stir in cheese. Set aside. Mix flour and salt; cut in lard till mixture resembles size of small peas. Sprinkle water, *1 tablespoon* at a time, over flour mixture; toss with a fork; push to side of bowl. Repeat till all is moistened. Form into a ball. Roll on floured surface to 1/8-inch thickness; cut into 4-inch circles. Place scant tablespoonful filling on half of each circle. Fold over in half-moon shape; seal edges with fork. In a heavy skillet, heat 1/4 inch fat to 375°. Fry pies till brown, 3 to 4 minutes per side. Drain well on paper toweling. Sprinkle with powdered sugar, if desired. Makes 18 to 20.

Eve's Pudding

6 tart apples
6 beaten eggs
4 cups soft bread crumbs
2/3 cup sugar

2/3 cup dried currants
1/4 teaspoon salt
1/8 teaspoon ground nutmeg
Rum Sauce

Peel, core, and finely chop apples. Combine apples, eggs, bread crumbs, sugar, currants, salt, and nutmeg. Turn into greased and floured 6-cup mold (not ring mold); cover with foil and tie with string. Place mold on rack in deep kettle; add boiling water to kettle to depth of 1 inch. Cover kettle and steam for 3 hours. Remove from kettle. Let stand 15 minutes. Unmold. Serve warm Rum Sauce over warm pudding. Makes 6 to 8 servings.
Rum Sauce: In small saucepan melt 2 tablespoons butter; remove from heat. Stir in 1/2 cup sugar and 4 teaspoons cornstarch; add 1 cup water and 1 tablespoon rum all at once. Cook and stir till thickened and bubbly.

Moravian Sugar Cake

1 small potato, peeled and
   cubed
1 package active dry yeast
1/3 cup granulated sugar
1/3 cup lard, melted
1 1/2 teaspoons salt

3 to 3 1/2 cups all-purpose
   flour
2 tablespoons butter
1/2 cup packed brown sugar
1/2 teaspoon ground cinnamon

In saucepan cook potato in 1 cup water till tender. Cool to lukewarm. Set aside 1/4 *cup* cooking liquid. Mash potato in remaining liquid, adding water if needed to make 1 cup potato mixture. Soften yeast in reserved cooking liquid. Combine potato mixture, yeast mixture, granulated sugar, lard, and salt; mix well. Stir in *1 cup* flour; beat well. Let rise in warm place till spongy (30 to 45 minutes). Stir down; add enough remaining flour to make a soft dough. Turn out on floured surface; knead lightly, about 4 minutes. Shape into a ball. Place in lightly greased bowl; turn once. Cover; let rise in warm place till double (about 45 minutes). Punch down; turn out on floured surface. Divide in half. Cover; let rest 10 minutes. Roll into two 8-inch squares. Pat into two greased 8x8x2-inch baking pans. Cover; let rise in warm place till double (about 45 minutes). With finger, make indentations in top at 1 1/2 inch intervals. Dot with butter. Top with mixture of brown sugar and cinnamon. Bake at 375° till golden brown, 20 to 25 minutes. Makes 2.

Syllabub *(see photo, page 99)*

1 cup dry white wine	1 tablespoon lemon juice
¼ cup sugar	2 cups whipping cream
¼ cup brandy	

The name Syllabub *comes from the wine used to make it (imported from Sillery, France, in colonial times) and from "bub" an Elizabethan word for a bubbly drink.*

Mix all ingredients except cream. Let stand till sugar is dissolved. Add cream; whip till soft and fluffy. Spoon into dessert glasses. Serves 8.

Chatham Artillery Punch

2 cups Catawba wine	⅓ cup gin
2 cups strong tea	⅓ cup brandy
⅔ cup rum	⅓ cup lemon juice
½ cup packed brown sugar	1 ⅘-quart bottle dry
½ cup rye whiskey	champagne
½ cup orange juice	

The Chatham Artillery is the oldest military organization in Georgia. It was founded by Revolutionary war veterans living in Chatham County. Regimental functions always livened up when the potent Chatham Artillery Punch *was served.*

Mix wine, tea, rum, sugar, rye, orange juice, gin, brandy, and lemon juice. Cover. Refrigerate 1 week. Stir in champagne. Makes 20 (4-ounce) servings.

Philadelphia and the Founding Fathers

Philadelphia was famous for its elegant living and good food, but it was also a leader in another area, city planning. Cities all over America copied its design. Large rectangular plots for homes interspersed with rectangular parks were used even in such cities as Winston-Salem where its hilly topography made the plan impractical. Another Philadelphia custom copied by hundreds of city planners was the practice of naming streets after popular trees such as chestnut, walnut, or locust rather than after famous people.

The city of Philadelphia, located centrally between the northern and southern colonies, was a logical choice as a meeting place for the Continental Congress. Fortunately for the delegates, it was the most cosmopolitan, the cleanest, the most conveniently laid out, and above all, the best provisioned city in North America. "One of the most beautiful cities in the world"[37] was the verdict of the Frenchman La Rochefoucauld-Liancourt, who visited it soon after the Revolution. For a Parisian, this was the most generous of comments and may well have had to do with the excellent meals and pleasant company he enjoyed in Philadelphia.

In 1776 Philadelphia had thirty thousand inhabitants and was the largest city and the busiest port in colonial America. Much of its population was of British and German origin. On market days the city swelled with the farm families who came into town, driving their heavy wagons loaded with luscious, fresh farm produce as well as meats such as beef, veal, and mutton known far and wide for their succulence.

The market, an arcaded, one-story affair, was the biggest in America, occupying nearly half a mile along the principal street. Market days were Wednesday and Saturday and the public was reminded of them by the ringing of a church bell — known as the butter bell — on the preceding evenings. In those days, and for decades afterward, the man of the family often did the marketing; and one can imagine that along High Street there was much political talk intermixed with discussions of the price of beans.

The fifty-five gentlemen who made history by signing the Declaration of Independence reacted in various ways to the lavish and excellent food of the Quaker City. John Adams was not sure he approved. "A most sinful feast again," he wrote. "Curds and cream, jellies, sweetmeats, twenty sorts of tarts, fools, trifles, floating island, whipped sillibubs. Parmesan cheese, punch, wine, porter, beer...."[38] But, somehow, Mr. Adams managed to get used to it: After attending a dinner given for Congress by the Pennsylvania House of Representatives, he reported he had eaten baked oysters and drunk "Madeira at a great rate and found no inconvenience in it."[39] In fact, he had to admit that it was a most elegant entertainment.

Benjamin Franklin not only found no inconvenience in the pleasure of the table, but was convinced that drinking had the express approval of the Deity. "Reflect on the position God has given the elbow," he wrote. "We see it is designed so that we can drink at our ease, the glass comes just to the mouth. Let us then adore, glass in hand, the wise benevolence...."[40]

But of all the delegates, Thomas Jefferson was probably the most dedicated to gastronomy. In 1776 he was a thirty-three-year-old gentleman farmer, and had it not been "times to try men's souls,"[41] he might well have spent the rest of his life that way. In his "garden book" he enjoyed recording the planting and harvesting of many kinds of fruits and vegetables at his Virginia estate, Monticello. He was aware of every detail of life there — including the abundance of game. According to his overseer, "He knew the name of every tree, and just where one was dead or missing."[42] Jefferson must have enjoyed the many dinners and levees in Philadelphia; he made no bones about saying, "I am an Epicurean."[43]

During the War of the Revolution, Philadelphia suffered from food shortages and was not quite the exciting place it had been. Legend has it that while General Washington was at Valley Forge, his Pennsylvania Dutch cook one day took the ingredients he had at hand — tripe, fatback, vegetables, and pepper — and created the classic, Philadelphia pepper pot soup.

After the peace and before the government moved to Washington, Philadelphia enjoyed about a decade as the seat of government. The excellence of the local cuisine was further enhanced by the arrival of aristocratic refugees from the revolutions then in progress in France and in the French West Indies — and their cooks. Among the many delectable French recipes they introduced was one for the best ice cream yet tasted in America. Records show President Washington bought a "Cream Machine for Making Ice."

Veal Roast with Madeira Sauce

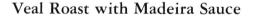

1 1½- to 2-pound veal blade
    roast
2 tablespoons butter
1 cup beef broth
2 small onions, sliced
1 teaspoon salt
½ teaspoon dried thyme,
    crushed

1 bay leaf
3 carrots, sliced
½ cup cold water
3 tablespoons all-purpose
    flour
½ cup sliced fresh
    mushrooms
¼ cup Madeira wine

In Dutch oven brown roast on all sides in butter. Add broth, *half* the onions, salt, thyme, bay leaf, and dash pepper. Cover; simmer 45 minutes. Add remaining onions and carrots. Simmer, covered, till meat and vegetables are tender, 25 to 30 minutes. Remove meat and vegetables to platter; keep warm. Skim off fat. Measure pan juices; add water to make 1 cup. Blend ½ cup cold water into flour; add to pan juices. Add mushrooms. Cook and stir till thickened. Stir in wine. Season to taste. Serve with veal. Serves 6.

The early Quakers of Philadelphia were not the somber, prohibitionists of later generations. Many were wealthy and enjoyed good living. And good living often includes wine. William Penn, himself, fostered Philadelphia's interest in wine by bringing French and Spanish grape vines with him. Of all the wines in colonial Philadelphia, one of the most widely served at fashionable dinner parties was Madeira. In this recipe Madeira is the base for an elegant sauce for veal.

Delegates and visitors to the Continental Congress were impressed by the grid design of Philadelphia's streets. This orderly arrangement did not just happen. Shortly after William Penn received his deed to the land, he dispatched a surveyor to lay out the plan of the town before the colonists arrived.

For its distinction as the busiest port in colonial America, Philadelphia had William Penn to thank. He and his friends set up trade with other colonies and the West Indies to export grain, lumber, meat, wool, tobacco, and horses. They also organized whale fishing in Delaware Bay.

Panned Beef Steaks

4 beef rib eye steaks,
   cut ½ inch thick
Coarsely ground black
   pepper

2 tablespoons butter
Salt
¼ cup chopped shallots *or*
   green onions

Sprinkle steaks with pepper. Melt *half* of the butter in skillet. Cook steaks over medium-high heat till desired doneness. *Total* cooking time is 5 minutes for rare; 7 minutes for medium rare; and 12 to 14 minutes for well done. Season with salt. Remove to platter; keep warm. Add remaining butter to skillet. Cook shallots 1 to 2 minutes. Spoon mixture over steaks. Serves 4.

Fish House Punch

1 cup packed brown sugar
2 cups rum
1 cup unsweetened pineapple
   juice

1 cup lemon juice
1 cup brandy
¼ cup peach brandy
Ice ring

Dissolve brown sugar in 8 cups water. Stir in rum, juices, and brandies. Chill. Serve in punch bowl with ice ring. Makes 25 (4-ounce) servings.

The most famous of Philadelphia's elegant eating clubs is the State in Schuylkill or the Fish House. Founded in 1732 by a group of Quakers, the club was a place where hunters and fishermen could relax and drink Fish House Punch.

Philadelphia Pepper Pot Soup

2 pounds honeycomb tripe
1 1½-pound veal knuckle
3 medium carrots, sliced
1 large onion, sliced
½ cup sliced celery
2 tablespoons snipped
   parsley
1 teaspoon dried marjoram,
   crushed
1 teaspoon dried summer
   savory, crushed

1 teaspoon dried basil,
   crushed
½ teaspoon dried thyme,
   crushed
½ teaspoon whole black
   pepper
⅛ to ¼ teaspoon cayenne
4 whole cloves
2 bay leaves
2 medium potatoes, peeled
   and cut in ½-inch cubes

In Dutch oven cover tripe with water. Add 1 teaspoon salt for each quart of water used. Simmer, covered, till tripe has clear, jellylike appearance, 3 to 4 hours. Drain; cut tripe into ½-inch pieces. Refrigerate. Meanwhile, in 4-quart Dutch oven place veal knuckle, carrots, onion, celery, parsley, remaining seasonings, and 1 teaspoon salt. Cover with 6 cups water. Simmer, covered, till meat comes off bone, about 2 hours. Strain, discarding bones and vegetables; refrigerate. Skim fat from broth. Heat 4 cups of veal broth; add tripe and potatoes. Simmer till potatoes are tender, 15 minutes. Serves 6.

Philadelphia was a thriving city and its residents enjoyed good living even before the Continental Congress came to town. The city happily puts its name on several tasty dishes which may or may not have originated there. Two examples are Philadelphia Pepper Pot Soup and Philadelphia Scrapple.

Some would claim that pepper pot was hastily concocted to feed General Washington's troops. The story may be true, but don't count on making this soup in a hurry. It takes long, slow cooking to prepare the broth and bring out the flavor, especially of the two kinds of pepper.

Scrapple was a thrifty way to use small pieces of pork at butchering time. Cooked with cornmeal and seasonings, this meaty mush was sliced and fried up crisp for breakfast. It probably came to town via the German farmers who brought meat and produce to the city.

Philadelphia Scrapple

1½ pounds boneless pork
   shoulder, cubed
1½ cups cornmeal
½ teaspoon salt

½ teaspoon dried sage,
   crushed
All-purpose flour
Fat for frying

Simmer pork in salted water to cover till meat is tender, about 1 hour. Drain; reserve broth. Measure broth; add water to make 4 cups. Return liquid to saucepan. Shred meat. Stir into broth with cornmeal, salt, sage, and ¼ teaspoon pepper. Bring to boiling, stirring constantly. Cook and stir till thick enough to make a cross with spoon, about 5 minutes. Pour into greased 9x5x3-inch loaf pan. Cover; chill till firm. Unmold; cut into ½-inch slices. Dust with flour. Brown in small amount of hot fat on both sides, about 10 minutes. Serve with warm maple syrup, if desired. Makes 8 servings.

Next time you see a picture of our national emblem remember— it would have been a turkey instead of an eagle if Ben Franklin had had his way. He thought the wild turkey a better choice because "it is a true native of America."[44] *The turkey didn't make it to the Great Seal of the United States, but it was a favorite at the Franklin dinner table—and ours.*

Philadelphia's location assured a plentiful supply of fish and seafood. Perch, rockfish, and catfish came from the Schuylkill River, while the Delaware River provided shad and salmon. Nearby Chesapeake Bay was an almost never-ending source of oysters, crabs, terrapin, and herring. Delicate Salmon Mousse *and* Fish à la Reine, *considered gourmet food today, were regular fare in even modest households.*

Oyster Sauce for Turkey

1 pint shucked oysters
2 tablespoons butter
3 tablespoons all-purpose
   flour
Dash ground nutmeg

¾ cup milk
2 teaspoons lemon juice
   • • •
Hot sliced cooked turkey

Drain oysters, reserving ¼ cup liquid. Cut up large oysters. Simmer oysters and reserved liquid, stirring constantly, till oysters curl, about 5 minutes. Set aside. Melt butter; blend in flour, nutmeg, ½ teaspoon salt, and dash pepper. Add milk. Cook and stir till thickened and bubbly. Stir in oyster mixture and lemon juice. Heat through. Serve with turkey. Makes 2 cups.

Salmon Mousse

2 egg yolks
¼ cup butter
¼ cup all-purpose flour
¾ teaspoon salt
⅛ teaspoon white pepper
1½ cups light cream
1 16-ounce can salmon,
   drained and finely
   flaked
1 tablespoon lemon juice
1 teaspoon grated onion
4 stiffly beaten egg whites

1 small onion, thinly
   sliced
2 tablespoons butter
2 tablespoons all-purpose
   flour
1 bay leaf
1 whole clove
1 cup milk
3 chopped hard-cooked eggs
2 teaspoons capers
¼ teaspoon salt
Dash white pepper

Beat egg yolks slightly with a fork. Melt ¼ cup butter in saucepan; blend in ¼ cup flour, ¾ teaspoon salt, and ⅛ teaspoon white pepper. Add cream all at once. Cook and stir till thickened and bubbly. Remove from heat. Stir a moderate amount of hot mixture into egg yolks. Return to hot mixture. Cook and stir 2 minutes more. Stir in salmon, lemon juice, and grated onion. Fold in stiffly beaten egg whites. Turn into an ungreased 1½-quart soufflé dish. Bake at 325° for 50 to 55 minutes. Serve immediately.

Meanwhile, in saucepan cook sliced onion in 2 tablespoons butter till tender; stir in 2 tablespoons flour. Add bay leaf and clove. Stir in milk all at once. Cook and stir till thickened and bubbly. Remove from heat; strain into saucepan. Add chopped eggs, capers, ¼ teaspoon salt, and dash pepper; heat through. Serve warm sauce over mousse. Makes 4 to 6 servings.

Fish à la Reine

½ cup chopped fresh
   mushrooms (2 ounces)
2 tablespoons butter
2 tablespoons all-purpose
   flour
¾ teaspoon salt
⅛ teaspoon white pepper
1¼ cups milk
1 cup fish stock*

2 beaten egg yolks
1 pound fish, cooked and
   broken into small
   pieces (2 cups)
2 tablespoons snipped
   parsley
   • • •
6 frozen patty shells,
   baked

In medium saucepan cook the mushrooms in butter till tender. Blend in flour, salt, and white pepper. Add milk and fish stock all at once. Cook quickly, stirring constantly, till mixture thickens and bubbles. Remove from heat. Gradually blend a moderate amount of milk mixture into egg yolks. Return mixture to saucepan and cook 2 minutes more, stirring constantly. Fold in cooked fish and snipped parsley. Cover and cook over low heat till heated through. Serve fish mixture in prepared patty shells. Makes 6 servings.

*Note: Milk may be substituted for fish stock, if desired.

Strawberry Flummery *(see photo, page 99)*

⅓ cup sugar
¼ cup cornstarch
3 cups milk
1 beaten egg yolk

2 teaspoons vanilla
2 tablespoons sugar
2 cups fresh strawberries,
  halved

In a saucepan combine ⅓ cup sugar, cornstarch, and ¼ teaspoon salt. Blend in milk. Cook and stir till mixture thickens and bubbles. Stir a moderate amount of hot mixture into egg yolk; return to saucepan. Cook and stir till thickened, about 2 minutes more. Remove from heat; stir in vanilla. Pour into 1½-quart serving bowl. Cover surface with plastic wrap; cool. Chill 2 hours. Sprinkle remaining sugar over berries. Place atop flummery. Serves 6.

Trifle *(see photo, page 99)*

8 cups sponge cake cubes
  (1-inch cubes)
¾ to 1 cup sherry
½ cup strawberry, apricot,
  or raspberry jam
2 eggs
1 egg yolk
1¾ cups milk

¼ cup granulated sugar
1 egg white
1 tablespoon powdered sugar
1 cup whipping cream
¼ teaspoon vanilla
• • •
¼ cup slivered almonds

Place *half* of the cake cubes in bottom of 2-quart clear glass bowl. Moisten with some of the sherry. Cover with jam. Top with remaining cake cubes. Add enough additional sherry to moisten cake well. In saucepan beat eggs and egg yolk. Stir in milk and granulated sugar. Cook and stir till custard coats a metal spoon. Remove from heat. Cool at once in ice water; stir occasionally. Spoon cooled custard over cake. Beat egg white to soft peaks. Gradually add powdered sugar, beating till stiff peaks form. Whip cream with vanilla. Fold into egg white. Pile mixture atop custard. Refrigerate 6 hours or overnight. Garnish with slivered almonds. Serves 10 to 12.

Floating Island *(see photo, page 99)*

Separate 3 eggs; set yolks aside. Beat whites till soft peaks form. Gradually add ⅓ cup sugar, beating till stiff peaks form. In 10-inch skillet heat 3 cups milk to simmering. Drop egg white mixture in 8 portions into milk; simmer, uncovered, till firm, about 5 minutes. Lift from milk. Reserve milk for custard. Drain meringues on paper toweling. Chill. For custard, slightly beat reserved yolks with 2 more eggs. Add ½ cup sugar and dash salt. Stir into reserved slightly cooled milk. Cook and stir over low heat till custard coats a metal spoon. Cool quickly in ice water. Stir in 1½ teaspoons vanilla; chill. Top with meringues and a few slivered almonds. Serves 8.

Plumb Gingerbread

½ cup butter
½ cup sugar
½ cup molasses
2 eggs
2 cups all-purpose flour

1 tablespoon ground ginger
¾ teaspoon baking soda
¾ cup milk
½ cup raisins*
½ cup dried currants*

In mixing bowl cream butter and sugar together. Add molasses and eggs; beat thoroughly. Stir flour, ginger, and baking soda together. Add dry ingredients to creamed mixture alternately with milk, beating after each addition. Stir in raisins and currants. Turn into greased and lightly floured 13x9x2-inch baking pan. Bake at 350° till done, 25 to 30 minutes.

Note: All raisins or all currants may be used in gingerbread, if desired.

Desserts played an important part in elegant menus right into the Federal period. After the meal, dishes and tablecloth were removed and an assortment of cakes, tarts, or custards was served. To enhance the elegance of this collection, serving dishes were formally balanced and figurines served as centerpieces.

In 1790 the Capitol moved from New York to Philadelphia and stayed about 10 years. George Washington completed his presidency there and John Adams began his. The First Families were expected to entertain often. Abigail Adams tells about it in a letter dated June 23, 1797.

"Today will be the 5th great dinner I have had, about 36 gentlemen today, as many more next week and I shall have got through the whole of Congress and their appendages. Then comes the 4th of July which is a still more tedious day, as we must have then not only all Congress but all the Gentlemen of the city, the Gouvernour and officers and company, all of whom the late President used to treat with cake, punch and wine. What the house would not hold used to be placed at long tables in the yard. As we are here we cannot avoid the trouble or expense...I hope the day will not be hot. I am like to be favoured with a cool one today at which I rejoice, for it is no small task to be sit at table with 30 gentlemen."[45]

Pictured opposite: This lavish display of desserts is but a sampling of those enjoyed well into the Federal Period. Front to back: *Trifle, Maids of Honor, Strawberry Flummery,* apricot-sauced *Blancmange,* wafers, *Floating Island,* and *Syllabub.* (See index for pages.)

"Unflavored" gelatin in granular form was unknown until 1890. Until then homemakers made their own gelatins by boiling calves' or pigs' feet or preparing isinglass. The latter, not to be confused with mica, is a whitish, semitransparent gelatin found in the air bladders of certain fish. Since neither of the homemade products was exactly tasteless, large amounts of suitable herbs or spices were often used both to add new flavor and to cover up the original one.

General Washington was especially fond of Beef and Kidney Pie. *On one occasion, a small dinner planned at his West Point headquarters in 1779, he was glad to have the pies to help fill up the table. Although ham and roast beef would be at the head and foot, he commented that the presence of two* Beef and Kidney Pies, *one on either side of the center dish, would reduce the distance between other serving dishes to six feet, else the distance would be almost twelve feet.*

Philadelphia Vanilla Ice Cream

In saucepan mix 1 cup light cream; 1 cup sugar; 1 vanilla bean, split in half; and ¼ teaspoon salt. Cook and stir over low heat 10 minutes. *Do not let mixture boil.* Remove from heat. Remove vanilla bean. When cool enough to handle, scrape out seed and soft part from inside bean; stir into cooked mixture. Discard pod. Chill well. Stir in 2 cups whipping cream and 1 cup light cream. Pour into ice cream freezer. Freeze according to manufacturer's directions. After freezing, let ripen 4 hours. Makes 1 quart.

Blancmange

½ pound whole almonds,*
  blanched
¼ cup milk*
1 envelope unflavored
  gelatin

½ cup sugar
1 tablespoon rum *or* kirsch
1 cup whipping cream
• • •
Brandied Apricot Sauce

Pound almonds in a mortar or blend in covered blender container till very fine. Stir milk and 2 cups hot water* into almonds; let stand 15 minutes. Strain mixture through several thicknesses of cheesecloth, squeezing out as much liquid as possible (about 1½ cups). Reserve liquid. In saucepan mix unflavored gelatin and sugar; add almond liquid. Cook and stir over low heat till gelatin is dissolved. Chill till partially set; add rum or kirsch. Whip till frothy. Whip cream; fold into almond mixture. Turn into oiled 3-cup mold. Chill till firm, about 3 hours. Serve with Brandied Apricot Sauce. Makes 6 to 8 servings.

Brandied Apricot Sauce: Halve the apricots from one 8¾-ounce can unpeeled apricots. In saucepan simmer undrained apricots 5 minutes. Stir in 1 tablespoon apricot brandy. Cool.

*1⅓ cups milk and ¾ teaspoon almond extract may be substituted for almonds, milk, and water. Omit straining step.

Beef and Kidney Pie

1 pound beef *or* veal kidney
1 medium onion, sliced
⅓ cup dry red wine
4 bay leaves
3 whole black peppercorns
2 pounds beef round steak,
  cut in 1-inch cubes
½ cup all-purpose flour
½ cup chopped onion
3 tablespoons lard, melted

¼ cup snipped parsley
¼ cup chopped celery leaves
1 teaspoon dried marjoram,
  crushed
1 cup sliced fresh
  mushrooms
2 tablespoons all-purpose
  flour
Pastry Topper
Milk

Remove any membrane and hard white parts from kidney; cut in 1-inch pieces. Mix kidney, sliced onion, wine, *three* bay leaves, peppercorns, and ½ teaspoon salt; marinate at room temperature for 1 hour. Coat steak cubes with *part* of the ½ cup flour. In Dutch oven brown steak cubes and chopped onion in lard. Drain kidney, reserving ⅓ cup marinade. Strain marinade; set aside. Coat kidney with remainder of ½ cup flour. Add to beef. Cook, uncovered, 5 minutes. Stir in parsley, celery leaves, marjoram, remaining bay leaf, and 1½ cups water. Cover; simmer till meat is tender, about 1 hour. Stir in mushrooms; cook 5 minutes. Blend reserved marinade into 2 tablespoons flour. Stir into meat mixture. Cook and stir till thick and bubbly. Remove bay leaf. Pour into 2-quart casserole. Top with Pastry Topper. Cut slits for escape of steam. Turn under edge and flute. Brush top with milk. Bake at 450° about 20 minutes. Makes 6 servings.

Pastry Topper: Stir together 1 cup all-purpose flour and ½ teaspoon salt. Cut in ⅓ cup lard till mixture resembles small peas. Sprinkle 3 tablespoons cold water, 1 tablespoon at a time, over mixture, tossing gently with fork and pushing to side of bowl. Form into ball; roll to a circle ½ to 1 inch larger than casserole.

Although presented by the committee (center) of John Adams, Roger Sherman, Robert Livingston, Thomas Jefferson, and Benjamin Franklin, the Declaration of Independence was mainly the result of two weeks' effort by Thomas Jefferson. Congress cut about one-fourth of his original draft and corrected his repeated misspelling of "its" as "it's."

*Long before the Founding Fathers
met to launch the nation,
kitchen and farm gardens had gone
beyond corn, beans, and squash.
A profusion of vegetables were grown,
including French artichokes,
cucumbers, cauliflower, peppers,
asparagus, beets, peas, lettuce,
and salad greens, and good cooks
served sophisticated soups
as this one made with cucumber.*

Chocolate Pots de Crème

2 4-ounce packages sweet
   cooking chocolate
2 cups light cream

2 tablespoons sugar
6 beaten egg yolks
1 teaspoon vanilla

Break up chocolate. Place *half* of the chocolate in blender container. Cover; blend till chocolate is grated. Repeat with remaining chocolate. In saucepan mix cream, sugar, dash salt, and chocolate. Cook and stir over low heat till blended and satin smooth. (Mixture should be *slightly thick but not boiling.*) Slowly pour into egg yolks, beating well. Stir in vanilla. Pour into 10 pots de crème cups or *small* sherbets. Cover; chill till firm. Serves 10.

Cucumber Soup

4 large cucumbers
1 tablespoon finely chopped
   onion
1 tablespoon butter

3 cups chicken broth
1 cup light cream
2 beaten egg yolks
  White pepper

Reserve *half* a cucumber for garnish; peel, seed, and finely chop remaining cucumbers to make 3½ cups. Cook onion in butter till tender. Add chopped cucumber and chicken broth. Simmer, covered, till cucumber is tender and transparent, about 10 minutes. Press mixture through sieve or food mill. Heat through. Mix cream and egg yolks. Stir a moderate amount of hot mixture into egg mixture; return to hot mixture. Cook and stir till slightly thickened. Season to taste with white pepper and ¾ teaspoon salt. Serve hot or chilled, garnished with slices of reserved cucumber. Makes 6 cups.

Roast Suckling Pig

Scrub one 12- to 14-pound suckling pig with a stiff brush, rinse cavity, and pat dry. Close opening with skewers and string, lacing closely and tightly. Truss by bringing feet forward and tying in kneeling position with string. Place firm ball of foil in pig's mouth and cover nose, ears, and tail with foil. Insert meat thermometer in thigh muscle. Roast at 325° till meat thermometer registers 170°, 3 to 4 hours. Makes 8 servings.

Roast Leg of Lamb

Season one 5- to 7-pound leg of lamb with salt and pepper. Place, fat side up, on a rack in shallow roasting pan; do not add water. Insert meat thermometer. Roast at 325° till thermometer registers 170° to 180°, 2½ to 3½ hours. Let stand 15 minutes before carving. Makes 2 or 3 servings per pound.

The colonists liked their roasted meat "done to a turn" and the phrase was meant literally since all large cuts were cooked on a turning spit in the fireplace. Many systems were invented to make the job easier. One was a reflector oven. It was open on the side toward the fire and the spit was rotated by hand at intervals by means of a ratchet. (See Chapter 3, Early American Kitchens for more information.)

Albemarle Peach Chutney

12 cups sliced, peeled fresh peaches (5 pounds)
4½ cups packed dark brown sugar (2 pounds)
2 cups vinegar
5 cups diced peeled tart apples (6 medium)
2 cups raisins
½ cup finely chopped onion
2 teaspoons grated lemon peel
⅓ cup lemon juice
1 tablespoon mustard seed
2 teaspoons ground ginger
2 teaspoons ground cumin
1 teaspoon paprika

Mix peaches, sugar, and vinegar. In 6-quart kettle mix apples, raisins, onion, lemon peel, lemon juice, mustard, ginger, cumin, and paprika. Cook, covered, over medium heat for 10 minutes; stir often. Add peach mixture. Bring to boil; reduce heat. Boil gently, uncovered, till slightly thickened, about 30 minutes. Pack into hot pint jars, leaving ½-inch headspace. Wipe jar rims; adjust lids. Process in boiling water bath 20 minutes (start timing when water returns to boiling). Makes 7 or 8 pints.

History counts many prominent Virginia planters as Founding Fathers; and, naturally, these men talked horticulture along with politics. Thomas Jefferson whose home Monticello was in Albemarle County shared more than views on a bill of rights with his friend George Mason of Gunston Hall. His papers include the letter Mason sent him in 1780 along with "rare-ripe peach stones" and instructions for planting them.

Spiced Peaches

12 inches stick cinnamon
5 cups sugar
2 cups water
1 cup vinegar
2 teaspoons whole cloves
2½ pounds fresh peaches

Break cinnamon. In 4- to 6-quart kettle combine sugar, water, vinegar, and spices. Heat to boiling. Keep hot but not boiling. Wash peaches well; peel, halve, and pit. Add peach halves to sugar syrup as soon as they are cut. Heat peaches in sugar syrup 5 minutes. Pack fruit and syrup into hot pint jars, leaving ½-inch headspace. Adjust lids. Process in boiling water bath 20 minutes (start timing when water returns to boiling). Makes 3 pints.

Julienne Soup

6 cups beef broth
2 carrots, cut in julienne strips
1 medium potato, peeled and cut in julienne strips
1 small turnip, peeled and cut in julienne strips
1 small onion, cut in thin wedges
½ teaspoon dried marjoram, crushed

In saucepan bring broth, carrots, potato, turnip, onion, marjoram, and ¼ teaspoon salt to boil. Cover; reduce heat. Simmer till vegetables are tender, 15 to 20 minutes. Top with seasoned croutons, if desired. Serves 8.

While the Constitutional Convention was in progress in Philadelphia, Thomas Jefferson was serving his country in France as Minister Plenipotentiary. His daughters were with him, and when they came home, a French governess, Annette, came with them. Julienne Soup is a recipe Annette brought with her.

Chapter 3

Early American Kitchens

A basic New England fireplace with hearth and built-in oven

The first permanent homes of the New World settlers were one- or two-room affairs with an enormous fireplace occupying one wall. Eventually houses acquired more rooms, even a separate kitchen, but the cooking fireplace, with hearth and beehive oven changed very little until the cookstove took over in the mid 1800s. In the Southwest fireplaces were made of adobe and might have a raised hearth. (See photo, page 43.) Elsewhere they were usually stone or brick, and the oven was either part of the fireplace or located nearby.

Fireplaces in New England ranged in height from four or five feet to high and wide enough for a person to stand in it. A mantel made from a heavy beam used as a lintel supported the masonry above it. The mantel darkened from the heat and smoke, but it seldom actually burned. The early lug poles didn't fare as well. These poles supported the cooking pots that hung over the coals. Until foundries could be established, all metal had to be imported, so in the first fireplaces the lug poles were of green wood that were serious fire hazards when they dried, charred, and finally collapsed or burst into flame. Wooden lug poles had to be changed frequently or kettles would drop into the fire splashing boiling food over anyone nearby. Everyone had to know first aid for burns.

Roaring fires are for the romantics; serious cooking was done over a small fire of carefully managed coals fed continually by short, split logs. Since the hearth was large and extended a foot or more into the room, it provided ample space for what we'd call top burner cooking. The cook lifted a scoopful of live coals from the main fire to make a small pile on the hearth. On top of the mound she set a footed skillet or small Dutch oven. Depending upon the menu, there might be two or three mounds of coals going at once and the cook would have to step nimbly between them.

FIREPLACE EQUIPMENT

Certain basic items were standard; they reappeared in household inventories throughout the colonial and pioneer years or as long as people depended on the fireplace for cooking. A wealthier family might have a greater number of items but the specific pieces remained the same.

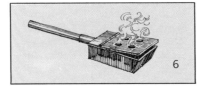

Cooking pots (1) of brass, iron, or a bell-metal type of bronze came in many sizes with capacities ranging from one or two quarts to twenty gallons. They were equipped with a handle for hanging over the fire and feet for standing on the coals.

Devices to raise and lower cooking pots were (2) a notched rack called a trammel or (3) interlocking pot hooks. These hangers were suspended from the lug pole or from a crane (4). Cranes were built into new fireplaces when the oven became a separate compartment.

A Dutch oven (5) was a three-legged pot that stood over the coals and had a flanged lid on which coals could be heaped. Later models had swivel handles so the oven could be turned around for even heating.

A fire pan (6) or box for carrying "borrowed" coals needed perforations for air to circulate so the coals didn't die out on the way home.

BURN REMEDY

"If a person who is burned will patiently hold the injured part in water, it will prevent the formation of a blister. If the water be too cold, it may be slightly warmed, and produce the same effect. People in general are not willing to try it for a sufficiently long time. Chalk and hog's lard simmered together are said to make a good ointment for a burn."

Child, *American Frugal Housewife*, 1832

TO ROAST IS NOT TO BAKE

The colonial cook roasted meat by placing it near a bed of glowing coals, not by shutting it in an oven as we do today. She would have called our way "baking." In the earliest days the meat was hung on a stout cord from the lug pole in the fireplace. She couldn't hang the meat and walk away, however. The "roasting string" must be twisted often and constant vigilance was required lest the meat catch fire or drop onto the hot coals. When fireplaces could be equipped with andirons, the meat was balanced on a metal spit between them and turned by hand or by a system of weights.

The reflector oven or tin kitchen, as it was sometimes called, was another step forward for roasting meat in the fireplace. The oven was open on the side facing the fire. The shiny surface of the curved side farthest from the fire reflected the heat and hastened cooking. Some models had a small door on the back so the cook could peek at the meat or baste it during cooking. The spit inside was turned at intervals on a ratchet. When the spit had come full circle, the meat was "done to a turn."

COOKING ACCESSORIES

Andirons (7) not only held the wood in the fireplace, but they also could be fitted to support a metal spit for roasting meat. Turning the spit by hand was a hot, tedious job, so many ingenious weights and pulleys were contrived to make the job easier.

The long-handled skillet on legs (8) was commonly called a spider, and was used on a small bed of coals pulled out from the main fire. Saucepots and griddles were also available on legs and with long handles.

Heat from the cooking fire was regulated not only by the amount of wood but also by moving the food closer or farther away from the coals. One useful device was a trivet (9) on long legs. A well-equipped household might have several of different heights. Trivets low enough to fit inside a Dutch oven doubled as a rack when the kettle was used for baking.

The toaster (10) was a metal grid that held one or more slices of bread. It, too, had a long handle and boasted a swivel action at the base so the toast could be turned. Some toasters were fairly simple in design, but some makers of toasters were artists, too, and their products could be ornate as well as utilitarian.

Managing the fire, or "Don't let the fire go out!"

Matches were a rarity until well into the nineteenth century. Thus, banking the fire properly at night and keeping it going in the daytime were responsibilities not to be taken lightly. The alternatives were (a) to direct sparks, struck with a piece of flint, at wood shavings or dry tinder until they caught fire, or (b) to send one of the children to a neighbor's house to "borrow" hot coals. The latter was easy if neighbors were not too distant, but sometimes the tediousness of the flint was the only way.

Ashes, the by-products of a wood fire, were a valuable commodity too. They cleaned the hearth, absorbed spilled grease, and were a source of lye for homemade soap. In New England any excess soap or ashes could be traded at the country store for necessary provisions not produced at home. Many early village stores had their own asheries where wood ashes were collected for export. Potash for industrial use was in short supply in England and the ashes were an important return cargo for ships bringing supplies to the colonies.

UTENSILS AND GADGETS

Space was limited on the vessels bringing colonists to this country; so too was the number of household goods each family could carry. In the first months and years "make do" was a way of life. Wood was carved into bowls and buckets, shells were attached to handles for spoons, and gourds made satisfactory dippers. As a family accumulated brass, tin, or pewter objects, and made or traded for pottery, the makeshift utensils became obsolete. The establishment of forges and foundries also increased the variety of items available.

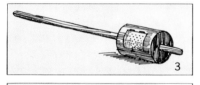

Wood was plentiful up and down the eastern coast. Large mixing bowls (1) such as this one on legs were fashioned at home. The legs weren't luxuries—tables for work space were sadly lacking in early houses and these bowls eased the problem. Wooden buckets (2) were necessary both indoors and out. The design has changed over the years, but not their usefulness.

Those who favored coffee and could afford it roasted the green beans near the fire in a coffee roaster such as the one shown (3). Roasted beans were ground in a coffee mill for each brew.

As time went on gadgets became more specialized. This long-handled oyster roaster (4) with slots for six of the succulent shellfish was standard equipment in a southern kitchen in the nineteenth century.

Black pot specialties

For several reasons the black pot hanging over the coals was most practical. Cooking in a liquid was necessary to rehydrate the dried corn for the ever-present porridge or mush—hasty pudding was by no means instant. And, soups and stews of the day needed a long slow cooking to blend flavors and make the meat tender—mostly the latter. Dumplings could be added to the pot to use up the gravy, to stretch the meal, and to make the finished dish look pretty.

More importantly, the housewife simply didn't have time for pot watching. The slow cooking freed her for her other household chores. Occasionally she'd have to add water to the mixture in the pot to replace liquid that had boiled away. Early hand-written recipes call for more liquid than we would think advisable, but those cooks knew how much would evaporate.

It wasn't only the main course that went into the pot. Heating up the big oven was a once-a-week job, but you could boil a pudding any day in the black pot. Puddings were usually made of cornmeal or leftover bread, sweetened with molasses and dressed up with raisins. The dough was tied loosely—to allow for expansion—in a floured cloth and dropped into boiling water till done. Thus today's boil-in-the-bag is not a new idea if you count the pudding bag. This technique of making boiled pudding went west with the pioneers and on the trail with the cowboys (see *Son-of-a-Gun-in-a-Sack* on page 207.)

Using the Dutch oven

Between baking days the colonial cook used a Dutch oven (see drawing, page 102). It was an indispensible pot—she could bake in it or cook stew.

The oven was wide enough to accommodate only one baking pan or pie dish. These had to be relatively shallow to allow room for a trivet on the bottom and head space between the pan and the flanged lid. Large Dutch ovens were suspended over the coals and turned at intervals to regulate the heat. Smaller versions were set in the coals. Either way heat on top came from coals on the lid. If a long baking time was needed, the fresh coals would replace dying ones.

WAFFLES AND WAFERS

There was quite a knack to wielding either a waffle iron or wafer iron. First the closed iron was heated in the coals for several minutes. When hot, the hinged end was rested on a thick wooden board and the iron was

opened by dropping the lower handle and anchoring it with one knee. A small amount of dough was spooned onto the iron, it was closed quickly, and the waffle cooked while the iron rested on the board. The iron wasn't returned to the coals with the waffle in it. In fact, a skillful waffle maker could cook more than one waffle from a single heating of the iron.

Using a beehive oven

Once a week (twice if you had a big family) a day was devoted to baking. The brick or stone oven was heated by letting a fire burn for several hours.

When the oven was hot, the ashes and coals were quickly removed, the oven swept clean, and the food placed inside. Speed was important because the baking was done on retained heat. Dishes that needed the longest cooking went to the rear. Others were arranged to avoid hot spots. As soon as the food was in the oven, the door was set in place to contain the heat.

Since the side of the oven nearest the fireplace was hotter than the outer side, the cook needed to be something of a magician to get her bread and cakes to bake evenly. A cake that came out higher on one side was called a "sad cake."

Occasionally some dish such as baked beans would be cooked overnight in the oven. Any cracks around the door could be sealed with mud or clay to hold in the heat.

This colonial housewife is removing loaves of freshly baked bread from the oven with the aid of a peel. The long-handled wooden or metal paddle was used to retrieve hot foods from the beehive oven.

BAKING DISHES

By the mid 1600s crude pottery was being made in Virginia, and soon in other locales that had suitable clay and a "pot baker" among its settlers. Nearly a hundred years passed before domestic pottery was common.

The covered beanpot (1) was typical of the plain, yet functional, earthenware containers so well suited to brick-oven baking. Since the handles on these pots were more decorative than practical, some pots had only one. Even a simple redware bowl (2) might carry a bit of decoration, perhaps a yellow zigzag pattern around the rim. Some potters glazed only the interior of the bowl, the rim, and a short distance down the outside. No need to waste glaze where a smooth surface wasn't needed. Besides, the contrast in color and texture was pleasing to the eye.

The pudding dish (3) has all but disappeared from the American kitchen. Deeper than today's pie plate, it was used for *Indian Pudding*, *Green Corn Pudding*, chicken puddings, plus a variety of two-crust meat pies. (See index for pages.)

The handy salamander

No matter how well the cook knew her oven—its hot spots and downdrafts—sometimes it simply wouldn't stay hot long enough to brown bread or pies satisfactorily. She solved the problem with a salamander, a long-handled browning iron. It was heated in the coals and then held over the food much the way we'd run something under the broiler to brown it. Unfortunately this affected only the top crust. The bottom crust of a pie would be "doughy" to our palates.

Not all the uses of a salamander were cosmetic. It could be counted on to melt cheese on pieces of bread or to set the sugary glaze on a cake. In fact, this is the way the *Orange-Raisin Cake* was originally prepared. (See recipe, page 54.)

IF THE OVEN BE SLACK

Any housewife worth her salt (and salt was worth a lot) took advantage of the heat left after baking was completed. In the slowly cooling oven she sometimes made meringues or dried bunches of herbs or roasted nuts and seeds. If the oven was very warm, she might experiment with a pan of cookies or biscuits for the children. She couldn't do many batches for each time the oven was opened, more heat escaped.

Kitchen staples

Let us assume the housewife has mastered the technical side of managing the fire and cooking, and examine what basic ingredients she had.

Cornmeal: At first cornmeal was made at home from cooked and dried corn kernels using a process learned from the Indians. The kernels were placed in a hollowed stump and pounded with a pestle and just fitted into the hollow. The other end of pestle was tied to a bent sapling so that it needed only to be pounded down and the springy sapling did the lifting. Later, when windmills and waterwheels powered grinding stones, corn was brought to the nearby mill.

Flour: Wheat and rye were slow to take hold in the New World, but with perseverance strains were developed that were hardy enough for even New England's rugged climate. These grains, too, were ground at the mill.

Salt: This seasoning and preservative was hard to come by. The housewife traded soap, or eggs, or homemade goods for it at the country store. If the salt were not imported, it had to be distilled from seawater, obtained from the salt licks in the forest, or mined from underground deposits.

Spices: These were the kitchen staples the early American housewife could least do without. Colonial taste buds were accustomed to large amounts of flavoring which suppressed any less pleasant tastes that might be present.

Nutmeg, mace, pepper, cloves, ginger, and cinnamon were the six spices that went into practically everything —meat, fish, vegetables, fruits, bread, and sweets. Pepper might be withheld from sweets, but otherwise all six were used together.

SWEETENINGS

Maple sugar and syrup: In areas where the sugar maples grew, the colonists learned from the Indians how to make maple syrup. Trees were tapped in the spring when the sap began to rise. A V-shaped gash was cut in the bark and a wooden spout inserted. A pail was set underneath it to catch the sap. Each tree might yield two gallons of sap in a twenty-four hour period. The sap was collected into large vats and boiled down to a thick syrup over slow-burning fires. When the syrup was the desired thickness, it was poured into molds and allowed to harden and crystallize into sugar. A portion of the sap was cooked a shorter time to produce maple syrup, another favorite for table use.

Molasses: Molasses came to the colonies from the West Indies by the barrelful—and fine New England barrels they were. A product of the sugar cane industry, molasses was less expensive to produce than refined sugar and had more uses. Its principal use was as an ingredient for making rum. However, large enough quantities were imported so that molasses was readily available for culinary purposes too.

Sugar: Because sugar required more labor in processing and refining, it was more expensive to import, and for many years was a luxury item to be used sparingly. It came from the Indies in cones wrapped in blue paper. (Thrifty housewives saved the paper and soaked it to extract the blue dye.) Women trading at the general store would buy a whole cone or have the storekeeper nip off the desired amount. The sugar cone was very hard and a special tool was needed to break it up. Pieces were pulverized with a pestle in a mortar before using in a recipe.

Honey: Bees were not native to the New World, but colonists were quick to bring them here. The Spanish missionaries raised them to obtain beeswax to make devotional candles. The English farmers along the eastern

seaboard imported the bees to pollinate fruit trees they intended to grow. Both groups made good use of the delicious honeys that were a by-product of beekeeping.

Sorghum: This cane-type grass is related to corn but, like sugar cane, it yields a thick syrup when crushed and boiled. Called "long sweetening," sorghum is still popular in parts of the United States.

TWO SPICES FROM ONE TREE

The nutmeg tree produces both mace and nutmeg. Mace comes from the netlike membrane that covers the shell around the nutmeg seed. After harvesting, the mace membrane is removed before the shell is cracked and the nutmeg released. In colonial times, mace was dried and ground before packaging and nutmegs were sold whole and grated as needed.

Gentlemen carried nutmegs and silver nutmeg graters in case they found themselves in a tavern or home where the drinks were not sufficiently spiced. Remember "Don't take any wooden nickels"? Colonists probably said the same about nutmegs because everyone just knew that wooden ones were being sold by itinerant peddlers. It hardly seems likely, however, that the time-consuming carving would have proved profitable.

Tendrils of mace encircle the seed of the nutmeg tree. When ground, both the mace and the nutmeg seed are popular spices.

MEAT FOR THE TABLE

Early settlers and visitors alike commented on the abundance of wild game. Nevertheless, the colonists wanted meat like they had at home. Pigs, chickens, sheep, and cattle made the long voyage almost as soon as the colonists did. But, the woods and the wilds here were a far cry from the carefully tended pastures of the Old World. Here the livestock ran loose and foraged for themselves, and not just in the rural areas, either. For it was not uncommon to see cattle and pigs roaming city streets.

The animals' freewheeling mobility was a mixed blessing. The exercise tended to make the meat tough. Yet in areas where pigs feasted on acorns and ground nuts, the hams and bacon developed a particular succulence.

Most animals served more than one purpose. The idea of special breeds for special purposes was a long time taking hold. Sheep, for example, were more useful perhaps for the wool they provided for clothing than for the mutton in the cooking pot. As a result, they were usually not slaughtered for meat until they were very old. And, since chickens provided eggs, they too were spared from the skillet till their laying days were over.

Pigs were a source of meat and fat for both cooking or soapmaking. Pork was salted down, smoked, or made into sausage. The trimmings were rendered for fat. Nothing was wasted. Pork tidbits went into head cheese, the intestines became sausage casings and the feet made gelatin.

Cattle were, first, work animals, second, a source of milk for cheese, third, a source of hides, and lastly, meat. Consequently, the animals were usually butchered only after they were too old to work or supply milk. If a calf was butchered, the stomach provided rennet for making cheese and the feet were another source of gelatin.

What made the dough rise

Yeast: Most breads and cakes depended on yeast for lightness. But yeast wasn't store-bought. It was made at home from the yeast spores in the air acting on a "starter" and some starter was saved for the next batch. The starter medium was water—often from cooked potatoes—combined with flour, sugar, and salt. The term salt-rising bread comes from this mixture. The name "sour dough" came later, but the procedure was very old.

The colonial cook didn't always have to rely on the capriciousness of yeasts in the air for her baking needs. Hops for beer were among the first crops planted. A by-product of beer making was a type of brewer's yeast. This could be added to the starter to be sure the bread would rise.

Saleratus and Pearl Ash: These were early forms of baking soda and baking powder respectively. Both were strongly alkaline and reacted with sour milk or molasses to leaven biscuits and gingerbread. Proportions were very difficult to judge accurately. Too much of either saleratus or pearl ash gave the food a bitter taste and unpleasant yellowish-green streaks.

Eggs: Good cooks, including early American homemakers, have long taken advantage of the foaming properties of beaten eggs, especially egg whites, to make sponge cakes, meringues, and floating islands.

Air is the actual leavening agent. It is trapped in the egg whites by beating them until they are stiff. Then the egg whites are carefully folded into the batter. The air expands during baking and gives the cake its lovely light, airy texture.

Making gelatin

Gelatin was prepared by boiling calves' feet or melting isinglass obtained from the swimming bladders of certain fish. With it fruit jellies or molded custards were made. It took prodigious amounts of spices, rose water, and sweet wine sauce to subdue the rather indelicate meat or fish flavor. If the cook wanted a colored jelly, she could make it green with spinach juice or young grass; yellow with extract from marigolds; or red from crushed conchineal. Since each color added its own flavor, more disguising was needed.

Woman's work was never done

Not just the cooking, cleaning, and gardening occupied a woman's day. She had to produce the materials for many of her household projects. For example, she didn't have shortening for cooking without rendering lard

or churning butter. There was no rennet for cheese unless she took it from the newly butchered calf's stomach. And no sausage if she didn't take time at hog butchering to save and clean intestines to use for casings.

Like "the house that Jack built" to clean she had to make soap, to make soap she had to leach out lye, to leach out lye she had to save ashes, to save ashes....

TO MAKE SOAP

"Put on the fire any quantity of lye you choose that is strong enough to bear an egg—to each gallon, add three quarters of a pound of clean grease; boil it very fast, and stir it frequently—a few hours will suffice to make it good soap. When you find by cooling a little on a plate that it is a thick jelly, and no grease appears, put in salt in the proportion of one pint to three gallons—let it boil a few minutes, and pour it in tubs to cool....Next day, cut out the soap, melt it, and cool it again; this takes out all the lye, and keeps the soap from shrinking when dried."

Randolph, *Virginia Housewife*, 1860

KITCHEN GARDENS

Regardless of nationality, location, or station in life, each early settler had a garden strategically placed near the kitchen door. The garden was not planted for its aesthetic value. It was a vital source of fresh fruits and vegetables for the table and herbs for flavoring or medicinal purposes. Fruit trees were planted singly or in orchards as soon as seeds, seedlings, or cuttings could be shipped from home. In fact, much of the correspondence between the colonists and their agents at home concerned orders for seeds and plants of all kinds. The wealthier colonists could request special shipboard treatment for the plants being sent to them to insure their safe arrival.

English vegetables such as peas, onions, turnips, cabbage, cauliflower, carrots, cucumbers, and radishes thrived along with native corn, squash, pumpkin, beans, and sweet potatoes. Many of these crops were being cultivated in Virginia gardens in 1610. All were growing in Massachusetts Bay Colony settlements by 1634. The Dutch and Swedish settlers had much the same taste in vegetables as did their English neighbors. Records show that their gardens also included both head and leaf lettuce, beets, and red peppers. Of course, not all families planted everything in these lists, but a considerable variety was available.

The larger the household, the bigger the garden. Estates such as Mount Vernon and Monticello benefited from the moderate Virginia climate and a long growing season. The kitchen garden in these locations could be counted on for more than one planting in each plot each season and careful records were kept from year to year.

Apple and other fruit trees were not growing in America when the first colonists arrived. But by 1615 Jamestown settlers could enjoy apples and pears raised locally from stock sent from home. Quince was added to the list and grew throughout all of New England by 1634. The great variety of native berries and melons also did well everywhere. Strawberries, long cultivated by the Indians, grew wild in many areas. The hardy plants were quickly transferred to the kitchen gardens. There were wild currants, too, but for all the colonist's careful seeding, grafting, and transplanting, the favored English varieties were a horticultural problem for many years and had to be shipped across the Atlantic.

The kitchen garden grew a delicious assortment of herbs and vegetables for the table.

Cooking with flowers

Another important source of kitchen ingredients is one scarcely put to culinary use today: the flower garden. Distilled rose water and orange water were particular favorites added to cakes or desserts like extracts are used today. Rose petals, wild violets, and the leaves of mint were sugared and eaten as candy.

Marigold and chrysanthemum blossoms among others were dipped in batter and lightly fried. Tansy was especially enjoyed as a dessert, a salad, or fried with eggs. Gillyflowers (phlox), pinks, clover, and other flowers were added to many dishes.

To release the full flavor of herbs, the cook put them in the trough and crushed them by pulling the roller back and forth.

Cooking with herbs

Herbs were universally used for flavoring and for them the housewife need go no farther than her own garden. A knot garden, as herb gardens were sometimes called, grew right outside the kitchen door. Many were laid out in a formal pattern, while others were set in rows for easy tending. Some gardeners preferred to intersperse the more fragrant herbs among other plants as a kind of natural insect repellent.

The most common of the culinary herbs were sage, thyme, parsley, chives, rosemary, marjoram, chervil, and sorrel. Other herbs that were common have now been all but forgotten. These were bugloss, hyssop, pennyroyal, and rue. The woods yielded indigenous flavorings that the settlers adopted—sassafrass, wintergreen, and checkerberry. Many were transplanted to home gardens.

Throughout the summer, herbs were picked fresh from the garden. At the end of the growing season, they were gathered and dried.

Kitchen as a family room

By 1700 there were many improvements in kitchens and the art of cookery. In the South, because of hot summers, anyone who could afford it built a kitchen separate from the house, sometimes with a connecting passage. But in the North, heat was more often wanted than avoided, and the kitchen remained the center of family life. Even when houses grew larger, there was, at least, one bed in the kitchen, as well as a cradle and a spinning wheel. Seats, called inglenooks, were built into the sides of the chimney corner, so that aged people might sit there, warm and out of drafts. In front of the fire there was a settle whose high back retained heat.

Mealtimes and menus

The hours and menus of breakfast, dinner, and the evening meal were more or less governed by climate and class. In New England, the average family ate breakfast at dawn or earlier. Cornmeal porridge and hard cider were usual. In the eighteenth century other things were added, such as apple pie, sausage, hot cakes, and rum. A bracing meal like this gave all members of the family the calories they needed for a morning of hard work. Dinner, served at noon, was the main meal of the day and consisted of meat, vegetables—if available—bread, and pudding of bread or cornmeal, sweetened with maple sugar or molasses. Families in modest circumstances made a habit of eating the pudding first—to dampen the appetite for meat which might be in short supply. Supper (or tea, as it was called later) was a lighter meal—porridge again, with or without stewed fruit.

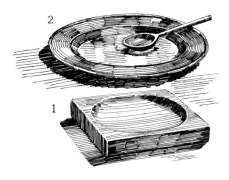

Wood before pewter before china was the order. Thus, wooden trenchers (1) preceded pewter *chargers* (2) and china plates.

Cider or beer accompanied all meals. Children drank milk if there was any, but they also drank cider and beer. Water was regarded as a last resort, to be approached with caution and only if nothing else was on hand.

In the South the food was similar to that in the North, but the schedule was different. The plantation owner rose early, fortified himself with beer, cider, or mint julep, and inspected his property during the early-morning hours. At ten there was a large breakfast, and in midafternoon an even larger dinner. A third, lighter meal was served by candlelight in the evening. But this schedule was for the well-to-do. Simpler families did with two meals a day, breakfast and midafternoon dinner and settled for bread or cheese after the day's labors.

In modest homes the dining table consisted of boards on trestles and was dismantled when not in use. During the early years, chairs were luxuries. A family might have brought one or two along, but space on sailing vessels was better used for essential food such as bags of flour or peas.

If there was a chair, the master of the house sat in it. If there was another, his wife sat beside him, or offered it to a guest. Everyone else sat on benches. According to a custom from medieval times, a large saltcellar occupied the middle of the table and those who sat "above the salt" had more prestige than those below. Thus the wife sat at her husband's side and the children and servants were all "below the salt."

MESS IT FORTH

"Mess it forth," said colonial cooks, meant "serve it." Now "mess" applies only to meals of the military. In other times it was a synonym for dinner or a bunch of greens. There was good-natured competition about picking the first mess of spring greens.

In all homes, rich and poor, the entire meal was brought to the table at once. The notion of serving meals in courses (with the sweet course last) came from France and did not become standard practice in this country until well into the nineteenth century. If there were a great many dishes, as at Christmas or a wedding feast, they might be placed on the table in two or more shifts.

Judge Samuel Sewall, an eighteenth century Bostonian, recorded a feast at which he ate the following dishes, apparently in no particular order: boiled pork, boiled pigeons, boiled venison, salmon, oysters, fish and oil, cunners, leg of pork, hog's cheek and suet, mince pie, green peas, barley, corn in milk, cherries, strawberries, raspberries, roast beef, roast lamb, roast fowl, gingerbread, sugared almonds, glazed almonds, honey, curds and cream, sage cheese, chocolate, shaddocks and quinces.

PLATES, SPOONS, AND KNIVES

China, silver, and glass rarely appeared on the earliest colonial tables—though in the eighteenth century they were eagerly acquired by the well-to-do. In ordinary homes, those at the head of the table might each rate a pewter plate, but the lower-ranking diners ate from wooden trenchers, rectangular shaped so that two could conveniently share one. No second clean plate was offered, but it was quite *de rigueur* to turn one's trencher face down and eat from "the pie side."

Not until the nineteenth century was it bad manners to use one's knife. As for forks, Governor John Winthrop of Massachusetts Bay Colony brought one with him across the ocean and for years it was probably the only fork in New England. Everyone else ate with spoons—pewter ones or perhaps clamshells fastened to wooden handles.

Most meat was served as "spoon meat," that is, cut small and pounded by the cook and boiled for hours in hope of making it tender. Even roasts, which came to the table on huge pewter *chargers*, were first cut into bite-size pieces, suitable for spearing with the point of a knife.

The Developing Nation

Chapter 4

The Developing Nation

The period between the founding of the United States and 1900 was an exciting time for the citizens of the young nation. Optimism was in the air they breathed; and they were on the move—to the West in Conestoga or smaller farm wagons to seek new lands, new life—to the cities to test the unprecedented opportunities in commerce and trade. Shipping, too, was growing (especially after the War of 1812) and many youths responded to the lure of the sea and the tall ships.

There were other kinds of movement, too. It was a time of spiritual and intellectual innovation. The Shakers were establishing their communal settlements in New Lebanon, New York, throughout New England, and in Ohio and Indiana. There were experimental communities in the as yet "uncorrupted" new nation, such as Robert Owen's secular New Harmony, Indiana, and Bronson Alcott's transcendentalist farm in Massachusetts; there was the Mormons' great trek westward to Illinois, through Missouri, and finally on into the valley of the Great Salt Lake.

In little more than half a century, new inventions of all kinds changed radically the daily life of every citizen. Among the most significant were the cotton gin, the steamboat, the railroad, the mechanical reaper, the sewing machine, the Colt revolver, the telegraph, the phonograph, and the telephone; but there were many lesser inventions that made life simpler, safer, and more comfortable. These included the safety pin; matches; rubber overshoes, raincoats, and bottle nipples; oil lamps; gas street lamps; bed springs; and much else.

However, if one had to name a single factor that contributed more than any other to the development of the nation, it would surely be improved transportation. At the close of the Revolution there were very few roads connecting the states. It was, for instance, much easier to travel from Boston to New York or from New York to Charleston by sea than over land, in spite of storms and reefs. The existing roads were little more than widened trails, originally blazed by Indians. The new United States government attached great importance to the development of better ways of travel, both by land and by inland waterway. Without such facilities there could be neither commercial growth nor any great mobility for people. "Open *all* the communication which nature has afforded between the Atlantic States and the Western territory," wrote George Washington, "and encourage the use of them to the utmost...."[1]

In the closing years of the eighteenth century, Americans were a rural people. At least nine out of ten drew their living from the land, while less than 4 percent lived in communities of more than eight thousand inhabitants. In general, the only farmers who could make a substantial income from cash crops were the big planters of the South who raised tobacco, rice, indigo, sugar, or cotton (depending on the latitude and terrain) with the aid of slave labor; and the farmers of the Middle Atlantic states who were near water transportation and could ship wheat abroad or to the South. But in New England and in the back country of the South there were a great number of subsistence and semisubsistence farms, isolated from markets and too poor to afford extra hands. Their owners knew nothing of agronomy, and, inevitably, their soil "wore out." Thus, interest was great in opening new lands to the west for settlement and in finding new ways for people to get there.

The 1790s saw the beginning of the Turnpike Era. The first turnpike ran from Philadelphia to Lancaster, Pennsylvania, with a tollhouse every eight to ten miles. This venture, financed by the state, proved so successful that others soon followed. The first great highway that was substantially toll-free was the Cumberland Road, also known as the National Road, which wound its way through the Allegheny Mountains from Cumberland, Maryland, to Wheeling, West Virginia (and eventually winding up near St. Louis). Completed as far as Wheeling in 1817, it was the busiest thoroughfare in the country for two decades. Stage and freight lines, express wagons, droves of cattle and pigs, and lumbering Conestoga wagons loaded with migrating families rumbled their way along it.

River commerce in America dates back to colonial days when onions and potatoes and live cattle and horses destined for the Caribbean were sent down the Connecticut River. In tidewater Virginia and Maryland, every large plantation had its own wharf to accommodate oceangoing ships. After the Revolution, flatboats and keelboats began to ply the Ohio and the Mississippi laden with barrels of flour, bacon, potatoes, whiskey, and peach brandy for the New Orleans market.

The invention of the steamboat revolutionized the transport of foodstuffs from the moment Robert Fulton's **Clermont** made her first run up the Hudson in 1807 — an event described by one onlooker as "the devil going upriver to Albany in a sawmill."[2] Steam-driven riverboats meant that farmers and merchants could count on regularly scheduled shipments, even traveling upstream. By 1848 American steam tonnage was three times that of Great Britain and most of it traveled on inland waterways.

B ut what to do where nature failed to provide waterways? The answer — typical for that self-confident, ebullient generation — was "make them." And the Canal Era followed hard upon the turnpike boom. The first of the important canals was the Erie, connecting the Hudson River with the Great Lakes. Constructed between 1817 and 1825, at great cost both in dollars and in human life, the Erie Canal brought prosperity and development to western New York by enabling farmers and cattlemen to reach markets in eastern cities, and even more important, it opened a path to the west via the Great Lakes. Of course, the canals made passenger travel easier, and the owners of canal boats went to great lengths to please their customers. A noonday meal on an Erie Canal boat included pike, bass, steak, bacon, sausage, ham, scrambled eggs, baked potatoes, boiled cabbage, squash, white and corn bread, wheat and buckwheat pancakes, sorghum, maple syrup, molasses, honey, coffee, tea, milk, and skimmagig.

The next great canal, this one in Pennsylvania between Philadelphia and Pittsburgh, was an astonishing engineering achievement. The route crossed the Allegheny Mountains and at one point the canal boats were actually carried over — hauled up one side and down the other. One traveler who made this journey wrote that the boat in which he was a passenger rested for the night at the top of the mountain "like Noah's Ark on Ararat."

The thousands of jobs created by canal building precipitated a great surge of immigration, particularly from Ireland. The men who worked on these prodigious ditches (the Erie was deep enough for boats with a six-foot draught) often died of disease and the backbreaking labor. But the canals they built enabled many thousands to reach the Middle West, to develop farms there, and to ship their produce back East.

While the case Gibbons v. Ogden *is known to most students of the law as the decision that gave Congress power to regulate interstate commerce, it also helped promote the use of the steamboat. After Fulton and his financial backer, Robert Livingston, had successfully launched the* Clermont, *they quickly obtained from New York legislature the privilege of being the only people allowed to run a steamboat on New York waters. Later, the Territory of Orleans (soon to be Louisiana) gave them the same privilege. This monopoly severely limited the number of steamboats, and for many years the descendants of Livingston and would-be competitors were involved in a series of lawsuits. The issue was finally resolved when Chief Justice John Marshall ruled in* Gibbons v. Ogden *that the monopoly laws of New York were invalid, thus opening up steamboat traffic. He also ruled that Congress had the power to legislate other types of commerce between the states. Since then the doctrine that Marshall set down has been applied to the railroad, telegraph, telephone, and air travel.*

The possibility of journeying across country by rail became reality for travelers (like those pictured above) at Promontory Point, Utah, in 1869. The official linking of the east and west railroads called for driving a golden spike into the connecting rail. Came the great moment: a telegraph operator, perched on a high pole, tapped out "stand by" to the waiting nation. The band stopped playing. The governor of California, Leland Stanford, swung at the spike — and missed. But the telegrapher had already flashed the news which brought a hundred-gun salute in New York and the ringing of the Liberty Bell in Philadelphia.

The story of the building of the railroads is also woven into the fabric of our history. One of the first railroads, The Granite Railway Company, applied for a charter from the Massachusetts legislature in order to bring the granite needed for the Bunker Hill Monument from the quarry at Quincy to a wharf on the Neponset River. The line was three miles long, cost over $11,000 a mile to build, and the train had no engine. It was pulled by two horses when it was put into operation in 1826. In 1828 the city of Baltimore dared to finance a railroad through the Alleghenies to the Ohio River. It took twenty-five years to reach its goal. By then the floodgates had opened and rail lines were being laid all over the country. Then, May 10, 1869, the great day. Union Pacific Railroad working west from Omaha and Southern Pacific Railroad working east from Sacramento joined their lines at Promontory Point in Utah. The first transcontinental railroad was completed.

Railroads. Canals. Steamboat traffic on the rivers and Great Lakes. Turnpikes. The nation was humming with efficient forms of transportation that enabled no less than 200,000 new farms to be established between 1830 and 1850 in the states of Ohio, Indiana, and Illinois.

As the Mississippi valley was taken over by more and more farms, and a three-tiered transport system — railroad, canal, highway — became established, a need was created for certain cities to function as centers for the collection and distribution of farm produce.

One of the earliest collection points, Cincinnati — nicknamed "Porkopolis" — was a great meat-packing center. Some of the corn produced by the thousands of new midwestern farms was fed to hogs, many of which were then slaughtered at Cincinnati. (It has been said that pork is corn that walks to market.) The meat was salted and shipped on the Ohio and Mississippi rivers. Cincinnati retained its domination of the industry until the Civil War when trade with the South was totally disrupted. After the war, Chicago, having become the hub of midwestern railroads, captured the leadership in meat-packing. Later, Kansas City and Omaha also became important in the packing and distribution of meat.

As places such as Cincinnati, Pittsburgh, Chicago, St. Louis, and Denver grew into cities, there were those who helped promote the growth. William B. Ogden helped make Chicago a metropolis by establishing the Galena and Chicago Union Railroad, the Pittsburgh, Fort Wayne, and Chicago Railroad, the Chicago, St. Paul, and Fond-du-Lac Railroad (later the Chicago and Northwestern Railroad), and the Union Pacific Company — all with Chicago as the hub. Dr. Daniel Drake realized his dream of making Cincinnati a medical center by founding what later became the University of Cincinnati Medical College. William Larimer helped bring the first stage line into Denver and in addition promoted stores, hotels, sawmills, and newspapers. With help from men like these, American cities grew quickly and ushered in the age of urban America.

As the thriving businesses drew more and more people to the cities, the hotels and inns not only expanded, but took on uniquely American characteristics. Writer Anthony Trollope describes the hotels of the mid-1800s, "The American inn . . . is altogether an institution apart and a thing of itself. Hotels in America are very much larger and more numerous than in other countries. They are to be found in all towns, and I may almost say in all villages. In England and on the continent we find them on recognized routes of travel and in towns of commercial or social importance. . . . But in the States of America the first sign of an incipient settlement is an hotel five stories high, with an office, a bar, a cloakroom, three gentlemen's parlours, two ladies' parlours, a ladies' entrance, and two hundred bedrooms. . . . When the new hotel rises up in the wilderness, it is presumed that people will come there with the express object of inhabiting it. The hotel itself will create a population — as the railways do. With us railways run to the towns; but in the States the towns run to the railways. It is the same thing with the hotels."[3]

In addition to commerce in the cities, ocean commerce increased steadily. New England exported more fish than ever before. After 1830 the wholesale markets of New York, New Orleans, and a few other ports were supplied with oranges and lemons from Italy, as well as with pineapples and bananas from the Caribbean. However, inland from the seaboard these delicacies were expensive and not ordinarily available. The average American diet, while somewhat more varied than it had been in colonial times, was still heavy in meat and breadstuffs and light in fresh fruits and vegetables. Not until the mid-1800s were ways found to bring year-round variety and flexibility to the diet, as well as to improve quality.

The nineteenth century was a time of growth and change for Americans — on all fronts. The government grew from its shaky beginnings to an established power, surviving a Civil War in the process. Cities that were mere settlements in 1800 were transformed into large metropolises, and the economy switched from one based on agriculture to an industrial one. Keeping in step with the rest of American life, the food changed too. The recipes in this chapter reflect the variety of peoples and life of the developing nation.

The words "taverns," "inns," and "ordinaries" were all used to describe important gathering places of early America. In New England and New York they were taverns, in Pennsylvania the same establishments were called inns and in the South the slang name was ordinaries. However designated, these institutions were meeting places for all types of people, as E. L. Bynner describes. "They were the centers of so much of its life and affairs, the resort at once of judge and jury, of the clergy and the laity, of the politician and the merchant; where the selectmen came to talk over the affairs of the town, and higher officials to discuss the higher interests of the province; where royal governors and distinguished strangers were entertained alike with the humblest wayfarer and the meanest citizen; where . . . the frowning Puritan, the obnoxious Quaker, the Huguenot refugee, and the savage Indian chief from the neighboring forest might perchance jostle each other in the common taproom."[4]

Developing The Nation

To be part of the American scene during the years between the end of the American Revolution and 1900 was exciting. The United States was growing from the thirteen states nestled on the Atlantic coast to a sprawling nation stretching clear to the Pacific. One giant step in the growth of the nation was the Louisiana Purchase which added more than a million square miles to American holdings. With this vast expanse of land to be conquered, good transportation was a must, and Americans worked hard to develop canal, railroad, and stagecoach travel as fast as possible. Along with the improvements in transportation came a new interest in better ways of doing everything from harvesting cotton to sewing clothing. This interest spawned such inventions as the cotton gin, sewing machine, and telegraph during this century. The Civil War interrupted the growth of the country, but out of the turmoil of the period came many social and technological changes which set the stage for the America we know today.

New Orleans celebrates news of the Louisiana Purchase on December 20, 1803.

Eli Whitney and Catherine Littlefield Greene developed the cotton gin which revolutionized the cotton industry.

Soldiers in the Civil War fall in line for their daily ration of soup.

While boats on the Erie Canal wait for locks to open, passengers walk on the shore.

Before trains had dining cars, they stopped for only twenty minutes so passengers could gulp down a quick meal.

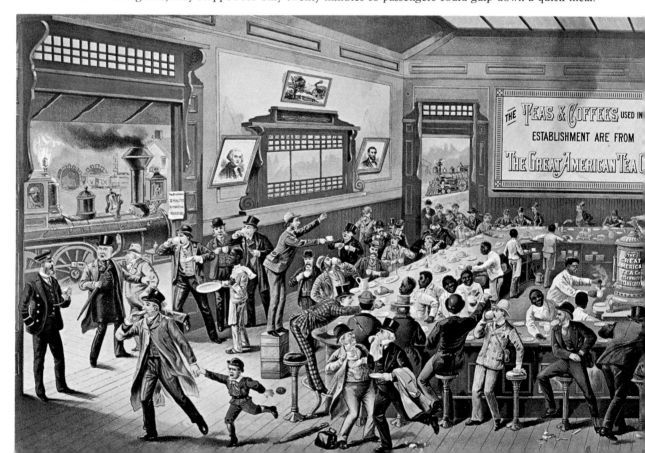

Five hundred dollars was the prize offered in a public contest to design the president's home in the new capital. Entries came in from Thomas Jefferson and a number of others, but the winner was an Irish-American resident of Philadelphia, James Hoban. The cornerstone was laid October 12, 1792. The white limestone building was in striking contrast to the red brick of other public buildings and probably accounts for its later nickname, the White House. But the story is also told that some of President Jackson's opponents felt he was not worthy of an executive mansion, so they dubbed his home the White House.

Who could possibly live in a damp mansion where there were not enough lamps, the main staircase was not yet built, and thirty servants had to be hired? If anyone could it was Abigail Adams. She used her Yankee ingenuity, turned the unfinished East Room into a room for drying laundry, and wrote to her daughter, "If they will put me up some bells and let me have wood enough to keep fires, I design to be pleased." She added, "You must keep all this to yourself, and when asked how I like it, say that I write you the situation is beautiful, which is true."[5]

White House Dining

Ever since the office of president was created, an invitation to dine at the President's House (later called the White House) has been considered a great privilege. An invitation to the first New Year's Day reception ever held on Pennsylvania Avenue was no exception. This legendary 1801 party was given by plucky Abigail Adams under the worst circumstances — the mansion was still under construction, there was little furniture, and most of the china had been broken in the move to Washington.

Conditions were considerably better for Thomas Jefferson who succeeded John Adams that year. Since Jefferson was a widower, he had to superintend his own household, with the help of his daughter, Martha. Fortunately, he enjoyed it. His years as American minister in France had enabled him to develop his natural taste for good food, and he had brought back a French chef and lots of European recipes. Among these were "French fries," pasta dishes, and ice cream served in a hot pastry shell. For his garden he brought seeds of broccoli and other European vegetables, and he introduced the culture of olives and dry rice to the South, rating this achievement as equal in importance to writing the Declaration of Independence.

Jefferson's dining table accommodated sixteen, and there was rarely an empty place at his four o'clock dinners. After the cloth was removed and the wine and nuts brought in, conversation continued for hours.

Jefferson is often rated the most convivial host of all our presidents. The honor of most talented White House hostess is usually accorded to Dolley Madison. "Mrs. Dolley" knew how to achieve the perfect balance between dignified elegance and democratic cordiality, and her entertainments gave the raw capital city a new polish. It was said that even the most casual visitor was offered refreshments, while the Madison dinner table was lavish with French dishes and fine wines. A guest at one of Mrs. Madison's balls, in 1813, wrote, "I am sure not ten minutes elapsed without refreshments being handed. 1st, coffee, tea, and kinds of toasts and warm cakes; 2d, ice-creams; 3d, lemonade, punch, burgundy, claret, curacoa, champagne; 4th, bonbons, cakes of all sorts and sizes; 5th, apples, oranges; 6th, confectionary...; 7th, nuts, almonds, raisins; 8th, set supper, composed of tempting solid dishes, meats, savory pasties garnished with lemon; 9th, drinkables of every species; 10th, boiling chocolate."[6]

The White House was burned during the War of 1812, and during its reconstruction the Madisons lived in Octagon House. The task of ordering new furnishings fell to the next presidential couple, James and Elizabeth Monroe. Some of the first items they purchased were handsome table fittings from Paris. Many of these are still in use today.

The chief contribution of the John Quincy Adamses was a two-acre garden. Adams wrote that it contained "forest and fruit-trees, shrubs, hedges, esculent vegetables, kitchen and medicinal herbs, hot-house plants, flowers and weeds to the amount, I conjecture, of at least one thousand."[7]

Andrew Jackson, another widower in the White House, was the first president to invite the public to his levees. He also gave elegant parties to which a thousand or more were invited. Jessie Benton Fremont, then a little girl, remembered "The gorgeous supper-table shaped like a horse shoe, and covered with every good and glittering thing French skill could devise, and at either end was a monster salmon in waves of meat jelly."[8]

The next resident of the White House, Martin Van Buren, had luxurious tastes. His bills for French china and gold-plated knives and forks were gleefully attacked by the opposition and cost him votes in the next election. Even his garden—"fine Neshanock potatoes, honest drumhead and early York cabbages, white and red sugar and pickle beets, marrowfat peas, carrots, parsnips, etc. etc., with an abundance of the strawberry, dewberry, raspberry, etc."[9]—was derided in Congress for being altogether too grand.

Perhaps because of the criticism leveled at Van Buren, the next few incumbents were unpretentious. Not until four years before the Civil War was there another *bon vivant* in the White House. President James Buchanan, a bachelor, put his social calendar into the hands of his niece, Miss Harriet Lane, who handled the job well, especially such taxing assignments as glittering receptions for the Prince of Wales, thirty Indian chiefs, and the first official ambassadors ever to arrive from Japan.

In contrast, the next president, Abraham Lincoln, focused most of his attention on the problems of the Civil War. His wife, Mary Todd Lincoln, however, used her Southern background to help her entertain and lighten those difficult years. During the Lincoln administration, the White House was always open for evening levees, afternoon teas, and elegant receptions.

After the war, the flamboyant style of Ulysses Grant dominated the Washington scene. The social event of the Grant administration was the marriage of his daughter, Nellie, to Algernon Charles Frederick Sartoris.

Chester Arthur, like his predecessors Jefferson and Van Buren, had an avid interest in gourmet food. His official dinners were models of refinement. Prepared by a chef whom Arthur imported from France and presided over by his younger sister, Mary McElroy, they featured the finest in continental cuisine and often included as many as six wines.

While the food served at the White House frequently included the finest in the country, not all our Presidents were renowned for their epicurian tastes. The recipes in this section spotlight only those presidents who did have a flair for entertaining and a special interest in food. These recipes are the best of White House dining in the 1800s.

The first stove to grace the White House Kitchen arrived during the Millard Fillmore administration and caused quite a stir— of opposition. The situation is described by a contemporary. "The old black cook who had served many years at the White House was greatly upset when a range of small hotel size was brought to his quarters. He had managed to prepare a fine State dinner for thirty-six people every Thursday in a huge fireplace, with the cranes, hooks, pots, pans, kettles, and skillets; but he could not manage the draughts of the range, and it ended in a journey of the President to the Patent Office to inspect the model and to restore peace in the kitchen."[10]

Raspberry Shrub

Thaw one 10-ounce package frozen red raspberries. Place berries in blender container; cover and blend till smooth. Strain, reserving the juice; discard seeds. Add ¼ cup sugar to 1 cup boiling water; stir till sugar dissolves. Combine reserved juice, sugar mixture, ½ cup brandy, and ¼ cup light rum. Chill well. Serve over ice cubes. Makes 6 (4-ounce) servings.

Abigail Adams Beggar's Pudding with Sack Sauce

1 beaten egg
1 cup milk
½ cup packed brown sugar
1 teaspoon rosewater
¼ teaspoon ground ginger
¼ teaspoon ground nutmeg
⅛ teaspoon salt
10 slices firm-textured bread, cut in 1-inch cubes (6 cups)
½ cup dried currants
Sack Sauce

In a large bowl combine beaten egg, milk, brown sugar, rosewater, ginger, nutmeg, and salt. Stir in bread cubes and currants. Turn into a greased 8x1½-inch round baking dish. Bake, covered, at 350° till knife inserted halfway between center and edge comes out clean, about 25 minutes. Spoon the hot Sack Sauce over hot pudding. Serve immediately. Makes 6 servings.

Sack Sauce: In a small saucepan melt ¼ cup butter or margarine over low heat. Continue heating, stirring constantly, till the butter starts to brown; immediately remove from the heat. Add 1 tablespoon packed brown sugar and stir till the sugar dissolves. Stir in ½ cup dry sherry, 1 tablespoon lemon juice, and 1 teaspoon grated lemon peel.

Epigrammes of Lamb

President Jefferson had an active interest in sampling different types of food and spent money freely to set the most prodigal table in Washington. He is credited with introducing many European delicacies and was particularly fond of intricate and elaborate dishes. Of all the presidents, Jefferson was the greatest connoisseur of fine foods and wines.

2½ pounds lamb shoulder, cut in 4 pieces
1 cup chopped onion
½ cup chopped carrot
½ cup chopped celery
2 tablespoons snipped parsley
2 teaspoons salt
1 teaspoon dried oregano, crushed
1 teaspoon dried tarragon, crushed
1 bay leaf
1 beaten egg
¼ cup fine dry bread crumbs
2 tablespoons butter *or* margarine
4 lamb rib chops, cut ¾ inch thick
Tarragon Sauce

In large kettle or Dutch oven combine lamb shoulder, onion, carrot, celery, parsley, salt, oregano, tarragon, and bay leaf. Add 6 cups water; cover and simmer till meat is tender, about 1 hour. Remove meat from broth. Strain broth, reserving ¾ cup cooking liquid; cover and refrigerate till needed to make the Tarragon Sauce.

When lamb is cool enough to handle, remove meat from bones. Discard fat and bones. Dice meat. Arrange the meat in four mounds of ¼ cup each between two pieces of clear plastic wrap. Pound to 2½- to 3-inch patties. Carefully peel off wrap. Shape patties to an even thickness and place in shallow pan; cover and refrigerate several hours or overnight.

Dip the chilled patties in beaten egg and then in bread crumbs. Melt butter in skillet. Cook patties till lightly browned on both sides, about 5 minutes per side. Meanwhile, place lamb chops on rack in broiler pan; broil 3 to 4 inches from heat for 5 to 6 minutes. Turn chops; broil 5 to 6 minutes more. Arrange patties atop chops on warm serving platter. Serve with Tarragon Sauce. Makes 4 servings.

Tarragon Sauce: In small saucepan melt 1 tablespoon butter or margarine; blend in 1 tablespoon all-purpose flour. Stir in the reserved ¾ cup cooking liquid, 2 tablespoons dry sherry, 1 teaspoon sugar, and ¼ teaspoon dried tarragon, crushed. Cook, stirring constantly, till thickened and bubbly. Stir a moderate amount of hot mixture into 1 beaten egg yolk; return to the hot mixture. Cook and stir sauce 1 to 2 minutes more.

Dolley Madison's Hospitable Bouillon *(see photo, page 122)*

1 pound beef stew meat
1 beef knuckle
1 cup chopped carrot
½ cup chopped onion

½ cup chopped turnip
½ cup snipped parsley
2 teaspoons salt
⅛ teaspoon cayenne

In large saucepan or Dutch oven combine stew meat, beef knuckle, carrot, onion, turnip, parsley, salt, cayenne, and 12 cups water. Cover; simmer 2 hours. Strain the broth. Season to taste. Serve hot. Makes 10 servings.

Madison Cakes *(see photo, page 122)*

1 cup sliced potato
3¾ to 4 cups all-purpose
    flour
1 package active dry yeast

3 tablespoons butter
2 tablespoons sugar
1 egg
Butter, melted

In saucepan cook potato, covered, in 1 cup water till tender, 15 to 20 minutes. Drain, reserving liquid. Add water, if necessary, to equal ¾ cup liquid. Mash potato; set aside. In large mixing bowl combine *1 cup* of the flour and the yeast. In saucepan heat the reserved potato liquid, 3 tablespoons butter, sugar, and 1½ teaspoons salt just till warm (115-120°); stir constantly. Add to dry mixture; add egg and mashed potato. Beat at low speed of electric mixer for ½ minute, scraping sides of bowl constantly. Beat 3 minutes at high speed. By hand, stir in enough of the remaining flour to make a moderately stiff dough.

Turn out onto lightly floured surface; knead till smooth (5 to 8 minutes). Place in lightly greased bowl; turn once. Cover; let rise in warm place till nearly double (about 35 minutes). Punch down. Cover; let rest 10 minutes. Roll dough to ½-inch thickness. Cut with floured 2½-inch round cutter. Place on greased baking sheets. Cover; let rise till nearly double (about 20 minutes). Bake at 350° for 18 to 20 minutes. Brush tops with melted butter. Makes 18 rolls.

Mint-Flavored Punch

⅔ cup sugar
½ cup lightly packed fresh
    mint leaves, snipped
2 cups red grape juice,
    chilled

2 cups orange juice,
    chilled
¾ cup lime juice, chilled
Crushed ice
Fresh mint leaves

Combine sugar, mint, and 2 cups boiling water; stir till sugar dissolves. Chill. Strain, reserving liquid; discard leaves. Stir together reserved liquid, grape juice, orange juice, and lime juice. Serve over crushed ice. Garnish with fresh mint leaves. Makes 13 (4-ounce) servings.

Monroe's Mock Turtle Soup

2 cups dry black beans
¼ cup chopped onion
¼ cup butter *or* margarine
2 stalks celery, cut up

¼ cup dry sherry (optional)
2 hard-cooked eggs, finely
    chopped
1 lemon, thinly sliced

Cover beans with water. Soak overnight. Drain; rinse well. In large saucepan cook onion in butter till tender but not brown. Add beans, celery, and 10 cups water. Cover; simmer till beans are soft, 3 to 3½ hours. Remove from heat. Place part of bean mixture at a time in blender container; cover and blend till smooth. Return blended mixture to saucepan; stir in 2½ teaspoons salt and dash pepper. Heat soup just to boiling. Stir in sherry. Garnish each serving with chopped eggs and lemon slices. Makes 8 servings.

The hospitable and charming Dolley Madison is the most renowned hostess of all the presidential First Ladies. Dolley graciously welcomed everyone who visited the White House, and thereby, gained a reputation for generous and warm hospitality. One of Dolley's most appreciated customs was serving her guests hot bouillon as they arrived and before they left when the weather was cold and dreary.

At Oak Hill, the family plantation in Virginia, President James Monroe sipped this refreshing Mint-Flavored Punch. It was his favorite thirst-quenching beverage on hot summer afternoons.

Tyler Coconut Pie

3 beaten eggs
1 cup sugar
¼ cup butter, melted
⅔ cup freshly grated
    coconut *or* flaked
    coconut

½ cup light cream
1 teaspoon vanilla
1 unbaked 8-inch pastry
    shell (see recipe,
    page 351)

In mixing bowl combine beaten eggs, sugar, and butter; beat well. Stir in coconut, light cream, and vanilla.

Pour into unbaked pastry shell. Bake at 350° till knife inserted off-center comes out clean, 45 to 60 minutes.

Pictured opposite: Always concerned about the comforts of her guests, Dolley Madison made a practice of serving cups of *Dolley Madison's Hospitable Bouillon* during the cold months. *Golden Madison Cakes* are a fitting accompaniment. (See recipes, page 121.)

Old Hickory Nut Cake

1 cup sugar
½ cup butter *or* margarine
3 egg yolks
2 cups all-purpose flour
1 teaspoon ground cinnamon
½ teaspoon baking soda
½ teaspoon ground nutmeg

⅓ cup bourbon
⅓ cup milk
1 cup chopped hickory nuts
    or pecans
1 cup raisins
3 stiffly beaten egg whites
3 tablespoons bourbon

Cream sugar and butter together till fluffy. Add egg yolks, one at a time, beating well after each. Stir together flour, cinnamon, soda, nutmeg, and ¼ teaspoon salt; add to creamed mixture alternately with ⅓ cup bourbon and

milk. Stir in nuts and raisins. Gently fold in egg whites. Bake in greased 9x5x3-inch loaf pan at 350° for 60 to 65 minutes. Cool. Brush entire cake surface with 3 tablespoons bourbon. Wrap in foil; store overnight.

One of the most heartwarming affairs President Jackson, or Old Hickory as he was called, gave during his term was a memorable Christmas party for about one hundred Washington children. Jackson and his family played games with the young guests in the East Room. Afterward, the children were ushered to the State Dining Room for a grand feast of frozen fruits, candies, cakes, and fresh pastries.

Salade à la Volaille

½ teaspoon salt
¼ teaspoon dry mustard
⅛ teaspoon paprika
    Dash cayenne
1 egg yolk
1 tablespoon white wine
    vinegar
1 cup salad oil
1 tablespoon lemon juice
6 cups torn lettuce

1½ cups cooked turkey *or*
    chicken cut in strips
1 7-ounce can artichoke
    hearts, drained and
    halved
½ cup sliced pitted ripe
    olives
6 anchovy fillets, halved
2 tablespoons capers,
    drained

In small mixing bowl combine salt, mustard, paprika, and cayenne; blend in egg yolk. Add vinegar; mix well. Add oil, a teaspoonful at a time, beating constantly with electric mixer till 2 tablespoons have been added. Add remaining oil in increasing amounts,

alternating the last ¼ *cup* with lemon juice. Chill. In large salad bowl combine lettuce, turkey, artichokes, olives, anchovies, and capers. Toss with enough of the dressing to coat. (If desired, thin dressing with a little milk.) Makes 6 servings.

Van Buren entertained the elite of Washington's diplomatic and political society with small intimate dinners. The ostentatiousness of the food and table appointments at these select dinners was harshly criticized by bitter political opponents. This criticism helped undermine Van Buren's popularity and contributed to the failure of his bid for re-election.

Laplands

2 egg yolks
⅔ cup all-purpose flour
⅔ cup milk

1 tablespoon sugar
1 tablespoon butter, melted
2 stiffly beaten egg whites

Beat egg yolks till thick and lemon-colored, 4 to 5 minutes. Blend in flour, milk, sugar, butter, and ¼ teaspoon salt. Beat 2 to 3 minutes. Gently

fold in egg whites. Fill well-greased 2-inch muffin pans ⅔ full. Bake at 375° for 30 to 35 minutes. Serve with butter and jam, if desired. Makes 10.

Leading historians rank Polk as one of our most forceful and dynamic presidents. During his administration, the First Family banned dancing, card playing, and fancy cooking. So, while official dinners were formal, they offered simple and unadorned food.

For his last reception, President Andrew Jackson invited the public to share the 1,400-pound cheese he had received from New York dairymen. Measuring three feet thick and four feet in diameter, the cheese had been kept in the White House cellar for a year to age and ripen. The result was described by some as "an evil-smelling horror." Nonetheless, shops and offices declared a holiday and 10,000 cheese-lovers marched on—or should we say, stormed—the White House. By the time the last guest had gone the cheese stand was empty, and the cheese had been transferred to the carpets, the walls, drapes, and furniture. The scent remained in the East Room for a month.

Elaborate entertaining was definitely a trademark of President Buchanan's administration. The most talked-about event of his presidential term was a festive reception honoring the first official delegation visiting our country from Japan.

Duchess Potatoes

3 tablespoons butter *or* margarine
1 beaten egg
Salt

Pepper
4 medium potatoes, cooked and mashed (4 cups)

Beat *1 tablespoon* of the butter, egg, salt, and pepper to taste into mashed potatoes. Using pastry bag with large star tip, pipe 2-inch rosettes onto greased baking sheet. Melt remaining 2 tablespoons butter; drizzle butter atop potato rosettes. Bake at 500° for 10 to 12 minutes. Serves 6 to 8.

It is said that President Abraham Lincoln took little interest in food and eating. However, this delicious cake was an exception, and he pronounced it the best dessert he ever ate.

Mary Todd Lincoln's Vanilla-Almond Cake

1½ cups sugar
1 cup butter *or* margarine
1 teaspoon vanilla
2¾ cups sifted cake flour
1 tablespoon baking powder

1⅓ cups milk
1 cup finely chopped almonds
6 stiffly beaten egg whites
White Frosting

Cream together sugar, butter, and vanilla. Stir together the cake flour and baking powder; add to the creamed mixture alternately with milk. Stir in almonds. Gently fold in the egg whites. Pour into two greased and lightly floured 9x1½-inch round baking pans. Bake at 375° for 28 to 30 minutes. Cool 10 minutes; remove from pans. Fill and frost with White Frosting.

White Frosting: In a saucepan combine 1 cup sugar, ⅓ cup water, ¼ teaspoon cream of tartar, and dash salt. Bring mixture to boiling, stirring till the sugar dissolves. In mixing bowl place 2 egg whites; very slowly pour the hot sugar syrup over, beating constantly with electric mixer till stiff peaks form, about 7 minutes. Beat in 1 teaspoon vanilla.

Romaine Punch

1⅔ cups cold water	2 jiggers brandy (3 ounces)
⅓ cup sugar	2 jiggers light rum
⅓ cup lemon juice	(3 ounces)

Combine water and sugar; stir till sugar dissolves. Stir in lemon juice. Freeze at least 3 hours. Remove from freezer about 1 hour before serving; thaw sugar mixture to a slush. Divide the slush mixture evenly among four glasses. Combine brandy and rum; pour *1 jigger* of the mixture into each glass. Stir well to mix. Freeze till served. Makes 4 (5-ounce) servings.

Nesselrode Pudding

1¼ cups crumbled soft coconut macaroons (8 macaroons)	¼ cup toasted almonds, chopped
¼ cup finely chopped mixed candied fruits and peels	3 eggs
	2 cups milk
¼ cup raisins, chopped	⅓ cup sugar
	2 tablespoons rum
	½ teaspoon vanilla

Combine the crumbled macaroons, candied fruits and peels, raisins, and almonds. Divide the mixture evenly among six 6-ounce custard cups.

Beat eggs slightly with a fork; stir in milk, sugar, rum, vanilla, and ⅛ teaspoon salt. Pour over macaroon mixture in custard cups. Set the cups in a shallow baking pan on oven rack. Pour hot water around cups in pan to depth of 1 inch. Bake at 325° till knife inserted just off-center comes out clean, 30 to 35 minutes. Cool 15 minutes; loosen with knife and invert on individual serving plates. Serve warm or chilled. Makes 6 servings.

President and Mrs. Grant held an elaborate breakfast in the State Dining Room after the marriage ceremony of their daughter, Nellie, to Algernon Sartoris. Here is part— only a part—of Nellie Grant's wedding breakfast menu:

Menu

Soft Crabs on Toast
Croquettes of Chicken
Côtelettes d'Agneau
Aspic de Langue-de-Boeuf
Woodcocks and Snipes on Toast
Broiled Spring Chicken
Salade Sauce Maillenaise
Bride's Cake
Strawberries with Cream
Charlotte Russe
Epigraphe la Fleur
Pudding à la Nesselrode
Blancmange à la Napoleon
Plombieres Garnies de Fruits
Ice Cream   Water Ices
Small Cakes
Punch à la Romaine
Coffee   Chocolate

Food Away From Home

"**G**obble, gulp, and go." That was one foreign visitor's description of American eating habits in public places. Perhaps because much of the country was constantly busy and moving, many people regarded eating as little more than a bothersome necessity. A Scotsman in 1820 noted that when the hotel dinner bell rang, everyone took their seats instantly—"and in little more than a quarter of an hour, most of them are ready to leave the table."[11] The speed with which Americans ate meals was marveled at repeatedly by visitors from abroad. And the meals were always substantial. One Englishman reported sharing a table on a trans-atlantic ship with two young ladies who each ate a beefsteak every morning "while they were considering what they would order for breakfast."[12]

Most travelers in early America had mixed luck when it came to dining. A traveler in New York in 1826 spoke of second helpings of turtle soup "without extra charge," good beef, and excellent chicken. Charles Dickens in 1842 praised the oyster cellars in New York for their "wonderful cookery of oysters, pretty nigh as large as cheese-plates...."[13]

He also stayed at the Planter's House in St. Louis and spoke kindly of it. "We went to a large hotel, called the Planter's House.... It is an

One uniquely American phenomenon was the many people who made hotels and boardinghouses their permanent homes in the 19th century. This was due to the frequency with which a man might change his job and move from place to place; to the problems of housekeeping; to the difficulty of procuring good servants; and to the fact that many young brides had not been taught to cook or keep house or were too frail to do so. These hotel residents were aptly called "permanents."

Pictured opposite: Among the more elegant main courses offered to those who frequented the best eating establishments were *Trout Amandine, Bouilli of Beef with Horseradish Sauce* (see recipe, page 128), and *Crown Roast of Lamb with Vegetables* (see recipe, page 129).

The Barcelona Inn established in 1827 in Westfield, New York, is a historic eating place on Lake Erie. It was constructed shortly after the building of the Erie Canal which brought a flood of settlers through the area. Most customers ordered fresh fish at the inn.

The Sun Inn, founded in 1715 by Moravians in Bethlehem, Pennsylvania was noted for its good food and hospitality.
The Marquis de Chastelleux in his book Travels in North America, *1787, wrote of the Sun Inn: "This inn from its external appearance and its interior accommodations is not inferior to the best of the large inns in England. We were supplied with luxuriant asparagus, and the best vegetables, in short...we were here regaled with wine and brandy of the best quality...."*[14]

excellent house, and the proprietors have most bountiful notions of providing the creature comforts. Dining alone with my wife in our own room, one day, I counted fourteen dishes on the table at once."[15]

On the other hand, Frederick Law Olmstead, who journeyed through Texas in 1859, reported that he could get almost nothing but corn bread and pork for six months. (Meals like these were known as "cornbread and common doings.") Most food was fried in either lard or butter that had traveled from New York State and had not survived the journey too well.

The best inns encountered by Olmstead were run by German immigrants. At one he was offered "two courses of meat, neither of them pork and neither of them fried, two dishes of vegetables, salad, compote of peaches, coffee with milk, wheat bread from the loaf and beautiful and sweet butter."[16] One German-owned inn of early Texas was the Nimitz, founded by the grandfather of Admiral Nimitz. Another which still survives, was the Menger Hotel in San Antonio.

On the whole, standards of public cookery in the nineteenth century were highly variable. Indeed, many inns or "ordinaries" left a great deal to be desired. But there were also many fine establishments, and the recipes in this section are the best of early American food away from home.

Trout Amandine

4 to 6 pan-dressed trout (about 8 ounces each)	2 tablespoons cooking oil
Salt	2 tablespoons butter *or* margarine
Pepper	1/4 cup slivered almonds
1 beaten egg	1/4 cup butter *or* margarine, melted
1/4 cup light cream *or* milk	2 tablespoons lemon juice
1/4 cup all-purpose flour	

Bone trout, if desired. Season trout with salt and pepper. Mix together the egg and cream. Dip the trout in flour, then in the egg-cream mixture. Heat together the oil and the 2 tablespoons butter; fry trout in hot fat till golden and flakes easily, 8 to 10 minutes, turning once. In a skillet cook almonds in the 1/4 cup melted butter till almonds are golden brown. Remove from heat and stir in lemon juice. Place trout on a warm serving platter; pour almond mixture over and serve immediately. Serves 4 to 6.

Asparagus with Lemon-Mint Sauce

2 pounds fresh asparagus *or* 2 10-ounce packages frozen asparagus spears	1/4 teaspoon dried mint, crushed
1/2 teaspoon salt	1/4 teaspoon salt
2/3 cup light cream	• • •
2 tablespoons butter	1 slightly beaten egg yolk
	1 tablespoon lemon juice

Wash fresh asparagus; cut off and discard woody base of stalks. Cook asparagus in small amount boiling water with 1/2 teaspoon salt. Cook, covered, till tender, 10 to 15 minutes. (Or, cook frozen asparagus according to package directions.) Drain.

Meanwhile, in small saucepan combine the cream, butter, dried mint, and 1/4 teaspoon salt. Heat and stir till butter melts and mixture is hot. Stir a moderate amount of the hot mixture into the egg yolk. Return to saucepan; cook and stir till thickened, 1 1/2 to 2 minutes more. Remove from heat, stir in lemon juice. Serve sauce over cooked asparagus. Makes 6 servings.

Bookbinder's Snapper Soup

Specializing in seafood, the Old Original Bookbinder's has been a Philadelphia landmark since 1885. World famous for snapper soup, the restaurant daily serves 125 quarts of the specialty. Delicately laced with dry sherry, this classic has managed to survive unchanged for more than one hundred years.

1½ pounds beef *or* veal knuckle, cut in 2-inch pieces
1 cup chopped onion
½ cup chopped celery
½ cup chopped carrot
¼ cup butter *or* margarine, melted
½ teaspoon salt
¼ teaspoon dried thyme, crushed
1 small bay leaf

1 whole clove
¼ cup all-purpose flour
2 10½-ounce cans condensed beef broth
1 8-ounce can tomatoes
2½ to 3 pounds frozen turtle, cut up*
6 cups water*
½ cup dry sherry
1 lemon slice
Dash bottled hot pepper sauce

In a shallow pan combine beef or veal knuckle, onion, celery, carrot, butter, salt, thyme, bay leaf, clove, and ¼ teaspoon pepper. Bake at 400° for 30 minutes. Push bones to one side; blend in flour. Bake at 350° for 30 minutes more. Transfer to kettle; add broth and tomatoes. Cover; simmer 45 minutes. Strain; chill. Remove fat from surface.

In large kettle combine turtle and water.* Cook, covered, till tender, about 1 hour. Remove meat; reserve

2 cups cooking liquid. Cut meat off bones and dice (should have 2 to 2½ cups); discard bones. In saucepan mix turtle meat, reserved cooking liquid, beef mixture, sherry, lemon slice, and hot pepper sauce. Cover and simmer 10 minutes. Remove lemon. Season with salt and pepper. Serves 6.

*Note: To use boneless frozen turtle meat, dice 1 pound meat. Cook turtle meat, covered, in 3 cups water till tender, about 1 hour. Proceed as above.

Bouilli of Beef with Horseradish Sauce *(see photo, page 127)*

Of all the restaurateurs of early America it was Samuel Fraunces whose name is the most prominent. The solemn dinner where George Washington bade his officers farewell was held at Fraunces Tavern in New York City in 1783.

In a 4-quart Dutch oven combine one 3- to 4-pound boneless beef brisket; 2 cups water; ½ cup chopped onion; 2 cloves garlic, minced; and 2 bay leaves. Cover and simmer till meat is tender, 2½ to 3 hours. Drain meat; slice. Meanwhile, in a bowl mix 3 tablespoons

grated fresh horseradish, 2 tablespoons vinegar, 1 tablespoon prepared mustard, ½ teaspoon salt, dash cayenne, and dash paprika. Whip ½ cup whipping cream till soft peaks form; fold in horseradish mixture. Serve with the sliced beef brisket. Makes 6 servings.

Peach Charlotte

2 cups chopped peeled fresh peaches
1 envelope unflavored gelatin
½ cup sugar
1 cup water
1 tablespoon lemon juice

⅛ teaspoon almond extract
2 egg whites
24 ladyfingers, split lengthwise
½ cup peach preserves
1 cup whipping cream

Press peaches through a sieve with the back of spoon, put through a food mill, *or* puree in a blender. In a small saucepan combine gelatin and sugar; add water. Heat and stir till sugar and gelatin dissolve. Add pureed peaches, lemon juice, and almond extract; gradually stir into unbeaten egg whites. Cool to room temperature. Meanwhile, spread *half of the ladyfinger halves* with peach preserves; top with remaining ladyfinger halves. Arrange *4 sandwiches* lengthwise on bottom of a waxed paper-lined 9x5x3-inch loaf pan. Stand *16*

ladyfinger sandwiches around sides of loaf pan. Set remaining 4 sandwiches aside. Whip gelatin mixture till light. Whip cream till soft peaks form; fold into gelatin mixture. Chill till mixture mounds, stirring occasionally. Carefully turn *half* the gelatin mixture into the ladyfinger-lined pan. Place remaining 4 sandwiches lengthwise atop; top with remaining gelatin mixture. Cover and chill 6 to 8 hours or overnight. Invert pan onto serving platter; remove pan. Remove waxed paper. Garnish with peach slices, if desired. Serves 16.

Crown Roast of Lamb with Vegetables *(see photo, page 127)*

1 4½-pound crown roast of
    lamb (16 to 18 ribs)
1 clove garlic, halved
1½ teaspoons salt
1 teaspoon dried rosemary,
    crushed
18 new potatoes, peeled
    (about 1½-inch diameter)

2 10-ounce packages frozen
    peas
2 tablespoons butter
2 teaspoons finely chopped
    fresh mint *or* ½ tea-
    spoon dried mint,
    crushed
Sprigs of fresh mint

Rub lamb with garlic. Combine salt, rosemary, and ¼ teaspoon pepper; pat onto meat. Wrap ends of bones in foil; stuff center of crown with foil to keep its shape. Place roast on rack in shallow roasting pan. Roast at 325° for 75 minutes. Roll potatoes in lamb drippings in pan and arrange around lamb; continue roasting till meat thermometer registers 170° to 180°, about 1½ to 1¾ hours more. Baste potatoes occasionally. Transfer lamb to large platter; remove foil and strings. Let stand 10 minutes. Meanwhile, cook peas; drain. Add butter and chopped fresh mint or dried mint. Place some peas in center of crown as garnish; serve remaining peas in bowl. Arrange roasted potatoes around crown roast; garnish with sprigs of mint. Makes 8 servings.

The modern, luxurious hotels that replaced the rustic taverns and inns of colonial America in the 1800s were a dramatic change. When the Tremont House opened in Boston in 1829, it was considered the prototype of modern "first class" hotels in the United States. The guests enjoyed magnificent marble fireplaces, carpeted and curtained rooms and corridors, imported furniture, and crystal chandeliers. The era of opulent hotels and restaurants was becoming firmly established.

Pecan Brittle

Spread 1½ cups coarsely chopped pecans in a shallow baking pan; toast in a 350° oven for 10 minutes. Grease a 15½x10½x1-inch shallow pan or marble slab. In a heavy skillet, heat 2 cups sugar over medium-low heat, stirring constantly with a wooden spoon, till sugar melts and has a golden color, 18 to 20 minutes. Stir in the pecans. Immediately pour into greased pan or onto marble slab. Quickly spread using a greased spatula. Cool till solid; break into pieces. Makes about 1½ pounds candy.

Everyone who dined on the J. M. White steamboat remembered the delicious pyramids of nougat. It was not the foamy delicacy that we know as nougat today; but a crunchy brittle with nuts throughout.

Elegant Beef Tenderloin

4 beef tenderloin steaks,
    cut ½ inch thick
1 tablespoon butter
¼ cup brandy
½ cup dairy sour cream
2 tablespoons catsup

¼ teaspoon salt
2 dashes Worcestershire
    sauce
2 drops bottled hot
    pepper sauce
Dash ground thyme

In skillet brown the steaks in butter on both sides till desired doneness. (Allow 6 to 8 minutes total for medium-rare.) Remove from heat; pour *half* the brandy over. Place steaks on warm platter; keep warm. Combine sour cream, catsup, salt, Worcestershire, hot pepper sauce, thyme, and remaining brandy; add to same skillet. Heat, stirring constantly, just till heated through. Spoon some sauce over steaks; pass remainder. Serves 4.

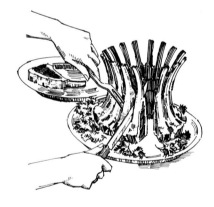

Cream of Mushroom Soup

1 cup sliced fresh
    mushrooms
2 tablespoons chopped
    onion
2 tablespoons butter
2 tablespoons all-purpose
    flour

2 cups chicken broth
• • •
1 cup whipping cream
¼ teaspoon salt
¼ teaspoon ground nutmeg
⅛ teaspoon white pepper

Cook mushrooms and onion in butter till tender but not brown, about 5 minutes. Blend in flour; add broth. Cook and stir till slightly thick and bubbly. Stir in cream, salt, nutmeg, and pepper. Heat through. Makes 4 to 6 servings.

Partridge in Red Wine

By the 1880s the Windsor Hotel in
Denver was celebrated for
the wild game on its menu. One could
order bear paws, buffalo,
doves, quail, duck, or partridge.
The hotel boasted another
unusual feature. It had the first
"ladies' ordinary" in the
West—that is, the first restaurant
to serve unescorted women.

3 tablespoons all-purpose
  flour
2 1-pound ready-to-cook
  partridges *or* Rock
  Cornish game hens

2 tablespoons butter
1 cup beef broth
2 tablespoons finely
  chopped onion
½ cup Burgundy *or* claret

Mix flour and ½ teaspoon salt. Halve birds; coat with flour mixture. In skillet brown birds in butter. Add broth and onion. Cook, covered, over low heat till tender, 45 to 55 minutes.

Transfer to a serving platter; keep warm. Skim off fat. Stir wine into skillet. Boil vigorously till liquid is reduced to ½ cup, about 10 minutes. Spoon over birds. Makes 2 servings.

Veal in Cream

½ cup chopped onion
1 clove garlic, minced
6 tablespoons butter
6 veal cutlets, cut ½ inch
  thick

1 cup whipping cream
½ pound fresh mushrooms,
  sliced
3 to 4 tablespoons brandy
Hot cooked noodles

Steamboating was not simply a means of transportation. It was also a source of entertainment during the 1800s. Captains often rented their ships for excursion parties or group meetings.

In skillet cook onion and garlic in *4 tablespoons* butter till onion is tender but not brown; add veal and cook till almost done, 6 to 7 minutes. Add 1 teaspoon salt and dash pepper. Add

cream; simmer, covered, 10 minutes more. Meanwhile, cook mushrooms in remaining butter 2 to 3 minutes. Add mushrooms and brandy to veal. Serve with noodles. Makes 6 servings.

Shaker Cooking

"**P**ut your hands to work and give your hearts to God,"[17] said the founder of the Shakers, Mother Ann Lee.

Born in Manchester, England, in 1743, this daughter of an illiterate blacksmith founded a new sect, an offshoot of the Quakers. This sect taught that God's kingdom could be achieved here on earth and the second coming of Jesus Christ would take place in the individual souls of those who withdrew from the world and lived in celibate, self-sufficient communities. Members of the group were called Shakers because of a peculiar ceremonial dance they did as part of their worship.

Mother Ann was persecuted in England, and in 1774, with seven followers, she emigrated to America. Before the eighteenth century ended thousands of converts joined the Shakers, and eleven communities were founded in New England and New York. As the west opened up, other Shaker communities located in Ohio, Kentucky, and Indiana.

But what place has all this in a cook book? The Shakers were among the best cooks we've ever had. And not only did they cook, they also preserved, smoked, canned, farmed, gardened, and were responsible for many simple but ingenious inventions to lighten household work. Examples of the latter are a circular saw, a pea sheller, a kernel-cutter for corn, a threshing machine, a washing machine, a flat broom, a screw propeller, and a revolving pie oven for even distribution of heat. Gail Borden, who later put evaporated milk on the market, developed his idea from a process devised by the Shakers. They also made furniture, boxes, shaving mugs, fire irons, and other useful household items. They established nurseries and were the first to package garden seeds and dried herbs and sell them commercially.

In Shaker communities the women did the cooking and the men did the farming. Their kitchens were large, for there were often hundreds to be fed, including homeless children whom the Sisters and Brethren raised. "There is no dirt or filth in Heaven,"[18] Mother Ann had said, and the kitchens were spotless, with running water (before most people had any) and stone sinks. Some of their ideas about cooking were remarkably modern. For example, they cooked vegetables in small amounts of water and avoided the then-common practice of boiling them too long. The cooking water was saved for gravies and soups. They preferred their stewed fruits unpeeled and their flour unbolted (that is, with the wheat germ intact).

Shaker cooking included some delicious meatless dishes using nuts, mushrooms, lentils, rice, and cheese. Many are favorites today among vegetarians. From their well-tended orchards, the communities harvested apples for cider, apple butter, dried apples, and applesauce. Shaker preserves, relishes, and pickles were much in demand, and so were their homemade extracts—rosewater, orange-flower water, and lemon extract. They also made and marketed sarsaparilla, as well as "charged water" flavored with fruit juice, and an old-fashioned drink called switchel, made of water, molasses, ginger, and sugar or maple syrup.

Today, the Shaker community founded in 1794, at Sabbathday Lake, Maine, is the only one surviving. A number of former communities are preserved as historic landmarks and museums. Meantime, their simple, well-made crafts and their delicious recipes have become an American tradition.

For a decade after 1837 a ban on meat was observed by all Shakers. But the ban proved difficult to enforce, so later, tables were earmarked in Shaker communities for those believing in "the Bloodless diet" and other tables were reserved for those on the "regular" diet. Although the ban lasted only ten years, the belief persisted in the propriety of a diet of grains, fruits, vegetables, eggs, and dairy products. Hester A. Pool describes the food she saw at the Shaker settlement in Mt. Lebanon in 1888. "The food is of the best quality and generous in quantity. Almost no use is made of flesh food and homegrown and ground cereals are cooked to perfection. Such vegetables plucked within the hour, and such pies shortened with sweet cream and filled with fresh fruit or that preserved by their own peculiar process, we mutually confessed to have never tasted before...."[19]

Shakers had a reputation for strict adherence to "family" rules and dinner time was no exception. According to the account written by Shaker Hervey Elkins, they entered their dining hall all at one time: the Sisters entering by one door and the Brethren by another. Each group had its own tables. They took their places and knelt in silent prayer. Then they were seated and the meal began. Another account by David R. Lamson continues, "All conversation in the dining room was strictly forbidden. The sisters who prepared the food also waited on table — and when an individual wished anything which was not before him, he beckoned a sister who was in waiting and made known to her his wish in a low whisper."[20] Shaker meals were eaten quickly, often in fifteen minutes or less. After the meal the members again prayed and quietly filed out.

Prune Loaves

2 cups water
1 cup snipped pitted dried
   prunes (8 ounces)
• • •
1 cup sugar
¼ cup shortening
1 egg

1 cup buttermilk
2 cups all-purpose flour
1 cup whole wheat flour
1 teaspoon baking soda
½ teaspoon salt
¼ teaspoon baking
   powder

In a small saucepan combine the water and snipped prunes; bring to a boil. Cover and simmer 3 minutes. Drain, reserving ⅓ cup liquid. Set aside. Cream together the sugar and shortening till light and fluffy; beat in egg. Combine the buttermilk and the reserved prune liquid. Stir together thoroughly the all-purpose flour, whole wheat flour, baking soda, salt, and baking powder; add to the creamed mixture alternately with buttermilk mixture. Fold in cooked prunes. Turn batter into 2 greased 7½x3½x2-inch loaf pans. Bake at 350° till done, about 1 hour. Cool in pans 10 minutes. Remove from pans; cool on wire racks. Wrap and refrigerate overnight. Makes 2.

Crackers

1 cup all-purpose flour
1 teaspoon baking powder
¼ teaspoon salt

¼ cup butter *or*
   margarine
¼ cup milk

Stir together thoroughly the all-purpose flour, baking powder, and salt. Cut in butter or margarine till the mixture resembles coarse crumbs. Add milk; stir till the mixture forms a ball. Turn dough out onto lightly floured surface. Knead dough gently 8 to 10 strokes. Roll the dough to ¼-inch thickness. Dip a 2½-inch biscuit cutter in all-purpose flour; cut dough straight down. Place dough rounds on greased baking sheet. Bake at 400° for 10 minutes. Split the hot crackers with a knife. Return to oven and bake at 400° till golden brown, 4 to 6 minutes longer. Makes 24 crackers.

Wheaten Bread

4 to 4⅓ cups whole wheat
 flour
2 packages active dry yeast
1¾ cups milk

⅓ cup molasses
2 tablespoons lard
2 teaspoons salt

In a large mixing bowl combine *2 cups* of the whole wheat flour and the yeast. In saucepan heat milk, molasses, lard, and salt just till warm (115-120°), stirring constantly. Add molasses mixture to dry mixture in mixing bowl. Beat at low speed with electric mixer for ½ minute, scaping the sides of the bowl constantly. Beat 3 minutes at high speed. By hand, stir in enough of the remaining whole wheat flour to make a moderately stiff dough. Turn dough out onto lightly floured surface and knead till smooth and elastic (4 to 5 minutes). Shape into a ball. Place in a lightly greased bowl, turning once to grease surface. Cover; let rise in warm place till double (1 to 1½ hours). Punch dough down; turn out on lightly floured surface. Cover; let rest 10 minutes. Shape in a loaf; place in greased 9x5x3-inch loaf pan. Cover and let rise in warm place till double (about 30 minutes). Bake at 375° till done, 35 to 40 minutes. Remove from pan and cool on wire rack. Makes 1 loaf.

Old-Fashioned Whipping Cream-Nut Cake

1½ cups sifted cake flour
1½ teaspoons baking powder
½ teaspoon salt
• • •
2 eggs

¾ cup whipping cream
1 cup sugar
½ cup chopped walnuts
 Golden Butter Frosting

In a bowl sift together the cake flour, baking powder, and salt. In large mixing bowl combine the eggs and cream; beat with rotary beater or electric mixer till well blended. Beat in sugar; continue beating till thickened (about 5 minutes). Stir in the flour mixture. Stir in the walnuts. Pour the batter into a greased and floured 9x9x2-inch baking pan. Bake at 350° till the cake tests done, 25 to 30 minutes. Cool. Frost with Golden Butter Frosting.

Golden Butter Frosting: In a small saucepan melt ¼ cup butter *or* margarine; keep over low heat till butter is golden brown. (Watch carefully to prevent scorching.) Remove from heat. Place 2 cups sifted powdered sugar in a mixing bowl. Beat in the melted butter. Add ½ teaspoon vanilla. Blend in enough light cream to make frosting of spreading consistency (about 2 tablespoons). Quickly spread frosting on top of cooled cake.

Although the Shakers are known for their simple foods, not everything they ate was home-style. On holidays or for special occasions, they served rich dishes such as Old-Fashioned Whipping Cream-Nut Cake.

Brown Sugar Rhubarb Pie

1 to 1¼ cups packed brown
 sugar
¼ cup all-purpose flour
¼ teaspoon salt
4 cups rhubarb cut in ½-
 inch slices
• • •
2 beaten egg yolks
1 tablespoon lemon juice

1 unbaked 9-inch pastry
 shell (see recipe,
 page 351)
3 egg whites
½ teaspoon vanilla
¼ teaspoon cream of tartar
6 tablespoons granulated
 sugar

In bowl combine brown sugar, flour, and salt; stir in rhubarb. Let stand 15 minutes. Combine egg yolks and lemon juice; stir into rhubarb mixture. Turn into unbaked pastry shell. Bake at 400° for 20 minutes. Reduce heat to 350°; continue baking till knife inserted off-center comes out almost clean, about 20 minutes (cover edges with foil if necessary). Beat egg whites with vanilla and cream of tartar till soft peaks form. Gradually add granulated sugar, beating till stiff peaks form. Spread over hot filling; sealing to the edge. Bake at 350° till meringue is golden brown, 12 to 15 minutes.

Mother Ann's Birthday Cake

Ann Lee, the founder of the Shakers, was born on February 29, 1736. Her birthday was always celebrated on March 1st with this special peach cake. It was served at supper, following the meeting commemorating Mother Ann. In the original recipe a twig was cut from a peach tree and used to beat the cake batter, giving the cake a delicate peach flavor.

1½ cups sugar
¾ cup butter *or* margarine
3 egg yolks
½ teaspoon vanilla
2¼ cups sifted cake flour
1 tablespoon baking powder
¼ teaspoon salt

1 cup milk
3 egg whites
• • •
1 10- or 12-ounce jar
    peach preserves
Lemon-Butter Frosting

In a bowl cream the sugar and butter till light and fluffy. Add egg yolks and vanilla; beat well. Sift together the cake flour, baking powder, and salt; add to creamed mixture alternately with milk, beating well after each addition. Beat egg whites till stiff peaks form; fold into batter. Turn into 2 greased and floured 8x1½-inch round baking pans. Bake at 350° for 30 to 35 minutes. Cool. Split each layer in half. Spread *three* of the halves with preserves; stack and top with remaining half. Frost top and sides of cake with Lemon-Butter Frosting.

Lemon-Butter Frosting: Cream 6 tablespoons butter *or* margarine; gradually add 2 cups sifted powdered sugar, blending thoroughly. Beat in 1 egg yolk, 1½ teaspoons vanilla, and 1 teaspoon grated lemon peel. Gradually blend in another 2 cups sifted powdered sugar. Add enough milk (about 3 tablespoons) to make of spreading consistency.

Cranberry Pie

3 cups cranberries
    (12 ounces)
1 cup raisins
1 cup water
1½ cups sugar

¼ cup all-purpose flour
1 teaspoon vanilla
Pastry for 2-crust
    9-inch pie (see
    recipe, page 351)

In saucepan combine cranberries, raisins, and water. Bring to boil; cook 3 minutes. Mix sugar and flour. Stir into hot cranberry mixture. Cook and stir till thickened and bubbly. Stir in vanilla. Line 9-inch pie plate with pastry. Spoon in hot cranberry mixture. Adjust top crust, cutting slits for steam to escape. Seal edges; flute. Bake at 400° for 30 to 35 minutes. (Cover edges with foil to prevent overbrowning, if necessary.) Cool before serving.

Shaker Fruit Shrub

2 10-ounce packages frozen
    red raspberries, thawed
1½ cups water

¼ cup lemon juice
Sugar
Ice cubes

In saucepan crush raspberries. Stir in water. Bring to boil; boil gently for 3 minutes. Press through sieve; chill. Stir in lemon juice. Add enough sugar to taste. Serve over ice cubes. Makes 4 (6-ounce) servings.

Ohio Lemon Pie

Pies are fundamental to Shaker cooking. Depending on the filling, there are Shaker pies for any part of any meal. One favorite for dessert is Ohio Lemon Pie. It is unique because it does not have a filling made with lemon juice. Whole lemons, peeled and sliced paper-thin, are used.

Pastry for 2-crust
    8-inch pie (see
    recipe, page 351)

2 lemons
1¾ cups sugar
4 eggs

Line an 8-inch pie plate with pastry. Set aside. Shred peel from lemons to make 2 teaspoons; set aside. Peel lemons, removing all white membrane; cut lemons into very thin slices. Remove seeds. In bowl mix lemon slices, peel, and sugar. Let stand 20 minutes, stirring occasionally. Beat eggs well. Stir into lemon mixture; pour into pastry-lined plate. Adjust top crust; cut slits for steam to escape. Seal and flute edges. Bake at 400°, till done, 35 to 40 minutes. (Cover edges with foil to prevent overbrowning, if necessary.)

Apple Dumplings

Mix 2¼ cups all-purpose flour and ½ teaspoon salt. Cut in ⅔ cup chilled shortening till mixture resembles coarse crumbs. Sprinkle 6 to 8 tablespoons cold water over, a little at a time; mix till moistened. Form into ball; roll out on floured surface to 18x12-inch rectangle. Cut into six 6-inch squares. Using 6 small tart apples, peeled and cored; place one apple on each square.

Mix ⅔ cup sugar and ¼ cup light cream; spoon into apple centers. Moisten edges of pastry. Fold up corners to center; pinch. Place, not touching, in ungreased 11x7½x1½-inch baking pan. Bake at 450° for 15 minutes. Reduce heat to 350°. Baste with ¾ cup hot maple *or* maple-flavored syrup. Bake till done, about 30 minutes, basting every 15 minutes. Serves 6.

For Shaker cooks, the pastry dough had to be just the right kind to complement the filling. They used rye or white flour pastry for meat pies or dumplings and puff pastry for tarts or delicate pies. One hearty pastry dessert was *Apple Dumplings,* often served with maple syrup.

Fresh Applesauce

4 pounds tart apples, peeled, cored, and thinly sliced

1 cup sugar
¾ teaspoon ground cinnamon

In large Dutch oven or kettle mix apples, sugar, and cinnamon. Let stand 30 minutes till juices start to form; stir once or twice. Cook, covered, over *very low* heat till quite juicy, about 10

minutes. Continue cooking over medium heat, to desired thickness, stirring often, about 20 minutes for chunk-style applesauce or 30 minutes for smooth applesauce. Makes 5½ cups.

Fresh Applesauce *is special; it needs no water. It can be prepared either as a chunky or a smooth sauce.*

As early as 1811, Shaker communities were selling a variety of jellies, relishes, sauces, and preserves to neighbors. As with everything they did, the Shakers strove for the highest quality in their canned products— and they attained it. Thousands of bushels of fruits and vegetables were canned during the harvest season each year.

Corn Relish

16 to 20 ears corn
4 cups chopped celery
2 cups chopped sweet red pepper
2 cups chopped green pepper
2 cups sugar

2 cups vinegar
1 cup chopped onion
2 teaspoons celery seed
¼ cup all-purpose flour
2 tablespoons dry mustard
1 teaspoon ground turmeric

Cook corn in large amount boiling water 5 minutes; plunge into cold water. Drain. Cut corn from cobs; do not scrape cobs. Measure 8 cups corn. In large kettle or Dutch oven combine celery, peppers, sugar, vinegar, onion, celery seed, 2 cups water, and 2 tablespoons salt. Bring to boiling. Boil 5 minutes, stirring occasionally. Mix flour, dry mustard, and turmeric. Blend ½ cup cold water into flour mixture. Add with corn to vegetable mixture. Return to boiling; cook and stir 5 minutes. Pack into hot pint jars, leaving ½-inch headspace. Adjust lids. Process in boiling water bath 15 minutes. (Start timing when water returns to boiling.) Makes 7 pints.

Sausage Cooked in Cider

1 12-ounce package pork sausage links
¼ cup chopped onion
1 tablespoon all-purpose flour

1 cup apple cider *or* apple juice
2 teaspoons finely snipped parsley
Honeyed Apple Rings

Prick sausage links with fork. In skillet cook links in ¼ cup water, covered, 5 minutes. Drain. Cook, uncovered, till sausage is browned. Drain off fat; reserve 2 tablespoons fat. Set links aside. Cook onion in fat till tender; blend in flour and ¼ teaspoon salt. Add cider. Cook and stir till thick and bubbly; stir in parsley. Return sausage to skillet. Cover; heat through. To serve, place sausage on platter; surround with Honeyed Apple Rings. Spoon some sauce over; pass remaining sauce. Makes 3 or 4 servings.

Honeyed Apple Rings: Wash and core 4 apples. Cut unpeeled apples in ½-inch rings. Mix ½ cup honey, 2 tablespoons vinegar, ¼ teaspoon salt, and ¼ teaspoon ground cinnamon; bring just to boiling. Add apple rings. Cook till apple rings are transparent, turning often, about 10 to 12 minutes.

Shaker Fish Pie

1 pound fresh *or* frozen fish
1 unbaked 9-inch pastry shell (see recipe, page 351)
1 cup chopped onion
½ cup chopped celery
3 tablespoons butter
1 tablespoon snipped parsley

½ teaspoon dried marjoram, crushed
2 tablespoons all-purpose flour
1 teaspoon salt
Dash pepper
1 cup light cream
⅓ cup fine dry bread crumbs
2 tablespoons butter *or* margarine, melted

Thaw frozen fish. Cook fish in boiling salted water to cover till fish flakes easily when tested with a fork. Remove fish. Bake pastry shell at 450° for 5 minutes (do not prick pastry). Remove from oven and set aside. Reduce the oven temperature to 325°. Meanwhile, cook onion and celery in 3 tablespoons butter till tender but not brown. Stir in parsley and marjoram. Blend in flour, salt, and pepper. Add cream all at once. Cook and stir till the mixture is thickened and bubbly. Remove from heat; stir in the cooked fish. Pour the fish mixture into the partially baked pastry shell. Sprinkle with a mixture of bread crumbs and 2 tablespoons melted butter. Bake at 325° for 30 to 35 minutes. Let stand 5 minutes before serving. Makes 6 servings.

Shaker Squash

1 2½- to 3-pound Hubbard
    squash, cut in
    large pieces
2 tablespoons maple *or*
    maple-flavored syrup

2 tablespoons butter
1 teaspoon salt
1 tablespoon snipped
    parsley *or* sliced
    green onion

Place squash pieces in large baking pan. Bake, covered, at 350° till tender, about 1¼ hours. Remove pulp; press through sieve. Place pulp in saucepan; stir in syrup, butter, salt, and dash pepper. Heat through. (If thin, cook and stir till desired consistency.) Top with parsley or onion. Serves 6 to 8.

Pork Chops with Cabbage

Trim excess fat from 4 pork shoulder chops, cut ½ inch thick; cook trimmings in skillet till 1 tablespoon fat accumulates. Remove trimmings. Season chops with salt and pepper. Brown in hot fat. Remove chops and set aside. In same skillet combine 8 cups coarsely chopped cabbage and ⅓ cup chopped onion. Add ½ cup apple cider *or* apple juice, ½ teaspoon rubbed sage, and ¼ teaspoon salt; top with chops. Cover tightly; cook over low heat till meat is tender, 40 to 45 minutes. Remove chops; keep warm. Slowly blend ½ cup light cream into 1 tablespoon all-purpose flour; stir into skillet. Cook and stir till thick and bubbly. Turn onto platter. Place chops atop cabbage. Garnish with snipped parsley; sprinkle with paprika. Makes 4 servings.

Probably the Shaker enterprise that was best known to outsiders was their herb and seed business. After learning about wild herbs from the Indians, the Shakers successfully gathered, transplanted, cultivated, and sold the plants to people throughout the country. By the Civil War era, this thriving venture was advertising more than 300 kinds of herbs (both medicinal and flavoring herbs) and seeds.

Louisiana-New Orleans' Food Heritage

It may have been the greatest bargain of all time—over a million square miles for $15 million, or about three cents an acre. Thomas Jefferson, who, in 1803, negotiated the Louisiana Purchase, sent out the Lewis and Clark expedition to scout this vast new possession and, among other things, bring back seeds or cuttings of new food plants. Nobody was quite sure where the northwest boundaries of the Louisiana Territory were—perhaps at the Continental Divide (wherever that was). But one thing was certain; the colorful, bustling port city of New Orleans, which had been settled by the French in 1718, turned over to the Spanish in 1762, and returned to the French in 1800, was now going to be American.

There were ninety thousand people in the Louisiana Territory, and half of them lived in New Orleans. Those who were French or Spanish or a mixture of both were called Creole. The French predominated. There were also many Negro slaves and "free people of color," as well as remnants of the Indian tribes that had formerly lived in the area. After 1760, when the British vanquished the French in Canada, French-speaking refugees from Acadia (in Nova Scotia), settled in the bayou country southwest of New Orleans. They were the ancestors of the people now known as Cajuns. A few Germans and Irish had also immigrated to southern Louisiana, as did people who had been Tories during the Revolution. American traders

Natchitoches has the distinction of being the oldest town in Louisiana. The settlement was established about 1714 by the French. It became a flourishing trading post where hides and bars of silver were exchanged for tobacco, guns, medicine, and liquor brought up the Red River. But as luck would have it, the Red River changed its course leaving Natchitoches with no water transportation, thus destroying the hope that the rapidly growing city would rival its southern trading sister, New Orleans.

had been visiting New Orleans for some time, and as soon as the purchase was completed there was an influx of American families.

The heterogeneous population, plus the abundant and excellent cooking ingredients available in New Orleans markets produced a unique and delectable cuisine. The French contributed an essential flair for cooking, along with some traditional French recipes — *daube glacé, bouillabaisse,* frogs' legs, fish poached in *court bouillon,* and the kind of savory soups that thrifty French cooks make from leftovers. From Africa came okra, a favorite Louisianian vegetable and a necessary ingredient for the thick stew called gumbo. The word "gumbo" is of African origin, but the very special flavor of this stew is imparted by *filé* powder, an invention made from sassafras by the Choctaw Indians. A gumbo may contain crabs, shrimp, oysters, chicken, or ham, but if it lacks both okra and *filé* powder, it isn't gumbo.

Rice, universally enjoyed in Louisiana, is the main ingredient in a number of famous local dishes. Red beans, simmered with a little meat and a lot of garlic, combined with rice make one nourishing and economical dish. Another, jambalaya, is perhaps the most well known of the rice dishes. It is a mixture of spicy sausage, chicken, and shrimp served over rice.

Jambalaya and many other Creole dishes depend on liberal dashes of hot pepper sauce. One of these, Tabasco, has been made commercially in Louisiana since 1868. Another sauce that combines tomatoes and green peppers is now well known far and wide as "Creole sauce."

Rice is the chief ingredient for *calas tout chauds* — rice cakes, deep fried and dipped in powdered sugar — these were sold by street vendors and at the French Market. Street vendors also sold a sort of oyster sandwich called *la médiatrice* (peacemaker) comprised of a small loaf of French bread, hollowed and filled with hot oysters.

Among the many delicious sweets are French doughnuts, orange-flower macaroons, sweet potato cake, and, of course, the renowned praline, the delicate concoction of sugar, cream, and Louisiana's prized pecans.

Famous New Orleans drinks are *café au lait, grand brûlé* — coffee with burned spiced brandy, sugar, and citrus peel — and several cocktails. The New Orleans version of the naming of cocktails says that the first cocktails were made in New Orleans and served in an egg cup or *coquetier.* Over the years, cocktails became a specialty in antebellum days of the St. Charles Hotel bar, which could accommodate one thousand customers.

French Doughnuts

2¾ to 3¼ cups all-purpose flour
1 package active dry yeast
½ teaspoon ground nutmeg
1 cup milk
¼ cup granulated sugar
¼ cup cooking oil
1 egg
Fat for frying
Sifted powdered sugar

In mixing bowl mix *1½ cups* flour, yeast, and nutmeg. Heat milk, granulated sugar, oil, and ¾ teaspoon salt just till warm (115-120°). Add to dry mixture; add egg. Beat at low speed of electric mixer for ½ minute, scraping bowl constantly. Beat 3 minutes at high speed. By hand, stir in enough remaining flour to make a soft dough. Place in greased bowl; turn once. Cover; chill. Turn dough out on floured surface. Cover; let rest 10 minutes. Roll to 18x 12-inch rectangle. Cut into 3x2-inch rectangles. Cover; let rise for 30 minutes (dough will not be doubled). Fry in deep hot fat (375°) till golden, turning once, about 1 minute. Drain. Sprinkle with powdered sugar. Makes 36.

French Quarter Oyster Sandwich *(see photo, page 139)*

(see photo, page 139)

In New Orleans, the husband who stayed out too late at the Chess Club — or otherwise diverting himself in the French Quarter — would stop by the Old Market to pick up an oyster sandwich called La Médiatrice *(mediator), to act as peacemaker at home. Wrapped in layers of heavy brown paper it was still crisp and hot on arrival home.*

½ pint shucked oysters
⅓ cup all-purpose flour
½ teaspoon salt
⅛ teaspoon pepper
• • •
1 beaten egg

1 tablespoon water
½ cup fine dry
   bread crumbs
½ cup butter *or* margarine,
   melted
1 small loaf French bread

Drain oysters; dry with paper toweling. In a bowl combine flour, salt, and pepper. Coat oysters with flour mixture. Dip oysters into a mixture of egg and water; roll in bread crumbs. In skillet fry oysters in *half* the melted butter till golden, about 5 minutes. Mean-while, remove a thin slice from top of bread. Hollow out loaf, leaving about ½ inch bread on all sides. Brush with remaining melted butter; bake at 400° till golden, about 5 minutes. Fill with the fried oysters. Top with bread top. Makes 3 or 4 servings.

Little Ears *(see photo, page 139)*

(see photo, page 139)

These age-old Acadian favorites are an elegant sweet pastry served with a Praline Sauce. *This crisp confection has been dubbed* Les Oreilles de Cochon *or* Little Ears.

2 cups all-purpose flour
2 tablespoons sugar
2 teaspoons baking powder
½ teaspoon salt
¼ teaspoon ground nutmeg
2 well-beaten eggs
¼ cup butter *or* margarine,
   melted

¼ cup milk
1 teaspoon grated orange
   peel
• • •
Fat for frying
Praline Sauce
   (see recipe below)

In a mixing bowl combine the flour, sugar, baking powder, salt, and nutmeg; make a well in the center of the dry ingredients. Stir together the eggs, butter or margarine, milk, and orange peel; add all at once to dry ingredients. Mix till well combined. Cover and chill thoroughly, about 2 hours. Roll out *half* the dough at a time to ⅛-inch thickness. Cut dough into 4-inch rounds. Fry 3 or 4 dough rounds at a time in deep hot fat (375°) till puffed and light golden, 1 to 2 minutes on each side. Drain well on paper toweling; keep warm. Serve with warm Praline Sauce. Makes 16.

Praline Sauce

1 cup dark corn syrup
3 tablespoons packed brown
   sugar
3 tablespoons water

½ cup coarsely chopped
   pecans
¼ teaspoon vanilla

In a saucepan combine the corn syrup, brown sugar, and water. Cook and stir over medium heat till mixture boils; boil 1 minute. Remove from heat. Stir in nuts and vanilla. Drizzle over the Little Ears. Makes about 1⅔ cups.

Pain Perdu

The French Pain Perdu *means "lost bread," so named because it is prepared with day-old bread that might otherwise go to waste. It is really our familiar French toast, but made intriguing by adding a bit of lemon.*

⅔ cup milk
2 beaten eggs
2 tablespoons sifted
   powdered sugar
1 teaspoon grated lemon
   peel

Dash salt
8 1-inch-thick slices
   day-old French bread
Butter *or* margarine
Sifted powdered sugar
Maple syrup *or* honey

In mixing bowl combine milk, eggs, 2 tablespoons sugar, lemon peel, and salt; mix well. Dip the bread in egg mixture, coating both sides. In a skillet over low heat, brown bread in butter on both sides. Sprinkle with powdered sugar. Serve hot with syrup or honey. Makes 4 servings.

Shrimp Étouffé

1½ pounds fresh *or* frozen
    shelled shrimp
2 tablespoons all-purpose
    flour
¼ cup butter *or* margarine
¼ cup finely chopped celery
2 tablespoons sliced green
    onion with tops

1 clove garlic, minced
1 cup water
2 tablespoons snipped
    parsley
1 teaspoon salt
    Dash cayenne
    Hot cooked rice

Thaw frozen shrimp. In saucepan cook flour in butter till golden brown, about 5 minutes; stir often. Stir in celery, onion, and garlic; cook and stir for 3 to 4 minutes. Add water, parsley, salt, cayenne, and shrimp. Simmer, covered, 15 minutes. Serve over hot cooked rice. Makes 6 servings.

Shrimp Jambalaya

½ cup celery leaves
2 tablespoons vinegar
1 slice onion
2 teaspoons salt
1 teaspoon seafood
    seasoning
1½ pounds fresh *or* frozen
    shrimp in shells *or*
      1 pound frozen shelled
      shrimp
½ cup chopped onion
½ cup chopped celery
1 clove garlic, minced
¼ cup butter *or* margarine

1 16-ounce can tomatoes,
    cut up
1 6-ounce can tomato paste
1 teaspoon sugar
1 teaspoon Worcestershire
    sauce
½ teaspoon seafood
    seasoning
    Several dashes bottled
      hot pepper sauce
1 cup sliced fresh
    mushrooms
1 teaspoon filé powder
    Hot cooked rice

In a large saucepan mix celery leaves, vinegar, onion slice, salt, 1 teaspoon seafood seasoning, and 4 cups water; bring to boiling. Add shrimp in shells*; return to boiling. Simmer till shrimp turn pink, about 3 minutes. Drain. Peel shrimp under running water; remove vein that runs down the back. Cook chopped onion, celery, and garlic in butter till tender. Add tomatoes, tomato paste, sugar, Worcestershire sauce, ½ teaspoon seafood seasoning, pepper sauce, 1½ cups water, and ½ teaspoon salt. Simmer, covered, 30 minutes. Add shrimp and mushrooms; simmer till shrimp are heated through and mushrooms are tender. Stir in filé powder; serve over rice. Serves 6.

Note: For frozen shelled shrimp, thaw shrimp; omit cooking.

The Creole name jambalaya, is derived from the French word for ham (jambon). This is just one of the ingredients that can go into the pot. Seafood, vegetables, and any leftover meats are also acceptable jambalaya ingredients.

Cream-Sauced Frog Legs

2 pounds fresh *or* frozen
    frog legs
⅓ cup all-purpose flour
1½ teaspoons salt
½ teaspoon dried tarragon,
    crushed
¼ teaspoon pepper

¼ cup butter *or*
    margarine
2 tablespoons finely
    chopped onion
1½ cups light cream
2 tablespoons snipped
    parsley

Thaw frozen frog legs. Separate into individual legs. In paper or plastic bag combine flour, salt, tarragon, and pepper; shake frog legs in flour mixture, a few at a time, to coat thoroughly. Reserve 1 tablespoon flour mixture. In a large skillet brown frog legs in butter. Cook, covered, till tender, about 25 minutes. Remove legs to serving platter; keep warm. In same skillet cook onion till tender but not brown. Blend in reserved flour mixture. Stir in light cream; cook and stir till thickened and bubbly. Spoon over frog legs. Garnish with the snipped parsley. Makes 6 servings.

Crayfish Bisque

4 to 4½ pounds live
    crayfish *or* two 8-ounce
    packages frozen
    lobster tails
½ cup chopped celery leaves
2 bay leaves
2 sprigs parsley
2 teaspoons vinegar
1½ teaspoons salt
¼ teaspoon dried thyme,
    crushed
¼ teaspoon dried basil,
    crushed
¼ teaspoon dried marjoram,
    crushed
1 cup chopped onion
2 cloves garlic, minced
¼ cup butter *or* margarine
⅓ cup all-purpose flour

1 8-ounce can tomatoes
½ cup sliced parsnip
¼ cup shredded carrot
1 teaspoon salt
¼ teaspoon sugar
⅛ teaspoon pepper
    Dash bottled hot pepper
    sauce
1 tablespoon snipped
    parsley
1½ teaspoons lemon juice
½ teaspoon salt
    Dash bottled hot pepper
    sauce
1 beaten egg
¼ cup fine dry bread crumbs
1 tablespoon butter *or*
    margarine, melted
    Hot cooked rice

Rinse crayfish or lobster in cold water. In large kettle mix 6 quarts water, celery leaves, bay leaves, parsley sprigs, vinegar, 1½ teaspoons salt, thyme, basil, and marjoram. Bring to boiling; add crayfish or lobster. Return to boiling; cook till red, about 5 minutes for crayfish and 8 minutes for lobster. Remove shellfish; strain and reserve 3⅔ cups liquid. Set reserved liquid aside. Snip along underside of thin shell of the body or tail of shellfish. Remove undershell; discard. Remove meat, chop, and set aside. Reserve crayfish shells or lobster tails.

Cook ½ *cup* onion and *1 clove* garlic in *3 tablespoons* of the butter till onion is tender. Blend in flour; cook and stir over low heat till mixture browns.

Remove from heat. Add *3 cups* of the reserved liquid, the undrained tomatoes, parsnip, carrot, 1 teaspoon salt, sugar, pepper, and dash pepper sauce. Simmer for ½ hour.

Cook remaining ½ cup onion and 1 clove garlic in remaining 1 tablespoon butter till tender. Add remaining ⅔ cup reserved liquid, snipped parsley, lemon juice, ½ teaspoon salt, and dash pepper sauce. Bring to boiling. Stir a moderate amount of hot mixture into egg; return to saucepan. Cook and stir 1 to 2 minutes. Stir in crumbs and shellfish. Stuff reserved shells with mixture. Place in shallow baking dish. Drizzle 1 tablespoon melted butter atop. Bake at 350° for 20 minutes. Serve with sauce over rice. Serves 4 to 6.

Bouillabaisse Louisiane

2 pounds fresh *or* frozen
    red snapper fillets
3 tablespoons snipped
    parsley
1 clove garlic, minced
1 bay leaf, crumbled
¾ teaspoon dried thyme,
    crushed
½ teaspoon salt
¼ teaspoon ground allspice
1 teaspoon cooking oil

½ cup chopped onion
1 tablespoon cooking oil
1 16-ounce can tomatoes,
    cut up
½ lemon, sliced
1 teaspoon instant chicken
    bouillon granules
¼ teaspoon ground hot red
    pepper
⅛ teaspoon ground saffron
    Hot cooked rice

Thaw frozen fish. Cut fish into six portions. Pat dry on paper toweling. Mix parsley, garlic, bay leaf, thyme, salt, and allspice. Stir in 1 teaspoon oil. Spread mixture over top of each fillet; set aside. In large skillet cook onion in 1 tablespoon oil till tender.

Stir in tomatoes, lemon slices, bouillon granules, red pepper, and saffron. Bring to boiling. Add fish; cover. Reduce heat. Poach till fish flakes easily, about 10 minutes. Remove lemon slices; serve in bowls over hot cooked rice. Makes 6 servings.

Creole Gumbo

3 tablespoons butter
3 tablespoons all-purpose
  flour
½ cup chopped onion
1 clove garlic, minced
1 16-ounce can tomatoes,
  cut up
½ cup chopped green pepper
2 bay leaves
1 teaspoon dried oregano,
  crushed

1 teaspoon dried thyme,
  crushed
¼ teaspoon bottled hot
  pepper sauce
2 4½-ounce cans shrimp,
  drained and cut up
1 7½-ounce can crab meat,
  drained and cartilage
  removed
1 tablespoon filé powder
Hot cooked rice

In large saucepan melt butter; blend in flour. Cook and stir till golden brown, 7 to 8 minutes. Stir in onion and garlic; cook till onion is tender but not brown. Stir in undrained tomatoes, green pepper, bay leaves, oregano, thyme, hot pepper sauce, 1½ cups water, and ½ teaspoon salt. Bring to boiling; reduce heat and simmer, covered, about 20 minutes. Remove bay leaves. Stir in shrimp and crab; heat through. Remove from heat. Blend moderate amount hot liquid into filé powder. Return to remaining hot mixture in saucepan, stirring till combined. Serve over rice in soup bowls. Pass additional bottled hot pepper sauce, if desired. Serves 5 or 6.

A roux is used extensively in French and Creole cooking to thicken sauces or gravy. In making a roux, flour and fat are mixed in equal parts. Then the mixture is cooked, stirring constantly to prevent scorching. It may be cooked to three different stages depending upon its use. A light roux is used in making light-colored sauces such as veloute; golden roux for slightly darker sauces and in recipes such as Creole Gumbo; *and a rich brown roux is used to make brown sauces.*

Café au Lait

Measure 3 cups cold water into percolator. Measure ¾ cup chicory-blend coffee into basket. Cover; place over heat. Bring to boiling; reduce heat and perk gently 6 to 8 minutes. Remove basket; keep coffee hot over very low heat till ready to serve. Meanwhile, heat 3 cups light cream *or* milk over low heat. Beat with rotary beater till foamy. Transfer to a warmed container. Pour coffee and cream in equal amounts into serving cups. Serves 10.

From this field of color 125 miles west of New Orleans comes the hot sauce once known only to southern Louisiana cooks, but now marketed worldwide as Tabasco. The fully ripe red peppers are harvested in the fall, then ground, sprinkled with salt, and placed in oak casks. After a three-year fermentation period, the peppers are churned with vinegar for 30 days and finally bottled. An ingenious technological device sucks the air out of the bottle, creating a vacuum inside so that the sauce is automatically drawn in through the tiny nozzle hole.

Louisiana Red Beans and Rice

The dish, red beans and rice, is so popular in Louisiana that it has become a tradition to serve it every Monday — even in restaurants. The special bean mixture is often simmered with the ham bone left over from Sunday's ham dinner. You may wish to substitute a ham bone for the salt pork in this recipe; either way the dish has a remarkable flavor.

½ pound dry red beans
   (1¼ cups)
4 cups water
• • •
¼ pound salt pork,
   diced
1 cup chopped onion
1 cup finely chopped celery

2 tablespoons snipped
   parsley
¼ to ½ teaspoon crushed
   dried red pepper
1 large clove garlic,
   minced
1 bay leaf
Hot cooked rice

Rinse beans. Place beans in large Dutch oven; add the water. Bring to boiling; reduce heat and simmer 2 minutes. Remove from heat. Cover; let stand 1 hour. (Or, combine beans and water; soak overnight.) Do not drain.

Add salt pork, onion, celery, parsley, red pepper, garlic, and bay leaf. Bring to boiling; cover and simmer 1 hour and 45 minutes, stirring once or twice. Remove bay leaf. Mash beans slightly. Serve over hot cooked rice. Serves 6.

New Orleans Dirty Rice

Creole cooks invented this rich rice dish and refer to it as dirty rice. The "dirty" appearance comes from the pieces of chicken livers and dark beef broth that are cooked with the rice till not a white grain is visible. A rather unpalatable name for such a savory and delicious dish.

1 14-ounce can beef broth
¾ cup regular rice
3 tablespoons butter *or*
   margarine
3 tablespoons all-purpose
   flour
1 cup finely chopped onion
½ cup finely chopped celery

½ cup finely chopped green
   pepper
½ teaspoon garlic powder
½ teaspoon salt
⅛ teaspoon cayenne
1 pound chicken livers
1 3-ounce can sliced
   mushrooms

In saucepan combine beef broth and rice; bring to boiling. Cover and cook according to rice package directions. Meanwhile, in another saucepan, melt butter; stir in flour. Cook and stir till golden brown. Stir in onion, celery, green pepper, garlic powder, salt,

and cayenne. Cook till onion is tender. Coarsely chop chicken livers. Stir livers and undrained mushrooms into onion mixture. Cover; cook over low heat till livers are tender, 6 to 8 minutes, stirring often. Fold liver mixture into hot cooked rice. Makes 6 servings.

Calenda Cabbage

Congo-born Marie Therese Coincoin overcame the oppression of slavery to achieve her freedom and to liberate her 14 enslaved children. From a small tract of land given to her, she and her children worked hard and acquired more land. The next three generations of her descendants worked equally hard to develop the estate known as Melrose plantation, one of the few Southern plantations on which Blacks were wealthy property owners and masters over Black slaves. Out of the kitchens of Melrose came famed recipes such as this delicious cabbage main dish served with a cheese sauce.

1 small head cabbage
⅓ cup regular rice
1 cup chopped cooked
   chicken

½ cup finely chopped
   fully cooked ham
Cheese Sauce
Paprika

Core cabbage. In large saucepan cover whole cabbage with water and season with salt. Cover pan and cook cabbage till tender, 15 to 20 minutes. Drain, reserving ½ cup cooking liquid; cool cabbage. Meanwhile, combine rice and ⅔ cup water; bring to boiling. Cover and cook 12 minutes. Combine cooked rice, chopped chicken, ham, ½ teaspoon salt, and dash pepper.

Beginning at the outside of the cabbage, gently open the leaves. Then, starting at center fill the space between the layers of leaves with rice-meat mixture; press back. Tie the cabbage firmly with a piece of string. Return stuffed cabbage to pan. Add

the ½ cup reserved cooking liquid. Cover, cook till heated through, about 20 minutes. Drain. Place on warm serving platter, remove string. Spoon a little Cheese Sauce over cabbage. Sprinkle with paprika. Pass remaining Cheese Sauce. Makes 6 servings.
Cheese Sauce: In a small saucepan melt 2 tablespoons butter *or* margarine. Blend in 2 tablespoons all-purpose flour, ¼ teaspoon salt, and dash pepper. Add 1¼ cups milk all at once. Cook, stirring constantly, till mixture is thickened and bubbly. Stir in ½ cup shredded sharp American cheese (2 ounces). Heat till cheese is completely melted, stirring constantly.

Cooking on the Plantation

Question: What do strawberry shrub, cracklin' bread, dirty rice, she-crab soup, pot liquor, hoppin' John, collards, goobers, roast oysters, Brunswick stew, scuppernong wine, cow peas, molasses pie, clam fritters, chitlins, beaten biscuits, chess pie, Chickasaw peas, hog jowls, flannel cakes, crab cakes, poke salad, baked grits, sweet potato pone, benne brittle, persimmon pudding, and 'possum have in common?

Answer: They are all delicious things to eat or drink and were all served on Southern plantations either at the big house or in the slave quarters. Southern cooking, like Southern hospitality, has become a legend. Like all legends it is partly myth. For certainly, not every plantation had good cooks, nor was every planter hospitable. Nevertheless, every region of the South, from Maryland to Louisiana, has its rich tradition of culinary lore.

Unlike the one-crop colonial plantations, most plantations by the mid-1800s were self-contained kingdoms. Although there might be imported delicacies on the master's table — potted shrimp from England, marmalade from Scotland, and the best French and Spanish wines — most of the food was grown and processed on the spot. For example, the second course of a three-course dinner served at Andrew Jackson's plantation, The Hermitage, near Nashville, is described as follows: sheep rumps, blancmange, woodcocks, apple puffs, crocant (a sweet), lemon tart, hare, a dish of jelly (perhaps calves'-foot jelly, a favorite of Jackson's), lambs' ears, oyster loaves, and ragooed lobster. All except the last two — and the lemon for the tart — undoubtedly came from the pastures and forests of The Hermitage. The shellfish, unless it was smoked, was probably rushed in by fast stage. All eleven dishes were placed on the table at once and "garden stuff" was served from a sideboard.

Because plantation houses were far apart, dinner guests often stayed overnight and might even linger for several weeks. A wedding brought whole families complete with cousins, children, nurses, and ladies' maids. The whole countryside entertained the bride and groom with party after party. Near the seashore, oyster and crab roasts were popular, with mountains of the shellfish cooked over huge pits of hickory coals. Even a simple breakfast might consist of a dozen or more dishes, and some of the gentlemen might have prepared for it with a mint julep or two.

Corn and pork were Southern staples of diet for both master and slave. The master might have delicate puddings and hot breads, rich with eggs and cream, and thin slices of choice smoked ham, while his slaves ate mush and chitlins; but it was still corn and pork. The rations issued in "The Quarters" were likely to be light on meat, with hominy or sweet potatoes added to the ration of cornmeal. On some plantations work was assigned by the task. Workers who finished early might have the rest of the day to fish or hunt, to work in their own vegetable gardens, or to tend their own livestock, varying, when possible the monotonous rations. From the big house rations plus what the slaves could grow, hunt, or catch for themselves, grew the beginnings of the cuisine we today call "soul food."

Entertaining must be effortless — or seem so. So decreed Southern society and it was up to the lady of the house to carry out that edict. When she presided over the drawing room in the evening, exquisitely dressed and languidly waving her fan, no one was supposed to guess that she had been up since dawn, acting (as Thomas Nelson Page wrote of a Virginia lady) as "mistress, manager, doctor, nurse, counselor, seamstress, teacher, housekeeper, slave, all at once."[21] Jessie Benton Fremont described her aunt hostessing a three-hour dinner party, smiling and conversing graciously while a wasp, entrapped in her lace shawl, stung her time after time. To have mentioned it would have been bad manners.

Households that lacked such model mistresses were often run magnificently by slave housekeepers and butlers. Many a Black cook, never taught to read or write, had a head full of recipes for which kings would have paid a mighty ransom.

Clam Fritters with Wine Sauce

1 7½-ounce can minced clams
Milk
1 cup all-purpose flour
2 teaspoons baking powder

½ teaspoon salt
1 beaten egg
Fat for frying
Creamy Wine Sauce

Drain clams, reserving liquid. Add milk to liquid to equal ⅔ cup. Stir together flour, baking powder, and the salt. Combine the milk mixture, drained clams, and beaten egg. Stir into the dry ingredients just till moistened.

Carefully drop by tablespoonfuls into deep hot fat (365°). Fry six to eight fritters at a time till golden, 2 to 3 minutes. Drain on paper toweling. Serve immediately with Creamy Wine Sauce. Makes 6 servings.

Creamy Wine Sauce: In small saucepan melt 2 tablespoons butter *or* margarine. Blend in 3 tablespoons all-purpose flour and ¼ teaspoon seasoned salt. Add 1 cup light cream *or* milk all at once. Cook, stirring constantly, till mixture is thickened and bubbly. Stir some of the hot mixture into 1 slightly beaten egg yolk; return to remaining hot mixture. Stir in 3 tablespoons dry white wine and 2 tablespoons chopped canned pimiento. Heat through.

Pictured opposite: Good eating in the big house began with a huge breakfast that included *Old Southern Beaten Biscuits* (see recipe, page 149). A vinaigrette-topped salad combination called *Salmagundi* might be served for lunch or as an appetizer for dinner. *Roast Squab with Oyster-Giblet Dressing* was a year-round choice for the main course at dinner.

Roast Squab with Oyster-Giblet Dressing

Giblets from squabs *or*
  Rock Cornish game hens
½ cup chopped celery
⅓ cup finely chopped
  onion
¼ cup butter *or*
  margarine
½ pint shucked oysters
2 tablespoons snipped
  parsley
¼ teaspoon salt
⅛ teaspoon pepper

⅛ teaspoon dried rosemary,
  crushed
⅛ teaspoon dried thyme,
  crushed
3 cups dry bread cubes
      • • •
6 12- to 14-ounce
  ready-to-cook squabs
  or Rock Cornish
  game hens
Cooking oil
⅓ cup dry white wine

Chop the giblets from the squabs or Rock Cornish game hens. In large saucepan cook chopped celery, onion, and giblets in the butter or margarine till tender, about 10 minutes. Stir in the undrained oysters and snipped parsley; cook 5 minutes more. Stir in salt, pepper, rosemary, and thyme. Add dry bread cubes; mix thoroughly. Sprin-

kle the inside of squabs or hens with salt. Stuff each of the birds with some of the dressing; brush skin with cooking oil. Place the stuffed birds, breast side up, on rack in shallow roasting pan. Roast, uncovered, at 400° till done, 40 to 50 minutes; baste the birds frequently with the dry white wine. Makes 6 servings.

In the South the master's plantation home was referred to as the big house. Here his slaves did all the necessary housework and cooking, to maintain its elegance.

The slave quarters in comparison were mud-daubed log cabins built in long rows. The cabins were sometimes called shotgun houses because each had three rooms, one right behind the other, so that a shotgun fired into the doorway could scatter shot through all rooms. However, most slaves lived in one-room cabins. The chimneys were made of sticks and mud and would often catch on fire. Slave cabins didn't have glass windows. Instead they used plain plank shutters for blinds and the doors were rough planks.

Salmagundi

12 tiny whole onions
4 cups shredded lettuce
3 cups cooked chicken cut
  in julienne strips
1 cup seedless green grapes
4 hard-cooked eggs, cut up
6 anchovy fillets

2 tablespoons snipped
  parsley
½ cup salad oil
¼ cup white wine
  vinegar
½ teaspoon salt
Dash pepper

In saucepan cook the onions in large amount of boiling salted water till just tender, about 10 minutes. Drain and refrigerate till chilled, at least 2 hours. At serving time arrange lettuce, chicken, grapes, eggs, anchovies, snipped parsley, and the chilled onions

in salad bowl. In a screw-top jar combine the salad oil, white wine vinegar, salt, and the pepper. Cover jar tightly and shake vigorously till dressing is thoroughly mixed. Pour over the lettuce-chicken mixture. Toss lightly to coat. Makes 6 servings.

HOEING

The establishment of the slave-labor system went hand in hand with the growth of the Southern plantations. Some slaves were fairly well treated, if for no other reason than they worked more efficiently when adequately fed and cared for.

Sesame seed was introduced to America by the early African immigrants. Also known as benne seed, it was a token of good luck and good health.

Rabbit Brunswick Stew

1 2-pound ready-to-cook rabbit, cut up	2 medium potatoes, peeled and cubed
1½ teaspoons salt	1 16-ounce can tomatoes, cut up
⅛ teaspoon pepper	1 8¾-ounce can whole kernel corn, drained
• • •	
2 cups water	1 8½-ounce can lima beans, drained
2 medium onions, sliced	¼ cup cold water
2 slices bacon, cut up	2 tablespoons all-purpose flour
½ teaspoon dried rosemary, crushed	
½ teaspoon dried basil crushed	

Sprinkle rabbit generously with the salt and pepper. Place rabbit pieces in large kettle or Dutch oven; add 2 cups water. Stir in the sliced onions, bacon, rosemary, and basil. Bring to boiling. Cover and reduce heat; simmer for 45 minutes. Stir in the potatoes, undrained tomatoes, whole kernel corn, and lima beans. Cover; simmer till meat is done and potatoes are tender, about 30 minutes longer. Blend ¼ cup cold water slowly into flour; stir into hot stew. Cook and stir till thickened and bubbly. Serves 5 or 6.

Benne Brittle

Spread two 1⅞-ounce cans sesame seed (benne) in large baking pan. Toast in 350° oven till lightly browned, 15 to 20 minutes; stir occasionally. In heavy saucepan cook and stir 1 cup sugar over low heat till melted. Remove from heat; quickly stir in sesame and ½ teaspoon vanilla. Pour onto well-buttered baking sheet; spread thin. Cool; break up. Makes ½ pound.

Bittersweet Chocolate Soufflé

3 egg yolks
• • •
2 tablespoons butter *or*
   margarine
2 tablespoons all-purpose
   flour
¼ teaspoon salt
¾ cup milk

2 1-ounce squares
   unsweetened chocolate,
   melted and cooled
½ cup sugar
2 tablespoons hot water
3 egg whites
½ teaspoon vanilla
   Sweetened whipped cream

Beat egg yolks till thick and lemon-colored; set aside. In saucepan melt butter or margarine. Stir in the flour and salt. Add the milk all at once. Cook, stirring constantly, till mixture is thickened and bubbly. Stir moderate amount of hot mixture into beaten egg yolks; mix well. Return to remaining hot mixture in saucepan; cook and stir 2 minutes more. Remove from heat. Stir together cooled chocolate,

¼ *cup* sugar, and hot water. Stir chocolate mixture into egg mixture. Beat egg whites and vanilla till soft peaks form; gradually add remaining sugar, beating to stiff peaks. Fold the egg whites into chocolate mixture. Turn into 1½-quart soufflé dish. Bake at 325° till knife inserted just off-center comes out clean, 55 to 60 minutes. Serve immediately with sweetened whipped cream. Makes 6 servings.

To prevent slaves from sampling the food, they were required to whistle as they carried the hot prepared dishes from the outside kitchens to the master's dining table. This route was called "whistler's walk."

Lemon Cake

1½ cups granulated sugar
½ cup butter *or* margarine
1½ teaspoons grated lemon
   peel
3 eggs
2½ cups all-purpose flour
½ teaspoon baking soda

½ cup milk
¼ cup lemon juice
• • •
2 cups sifted powdered
   sugar
½ teaspoon vanilla
   Milk

In mixing bowl cream together granulated sugar, butter, and *1 teaspoon* lemon peel till fluffy. Add eggs, one at a time, beating well after each addition. Stir together flour and soda; add to the creamed mixture alternately with the milk, beating after each addition. Beat in the lemon juice. Turn the mixture into a greased and lightly

floured 13x9x2-inch baking dish. Bake at 350° till cake tests done, about 25 minutes. Cool thoroughly.

Stir together sifted powdered sugar, remaining lemon peel, and vanilla; stir in enough milk (about 2 tablespoons) to make glaze of spreading consistency. Spread the glaze on cooled cake. Makes 1 cake.

Old Southern Beaten Biscuits *(see photo, page 146)*

2 cups all-purpose flour
1 teaspoon sugar
½ teaspoon salt
¼ teaspoon baking powder

⅛ teaspoon cream of tartar
¼ cup lard
¾ to 1 cup ice water
   Butter

In a small mixing bowl thoroughly stir together the all-purpose flour, sugar, salt, baking powder, and cream of tartar. Cut in the lard till mixture resembles coarse crumbs. Make a well in center of dry mixture. Add ¾ cup of the ice water all at once; stir well. Stir in enough additional ice water to make a stiff dough.

Turn the dough out onto a lightly floured surface. Beat vigorously with the flat side of a wooden or metal mal-

let for 15 minutes, turning and folding the dough constantly. Roll or pat the dough to ¼-inch thickness. Cut the dough with floured 2-inch biscuit cutter; dip the cutter in flour between cuts to prevent sticking.

Place the biscuits on ungreased baking sheet. Prick the tops of each biscuit 3 times with a fork. Bake at 400° till crisp and lightly browned, about 20 minutes. Serve biscuits warm with butter. Makes about 24.

Beaten biscuits were a breakfast specialty in the Deep South before the Civil War. However, they were allowed for slaves only on Sunday. Unlike other biscuits, beaten biscuits are kneaded by repeatedly pounding the dough with a hammer, mallet, or even an iron rod. Slave cooks often timed the steady strokes of beating the dough to the rhythm of a spiritual.

'Possum Supper

Often the slaves were forced to supplement their rations by hunting or trapping wild animals. Since hunting was usually restricted to after work when it was dark, opossums were a frequent catch.

1 1½- to 2-pound ready-to-
  cook opossum
Salt
Pepper
2 medium sweet potatoes
  (about 1½ pounds)

½ cup water
¼ cup butter, melted
Salt
Cayenne
• • •
Butter, melted

Wash opossum; trim off excess fat. Season cavity with salt and pepper. Close with skewers; tie legs together. Scrub potatoes; do not peel. Place opossum and potatoes in shallow roasting pan. Add water. Brush meat and potatoes with melted butter. Sprinkle with salt and cayenne. Cover and bake at 350° till meat and potatoes are tender, about 1¼ hours, basting occasionally with butter. Uncover; bake till brown, basting often. Serves 2.

Molasses Taffy

For the slaves, Christmastime was exciting because there were good things to eat that weren't available the rest of the year. One was pulled syrup candy. Molasses Taffy is similar to the slaves' Christmas treat, except that they used cane syrup and molasses as sweetening.

Butter
2 cups sugar
1 cup light molasses
⅓ cup water

2 teaspoons vinegar
2 tablespoons butter
½ teaspoon baking soda

Butter sides of heavy 3-quart saucepan. In it mix sugar, molasses, and water. Heat slowly, stirring constantly, till boiling. Stir in vinegar, cook to soft crack stage (270°). Remove from heat. Add 2 tablespoons butter; sift in soda and mix. Pour into buttered 15½x 10½x1-inch pan. Cool till easy to handle. Butter hands; gather taffy into ball. Pull. When golden and hard to pull, cut in fourths. Pull into strands about ½ inch thick. With buttered scissors, snip into bite-size pieces. Wrap in waxed paper. Makes 1¼ pounds.

Civil War Cooking

Confederate soldiers knew many recipes using cornmeal. One called Indian sagamite was made from this recipe. "Three parts of Indian meal and one of brown sugar, mixed and browned over the fire, will make the food known as "sagamite." Used in small quantities, it not only appeases hunger but allays thirst, and is therefore useful to soldiers on a scout."²²

While the recipes of war years are usually quickly—and best—forgotten, these that resulted from the shortages of the Civil War years illustrate American ingenuity—both Yankee and Rebel. Admittedly, the soldiers in the field did not have much to work with. In the Union army the standard daily ration consisted of meat (either twelve ounces of pork or bacon, or one and a quarter pounds of salted or fresh beef); plus one pound and six ounces of either soft bread or flour, or a pound of hard crackers (called hardtack), or a pound and a quarter of cornmeal. Each soldier was also supposed to receive stipulated amounts of dried beans or peas, rice or hominy, coffee or tea, sugar, salt, pepper, and molasses. Dried fruits were issued when available, and so were potatoes and vegetables, dehydrated and compressed for easy transportation. All this was enough to keep a fighting man alive, if not exactly well-nourished.

At the outset of the war, bread for the army of the Potomac was baked in ovens installed under the west terrace of the Capitol in Washington. Later, when the battlefront shifted, ovens had to be set up in the field or in nearby towns. When time or equipment was lacking and ovens were not available, the soldiers made do with hardtack because it was easier to keep than soft bread. The taste was dismal, but the soldiers improvised by heating it in pork grease or soaking it in coffee.

The meat issued in both Union and Confederate armies was likely to be of dubious age and quality. If salted, it was so permeated with saltpeter that even an all night soak in a brook had little effect. Dried beans and peas were the soldiers' best bet. Robert E. Lee is said to have called the humble field pea "the Confederacy's best friend." Northerners made Boston baked beans by the ancient hole-in-the-ground method.

Desiccated or dehydrated vegetables were used to best advantage in soups. Even so, the men were likely to refer to them as "desecrated vegetables." Although the canning industry received a healthy impetus from its sales to the Union army, the output of cans was still small and it was a rare soldier who ever saw one. Dried fruit, rice, and fresh potatoes were welcomed — if they survived the ministrations of company cooks.

Union army rations may not have been taste-tempting, but the soldiers seldom went hungry. The Confederates, on the other hand, suffered terribly from food shortages caused by a deteriorating railroad system and insufficient barrels, boxes, and other food containers. Food was being produced, but did not reach the soldier since Union advances cut transportation lines.

Corn bread — coarse, dry, and minus salt or butter — was the basis of a Southern soldier's diet. His beef and pork, when he could get them, were notoriously bad. In the absence of coffee, various substitutes were devised: parched peanuts, potatoes, peas, dried apples, and ripe acorns. Even pots and pans became scarce. One Southern colonel complained in 1863, "I cannot fight more until I get something to cook in."[23]

Both Yanks and Rebs supplemented their rations whenever possible by hunting and fishing or by "foraging" — begging, stealing, or taking by force any foodstuffs they found in the hands of civilians.

In the North, the civilian population did not suffer greatly from shortages; but Southerners had to grow their own food, and if this was given to Southern soldiers or appropriated by Northern ones, great hardships ensued. Ingenious Southern cooks used rice or potato flour to make bread; crackers and tartaric acid instead of apples in apple pie; or a white of an egg and a little butter whipped up together as a substitute for cream in coffee. "Confederate cush" was an improvisation that could be rather tasty if carefully made: bits of cooked beef were fried in bacon grease and then stewed with crumbled hardtack or cornmeal mush, flavored with garlic. Other improvisations were *Mock Oysters* and *Rose Geranium Cake*.

One Mississippi soldier probably summed up the feelings of both armies when he wrote home that while he hoped someday to have a pleasant house and a carriage and other niceties, "having plenty of good things to eat ... is ... worth all the rest."[24]

To many soldiers, coffee was the most important ration of all. One old campaigner wrote, "How often, after being completely jaded by a night march ... have I had a wash, if there was water to be had, made and drunk my pint or so of coffee, and felt as fresh and invigorated as if just arisen from a night's sound sleep."[25] At noonday halts or at the end of a day's march, soldiers habitually brewed coffee as soon as they could kindle a campfire. Sugar was issued simultaneously with coffee, and a man learned to mix the two together at once before the sugar could get wet, spilled, or stolen. The Union army bought large quantities of Gail Borden's new invention, condensed milk, but it was seldom available to troops on the march, and they learned to drink their coffee black. Army life introduced coffee to many who had never seen it before. After the Civil war it became America's national drink.

☐ Union States
☐ Confederate States

Claret Punch

2 ⅘ quart bottles claret,
    chilled
¾ cup sugar
½ teaspoon ground nutmeg

3 7-ounce bottles
    carbonated water,
    chilled

In punch bowl mix claret, sugar, and nutmeg till sugar dissolves. Slowly pour in carbonated water. Makes about 15 (5-ounce) servings.

Claret Punch was a frequently served beverage at official army functions. It was used often during the Civil War because it was available, while most other spirits were not.

The fragrant and delicately flavored *Rose Geranium Cake* was one answer to the shortages during the war. Rose geranium leaves, it was found, provided a tasty substitute for the more common, but unavailable, flavorings. Today, this geranium variety, known as *Pelargonium Graveolens*, is available in either seed or plant form from local or mail-order greenhouses in the spring.

Rose Geranium Cake

12 rose geranium leaves
1 cup butter *or* margarine
(2 sticks)
1¾ cups sugar
6 egg whites

3 cups sifted cake flour
4 teaspoons baking powder
¾ cup milk
½ cup water
Rose Frosting

Rinse leaves. Wrap 6 leaves around each stick of butter; wrap and chill overnight. Remove leaves; rinse and set aside. Cream butter and sugar till light. Add egg whites, two at a time; beat well after each addition. Sift together flour, baking powder, and ½ teaspoon salt. Mix milk and water. Alternately add flour mixture and liquid to butter mixture; begin and end with flour mixture. Beat smooth after each addition. Grease and flour two 9x1½-inch round baking pans. Arrange 6 leaves in each pan; spoon batter over. Bake at 350° for 30 to 35 minutes. Cool 10 minutes.

Remove from pans; cool on racks. Gently remove leaves from cakes; discard. Fill and frost with Rose Frosting.

Rose Frosting: In top of double boiler (not over heat) stir together 1½ cups sugar, 2 egg whites, ⅓ cup cold water, ¼ teaspoon cream of tartar, and dash salt. Beat 1 minute with rotary or electric beater. Place over boiling water. (Upper pan should not touch water.) Cook, beating to stiff peaks, about 7 minutes (do not overcook). Remove from boiling water. Add 5 drops red food coloring; beat till of spreading consistency, about 2 minutes.

Mock Oysters

Before the Civil War was two years old, Southerners were feeling the pinch of shortages, and were devising many new recipes as well as reviving old ones such as Mock Oysters.

Husk and silk 6 ears corn. With a sharp knife make cuts down through center of kernels on each row of corn; scrape cob. In a bowl mix corn; 1 beaten egg; 2 tablespoons butter *or* margarine, melted; ¾ teaspoon salt; and ⅛ teaspoon pepper. Stir in ⅔ cup all-purpose flour. In a heavy skillet pour cooking oil to a depth of ½ inch. Heat oil. Carefully drop the corn mixture by tablespoonfuls into hot oil. Fry till golden, turning once. Makes about 36.

Sweet Potato Pie

1 pound sweet potatoes *or*
  1 18-ounce can sweet
  potatoes
¾ cup packed brown sugar
1 teaspoon ground cinnamon
½ teaspoon salt
3 eggs

1¾ cups milk
1 tablespoon butter *or*
  margarine, melted
1 unbaked 9-inch pastry
  shell (see recipe,
  page 351)

Cook fresh potatoes, covered, in boiling water till tender, about 30 minutes. Peel and mash. (Or, drain and mash canned potatoes.) Measure 1½ cups. Combine potatoes, sugar, cinnamon, and salt. Beat eggs slightly with fork. Stir eggs, milk, and butter into potato mixture. Spoon into pastry shell. Bake at 400° till knife inserted just off-center comes out clean, 45 to 50 minutes.

Stretching the meager supplies available during the war was a challenge. Southerners often boiled down the dirt gathered from under old smokehouses to get salt, and soda was made from burnt corncobs. Sweet potatoes, long a Southern staple, were used in all sorts of ways, from vegetable dishes to what has since become a classic dessert, Sweet Potato Pie.

Mock Apple Pie

Prepare pastry for 2-crust 9-inch pie (see recipe, page 351). Roll pastry for bottom crust; fit into 9-inch pie plate. Coarsely break 36 round cheese crackers into pie plate. In saucepan mix 2 cups sugar, 2 cups water, and 2 teaspoons cream of tartar; bring to boiling. Simmer, uncovered, 15 minutes.

Remove from heat. Stir in 1 teaspoon grated lemon peel and 2 tablespoons lemon juice; cool. Pour syrup over crackers. Dot with 2 tablespoons butter; sprinkle with ground cinnamon. Adjust top crust; cut slits for escape of steam. Seal and flute. Bake at 425° till golden, 30 to 35 minutes. Serve warm.

Salt Pork with Cream Gravy

1 pound salt pork
¼ cup yellow cornmeal
2 tablespoons all-purpose
  flour

Dash pepper
1½ cups milk
Toast

Remove the rind from salt pork. Slice pork ¼ inch thick. Place in saucepan with enough water to cover; bring to boiling and drain well. Coat slices with cornmeal. In a skillet brown salt pork on both sides, about 15 minutes. Spoon off drippings; reserve 3 tablespoons. Remove salt pork. Return reserved drippings to skillet; stir in flour and pepper. Add milk all at once. Cook and stir till thickened and bubbly. Add salt pork and heat through. Season to taste with pepper. Serve on toast. Makes 4 servings.

Brown Rice Bread

2½ to 3 cups unbleached
  white flour
1 package active dry yeast
1 cup milk
2 tablespoons honey

2 tablespoons cooking oil
2 teaspoons salt
1 egg
½ cup brown rice flour

In large bowl combine *1½ cups* white flour and yeast. In saucepan heat milk, honey, oil, and salt just till warm (115-120°). Add to dry mixture; add egg. Beat at low speed with electric mixer for ½ minute, scraping sides of bowl. Beat 3 minutes at high speed. By hand stir in brown rice flour and enough of the remaining white flour to make a soft dough. Turn dough onto lightly floured surface; knead till smooth and elastic (8 to 10 minutes). Shape in ball. Place in lightly greased bowl; turn once. Cover; let rise in warm place till double (1 to 1½ hours). Punch down; turn out onto lightly greased surface. Cover; let rest 10 minutes. Shape into a loaf. Place in greased 8½x4½x2½-inch loaf pan. Cover; let rise till double (about 45 minutes). Bake at 375° about 30 minutes. Remove from pan. Cool on rack. Makes 1.

City Life

As the cities grew, so did the problem of providing their people with acceptable food and drink. During the growing season, farmers from the outlying countryside brought their produce into town. They traveled at night, when the weather was cool, to avoid or delay spoilage. An open-air market area in the early morning was chaos—a bedlam of farmers' carts, makeshift wooden stalls, and buyers and sellers milling together. Boston in 1826 was one of the first cities to provide its citizens with a clean, organized, covered market. Bold city-planners took radical action. They filled in the old town dock and built a handsome, two-story market house on top of the fill. Two new streets and a couple of well-designed granite warehouses flanked the market, and the whole complex was not only useful but beautiful.

In Washington, there was a large, tumultuous open market on Pennsylvania Avenue, on the site of the present National Archives Building. Gentlemen often did their own marketing (either they were bachelors or their wives shrank from the jostling and noise of the market). Daniel Webster, accompanied by his Black cook, was often seen concentrating the force of his great mind on choosing a terrapin or a brace of ducks or on the number of soft-shelled crabs he would need for a party of eight. President William Henry Harrison is said to have caught the cold that became pneumonia and killed him because he walked from the White House to the market on a blustery March day. After the Civil War, a palatial Victorian brick building, covering three acres, replaced the old open market, and included a cafe, an icemaking plant, and a cold storage. A contemporary account of it mentioned "superb carriages and turnabouts coming and going, with their occupants of wealth, beauty, and station. In no other city has marketing been made so attractive to the favorites of fortune."[26]

Before the days of refrigerated railroad cars, animals destined for city consumption had to walk to market, to be butchered at a nearby slaughterhouse. In seaboard cities, fish was an important commodity, and markets often provided a rough "oyster bar," offering the mollusk fresh-shucked, along with vinegar, pepper, and oyster crackers for the enthusiasts who couldn't wait for a feast.

Caveat emptor, the buyer beware, was the unspoken motto of city markets. A wary customer had to dig into a crock of butter to test its freshness; gaze into a fish's eyes to determine their fresh brightness or sunken glaze; sniff the meat; and watch the grocer's hand on the scales when he weighed purchases.

Nevertheless, there were wonderful things to buy in a city market—things that country dwellers seldom saw: pineapples from the West Indies, oranges and lemons from Sicily, tinned delicacies from France (prized above American ones until the late nineteenth century); and deep-sea fish caught just that morning and still giving an occasional flop to prove it.

One advantage of city living was that bakers would deliver fresh bread each morning before breakfast. Women heavily burdened with housekeeping cares found this a relief, for home bake-ovens were troublesome and hard to regulate. For years, commercial bakers prepared their dough by hand and baked it in egg-shaped ovens whose design had remained unchanged for countless centuries. The first attempts at mechanized bakeries were made in France in the 1840s, but the large, automated bread factory developed by degrees and was not perfected until less than fifty years ago.

The advent of the Industrial Age brought radical changes in everyday city eating habits. Colonial working people, self-employed or working within walking distance of their houses, had always eaten the main meal of the day at noon. But after heads of families began to work far from their homes, it eventually became customary to serve the main meal in the evening. Middle-class businessmen also began to follow this pattern, eating lunch near their offices and a hearty evening meal with their families.

In polite colonial society, the practice at dinnertime had been to place twelve or fifteen dishes on the table all at once. Each guest would help himself to the dish nearest him and serve others from it. Later, as more prosperous city folk visited Europe, the new French custom of table service became fashionable. This meant that all the dishes were carried around the table by servants and offered to each guest. There were many separate courses; eight or nine was not unusual.

Old-timers sniffed at this sort of thing. "Un-American," they said. But the new fashion persisted. And what was accepted in New York one year was likely to be adopted the next in Pittsburgh, Cleveland, and Chicago.

The neighborhood saloon — that home away from home for some. Few memories of 19th-century city life evoke deeper sighs of nostalgia. The swinging doors, the free lunches, have passed into folklore and history. A typical saloon had a dark, richly carved bar running lengthwise along one side. The floor was covered with sawdust to absorb any spills, and a slot machine was likely to be in one corner. The bartender could provide as many as 150 different kinds of drinks, but the beverages ordered most were beer, bourbon, or rye.

Cecils of Cold Meat

1 beaten egg
1 tablespoon milk
2 cups finely chopped
    cooked beef
2 tablespoons fine dry
    bread crumbs
1 tablespoon grated onion
½ teaspoon salt

¼ teaspoon ground nutmeg
⅛ teaspoon pepper
• • •
1 beaten egg
⅓ cup fine dry bread crumbs
    Cooking oil
    Béchamel Sauce

In saucepan combine 1 beaten egg and milk. Add cooked beef, 2 tablespoons crumbs, onion, salt, nutmeg, and pepper. Cook and stir over medium heat till heated through. Cool. Form into 1½-inch balls. Dip in 1 beaten egg; roll in ⅓ cup crumbs. In heavy skillet fry balls in ½ inch hot oil till golden. Serve with Béchamel Sauce. Makes 10.

Béchamel Sauce: In saucepan melt 1 tablespoon butter *or* margarine. Blend in 1 tablespoon all-purpose flour, ¼ teaspoon salt, and dash pepper. Add 1 cup milk all at once. Cook and stir till thickened and bubbly. Blend moderate amount hot sauce into 1 beaten egg yolk. Return to remaining hot sauce. Cook and stir 1 minute more.

According to Sarah Rorer, principal of the Philadelphia Cooking school this leftover meat dish was quite acceptable for breakfast. A menu for breakfast in 1885 might have included the following:

Menu

Fried Indian Mush   Maple Syrup
Cecils of Cold Meat
Saratoga Potatoes
Flannel Cakes
Cocoa
Fresh Fruit

Rice-Cornmeal Muffins

1 cup milk
1 tablespoon butter *or*
    margarine
½ cup yellow cornmeal
½ cup cooked rice
1 egg yolk

¾ cup all-purpose flour
2 tablespoons sugar
1 tablespoon baking powder
¼ teaspoon salt
1 stiffly beaten egg white

Heat milk and butter or margarine. Stir into cornmeal. Let stand 5 minutes. Stir in rice and egg yolk. Stir together flour, sugar, baking powder, and salt. Add cornmeal-rice mixture all at once to dry ingredients. Stir just till moistened. Fold in beaten egg white. Fill greased 2-inch muffin pan ⅔ full with batter. Bake at 400° for 20 to 25 minutes. Makes 8 muffins.

Poached Eggs with Spinach

*City living became more comfortable
and new businesses, including
restaurants, helped make it so. As
elegant restaurant dining
became fashionable, cooking at home
also became more sophisticated
and dishes such as* Poached Eggs
with Spinach *were not unusual.*

2 tablespoons finely
 chopped onion
¼ cup butter *or* margarine
3 tablespoons all-purpose
 flour
¼ teaspoon salt
⅛ teaspoon dry mustard
2¾ cups milk

1 cup shredded sharp
 American cheese
6 eggs
1 10-ounce package frozen
 chopped spinach
3 English muffins, split,
 toasted, and buttered

In large skillet cook onion in butter till tender, about 5 minutes. Blend in flour, salt, and dry mustard. Stir in milk; cook and stir till thick and bubbly. Add *half* the cheese; stir till cheese melts. Reduce heat; slip eggs, one at a time, into sauce. Simmer, covered, till eggs are set, 12 to 15 minutes. Meanwhile, cook frozen spinach according to package directions; drain well. Place hot cooked spinach atop English muffin halves; top with eggs and hot cheese sauce. Sprinkle with remaining cheese. Makes 6 servings.

Manhattan Clam Chowder

*"If the tomato doesn't poison you, it
will make you fall in love,"
said common-sensed people in colonial
times. They called it "love
apple." Spanish explorers knew
Indians ate tomatoes, but
for much of Europe and the New
World, until the early
1880s, it was merely an ornamental
plant. Once the tomato had
gained acceptance it quickly became
a favorite, especially,
as an ingredient in soups.*

2 dozen medium quahog clams
 or 2 7½-ounce cans
 minced clams *or* 1 pint
 shucked clams
3 slices bacon, finely
 diced
1 cup finely chopped celery
1 cup chopped onion
 • • •
1 16-ounce can tomatoes,
 cut up, undrained

3 cups water
2 cups diced potatoes
1 cup finely diced carrot
1½ teaspoons salt
¼ teaspoon dried thyme,
 crushed
Dash pepper
2 tablespoons all-purpose
 flour
2 tablespoons cold water

For clams in shell, place in large kettle; add 1 cup water. Cover and bring to boiling. Reduce heat; steam just till shells open, 5 to 10 minutes. Remove clams from shells. Dice clams. Strain liquid; reserve ½ cup. (*Or,* drain minced or shucked clams; reserve ½ cup liquid. Cut up large clams.) Partially cook bacon. Add celery and onion; cook till tender. Add clam liquid, tomatoes, 3 cups water, potatoes, carrot, salt, thyme, and pepper. Cover; simmer 35 minutes. Blend 2 tablespoons cold water into flour. Stir into chowder; cook and stir till boiling. Add clams; heat through. Serves 6 to 8.

Savory Tomato Soup

1 pound beef stew meat,
 cut in 1-inch cubes
1 small beef soup bone
2 tablespoons shortening
1 28-ounce can tomatoes,
 cut up *or* 2½ pounds
 fresh tomatoes, peeled
 and cubed
1 cup chopped celery
1 cup sliced carrot
¼ cup snipped celery
 leaves
1 tablespoon salt

½ teaspoon dried marjoram,
 crushed
½ teaspoon dried basil,
 crushed
¼ teaspoon dried savory,
 crushed
¼ teaspoon dried thyme,
 crushed
⅛ teaspoon ground mace
1 small whole dried hot
 red pepper *or*
 ⅛ teaspoon bottled
 hot pepper sauce

In 4½-quart Dutch oven brown stew meat and soup bone in hot shortening. Stir in undrained tomatoes, celery, carrot, celery leaves, salt, marjoram, basil, savory, thyme, mace, red pepper, and 4 cups water. Cover; simmer 4 to 5 hours. Skim off fat. Remove bone. Makes 8 servings.

Mrs. Rorer's Cooking School Sauce

Cream together ½ cup sugar and ⅓ cup butter *or* margarine; beat in 2 egg yolks till light and fluffy. Blend in ⅓ cup boiling water, ⅓ cup dry white wine, and dash ground nutmeg. Transfer mixture to top of double boiler; place over boiling water. (Upper pan should not touch water.) Cook, stirring constantly, till slightly thickened, about 5 minutes. Serve warm or chilled over fresh fruit *or* well-drained juice-pack fruit. Makes 1½ cups sauce.

Ideally located where the Monongahela and Allegheny rivers unite to form the Ohio, Pittsburgh met all the qualifications for a successful inland port. Fresh produce from the local area as well as from distant fields made the Pittsburgh market of the 1870s a gourmet's delight.

Summer Fruit Platter

> 1 whole pineapple
> 2 apples, cored and cubed
> 2 pears, cored and cubed
> 2 cups fresh blueberries
>   *or* frozen blueberries,
>   thawed
> 2 oranges
> 2 bananas
> 12 pitted dried prunes,
>   cooked and drained
>   Fresh mint
>   Lime-Honey Dressing

Chill fruit. Halve pineapple lengthwise; remove hard core. Remove pineapple and cut into chunks. Reserve shells. Lightly toss pineapple, apples, pears, and blueberries together. Pile into the shells. Peel oranges and bananas; slice crosswise. Arrange on a tray with filled shells and prunes. Garnish with fresh mint. Serve with Lime-Honey Dressing. Makes 6 servings.

Lime-Honey Dressing: Mix ½ cup honey, ¼ cup lime juice, and dash salt.

"*Success in entertaining is accomplished by magnetism and tact. It is the ladder to social success. If successfully done, it naturally creates jealousy. The success of the dinner depends as much upon the company as the cook.*"[27] That is the advice of Ward McAllister, well-known member of New York's Four Hundred. The cook's importance for a successful dinner party is evident in this menu from his 1890 book, **Society As I Have Found It.**

Turtle Soup
Ham Mousse   Poached Salmon
Filet of Beef   Russian Salad
Crown Roast of Lamb
Asparagus with Hollandaise
Paté en Bellevue   Sorbet
Camembert Cheese with Crackers
Nesselrode Pudding   Demitasse

During the 1800s, the prevalence of men's clubs reached a peak. In Philadelphia, the Farmer's Club was established for country estate owners. Members delighted in elegant dining and the group became known for its spectacular dinners. When they were in season, strawberries were often part of the menu for these dinners.

Chicken Salad Sandwiches

2 cups finely chopped cooked chicken	1 teaspoon lemon juice
¾ cup mayonnaise	½ teaspoon salt
¼ cup chopped toasted almonds	Dash cayenne
	20 slices sandwich bread
	Snipped parsley

Mix chicken, mayonnaise, almonds, lemon juice, salt, and cayenne. Chill well. With serrated knife, trim crusts from bread (stack 3 slices for easier trimming). Flatten each slice with rolling pin; cut in half diagonally. Spread each bread triangle with about 2 teaspoons chicken mixture. Fold into cornucopias. Garnish openings with snipped parsley. Place on flat pan, seam side down; cover and chill till ready to serve. Makes 40 tea sandwiches.

Elegant Poached Salmon

1 4- to 5-pound fresh *or* frozen dressed salmon	1 bay leaf
6 cups water	1½ cups chicken broth
3 tablespoons vinegar	1 envelope unflavored gelatin
1 small onion, sliced	¼ cup lemon juice
1 small lemon, sliced	Sliced unpeeled cucumbers
⅓ cup sliced celery	Sliced radishes
⅓ cup sliced carrot	2 8-ounce packages cream cheese, softened
3 whole cloves	5 to 6 tablespoons milk
3 whole black peppercorns	

Thaw frozen salmon. In a fish poacher combine the water, vinegar, onion, sliced lemon, celery, carrots, cloves, peppercorns, bay leaf, and 1 teaspoon salt. Bring to boiling. Simmer, covered, 10 minutes. Add salmon. Simmer, covered, till thickest part of fish flakes easily when tested with a fork, 30 to 35 minutes. Remove from poacher. With sharp knife remove skin. Place on serving platter. Cover; chill.

In saucepan mix chicken broth and gelatin; dissolve over low heat. Stir in *half* the lemon juice. Chill till slightly thickened. Spoon small amount gelatin mixture over surface of cold salmon. Place cucumber and radish slices atop in overlapping rows. Spoon remaining gelatin over all; chill. Remove any gelatin from edges of platter. Mix cream cheese and remaining lemon juice; beat in *2 tablespoons* milk. Using *half* the cream cheese mixture and a pastry tube, pipe a border around fish. Thin remaining cream cheese with remaining milk. (Mixture stiffens when chilled.) Chill fish and cream cheese. Serve fish with thinned cream cheese mixture. Garnish platter as desired. Makes about 24 servings.

Strawberry Meringues Chantilly

Meringue Shells	2 tablespoons sifted powdered sugar
1 quart fresh strawberries	2 tablespoons brandy
1 cup whipping cream	

Prepare Meringue Shells. Set aside 8 whole berries. Hull and slice remaining berries; sweeten if desired. In chilled bowl combine cream, sugar, and brandy; whip till soft peaks form. Fill Meringue Shells with sliced berries. Top with whipped cream mixture. Garnish with whole berries. Serves 8.

Meringue Shells: Cover baking sheets with brown paper. Draw eight 3-inch diameter circles spaced 2 inches apart on paper. Have 3 egg whites at room temperature. Add 1 teaspoon vanilla, ½ teaspoon cream of tartar, ¼ teaspoon almond extract, and dash salt. Beat to soft peaks. Gradually add 1 cup granulated sugar, beating to very stiff peaks. Divide among the 8 circles, using about ⅓ cup for each. Using back of spoon shape into shells. Bake at 300° till light beige, 35 to 45 minutes. Cool. Peel off paper. (If not used immediately wrap in waxed paper; store in cool dry place.)

By the 1820s formal evening parties
were quite the thing, even
in frontier cities. The food was rich
and plentiful. The center
of attraction might be an exceedingly
sophisticated dish, perhaps
Filet of Beef à la Bearnaise. After
dinner, the entertainment
was provided by the young
ladies present who often sang or
played piano.

We call them brunches and think
them quite modern. But in
the late 1880s, they were called
company breakfasts, and
in the cities they were a stylish way
of entertaining in literary
and artistic circles. These brunches
comprised many courses
including several main dishes such
as Chicken Cutlets with
Mushroom Sauce.

San Francisco was growing; it was
no longer a rough frontier
town, and one of its citizens, Francois
Pioche decided the city's
cuisine should reflect its new elegance
and sophistication.
Accordingly, he sent for a number
of French chefs, who were
skilled in preparing everything
from delicate sauces to Choux or
Cream Puffs.

Filet of Beef à la Bearnaise

6 beef tenderloin steaks,
   cut ¾ inch thick
· · ·
3 tablespoons tarragon
   vinegar
1 teaspoon finely chopped
   shallots *or* green onion
   with tops

¼ teaspoon freshly ground
   black pepper
1 tablespoon cold water
4 egg yolks
½ cup butter, softened
¼ teaspoon dried tarragon,
   crushed

Place steaks on cold rack in broiler pan. Broil 3 inches from heat till desired doneness, turning once. (Allow 10 to 12 minutes for medium.) Season with salt and pepper. Meanwhile, in a saucepan mix tarragon vinegar, shallots or green onion, and pepper; simmer 2 minutes. Add water. Beat egg yolks in top of double boiler (not over boiling water). Slow add vinegar mixture. Stir in *a few tablespoons* butter; place over boiling water (upper pan should not touch water.) Keep adding butter and stirring till all the butter has been used and sauce is smooth and thick. Remove from heat. Salt to taste; stir in crushed tarragon. Serve sauce over steaks. Makes 6 servings.

Chicken Cutlets with Mushroom Sauce

4 large chicken breasts,
   skinned, boned, and
   halved lengthwise
¼ cup all-purpose flour
2 beaten eggs

2 tablespoons milk
1 cup fine dry bread crumbs
¼ cup cooking oil
   Mushroom Sauce

Pound halved chicken breasts to ½-inch thickness. Coat with flour. Dip in a mixture of eggs and milk. Coat with fine dry bread crumbs. Fry cutlets, four at a time, in hot oil till golden brown, about 5 minutes per side. Remove to warm platter; keep warm. Serve with Mushroom Sauce. Serves 8.

Mushroom Sauce: Cook ½ cup sliced fresh mushrooms and ¼ cup chopped onion in 2 tablespoons butter till tender. Stir in 1 tablespoon all-purpose flour. Add 1 cup milk, ½ teaspoon salt, and ¼ teaspoon pepper. Cook and stir till boiling. Stir in ½ cup dairy sour cream. Heat through; *do not boil.*

Cream Puffs

In saucepan melt ½ cup butter in 1 cup boiling water. Add 1 cup all-purpose flour and ¼ teaspoon salt; stir vigorously. Cook and stir till mixture forms a ball that doesn't separate. Cool slightly. Add 4 eggs, one at a time; beat after each till smooth. Drop by rounded tablespoonfuls onto greased baking sheet. Bake at 400° till golden brown and puffy, about 30 minutes. Remove from oven. Split; cool on rack. (For a crisp, hollow puff, remove excess center membrane before cooling.) Fill as desired. Makes 12.

Cranberry Sherbet

1 16-ounce package
   cranberries (4 cups)
2 cups sugar

1 teaspoon unflavored
   gelatin
2 cups ginger ale

In large saucepan combine cranberries and 2 cups water. Cook, uncovered, till skins pop. Press through a food mill or sieve. Combine sugar and gelatin; stir into cranberry mixture till sugar and gelatin dissolve. Cool. Stir in ginger ale. Pour into two 3-cup refrigerator trays; freeze till partially frozen. Break into chunks in chilled mixing bowl. Beat till smooth with electric mixer. Pour into cold refrigerator trays or paper cups. Freeze firm. Serve as a main dish accompaniment or as a dessert. Makes 5 cups.

Wild Duck in Wine

2 1½- to 2-pound ready-to-
    cook wild ducks,
    quartered
    • • •
2 tablespoons butter *or*
    margarine
2 tablespoons all-purpose
    flour
1 cup beef broth

½ cup sliced fresh
    mushrooms
¼ cup Burgundy
2 tablespoons chopped
    onion
1 bay leaf
½ teaspoon salt
    Dash pepper
    Snipped parsley

In a large saucepan simmer ducks in small amount of salted water 20 to 30 minutes; drain. In large skillet brown ducks in butter; transfer to a 12x7½x 2-inch baking dish. Blend flour into pan drippings. Stir in broth, mushrooms, Burgundy, onion, bay leaf, salt, and pepper. Cook and stir till thick and bubbly. Pour sauce over ducks. Cover; bake at 350° till tender, 1¼ to 1½ hours. Remove ducks to platter. Remove bay leaf; skim off fat. Drizzle sauce over ducks; sprinkle with parsley. Makes 4 servings.

The most unusual gentlemen's society in Maryland was the Tuesday Club of Annapolis. When members gathered for dinner each Tuesday, they were bound by the rule of the club that any "discussions that level at party matters of the administration of the government... or any matter disagreeable to this club shall be silenced by vociferous and roaring laughter." [28] *In addition to lively discussions, the members also enjoyed dinners specializing in recipes such as* Wild Duck in Wine.

Garden Vegetable Skillet

4 ears corn *or* 1 10-ounce
    package frozen whole
    kernel corn
2 tablespoons butter *or*
    margarine

1 pound zucchini, sliced
    (4½ cups)
½ cup chopped onion
⅓ cup chopped green pepper
½ teaspoon dried dillweed

For fresh corn, cut corn from cob; do not scrape cob. In skillet melt butter; stir in corn, zucchini, onion, green pepper, dillweed, and ¾ teaspoon salt. Cook, covered, till vegetables are tender, 12 to 15 minutes. Serves 6.

Hot Apple Toddy

4 cups apple juice
2 tablespoons packed
    brown sugar
12 whole cloves
3 inches stick cinnamon
⅛ teaspoon ground nutmeg

2 large apples, peeled,
    cored, and quartered
1 cup brandy
¾ cup dark rum
    Butter

In saucepan mix apple juice, sugar, and spices. Simmer, covered, 20 minutes. Add apples. Simmer, covered, till tender, 10 minutes more. Strain. Return liquid to saucepan; add liquors. Heat through. Place an apple quarter and a dot of butter in each mug. Pour in toddy. Makes 7 (6-ounce) servings.

The Ancient South River Club in Maryland was one of the first social clubs organized in America. Dinners always included Hot Apple Toddy *and, according to the 10th rule of the body, the steward was supposed to appear by one o'clock "...with two and a half gallons of spirit, with ingredients for toddy...and a sufficient dinner with clean pipes and tobacco."* [29]

Lamb with Caper Sauce

1 4- to 5-pound whole
    lamb leg
1 clove garlic, sliced
½ cup chopped onion
3 tablespoons all-purpose
    flour

¼ teaspoon salt
1 cup water
½ cup light cream
3 tablespoons capers,
    drained

Trim fat from lamb. Cut slits in side of leg; insert garlic slices. Place meat, fat side up, on rack in shallow roasting pan. Top with onion. Season with salt and pepper. Roast at 325° till meat thermometer registers 170° to 180°, about 3½ hours. Remove to platter. Pour ½ cup pan juices into saucepan; stir in flour and salt. Add water and cream; cook and stir till thick and bubbly. Stir in capers. Serve with lamb. Makes 10 to 12 servings.

Trading at the General Store

Many general stores advertised
their wares with
newspaper ads such as this one.

*"Cloths middling, coarse, and
superfine,
Figs, raisins, sugar candy,
Sago and rice, pepper, allspice,
Madeira, wine and brandy.*

*Good corduroy for men and boys,
Excellent Irish linen;
Jeans, and jeanets, and velverets,
And cloth of Joan's spinning.*

*Cloves, ginger, prunes, and
silver spoons,
Both wax and tallow candles;
Bottles and corks, and knives
and forks,
With horn and ivory handles.*

*Starch, mustard, snuff, all cheap
enough,
Gloves, ribbons, gauze, and laces,
Good castile soap, all kinds of
rope,
Bed cords, plough-lines, and
traces....*

*Neat coverlids for feather beds,
And clarified honey;
Good calicoes and cotton hose,
All cheap for ready money.*

*Sweet Muscadine and Fayal wine,
Venetian red and umber,
Brass curtain rings, and many
things
Too tedious here to number."*[30]

The general store emerged during the eighteenth century as a typically American institution to supply those essential or much wanted items that families could not produce at home. It carried salt, spices, sugar, molasses, raisins, dried beans, tea, salted meat and fish; also wine, coffee, and chocolate for those who could afford them. In addition, there was butter, eggs, vegetables, and fruit—the produce from the nearby countryside.

Man does not live by bread alone, so there was likely to be pots, pans, kettles, axes, shovels, shoes, saddles, and harnesses; and a drug section filled with patent medicines, epsom salts, paregoric, physics, and sedatives. The whiskey or rum (popular items), however, were usually kept out of sight. Another part of the store was the dry goods section which featured everything from bed ticking to superfine cassimeres.

And can you imagine a general store without some heating source around which the customers gathered to warm themselves? The earliest stores had fireplaces. Later these were replaced by Franklin heaters, tin-plate stoves, and finally, the pot-bellied stove.

In colonial times, the store's business was usually for credit or barter rather than for cash. A farm wife might bring eggs and trade them for dried blueberries, which one of her neighbors had bartered to the store-keeper for lye soap. The storekeeper, in turn, might have received the soap in trade from another housewife, in exchange for flour and molasses.

Of all the tradesmen in town, the millers were the most apt to go into storekeeping—because the village gristmill was in a central location, frequented by everyone. After the United States postal system was established, the small town post office was customarily housed in the general store. The storekeeper also acted as middleman between farmers and city wholesalers. In addition, since he was often one of the few within miles who could read and write, he acted as lawyer and magistrate.

As the frontier moved west, no new town was worthy of the name until it had a general store. Settlers who had any cash developed the habit of leaving it with the storekeeper for safekeeping and drawing against it in purchases. Thus the storekeeper also became a banker; and since he knew everybody for miles around, he was in a good position to run for public office. As he prospered, he often traveled to buy supplies. In the West, a once-a-year journey to New Orleans or back East was usual.

Most of the foodstuffs in a general store were displayed in bulk. There were pickle barrels, beer and whiskey barrels, molasses barrels, and the famous cracker barrels, which became symbolic of a place where friends gathered to talk politics, farming, and news. The word "cracker," like the general store itself, is American. Also called pilot biscuits, crackers were first made commercially at a bakery in Newburyport, Massachusetts, in 1794. Later, they became part of the standard army ration. The word "biscuit" comes from Latin, and means baked twice, as similar biscuits were in the days when Roman legions ate them.

Baker's chocolate was the first American packaged food to appear on the market in 1765. But, in general, the early Americans did not care for

packaged foods. They liked to see what they were getting — and often with good reason, since packaged green tea, from China, was likely to contain filings, gypsum, and Prussian blue (a poisonous coloring), while packaged ground coffee often included bits of bark, sawdust, and other items that were definitely not coffee.

Machinery for making candy was invented in the 1840s, and after that general stores sold gumdrops, lozenges, and jujube paste. The famous "penny candy" came much later in the century. Many older people today remember the agony of deciding how to spend that terribly important penny. Should it pay for licorice sticks, magenta or mauve jawbreakers, chocolate "babies," Necco wafers, saltwater taffy, or some other sticky treat? Some of those time-honored confections may still be had, although now a penny scarcely pays for a bite.

When small towns grew into cities, the general stores gradually disappeared and their place was taken by grocery stores, candy stores, dry goods stores, hardware stores, drugstores, chemists, post offices, social clubs — and, in modern times, by shopping centers. In an effort to re-create the spirit of the general store, the recipes in this section feature many of the foods our grandparents and great-grandparents bought there.

A trip to the general store was an exciting event for farm families. The children waited anxiously while the home products were traded for other necessities and purchases made. Would there be a penny left over for a special treat? There might be mail waiting and always there was news to exchange with the storekeeper and other shoppers.

In 1869 general store customers could purchase prepared horseradish. It was packed by Henry J. Heinz in glass bottles so customers could see that it had no turnip filler.

Horseradish Butter

Cream together ½ cup butter, softened; 2 teaspoons prepared horseradish; ½ teaspoon dry mustard; ½ teaspoon salt; and dash pepper. Top with snipped parsley. Serve with hot cooked corn on the cob. Makes ½ cup.

Apple Jelly

Wash 3 pounds tart apples; remove blossom ends and stems. Do not peel or core. Cut apples in small chunks. In 8- to 10-quart kettle or Dutch oven combine apples and enough water to cover (about 5 cups). Cover; bring to boiling over high heat. Reduce heat; simmer till apples are soft, 20 to 25 minutes. Strain apples and liquid through jelly bag; measure 4 cups juice. In kettle mix apple juice and 3 cups sugar till dissolved. Bring to full rolling boil. Boil hard, uncovered, till syrup sheets off metal spoon, 10 to 12 minutes. Remove from heat; quickly skim off foam. Ladle into hot sterilized jars to within ½ inch of top. Wipe rims. Seal with metal lids and screw bands. Invert jars; turn upright and cool. Makes 3 half-pints.

Today's fine white granulated sugar is a relatively new innovation. Sugar in colonial times was sold in cones and cut with a special tool. The sugar sold just after the Civil War was coarse, slightly brown, and so hard it had to be loosened with a particular kind of augur and ground in a sugar mill.

Rolled Sugar-Mace Cookies

1 cup sugar
½ cup butter, softened
1 egg
¼ cup milk
½ teaspoon vanilla
2¼ cups all-purpose flour
2 teaspoons baking powder
½ teaspoon ground mace

Cream sugar and butter. Add egg, milk, and vanilla; beat well. Stir together flour, baking powder, mace, and ½ teaspoon salt; blend into creamed mixture. Divide in half. Cover; chill 1 hour. On lightly floured surface, roll *each half* to ⅛-inch thickness. Cut with cookie cutters. Bake on ungreased cookie sheet at 375° for 7 to 8 minutes. Makes about 52.

After the Civil War fresh fruits were often shipped to general stores by the new transcontinental railroad—a frequently expensive mode of transportation. For instance, the shipping charges for one carload of grapes and three carloads of fresh pears that were transported from California to New York in ventilated cars in 1869 was $1,200.

Pear Cobbler

1 cup all-purpose flour
2 tablespoons granulated sugar
1½ teaspoons baking powder
5 tablespoons butter
1 beaten egg
¼ cup milk
½ cup packed brown sugar
4 teaspoons cornstarch
¼ teaspoon ground cinnamon
1 tablespoon lemon juice
4 cups sliced peeled pears

Stir together flour, granulated sugar, baking powder, and ¼ teaspoon salt. Cut in *4 tablespoons* butter till resembles coarse crumbs. Mix egg and milk; stir into flour mixture just till moistened. Set aside. In saucepan mix brown sugar, cornstarch, and cinnamon. Stir in lemon juice, remaining butter, and 1 cup water. Cook and stir till thickened. Add pears. Cook about 5 minutes. Pour into 8x1½-inch round baking dish. Immediately spoon on flour mixture in 6 mounds. Bake at 400° for 25 to 30 minutes. Serves 6.

Dried fruits were a luxury for most customers at the general store. One farmer in 1857 was paid $13.78 for 110½ pounds of dried peaches and $12.35 for 247 pounds of dried apples. Does this sound low? Most farmers earned only $200 in a whole year.

Poor Man's Fruitcake

1⅓ cups raisins
1 cup packed brown sugar
¼ cup lard
1½ cups all-purpose flour
½ teaspoon baking soda
½ teaspoon salt
½ teaspoon ground cinnamon
½ teaspoon ground cloves

Heat raisins, sugar, lard, and 1 cup water till sugar dissolves and lard melts. Cool. Stir together flour, soda, salt, and spices. Add to lard mixture; beat smooth. Pour into greased and floured 8½x4½x2½-inch loaf pan. Bake at 350° for 45 to 50 minutes. Cool in pan. Wrap; store overnight. Makes 1.

Chow Chow Pickles

1½ pounds 2-inch cucumbers,
  halved lengthwise
6 green peppers, cut in
  strips
4 cups green beans cut in
  ¾-inch pieces
1 small head cauliflower,
  broken into flowerets

2 cups small onions
4 cups water
1 cup pickling salt
4 cups packed brown sugar
3 cups vinegar
¼ cup dry mustard
2 teaspoons ground turmeric

In large kettle combine cucumbers, green peppers, green beans, cauliflowerets, and onions; stir in the 4 cups water and pickling salt. Let stand in cool place for 2 to 3 hours. Drain; cover with boiling water. Let stand 10 minutes; drain. Combine brown sugar, vinegar, dry mustard, and turmeric; cook and stir till sugar is dissolved.

Add to vegetables; heat to boiling. Pack hot vegetables into hot pint jars, leaving ¾-inch headspace. Fill with vinegar mixture, leaving ½-inch headspace. Carefully wipe jar rims; adjust lids. Process in boiling water-bath canner for 5 minutes (start timing when water covering jars returns to boiling). Makes 5 pints.

Vinegar for making pickles was a staple in most early American homes and, of course the local general store was sure to carry it. It came to the store in huge barrels often weighing 200 pounds or more. The grocer set a vinegar barrel in a low cradle and inserted a spigot at one end. In the bunghole at the top of the barrel he would insert a burlap-wrapped bung. To draw vinegar for a customer the storekeeper used a tool called a bung starter to remove the bung from the hole and to let in enough air to allow the liquid to flow through the spigot.

Maple Brownies

2 eggs
¾ cup granulated sugar
1 teaspoon vanilla
½ cup maple-flavored syrup
6 tablespoons butter *or*
  margarine

2 1-ounce squares
  unsweetened chocolate
¾ cup all-purpose flour
½ teaspoon baking powder
½ cup chopped walnuts
  Sifted powdered sugar

Beat together eggs, granulated sugar, and vanilla. Add syrup; mix well. Melt butter and chocolate over low heat; remove from heat. Blend in egg mixture. Stir together flour, baking

powder, and ¼ teaspoon salt; stir into chocolate mixture. Stir in nuts. Spread in greased 9x9x2-inch baking pan. Bake at 350° for 25 to 30 minutes. Cool; dust with powdered sugar. Makes 24.

As each was perfected, chocolate products were eagerly sought at the general store. In 1765 a man named James Baker, in partnership with John Hannon, opened the first chocolate mill in America and produced fine chocolate throughout the Revolutionary War. Later, Baker's grandson Walter collaborated with a man named German to create a sweet baking chocolate that is sometimes known as German sweet chocolate. In 1828 Conrad Van Houten in Holland discovered a way to remove cocoa butter from cocoa beans, thus helping to create cocoa powder. It wasn't until 1876, however, that Daniel Peters in Switzerland invented milk chocolate for candy bars.

Chocolate Waffle Drops

1 cup granulated sugar
½ cup butter *or* margarine,
  softened
2 eggs
1 teaspoon vanilla
1¼ cups all-purpose flour

¼ cup unsweetened cocoa
  powder
1 teaspoon baking powder
½ teaspoon ground cinnamon
½ cup chopped nuts
  Powdered sugar

Cream granulated sugar and butter till fluffy. Add eggs and vanilla; beat well. Stir together flour, cocoa, baking powder, cinnamon, and ½ teaspoon salt; stir into creamed mixture. Stir in nuts.

(Mixture will be stiff.) Drop by teaspoonfuls 2 inches apart on preheated waffle baker; bake about 1½ minutes. Cool on rack. Sift powdered sugar over. Makes about 48.

Honeyed Chocolate

1 4-ounce package sweet
  cooking chocolate
¼ cup honey

½ teaspoon salt
7 cups milk
1 teaspoon vanilla

Chop chocolate. In a 3-quart saucepan combine chocolate, honey, salt, and 1 cup water. Cook and stir chocolate mixture over low heat till smooth.

Gradually stir in milk. Cook and stir till mixture is heated through. Stir in vanilla. Serve hot in small mugs. Makes 16 (4-ounce) servings.

Spicy Meat Loaf

2 beaten eggs
½ cup milk
2 cups soft bread crumbs
    (about 2½ slices)
½ cup chopped onion

½ teaspoon ground nutmeg
½ teaspoon ground allspice
⅛ teaspoon ground ginger
1½ pounds ground beef
½ pound ground pork

Combine eggs, milk, bread crumbs, onion, spices, 1 teaspoon salt, and ¼ teaspoon pepper. Add beef and pork; mix well. Shape into an 8x4-inch loaf. Place in a shallow baking pan. Bake at 350° for 1½ hours. Makes 8 servings.

Pictured opposite: The Asa Knight Store in Old Sturbridge Village re-creates the shopper's world of yesterday when sugar was sold in cones wrapped in blue paper. The paper was later soaked in water so that the indigo dye could be retrieved. Purchased or homemade, *White Sugar Gingerbread* was a special treat.

Savory Rabbit-Chicken Pie

1 1½- to 2-pound ready-to-
    cook rabbit
½ cup finely chopped celery
¼ cup finely chopped onion
¼ cup snipped parsley
3 tablespoons butter
3 tablespoons all-purpose
    flour
½ teaspoon ground savory
¼ teaspoon ground nutmeg

¼ teaspoon pepper
¼ teaspoon ground thyme
⅛ teaspoon ground cloves
1½ cups chicken *or* turkey
    broth
2 cups diced cooked chicken
    or turkey
Pastry for 2-crust 9-inch
    pie (see recipe,
    page 351)

Simmer rabbit in large amount boiling salted water till tender, about 1 hour. Set aside to cool. Remove meat from bones; dice. Cook celery, onion, and parsley in butter till tender. Stir together flour, savory, nutmeg, pepper, thyme, cloves, and 1 teaspoon salt. Stir into celery mixture; stir in broth. Cook and stir till thickened and bubbly. Add rabbit and chicken or turkey. Line 9-inch pie plate with pastry; spoon in meat mixture. Adjust top crust; seal. Cut slits for escape of steam. Bake at 375° till done, about 40 minutes. Cover edges with foil if needed to prevent overbrowning.

Many early American recipes made generous use of spices. But most often they were used to cover up off-flavors in meat — no refrigeration, you know. So, spices were always in demand and were a profitable item in the general stores. One of the most lucrative of colonial spices was black pepper. Yankee ship owners often made as much as 700% profit on shiploads of pepper. Elihu Yale, for one, made his fortune by selling spices, especially pepper. Later, this wealth was used to start Yale University.

White Sugar Gingerbread

1½ cups sugar
¾ cup butter *or* margarine
3 eggs
3 cups all-purpose flour
1½ teaspoons baking powder

1 teaspoon salt
1 teaspoon ground ginger
½ teaspoon baking soda
⅛ teaspoon ground nutmeg
1½ cups buttermilk

Cream sugar and butter till light, 5 to 7 minutes. Add eggs, one at a time, beating well after each. Stir together flour, baking powder, salt, ginger, soda, and nutmeg. Add to creamed mixture alternately with buttermilk; beat after each addition. Pour into greased and floured 13x9x2-inch baking pan. Bake at 350° for 40 to 45 minutes. Cool. Cut in squares. Serves 18.

A well-stocked general store sometimes carried baked goods. At least one store we know featured two kinds of gingerbread. Upper-shelf gingerbread, kept on a top shelf (out of reach?), was more expensive because it was made with white sugar. Lower-shelf gingerbread, on the other hand, was your everyday, molasses gingerbread.

Sorghum Drop Cookies

¼ cup packed brown sugar
¼ cup butter *or* margarine
½ cup sorghum
1 egg
1¼ cups all-purpose flour
½ teaspoon baking soda

½ teaspoon ground cinnamon
½ teaspoon ground ginger
⅛ teaspoon ground cloves
⅛ teaspoon salt
⅓ cup buttermilk
¼ cup raisins

Cream sugar and butter; beat in sorghum and egg. Stir together flour, soda, spices, and salt. Add to creamed mixture alternately with buttermilk; beat after each addition. Drop by tablespoonfuls onto greased cookie sheets. Top each with one or two raisins. Bake at 350° for 7 to 10 minutes. Makes 36.

Sorghum was an especially important staple in Southern general stores. During and after the Civil War, sorghum syrup and sorghum sugar were widely used as a substitute for cane sugar in everything from baked goods such as Sorghum Drop Cookies to alcoholic beverages.

Lamb Shanks and Bean Stew

Dried legumes were a valuable commodity. One general store kept them in paper-lined bushel baskets on the floor. The customers were free to choose from a selection that included navy beans, kidney beans, lima beans, split peas, dried peas, and marrowfat beans. Most likely the homemakers of the day used them in recipes such as Lamb Shanks and Bean Stew.

1½ cups dry navy beans
6 lamb shank crosscuts
2 tablespoons cooking oil
½ cup chopped onion
2 cups sliced carrot
1 13¾-ounce can chicken
  broth
1 teaspoon salt

1 bay leaf
¼ teaspoon dried thyme,
  crushed
¼ teaspoon dried rosemary,
  crushed
Dash pepper
2 tablespoons all-purpose
  flour

Rinse beans; in large kettle combine beans and 3½ cups water. Bring to boiling; simmer 2 minutes. Remove from heat; let stand 1 hour. (Or, add beans to water and soak overnight.) Drain. Brown shanks in hot cooking oil for 25 to 30 minutes; remove from pan. Drain off fat, reserving 2 tablespoons in skillet. Cook onion in drippings till tender. Stir in beans, carrot, broth, salt, bay leaf, thyme, rosemary, and pepper. Place shanks on top. Bring to boiling. Cover; simmer till shanks and beans are tender, about 1½ hours. Remove shanks to platter. Remove bay leaf. Skim off fat. Blend ¼ cup cold water into flour. Stir into vegetables; bring to boiling. Serves 6.

Vanilla Cream Pie

In the mid 1800s, one of the newer products was vanilla extract. Joseph Burnett (a specialist in household remedies) created it in 1847 in response to a lady's request for a simplified method of flavoring with vanilla. She loved the flavor, she said, but not the involved process of cutting up whole vanilla beans, putting the pieces in a sack, and immersing the sack in the food.

¾ cup sugar
⅓ cup all-purpose flour *or*
  3 tablespoons
  cornstarch
2 cups milk
3 beaten egg yolks

2 tablespoons butter
1 teaspoon vanilla
1 *baked* 9-inch shell,
  cooled (see recipe,
  page 351)
Whipped cream

Mix sugar, flour or cornstarch, and ¼ teaspoon salt; stir in milk. Cook and stir till thickened and bubbly. Cook and stir 2 minutes more. Remove from heat. Stir moderate amount of hot mixture into yolks; immediately return to hot mixture. Cook and stir 2 minutes. Stir in butter and vanilla. Pour into pastry shell. (To prevent skin from forming on filling surface, put waxed paper directly atop hot filling.) Chill. Serve with whipped cream.

Molded Butterscotch Pudding

Cornstarch was often used in such desserts as Molded Butterscotch Pudding *since the fancy molds needed to make these desserts were given away by cornstarch manufacturers.*

1 cup packed dark brown
  sugar
½ cup cornstarch

4 cups milk
2 tablespoons butter
1 teaspoon vanilla

In saucepan mix brown sugar and cornstarch. Stir in milk. Cook and stir till mixture thickens and bubbles. Cook 2 minutes longer. Stir in butter and vanilla. Pour into 5-cup mold. Chill till firm. Unmold. Makes 8 servings.

Cheese Loaves

Cheese was one of the first products to be sold at the general store. By the 1800s farmers' wives were making cheese to trade in exchange for other goods. Later, cooks used the cheese in recipes such as Cheese Loaves.

In mixing bowl mix 2 cups all-purpose flour and 2 packages active dry yeast. In saucepan heat and stir 2 cups shredded sharp Cheddar cheese, 2 cups milk, 2 tablespoons sugar, 2 tablespoons lard, and 2 teaspoons salt just till warm (115-120°). Add to dry mixture. Beat at low speed of electric mixer for ½ minute, scraping bowl. Beat 3 minutes at high speed. By hand stir in enough of 3½ to 4 cups all-purpose flour to make a soft dough. Turn onto floured surface; knead till smooth and elastic (5 to 8 minutes). Place in greased bowl; turn once. Cover; let rise in warm place till double (45 to 60 minutes). Punch down; turn out on floured surface. Divide in half. Cover; let rest 10 minutes. Shape into 2 loaves; place in two greased 8½x4½x2½-inch loaf pans. Cover; let rise till nearly double (30 to 45 minutes). Bake at 375° for 30 to 35 minutes. Remove from pans; cool on rack. Makes 2.

Baking Powder Biscuits

2 cups all-purpose flour
1 tablespoon baking powder
½ teaspoon salt

⅓ cup shortening
¾ cup milk

Stir together flour, baking powder, and salt. Cut in shortening till resembles coarse crumbs. Make a well; add milk. Stir quickly with fork just till dough follows fork around bowl. Turn onto lightly floured surface. (Dough will be soft.) Knead gently 10 to 12 strokes. Roll or pat dough ½ inch thick. Dip 2½-inch biscuit cutter in flour; cut dough straight down. Bake on ungreased baking sheet at 450° for 12 to 15 minutes. Makes 10.

Spicy Cake Doughnuts

3¼ cups all-purpose flour
2 teaspoons baking powder
½ teaspoon ground cinnamon
¼ teaspoon ground nutmeg
Dash salt
2 eggs
⅔ cup sugar

1 teaspoon vanilla
⅔ cup light cream
¼ cup butter *or* margarine, melted
½ cup sugar
½ teaspoon ground cinnamon
Fat for frying

Stir together thoroughly the all-purpose flour, baking powder, ½ teaspoon ground cinnamon, ground nutmeg, and salt. Beat together eggs, ⅔ cup sugar, and vanilla till thick and lemon-colored. Combine light cream and melted butter or margarine; add to egg mixture alternately with dry ingredients, beating just till blended after each addition. Chill dough 2 hours. Roll dough ⅜ inch thick on floured surface; cut with floured doughnut cutter. Fry in deep hot fat (375°) till golden, turning once. (Allow about 1 minute per side.) Drain on paper toweling. Shake warm doughnuts in a mixture of the ½ cup sugar and ½ teaspoon cinnamon. Makes about 20 doughnuts.

Corn-Potato Chowder

2 medium potatoes, peeled and diced
1 medium onion, thinly sliced and separated into rings
½ cup chopped celery
½ cup water
1 teaspoon salt

1 17-ounce can whole kernel corn
1½ cups milk
¼ teaspoon dried marjoram, crushed
5 slices bacon, crisp-cooked and crumbled
Butter *or* margarine

In saucepan combine potatoes, onion, celery, water, and salt. Cover; cook till vegetables are tender, 15 to 20 minutes. Stir in undrained corn, milk, marjoram, and dash pepper. Heat through. Serve in warmed soup bowls; top with crumbled bacon and a pat of butter or margarine. Makes 6 servings.

Ham-Bean Bake

2 cups cubed fully cooked ham
2 16-ounce cans pork and beans in tomato sauce
2 tablespoons molasses
2 tablespoons catsup

2 teaspoons instant minced onion
2 teaspoons Worcestershire sauce
1 teaspoon prepared mustard

In mixing bowl combine ham, pork and beans, molasses, catsup, instant minced onion, Worcestershire, and mustard. Spoon into 6 individual casseroles. Bake, uncovered, at 375° till heated, 25 to 30 minutes. Serves 6.

Some old ways die hard. Women were accustomed to leavening their cakes and biscuits by using sour milk and molasses, or pearl ash, or saleratus (a commercial preparation of potassium bicarbonate). When the wrong amount of the latter was used, the finished cake or biscuit was streaked yellowish green and had an alkaline taste. Nevertheless, it took a couple of decades for housewives to see the value of baking powder, first available commercially in the late 1860s. Baking powder (Royal is the longest selling brand) was made of cream of tartar and soda in a carefully measured ratio. Cooks finally realized that their baked goods were much more successful with baking powder. Probably because of it, the 1880s witnessed a flood of new recipes for light, wonderful baked goods.

The canning industry developed with the growth of the general store. Or was it the other way around? Before the Civil War less than 5 million cans of food were produced annually, but by 1870 the figure had skyrocketed to 30 million. Canned corn, one of the earliest successful products, dropped from 27¢ for a two-pound can in 1869 to 18¢ in 1873 because of improvements in canning technology.

The first successful canned convenience product was baked beans in tomato sauce. The credit belongs to Gilbert and Frank Van Camp, who, in 1861 began processing the popular vegetable combination.

Chapter 5

Preserving Food at Home

Feast or famine—such were the choices in the earliest days of mankind. When there was fresh food, people gorged themselves; when there was none, they stoically went hungry. Then, slowly, by trial and sometimes fatal error, various ways of preserving food became standard practice. These were drying, salting, pickling, smoking, preserving with sugar or spices, storing in root cellars, and cooling or freezing with cold water or ice. Cheese preserved milk and cider preserved apples.

All these methods begun by ancient civilizations were still being used in 1800. The only recent discovery was that meat would keep for a short time if protected by layers of fat.

People living where winters were cold knew that food froze when stored in unheated places between November and April. But storage chests (freezers) that maintain 0° were still a century away. After World War I technology and refrigeration equipment caught up with Clarence Birdseye and the development of the frozen food industry. (See Chapter 10.)

Thus, in the 1800s, until canning was invented, every cook had to master the techniques of drying, pickling, and preserving food. The alternative was to see her family suffer either from hunger or from food poisoning. Even so, digestive illnesses were common. Often, the question was not whether the food was tainted, but whether it was so far gone it would poison the diners. Every housewife had a private store of tricks for disguising the taste and smell of dubious pieces of fish or for curing musty corn.

Today, home food preservation is more the exception than the rule. Technology has both eased the work and has increased the safety of the food supply. It also fosters respect for the resourcefulness of the women who coped before refrigerators, pressure canners, and supermarkets.

DRYING FOOD FOR THE DAYS AHEAD

In the dim, dark past, people had learned that many foods would keep almost indefinitely if they were exposed to warm sunshine until the moisture was drawn out. The arid climates of the American Southwest were well suited for drying foods outdoors. Along the humid eastern shores of the country, however, the heat of hearth or oven was needed to help the drying process along.

Drying was particularly useful for fruits and vegetables. Apples, pumpkins, and other garden products were sliced, strung on a thread, dried, and hung in a cool place. When the cook wanted to use them she cooked the pieces with liquid until they were the right consistency. Small fruits and berries were often dried without sugar. White sugar was either too expensive or nonexistent. Brown sugar, molasses, or maple sugar were used sparingly because they changed the color or flavor of the food.

Hunters, travelers, and other people on the move knew well the practicality of carrying lightweight foods of concentrated strength. Both jerky —strips of dried meat (see recipe, page 197) and Indian pemmican met that test. The latter was usually made from dried buffalo meat pounded or mashed with meat fat and flavored with wild berries.

Soup-in-his-pocket

One clever colonial use of drying or dehydration was a portable soup—the equivalent of our modern bouillon cubes. Veal bones were boiled to a glue-like jelly, then put into small molds (teacups would do) and dried in the sun or squeezed in a flannel cloth until all the moisture was gone. Thus dried, it would keep until reconstituted in boiling water. One of Virginia's leading planters, William Byrd, took some with him on a journey in the wilderness and afterward wrote, "If you should faint with fasting or fatigue, let a small piece of this glue melt in your mouth and you will find yourself surprisingly refreshed."[1]

cutaway view

TO DRY CHERRIES WITHOUT SUGAR

"Stone and set them over the fire in the preserving pan: let them simmer in their own liquor; and shake them in the pan. Put them by in China common dishes. Next day give them another scald, and put them, when cold, on sieves to dry, in an oven of a tempered heat.* Twice heating, an hour each time will do them. Put them in a box, with a paper between each layer.
*Lay them on a hot hearth, or in an oven, when either are cool enough to dry without baking them."

Rundell, *A New System of Domestic Cookery*, 1807

The smokehouse fire of corncobs or hardwood was built on the dirt floor. Smoke swirled around hams suspended from beams and then went out a vent.

Putting down meat

Salting, pickling, and corning are really variations of the same process. All use great quantities of salt and "put the meat down" in a barrel or down in the cellar or both. The differences are a matter of how much salt, for how long, and what else is mixed with the salt. Many early cook book writers use the terms interchangeably. In general, however, beef, pork, and legs of lamb were salted. Pork was pickled and beef was corned.

Don't let the word "pickle" (which today usually means cucumbers pickled in vinegar) throw you. Few families pickle meat at home any more and so are unfamiliar with a sweet pickling mixture of salt with molasses or brown sugar.

Salting and pickling were methods of keeping meat a long time. (The word "curing" was sometimes used to describe the processing of meat, usually hams, destined for the smokehouse.) Individual pieces of meat were either packed in layers of salt or submerged in a brine solution. The rule of thumb for the brine was that it must be strong enough to float an egg. Either way saltpeter was usually added with the salt.

At this point the cook's ingenuity took over and recipes changed to suit family preferences and what was available. Some added only 'molasses. Others added only brown sugar. The pickling solution might be flavored with beer or ale. The filled barrels were stored in a cool place, and

Harvesting ice in New England for summer use at home or to ship abroad.

checked often for spoilage and to be sure the contents stayed under the brine. Any scum that rose was skimmed off and more "pickle" added. Then, oh, the scrubbing and soaking necessary to wash out the salt before the meat was cooked.

Corning was the shortest method and was used primarily for beef. Mrs. Child in the *American Frugal House-wife,* dated 1832, observes, "When you merely want to corn meat you have nothing to do but rub in salt plentifully, and let it set in the cellar a day or two. If you have provided more meat than you can use while it is good, it is well to corn it in season and save it. In summer, it will not keep well more than a day and a half; if you are compelled to keep it longer, be sure and rub in more salt, and keep it carefully covered from cellar flies."[2]

Ice Before Iceboxes

Where the winter climate was very cold, icehouses were located near rivers and ponds. But elsewhere ice was not available until after 1831 when Bostonian Frederic Tudor succeeded in shipping ice from New England to Martinique by packing the blocks in sawdust.

But Tudor then faced the problem of hacking huge quantities of ice from the pond to meet the growing demand. A fellow New Englander, Nathaniel Wyeth, invented an ice cutter with parallel saw-toothed runners like those on a sleigh. Pulled by horses over a frozen pond, this contrivance incised the ice into squares, which workmen cut and floated into water and into Tudor's icehouses. Plentiful supplies of cheap ice eventually made home iceboxes practical for most families.

SMOKING MEAT IN THE SMOKEHOUSE

Though used only seasonally, the smokehouse was a necessity in rural America right into the twentieth century. Fall with its cool days and prospects for colder weather ahead was an ideal time for hog-butchering. After butchering, the fresh hams, the picnic shoulders, and the bellies for bacon were cured. That is, they were rubbed with salt or put in a brine for several weeks before smoking.

In the smokehouse, local hardwoods such as hickory or maple provided the smoke. They are the aromatic woods nostalgically associated with old-fashioned hams and bacon. But corncobs also gave the desired slow smoking. Since corncobs were plentiful, what better way to use them up? The freshly cured hams and bacon hung in the smokehouse at least a week. Some country-style hams, especially those from Virginia, Maryland, and Tennessee, received an extra long smoking. Smithfield hams still do today.

Once out of the smokehouse, the hams were rubbed with pepper, wrapped or sewn in muslin, and allowed to hang in a barn or storeroom till needed. Where butchering was a once-a-year project, some hams would hang and age the full year before being cooked.

Cold storage

For winter there was the *root cellar* located under the house or dug out of a hill not far from the kitchen door. Here apples, carrots, onions, potatoes, and other garden bounty stayed dry and firm for months. (In areas where tornadoes occurred, the root cellar doubled as a storm cellar.)

In warm weather perishables went to the *springhouse* if the farm was lucky enough to have one. It was so named because a spring flowed over the stone floor. Crocks of milk and butter set in the water escaped the midday heat.

Cheesemaking at home

Cattle were work animals rather than dairy breeds and it might take several milkings to collect enough milk to make cheese. One reason cheese flavor varied so much from batch to batch was the milk often soured before the cheese could be made.

The cheesemaker heated the milk over a low fire or by adding a small amount of hot water. Lacking today's thermometer, how did the cook test the milk for that all important temperature? Why, with her elbow or wrist, of course.

The rennet necessary to curdle the milk came from the lining of a calf's stomach. (Obtaining rennet was another food preservation job for the farm wife.) Whenever a calf was butchered, she cut the calf's stomach lining that contained the rennet into thin strips to dry till needed. At cheesemaking time, she selected one that was neither moldy nor spoiled.

How long the strip of rennet stayed in the milk depended on the eye and judgment of the cheesemaker. As the curd formed, it sank to the bottom. The whey at the top was poured off.

The next step was transferring the curd to a cheesecloth-lined press, usually a round and fairly simple device. Holes in the bottom let out the whey and a plunger pressed down on the curd. The cheese stayed in the press up to a week, then was greased with lard or butter and left to cure in a cool, dry place. Good cheese would keep up to a year.

HOW APPLE CIDER WAS MADE

Apples were cored and crushed into a coarse applesauce called pomace. (In the early days not everyone bothered to remove cores and seeds.) This pomace was transferred to a press and the juice extracted. Both the crushing and the pressing took considerable physical strength. On the farm it might be done manually, but it was not uncommon to hitch up a horse or even a waterwheel to the press.

The pressed juice was strained into barrels and allowed to ferment, relying on the action of the natural sugar in the apples and the yeasts in the air. The rate of fermentation was regulated by a bunghole at the top of the barrel. Processing was slowed down as much as possible to improve the flavor of the cider. Besides, if fermentation was too fast, the barrel might burst. As the process continued, cider was periodically drawn off through the bunghole into new casks until fermentation stopped. The casks were finally sealed and allowed to stand to mellow the cider.

Preserving apples

Whole fruit would keep several months in a cool, dry place, while sliced apples could be strung and dried. But most of the crop went into cider. In the early days of this country cider meant hard cider and every member of the family drank it.

Boiled Cider: In rural New England, especially Vermont, sweet cider was boiled down into a syrup of many cooking uses, the most notable being *Cider Pie*, (See recipe, page 195.) Sometimes brown or maple sugar might be added during boiling. The resulting syrup was bottled and stored.

Vinegar: Nature's action could turn sweet cider to vinegar just as easily as to hard cider. Homemade vinegar was important for cooking and preserving food. The process could be speeded up by adding "mother of vinegar"—the brown mat of bacteria in old vinegar. It was removed when the vinegar was the right strength.

To Prepare Vinegar for Green or Yellow Pickle

"One pound of ginger sliced and dried, one of horseradish scraped and dried, one of mustard seed washed and dried, one ounce long pepper, an ounce of mace and one of nutmegs finely pounded; put all these ingredients in a pot, pour two gallons of strong vinegar on, and let it stand twelve months, stirring it very frequently. When this vinegar is used for pickles, put two gallons more vinegar with some mace and nutmegs and keep another year. When the prepared vinegar is poured from the ingredients, do it very carefully, that it may be quite clear. Pickles keep much better when the vinegar is not boiled. Should the green pickles at any time lose their colour, it may be restored by adding a little more turmeric. All pickles are best, when one or two years old."

Randolph, *The Virginia Housewife,* 1860

A fruit-packing bee in the orchard—the processing was done back home.

Putting up fruits and vegetables

Today this means jams, jellies, pickles, and home-canned or frozen produce. It was not always so. Before scientists knew that pectin in apples made sweetened fruit syrup set up or gel, or that heat processing would save food in a can, putting up was limited to making jams, preserves, and pickles.

The chief distinction between jams and preserves is that the latter are made with whole fruit, while jams use crushed. Both rely on quantities of sugar as a preservative.

Jams and preserves were stored in clean (not sterilized) glasses or pots and sealed by fitting a piece of brandy-soaked paper on the surface of the fruit. (Paraffin came later as a by-product of kerosine.) Some preserves did spoil—but, some fortunately, did not.

PRESERVES

"A pound of sugar to a pound of fruit is the rule for all preserves. The sugar should be melted over a fire moderate enough not to scorch it. When melted, it should be skimmed clean, and the fruit dropped in to simmer till it is soft. Plums, and things of which the skin is liable to be broken, do better to be put in little jars, with their weight of sugar, and the jars set in a kettle of boiling water, till the fruit is done."

Child, *American Frugal Housewife,* 1832.

Many small, young vegetables were pickled. Nuts of all kinds also went into a spicy brine, as did nasturtium seeds, a colonial substitute for capers. Another favorite was "American citron," better known as pickled watermelon rind.

For all the potent vinegar described on the previous page, pickled food frequently spoiled. For protection, jars or crocks were covered closely with a cork or pig's bladder. Since "closely" was not "hermetically sealed," the upper third was apt to spoil.

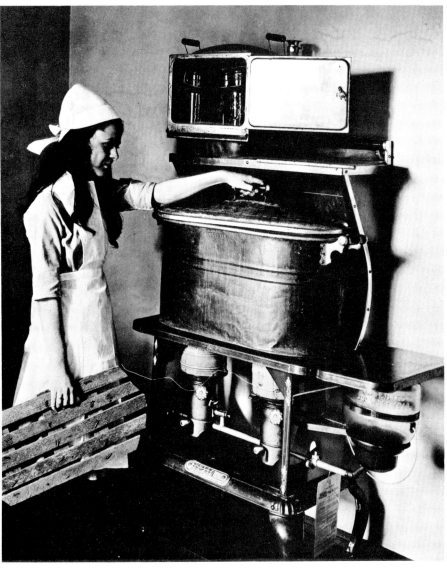

A new use for the family wash boiler—turn it into a water-bath canner.

Home canning

How to feed his army so vexed Napoleon that he offered a prize for a method of preserving food. Nicolas Appert, a Paris confectioner, won the award in 1810 by demonstrating that cooked food packed in glass bottles, heated, and sealed would keep for months—even years. Just why wasn't understood until Louis Pasteur's work more than a half century later.

Once the effect of heat on bacteria was understood, canning techniques improved. John Mason's jar in 1858 helped, too. A rubber gasket fitted the shoulder on his jar and a zinc lid screwed down tight. A later jar had a glass lid, rubber gasket, and a wire bale arrangement. Today's jars use a two-piece metal lid. The flat center portion seals against the glass and a removable screw band holds it.

Water-bath canning of fruits requires only a large, deep kettle with a rack and cover. Filled jars simmer covered with boiling water. Introduction of a kitchen-size pressure canner just before World War I made possible a safe method for canning low-acid vegetables and meats at home.

During two world wars canning was vital in preserving food from victory gardens. Centers were set up in schools and church basements. Some operated long after the emergency. By the 1950s, however, home freezers and a population shift to cities made canning a lost art for many people. Now, as home gardens sprout again, homemakers once again face the problems of preserving food at home.

The
Beckoning West

Chapter 6

The Beckoning West

Tales of the deeds of fur traders and buffalo hunters were celebrated in the folklore and legends of the West, but the economic function they served was a real one. In the 19th century beaver pelts and buffalo hides meant money. Beaver pelts, for example, were used for men's hats. First, the soft underfur from the skins was stripped by hand and then the fur was matted into felt using hot water. Finally the felt was shaped into a hat over a wooden mold. Hats such as these sold for as much as fifty dollars in both the eastern United States and Europe. Buffalo hides were used for lap robes in buggies and sleighs. Fashionable people in the East would not be caught traveling without one.

The history of our country from colonial times until the end of the nineteenth century is one of frontier succeeding frontier. Explorers were always first, then trappers and fur traders, then men who, for various reasons, were dissatisfied with their lot at home and were seeking a better life, either alone or with their families. Some hoped for wealth from minerals; some from commercial ventures; and others — the majority — hoped to obtain a good life from the wealth of the soil.

In the early 1800s, while this process was developing east of the Mississippi in what was then called the Northwest Frontier and the Southwest Frontier, the vast regions between the Mississippi and the Pacific were largely unexplored. After the Louisiana Purchase in 1803, President Jefferson sent an expedition, headed by Meriwether Lewis and George Clark, to report on the nature of the huge grab bag package we had bought. The party set out from St. Louis in May 1804 with the immediate objective of following the Missouri River to its headwaters. Their explorations were not over until September 1806, by which time they had been all the way to the Pacific and had explored large parts of the northern plains and Rockies.

During much of this time, they were able to use such basic provisions as flour, sugar, salt, and coffee; but as often as possible they caught game, especially bear, buffalo, and deer. Sometimes they ate well; other times they had to make do. On Christmas Day 1805, somewhere near the Columbia River, Clark recorded that "our Diner concisted of pore Elk, so much Spoiled that we eate it thro' mear necessity, Some Spoiled pounded fish, and a fiew roots."[1]

The trapper-traders followed the explorers. The "Mountain Men," of whom Kit Carson is perhaps the best known, were a tough breed of loners and adventurers who roamed the Rockies, usually trapping beaver and hoping to find mines, and living a rather planless life. Like nomadic Indians, they too, carried basic cooking supplies, but when these ran out and game was scarce, they knew how to survive on wild greens and berries, and if need be, on things that most men would shudder at: ants and crickets; the leather ties of moccasins, softened by boiling; reptiles, vultures, and worse. Like the Indians, they did not waste meat when they had it. Of the buffalo, they ate not only the choice meat including the hump and tongue, but the fresh blood, raw liver, and the thick layer of fat that lay just under the skin. "Trapper's butter" was marrow mixed to a spreadable consistency with boiling blood and water. A special treat, to which the French trappers gave the name *boudins* (sausages), were coils of roasted buffalo intestines.

Hard on the heels of the trapper-traders and explorers came the land speculators and the traders of miscellaneous goods. Among the latter, many were town-bred and some were recent immigrants, and they needed unusual courage to brave the hazards of the wilderness. Prospects of profits up to 2000 percent provided an irresistible incentive. From 1825 until the early 1840s, traders with their goods loaded on pack animals, traveled annually from St. Louis to a prearranged rendezvous point in the northern Rocky Mountains. There they met hundreds of Mountain Men from all over the West, whose mules were laden with beaver skins. Since beavers were seemingly in limitless abundance and their skins sold for three to six dollars each, the trappers did not balk when they were charged exorbitant prices:

two dollars a pound for sugar and coffee or five dollars for a pint of whiskey. At the end of the "Rocky Mountain Fair," as this assemblage was called, most of the trappers had gambled and drunk their profits and were ready for another year of hunting and trapping in the wild.

In the Southwest, Spain cast a suspicious eye on American traders and trappers. However, after the revolution of 1821, the new, independent Mexican government was glad to welcome traders. First to cash in on this welcome was a Missourian named William Becknell, the "father" of the Santa Fe trade. In 1822 he pioneered the Cimarron Cut-Off on the Santa Fe Trail. This route saved days of travel — that is, if one did not die of thirst in the Cimarron Desert, as Becknell's party very nearly did. Between that time and the completion of the last transcontinental section of railroad in the Southwest in 1880, thousands of merchants packed their cumbersome wagons with goods to please the Spanish taste and headed for Santa Fe. Many also went on for another six hundred miles or so, along the Camino Real, which led down the Rio Grande to El Paso and on to Chihuahua, Mexico.

Experience taught them to bring only the most basic food supplies. For the eight- or nine-week journey from Independence to Santa Fe, each man brought fifty pounds of flour, fifty pounds of bacon, ten of coffee, twenty of sugar, and some salt. Josiah Gregg, a trader who made more than forty trips to Santa Fe, wrote that prairie travel produced an insatiable appetite, buffalo being the favorite food. Each evening, "the fires had scarcely been kindled when the fumes of broiling meat pervaded the surrounding atmosphere; while all huddled about, anxiously watching their cookeries, and regaling their senses in anticipation upon the savory odors which issued from them."[2] A great quantity of coffee was consumed, but such items as tea, rice, and crackers were considered dispensable, for the traders wanted to use every possible inch of space in their wagons for merchantable goods rather than provisions for themselves.

"The Permanent Indian Frontier," so designated by Congress about 1825, was an imaginary line that meandered northward from Louisiana to Lake Superior, most of the line lying a few hundred miles west of the Mississippi. It was then generally believed that most of the land between that frontier line and the Rockies was unsuitable for settlement and therefore might "generously" be left to the Indians. Maps of the day labeled that region, or parts of it, "The Great American Desert." However, no sooner was the line established than pioneers began to disregard it. At first their destination was either the Northwest, via the Oregon Trail, or Stephen Fuller Austin's settlements in Texas. Then, in 1846, Brigham Young led his first band of Mormons across the prairie and plains to the Salt Lake Valley. Through hard work and brilliant organization they overcame the drawbacks of an arid, almost treeless country. They used mountain streams for irrigation. Unlike other frontier settlers, they established and strictly obeyed controls over the activities of every family: what they planted, how much wood they might cut, what they might do with their money, and so on. The thousands of California-bound travelers crossing their land during the Gold Rush gave a tremendous boost to Mormon economy, and during the 1850s a string of Mormon communities was founded from the Salt Lake Valley in Utah all the way to San Diego. This was known as the Mormon Corridor and it became known for its great agricultural prosperity.

The potential richness of the "desert" was now apparent and the idea of a Permanent Indian Frontier was forgotten by all but the betrayed, dispossessed Indian tribes whose homes were in that region.

The prairie was a lonely place and a visitor was a rare occurrence. Pioneers gladly opened their homes to the stranger and shared what they had as this description illustrates: "If a stranger calls to take supper ... the good woman of the house will make ready quickly three measures of fine meal, if necessary, and knead it, and make cakes upon the hearth, probably in a tin oven set down before the fire. She will then produce her clean white cloth and set out the table. One by one, around the sides of the tea table will come on the cups and saucers in company with as many plates as guests, each plate containing a piece of apple and a piece of custard pastry. In the midst, peering proudly over all, stands the tea-pot; and in its neighborhood, sugar and milk to season the tea, and the jug of hot water to dilute it .... Not far off .... May be seen dried beef cut up into slices, a dish of nut-cakes, sauces, etc."[3]

The great Mormon goal was to turn the vast expanse of the basin of the Great Salt Lake into home. They found a number of foods growing wild including grapes, cherries, persimmons, and all sorts of berries. But the Mormon dream was to provide for all their own needs, and this meant growing corn, wheat, potatoes, and other crops. In fact, the direction Brigham Young gave his followers was to "...prosecute the route as you have hitherto done until you arrive at some point in the Basin where you could hear the potatoes grow, if they had only happened to be there."[4] The Mormons did exactly that and in the process, built the Mormon Corridor.

In the eastern woodlands and on parts of the prairie, settlers had no trouble finding wood for fuel and for building cabins. Farther west, however, wood was scarce and they had to resort to dugouts and houses made of blocks of sod. Attempting to solve the ever-present fuel problem, Mennonite immigrants from Russia introduced hay-burning stoves, using hay twisted into logs—an inconvenient, quickly consumed, and hazardous fuel. Another make-do fuel was pressed cornhusks.

Frame houses were, of course, very preferable to sod ones. Because of the great westward expansion after the Civil War, the need for wood on the prairies and plains made lumbering an important enterprise in the forests of Michigan, Wisconsin, and Minnesota. These regions became known as the Lumberjack Frontier. As was the case back east in the woods of Maine and the Adirondacks, many of the lumberjacks were French Canadians. Cutting wood all day in the cold northern air made a man extremely hungry, and bosses soon learned the importance of a good camp cook. Besides plenty of roasted meat, lumberjacks liked salted or smoked cod, savory stews and chowders, split pea soup, pancakes, gingerbread, and bean-hole beans. For the latter dish, a sealed pot of beans, flavored with onion, pork, and molasses, was buried in a preheated hole in the ground beside the campfire. Another fire was kindled on top of it and kept going for twenty-four hours.

By 1850 the frontier had developed beyond Illinois into southern Michigan and Wisconsin and southeastern Iowa. The western parts of Missouri, Arkansas, and Louisiana were now thinly settled. The 1850s brought many more pioneers, some from back east and many more directly from northern and middle Europe. Like pioneers before them, they sought good land and a better life. Some obtained land through squatters' rights; some bought from land speculators; and others were lured by the propaganda of the railroad companies, who advertised in eastern and European newspapers. At four dollars and up an acre, and with ten years to pay, railroad land was indeed a tremendous bargain, especially since there was bound to be a town close by, offering a market or transportation to a market.

After the Texas Revolution in 1836, and again after the Mexican War ten years later, there was a rush of pioneers to Texas. In 1849, another westward rush brought thousands of fortune seekers to California in search of the gold discovered there. Because of the tremendous hardships of the journey to the Pacific coast, these "forty-niners" usually went alone and sent for their families later. Mining towns sprang up in California with nearly all-male populations and were considerably rougher and wilder than anything previously seen on the frontier. Whether the miners came across the continent, or by ship around the Horn, or from port to port in Panama, they had suffered much to get there. Gold was their object and they cared little about the amenities. Some "Argonauts," as they were sometimes called, did not hesitate to steal foods from the Spanish *rancheros,* sometimes slaughtering their cattle and destroying other property. The once-generous hospitality of the Spanish landowners and the leisurely charm of their traditional ways were casualties of the violent changes in California.

Gold miners who had struck it rich seldom minded throwing money around. Hangtown Fry is a dish said to have been invented for a miner who, having just made a strike, walked into the hotel in Hangtown and said he'd like the most expensive items on the menu. These happened to be oysters and eggs, which the chef ingeniously combined.

By the Civil War, pioneering was taking place from the Pacific coast eastward as well as from the settled East westward. As a result, the Indians who lived in the last unsettled regions were caught in a vise and were finally forced to accept the meager land that the government designated as tribal reservations.

Unlike the Indian, the white settler had a number of ways to obtain good land legally. Perhaps the best-known avenue was the Homestead Act of 1862 under which adult males or females could acquire 80 to 160 acres of land free of charge. The only provisions were that the homesteader be native born, naturalized, or intending to become a naturalized citizen, and pay a ten-dollar fee to record the claim. In order to keep the claim, he or she had to live there for five years, cultivate the land, and improve it. Although these provisions at first glance seemed easy to comply with, the homesteaders soon found the loneliness of living on a claim often miles from town or neighbors and the inconvenience of makeshift housing were serious handicaps. Nonetheless thousands of homesteaders rushed for land when new sections were opened. Nebraska and Kansas were homesteaded first; later North and South Dakota and Colorado; and last of all Oklahoma.

Pioneer cooking meant working with limited ingredients and a lot of imagination. For example, when sugar was scarce and even sorghum molasses was in short supply, pumpkin or watermelon juice boiled to a syrup might be substituted. During a blackbird plague, blackbirds took a prominent place on the menu. A Nebraska farm paper of 1862 lists thirty-three different recipes using corn. As for coffee, it might be made of parched barley, okra seeds, carrots, or cornmeal and molasses that had been fried, powdered, and semiburned; but it seldom had anything to do with a coffee bean. Most households owned a coffee grinder, but used it to grind corn.

There were also many varieties of bread to be made from a basic recipe — streusel, crumpets, cracklin' bread, and so on — depending on the ethnic origin of the cook. Most bread started with cornmeal, but might also include rye, wheat, or acorn flour. Wild greens, such as sheep sorrel and buffalo peas, were eaten in summer, but in winter there were only a few root vegetables like potatoes or turnips. The cow, a victim of malnutrition during the winter months, usually went dry, so there was no milk then. Eggs were carefully conserved by immersing them in water glass (water mixed with potassium silicate or sodium silicate), covered, and kept cool. Game on the prairie had greatly diminished by the homestead era, and by the mid-70s, the buffalo was nearly extinct everywhere. Because fuel was a constant problem, sod-house cooking was done with the help of a hot box — a covered wooden box big enough to hold a boiling pot and retain its heat so that it continued to cook for a while without needing more fuel.

Beset by drought, tornadoes, and plagues of insects, the pioneers battled to provide for their families. But no matter how difficult times were, these indomitable cooks somehow managed to serve up savory meals.

Life became easier once the pioneers established their homesteads, and the meagerness of the meals of the early days disappeared. As soon as possible, they planted gardens. Before long, dinner tables groaned under the weight of tomatoes, corn, peas, and onions. The first freeze signaled butchering time and smokehouses bulged with curing hams and sausages. With better crops, more feed was given to the cows and they produced milk for dairy products year round. Over the years, the bounty of these homesteads led to the heartiest fare of our national cuisine. The recipes in this chapter invite you to sample Western home-style cooking.

The cattle baron was a distinctive personality in the beckoning west. One baron was German immigrant Conrad Kohrs. Beginning as a cabin boy on a ship, he progressed to raftsman and finally switched to gold mining. He soon decided, however, that there was more money in selling to miners than in being one. Over the years he accumulated over a million acres of ranchland in eastern Montana by selling beef to the miners in Bannack and Virginia City, Montana.

The blending of the worlds of the red man and the white man is shown idealistically in this scene at Fort Laramie, Wyoming.

The first settlers on the prairie, often lacking wood, built houses and cellars from sod.

During rest stops on the trail, the pioneers often found time to swap tales.

The Lure of the West

People of all types answered the call of the beckoning West. First came the trailblazers—the explorers, trappers, and fur traders. Then came those in search of more land or a new life. And finally, came those in search of gold. All found a land that was rough and wild. But slowly, mile by mile, they tamed the rugged frontier. The first settlers came individually, but later pioneers formed into wagon trains that eased the way over natural barriers, such as dangerous river crossings, and, offered protection against the hazards of being alone in the wilderness. Once out West, some pioneers staked claims to land or a mining site and went to work. Others found jobs on the railroads or as cowboys on ranches. The results of all this hard work were mixed. Many (especially the gold miners) failed, but many successfully built a new life. Both the successes and the failures contributed to the lore of the West.

Wagons wait in line to cross the Missouri River at Council Bluffs, Iowa.

Gregory Gulch, Colorado, was a site that lured men with gold fever.

Pioneers rush to stake claims for land in Oklahoma's Cherokee Strip.

Breaking the Way

As the New World appeared attractive to many Europeans, so the land west of the Alleghenies beckoned those colonists who were restless. Well before the Revolution, despite official prohibitions, pioneers, singly or in families, began to probe the Indian-ruled wilderness. Then, between 1783 and the War of 1812, there was a massive thrust into western Pennsylvania, Ohio, southern Michigan, Indiana, Illinois, West Virginia, Kentucky, and Tennessee; that is, the old northwest and old southwest frontiers.

Traveling was made easier by the new turnpikes and by river waterways using flatboat and keelboat. Families often traveled alone with all their possessions in one wagon and perhaps a cow trailing behind. As they journeyed, they kept an eye open for rich soil, water, and a way to build a shelter. Sometimes this shelter was made of logs; often, if timber was scarce, it was a sod house or a dugout cut into a hillside.

A location close to a creek and a wooded area was best. But if there was no flowing water close by, they looked for a small spring or dug a shallow well. Working from dawn to dusk, they cleared the land by cutting down or girdling trees, digging and burning out stumps, and moving rocks. Often a season passed before sufficient land was cleared and the soil tilled to plant crops for the following year. Thus the first year's diet was usually limited to wild game and the food the people brought with them.

The first crop planted was usually corn. Before it was ripe but as soon as the kernels were milky, some of it was "gritted"—that is, rubbed on a perforated piece of tin to produce coarse meal. This meal was made into "gritted bread," which was much like spoonbread. Once the corn was ripe, it was ground into cornmeal. This important staple appeared at least once a day as mush, johnnycake, bread, or even whiskey; and there were many variations of hominy and hominy grits.

Preparing food in the wilderness was a challenge. In the wintertime, eating was monotonous; meals often consisted of no more than cornmeal mush or corn bread sweetened with molasses, a few potatoes or turnips, or perhaps a bit of salt pork. But with the coming of summer, things changed and cows began producing milk again. That meant the families could have milk, butter, and cheese—if they were lucky enough to own a cow. Also, many healthful foods could be found growing wild in the summer woods—wild honey; berries, plums, persimmons, and other fruits; and greens, such as plantain, pokeweed, dandelion, and lamb's-quarters. Green hickory nuts, crushed, produced a buttery substance which, in the absence of butter, tasted good on corn bread—a trick the early pioneers learned from the Indians. The sap from burning hickory logs was saved for the children, who called it a hickory goody.

As one area became populated, settlers pushed farther west. Not only were new wagons passing settled areas, but old ones were also being repacked for another move west. Pioneers were restless souls and often moved more than once. Daniel Boone's father loaded his large family into wagons and took them from Virginia to North Carolina; later, Daniel would explore Kentucky and lead settlers there. Abraham Lincoln's father, born in Virginia during the Revolution, moved to Kentucky, where he married, then to Indiana, where Abe grew up, and finally to Illinois.

Corn Bread-Stuffed Trout

1 3-pound fresh *or* frozen
   dressed trout
  Salt
1 cup coarsely crumbled
   dry corn bread
1 cup soft bread crumbs
   (1½ slices)
½ cup chopped celery
¼ cup finely chopped onion

2 tablespoons finely
   chopped green pepper
½ teaspoon salt
¼ teaspoon ground sage
  Dash pepper
¼ cup water
3 tablespoons butter *or*
   margarine, melted

Thaw frozen fish. Sprinkle fish generously with salt. Place in a well-greased shallow baking pan. Mix crumbled corn bread, soft bread crumbs, celery, onion, green pepper, ½ teaspoon salt, sage, and pepper. Gradually add water to bread mixture, tossing to coat. Stuff fish loosely with mixture. Brush fish generously with melted butter or margarine and cover with foil. Bake at 350° till fish flakes easily when tested with a fork, 45 to 60 minutes. Remove stuffed fish to serving platter. Makes 6 servings.

Families that settled near water depended on fish to supplement the meager diet until they could plant crops or a vegetable garden. Fish was prepared in the fashion learned from the Indians. It was placed on a wide strip of wood or plank which was then secured at the edge of the fire so that it angled in close to the heat.

Stuffed Venison Steaks

2 pounds venison steak, cut
   ¾ inch thick
1½ cups milk
6 slices bacon
⅓ cup sliced green onion
   with tops

  Salt
  Pepper
½ cup water
½ cup cold water
¼ cup all-purpose flour

Cut venison steak into six serving-size pieces. Place in a shallow pan; pour milk over meat. Cover and refrigerate overnight, turning meat several times. Drain meat; pat dry with paper toweling. Cook bacon till crisp. Drain, reserving 2 tablespoons drippings. Crumble bacon and set aside. With sharp knife, carefully cut a pocket in one side of each piece of meat. Mix bacon and green onion. Stuff onion mixture into pockets in meat. In 10-inch skillet brown steaks in reserved bacon drippings. Season with salt and pepper. Add ½ cup water. Cover and simmer over low heat till tender, 45 to 60 minutes. Remove meat to platter.

For gravy, measure pan juices; add enough water to make 1½ cups. Blend ½ cup cold water slowly into flour. Stir into pan juice mixture. Cook, stirring constantly, till mixture thickens and bubbles. Season to taste with salt and pepper. Makes 6 servings.

Before the great surge of settlers moved in, deer, bear, and elk were abundant on the frontier. The hunter lucky enough to shoot one could feed his family for a long time.

The pioneer cook had several ways of removing the "wild game taste." One method was to soak the meat overnight in salted water. For the very tough cuts, the meat was soaked in a mixture of vinegar, water, and spices sometimes for as long as several days. Another method, which is more suited to modern tastes, is to soak the meat in milk as in this recipe for Stuffed Venison Steaks.

Smothered Pheasant

2 tablespoons all-purpose
   flour
½ teaspoon salt
⅛ teaspoon pepper
1 1- to 3-pound ready-to-
   cook pheasant, cut up
2 tablespoons lard
2 medium onions, sliced

1 cup water
¾ cup milk
2 tablespoons all-purpose
   flour
1 teaspoon salt
  Dash pepper
  Paprika

In plastic bag combine 2 tablespoons flour, ½ teaspoon salt, and ⅛ teaspoon pepper. Add pheasant pieces, a few at a time; shake to coat. In skillet brown pheasant slowly in hot lard. Arrange onions atop pheasant; add 1 cup water. Cover tightly; cook over low heat till tender, 45 to 60 minutes. Remove pheasant; measure liquid in pan. Add water, if necessary, to equal 1 cup. In screw-top jar shake milk, 2 tablespoons flour, 1 teaspoon salt, and dash pepper till blended. Stir into pan liquid. Cook, stirring constantly, till thickened and bubbly. Cook and stir 2 to 3 minutes more. Before serving, sprinkle pheasant with paprika. Pass gravy with pheasant. Makes 2 to 4 servings.

In addition to big game, there were also a great number of wild birds on the frontier. The prairie hen, duck, wild turkey, and goose were the most common. They were usually prepared by braising in a skillet as in the recipe for Smothered Pheasant. But frontier people never heard of a pheasant. The first time Americans saw what has become a most popular game bird was when pheasants were brought from China in 1880.

Roast Wild Duck or Goose

Remove wing tips and first joint of ready-to-cook wild duck or goose; salt cavity. Stuff with quartered onions and apples. Tie legs together; tie to tail. Place, breast side up, on rack in shallow pan. (*For goose only,* lay bacon slices over breast or rub with oil.) Roast, uncovered, at 400° till done. Allow 60 to 90 minutes for 1- to 2-pound duck; 1½ to 3 hours for 2- to 4-pound goose; 3 to 4 hours for 4- to 6-pound goose. Cap with foil to prevent overbrowning. Discard stuffing. Allow 1 to 1½ pounds per serving.

Note: If bird has had a fish diet or is old, stuff with carrot or potato; simmer bird in water for 10 minutes. Discard stuffing. Prepare as above.

Pioneer Mock Lemon Pie with Raisins

The first women on the frontier lacked many cooking ingredients that they had been used to back East. One was lemon juice. Not to be outdone by the hardships of frontier life, these resourceful women developed a recipe for lemon pie using homemade vinegar instead of lemon juice. Pioneer Mock Lemon Pie with Raisins *is an excellent example of one of those early pies.*

½ cup raisins
  Boiling water
1½ cups sugar
  3 tablespoons cornstarch
  3 tablespoons all-purpose flour
  3 slightly beaten egg yolks

2 tablespoons butter *or* margarine
¼ cup cider vinegar
1 *baked* 9-inch pastry shell, cooled (see recipe, page 351)
Meringue

Cover raisins with boiling water; cool. Drain. In saucepan mix sugar, cornstarch, flour, and dash salt. Stir in 1½ cups water. Cook and stir over high heat till boiling. Reduce heat; cook and stir 2 minutes more. Remove from heat. Stir moderate amount hot mixture into egg yolks; return to hot mixture in saucepan. Bring to boiling; cook and stir 2 minutes. Add butter.

Slowly stir in vinegar. Stir in raisins. Pour into pastry shell. Spread Meringue over hot filling, sealing to edge of pastry. Bake at 350° for 12 to 15 minutes. Cool before cutting.

Meringue: Beat 3 egg whites with ½ teaspoon vanilla and ¼ teaspoon cream of tartar till soft peaks form. Gradually add ⅓ cup sugar, beating till stiff peaks form and sugar is dissolved.

Generous portions are sure to be welcome when *Deep-Dish Plum Pie* is dessert. This brown-sugar-sweetened fresh plum pie is at its best served warm from the oven topped with cream or ice cream.

Mint Tea

Crush ½ cup lightly packed fresh mint leaves (should have about 2 tablespoons crushed). Place mint in teapot heated by rinsing with boiling water. Bring 4 cups cold water to full rolling boil. Pour over mint; steep for 5 minutes. Stir briskly; pour through tea strainer into cups. Pass sugar. Serves 6.

Blackberry Jam Cake

½ cup sugar
¼ cup butter *or* margarine
2 eggs
1 cup all-purpose flour
1 teaspoon ground cinnamon
½ teaspoon baking soda
¼ teaspoon ground cloves
¼ teaspoon ground nutmeg
⅓ cup buttermilk
½ cup seedless blackberry
    jam *or* preserves
¼ cup chopped walnuts
    Caramel Icing

Cream together sugar and butter or margarine. Beat in eggs. Stir together flour, cinnamon, soda, cloves, and nutmeg; add to creamed mixture alternately with buttermilk, beating just till blended after each addition. Fold in blackberry jam and nuts, leaving swirls of jam. (Do not overmix.) Turn into a greased and lightly floured 9x9x2-inch baking pan. Bake at 350° till done, about 25 minutes. Cool completely. Frost with Caramel Icing.

Caramel Icing: In saucepan melt 2 tablespoons butter or margarine; stir in ½ cup packed brown sugar. Cook, stirring constantly, till mixture bubbles; remove from heat. Cool 5 minutes. Stir in 3 tablespoons milk. Blend in 1¾ cups sifted powdered sugar; beat till spreading consistency.

Hickory Nut Custard Pie

1 cup sugar
2 tablespoons cornstarch
¼ teaspoon salt
1 cup water
½ cup molasses
4 slightly beaten eggs
1 teaspoon vanilla
1 unbaked 9-inch pastry
    shell (see recipe,
    page 351)
¾ cup coarsely broken
    hickory nuts *or* pecans
    Whipped cream

In a medium saucepan combine the sugar, cornstarch, and salt. Stir in the water and molasses. Cook and stir till thickened and bubbly. Gradually stir the hot mixture into the eggs. Add vanilla. Bake *unpricked* pie shell at 350° for 5 minutes. Remove from oven. Pour in egg mixture; top with nuts. Return pie to oven. Bake at 350° till a knife inserted just off-center comes out clean, about 30 minutes. Cool. To serve, top the pie with whipped cream.

Deep-Dish Plum Pie

5 cups halved pitted fresh
    purple plums (2 pounds)
¾ cup packed brown sugar
2 teaspoons quick-cooking
    tapioca
¼ teaspoon ground cinnamon
    Dash ground nutmeg
    Dash salt
1 tablespoon butter *or*
    margarine
    Pastry for 1-crust
    9-inch pie (see
    recipe, page 351)
    Light cream *or* ice cream

In a large bowl combine the purple plums, brown sugar, tapioca, cinnamon, nutmeg, and salt. Let stand 15 minutes. Turn mixture into an 8x1½-inch round baking dish. Dot with butter. Roll pastry to a 9-inch circle. Place over filling. Trim; flute edges to seal. Cut slits for escape of steam. Using pastry trimmings, garnish top of pie with pastry cutouts, if desired. Bake at 375° for 40 to 45 minutes. Serve warm with light cream or ice cream.

Hot drinks and medicines for the pioneers were made from wild roots, barks, and leaves such as sassafras and mint. Hot Mint Tea, *said many a pioneer mother, was especially good for digestive upsets and colic.*

On early frontier homesteads, before the crops had been harvested, the pioneers depended heavily on the wide assortment of fruits and nuts that grew wild. Plums, strawberries, blueberries, raspberries, blackberries, grapes, currants, and elderberries were gathered and either used fresh as in this recipe for Deep-Dish Plum Pie, *or carefully preserved. Some fruits were preserved by drying in the sun and others were made into jellies, jams, or sauces. The jellies and jams were served on bread or used in recipes such as* Blackberry Jam Cake. *Nuts, including hickory nuts, walnuts, pecans, butternuts, and hazelnuts, were dried and eventually found their way into all sorts of breads, cakes, and pies such as* Hickory Nut Custard Pie.

Hominy in Sour Cream

2 tablespoons butter
2 14½-ounce cans golden
    hominy, drained

1 cup dairy sour cream
½ teaspoon salt
Dash pepper

Melt butter in a heavy skillet. Add drained hominy and sour cream. Season with salt and pepper. Heat through, stirring often. Makes 8 to 10 servings.

Cornmeal Pancakes

Corn in the morning. Corn at night. It was one of the first crops frontier folks planted, and it was the food they were most likely to have when all other food was gone. As a result, the pioneers were always looking for new ways to use corn. One Nebraska farm paper in 1862 published 33 different recipes for using corn. One of its uses was for Cornmeal Pancakes.

1½ cups all-purpose flour
½ cup yellow cornmeal
2 tablespoons sugar
1 teaspoon baking soda
1 teaspoon salt

2 cups buttermilk
2 beaten eggs
2 tablespoons butter *or*
    margarine, melted

Stir together flour, cornmeal, sugar, soda, and salt. Add buttermilk, eggs, and butter. Stir just till flour is moistened. Using ¼ cup batter for each pancake, bake on a hot, lightly greased griddle. Makes sixteen 4-inch pancakes.

Puffy Noodles

Mix 1 beaten egg and 1 tablespoon milk. Stir together ¾ cup all-purpose flour, 1 teaspoon baking powder, and dash salt. Stir into milk mixture to make a stiff dough. Roll to a 12x12-inch square on lightly floured surface. Roll up; slice into ¼-inch wide strips. Unroll. Cut strips into desired lengths. *To cook noodles,* drop into boiling chicken broth or boiling salted water. Cook, uncovered, 10 to 12 minutes. Makes 2½ cups cooked noodles.

Brown Pudding

Dishes were at a premium in the West. So valuable were they, that one man is reported to have nailed his dishes (tin, most probably) onto the table. Washing the dishes was no problem for him. He simply turned the table on its side and washed them with a broom and hot water.

2¼ cups soft bread crumbs
    (3 slices)
1 cup buttermilk
1 cup packed brown sugar
¼ cup butter *or* margarine
1 egg
1 cup all-purpose flour

1 teaspoon baking soda
1 teaspoon ground cinnamon
¼ teaspoon salt
1 cup raisins
½ cup finely chopped
    walnuts
Sifted powdered sugar

Soak bread crumbs in buttermilk for 5 minutes. Cream together brown sugar and butter; add egg and bread mixture. Beat till smooth. Stir flour, soda, cinnamon, and salt together thoroughly; blend into creamed mixture. Stir in raisins and walnuts. Turn into a greased and lightly floured 6-cup ring mold. Cover with foil; tie with string. Place on rack in deep kettle; add boiling water to depth of 1 inch. Cover and steam till done, 2¼ to 2½ hours, adding water if needed. (Keep the water boiling.) Remove from kettle. Let stand 15 minutes; unmold. Dust with powdered sugar. Serves 6 to 8.

Cry Babies

1 cup butter *or* margarine
1 cup sugar
1 cup molasses
1 egg

4 cups all-purpose flour
1 teaspoon baking soda
1 teaspoon ground ginger
1 cup milk

Cream butter and sugar till light. Add molasses and egg; beat till smooth. Stir together flour, soda, and ginger. Add to creamed mixture alternately with milk, beating after each addition. Drop by teaspoonfuls onto greased cookie sheet. Bake at 350° till lightly browned, 10 to 12 minutes. Makes 60.

Buttermilk Doughnuts

2 eggs
1 cup granulated sugar
¼ cup cooking oil
1 teaspoon vanilla
4 cups all-purpose flour
4 teaspoons baking powder

¾ teaspoon salt
¼ teaspoon baking soda
1 cup buttermilk
Fat for frying
Sifted powdered sugar
   (optional)

In large mixing bowl beat eggs till thick and lemon-colored. Add the granulated sugar and beat till smooth. Stir in the oil and vanilla. Thoroughly stir together flour, baking powder, salt, and soda. Add to egg mixture alternately with buttermilk. Turn out onto a lightly floured surface and roll to ½-inch thickness. Cut dough with floured doughnut cutter. Fry in deep hot fat (375°) till golden brown, about 3 minutes, turning once. Drain on paper toweling. Serve plain or sprinkled with powdered sugar. Makes 24.

According to an old story of the 1850s, an Indian tried to buy the wife of a pioneer because he liked the way she made doughnuts. Through a misunderstanding, the Indian was prepared to trade three Indian women for the young wife. As the legend goes, it took a council of war and a bushel of doughnuts to save the doughnut maker.

Spiced Prune Sauce

1½ cups water
1 cup chopped pitted dried
   prunes
¼ teaspoon ground cinnamon

⅛ teaspoon ground cloves
⅛ teaspoon ground allspice
2 tablespoons packed brown
   sugar

In saucepan combine water, prunes, cinnamon, cloves, and allspice. Bring to boiling; reduce heat. Cover and simmer gently for 10 minutes. Stir in brown sugar. Cook 5 minutes more. Serve warm. Makes about 1½ cups.

A breakfast favorite of the lumberjacks of the northern frontier was "sweat pads" (pancakes) spread with bacon grease or molasses and topped with sausages and Spiced Prune Sauce. *It was a meal to keep a man going—at least till lunchtime.*

Settling In

Once the Westward Movement was started, it spread like a prairie fire. News traveling back East told of vast stretches of land and a rich bounty of native foods available practically for the taking. The West offered land for those who had none, adventure for those who were dissatisfied with the tameness of the settled East, and a new start in life for those who weren't prospering in the eastern cities and on the farms. Letters written from the West to relatives and friends back home encouraged more families to pack up their wagons and head for the western lands. The eagerness of the early pioneers for land caused the vast middle region of the continent to become populated rapidly.

When the pioneer arrived, the first job was to build a shelter. Then the tough prairie sod had to be conquered. Though enormously fertile, the roots of the native grasses drove deep into the soil and its texture was heavy and full of clay. Even the strong ox teams could scarcely pull an old-fashioned wooden plow through it, and every few feet the plowshare had to be cleaned. In 1847 a young man from Illinois, John Deere, devised a steel plowshare that was strong enough to cut through the prairie sod and not become clogged. Deere's invention was an important step toward the conquest of the seemingly limitless Great Plains.

After a pioneer had his corn planted, he turned to the next priorities. Of primary importance was breaking more land for additional crops: wheat

Pictured opposite: Threshing day meant extra cooking. After extending plank tables as far as possible and laying boards across the chairs to give more seating, the food would be set out — steaming platters of *Chicken-Fried Steak* and *Chicken and Homemade Noodles,* plus bowls heaped with boiled new potatoes, *Nutmeg Squash,* bacon-topped green beans, *Cabbage Slaw,* and sliced cucumbers and onions in vinegar. Freshly sliced tomatoes from the garden and thick slices of homemade bread, plus jelly and jam were also included. *Red Cherry Pie* and other favorites were offered for dessert. Since the men often ate in shifts, as soon as one man finished, his plate would be quickly washed and made ready for another. See index for recipe page numbers.)

One problem in opening up the prairie was that wheat did not grow well there. Then in the early 1870s, members of the German religious sect called Mennonites, who had been living in the Crimea, immigrated to Kansas. Each family brought along carefully selected seed wheat of the kind they had been growing in Russia and which had come originally from Turkey. Known as Turkey Red, it was hard winter wheat that took well to the climate of the Great Plains, thriving where other varieties failed.

Growing corn was also a problem on the prairie at first. Nothing seemed to work. Flint corn from New England was too low-yielding and the gourd-seed type from Virginia and Kentucky matured too late in the season. Before long, however, Yankee ingenuity developed a hybrid of the two called Redie's Yellow Dent. Not until the 1920s was a better hybrid developed.

and oats and a very complete vegetable garden. He also turned his attention to building a more permanent home, shelters for horses and oxen, fences for the garden, and rough furniture for the house. Like the colonial settlers, pioneer families salted and smoked meat and fish, dried some vegetables and stored others in attic or cellar to last the winter.

These families were still isolated and life in the woods or on the prairie was lonely. However, as each passing day brought more settlers, neighboring farms soon were not so distant. Towns sprang up where a large number of pioneers had settled (although sometimes it was the other way around; railroads planned towns before there were people to live in them).

Now, a pioneer farmer could count on a trip into town at least a few times a year to barter for items at a general store. Hides and furs, obtained and seasoned throughout the winter months, might be traded for calico, nails, salt, store sugar, crackers, candy, or a plow. If the family lived near a major river — the Ohio, Missouri, or one of their tributaries — they might buy sugar, coffee, and other luxuries from traders who had been down the Mississippi. Towns situated on rivers, especially at the fork where two rivers joined, grew very rapidly into major trading centers.

The pioneer family now had friends and neighbors with whom to trade work and to socialize. When a new family arrived to settle, the neighbors would gather to help them raise their house or barn. Chances were that they could also count on help in digging their well. At harvest time or when a lot of work needed to be done in a hurry, work bees were carried on — corn huskings, sewing and quilting, apple paring, sausagemaking, and soapmaking. Many customs grew out of these combination work and social bees. One, in particular, said that at a corn husking the first man to find a red ear of corn could kiss any girl present.

Also the Fourth of July was an important day for getting together; and as soon as a community had churches, there were church suppers and box socials. All these gatherings gave good cooks a chance to show off their talent by bringing their favorite dishes. And, except among teetotalers, there was likely to be considerable consumption of homemade liquor at these celebrations — corn whiskey, peach brandy, and hard apple cider.

Many who were brought up on a farm in the latter part of the nineteenth century fondly remember the splendid foods of the farm kitchen. Especially at threshing time, when there were neighbors to be fed, the meals were monumental. Favorites included chickens bursting with rich stuffing or stewed with noodles; standing rib roasts of beef; platters of steaming sweet corn; mashed potatoes, gently oozing butter and cream; candied sweets; fresh, crusty bread; juicy red tomatoes, just picked and still warm; and flaky-crusted pies — apple, peach, and cherry — over which, if you were still feeling a mite underfed, you could pour a river of cool, thick cream.

Ham with Red-Eye Gravy

Cut three ½-inch thick country ham slices *or* fully cooked ham slices in half. Trim the fat from ham slices, reserving trimmings. In skillet cook trimmings till crisp. Discard trimmings and brown the ham on both sides in the hot fat, 5 to 6 minutes per side. Remove ham to warm platter. Stir ⅔ cup boiling water and 1 teaspoon instant coffee powder into the drippings in skillet. If ham is mild-cured, add a few drops liquid smoke. Cook, scraping pan to remove crusty bits, for 2 to 3 minutes. Serve warm gravy over ham slices. Serve ham with grits, if desired. Makes 6 servings.

Menu

Chicken and Homemade Noodles
Chicken-Fried Steak
Nutmeg Squash
Buttered Green Beans
Buttered Potatoes
Cabbage Slaw
Sliced Tomatoes
Sliced Cucumbers and Onions
in Vinegar
Whole Wheat Bread
with
Butter and Jam
Red Cherry Pie
Apple Pie
Pumpkin Pie
Milk   Coffee

Chicken and Homemade Noodles *(see photo, page 189)*

Noodles
1 5- to 6-pound ready-to-cook stewing chicken, cut up, *or* 2 2½- to 3-pound ready-to-cook broiler-fryer chickens, cut up

1 medium onion, chopped
4 teaspoons salt
¼ teaspoon pepper
3 carrots, thinly sliced
2 tablespoons all-purpose flour

Prepare Noodles. Place chicken in kettle with enough water to cover (about 8 cups). Add onion, salt, and pepper. Cover; bring to boiling and simmer 1 hour for broiler-fryers *or* 2 to 2½ hours for stewing chicken. Remove chicken pieces; cool. Remove meat from bones; discard bones. Bring broth to boiling; add Noodles and carrots. Cover and simmer 10 minutes. Add chicken. Blend ¼ cup cold water into flour; add to chicken-noodle mixture. Cook and stir till slightly thickened. Makes 6 to 8 servings.

Noodles: Combine 2 beaten eggs, ¼ cup milk, and ¾ teaspoon salt. Add about 2 cups all-purpose flour to make a stiff dough. Divide dough in half. Roll very thinly on floured surface; let stand 20 minutes. Roll up loosely; slice ¼ inch wide. Unroll; cut into desired lengths. Let dry 2 hours.

Nutmeg Squash *(see photo, page 189)*

Cut 3 pounds Hubbard squash into chunks. Cook, covered, in boiling salted water till tender, about 25 minutes. Drain. Scoop pulp from rind. Mash pulp. If squash seems too thin, place in saucepan; cook, uncovered, till desired consistency. Stir in 2 tablespoons butter, 2 tablespoons packed brown sugar, ½ teaspoon salt, and ½ teaspoon ground nutmeg. Serves 6.

Cabbage Slaw *(see photo, page 189)*

6 cups shredded cabbage
1 cup shredded carrot
¼ cup chopped green pepper
1 cup mayonnaise

2 tablespoons sugar
2 tablespoons vinegar
1 teaspoon prepared mustard
1 teaspoon celery seed

Combine cabbage, carrot, and green pepper; chill. Blend together mayonnaise, sugar, vinegar, mustard, celery seed, and ½ teaspoon salt. Lightly toss vegetables with mayonnaise mixture. Makes 12 servings.

Red Cherry Pie *(see photo, page 189)*

3 cups canned pitted tart red cherries (water pack)
¾ cup juice from cherries
1 cup sugar
2 tablespoons quick-cooking tapioca

3 or 4 drops almond extract
10 drops red food coloring (optional)
Pastry for 9-inch lattice-top pie (see recipe, page 351)
1 tablespoon butter

Combine cherries and juice; stir in sugar, tapioca, almond extract, and dash salt. Add food coloring, if desired. Let stand 20 minutes. Line 9-inch pie plate with pastry. Fill with cherry mixture. Dot with butter. Trim crust ½ inch beyond edge of pie plate. Roll remaining dough ⅛-inch thick; cut strips of dough ½ to ¾ inch wide. Lay strips on pie at 1-inch intervals. Fold back alternate strips to center. Lay one strip crosswise 1-inch from edge. Return folded strips to original position. Repeat with alternate strips to form lattice. Trim lattice below outer rim of pie plate; fold lower crust over strips. Seal; crimp edges high. Bake at 400° till browned, 50 to 55 minutes. (Cover edges with foil to prevent overbrowning.)

Homemade Seasoned Sausage Patties

2 pounds boneless pork
    shoulder
4 ounces salt pork
• • •
⅔ cup water
⅓ cup finely chopped
    onion
2 tablespoons finely
    snipped parsley
4 teaspoons rubbed sage
1 teaspoon salt

1 teaspoon dried sweet
    pepper flakes
1 teaspoon chili powder
½ teaspoon dried thyme,
    crushed
½ teaspoon dried marjoram,
    crushed
½ teaspoon dried basil,
    crushed
2 cloves garlic, minced

Using coarse blade on food grinder, grind pork shoulder and salt pork together. Combine the ground meat, water, onion, parsley, sage, salt, pepper flakes, chili powder, thyme, marjoram, basil, and garlic; mix very well. Grind again. Divide mixture in half. On waxed paper, shape each half into a roll 6 inches long and 2 inches in diameter. Wrap in waxed paper or foil. Chill at least 2 hours. Just before cooking, slice into rounds ½ inch thick. Place a few sausage rounds in a cold skillet. Cover and cook slowly for 10 to 12 minutes, turning once. Drain on paper toweling. Makes 24 patties.

Noisy though they were with their rackety clanging and banging, machines like this combination harvester-thresher used around the turn of the century greatly reduced the time required to gather in the crop for winter storage. Neighboring farmers sometimes united to buy the expensive machine and then worked together to do the harvesting. The new time-saving machinery made it possible for farmers to increase the amount of land they could plant and harvest and so greatly increased production.

Pickled Ham

<table>
<tr><td>

2 cups cubed fully cooked
  ham
1 medium onion, cut up
3/4 cup water
1/2 cup vinegar

</td><td>

1 1/2 teaspoons mixed pickling
  spice
1 teaspoon sugar
1/4 teaspoon whole black
  pepper

</td></tr>
</table>

In a bowl mix ham and onion. In a saucepan heat the water, vinegar, pickling spice, sugar, and pepper till simmering. Pour over ham mixture. Cover and chill overnight. To serve, drain ham and onion. Makes 3 cups.

Mock Duck

<table>
<tr><td>

2 1 1/2-pound beef top round
  steaks (3/4 inch thick)
1 1/2 cups finely chopped
  celery
3/4 cup chopped onion
1/4 cup butter *or* margarine
4 cups dry bread cubes
3/4 teaspoon ground sage

</td><td>

1/2 teaspoon salt
1/8 teaspoon pepper
1 pound ground pork
2 tablespoons shortening
1/2 cup water
1 teaspoon instant beef
  bouillon granules
1/3 cup all-purpose flour

</td></tr>
</table>

Sprinkle steaks with salt and pepper; pound *each* to a 12x8-inch rectangle about 1/4 inch thick. Cook celery and 1/2 *cup* onion in butter till tender. Mix vegetables with bread cubes, sage, 1/2 teaspoon salt, and 1/8 teaspoon pepper. Add pork; mix well. Spread stuffing atop steaks. Roll up, from long side, jelly-roll style. Tie with string. In a 12-inch skillet brown meat on all sides in hot shortening. Remove from heat; spoon off fat. To skillet add water, bouillon granules, and remaining onion. Stir to dissolve bouillon. Cover and simmer till meat is tender, about 1 1/4 hours; spoon juices over meat often. Remove meat to platter; keep warm. Skim fat from pan juices; add water to make 2 1/2 cups liquid. Blend 1/2 cup cold water into flour. Stir into pan juices. Cook and stir till thick and bubbly. Serves 10 to 12.

Chicken-Fried Steak *(see photo, page 189)*

Pound 1 1/2 pounds beef top round steak 1/4 inch thick; cut in serving-size pieces. Mix 1 beaten egg and 1 tablespoon milk. Dip meat in egg, then in 1 cup finely crushed saltine crackers. In skillet brown meat in 1/4 cup cooking oil; turn once. Cover; cook over low heat 45 to 60 minutes. Serves 6.

Green Tomato Pie

<table>
<tr><td>

6 green medium tomatoes
  (1 3/4 pounds)
1 cup sugar
3 tablespoons all-purpose
  flour
1 teaspoon ground cinnamon
1 teaspoon grated lemon
  peel

</td><td>

1/2 teaspoon ground nutmeg
1/2 teaspoon salt
2 tablespoons butter *or*
  margarine
Pastry for 2-crust 9-inch
  pie (see recipe,
  page 351)
Sugar

</td></tr>
</table>

Dip tomatoes in boiling water 20 to 30 seconds; remove core and peel. Cut in 1/4-inch thick slices. Combine tomatoes and 1/4 cup water. Bring to boil; reduce heat. Simmer, covered, 5 minutes. With slotted spoon, remove tomato slices. Mix 1 cup sugar, flour, cinnamon, peel, nutmeg, and salt. Add to liquid in saucepan. Cook and stir just till boiling. Remove from heat; add butter. Gently stir in tomato slices. Cool 10 minutes. Line 9-inch pie plate with pastry. Spoon in tomato mixture. Adjust top crust; cut slits. Seal; crimp edges high. Sprinkle with sugar. Bake at 400° about 40 minutes.

The ancestors of the present-day Amana Society first banded together in 1714 in Hesse, Germany. The Society came to America seeking freedom to practice their religion. They purchased the Seneca Indian Reservation near Buffalo, New York, and under the name of Ebenezer Society set up a communal system. Later the Society moved to an 18,000-acre site along the Iowa River. Here the members developed their land holdings into communal farms. They also established communal kitchens. The foods served in the Ebenezer Society kitchens were excellent and their fame spread far and wide. Although no longer a communal organization, members of the Amana Society are still serving Amana recipes to family and tourists alike. You will see why when you taste their Pickled Ham.

Tomatoes were a prized food in the frontier home. So when frost threatened, the precious unripe tomatoes were quickly gathered. Some were wrapped and placed in a dark dry place to ripen, while some were eaten green. The pioneers prepared green tomatoes in several ways. Sometimes they just sliced and fried them, and other times they enjoyed them in recipes such as Green Tomato Pie.

Pan-Fried Cabbage

2 tablespoons bacon drippings	¼ cup water
1 small head cabbage, shredded (4 cups)	1 tablespoon sugar
¼ cup vinegar	½ teaspoon salt
	Dash cayenne

Heat drippings in skillet. Add cabbage, vinegar, water, sugar, salt, and cayenne. Cook over medium heat, stirring occasionally, till cabbage is lightly browned but still crisp, 10 to 12 minutes. Makes 4 servings.

Steamed Carrot Pudding

2 medium carrots, cut up	1 teaspoon vanilla
2 medium apples, peeled, cored, and cut up	1½ cups all-purpose flour
1 medium potato, peeled and cut up	1½ teaspoons baking soda
4 ounces suet, cut up	1 teaspoon ground cinnamon
• • •	1 teaspoon ground nutmeg
1 beaten egg	½ teaspoon ground cloves
1 cup sugar	½ teaspoon salt
⅓ cup orange juice	1 cup snipped pitted dates
	1 cup raisins
	Brown Sugar Sauce

Using coarse blade of food grinder, grind carrots, apples, potato, and suet together. Combine egg, sugar, orange juice, and vanilla. Stir into carrot mixture. Stir together flour, soda, spices, and salt. Stir into carrot mixture. Fold in dates and raisins. Pour into a well-greased 2-quart mold (not ring mold). Cover with foil; tie tightly with string. Place on rack in deep kettle; add water to depth of 1 inch. Bring to boiling. Cover; steam for 3½ hours, adding water if needed. Cool 10 minutes; unmold. Serve warm with Brown Sugar Sauce.

Brown Sugar Sauce: In heavy saucepan mix ½ cup packed brown sugar and 2 teaspoons cornstarch; stir in ⅓ cup water and 2 tablespoons butter *or* margarine. Cook, stirring constantly, till thickened and bubbly. Gradually stir hot mixture into 1 beaten egg; return to saucepan. Cook and stir 1 minute more. Stir in 1 teaspoon vanilla.

Mock Whipped Cream

In a bowl mix ¾ cup sifted powdered sugar; 1 egg white; 1 large tart apple, peeled and grated; and 1 teaspoon vanilla. Beat with electric mixer till consistency of whipped cream, 12 to 15 minutes. Makes about 3 cups.

Raisin Pastry Squares

1 cup raisins	¾ cup butter *or* margarine
Water	5 to 7 tablespoons milk
2 cups all-purpose flour	¼ cup sugar
½ teaspoon salt	Milk
½ teaspoon baking powder	Sugar

In saucepan cover raisins with water; bring to boiling. Remove from heat; let stand 5 minutes. Drain and set aside. Thoroughly mix flour, salt, and baking powder. Cut in butter till mixture is size of small peas. Gradually add 5 to 7 tablespoons milk, gently mixing with fork till all is moistened. Form into ball. On lightly floured surface roll to a 17x11-inch rectangle, rolling from center to edges. Spread raisins evenly over lengthwise half of dough; sprinkle ¼ cup sugar over raisins. Fold dough over to cover raisins; seal. Transfer to baking sheet. Brush with milk; sprinkle with sugar. Bake at 375° till golden, 30 to 35 minutes. Cool; cut in squares. Makes about 24.

Most frontier congregations could not afford to pay their ministers very well. In order to augment the minister's poor salary, church socials were often held with the proceeds going to his family. The food was donated by church members. Heaping plates of fried chicken and roast beef, bowls of steaming vegetables, home-canned pickles and fruits, and plenty of desserts were served on plank tables on the church lawn in summer and in the church basement in winter. The cost was usually 25 cents for adults and 10 cents for children. The food was served family-style and the rule was all-you-could-eat. There were definite rules for the division of labor at the social. Society matrons in the congregation presided at the cake table, while lesser members washed dishes and served the other food. All eyes were on unmarried couples because for a young man to escort a girl to one of these socials meant that most likely there would be a wedding soon.

Box lunches to carry to school have been a part of American life since pioneer times. In those days instead of fruit or cake or packaged desserts, the children were more likely to take Raisin Pastry Squares. These pastry squares were particularly well suited for box lunches because they were sturdy, carried so well, and were easy to eat.

Stack Cake was a traditional pioneer wedding cake made – at least, put together – right at the wedding celebration. Each guest brought a layer of cake. Applesauce made from either fresh or dried apples (depending on the time of year) was spread on each cake layer and the layers were stacked. The bride's popularity could be measured by the number of stacks she had and by the number of layers in each stack.

Since guests were apt to bring different types of cake, the stacks were often varicolored and flavored. Our recipe is for six layers of a simple molasses cake, typical of pioneer times.

Stack Cake

1 cup butter *or* margarine
1 cup sugar
1 cup molasses
3 eggs
4 cups all-purpose flour
1 teaspoon baking soda

1 teaspoon salt
1 cup milk
2 16½-ounce jars chunk-
    style spiced applesauce
Whipped cream
Chopped nuts

Cream together butter and sugar till light. Stir in molasses; add eggs, one at a time, beating after each. Stir together flour, soda, and salt; add to creamed mixture alternately with milk, beating after each addition. Grease and flour three 8x1½-inch round baking pans. Pour *1⅓ cups batter* into each pan. (Refrigerate remaining batter.) Bake at 375° till done, about 15 minutes. Cool 5 minutes; remove from pans and cool on rack. Wash pans; grease and flour. Repeat with remaining batter. Spread applesauce between layers. Spread whipped cream atop; sprinkle with nuts. Makes 24 servings.

Mincemeat Cookies

1½ cups sugar
1 cup butter *or* margarine
3 eggs
3 cups all-purpose flour

1 teaspoon baking soda
1 18-ounce jar prepared
    mincemeat
½ cup chopped walnuts

Cream sugar and butter till light. Add eggs; beat well. Stir together flour, soda, and ¼ teaspoon salt; stir into creamed mixture. Stir in mincemeat and nuts.

Drop by rounded teaspoonfuls onto greased cookie sheet. Bake at 350° about 15 minutes. Let stand 1 minute; remove from cookie sheet. Makes 72.

Apple Jonathan

6 to 8 tart apples, peeled,
  cored, and thinly
  sliced (6 cups)
½ cup pure maple syrup *or*
  maple-flavored syrup
½ cup sugar
¼ cup butter *or* margarine

1 egg
1 cup all-purpose flour
2 teaspoons baking powder
½ teaspoon salt
½ cup milk
  Light cream

In bowl toss apples with syrup till apples are coated. Spread evenly in 12x 7½x2-inch baking dish. Cream together sugar and butter till light. Beat in egg. Thoroughly mix flour, baking powder, and salt; add to butter mixture alternately with milk, beating after each addition. Pour over apples. Bake at 350° 30 to 35 minutes. Serve warm or cool. Pass cream. Serves 6 to 8.

Although folk hero Johnny Appleseed has often been given most of the credit for introducing apples to the West, he actually visited only a small part of the frontier. Born John Chapman, he began growing and selling apple trees at the age of twenty-seven. For 40 years he traveled Ohio and Indiana, making sure pioneers had apple trees — to grow apples they could use in recipes such as Apple Jonathan.

Cider Pie

1 unbaked 8-inch pastry
  shell (see recipe,
  page 351)
1 6-ounce can frozen apple
  juice concentrate,
  thawed

3 eggs
½ cup packed brown sugar
2 tablespoons butter *or*
  margarine, melted
¼ teaspoon salt
  Ground nutmeg

Bake *unpricked* pastry shell at 450° for 4 minutes. Remove from oven; reduce oven temperature to 350°. Meanwhile, beat together concentrate, eggs, sugar, butter, and salt. Pour into pastry shell. Sprinkle with nutmeg. Bake at 350° till knife inserted just off-center comes out clean, 25 to 30 minutes.

In the old West, homemakers made Cider Pie *by boiling apple cider down until it was very thick. Today frozen apple juice concentrate is a convenient substitute for boiled cider.*

Bishop's Bread

2½ cups all-purpose flour
1¾ cups packed brown sugar
1 teaspoon ground cinnamon
½ teaspoon salt
• • •
½ cup butter *or* margarine

½ cup chopped nuts
1 teaspoon baking soda
1 cup buttermilk
2 beaten eggs
½ cup raisins *or*
  dried currants

In a bowl stir together flour, brown sugar, cinnamon, and salt; cut in butter till mixture is crumbly. Stir in nuts. Reserve ½ cup crumb mixture for topping; stir soda into remaining crumb mixture. Mix buttermilk, eggs, and raisins. Stir into flour mixture. Mix just to moisten. Turn into two greased and floured 8x1½-inch round baking pans. Sprinkle reserved crumb mixture over tops. Bake at 350° till done, about 35 minutes. Makes 2 coffeecakes.

Most frontier settlements did not have a permanent clergyman for the church. Instead, circuit-riding bishops and other church officials came to the community for Sunday services. According to legend, one early Sunday morning a circuit-riding bishop in Kentucky dropped in on one family unexpectedly for breakfast. The resourceful hostess invented a quick fruit bread for the occasion. She named it Bishop's Bread *in honor of her guest.*

Poppy Seed Cake

1½ cups granulated sugar
¾ cup butter *or* margarine
4 egg yolks
⅓ cup poppy seed
1½ teaspoons vanilla
2 cups all-purpose flour

1 teaspoon baking soda
¼ teaspoon salt
1 cup dairy sour cream
4 stiffly beaten egg whites
  Powdered sugar

Cream granulated sugar and butter till light and fluffy. Beat in egg yolks, poppy seed, and vanilla. Thoroughly stir together flour, soda, and salt; add to creamed mixture alternately with sour cream, beating after each addition. Fold in egg whites. Turn batter into *greased* 10-inch tube pan. Bake at 350° for 45 to 50 minutes. To prevent over-browning, cover with foil last 5 to 10 minutes. *Do not invert* cake in pan. Cool. Remove; dust with powdered sugar.

Burgoo

Politicians have always resorted to all sorts of ways of getting votes. One of the more colorful was the political barbecue where voters were swayed more by what they ate and drank than by rhetoric. These vote-getting rallies were at their greatest during the 1840 presidential campaign of William Henry Harrison. The featured dish was often Burgoo, a hearty concoction of chicken, beef, and vegetables which took all night to prepare. As if to prove that the food was more important than the speeches, the rally itself was often called a burgoo.

1 3-pound ready-to-cook
   broiler-fryer chicken,
   cut up
2 pounds beef shank cross
   cuts
12 cups water
1 tablespoon salt
¼ teaspoon pepper
6 slices bacon
2 28-ounce cans tomatoes
2 cups cubed peeled
   potatoes
2 cups coarsely chopped
   carrots
1 cup chopped onion
1 cup chopped celery

1 cup chopped green pepper
2 tablespoons packed dark
   brown sugar
¼ teaspoon crushed dried
   red pepper
4 whole cloves
1 bay leaf
1 clove garlic, minced
4 ears corn
2 16-ounce cans butter
   beans
1 10-ounce package frozen
   cut okra
   • • •
⅔ cup all-purpose flour
½ cup snipped parsley

In 10-quart Dutch oven combine chicken, beef cross cuts, water, salt, and pepper. Cover; cook till meat is tender, about 1 hour. Remove chicken and beef from broth, reserving broth. Remove chicken and beef from bones; discard skin and bones. Cube beef and chicken. Set aside. Cook bacon till crisp; drain, reserving drippings. Crumble bacon; set aside. To reserved broth in Dutch oven add cubed beef, undrained tomatoes, potatoes, carrots, onion, celery, green pepper, sugar, red pepper, cloves, bay leaf, and garlic. Cover; simmer 1 hour, stirring often. Remove cloves and bay leaf. With knife, make cuts down *center of corn kernels* on each row; scrape cob. Add corn, cubed chicken, undrained beans, and okra to Dutch oven; simmer 20 minutes. Blend flour and reserved bacon drippings; stir into soup. Cook and stir till soup thickens. Salt to taste. Garnish with parsley and bacon. Serves 20.

Black Walnut and Honey Ice Cream

In saucepan blend 2 cups milk into ¾ cup honey. Cook and stir till hot *(do not boil)*. Remove from heat. Stir moderate amount of hot mixture into 3 beaten eggs; return to saucepan. Cook and stir 2 minutes longer. Cool to room temperature. Blend in 2 cups whipping cream and 1 teaspoon vanilla. Stir in 1 cup coarsely chopped black walnuts. Freeze mixture in ice cream freezer according to manufacturer's directions. Makes 2 quarts.

=== OREGON TRAIL
=== SANTA FE TRAIL
=== MORMON TRAIL
=== GILA RIVER TRAIL
=== CALIFORNIA TRAIL
▬ OLD SPANISH TRAIL

On the Trail

Pioneering families who wanted to migrate west by way of the Oregon, Santa Fe, or Mormon Trail had to travel in convoys. Tragic experience had shown that a high degree of organization was necessary for a wagon train to survive the hazards of terrain, weather, Indians, and food supply. Those who wished to make the trip on the Oregon Trail (the major trail) gathered at Independence, Missouri, in the late spring and joined a great caravan, sometimes of a thousand or more migrants. Before starting out, officials were elected by democratic vote — men who were seasoned guides and scouts. It was up to these leaders to choose camping sites, decide on the precise route, and generally keep order.

At the end of every day on the trail, the captain, riding ahead of the wagon train, decided on a campground for the night and marked out a circle. He knew just how large the circle must be in order to accommodate the wagons that would form the wall of a temporary fortress. The space inside the circle was large enough for tents and cooking fires.

The wagons — "prairie schooners" — were not the Conestogas of the East. They were farm wagons, built with extra-sturdy wheels and canvas tops that could be tied down tightly in bad weather or left flapping loose to admit air on a hot day. They were usually pulled by oxen because these animals were stronger, although much slower, than mules and horses. Each wagon in the train had to carry enough food to see its owners through the long trip. On the Oregon Trail each person was required to supply himself with enough flour, dry beans, rice, sugar, coffee, pork, and water for a trip that might last as long as three and a half months. On the trail, this fare had to be supplemented with game.

As soon as camp was made, everybody went to work: children hunted buffalo chips for fuel, the men pitched tents, and the women kindled fires and cooked the evening meal. This consisted of fresh roasted game, if there was any; otherwise, there was cornmeal and pork, and bread baked in Dutch ovens. Because getting a fire going could be a tiresome chore, they made sure to keep some coals alive for cooking breakfast.

Before dawn, a bugle sounded and the women made hot mush and bacon while the animals were rounded up, the tents struck, and everything stowed back in the wagons. Another bugle at seven and the cry, "Catch up!" had the wagon train on its slow, unwieldy way. At noon, there was a brief stop for some rest and a light meal of cold food. However, during hot weather, breakfast often was dispensed with in order to get an early start. On these occasions, the party would stop when the sun grew hot to rest the animals, eat a substantial meal, and, if possible, take a short nap in the shade. Thousands of pioneers crossed the plains this way without serious incident. Indians seldom attacked a well-organized wagon train, although they looked for stragglers and waited to seize stray animals.

In 1858 an alternative way of traveling west was offered by John Butterfield's overland stagecoaches. The route covered 2,800 miles: Memphis, St. Louis, Little Rock, El Paso, Yuma, and San Francisco. A more northerly route would have been shorter, but ran the risk of snow and storm. The journey could be made in twenty-one days, barring accident, highway robbers, washouts, and Indian attack. Meals along the stage route were taken at "road ranches" — taverns built along the road.

The end of trail life was signaled in May 1869, at Promontory, Utah, when the last spike was driven in the Union and Central Pacific Railroad, linking East and West. No longer did settlers need to travel months in a wagon; trains could speed them to their new homes in days.

Most of the pioneers who crossed the country in covered wagons did so safely, but some weren't so lucky. The story of the ill-fated Donner Party, lost in a blizzard in the High Sierra and driven to cannibalism is well-known. In addition, disease and accident accounted for many a lonely, anonymous grave on the prairie. Although Brigham Young's first "Pioneer Band" traveled without serious mishap from the Missouri along the Platte and into the Salt Lake Valley, a major disaster was suffered in 1856 by Mormon "hand-cart brigades." These were families traveling on foot and pushing carts laden with food and possessions. Overtaken by winter weather and sickness nearly 250 of these pioneers died on the trail.

Beef Jerky

Remove all fat from 1 pound beef top round steak. Freeze steak till icy. Cut in very thin strips, cutting *across grain* for crisp jerky and *with grain* for chewy jerky. Place in bowl in ½-inch thick layer. Sprinkle with salt, pepper, and liquid smoke. Repeat layers. Weight down with plate or heavy object; cover. Chill overnight. Drain; pat dry. Arrange on rack in shallow baking pan. Bake at 250° till dry, 3½ to 4 hours. Cool. Store in airtight container in refrigerator or at cool room temperature. Makes 8 to 9 ounces jerky.

Cooking on the trail was often
difficult, especially where fuel was
scarce. Hardwood made the
best fires, but in timberless country
the pioneers often had to
resort to hay, weeds, and sagebrush,
which burned very quickly
and produced a great many hot
ashes. Sometimes, cow or
buffalo chips were used as fuel.
But the odor of such a fire
was unpleasant and sometimes
affected the taste of the
food. In dry weather buffalo chips
made a hot fire, but burned
very quickly. When wet, they
would hardly burn at all
and had to be fanned to keep the
fire going. In spite of these
hardships, the pioneers on the trail
managed to enjoy recipes such
as Rabbit with Cream Gravy.

Rabbit with Cream Gravy

1 1- to 1½-pound ready-to-
cook rabbit, cut up
¼ cup all-purpose flour
¾ teaspoon salt
Dash pepper
2 tablespoons cooking oil
1 cup chopped onion
½ teaspoon ground allspice
⅛ teaspoon ground cloves

1 bay leaf
¼ cup water
1 tablespoon vinegar
Paprika
1 to 1¼ cups milk
2 tablespoons all-purpose
flour
1 tablespoon plum preserves
(optional)

Coat rabbit with mixture of ¼ cup flour, salt, and pepper. In skillet brown meat slowly in hot oil, about 15 minutes. Add onion, allspice, cloves, and bay leaf. Stir in water and vinegar. Cover; simmer till meat is tender, 45 to 60 minutes. Add more water if needed. Remove rabbit to serving platter; keep warm. Sprinkle with paprika. Remove bay leaf from drippings. In screw-top jar shake ½ *cup* milk with 2 tablespoons flour, ½ teaspoon salt, and dash pepper till blended; stir into pan drippings. Add ½ *cup* more milk and preserves, if desired. Cook and stir till thick and bubbly. If necessary, stir in additional milk to desired consistency. Serve gravy with rabbit. Serves 4.

Fried Apples with Salt Pork

1 ounce salt pork
4 tart apples, cored and
thinly sliced (4 cups)

2 tablespoons packed brown
sugar

Remove rind from salt pork; slice meat thinly. In skillet brown salt pork slowly. Add apples and sugar. Cover and cook till apples are tender and translucent, about 10 minutes, stirring occasionally. Serves 4 to 6.

Pioneer Lettuce Salad *(see photo, page 201)*

1 cup whipping cream
2 tablespoons sugar
¼ teaspoon salt

¼ cup vinegar
Leaf lettuce, torn

Whip the cream with sugar and salt till the mixture begins to thicken; stir in the vinegar. Toss with torn lettuce. Makes about 1½ cups dressing.

The Mormons, in establishing the
Mormon Trail, traveled 1,400
miles from Nauvoo, Illinois, to the
Salt Lake Valley. They
followed a route just north of the
Platte River so that they
would avoid unfriendly pioneers
traveling the Oregon Trail.
Their trip was meticulously planned.
The Mormons moved in small
groups. The first groups plowed
fields and planted crops and
gardens for those to follow. Later
groups harvested the crops
and planted new ones for those who
would follow them. Along
the trail they used their garden-
grown leaf lettuce to prepare
Pioneer Lettuce Salad.

Mormon Fish Chowder

2 pounds fresh *or* frozen
haddock fillets *or*
other fish fillets
4 ounces salt pork, diced
1 cup chopped onion
4 cups cubed, peeled
potatoes (6 medium)
2 cups water

2 teaspoons salt
¼ teaspoon pepper
2 cups milk
1 13-ounce can evaporated
milk
2 tablespoons all-purpose
flour

Thaw frozen fish. In large saucepan cook salt pork slowly till golden brown. Drain, reserving 1 tablespoon fat in pan. Set aside cooked salt pork. Add onion to pan; cook till tender but not brown. Stir in potatoes and water. Add fish fillets, salt, and pepper. Bring to boiling; cook over low heat till potatoes are tender and fish flakes easily when tested with a fork, 15 to 20 minutes. With slotted spatula, remove fish. Break fish into bite-size pieces; return to pan. Mix milk and evaporated milk. Slowly stir milk mixture into flour till smooth; add to fish mixture. Add cooked salt pork; cook over low heat till heated through (do not boil). Makes 8 servings.

Molasses Butter

1 cup molasses
2 tablespoons butter *or*
    margarine

¼ teaspoon ground nutmeg
    Dash baking soda
2 well-beaten eggs

Mix molasses, butter, nutmeg, soda, and dash salt in heavy saucepan. Bring to a boil over low heat. Stir moderate amount of hot mixture into eggs; return to pan. Cook and stir till thick, about 1 minute. Chill. Makes 1½ cups.

When the luxury of cream was available on the trail, it was put in the back of the wagon and the jogging over the rough trails churned it into butter. The butter was used on bread or extended by making Molasses Butter.

Pioneer White Bread

2½ to 3 cups all-purpose
    flour
1 package active dry yeast

1¼ cups water
1 tablespoon sugar
    Cornmeal

In large mixing bowl mix *1 cup* flour and the yeast. In saucepan heat water, sugar, and ¾ teaspoon salt just till warm (115-120°), stirring to dissolve sugar. Add to dry mixture. Beat at low speed of electric mixer ½ minute, scraping bowl. Beat 3 minutes at high speed. By hand, stir in enough remaining flour to make a soft dough. Shape into ball. Place in lightly greased bowl; turn once. Cover; let rise till double (about 1 hour). Punch down. Cover; let rest 10 minutes. Grease a 1-quart casserole; sprinkle with cornmeal. Place dough in casserole; sprinkle with cornmeal. Cover; let rise till double (30 to 45 minutes). Bake at 400° for 40 to 45 minutes. Cover loosely with foil if top browns too quickly. Remove from casserole; cool. Makes 1.

Hopes for a better life led many pioneers across the prairies to the unknown lands of the West. But hopes were not enough. Success demanded the skills and stamina to build a farm on virgin land. It also required the means to outfit the family for the journey. A stout wagon and a good team were of primary importance since the supplies and provisions recommended for four adults making a six-month trip often weighed close to 2,500 pounds.

Pictured opposite: Mormons traveling westward in the mid-1800s brought along their East-coast ways of cooking. A typical meal might have included a big kettle of *Mormon Split Pea Soup,* a loaf of *Whole Wheat Quick Bread* served with comb honey, and *Pioneer Lettuce Salad* (see recipe, page 198) topped with a favorite sweet-sour whipping cream dressing.

Lima Beans and Pork Sausage

1 pound dry lima beans (2½ cups)	2½ cups tomato juice
6 cups cold water	1 teaspoon dried basil, crushed
½ teaspoon salt	¼ teaspoon chili powder
1 pound bulk pork sausage	⅛ teaspoon pepper

Rinse beans. In kettle combine with water and salt. Bring to boiling and simmer 2 minutes; remove from heat. Cover; let stand 1 hour. (Or, add beans to water and salt; soak overnight.) Do not drain. Return to boiling. Cover; simmer till tender, 45 to 60 minutes. Drain. Cook sausage till browned; drain. Stir in tomato juice, basil, chili powder, pepper, and drained beans. Simmer, uncovered, till heated, about 10 minutes, stirring often. Serves 8.

Mormon Split Pea Soup

1 pound dry green split peas (2 cups)	¼ teaspoon pepper
8 cups cold water	1 pound ground pork
1 cup chopped onion	¾ teaspoon ground sage
½ cup chopped celery	¾ teaspoon salt
2 teaspoons salt	⅛ teaspoon pepper
½ teaspoon dried marjoram, crushed	3 medium potatoes, peeled and diced (3 cups)

Rinse split peas. In large kettle or Dutch oven combine split peas, cold water, onion, celery, 2 teaspoons salt, marjoram, and ¼ teaspoon pepper. Bring to boiling; cover and simmer till peas are tender, about 1 hour. Do not drain. Meanwhile, combine ground pork, sage, ¾ teaspoon salt, and ⅛ teaspoon pepper. Mix thoroughly. Shape into twenty-four 1-inch balls. Drop balls and potatoes into soup mixture; return soup to boiling. Cover; simmer 20 minutes longer. Season to taste. Serves 10 to 12.

During their first spring in the Salt Lake Basin, the Mormons planted wheat and corn to make into bread. Before the plants had a chance to grow, however, the fields were invaded by a swarm of crickets that threatened to eat everything in sight. Suddenly, sea gulls from the Great Salt Lake began eating the crickets, and feasted on them each day. The crops—at least some—were saved. This said the Mormons, was God at work, and the "miracle of the gulls" has become a firm part of Mormon tradition.

Whole Wheat Quick Bread

2 cups whole wheat flour	¼ cup honey
1 teaspoon baking powder	¼ cup butter *or* margarine, melted
1 teaspoon baking soda	½ cup chopped walnuts
1 teaspoon salt	½ cup raisins
1 beaten egg	
1¾ cups buttermilk	

In mixing bowl stir together whole wheat flour, baking powder, baking soda, and salt. Combine beaten egg, buttermilk, honey, and butter or margarine. Add to dry ingredients; stir just till moistened. Fold in walnuts and raisins. Turn into greased 9x5x3-inch loaf pan. Bake at 350° till done, 55 to 60 minutes. Remove from pan; cool on rack. Makes 1 loaf.

Pioneer Fruit Candy

3 cups raisins	Peel of ½ orange
1 12-ounce package dried figs	1 cup coarsely chopped walnuts
1 cup pitted dates	2 tablespoons orange juice
1 cup pitted dried prunes	Granulated sugar

Using coarse blade of food grinder, grind raisins, figs, dates, prunes, and orange peel together. Blend with nuts and orange juice. Shape into balls using 2 teaspoons for each. Roll in sugar. Store in covered container. Makes 96.

Chuck Wagon Chow

The great era of cattle-driving across the Texas plains to Kansas railheads only lasted twenty years (approximately from 1865 to 1885), but enough folklore, books, songs, and movies have come out of it to make it seem like major American history. There are people all over the world who couldn't tell you who John Adams or Thomas Jefferson were, but who know all about Wild Bill Hickok. Millions who can't speak English know the meaning of the words cowpuncher, trail boss, and chuck wagon.

The cattle drives of the West were by no means the first in this country. As early as the 1790s, herds were driven from western New York and Pennsylvania or along the Cumberland Road to New York City, Baltimore, and Richmond, to be slaughtered for meat. And even before that, butchers used to drive cattle from farm to farm, trading beef-on-the-hoof or their services as slaughterers in return for farm produce. On one occasion, during the 1850s, some enterprising Texans drove 150 head of cattle all the way to New York. The cattle drive took two years, but the profit was substantial enough to justify the trouble.

Then, in 1867, the Kansas and Pacific Railroad reached Abilene, Kansas, and cattle could be shipped to Chicago slaughterhouses, instead of driven there on the hoof. Later, as the rails moved westward, other towns in Kansas—notably Dodge City—took over from Abilene as the wild "cow towns."

Although the cowboys took their orders from the trail boss, the cook was the real keeper of the crew. Besides preparing three hot meals a day, he also served as doctor and barber. On starlit nights his last responsibility before turning in was to point the chuck wagon's tongue toward the North Star so the trail boss would have a sure compass heading the next morning.

On the trail, the chuck wagon went first, drawn by horses or oxen. Then came the lead steer, and then the herd of sometimes two or three thousand head of cattle. The trail boss and up to twenty cowhands rode ahead of, in the midst of, and behind the herd. They pushed hard for the first three or four days, covering up to thirty miles between dawn and late afternoon, in order to tire the rambunctious longhorns. After that, ten or fifteen miles was considered a good day's travel. Stampedes were the greatest hazard. One never knew when the herd would take fright. An unfamiliar sound, a bolt of lightning, or even the movement of a rabbit might send the longhorns thundering off across the boundless plains.

Indians were a constant concern. They rarely attacked the camp but were always ready to make off with stray stock. The Oklahoma Indians levied tolls for passage through their territory. Farther east, homesteaders who had fenced their land with barbed wire (invented in 1874) had to be bargained with. Sometimes they were glad to get the fertilizer and fuel left behind after the huge herds had passed; other times they refused permission to cross their properties and deadly fights often resulted.

The chuck wagon was guarded by the cowboys as if it carried bullion; and the cook was an honored citizen, even though his nicknames were hardly complimentary—"old lady," "gut robber," and the like.

The chuck wagon was the design of Charles Goodnight, the famous cattle king. A high box was built to fit the entire rear of an ordinary wagon. The box was divided into cupboards and shelves, with one large door to protect them in transit. At mealtime the door could be let down, like a tailgate, and used as the cook's worktable.

Thirty days' supplies could be carried in a chuck wagon: there were always beans, flour, cornmeal, molasses, vinegar, salt pork and bacon, coffee, and sourdough starter. These basics might be supplemented by dried apples, cheese, onions, and potatoes. Using the basic black pot, Dutch oven, and spider of colonial times, a talented cook could contrive considerable variety from these ingredients, plus beef and game. A good cook was a treasure on these hard and hunger-making journeys. Besides barbecued and fried meat, the chuck wagon cook could make a variety of cornmeal dishes; molasses or dried-apple pie; hot potato salad with bacon; hashed brown potatoes; and beans and chili. Today some of the old chuck wagon favorites, especially Tex-Mex chili and fried soda biscuits, have become part of our national cooking heritage.

There is an old saying, "Only a fool argues with a skunk, a mule, or a cook." This was especially true of the cooks on the cattle drives, for these men had earned a reputation for crankiness. If a cook wasn't cranky, said the old-time cowboys, it was because he hadn't cooked long enough. In most cases the chuck wagon cook had good reason to be cantankerous. He worked long, hard hours under difficult conditions. Often his fuel was short and what he did have was wet. And the wind or some animal usually kicked dust into the food. Most cowboy cooks took pride in their reputation for meanness and in their position as master of the chuck wagon. If a cowboy offended the cook, he was likely to find gravel in his beans, no salt on his steak, and his biscuits scorched. But if a cowboy helped the cook by bringing in fuel, he was likely to receive an extra helping of beans or a cup of coffee during nightwatch.

Cowboy Beans

1 pound dry pinto beans (2 cups)	1 6-ounce can tomato paste
7 cups cold water	1 4-ounce can green chili peppers, seeded and chopped
2 pounds smoked ham hocks	
½ cup chopped onion	2 tablespoons sugar

Rinse pinto beans thoroughly. Combine beans and cold water in kettle or Dutch oven. Bring to boiling. Simmer 2 minutes; remove from heat. Cover; let stand 1 hour. (Or, add beans to cold water; soak overnight.) Do not drain. Add ham hocks and onion. Cover; cook over low heat for 1 hour, stirring occasionally. Remove ham hocks. Remove meat from bones; dice. Discard bones. Return meat to beans. Add tomato paste, chopped chili peppers, and sugar. Cover and cook till beans are tender, about 30 minutes more, stirring occasionally. Add additional water, if needed. Makes 6 to 8 servings.

No range cook would start out on the trail without a good supply of dried beans. In fact, mealtime was often referred to as bean time. Some cooks placed their beans over a slow fire to cook at least five hours—a full day's cooking was even better. Others buried the bucket of beans in a hole, full of hot ashes, dug near the fire. If the cook was busy, cowboys who passed by would make sure the ashes were always hot.

Besides the cowboy cooks who worked on the trail, there were also cooks who fed the hands on the large ranches. Here, as on the trail, the cook reigned supreme over the cooking facilities. Usually he had more and better equipment than on the trail, and he didn't have to worry about wind, dust, or rain. The dining hall on a ranch was called the "feed trough," "nose-bag," or "swaller-an-git-out trough." The hands ate dishes like Short Ribs with Cornmeal Dumplings *and* Cowpuncher Stew *at long wooden tables. Eating was the main item of business and there was little conversation during meals. After supper, however, if the cook permitted, the boys might hang around for a storytelling session, each cowboy seeing if he could out-lie the next man.*

Leather Aprons

1 cup all-purpose flour
1/4 teaspoon salt
1/3 cup cold water

4 cups beef broth *or*
    chicken broth

Stir together flour and salt. Add enough of the cold water to form a stiff dough. Roll dough paper thin. Cut into 2-inch squares. Drop into boiling broth; cook 15 minutes, stirring often. Makes about 30.

Short Ribs with Cornmeal Dumplings

3 pounds beef short ribs,
    cut in serving-size
    pieces
Salt
Pepper
1 medium onion, cut in thin
    wedges
1 clove garlic, minced
1 28-ounce can tomatoes,
    cut up

1 12-ounce can beer
1 fresh *or* dried hot red
    chili pepper, seeded
    and chopped
2 tablespoons soy sauce
1 tablespoon sugar
3/4 teaspoon salt
1/4 teaspoon pepper
1/4 teaspoon ground nutmeg
    Cornmeal Dumplings

Trim excess fat from ribs. In Dutch oven brown short ribs on all sides; season with salt and pepper. Remove ribs. Drain off fat, reserving about 2 tablespoons. Add onion and garlic to reserved drippings; cook till onion is tender. Add tomatoes, beer, chili pepper, soy sauce, sugar, the 3/4 teaspoon salt, 1/4 teaspoon pepper, and nutmeg. Return meat to Dutch oven; bring to a boil. Reduce heat; simmer, covered, till meat is tender, 1 1/2 to 2 hours. Cool; skim off excess fat. Return to heat; bring to boiling. Meanwhile, prepare Cornmeal Dumplings.

Drop batter by rounded tablespoonfuls onto boiling stew mixture. Cover; simmer till dumplings are done, 10 to 12 minutes. Makes 6 to 8 servings.

Cornmeal Dumplings: In saucepan combine 1 cup water, 1/2 cup yellow cornmeal, and 1/2 teaspoon salt; bring to boiling. Cook and stir till thickened. Remove from heat. Stir moderate amount hot mixture into 1 beaten egg. Return to hot mixture. Stir together 1/2 cup all-purpose flour, 1 teaspoon baking powder, and dash pepper. Add to cornmeal mixture; beat well. Stir in one 7-ounce can whole kernel corn, drained.

Cowpuncher Stew

1 1/2 pounds beef stew meat,
    cut in 1-inch cubes
2 tablespoons all-purpose
    flour
1 teaspoon salt
2 tablespoons shortening
1 1/2 cups strong coffee
2 tablespoons molasses
1 clove garlic, minced
1 teaspoon salt
1 teaspoon Worcestershire
    sauce

1/2 teaspoon dried oregano,
    crushed
1/8 teaspoon cayenne
1 1/2 cups water
4 carrots, cut in 1/2-inch
    slices
4 small onions, quartered
3 medium potatoes, peeled
    and cut up
1/4 cup cold water
3 tablespoons all-purpose
    flour

Coat beef cubes with a mixture of 2 tablespoons flour and 1 teaspoon salt. In Dutch oven brown meat on all sides in hot shortening. Stir in the coffee, molasses, garlic, 1 teaspoon salt, Worcestershire, oregano, and cayenne. Cover; simmer over low heat till meat is almost tender, about 1 1/2 hours. Add the 1 1/2 cups water, carrot slices, onion quarters, and potato pieces. Simmer, covered, till vegetables are tender, about 30 minutes. Blend 1/4 cup cold water into the 3 tablespoons flour; add to stew mixture. Cook and stir till mixture is thickened and bubbly. Serve in bowls. Makes 6 to 8 servings.

The dining table on the range was anything the cowboy found usable. He used the ground, his lap, or his bedroll as a table. No one was allowed to use the cook's private workbench. The cowhand picked out his utensils, and then went from pot to pot helping himself to food and coffee. He took all he could eat at his first helping—just in case there wasn't enough for a second helping. Usually the cowboy was considerate of others, following a strict etiquette. When removing the lid from a pot for a helping, he was careful to place it so the lid wouldn't touch sand. Then he stood downwind so that any dust he kicked up wouldn't blow into someone's food. He never took the last pieces of food unless he was sure everyone was finished. It was against the rules to begin dishing up food until the cook called. It was also against custom to ride a horse into camp and to tie it to the chuck wagon—no one liked horse hair in the food. If a cowboy refilled his coffee cup and another hand called, "man at the pot," he was obliged to go around and fill any cups held out to him. Proper conduct around the wagon was as important to the cowboy as society etiquette was to his Eastern brother.

The range cook shaped soda biscuits by a different method from that used nowadays. Since he did not want to bother with a biscuit cutter, he merely pinched off pieces of dough about the size of an egg. He then rolled these pieces into balls with his hands and fried them in hot grease in the Dutch oven.

Texas-Style Chili

2½ pounds beef round steak, cubed
1 clove garlic, minced
3 tablespoons cooking oil
1 10½-ounce can condensed beef broth
1½ cups water
2 teaspoons dried oregano, crushed
2 teaspoons sugar
1 to 2 teaspoons cumin seed, crushed
½ teaspoon salt
2 bay leaves
1 4-ounce can green chili peppers, seeded and mashed
2 tablespoons cornmeal

In large skillet brown the beef cubes and garlic in hot oil; drain off excess fat. Add beef broth, water, oregano, sugar, cumin, salt, and bay leaves. Reduce heat and simmer till the meat is tender, about 1½ hours. Stir in the chili peppers and the cornmeal. Simmer 30 minutes, stirring occasionally. Remove bay leaves. Serve over corn bread, if desired. Serves 4 to 6.

Beef Pot Roast

Coat one 3- to 4-pound beef pot roast with all-purpose flour. In Dutch oven brown slowly on all sides in 2 tablespoons hot shortening. Season with salt and pepper. Remove from heat; add ½ cup water. Cover tightly; simmer till tender, about 2½ hours. Add additional water if needed to prevent sticking. If desired, the last 45 to 60 minutes of cooking add small potatoes, peeled and halved; small whole onions; and carrots, peeled and cut in 1-inch pieces. Remove roast to hot platter; skim off fat from juices. Add water to make 1½ cups liquid. Slowly blend ½ cup cold water into ¼ cup all-purpose flour; stir into juices. Cook and stir till thickened and bubbly. Simmer 2 to 3 minutes more; stir often. Season with salt and pepper. Serves 6 to 8.

Ranch Toast 'n Ham

½ cup all-purpose flour
1 tablespoon sugar
1 teaspoon baking soda
1 cup buttermilk *or* sour milk
2 eggs
6 1-inch thick slices bread
Fat for frying
6 ¼-inch thick slices ham, fried
Maple-flavored syrup

Mix flour, sugar, and baking soda. Add buttermilk and eggs; beat smooth with rotary beater. Dip bread in batter; let stand 1 minute on each side. Fry in 8-inch skillet in ¼-inch hot fat till crisp and golden, 2 to 3 minutes per side. Top toast with fried ham; serve with syrup. Makes 6 slices.

Fried Soda Biscuits

2 cups all-purpose flour
1 teaspoon baking soda
½ teaspoon salt
¼ cup shortening
¾ cup buttermilk *or* sour milk
Shortening

Stir together flour, soda, and salt. Cut in ¼ cup shortening till the mixture resembles coarse crumbs. Make a well in the dry mixture; add buttermilk or sour milk all at once. Stir just till the dough clings together. Knead gently on lightly floured surface 10 to 12 strokes. Melt enough shortening in deep skillet to give a depth of 1 inch. Heat to 375°. To shape each biscuit, cut off about 1 tablespoon of the dough and form into a ball about 1 inch in diameter; flatten slightly. Carefully place biscuits, a few at a time, in the hot shortening. Fry till golden, turning once, about 2 minutes per side. Drain on paper toweling. Serve hot. Makes about 24 biscuits.

Son-of-a-Gun-in-a-Sack

2 cups all-purpose flour
1½ cups soft bread crumbs
½ cup packed brown sugar
1 tablespoon baking soda
1 teaspoon salt
1 teaspoon ground cinnamon
¼ teaspoon ground cloves
¼ teaspoon ground nutmeg
1 cup raisins

1 cup ground suet
   (5 ounces)
½ cup chopped nuts
1 5⅓-ounce can evaporated
   milk (⅔ cup)
½ cup light molasses
   Sweetened whipped cream
   (optional)

In mixing bowl combine flour, bread crumbs, sugar, soda, salt, cinnamon, cloves, and nutmeg. Stir in raisins, suet, and nuts. Stir in milk and molasses; mix well. Arrange layers of cheesecloth to form a 16-inch square about ⅛ inch thick; set in a 1-quart bowl. Fill cheesecloth with pudding mixture; bring up sides of cheesecloth allowing room for expansion of the pudding; tie tightly with string. Place the "sack" in a colander. Place colander in kettle; add enough boiling water to cover the sack. Cover; boil gently for 2 hours. Remove colander from pan; remove cheesecloth from around pudding at once. Turn pudding, rounded side up, on plate. Let stand 30 minutes before serving. Serve warm with whipped cream, if desired. Serves 10 to 12.

When the ranch cook wanted to be especially nice to the cowhands he made a boiled pudding sometimes called Son-of-a-Gun-in-a-Sack. *Raisins or dried apples and suet were added to a soft dough. Following the old colonial method, the mass was placed in a cloth sack and boiled in a big kettle of water until done. Perhaps it got its name because it was so much trouble to make.*

Basque Shepherd's Pie

4 slices bacon
3 medium potatoes, peeled
   and thinly sliced
2 tablespoons sliced green
   onion with tops
1 tablespoon finely snipped
   parsley

¾ teaspoon salt
⅛ teaspoon dried thyme,
   crushed
   Dash pepper
4 eggs
2 tablespoons milk

In 8-inch skillet cook bacon till crisp; drain, reserving 2 tablespoons of the drippings. Crumble bacon and set aside. In same skillet combine reserved drippings, potatoes, onion, parsley, salt, thyme, and pepper. Cover tightly; cook over low heat till potatoes are barely tender, 20 to 25 minutes, stirring carefully once or twice. In small bowl beat together eggs and milk; pour over potato mixture. Cover and continue cooking over very low heat till egg is set in center, 8 to 10 minutes. With a wide spatula, loosen sides and bottom and slide potatoes out onto serving plate. (Or, serve from skillet.) Sprinkle crumbled bacon atop. Serve at once. Makes 4 servings.

Most Basques came to the West from the mountains between Spain and France in answer to a call from American sheep ranchers for herders. The lonely rigorous existence of a shepherd did not appeal to most Americans, but it was a traditional way of life for the Basques. Since these men often spent months in the mountains with their sheep, the foods they ate had to be hearty and uncomplicated. Recipes like Basque Shepherd's Pie *were prepared by many a herder forced to cook for himself.*

Baked Steak and Lima Beans

1 pound dry lima beans
6 cups water
4 slices bacon
2 pounds beef round steak,
   cut in 1-inch strips
¼ cup all-purpose flour
1 large onion, sliced

1 18-ounce can tomato juice
1 tablespoon packed brown
   sugar
1½ teaspoons salt
1 teaspoon dry mustard
⅛ teaspoon pepper

Rinse beans; add the 6 cups water. Bring to a boil; simmer 2 minutes. Remove from heat; let stand, covered, 1 hour. (Or, combine beans and water; soak overnight.) Do not drain. Cover; simmer for 25 minutes. Drain, reserving liquid. In oven-going Dutch oven, cook bacon till crisp. Drain, reserving drippings. Crumble bacon; set aside. Coat beef with flour. Brown beef in hot drippings; pour off excess fat. Stir in beans and onion. Combine tomato juice, sugar, salt, mustard, and pepper; pour over bean mixture. Bake, covered, at 325° till tender, about 1½ hours. Add some reserved bean liquid if mixture becomes dry. Stir in bacon before serving. Serves 8.

Chapter 7

Hearth to Microwave

The small size of modern ovens, especially the microwave, as compared to the open hearth of the 1700s, has drastically altered kitchen design. The space once devoted to the open hearth can now be put to better use in well-planned storage and work areas.

From fireplace to cookstove

The introduction of the cookstove greatly changed the American kitchen. Its story began in the late 1700s when an American-born experimenter and statesman, Count Rumford, demonstrated that a heat source contained in as small a space as possible provided the most efficient type of cooking. The first step toward enclosing the fire was a tablelike cooking unit set over the fire to hold pots. One such version owned by Martha Washington's granddaughter, Eliza Curtis Law, was aptly described as a "stove installed in the fireplace."[1]

Count Rumford designed a boxlike stove which completely enclosed the fire and so could be set away from the wall. Since it contained the heat source in a smaller space, it was more efficient and used less fuel than a fireplace. But it couldn't replace the brick bake oven and spit of the fireplace used in earlier days.

Count Rumford also devised a saucepan that fitted into the top of an almost funnel-shaped fire chamber. This design was improved by Phil P. Stewart, a missionary and educator. His Oberlin stove (named after the college he founded) is generally recognized as the starting point to which others added technical improvements. These included the ash chest, movable grates, and the placing of roasting and baking ovens on the top or side of the stove.

By the 1860s, the addition of the oven had rendered the fireplace superfluous for cooking. Later cookstove variations aimed for a more efficient placement of grates and flues.

The Franklin stove

An indefatigable experimenter, Benjamin Franklin designed a heating stove in the 1740s. It was set in the fireplace to utilize the unexhausted combustion gases and could raise the winter temperature in a Philadelphia room to as high as 50° Fahrenheit. It was also possible, he informs us, to prepare chocolate in his "iron fireplace."

The revolving top of the 1835 Stanley's Patent Cookstove held four raised burners and was worked by a hand crank on the side. The cylindrical oven in back was supported and heated on either side by smoke pipes from below.

Accessories for the cookstove

1. Kitchen Fire Set—including nickel-plated poker, lifter, shovel, tongs, and ornamental stand; total height is 18 inches.
2. Coal Hod—galvanized with a black japanned half-cover.
3. Coal Vase—Fifth Avenue style; black japanned; double-size.
4. Common sadiron—nonremovable handle.

MATCHES

Starting the cookstove was often one of the hardest parts in using it. The friction and safety matches developed in the 1800s were a definite improvement over earlier ones in which a sulfur-tipped splint had to be drawn through a folded, phosphorus-coated paper. Even so, the Lucifer, an early friction match, gave a shower of sparks when ignited and its label warned those with "delicate" lungs of the odor.

How to use the cookstove

Students in the late 1800s enrolled in Mrs. Mary Johnson Lincoln's Boston Cooking School received a list of no less than fifteen steps to follow when preparing the stove for cooking.

(1) Get kindlings and wood.
(2) Build fire.
(3) Regulate dampers.
    (Located under the range to let fresh air in and carbon out.)
(4) Empty ashes into sifter.
(5) Brush stove; blacken it with stove polish while it is cold.
(6) Light fire.
(7) Regulate dampers.
(8) As soon as the stove is warm and before it gets hot, polish it.
(9) Sift ashes; save half-burned coal.
(10) Add coal, wood, charcoal, or Franklin coal *gradually*. (If added too quickly, it will not ignite.)
(11) When coal is burning, shut the front damper.
(12) Regulate the heat of the fire by the damper in the stovepipe.
(13) Add more coal before the first burns out.
(14) Keep the fire at a uniform heat.
(15) Begin cooking.

To extinguish the fire: Add a little fresh coal. After two or three minutes, close the dampers.

To restart the fire: Open the dampers, remove the ashes, poke, add coal, and shake the grate.

Once a month: Clean away the ashes and soot that have accumulated at the back of the oven.

After undergoing a number of changes in shape and size, the cookstove had been improved nearly as much as possible by the late 1800s. This Garland stove manufactured in 1888 by the Michigan Stove Company, Detroit, featured an elevated warming oven in addition to the lower baking oven. Its six burners were flat rather than raised.

THE MAN WITH TWO NAMES

Known as Count Rumford or as Benjamin Thompson, the American-born inventor and statesman was a man of many interests and accomplishments.

As a youth he was apprenticed to a storekeeper in Salem, Massachusetts, where he developed an interest in chemical experiments and engraving. He served briefly in the New Hampshire militia, but was accused of being a Tory and fled to Boston where evacuating British troops sent him to England with important dispatches.

His reward was an appointment to the Foreign Office and a return trip to the colonies. There his inventive talents were put to use in the building of Fort Golgotha on the site of a former cemetery in New York. The gravestones were removed and used for the fireplaces and ovens. As a result, each loaf of bread baked on the stones bore the imprint of the inscriptions in reverse on the bottom crust.

At the age of thirty he retired. After receiving his knighthood a year later, he went to Austria where his social work with the industrial classes led to the development of the cookstove and to the founding of public soup kitchens. These featured an indirectly heated oven in which saucepans were set into sunken openings and so warmed by heat and smoke passing through the branching arrangement of flues.

For his accomplishments—he also reorganized the Bavarian army—he was made a count of the Holy Roman Empire. He chose the name Count Rumford from his wife's native home, now Concord, New Hampshire.

Coffee drinkers of today should also credit Count Rumford as the designer of many of the styles of percolators still in use. These were included in his essay, "Of the Excellent Qualities of Coffee and the Art of Making It in the Highest Perfection," along with several recipes and an opinion that coffee should become the beverage of the masses.

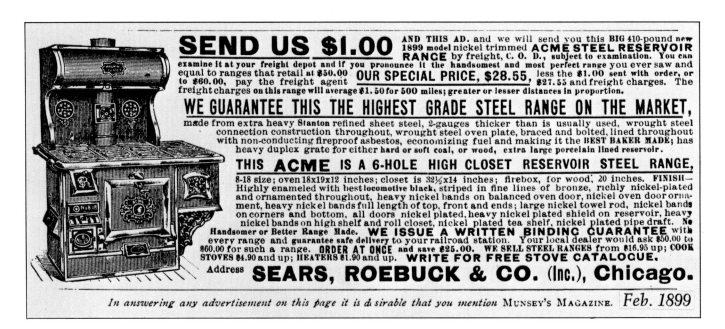

Gas ranges

Coal gas was quickly accepted as lighting fuel during the late 1800s, but not so as a cooking fuel. Promotion dinners featuring gas-cooked meals attempted to convert people to gas cooking, but only a few hotels and clubs installed the new stoves.

A forerunner of the American-developed tabletop range of the 1930s was shown at the Great Exhibition of 1851 in London. Its flat range top was cut by circular burners and set over the broiler and oven.

About 30 years later another English company displayed over 300 appliances that used gas.

Combination coal and gas ranges were still offered after World War I. The white porcelain enamel, eventually to envelop the entire unit, covered the range top and backsplash.

When gas ranges finally appeared to be coming into their own in the 1930s, the electric range emerged and stiffened the competition.

The physics of cooking

The development of the stove simply verifies Count Rumford's axiom that a closely contained heat source is more efficient.

As the source became smaller — from the enclosed fire to the gas jet to the electric current through a wire — the entire cooking unit became smaller. This in turn brought changes to the design of the kitchen itself.

"For eight years we have been manufacturing the Jewel. We were among the first to appreciate that gas was to be the fuel of the future. Is the use of gas for cooking purposes an extraordinary luxury? No, it is an economical necessity. The popular prejudice is gradually giving way."—Jewel Gas Stove Catalogue, 1889.[2]

The Garland Gas Range of 1910 had four burners with side oven and broiler.

Standard Electric range of 1913 had only two burners and an insulated warming pot on the range top. The oven unit was placed above the burners.

They've come a long way

Early gas and electric ranges copied the design of the cookstove. Even though no fire was needed under it, many of the new models stood over empty space on four fragile looking legs and viewers wondered if they were trying to imitate rare French antiques. Such designs did little to promote their sales.

Eventually the oven was placed beneath the burners. The legs became shorter until they disappeared altogether and a new look emerged to suit the new look of the kitchen.

As the design changed, so did the materials. The black cast iron gave way to gleaming white porcelain enamel casings. These were easier to clean and also offered the possibility of work space next to the burners and flush with the countertop.

In response to the demand for organized kitchens, more companies started marketing entire kitchen units in which their ranges blended into the counters and total kitchen design.

Today's cook can choose her range from a variety of colors and finishes. It can be built-in or freestanding. Self-cleaning ovens and ceramic cook tops have also been added.

Cooking by magic

The possibility of cooking by electricity appeared incredible to most viewers of the first electric kitchen exhibited at the Chicago World's Fair in 1893. They wondered how anything that did not have a flame could provide heat enough to cook meats or bake pies or bread. And wouldn't the foods have an "electric flavor?"

Still the electric range gained acceptance much more quickly than had the gas one, largely because the gas industry had already opened consumer's minds to the possibility of new cooking methods.

Public demonstration dinners might have convinced the public that electric cooking was safe. But they could not persuade them on cost. Besides being expensive, early electricity was not very reliable since currents and voltages varied with each household. So the total acceptance of electric cooking was delayed until standardization could catch up with the concept.

Better heat control

Today's automatic time and temperature ovens are refinements of the 1915 invention of an oven thermometer for regulating heat.

The quick-cooking microwave oven is the ultimate today in modern technology. Scientists working with radar during World War II noticed that some objects became very hot when exposed to the microwaves used as signals. Further experimenting showed that microwaves, which are actually high frequency radio waves, could be generated in a vacuum tube, or magnetron. When food is placed near the magnetron, the microwave energy penetrates the food causing its molecules to vibrate against each other. The resulting friction creates heat within the food making it cook quickly.

The problem of human rights

During the mid 1800s, most middle-class women wanted a house full of servants—since nobody "in society" did her own work. But servants in America did not want to remain servants all their lives, as their counterparts in Europe expected to do, they aimed higher. As the number of domestic helpers decreased, the time became right for the development and acceptance of mechanical "workers."

The Electrochef Electric Range of 1930 had six burners with ovens on each side.

The iceman's wagon was a familiar sight to nearly five generations of Americans as he made his daily deliveries about town.

The Leonard Icebox of 1881 was one of the first practical refrigerators in America.

Iceboxes

After the stove, the second most useful object in our kitchens is surely the refrigerator. The first ones were called iceboxes because they were lidless boxes containing a lump of ice. Later the top was closed and a separate compartment held the ice. The melting ice flowed through a pipe to a pan underneath the food compartment.

Both chest-style and upright iceboxes were available. Some featured walls insulated with ground cork and shelves made of slate, while others offered built-in water coolers. A few models even boasted matching sideboards and china closets.

The family-size icebox held ninety to one hundred pounds of ice. The iceman made regular deliveries of blocks of ice wrapped for insulation in thick newspaper or an old blanket. Occasionally the icebox had to be scoured and scalded.

What do you call an iceless icebox?

Four or five generations of icemen came and went before the first iceless icebox (called, of course, a refrigerator) was ready for home use. The principle of mechanical refrigeration developed from work done by Michael Faraday and, later, Ferdinand Carré. A prototype was shown at the Great Exhibition of 1862 in London, but viewers considered it a marvel, a fantasy, not a useful invention.

Gas and electric models were introduced in the United States in the early 1900s. Electric ones depended on the development of a small motor to make their size practical, but gas models required no motor since they worked on the principle of absorption.

As technology cut production costs and improved quality, sales of refrigerators were boosted. By 1923 there were twenty thousand refrigerators in the United States. But the numbers multiplied quickly and by 1943, refrigerators were as much a part of the American kitchen as gas or electric ranges and running water.

Streamlining

The refrigerator came at a time when "streamlining" was the pet word of businessmen as well as homemakers. Work processes were becoming more organized, while appliances, and even automobiles were designed with fewer flourishes, giving a smoother line.

Gas and electric companies had modernized their ranges by making the range surface countertop level. They had also discovered the advantages and popularity of easy-to-clean porcelain enamel casings.

Early refrigerators were still the proverbial sore thumb, since they had the same dark wood exterior as the iceboxes they were trying to replace. As more compact cooling methods were found, refrigerators also became streamlined and were given a porcelain enamel finish, later available in a choice of colors. Sizes and designs varied to suit the largest family kitchen to the smallest office or dorm-room minimodel.

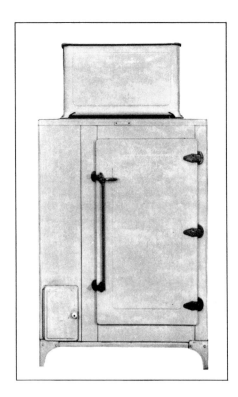

The millionth refrigerator manufactured by the General Electric Company was gold-plated and presented to Henry Ford in 1931 during a national radio broadcast.

Instead of large, disorganized kitchens, Catherine Beecher recommended specific work areas for preparation and cleanup. Each included storage space. Her idea of the continuous work surface is demonstrated by the flour barrel lid that fits flush with adjoining surfaces and by the molding board which forms another preparation area when turned over. Her concern for an organized kitchen reflected the New England Puritan's tendency to view homemaking as a vocation.

Efficiency enters the kitchen

As appliances became smaller and more efficient it was only natural that the total kitchen design should undergo a transformation also.

One of the earliest to offer a solution was Catherine Beecher whose ideas during the 1860s were nearly one hundred years ahead of her time. She introduced the idea that the kitchen was the core of the house around which other rooms were arranged. Included in her plan was the concept of continuous work surfaces coordinated with standard-sized built-in cupboards and shelves. She deplored the disarranged kitchens of the time and promoted instead the plan of a cook's galley on a steamship—quite literally, shipshape, with everything arranged to save steps and space.

About fifty years later, another woman, Christine Frederick furthered these ideas in her magazine articles on "bringing the science of efficiency to the home" which she expanded into a book in 1913. In it she translated the efficiency steps that had proved useful to industry into terms applicable to the kitchen. Her premise in organizing the work process was to set up an orderly arrangement of utensils and foodstuffs so that fewer motions were needed.

A reformer in the kitchen

The daughter of a New England minister and the sister of Harriet Beecher Stowe, author of *Uncle Tom's Cabin,* Catherine Beecher was a forward-looking woman. Her ideas are readily accepted today, but to nineteenth century audiences, they were new.

During a time when most middle-class women dreamed of having many servants, Catherine Beecher predicted a decline in numbers of domestic help and suggested that family members share household responsibilities whenever possible.

In a time when women's status was hardly considered, she urged that "domestic science" courses be offered in all schools. By receiving proper training for their "profession," women would have more self-assurance and confidence and so be able to make more contributions to society.

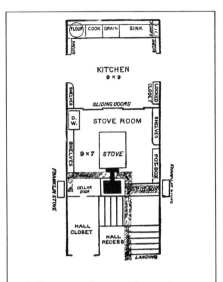

A floor plan designed by Catherine Beecher in 1869 placed the cast-iron range in its own room separated by glazed sliding doors.

INDUSTRY ENTERS THE KITCHEN

During the 1930s, gas and electric companies became interested in kitchen organization. Efficiency expert Lillian M. Gilbreth found that manufacturers did not know what the housewife needed. To help find out, special cooking institutes were opened by General Electric and Westinghouse. Expert staffs made time-and-motion studies. Today most companies dealing with kitchen-related items have a home economics staff to act as a go-between for consumers and designers. The American homemaker has changed since Gilbreth found that, "she herself seldom knows what she wants, much less what she needs." [3]

"The kitchen is the most carefully planned room in the house. It is fairly lined with built-in conveniences, and there is always a dining alcove, to save steps and time." Originally printed in *Better Homes and Gardens,* February 1925.

Change in cookware and kitchen utensils kept pace with the major appliances. New materials, mechanizations, and finally electricity brought improvements.

Tinware

Early cooking pots were available only in heavy cast iron or expensive copper or brass. So when the new lightweight tinware appeared in the mid 1700s it was quickly accepted. For a time, however, the best tinware had to be imported from England which made it costly. Tinsmiths soon immigrated to New England and set up shops, often in their homes. When their stocks built up they would take to the road to peddle their wares just as others peddled their family's surplus eggs or produce. The tin peddler, however, had a nonperishable product and soon expanded his territory and his products, to the dismay of local shopkeepers.

In 1883 a Spice Box Set cost 75 cents.

"Scuttles and cans,
buttons and bows,
I'll cure your ills,
and cheer your woes."[4]

So sang the peddler with his wagon or backpack full of useful and interesting items. Just as important, however, was the news he brought and the tales he told as he unpacked his treasures and offered them for trade.

In return for the wanted spices, medicines, gadgets, or whatever, family members offered feathers, rags (white ones were most valuable), or products of their own making.

America's standard cupboard-filler, the tin can, was accepted much more readily here in the United States than in England where the cans tended to rust in the damper climate.

STOP-A-LEEK

Repairs instantaneously without dirt or trouble

Granite Ware, Tin Ware, Iron, Copper, etc.

Mends from 75 to 125 leaks.

Simply hold part of vessel to be repaired over moderate heat "such as candle flame," apply STOP-A-LEAK to the inside of vessel by rubbing gently until enough is melted to stop the leak. Then remove the vessel from the heat and the solder will become as hard as iron and hold indefinitely.

No household should be without this invaluable article. It will pay for itself the first time used. Saves worry and expense.

3 oz.

Repair kits were a popular and, sometimes, often needed item.

Shiny new aluminum

Aluminum had been around since the 1880s when cheaper electrical methods of production had made it affordable. But nobody was interested. Manufacturers had to face the problem that aluminum was so light and so different from anything people were accustomed to that they resisted its use. Then by the late 1920s, homemakers seemed ready for something new in the cookware they used daily. The shiny newness of aluminum plus the fact that it didn't chip or rust suddenly made it universally desirable.

Britannia

In the 1850s a new alloy called Britannia was developed. It had the appearance of pewter but had a more silvery sheen and could be silver-plated. Near the end of the century, as more homemakers set their hearts on owning silver, the manufacturers responded to this demand by taking plain Britannia and silver-plating it.

Graniteware

Iron cookware enjoyed a return to popularity during the late 1800s and early 1900s because of a process developed by a German immigrant. In 1874 Jacob J. Vollrath started manufacturing porcelain-enameled cast iron. These utensils were cheap, sturdy, and available in speckled dark blue or gray.

Samples shown were extolled at the Philadelphia Centennial Exposition of 1876 as having all the advantages of glass plus the strength of metal. Variations soon appeared named agate-ware, graniteware, and enamelware.

Agate Iron Ware was one of the brands of graniteware made around the turn of the century. The name was especially suitable since the mottled design resembled the mineral agate. Many styles of cookware were available plus toilet articles, candlesticks and cruet sets.

Gadgets for every task

Mechanizing the common hand tasks involved in food preparation offered a gold mine of ideas to the inventor. One of the earliest gadgets to appear on the market was the mechanical apple parer. It is said that Eli Whitney began his career as an inventor at the age of thirteen by devising one in the 1770s. They became very popular since nearly every family who could do so had apple trees.

Mechanization of America

The discovery of electricity and the development of mass production technology were not exclusive to America. The same facts were known in Europe. But the new processes were not urgent there because they had a sufficient labor force. On the other hand, the size of America and the lack of servant labor demanded substitutes be found for manpower.

The new mechanical devices had to be simple and reliable since repairmen were hardly just a phone call away. The development of interchangeable parts led to mass production and lower prices. This, of course, also brought increased availability and sales.

In addition, Americans chose to promote home gadgets differently. This was noticed as early as 1851 when a German attending the Great Exhibition in London observed that "American domestic equipment breathes the spirit of comfort and fitness for purpose."[5] This was in contrast to the British attempts to promote new products as something else; for example, stoves disguised as furniture.

Technology catches up

One factor that hindered the acceptance of electrical appliances was the lack of a standardized electric current. The amount of power available to each user tended to vary greatly, since each had his own generator.

After the development of turbine and hydroelectric generators in the early 1900s, it was possible to set up power supply points with well-planned distribution networks, so that a standardized current could be supplied to all users no matter where they lived in the United States.

This 1895 cartoon predicts an electric "do-all" gadget by the 1920s.

IT'S ELECTRIC!

The pride of a modern kitchen (in addition to its cook, that is) is probably its electrical appliances. The invention of a small electrical motor late in the 1880s provided the power source needed for the development of a number of mechanical devices. By the end of the century, many manufacturers were offering a variety of pieces of electrical equipment including kettles, saucepans, frying pans, roasters, hot plates, ovens, coffee grinders, and toasters, as well as heaters and fans.

A drill for liquids – the eggbeater

One of the simplest and most useful of the new mechanical devices was the eggbeater. It has been compared to the drill, except that it drills liquids rather than solids. Earlier cooks had used a fork, wire whisk, narrow-slotted wooden paddle, or small broom.

One of the first crank-style beaters to appear was the Dover, patented in 1878. Well-advertised competitors' models followed. All were similarly made with tin blades and heavy iron cranks and handles. A lighter weight, all-tin model was patented in 1926. Some were even fitted with a tin cover and a glass bowl or measuring cup.

Wooden, push-handled whippers, patented in the 1900s, were designed to be held in the fist and pushed up and down. They were not too practical, however, as it was too easy to tip the bowl.

A later galvanized wire beater was operated by a thumb lever on the side which caused the spindle blades to turn one way and then the other.

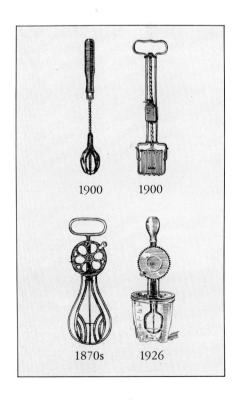

1900   1900

1870s   1926

The New Americans

Chapter 8

The New Americans

In three successive waves they came—tired, often impoverished, the immigrants crowded together in the early wooden sailing vessels or in large ships with such hopeful names as *Restaurationen.* These brave souls left home and family for a chance to work, to put down roots, to gain dignity, and to dream dreams.

Between 1820 and 1919 more than 30 million of these hopeful entrants stepped ashore. The first wave occurred immediately after the Napoleonic Wars and lasted for forty-five years (from 1815 through 1859); the second, shorter but more intense, was from 1860 to 1890; and the last and largest known migration ever (15 million people) took place between 1890 and 1920.

They were a motley group. Germans and Austrians (8.5 million of them) came to escape the harsh winter of 1829–1830, the rise of anti-Semitism, or the crop failures of the forties. Russian Jews arrived in long coats, clutching large strips of twisted cotton in which their meager belongings were gathered. Over 4 million Irish, their usually ruddy faces pale and drawn, came ashore, desperate for food (something they had little of after the potato famine) and, though they had been farmers, the majority were never to farm again. Three million-plus Italians, typified by black suits, white shirts, and colored blankets wrapped around their shoulders, made the journey determined to make a good living here and eventually send for the rest of the family. And 2 million English came with their expectations, fleeing their land because the Enclosure Act had resulted in exorbitant food prices, lowered farm wages, and an end to shareholding.

In smaller numbers came Belgians, Czechs, Hungarians, Chinese, Japanese, Indians (from Asia), and blacks (from Africa).

America meant many things to these diverse peoples. Some, fleeing persecution for religious beliefs, came seeking to overcome spiritual starvation. Others had heard of the "good life" in America and were anxious to try it out. But the overwhelming majority of the immigrants came for reasons related to food—or the lack of it. Initially, the doubling of the European population (brought about by an increased knowledge of medicine), a lowered mortality rate, effective development of crop yield, and a move toward concentrated agricultural production prompted many European farmers to turn from the land. And, too, the Industrial Revolution, so dramatically altering life in Europe and later in the United States, encouraged even more small farmers to abandon their farms for a job in a factory. If these weren't reasons enough to leave one's homeland, the series of crop failures in the mid-nineteenth century was the clincher. The potato famine in Ireland in 1846 was followed by three consecutive years of blight. This same blight took its toll in Germany from 1846 through 1855. Out of work and with little prospect of better times, they swarmed across the waters.

But it takes money to emigrate. Though early fares for passage were prohibitive for the bankrupt farmer or agricultural laborer, the increase in the eastward cargo trade and the centralizing of trading ports quickly brought about a scaling down of fares. Liverpool became the major port for emigrants from the British Isles; Le Havre, Bremen, and Hamburg vied for the German, Swiss, and Scandinavian trade. In 1816 the Liverpool-to-New-York fee was twelve pounds. Thirty years later, it was three pounds.

American travel companies, established by the middle of the century, had already adopted the "go now, pay later" concept, enabling adventurous young men to come ahead of the rest of the family and pay for their passage out of their American wages. In this way hundreds of thousands of Europeans made their way to their adopted land.

In their heads, in their hearts, in their way of life, the immigrants carried their food heritage — a way of cooking unique to a certain region — or even village — of one country, a special way of using an herb or spice, or a rare manner of combining ingredients. Lamb cooked on a spit — shish kebab from Turkey; a thick stew with vegetables, sour cream, beef or veal, and paprika — goulash from Hungary; lettuce, tomatoes, onion, vinegar, oregano, pepper, feta cheese, anchovy fillets, and ripe olives — salad from Greece; a mixture of shrimp, bean sprouts, water chestnuts, chicken broth, and soy sauce — chow mein from China; and spiced tomato sauces cascading over mounds of spaghetti from Italy — all these dishes, plus a multitude of others, added to a cuisine fast becoming the most cosmopolitan in the world.

The early newcomers, most of whom came to the United States unsolicited, tended to move where they could be guaranteed a job: the Welsh to the anthracite mines in East Pennsylvania; the Cornishmen from England to the copper, iron, or lead mines in Wisconsin, Illinois, and Michigan; the English Staffordshire potters to the potteries in East Liverpool, Ohio or Trenton, New Jersey; the Germans (in the ships from Le Havre following the cotton trade) to the Mississippi Valley; and the Irish (replacing the cargoes of New Brunswick timber delivered to Britain) to the New England States. Later, however, immigrants (from Austria, Hungary, Italy, Russia, Greece, Romania, and Turkey lured here by labor recruiters offering free passage) settled in the large cities in the East and Midwest. They avoided the farms and took work as unskilled laborers. And because of their unfamiliarity with the new life, they tended to group together, and by doing so preserved almost intact their great food traditions.

A sizable number of Poles, Bohemians, and Hungarians grouped together in Chicago; an equally large number of Italians and Jews settled in a part of New York City (today, New York has the largest Jewish population of any city in the world); the Chinese and Japanese opted for San Francisco and Los Angeles from where they set out to work as laborers on the transcontinental railroads; and the Irish molded Boston into the image they sought. Mid-twentieth-century surges of immigrants would be influenced by other conditions — the Hungarians who fled their native country in the 1956 uprising, the Czechs a decade later, the Koreans, and the Vietnamese, all tended to settle in an area where a common bond in language and custom could offer some security in a time of vast uncertainty.

When immigrants arrived at their destination, they all had first to find a place to live (often a single room in a ghetto shared with another family). The next step was to find some way to earn money. Then came the search for ingredients to prepare the foods they knew. They bartered for or bought, with what precious little money they had, the ingredients that were available. In more cases than not, the foodstuffs that ended up on their tables were not those that they had grown up with. So these hearty cooks improvised. They took their basic recipes and added an ingredient here, substituted an ingredient there, and by so doing helped create the American cuisine that we all know today.

A most trying aspect of the immigrant's journey across the sea was preparing meals on board ship. One new American describes the conditions. "It is an axiom of domestic science that no kitchen is large enough to hold two women, but around this fire a score or more of determined housewives pursued their different culinary purposes. One would be boiling coffee, another preparing a stew, a third with a bowl of batter in hand baking pancakes, when a sudden lurch of the vessel would mix coffee, stew, and batter into an unpremeditated combination. Since those awaiting their turn were impatient, the parent was obliged to take the mess to the waiting family as it was, nature perhaps adding a finishing touch by flavoring it with a dash of salt spray. Very often this joggling of elbows caused a serious physical encounter. No matter how dull life might be elsewhere on board, there was always fighting around the stove....Under such conditions breakfast was not ready until noon and dinner until night; and before the end of the journey both breakfast and dinner might be several days late."[1]

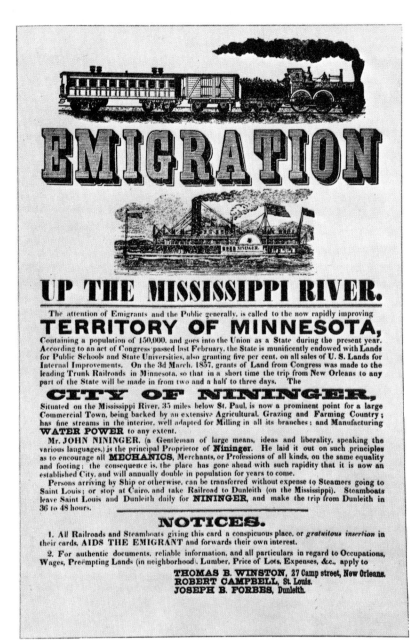

Posters proclaimed the opportunities that awaited immigrants out West.

In Search of Prosperity and a New Life

The New Americans came from all over the world—England, Germany, Hungary, Italy, and China to name a few countries—in search of prosperity and a new life. Most of them, after the journey across the ocean, landed at immigrant processing centers such as Ellis Island. From there, it was on to coastal cities such as New York or San Francisco. Gradually the immigrants worked their way inland and settled all over the country. The life the immigrants found in the United States was not the "streets paved with gold" fairy tale they had been led to expect. But these hearty souls learned to cope with the difficult work, the strange language, and the foreign culture they encountered. While learning Yankee ways, they also taught Americans a great deal about their varied cultures. Before long the ethnic festivals, foods, music, and art of the new Americans was a treasured part of the American scene.

Waiting on Ellis Island for the last boat trip before beginning a new life in America.

Soon-to-be Americans arriving in Omaha, Nebraska, waited in a special part of the depot for a Union Pacific train to the Black Hills.

One of the first jobs many new Americans found was selling foods from carts.

Immigrant passengers headed for America were often crowded together on board ship.

222

Four Cuisines
from the British Isles

The immigrants wrote to their relatives back home to regale them with stories of the strange ways of this altogether strange country. One woman from Yorkshire discusses the food she found in Illinois in 1831. "The Illinois settlers live somewhat differently from the English peasantry; the former have only three meals a day, and not much variety in them; bread, butter, coffee, and bacon, are always brought to the table, but fresh meat is a rarity, and is never obtained as in England by going to the butcher for it. In Illinois the farmers all kill their own cattle, and salt what is not used immediately; sometimes, however, they distribute portions among their neighbours, with the view of receiving as much again when they kill theirs. It is by no means uncommon for an old settler to have a couple of fowls, ducks, a goose, or a turkey to dinner; and generally speaking, everybody has plenty of plain good food....Indian corn is the only winter food used in Illinois..."[2]

The English have been called the Invisible Immigrants because they came here speaking English (although not "American"), have many similar traditions, and usually have had little difficulty making the transition from British subject to American citizen. Not only were a majority of the people of the original thirteen colonies English in ancestry, but about 4.5 million Britons, including those from Scotland and Wales, have disembarked since 1820. Surprisingly, the peak year was 1888.

Scots and Welsh, although officially included in the English statistics, do not, of course, wish to be considered English. Both have been coming to America in small but significant numbers since colonial days. The Welsh usually turn to farming and stockbreeding, while mining and skilled factory work, especially in textile mills, have attracted the Scot.

As for the Irish, 4.25 million of them appeared on these shores between 1820 and 1920, the largest number of immigrants from any one country — and a tiny country, at that, even smaller than the State of Maine. The first arrivals included some who could buy a little property. After 1846 if anyone could manage to board a ship, he came, fleeing the terrible potato famine. The peak years were the 1850s, when more than a million Irish crossed the ocean. The majority stayed in the port cities in which they landed, partly because life was easier among their fellow countrymen and partly because they lacked funds to go any farther. The men, if they could, got jobs working on canals, roads, and railroads.

Between 1880 and 1930, the Irish continued to pour in by the thousands but they were vastly outnumbered by people from southern and central Europe. Meantime, many of the earlier arrivals had managed to climb the social and economic ladder. They continued to do so until every area of American life — financial, industrial, intellectual, political, and more — numbered Irish-Americans among those at the top.

Sharing the cultural and culinary heritage of both the Irish and the Scots, but politically different from either are the Scotch-Irish. Originally from the lowlands of Scotland, they went to northern Ireland in the seventeenth century and were the ancestors of the present-day Ulster Protestants. In the eighteenth century, because of political unrest, crop failures, and discriminatory English laws that made it difficult to succeed in the linen trade, thousands of Scotch-Irish emigrated to America.

All of these immigrants from the British Isles added their traditional recipes to the American cuisine. The English brought foods typical of every region of their nation. From Yorkshire came beef with Yorkshire pudding; from Cornwall, beef pasties; from the shops of London, fish and chips; and from the colonies in India, mulligatawny. The Irish made famous their stew and taught Americans to enjoy everything from colcannon to Irish coffee. The Scots served up bowls of Scotch broth and contributed finnan haddie and oatcakes to the Yankee repertoire. The Welsh, not to be outdone, contributed bara brith (a fruit bread), Welsh rarebit, and Welsh white cookies to their American neighbors. The recipes on the following pages show the great variety of the four cuisines from the British Isles.

Angels on Horseback

8 slices bacon
16 shucked oysters
4 slices bread

Butter, softened
Lemon wedges

Cut bacon in half crosswise. Partially cook, drain. Wrap one piece of bacon around each oyster; secure with wooden picks. Place oysters on a rack in shallow baking pan. Bake at 450° till bacon is crisp, about 10 minutes. Toast bread; spread with butter. Cut diagonally into 4 triangles. Place one oyster on each toast triangle. Serve hot with lemon wedges. Makes 16.

Mulligatawny

¼ cup finely chopped onion
½ teaspoon curry powder
2 tablespoons shortening
1 cup diced cooked chicken
1 tart apple, peeled, cored, and chopped
¼ cup chopped carrot
¼ cup chopped celery
2 tablespoons chopped green pepper

3 tablespoons all-purpose flour
4 cups chicken broth
1 16-ounce can tomatoes, cut up
1 tablespoon snipped parsley
2 teaspoons lemon juice
1 teaspoon sugar
2 whole cloves

In large saucepan cook onion and curry powder in shortening till onion is tender. Stir in chicken, chopped apple, carrot, celery, and green pepper. Cook, stirring occasionally, till vegetables are crisp-tender, about 5 minutes. Sprinkle flour over chicken-vegetable mixture; stir to mix well. Stir in broth, undrained tomatoes, parsley, lemon juice, sugar, cloves, ¼ teaspoon salt, and dash pepper. Bring chicken-vegetable mixture to boiling, stirring occasionally. Reduce heat and simmer, covered, 30 minutes. Makes 6 servings.

Mulligatawny, *meaning "pepper water," was first eaten by British and Scottish soldiers serving in India. This hearty soup, flavored with curry powder (as you might expect from its birthplace) arrived here by way of the descendants of those fighting men.*

Beef with Yorkshire Pudding

1 8-pound beef standing rib roast
4 eggs

2 cups all-purpose flour
2 cups milk
1 teaspoon salt

Place roast, fat side up, in a shallow roasting pan. Season with salt and pepper. Insert meat thermometer avoiding bone. Roast, uncovered, at 325° till meat thermometer registers 140° for rare, 160° for medium, and 170° for well-done. (Allow about 3¼ hours for rare, 4 hours for medium, and 4¾ hours for well-done.) Remove meat from pan. Cover; keep warm. Reserve ¼ cup meat drippings. Increase oven temperature to 400°. Combine eggs, flour, milk, and salt. Beat 1½ minutes with electric mixer. Pour *half* the reserved drippings into *each* of two 9x9x2-inch baking pans. Pour *half* the batter into each pan. Bake at 400° for 30 minutes. Serve with roast. Serves 12.

Beef with Yorkshire Pudding *is perhaps the best very English dish. Two immigrant groups are definitely known to have brought it with them to America. One was the cooks of the English families who settled the colonies of the Carolinas and Maryland, and the other group was the English-Canadians who crossed the border into our northern states.*

Toad in the Hole

2 slices bacon
½ pound fresh pork sausage (8 or 9 links), cut in ½-inch pieces

1 cup all-purpose flour
1 teaspoon baking powder
1½ cups milk
3 eggs

Cook bacon till crisp; drain and set aside 2 tablespoons drippings. Crumble bacon; set aside. Brown sausage in same skillet; drain. Meanwhile, mix flour, baking powder, and 1 teaspoon salt. Add milk and eggs; beat till smooth. Spread bacon drippings in 10x6x2-inch baking dish. Place sausage in dish; top with bacon. Pour batter over. Bake at 400° for 30 to 35 minutes. Serves 4.

Toad in the Hole *is an adaptation of an old English entrée called froise which was prepared by dipping bacon in a batter and deep-frying it. Later, batter was poured over bits of leftover meat from the Sunday roast beef and the mixture was baked in the oven. Today almost any type of meat is used.*

A specialty of several national restaurant chains, *Fish and Chips* is now almost as big a favorite here as in England. But they don't taste truly English—or, at any rate, Londonish—unless you serve them in a cone made of newspaper lined with waxed paper.

A pasty is a whole meal wrapped up in pastry. It was brought to the United States by Cornishmen who came to work in the iron and copper mines in Michigan's Upper Peninsula. Before the age of the lunch pail, the miners carried their pasties to work in a cotton pouch called a crib bag. The miner reheated his pasty on a shovel held over the candle he wore on his hat.

Cornish Beef Pasties

3 cups all-purpose flour
1½ teaspoons salt
1 cup shortening
7 to 8 tablespoons cold
    water
• • •
2 or 3 medium potatoes
1 pound beef round steak,
    cut in ¼-inch cubes

1 medium turnip, peeled and
    cut in ¼-inch cubes
    (¾ cup)
½ cup finely chopped onion
1½ teaspoons salt
¼ teaspoon pepper
½ cup catsup (optional)
¼ cup water (optional)

In a large mixing bowl stir together thoroughly the flour and 1½ teaspoons salt. With a pastry cutter cut in the shortening till the mixture resembles coarse crumbs. Using the 7 to 8 tablespoons cold water gradually add to dry ingredients, 1 tablespoon at a time, tossing the ingredients with a fork till the mixture holds together. Form into a ball. If desired, cover and chill the dough 1 hour.

Meanwhile, prepare the meat-vegetable filling. Peel and coarsely chop the potatoes. In a bowl combine the cubed beef, chopped potato, cubed turnip, finely chopped onion, 1½ tea-

spoons salt, and the pepper. Set aside.

Divide the dough into five equal portions. On a lightly floured surface roll out each portion of dough to a 9-inch circle. Place about 1 cup meat-vegetable filling on one half of each circle of dough; fold the pastry over the filling to make a half-circle. Using tines of a fork seal the pastry edge; cut slits in the pastry for escape of steam. Carefully transfer pasties to an ungreased baking sheet. Bake pasties at 400° till golden brown about 45 minutes. If desired, in a small saucepan combine catsup and the ¼ cup water; heat through. Serve with pasties. Serves 5.

Fish and Chips

1 pound fresh *or* frozen
   fish fillets
1 pound baking potatoes,
   peeled (3 medium)
   Fat for frying
1/4 cup all-purpose flour
1/2 teaspoon salt

2 tablespoons water
1 tablespoon cooking oil
1 egg yolk
1 stiffly beaten egg white
1/4 cup all-purpose flour
   Salt
   Malt vinegar

Thaw frozen fish; cut into serving-size pieces. Pat dry with paper toweling. Cut potatoes in uniform strips slightly larger than French fries. Fry a few at a time in deep hot fat (375°) till golden, 5 to 6 minutes. Remove; drain and keep warm. In a bowl stir together 1/4 cup flour and salt. Make a well in center of dry ingredients. Add water, oil, and egg yolk; beat smooth. Fold in egg white. Dip fish in 1/4 cup flour and then in batter. Fry fish in deep hot fat (375°) till golden brown, 1 1/2 to 2 minutes on each side. To serve, season fish and chips with salt and drizzle with malt vinegar. Makes 4 servings.

Fish and Chips *became popular in England because factory workers needed cheap food that could be eaten quickly. Some restaurants featured combinations such as hot pies and peas or sausage and mashed potatoes, but fish and chips held its own because it could be eaten in the shop or on the street or at home. The immigrants in America brought a bit of England with them—their fondness for fish and chips.*

Lemon Curd Tarts

1 1/2 cups sifted all-purpose
   flour
1/2 teaspoon salt
1/2 cup shortening
4 to 5 tablespoons cold
   water
3 well-beaten eggs

1 1/4 cups sugar
1/2 teaspoon grated lemon
   peel (set aside)
1/3 cup lemon juice
1/4 cup butter *or* margarine
   Whipped cream
   Toasted slivered almonds

Stir together flour and salt; cut in shortening till pieces are size of small peas. Sprinkle *1 tablespoon* water over part of mixture. Gently toss with fork; push to side of bowl. Repeat till all is moistened. Form into ball. Flatten on floured surface by pressing with edge of hand three times in both directions. Roll from center to edge till 1/8 inch thick. Cut into 3-inch circles. Fit into small tart pans or fluted gelatin molds; press out bubbles. Prick dough. (Or, fit circles over inverted muffin pans. Pinch to make 4 corners; prick.) Bake at 450° till golden, 8 to 10 minutes. In saucepan mix eggs, sugar, lemon juice, and butter. Cook and stir over low heat till thick, about 15 minutes. Remove from heat; stir in peel. Chill. Fill shells with 2 to 3 teaspoons filling. Chill. Top with cream and almonds. Makes 30.

Shake Rag Street in Mineral Point, Wisconsin, was named after the custom of Cornish women shaking their dishrags from their kitchen doors to tell their families to "come and get it." It meant "the fire is glowing and the meal is on the table." The finishing touch to the meal might be Lemon Curd Tarts.

Crumpets

1 cup all-purpose flour
1 package active dry yeast
2/3 cup milk
1 tablespoon butter

1/4 teaspoon salt
1 egg
1/4 cup butter

In a small mixing bowl combine 1/2 *cup* of the flour and the yeast. In a saucepan heat milk, 1 tablespoon butter, and the salt just till warm (115-120°), stirring constantly. Add to dry ingredients in mixing bowl; add egg. Beat at low speed of electric mixer for 1 minute, scraping sides of bowl constantly. Stir in the remaining flour; beat till smooth. Cover and let stand in warm place till double (about 1 hour). In a large skillet or on griddle melt *half* of the remaining butter. Lightly brush egg poacher or crumpet rings with butter; place in skillet or on griddle. Pour *2 tablespoons* of batter into each ring; cook over medium heat till the crumpets are browned on one side, 4 to 5 minutes. Remove the ring and turn crumpet, cook 4 to 5 minutes more. After making 4 crumpets, remove the pan from heat and wipe pan and rings clean with paper toweling. Return pan to heat, melt remaining 2 tablespoons butter and repeat with remaining batter. Serve crumpets whole or split and toasted. Serve with butter and jelly, if desired. Makes 8.

Even without egg-poaching rings, you can make traditional English *Crumpets. Substitute open-topped cookie cutters or cans that are three inches in diameter and one to two inches tall. The eight-ounce pineapple or tuna cans work nicely. Be sure to remove the tops and bottoms of cans and wash them thoroughly.*

Hot Cross Buns *had their earliest beginnings in Greek and Roman times. These currant-filled buns served as a symbol of the sun, bisected by a cross into four seasons. Later in history these buns with their cross became associated with Easter and were formerly sold only on Good Friday. Now you need not wait for the holiday. Thanks to the English who brought this recipe to the United States they can be enjoyed anytime.*

Hot Cross Buns

3½ to 4 cups all-purpose
    flour
2 packages active dry yeast
½ to 1 teaspoon ground
    cinnamon
¾ cup milk
½ cup cooking oil

⅓ cup granulated sugar
¾ teaspoon salt
3 eggs
⅔ cup dried currants
1 slightly beaten egg white
Frosting

In a mixing bowl combine *2 cups* of the flour, yeast, and cinnamon. In saucepan heat milk, oil, sugar, and salt till warm (115-120°). Add to dry ingredients in mixing bowl; add eggs. Beat at low speed of electric mixer for ½ minute, scraping sides of bowl constantly. Beat 3 minutes at high speed. By hand, stir in currants and enough of the remaining flour to make a soft dough. Shape dough into a ball. Place in a greased bowl, turning once to grease the surface. Cover; let rise in a warm place till double (about 1½ hours). Punch dough down. Cover; let rest 10 minutes. Divide dough into 18 pieces; form into balls. Place on greased baking sheet 1½ inches apart. Cover; let rise till double (30 to 45 minutes). Cut a shallow cross on the top of each bun; brush tops with egg white (reserve any remaining egg white). Bake at 375° for 12 to 15 minutes. Using a pastry tube, pipe on crosses with Frosting. Makes 18 buns.

Frosting: Stir together 1½ cups sifted powdered sugar, ¼ teaspoon vanilla, dash salt, and reserved egg white till smooth. Add milk, if necessary, to make of piping consistency.

Colcannon

6 medium potatoes, peeled
    and quartered
4 cups shredded cabbage
1 cup chopped onion
¼ cup butter *or* margarine

½ to ¾ cup milk
1 teaspoon salt
⅛ teaspoon pepper
1 tablespoon snipped
    parsley

Cook potatoes in large amount of boiling salted water till tender, about 20 minutes. Drain. Meanwhile cook cabbage and onion together in small amount of boiling salted water for 15 minutes; drain. Mash potatoes using electric mixer. Beat in butter and as much milk as necessary to make fluffy. Add salt and pepper. Stir in cabbage and onion. Top with parsley. Serves 6.

Irish Coffee

1 jigger Irish whiskey
    (1½ ounces)
1 to 2 teaspoons sugar

Hot strong coffee
Whipped cream

Pour whiskey into serving glass or mug. Add sugar; stir to dissolve. Fill glass with hot coffee. Top with whipped cream. Makes 1 serving.

Irish immigrants, driven from their land by the potato famine, brought us Irish Soda Bread. Because there was a shortage of wood for fuel in Ireland, this bread was traditionally baked over a smoldering open peat fire. In America the recipe was changed slightly so it could be baked in an oven.

Irish Soda Bread

3 cups all-purpose flour
2 tablespoons packed brown
    sugar
2 teaspoons baking powder

1 teaspoon baking soda
½ cup dried currants
1 teaspoon caraway seed
1½ cups buttermilk

In a large bowl stir together the flour, brown sugar, baking powder, baking soda, and 1 teaspoon salt. Stir in the currants and caraway seed. Add buttermilk; stir till the dry ingredients are moistened. Turn into a greased 8x1½-inch round baking pan. Bake at 350° till browned, about 40 minutes. Cool 10 minutes in pan. Remove from pan and cool thoroughly. Makes 1 loaf.

Creamed Finnan Haddie

2 cups water
12 ounces smoked haddock
    fillets
1 teaspoon salt
2 tablespoons butter *or*
    margarine

2 tablespoons all-purpose
    flour
Dash pepper
1⅓ cups light cream
Patty shells *or* toast
    points

Bring the water to boiling in 10-inch skillet or fish poacher with tight-fitting cover. Sprinkle haddock with the salt. Place fish on a greased rack in the skillet or poacher so that fish does not touch water. Cover pan tightly; steam till fish flakes easily when tested with a fork, 3 to 4 minutes. Carefully remove fish. Skin and flake fish. Melt butter; stir in flour and pepper. Add cream all at once. Cook and stir till thickened and bubbly. Add flaked fish; heat through. Spoon into patty shells or over toast. Garnish with sieved hard-cooked egg yolk, if desired. Makes 4 servings.

Scotch Broth

1 pound lamb shanks
¼ cup pearl barley
1½ teaspoons salt
3 sprigs parsley, snipped
2 whole cloves

1 bay leaf
½ cup chopped onion
½ cup diced carrot
¼ cup chopped celery
¼ cup chopped turnip

In a 4-quart Dutch oven combine lamb shanks, barley, salt, parsley, cloves, bay leaf, and 5 cups water. Bring to boil; reduce heat. Simmer, covered, till meat is tender, about 1 hour. Remove shanks from soup. Remove meat from bones; discard bones. Cut meat into pieces; return to soup. Add vegetables; cook till tender, about 30 minutes. Remove bay leaf and cloves. Serves 4 or 5.

Oatcakes

1 cup quick-cooking rolled
    oats
2 tablespoons all-purpose
    flour
¼ teaspoon baking powder
¼ teaspoon salt

¼ cup hot water
2 tablespoons butter *or*
    margarine, melted
¼ cup quick-cooking rolled
    oats
Butter *or* margarine

Place ½ *cup* of the rolled oats in blender container; cover and blend till oats are a fine powder. Repeat with another ½ *cup* rolled oats. Combine the blended oats, flour, baking powder, and salt. Stir in hot water and the melted butter. Sprinkle board with remaining ¼ cup rolled oats; place dough on oat-covered board. Roll to a 10-inch circle; cut into 12 wedges. Place wedges on ungreased baking sheet. Bake at 350° for 15 minutes. Turn off heat and open oven door. Leave oatcakes in the oven till firm and crisp, 4 to 5 minutes. Serve with butter or margarine. Makes 12 wedges.

Scotch Shortbread

1 cup butter
½ cup sugar

2½ cups all-purpose flour

Cream butter and sugar till fluffy. Stir in flour. Chill several hours. Divide in half. On ungreased cookie sheet pat each half of dough into a 7-inch circle. With a fork prick *each* circle deeply to make 16 wedges. (Or, on floured surface, roll each half to ¼- to ½-inch thickness. Cut into 2x½-inch strips.) Bake on ungreased cookie sheet at 300° about 30 minutes. Cool slightly; remove from cookie sheet. Makes 32 wedges or about 42 strips.

The creation of finnan haddie came about quite by accident according to the way Scotch-Americans tell it. It seems there was a fire in a small fishing village in Aberdeen, Scotland, and the townspeople found that a quantity of salted haddock had been smoked in the fire. To avoid wasting the fish, or so the legend goes, Creamed Finnan Haddie was created. No one wished to burn down buildings of course, so from then on, fish was smoked over a fire made from seaweed. Today pine or oak chips are more likely to be used. Creamed Finnan Haddie lovers say the best way to serve it is topped with a pat of butter or a poached egg and accompanied by lots of brown bread.

Bannocks or Scottish Oatcakes are one of the foods Scotch-Americans traditionally serve at the New Year's Eve festival of Hogmanay. The cakes are made with oat flour and are shaped into a circle. The round is cut into wedges, called farls, that are baked and served with Mulligatawny (see recipe, page 223) or a chicken and leek soup called cock-a-leekie. Scottish immigrants have had to change the recipe slightly since American oatmeal is much too coarse. The Scotch solve the problem by grinding this oatmeal into a fine flour.

Welsh White Cookies

In a bowl cream together ½ cup butter *or* margarine and ½ cup sugar; add 1 egg, 1½ teaspoons vinegar, and ½ teaspoon vanilla. Beat till light and fluffy. Stir together 1 cup all-purpose flour, ½ teaspoon baking powder, ¼ teaspoon baking soda, and ¼ teaspoon salt; stir into creamed mixture. Chill thoroughly. Roll out thinly on lightly floured surface; cut with a 2-inch round cookie cutter.* Bake on ungreased cookie sheet at 375° till edges are golden, about 6 minutes. Cool on pan 30 seconds; remove to rack. Makes 48.

Note: Or, roll chilled dough into 1-inch balls. Place on ungreased cookie sheet. Flatten with glass dipped in sugar. Bake at 375° for 6 to 7 minutes.

Tea Scones

Tea Scones are a favorite of immigrants from all over the British Isles. The Scots take the credit for them, but immigrants of British and Welsh extraction claim them, too. The English call them singing hinnies because of the way they sizzle when they are cooked over an open fire.

2 cups all-purpose flour
2 tablespoons sugar
1 tablespoon baking powder
½ teaspoon salt
⅓ cup dried currants (optional)
6 tablespoons butter *or* margarine
1 beaten egg
½ cup milk
1 slightly beaten egg

In a bowl thoroughly stir together the flour, sugar, baking powder, and salt. Stir in the currants, if desired. Cut in butter till the mixture resembles coarse crumbs. Add 1 beaten egg and milk, stirring just till the dough clings together. Knead dough gently on lightly floured surface (12 to 15 strokes). Cut the dough in half. Shape each *half* into a ball and pat or roll to 6-inch circle, about ½ inch thick. With a sharp knife, cut each circle into 6 or 8 wedges. Place wedges on ungreased baking sheet (do not have sides of wedges touching). Brush scones with 1 slightly beaten egg. Bake at 425° till deep golden brown, 12 to 15 minutes. Makes 12 or 16 scones.

Afro-American Food Legacy

Afro-Americans have been developing a unique cuisine for over 300 years and one special ingredient of it is pork. True, you can't make a silk purse out of a sow's ear, but Afro-Americans have proved that you can make delicious dishes from every part of the pig. Chitterlings, hog snouts, barbecued spareribs—all are staples in the Afro-American diet and are dubbed soul food. American Indian, European, and Creole influences have all contributed to the development of this unusual cuisine.

Afro-Americans have had profound influence on many aspects of American culture, especially cooking. This heritage group came to America from many parts of Africa—including Zanzibar, Kenya, Nigeria, Burundi, Ethiopia, Dahomey, Chad, Guinea, Ghana, and the Congo. The majority came as slaves, but some also came as free men. Like migrants everywhere, they carried the memory of foods and dishes distinctive to their homeland.

The descendants of these first Afro-Americans used many traditional foods of Africa and adapted the time-honored dishes so that they were no longer African but Afro-American. Because of these culinary wizards, the red bean soup of Zanzibar, the bean stews of Kenya, the black-eyed peas of Nigeria, and the bean dishes of Burundi have been transformed into such dishes as ham hocks with black-eyed peas or hopping john. In addition, the African method of cooking spinach has been adapted to American turnip greens, kale, collards, or mustard greens. Also, the gumbos of Africa changed from bland stews with okra to the zippy American version incorporating filé powder, tomatoes, and rice.

Included in the Black heritage, but separate from Afro-American cooking, is what is commonly called soul food. This type of cooking comprises not only African traditions, but also the food influences of the American Indian and the European white sharecropper. It developed out of the limited resources of all these groups, which means it included lots of fresh vegetables, chicken, cornmeal, game, and whatever parts of the hog and cow were rejected by those who could afford to be choosy. Some of the most famous soul foods are chitterlings, hoecakes, and 'possum.

These two food heritages have only recently been published, having been passed down the generations by word of mouth. Thus, they are perhaps less well known to most Americans than other food customs. Both have added depth and variety to the national cuisine. The recipes that follow offer all Americans the chance to experience our Afro-American food legacy.

Watermelon Pickles

Trim the dark green and pink parts from 2 pounds watermelon rind. Cut rind in 1-inch cubes; measure 7 cups. Soak rind overnight in a solution of 4 cups water and ¼ cup pickling salt. (If more salt-water solution is needed to cover watermelon rind, use same proportions of salt to water.) Drain; rinse watermelon rind. Cover rind with cold water. Cook just till rind is tender. Meanwhile, in 6- to 8-quart kettle mix 2 cups sugar, 1 cup white vinegar, 1 cup water, 1 tablespoon broken stick cinnamon, and 1½ teaspoons whole cloves. Simmer 10 minutes; strain. Add watermelon rind and ½ lemon, thinly sliced. Simmer till rind is clear. Fill hot half-pint jars with mixture; leave ½-inch headspace. Adjust lids. Process in boiling water bath 5 minutes (start timing when water returns to boiling). Makes 5 half-pints.

Start your New Year off right. Serve *Ham Hocks and Black-Eyed Peas* (see recipe, page 230) on New Year's Day. Afro-Americans are just some of the many people who believe it will bring a whole year of good luck, health, and happiness.

Chicken Gumbo

1 4-pound ready-to-cook
  stewing chicken, cut up
7 cups water
1½ pounds fresh okra, thinly
  sliced (4 cups)

1 28-ounce can tomatoes
½ cup chopped onion
1 teaspoon sugar
¼ teaspoon pepper

Place chicken in 5-quart Dutch oven. Add water and ½ teaspoon salt; bring to boiling. Reduce heat; cover and simmer till barely tender, about 2 hours. Remove chicken; reserve 4 cups broth. When cool enough to handle, cut chicken from bones; cube meat. Skim off excess fat from broth. Return chicken to broth; add okra, undrained tomatoes, onion, sugar, pepper, and 1 teaspoon salt. Cover and simmer till okra is tender, about 30 minutes. Serves 8.

Ham Hocks and Black-Eyed Peas *(see photo, page 229)*

3 cups dry black-eyed peas
12 cups water
3 pounds smoked ham hocks
1¼ cups chopped onion
1 cup chopped celery

1 teaspoon salt
⅛ teaspoon cayenne
1 bay leaf
1 10-ounce package frozen
  cut okra

Rinse peas. In 6-quart Dutch oven combine water and peas. Bring to boiling; simmer 2 minutes. Remove from heat; cover and let stand 1 hour. (Or, combine water and peas; soak overnight.) Do not drain. Stir in hocks, onion, celery, salt, cayenne, and bay leaf. Bring to boiling. Cover; simmer till hocks are tender and beans are done, about 1½ hours. Stir in okra; cook till very tender, 10 to 15 minutes. Discard bay leaf. Season to taste. Serves 6.

Pan-Fried Fish

2 pounds fresh *or* frozen
  fish fillets *or* steaks,
  or 4 pan-dressed fish
  (8 ounces each)
1 beaten egg

2 tablespoons water
¾ cup finely crushed
  saltine crackers *or*
  cornmeal
Shortening

Thaw frozen fish. Cut fillets or steaks into 6 portions. Combine egg and water. Mix cracker crumbs or cornmeal, ½ teaspoon salt, and dash pepper. Dip fish into egg mixture, then roll in crumbs. Heat small amount of shortening in skillet; add fish in single layer. Fry over medium heat till browned on one side, 4 to 5 minutes. Turn; brown other side till fish flakes easily when tested with a fork, 4 to 5 minutes more. Drain on paper toweling. Makes 6 servings for fillets and steaks; 4 servings for pan-dressed fish.

Plantation Spareribs

½ cup sorghum
¼ cup prepared mustard
¼ cup vinegar
2 tablespoons
  Worcestershire sauce

½ teaspoon salt
½ teaspoon bottled hot
  pepper sauce
4 pounds pork spareribs

In small saucepan blend sorghum into mustard; stir in the vinegar, Worcestershire sauce, salt, and hot pepper sauce. Bring to boiling. Place spareribs, meaty side down, in shallow roasting pan. Roast at 450° for 30 minutes. Remove pan from oven; drain off excess fat. Turn ribs meaty side up. Reduce oven temperature to 350°; roast till tender, about 1 hour more. During the last 30 minutes of roasting, baste frequently with sorghum mixture. Garnish with parsley sprigs and candied kumquats, if desired. Makes 6 to 8 servings.

Turnip Greens with Cornmeal Dumplings

4 ounces salt pork with
   rind
3 quarts turnip greens
1 pound turnips
10 cups water
1 teaspoon salt
1½ cups white cornmeal

½ cup all-purpose flour
1 teaspoon baking powder
1 teaspoon sugar
½ teaspoon salt
3 tablespoons butter *or*
   margarine, melted
1 beaten egg

Dice salt pork, cutting to but not through rind. Wash and trim greens. Peel and quarter turnips. In large kettle bring the water to boiling. Add salt pork, greens, turnips, and 1 teaspoon salt. Simmer, covered, 2 hours. Remove 1 cup cooking liquid. Stir together the cornmeal, flour, baking powder, sugar, and ½ teaspoon salt; stir in butter or margarine and reserved cooking liquid. Stir in egg. Spoon 1 rounded tablespoon of batter at a time onto simmering greens. Cover and simmer 30 minutes. Makes 6 servings.

Salt pork is the key seasoning for many Afro-American vegetable dishes, particularly greens. Serving greens with the cooking liquid is not only tasty, but extra nutritious since the valuable nutrients from the greens are in this broth, sometimes called pot liquor.

Sweet Potato Pone

4 cups shredded raw sweet
   potato (1 pound)
1 cup water
½ cup packed brown sugar

½ teaspoon salt
¼ teaspoon ground ginger
2 tablespoons butter *or*
   margarine

Combine potatoes, water, sugar, salt, and ginger; turn into a 1-quart casserole. Dot with butter. Bake at 350° till potatoes are tender and caramelized, stirring occasionally, about 2 hours. Makes 4 servings.

The generous use of the sweet potato reflects strongly the use of similar vegetables, particularly the deep yellow potato-like tuber called a yam, in African cookery. Baked sweet potatoes or Sweet Potato Pone appear frequently on Afro-American menus. Try this version of pone either as a sweet vegetable course or as a dessert.

Chitterlings

10 pounds chitterlings
1 dried red pepper, cut up

1 clove garlic, minced
1 tablespoon salt

Wash chitterlings well. Trim fat, leaving a small amount on for seasoning. In large saucepan cover chitterlings with water. Add red pepper, minced garlic, salt, and 1 tablespoon pepper. Cook chitterlings till tender, 2 to 3 hours. Drain and cut in serving-size pieces. Serve at once. Makes 6 to 8 servings.

Pan-Fried Chitterlings: Dip boiled chitterlings in cornmeal. Fry in hot shortening till brown.

Deep-Fat-Fried Chitterlings: Dip boiled chitterlings in egg, then in crushed saltine crackers. Fry in deep hot fat (375°) till brown.

Peanut Soup

½ pound beef stew meat,
   cut in small cubes
1 tablespoon shortening
1½ cups water
1 cup chopped onion
1 teaspoon salt
⅛ teaspoon pepper
   Dash garlic powder
   Dash ground nutmeg
   Dash ground ginger

Dash ground cloves
Dash paprika
• • •
1 5⅓-ounce can evaporated
   milk (⅔ cup)
1 teaspoon cornstarch
1 8-ounce can tomatoes
½ cup finely chopped
   peanuts

In a 3-quart saucepan brown meat in hot shortening. Stir in water, onion, salt, pepper, garlic powder, nutmeg, ginger, cloves, and paprika. Simmer, covered, till meat is tender, about 1 hour. Slowly blend milk into cornstarch. Stir into soup and cook till slightly thickened and bubbly. Gradually add undrained tomatoes, stirring constantly; stir in peanuts. Serves 4.

Peanuts are an essential element of this cuisine. Evidence suggests they originated in Brazil and were probably introduced into Africa as payment for slaves. Peanuts are called groundnuts or goobers there, names often used in this country, also. From peanuts the Afro-Americans make such favorites as peanut cookies, peanut pie, and peanut butter. But one highlight of their cookery is Peanut Soup. Often okra and tomatoes are added to give it a special flair.

Our German-Austrian Heritage

Although Germany and Austria today are two distinct and separate nations, the immigrants who came to America from either one have traditionally been called Germans by their American neighbors. "A rose by any other name. . . ." These people, by whatever name, have had a deep and long-lasting effect on the American scene.

The first Germans to arrive in this country were Mennonites, recruited by William Penn for his colony of Pennsylvania. Not far behind them were Moravians, Pietists, and members of other religious sects. By 1776 Pennsylvania was nearly half German and Austrian, with numerous settlements that were German-speaking. Many of these people have maintained their heritage and are known today as the Pennsylvania Dutch.

During the eighteenth century, most German and Austrian immigrants came either as indentured servants (their labor contracted for in Europe) or as redemptioners — meaning that in return for their passage the captain of the ship that carried them had the right to sell their services to anyone for a period of up to six years. Great hardships resulted from this system, especially when some members of a family died at sea and the others had to serve their kinsmen's years of bondage as well as their own. In addition, five thousand Hessian soldiers, brought here to fight for the British during the Revolution, chose to remain after the war rather than to return to Hesse.

After 1830, German-Austrians began to cross the ocean by the thousands. In the next hundred years the total number was 6 million — more than any other nationality. Although they eventually settled everywhere in the United States, the first wave concentrated in the Middle West: Indiana, Illinois, Missouri, the Wisconsin side of Lake Michigan, the river towns of Iowa, and Cincinnati, Ohio. Many arrived in St. Louis via New Orleans, having taken passage on ships that had delivered cotton to European ports and gladly took passengers for the return trip.

The Republic of Texas (and, later, the State of Texas) was another center for Germans. Colonization societies had been started in Germany by people expecting to establish within Texas a new Germany, preserving their native language and culture. But such a scheme proved unworkable and before long the settlements joined the mainstream of American life.

The majority of German immigrants were literate and had skills to offer. They tended to interest themselves in politics and to exercise their vote. The German vote in Illinois and other states of the old Northwest was a factor in helping Lincoln win the presidency.

German and Austrian customs were different from those of the English. Their tradition of spending Sunday afternoons in social clubs and beer gardens, where they drank, sang, and listened to band concerts, drew many "tsk, tsks" at first. But their love of music, especially symphony orchestras, glee clubs, and choirs, proved infectious. Another German custom, the Christmas tree, was universally welcomed and became an American institution. German beer became a national drink, and a number of German-Austrian dishes captured the American fancy — especially *Wiener schnitzel,* German potato salad, apple strudel, and *springerle.*

Gugelhupf

1 package active dry yeast
¼ cup warm water (110°)
½ cup sugar
¼ cup butter *or* margarine
2 eggs
½ cup milk
2½ cups all-purpose flour
1 teaspoon salt

½ cup light raisins
1 teaspoon grated lemon
  peel
1 tablespoon butter *or*
  margarine, melted
3 tablespoons fine dry
  bread crumbs
Blanched whole almonds

Soften yeast in the warm water. In mixing bowl cream sugar and ¼ cup butter or margarine till light and fluffy; add eggs one at a time, beating well after each. Add softened yeast and milk. Stir together thoroughly all-purpose flour and salt; add to creamed mixture. Beat at medium speed of electric mixer till batter is smooth (about 2 minutes). By hand, stir in raisins and lemon peel. Cover; let batter rise in warm place till double (about 2 hours). Prepare a 1½-quart fluted tube pan by brushing the inside with the melted butter or margarine and sprinkling with the fine dry bread crumbs. Arrange whole almonds in a design in bottom. Stir down batter; spoon carefully into mold. Let rise till almost double (about 1 hour). Bake at 350° till done, about 25 minutes. Cool 10 minutes; remove mold. Makes 1.

Gugelhupf is an old world treasure that Austrians brought with them to America. This delicious tea bread, says the storyteller, was invented in Vienna in the 17th century to celebrate the defeat of Turkish invaders. Its traditional round shape with fluted edges and a hole in the center is said to be fashioned after a sultan's headdress.

Wiener Schnitzel

1½ pounds veal cutlets,
  cut ½ inch thick
    • • •
¼ cup all-purpose flour
1 teaspoon salt
¼ teaspoon pepper

1 beaten egg
1 tablespoon milk
1 cup fine dry bread
  crumbs
Cooking oil
Lemon wedges

Pound veal cutlets till about ⅛ inch thick. Cut small slits along edges of cutlets to prevent curling. Stir together thoroughly flour, salt, and pepper. Combine beaten egg and milk. Coat cutlets with flour mixture. Dip floured cutlets in egg mixture; then coat with fine dry bread crumbs. Cook cutlets in a small amount of hot cooking oil till tender, 2 to 3 minutes on each side. Serve cutlets with lemon wedges. Makes 4 servings.

Linzer Torte

¾ cup all-purpose flour
½ teaspoon ground cinnamon
¼ teaspoon baking powder
¼ teaspoon salt
¼ teaspoon ground cloves
4 ounces walnuts, ground
  (1 cup)
1 cup fine dry bread crumbs
½ cup butter *or* margarine

¾ cup sugar
½ teaspoon grated lemon
  peel
2 eggs
    • • •
¾ cup plum *or* raspberry
  preserves
¼ cup all-purpose flour

In a bowl stir together ¾ cup flour, cinnamon, baking powder, salt, and cloves. Add ground walnuts and fine dry bread crumbs; mix thoroughly and set aside. In mixing bowl cream butter or margarine and sugar till light and fluffy. Add grated lemon peel. Beat in eggs, one at a time. Stir in flour mixture. *Set aside ¾ cup dough.* Pat remaining dough evenly in bottom of a 9-inch springform pan, forming a rim around edge ½ inch wide and ¼ inch deep. Spread plum or raspberry preserves over dough in pan. On a lightly floured surface knead ¼ cup flour into the reserved ¾ cup of dough. Pat to ¼-inch thickness; cut dough into fancy shapes with small cookie or canape cutters. Place pieces atop preserves. Bake at 350° for 30 minutes. Cool; wrap tightly in foil and refrigerate at least two days before serving.

Viennese pastry: The pride of Austrian baking! The delight of cake connoisseurs! The skill of Austrian-American cooks! One can but sigh with pleasure. The Sacher Torte for example, is a rich chocolate sponge cake glazed with jam and chocolate frosting, the Dobos Torte is eight thin layers of sponge cake separated by chocolate buttercream filling and topped with caramel glaze. Competing with these is the Linzer Torte, two shortbread-like layers filled with preserves.

Pictured opposite: For a traditional German-American meal that's easy to make and fun to eat, serve *German-Style Meatballs* over hot cooked noodles. The subtle wine-lemon sauce gives these meatballs a special flavor.

Austrian Potato Salad

6 medium potatoes, peeled, sliced, and cooked	1 clove garlic, minced
1/4 cup chopped onion	1/4 cup wine vinegar
2 tablespoons snipped parsley	2 tablespoons olive oil
	1 teaspoon Dijon-style mustard

In a bowl place potatoes, onion, parsley, garlic, 1 teaspoon salt, and 1/4 teaspoon pepper. Heat wine vinegar, olive oil, and mustard; mix well. Pour over all; toss lightly. Chill thoroughly. Garnish with parsley if desired. Serves 8.

Königsberger Klops or German-Style Meatballs, says history, was named after the city of Königsberg in East Prussia. By a quirk of politics that city is now Kaleningrad and is part of the Soviet Union. The geography may be confusing, but the origin of this dish is clear. It is definitely German and features the slightly tart flavor that is so much a part of our German-American heritage.

German-Style Meatballs

1 2-ounce can anchovy fillets	1/2 pound ground pork
5 slices dry bread	3/4 cup sauterne
1 cup milk	4 whole cloves
1 1/2 cups chopped onion	4 whole black peppercorns
2 tablespoons butter *or* margarine	1 bay leaf
2 beaten eggs	2 tablespoons all-purpose flour
1 1/2 teaspoons salt	1 lemon, very thinly sliced
1/4 teaspoon pepper	1 tablespoon capers, drained
1 pound ground beef	Hot cooked noodles
1/2 pound ground veal	Snipped parsley

To desalt anchovies, soak in cold water 20 minutes; drain. Soak bread in milk. Cook onion in butter till tender but not brown. In a large bowl mix anchovies, bread mixture, onion, eggs, salt, and pepper. Add meats; mix well. Form into 24 meatballs. In large skillet mix sauterne, cloves, peppercorns, bay leaf, and 3/4 cup water. Add meatballs. Cover; simmer 25 to 30 minutes. Remove meatballs; strain liquid. Return liquid to skillet. Blend 1/4 cup cold water into flour. Stir into hot liquid; cook and stir till thick and bubbly. Add lemon slices, capers, and 1/4 teaspoon salt. Cook 1 or 2 minutes. Place meatballs on platter of hot cooked noodles. Top with sauce. Garnish with parsley. Serves 8.

Spaetzle, a cross between a curly noodle and a small dumpling, are a traditional German accompaniment to all types of roasts, especially sauerbraten.

Spaetzle

Mix 2 cups all-purpose flour and 1 teaspoon salt. Mix 2 eggs and 3/4 cup milk; stir into flour mixture. Place dough in coarse-sieved (1/4-inch holes) colander. Hold over kettle of boiling salted water. Press dough through colander to form spaetzle. Cook and stir 5 minutes; drain. Mix 1/2 cup fine dry bread crumbs and 1/4 cup butter, melted; spoon over spaetzle. Makes 4 cups.

Sweet-Sour Green Beans and Carrots is more traditionally called Blindehühn or blind hen by the immigrants from Westphalia who brought it to us. The original version is a casserole made with green and white beans, carrots, potatoes, onions, and apples. This American adaptation is minus the white beans and potatoes.

Sweet-Sour Green Beans and Carrots

1 cup chopped carrot	1 apple, peeled, cored, and sliced
1 9-ounce package frozen cut green beans	2 tablespoons vinegar
2 slices bacon	1 tablespoon sugar
1 medium onion, sliced	1/2 teaspoon salt

In saucepan cook chopped carrot, covered, in small amount boiling salted water till nearly tender, about 10 minutes. Add cut green beans and return to boiling. Cover and cook till the vegetables are tender, about 5 minutes more. Drain well. In a skillet cook bacon till crisp; drain, reserving 1 tablespoon drippings. Crumble bacon and set aside. Cook sliced onion in reserved drippings till tender but not brown. Add sliced apple, vinegar, sugar, and salt. Cover and cook just till apples are tender, 3 to 4 minutes. Add cooked beans and carrot; heat through. Sprinkle with the bacon. Serves 4 to 6.

Sauerkraut is a world traveler. It was first invented in Europe, but the process was somehow lost. Later, sauerkraut was introduced into Austria by the Tartars who, in turn, learned of it from the Chinese. The Austrians called it "sour plant" and passed it on to their German neighbors. Immigrants from both countries brought it to America. Over the years, however, the sauerkraut popular in the United States has become much coarser in texture and milder in flavor than that found in Europe.

Sauerkraut with Apples

1 27-ounce can sauerkraut
1 medium onion, sliced
2 tablespoons bacon
    drippings *or* cooking
    oil
3 medium apples, peeled,
    cored, and sliced

1 large potato, peeled and
    shredded
1 cup chicken broth
2 tablespoons packed brown
    sugar
1 teaspoon salt
1 teaspoon caraway seed

Drain and snip sauerkraut. Cook onion in bacon drippings or oil till tender. Add sauerkraut, apples, potato, broth, brown sugar, salt, and caraway; mix well. Cover and cook 15 to 20 minutes. Add more broth, if needed. Sprinkle with additional brown sugar, if desired. Makes 8 to 10 servings.

German Potato Salad

6 slices bacon
½ cup chopped onion
2 tablespoons all-purpose
    flour
2 tablespoons sugar
1½ teaspoons salt

1 teaspoon celery seed
    Dash pepper
½ cup vinegar
6 cups sliced cooked
    potatoes
2 hard-cooked eggs, sliced

In skillet cook bacon till crisp; drain and crumble, reserving ¼ cup drippings. Cook onion in the reserved drippings till tender but not brown. Blend in flour, sugar, salt, celery seed, and pepper. Add vinegar and 1 cup water. Cook and stir till thickened. Stir in bacon, potatoes, and eggs. Heat through, tossing lightly. Garnish with parsley, if desired. Serves 8 to 10.

Americans were always enthusiastic about bakeries run by German immigrants. Those bakeries in Wisconsin are claimed by some to be the very best. Today, they feature pretzels, rolls, coffee cakes, pumpernickel, and flavorful rye breads such as this one. In days gone by, these bakeries even had special delivery routes for their customers who lived out of town.

German Dark Rye Bread

3 cups all-purpose flour
¼ cup unsweetened cocoa
    powder
2 packages active dry yeast
1 tablespoon caraway seed

⅓ cup molasses
2 tablespoons butter
1 tablespoon sugar
3 to 3½ cups rye flour
    Cooking oil

In large bowl combine all-purpose flour, cocoa, yeast, and caraway seed. Heat and stir molasses, butter, sugar, 2 cups water, and 1 tablespoon salt till warm (115-120°). Add to dry mixture. Beat at low speed of electric mixer ½ minute, scraping bowl. Beat 3 minutes at high speed. By hand, stir in enough rye flour to make a soft dough. Turn out onto lightly floured surface; knead till smooth (about 5 minutes). Cover; let rest 20 minutes. Punch down; divide in half. Shape into two round loaves; place on greased baking sheets *or* in two greased 8-inch pie plates. Brush with small amount cooking oil. Slash tops with knife. Cover; let rise till double (45 to 60 minutes). Bake at 400° for 25 to 30 minutes. Remove from baking sheets; cool. Makes 2.

Who is not familiar with the German-Americans' fervid devotion to the pleasures of beer drinking? In many towns, beer was brought home from the local brewmaster or tavern in a covered bucket and served at mealtime, as an in-between refresher, and even in cheese spreads.

Beer and Cheese Spread

2 cups shredded sharp
    Cheddar cheese
2 cups shredded Swiss
    cheese
1 teaspoon Worcestershire
    sauce

½ teaspoon dry mustard
1 small clove garlic,
    minced
½ to ⅔ cup beer
    Assorted crackers *or*
    rye bread rounds

Have cheeses at room temperature. Combine cheeses, Worcestershire, mustard, and garlic. Beat in enough beer to make of spreading consistency. Serve at room temperature with crackers or rye rounds. Makes 2 cups.

Creamed Bratwurst

1 cup sliced fresh
    mushrooms
1 cup chopped onion
2 tablespoons butter *or*
    margarine
2 tablespoons all-purpose
    flour
	½ teaspoon salt
	2½ cups milk
	1 12-ounce package fully
	    cooked bratwurst,
	    sliced in ½-inch pieces
	¼ cup snipped parsley
	    Toast points

In skillet cook mushrooms and onion in butter till vegetables are tender but not brown. Stir in flour, salt, and ⅛ teaspoon pepper. Add milk all at once; cook and stir till mixture is thickened and bubbly. Stir in sliced bratwurst and parsley. Heat through. Serve on toast points. Makes 4 servings.

Lebkuchen

1 beaten egg
¾ cup packed brown sugar
½ cup honey
½ cup dark molasses
3 tablespoons brandy
½ teaspoon grated lemon
    peel
1 teaspoon lemon juice
4 cups all-purpose flour
1 teaspoon ground cinnamon
	½ teaspoon baking soda
	½ teaspoon ground cloves
	½ teaspoon ground ginger
	¼ teaspoon ground cardamom
	½ cup chopped almonds
	½ cup finely chopped mixed
	    candied fruits and
	    peels
	    Lemon Glaze

In a bowl combine egg and brown sugar. Beat till light and fluffy. Mix in honey, molasses, brandy, lemon peel, and lemon juice. Mix well. Stir together the flour, cinnamon, baking soda, cloves, ginger, and cardamom. Blend into molasses mixture. Stir in almonds and candied fruits and peels. Chill dough several hours. Divide dough in half. On a lightly floured surface, roll each half to a 14x9-inch rectangle; cut into 3x2-inch cookies. Bake on a lightly greased cookie sheet at 350° about 12 minutes. Cool slightly; remove from cookie sheet and cool on rack. While warm, brush with Lemon Glaze. Makes 42.

Lemon Glaze: In a bowl combine 1 beaten egg white, 1 tablespoon lemon juice, and dash salt. Stir in 1½ cups sifted powdered sugar till smooth.

Lebkuchen or ginger cookies are a perennial favorite among midwestern German-Americans, especially at Christmastime. The flavoring of these cookies is similar to that of a mild gingerbread and the lemon glaze adds just a hint of tartness.

Dakota-Style Kuchen

3 cups all-purpose flour
1 package active dry yeast
¾ cup milk
6 tablespoons butter
⅓ cup sugar
½ teaspoon salt
2 eggs
1 beaten egg
	3 tablespoons light cream
	    or milk
	1 cup sugar
	1½ teaspoons ground cinnamon
	2 cups thinly sliced peeled
	    apple,* sliced rhubarb,
	    sliced Italian plums,
	    or cottage cheese

In large bowl mix *1½ cups* flour and yeast. In saucepan heat ¾ cup milk, butter, ⅓ cup sugar, and salt just till warm (115-120°), stirring constantly. Add to dry mixture; add 2 eggs. Beat at low speed of electric mixer ½ minute, scraping sides of bowl often. Beat 3 minutes at high speed. By hand, stir in remaining flour. Divide dough in half. With lightly floured fingers, pat into two greased 9x1½-inch round baking pans. Cover; let rise till double (45 to 50 minutes). Combine the beaten egg and 3 tablespoons cream or milk. Stir in 1 cup sugar and cinnamon. (If cottage cheese is used, stir into sugar-cream mixture.) Arrange fruit atop risen dough. Carefully spoon sugar-cream mixture over fruit. Bake at 400° for 20 to 25 minutes. Cool slightly. Cut in wedges; serve warm. Makes 2.

*Note: If desired, cook apple slices for 3 minutes in boiling water. Drain, then arrange atop dough.

For homemakers who settled in the Dakotas a weekly baking was not complete without making at least one kuchen. If the homemaker was making a sweet dough, the kuchen had a sweet dough base; if not, a bit of bread dough was patted into the pan and topped with fruit or a custard mixture. At times cottage cheese was even substituted for the fruit. This version is an easy no-knead bread for those who want to bake just a kuchen and not do a whole week's baking all at once.

"Sunday" houses were an innovation of the German-Americans who settled around Fredericksburg, Texas. These settlers were for the most part ranchers and farmers. As a general rule, they would come to town to shop on Saturday, spend the night in their "Sunday" houses, and go to church on Sunday. After church before going back to the country, the women would serve large breakfasts in the German tradition. Sure to be among the dishes served was Apple Strudel.

Apple Strudel

3 cups all-purpose flour
½ cup butter *or* margarine
1 beaten egg
⅔ cup warm water
¾ cup butter, melted
⅔ cup granulated sugar*

2 teaspoons ground cinnamon
6 cups very thinly sliced
    peeled tart apples*
½ cup dried currants*
1 beaten egg white
Powdered sugar

Stir together flour and ½ teaspoon salt; cut in the ½ cup butter till crumbly. Mix beaten egg and water; add to flour and stir well. Turn onto lightly floured surface; knead 5 minutes. Halve dough. Cover and let stand 1 hour.

Cover large table with floured cloth. On cloth, roll *half* dough to 15-inch square. Brush with *2 tablespoons* melted butter; let stand few minutes. Starting from middle of square, *carefully* work underneath dough using backs of hands to gently stretch from one corner to the next till dough is *paper thin* and about 36 inches square. Brush dough with ¼ *cup* melted butter.

Mix granulated sugar and cinnamon. Trim edges of dough; put *half* the apples along one side, 6 inches from edge. Sprinkle *half* the sugar mixture over apples; top with *half* the currants. Gently fold 6-inch piece of dough over filling. Slowly and evenly raise cloth behind filling, making dough roll away from you into tight roll. Seal ends. Place on lightly greased 15½x10½x1-inch baking pan; curve slightly to form crescent. Repeat with remaining dough. Brush tops of strudels with beaten egg white. Bake strudels at 350° for 45 to 50 minutes. Remove from pan; cool. Top with powdered sugar. Makes 2.

*Note: For Cranberry Strudel, use one 16-ounce package cranberries, chopped, instead of apples; 2 cups sugar; and pecans instead of currants.

Cinnamon-Raisin Doughnuts

2¼ cups all-purpose flour
1 package active dry yeast
¾ cup sugar
½ cup milk
2 tablespoons cooking oil

¼ teaspoon salt
3 eggs
½ cup raisins
    Fat for frying
1 teaspoon ground cinnamon

Combine *1 cup* flour and yeast. Heat ¼ *cup* sugar, milk, oil, and salt just till warm (115-120°); stir constantly. Add to dry mixture; add eggs. Beat at low speed of electric mixer ½ minute; scrape bowl constantly. Beat 3 minutes at high speed. By hand, stir in raisins and remaining flour. Cover; let rise till double (about 2 hours). Stir down. Drop by level tablespoonfuls into deep hot fat (375°). Fry till golden, about 2½ minutes; turn once. Mix cinnamon and remaining sugar in bag. Shake doughnuts in sugar mixture. Makes 36.

One of the most prized possessions of many women who came from Germany was their richly carved wooden molds for making Springerle. *Originally these cookies were served in celebration of the winter solstice or Julfest.* Springerle, *meaning "little horse" was first made in the shape of a horse. Now the cookie dough is pressed into rectangular molds or rolled with a specially carved rolling pin.*

Springerle

4 eggs
2 cups sifted powdered
    sugar
    Few drops anise oil

3½ cups all-purpose flour
1 teaspoon baking soda
¼ cup butter, melted
    Aniseed

Beat eggs till light. Gradually add sugar, beating on high speed of electric mixer till like a soft meringue. Add anise oil. Combine flour, soda, and ¼ teaspoon salt; stir in butter. Blend into egg mixture, using low speed. Cover tightly; refrigerate 3 to 4 hours. Divide dough in fourths. On floured surface roll *each fourth* to an 8-inch square. Let stand 1 minute. Dust springerle rolling pin or mold with all-purpose flour; roll or press dough hard enough to make a clear design. Cut cookies apart. Place on floured surface; cover and *let stand overnight.* Grease cookie sheets and sprinkle each with 1½ to 2 teaspoons aniseed. Brush excess flour from cookies; rub underside of cookies lightly with cold water. Place on cookie sheets. Bake at 300° till light yellow color, 15 to 20 minutes. Makes 24 cookies.

Norwegian folk dancers in authentic costumes provide entertainment at Decorah, Iowa's yearly Nordic Fest. Similar festivals are held in many of the cities and towns of the upper Mississippi Valley where Scandinavians settled in large numbers.

Scandinavian-Style Cooking

Between 1820 and 1914 over 2 million Scandinavians settled in the United States. Soon other Americans were learning bits of their customs, languages, religions, and most especially their cooking traditions.

Of these immigrants, the Norwegians were the firstcomers, beginning in earnest in the 1840s and reaching a total of three-quarters of a million by World War I. Norway was second only to Ireland in loss of population to the United States. The shortage of land in Norway, together with a population explosion, was the principal cause of emigration—plus the efforts of land agencies in the United States to obtain good, hardworking, experienced farmers to develop the newly opened territories of the upper Mississippi Valley. To that part of the country traveled most of the pre-Civil War Norwegian immigrants; afterward, many more homesteaded in the Dakotas, Utah, and Washington. Those who did not become farmers found work as fishermen and seamen, miners, and railroad workers, as well as in skilled crafts. Norwegian women established a reputation as excellent cooks and servants, and through this means Norwegian cooking methods and recipes became part of American kitchen lore.

The great Swedish immigration to America began in the 1850s, for reasons similar to those in Norway. Minnesota was the destination of the majority of these immigrants, but some started their new homes in other parts of the upper Mississippi Valley, as well as in New England. The greatest number became farmers, while others found jobs as railroaders, carpenters, or in similar trades requiring skilled labor.

The Danes were the last of the three Scandinavian countries to migrate in large numbers, but after the Prussian wars of the 1860s about half a

As soon as a Swedish pioneer chose his land on the prairie he had to build a log cabin. The occasion was festive because all the neighbors helped. One immigrant describes the building of his cabin. "The work ...proceeded cheerfully and heartily.... Many adventures were told.... Jokes ...and laughter were the order of the day. A jug of whiskey had been placed by the side of a pail of fresh spring water with a teacup ready to be used in mixing a strengthening drink.... When the work was finished, we drank to the health of our neighbors, and it fell to my lot to thank them in a little oration, carried on in a mixture of Swedish and English that aroused much laughter. The filled teacup passed from hand to hand. The rest of the refreshments, simple and consisting only of a few sandwiches and a kind of ginger cookie, were eaten...."[4]

million Danes followed their Scandinavian brethren to Minnesota, Wisconsin, and other parts of the northern Midwest. Later, sizable contingents went west to Oregon and south to Texas.

Scandinavians usually arrived in this country with every intention of remaining; and of all non-English-speaking immigrants, they were perhaps most quickly and painlessly Americanized. They had an affinity for the bracing cold and the wide lakes and forests of the upper Midwest; and Americans discovered their affinity for Scandinavian cooking.

Once here, the Scandinavian cooks used the bounty of America's fertile farmland to reproduce their traditional recipes and in doing so they gave America a rare present. From the Swedish settlers we have learned to enjoy potato sausage, limpa rye bread, Swedish meatballs, and brown beans. From the Norwegian kitchens come *krumkake, lefse,* and rosettes. From the Danish pantry, we enjoy Danish pastry, the forerunner of the ubiquitous "Danish" — the pastry that daily accompanies millions of coffee breaks; and the open-faced sandwiches that feed so many guests at cocktail parties. Perhaps the most famous of all Scandinavian food customs, however, is the *smorgasbord* — that buffet meal which in modified form has reached into even the smallest town. The Scandinavians, through their cooking, have kept alive the spirit of their homelands. The recipes on these pages invite you to share that spirit. Try cooking Scandinavian-style.

Swedish Brown Beans

Swedish Brown Beans are favored by Swedish-Americans across the country. Recipes for it are legion since almost every Swedish kitchen in both Sweden and America has its own special version. This is just one of many, many delicious ways to make it.

1 pound dry Swedish brown beans	1/3 cup packed brown sugar
6 cups cold water	1/4 cup vinegar
3 inches stick cinnamon	2 tablespoons dark corn syrup
1 1/2 teaspoons salt	

Rinse beans; drain. Add the water. Bring slowly to boiling; simmer 2 minutes. Cover and let stand 1 hour. (Or, combine beans and water; soak overnight.) Stir in the stick cinnamon and salt. Cover and simmer till the beans are nearly tender, 1 1/2 to 2 hours. Stir in brown sugar and vinegar. Cook, uncovered, till beans are tender and of desired consistency, about 30 minutes; stir occasionally. Remove cinnamon. Stir in dark corn syrup. Serves 6.

Brown Sugar Cookies

Brown Sugar Cookies were called Pepparakaker *at the Swedish settlement of Bishop Hill, Illinois. The town was founded in 1840 by Eric Janson whose goal was to begin an austere way of life, free from the corruption of the church in Sweden. As time passed, the restrictions were softened, and the tables at Bishop Hill eventually reflected the bounty of the Illinois farmland. One of life's pleasures at Bishop Hill was Brown Sugar Cookies.*

1/2 cup packed brown sugar	1 1/2 teaspoons baking powder
1/2 cup dark corn syrup	3/4 teaspoon ground cinnamon
1/2 cup butter *or* margarine	1/4 teaspoon ground ginger
• • •	1/4 teaspoon ground cloves
2 eggs	1/4 teaspoon ground nutmeg
2 tablespoons milk	Granulated sugar
2 1/4 cups all-purpose flour	

In a 1-quart saucepan combine the brown sugar, corn syrup, and butter or margarine. Bring to boiling; boil 5 minutes. Cool completely. In a small bowl beat together the eggs and milk. Stir together the flour, baking powder, cinnamon, ginger, cloves, and nutmeg. In a large bowl combine the brown sugar mixture, egg mixture, and dry ingredients; mix well. Chill thoroughly (at least 2 hours). Roll the dough to 1/8-inch thickness on a lightly floured surface. Cut the dough with small fancy-shaped cookie cutters. Sprinkle each cookie with a small amount of granulated sugar. Bake on a greased cookie sheet at 400° for 5 to 6 minutes. Makes about 80 cookies.

Swedish Hash

1 pound pork *or* beef heart
1½ pounds boneless pork, cut
    in 1-inch cubes
3 cups water
2 teaspoons salt
½ teaspoon pepper
½ teaspoon ground allspice
½ teaspoon dried marjoram,
    crushed

¼ teaspoon celery seed
⅛ teaspoon ground cloves
    Dash ground ginger
1 cup quick-cooking barley
½ pound pork *or* beef liver
½ cup chopped onion
    Snipped parsley
    Fat for frying
    (optional)

Remove hard parts from heart and discard. Cut up heart. In 8-quart Dutch oven combine heart, pork, water, and seasonings. Simmer, covered, 1 hour. Stir in quick-cooking barley; cook till meat and barley are tender, about 45 minutes more. Strain; reserve liquid. Cool liquid; skim off fat. Measure 1½ cups liquid. In saucepan combine ½ *cup* reserved liquid and liver; cover and simmer till tender, about 10 minutes. Drain. Put meat mixture, liver, and onion through food grinder. Combine with remaining 1 cup cooking liquid. Heat through; serve hot. Garnish with parsley. (Or, line two 8½x 4½x2½-inch loaf pans with waxed paper. Fill with hash mixture. Cover; chill. Cut into 1-inch slices; fry in hot fat for 2 to 3 minutes per side.) Serves 10 to 12.

Swedish Hash, *or Polsa as Swedish-Americans refer to it, also won special favor at Bishop Hill. This dish was usually made in the fall at slaughtering time. It was first served hot as a thick, rich soup. The leftovers were often packed into small loaf pans and chilled. Then, it was sliced and fried for breakfast or lunch.*

Swedish Meatballs

¾ pound lean ground beef
½ pound ground veal
¼ pound ground pork
1½ cups soft bread crumbs
1 cup light cream
½ cup chopped onion
3 tablespoons butter

1 egg
¼ cup finely snipped
    parsley
1¼ teaspoons salt
    Dash ground ginger
    Dash ground nutmeg
    Gravy

Have meats ground together twice. Soak bread crumbs in light cream 5 minutes. Cook onion in *1 tablespoon* butter till tender. Mix meats, crumb mixture, onion, egg, parsley, salt, spices, and dash pepper. Mix thoroughly till well combined. Shape into 1-inch balls. (Mixture will be soft. For easier shaping, wet hands *or* chill mixture first.) In skillet brown meatballs in 2 tablespoons butter. Remove meatballs from skillet and prepare Gravy. Return meatballs to Gravy. Cover; cook *slowly,* about 30 minutes. Baste meatballs occasionally. Makes about 48.

Gravy: Melt 2 tablespoons butter in skillet with drippings. Stir in 2 tablespoons all-purpose flour. Dissolve 1 beef bouillon cube in 1¼ cups boiling water. Add bouillon and ½ teaspoon instant coffee powder to flour mixture. Cook and stir till thick and bubbly.

The smorgasbord, or bread-and-butter table is perhaps the most widely known of Swedish-American customs. In its traditional form, it comprised several different classes of dishes, each eaten from a separate plate. It often includes herring dishes; fish and egg recipes; cold meats and salads; hot dishes, such as Swedish Meatballs; *and rice pudding.*

Potato Sausage

    Sausage casings
1½ pounds boneless beef with
    fat trimmed
1 pound boneless pork with
    fat trimmed

6 potatoes, peeled and
    cut up
1 medium onion, cut up
1 tablespoon salt
1 teaspoon ground allspice

Rinse casings; soak at least 2 hours in water. Grind meats with coarse blade of meat grinder; combine with vegetables, salt, allspice, and ¼ teaspoon pepper. Attach sausage stuffer to grinder; push casings onto stuffer, letting some extend beyond end of attachment. Using coarse blade, grind meat-potato mixture into casings till firm but not overly full. When links are 18 inches long, tie ends with string. To cook links, prick with wooden pick in several places. In kettle combine sausage and enough water to cover; cook, covered, 30 to 40 minutes. Serve warm. Store leftovers covered with water in refrigerator; drain and reheat in skillet. Makes 5 pounds.

Swedish Potato Sausage *comes by the way of Swedish history: soldiers returning from duty in Prussia brought the potato home. Referred to as the earthpear, the potato was first used as animal feed. Later, the Swedes discovered it was good for humans, too, and to prove it, they ate it boiled, fried, creamed, and in potato sausage. Naturally, when Swedes settled in America they brought potato sausage recipes with them.*

Swedish Limpa Bread

In Swedish, the word limpa *means "a loaf of bread." Usually the bread referred to is made with rye flour, but* limpa *can also mean almost any type of bread. In America, the general meaning of the word has been changed. To Swedish-Americans* limpa *means a special type of rye bread with grated orange peel in it. Customarily this bread is not baked in a loaf pan, but is shaped into round loaves and is placed in the oven on baking sheets.*

Flaky Danish Pastry is bound to be the highlight of any coffee brunch. Try serving it the next time you have guests.

3½ to 4 cups all-purpose
   flour
2 packages active dry yeast
2 teaspoons caraway seed
½ teaspoon fennel seed
   (optional)
2 cups milk
½ cup packed brown sugar
2 tablespoons molasses
2 tablespoons butter *or*
   margarine
2 teaspoons salt
2 tablespoons grated orange
   peel
2½ cups rye flour

In a large mixing bowl combine 2½ *cups* of the all-purpose flour, the yeast, caraway seed, and fennel seed, if desired. In a saucepan combine the milk, brown sugar, molasses, butter or margarine, and salt; heat just till warm (115-120°), stirring constantly. Add to dry mixture in mixing bowl; add orange peel. Beat at low speed of electric mixer for ½ minute, scraping sides of bowl. Beat 3 minutes at high speed. By hand, stir in the rye flour and enough of the remaining all-purpose flour to make a moderately stiff dough.

Knead dough on a lightly floured surface till smooth and elastic (8 to 10 minutes). Shape dough into a ball. Place in greased bowl; turn once to grease surface. Cover; let rise in a warm place till double (1 to 1½ hours). Punch dough down; divide in half. Cover and let rest 10 minutes. Shape into 2 round loaves; place in two greased 8-inch pie plates or on greased baking sheets. Cover and let rise in a warm place till double (about 45 minutes). Bake at 375° about 30 minutes. Remove from pans; cool on rack. Makes 2.

Danish Pastry

1 cup butter *or* margarine
1/3 cup all-purpose flour
3¾ to 4 cups all-purpose
    flour
2 packages active dry yeast
1¼ cups milk

1/4 cup sugar
1 egg
1/2 teaspoon lemon extract
1/2 teaspoon almond extract
    Confectioners' Icing

Cream butter with 1/3 cup flour. Pat or roll butter mixture between 2 sheets of waxed paper to 12x6-inch rectangle. Chill well. In large mixing bowl combine *1½ cups* of remaining flour and the yeast. In saucepan heat milk, sugar, and 1 teaspoon salt just till warm (115-120°). Add to dry mixture in mixing bowl; add egg and extracts. Beat at low speed of electric mixer for 1/2 minute, scraping bowl often. Beat 3 minutes at high speed. By hand, stir in enough of the remaining flour to make a moderately soft dough. Knead on lightly floured surface till smooth (about 5 minutes).

Cover; let rest 10 minutes. On a lightly floured surface, roll dough to 14-inch square. Place chilled butter mixture on half the dough. Fold over other half, sealing edges well. Roll dough to 20x12-inch rectangle. Fold in thirds (making three layers). Roll again to a 20x12-inch rectangle. Fold again. If butter softens, chill after each rolling. Repeat rolling and folding twice more. Chill 30 minutes. Shape into *Almond Fans* and *Baby Bunting Rolls*.

Place on ungreased baking sheets. Let rise in warm place till almost double (45 to 60 minutes). Bake at 450° about 8 minutes. Brush with Confectioners' Icing. Serve warm. Makes 36.

Almond Fans: Cream 1/4 cup butter and 1/4 cup sugar. Add 1/4 cup finely chopped blanched almonds; mix well. Roll 1/3 of dough to 12x8-inch rectangle. Cut in 4x2-inch rectangles; place 1 level teaspoon almond filling along center of each. Fold lengthwise. Seal edges; curve rolls slightly. Snip side opposite sealed edge at 1-inch intervals.

Baby Bunting Rolls: In bowl combine 1/2 cup cooked dried pitted prunes; 1/4 cup sugar; 1 tablespoon all-purpose flour; 1 tablespoon lemon juice; and dash salt. Roll remaining 2/3 dough into 18x12-inch rectangle; cut in 3-inch squares. Place 1 level teaspoon prune filling in center of each square. Fold opposite corners of pastry to center; overlap edges and seal well.

Confectioners' Icing: Mix 1 cup sifted powdered sugar, 1/4 teaspoon vanilla, and enough milk to make of spreading consistency (about 1½ tablespoons).

Danish immigrants found they had quite a few problems when they tried to make their famous pastry here in America. To begin with, the flour was different; it did not hold up as well in paper-thin layers as European flour. Also, American butter usually had a higher water content and was more difficult to roll than the Danish version. Even the weather proved obstreperous in many places. Summers were so warm that a crust formed on the pastry while it was rising and the butter sometimes melted out. There was no hesitant "to be or not to be" for these Danes. That pastry was meant to be— and they worked at perfecting it. Now even kinfolk in Denmark would be proud of it.

Krumkake

3 eggs
1/2 cup sugar
1 teaspoon vanilla

1/2 cup butter *or* margarine,
    melted and cooled
1/2 cup all-purpose flour

Beat together eggs, sugar, and vanilla. Mix in butter. Beat in flour till smooth. Drop small amount batter onto *hot, ungreased* krumkake iron (for 6-inch iron use 1/2 tablespoon batter); close gently (do not squeeze). Bake till golden on one side, 15 to 20 seconds; turn

iron over and bake 15 to 20 seconds more. Remove cookie with narrow spatula; immediately roll into a cylinder on wooden or metal form. Cool, seam side down, for 30 seconds; remove form. Repeat with remaining batter. Makes about 24 cookies.

Krumkake is a Norwegian-American Christmas treat. This cookie is usually made with a special iron that has been engraved with Christmas and Nativity scenes.

Norwegian Lefse

Beat together 2 cups hot mashed potatoes, 2 tablespoons butter, 1 tablespoon milk, and 1 teaspoon salt. Cover; chill well. Turn out on lightly floured surface. Sprinkle potato mixture with 1/2 cup all-purpose flour. Knead 8 to 10 minutes, gradually kneading in another 1/2 cup all-purpose flour. Divide

into 8 *or* 16 portions; shape into balls. On floured surface, roll small balls to 6-inch circles, large balls to 9-inch circles. Roll around rolling pin; transfer to hot, greased skillet. Cook till lightly browned, 4 to 6 minutes; turn once. (Should be limp.) Repeat. Makes 8 large or 16 small.

Traditionally, small portions of Norwegian Lefse were wrapped around a piece of food such as a meatball. Today, however, many Norwegian-Americans butter their lefse, sprinkle it with sugar and cinnamon, and roll it up to eat as a type of bread.

Rosettes

2 eggs
1 tablespoon granulated
    sugar
    •   •   •
1 cup all-purpose flour

1 cup milk
1 teaspoon vanilla
    Fat for frying
    Powdered sugar

In bowl combine the eggs, granulated sugar, and ¼ teaspoon salt; beat well. Add flour, milk, and vanilla; beat smooth. Heat a rosette iron in deep hot fat (375°). Dip hot rosette iron into batter, *being careful* batter only comes ¾ of the way up the side of iron. Fry rosette in the hot fat till golden, about ½ minute. Lift iron out; tip slightly to drain off excess fat. With fork, carefully push rosette off iron onto paper toweling placed on a wire rack. Reheat iron; repeat. Sift powdered sugar over cooled rosettes. Makes 42.

Rommegrot

In large saucepan blend together 2 cups dairy sour cream and ½ cup water. Place over medium-low heat; cook and stir till sour cream separates, about 15 minutes. Mix ½ cup all-purpose flour and ½ teaspoon salt; blend in 1 cup cold water. Stir into the sour cream. Cook and stir over medium heat till thickened and bubbly. Gradually blend in 2 cups warmed milk. Pour into a bowl. Dot with 2 tablespoons butter *or* margarine; sprinkle with a mixture of ¼ cup sugar and ¼ teaspoon ground cinnamon. Serve warm. Serves 8.

Herring in Cream

1 pound dressed boned
    salt herring
½ cup dairy sour cream
¼ cup chopped onion

1 tablespoon snipped
    parsley
1 tablespoon lemon juice
½ teaspoon sugar

Cut herring in 1-inch pieces. Place in earthenware or glass container; cover with cold water. Soak 8 hours or overnight; change water 2 or 3 times. Drain. Mix with the remaining ingredients. Chill well. Makes 2 cups.

Dining with the French-Canadians

The French-Canadians in the United States are virtually all descendants of the French who colonized Canada in the seventeenth and early eighteenth centuries. These numbered 65,000 in 1763, when England took over Canada. Today, those 65,000 have over 5.5 million descendants. Despite their long separation from France, they treasure the French language and customs, the Roman Catholic religion, and the fact that they are *"Canadiens."*

Most of those who settled in the United States arrived between 1870 and 1900, intending to remain only long enough to save money and then return to Canada. But many stayed, chiefly in New England, but with clusters here and there in the upper Mississippi Valley. They became lumberjacks, textile workers, and more recently, auto workers. In New England they turned abandoned farms into profitable enterprises.

When they arrived in the United States, they made little attempt to become acculturated — which aroused resentment among the native-born. But they worked hard and well, had large, closely knit families, and became excellent citizens.

The cuisine of the French-Canadians is much like the people themselves — hardy with a blend of French, New England, and Canadian influences. It is a country cuisine based on many fresh products, especially corn, pork, and maple syrup. Typical of French-Canadian cooking are the robust soups. The French word for a hearty soup or stew, *chaudiere,* was long ago Americanized to chowder, and their split pea soup or cheese soup is served often on American tables. The French-Canadians also enjoy meat pies and two of the most famous dishes from this cuisine are *tourtière* and *cipâte* (French-Canadian pot pie). For dessert the French-Canadians are likely to choose something flavored with maple syrup or the ever popular *buche de Noel.*

The French-Canadians occupy a unique position in the list of immigrants who settled in America. Since they tended to settle in New England, the French-Canadians, like the Mexican immigrants who settled in the Southwest, were not separated from their homeland by a long distance. This proximity enabled them to keep their own customs and traditions intact easier than most of the other immigrant groups. Because there was much travel back and forth across the northern border, contacts with family and friends back home stayed strong. Also French-Canadian communities relied on Quebec to provide them with priests for their churches and teachers for their schools. As a result many of these communities remain faithful to the old traditions in spite of pressures to become Americanized.

Mashed Potatoes with Turnips

2 large turnips, peeled and
cut into chunks
4 large potatoes, peeled
and quartered
½ cup finely chopped onion

2 tablespoons butter *or*
margarine
¾ teaspoon salt
⅛ teaspoon white pepper

Cook turnips, covered, in small amount of boiling salted water for 10 minutes. Add potatoes and onion; cook till vegetables are tender, 15 to 20 minutes. Drain well; mash vegetables with butter, salt, and pepper. Season with additional salt. Serve hot. Makes 4½ cups.

Note: Chill leftover potato-turnip mixture. Shape chilled mixture into 2½-inch patties, using ⅓ cup mixture for each. Coat patties with fine dry bread crumbs. Cook patties in butter *or* margarine till lightly browned on both sides, about 4 minutes per side.

Tourtière

1 pound lean ground pork
1 cup water
½ cup finely chopped onion
½ cup fine dry bread crumbs
1 teaspoon salt
⅛ teaspoon ground sage

Dash pepper
Dash ground nutmeg
Pastry for 2-crust
9-inch pie (see
recipe, page 351)

Brown ground pork in skillet; drain off excess fat. Stir in water, onion, bread crumbs, salt, sage, pepper, and nutmeg. Simmer, covered, till onion is tender, about 20 minutes, stirring often. Line a 9-inch pie plate with pas-

try; fill with meat mixture. Adjust top crust; seal and flute. Cut slits in top. Bake at 400° till golden brown, about 30 minutes. Cover edges of pastry with foil, if necessary, to prevent over-browning. Makes 6 servings.

Tourtière is the traditional pork pie served by French-Canadians early Christmas morning after midnight mass. The heartiness of this dish makes it easy to see why it makes a festive meal on a cold winter morning. The name for the pie comes from the old pottery casserole, called a tourte in which the French-Canadians first baked this flavorful pie.

Canadian Cheese Soup

In saucepan combine ½ cup finely chopped carrot, ¼ cup finely chopped celery, ¼ cup finely chopped onion, and 2 tablespoons butter. Cover; cook over low heat till vegetables are tender. Stir in ¼ cup all-purpose flour.

Add 2 cups milk, 1½ cups chicken broth, and dash paprika. Cook and stir till thick and bubbly. Stir in 1½ cups shredded sharp American cheese till melted. *Do not boil.* Makes 4 or 5 main dish servings or 8 appetizer servings.

French-Canadian Split Pea Soup

1 pound dry green split
    peas
1 meaty ham bone
1 cup chopped onion
1 teaspoon instant chicken
    bouillon granules

1 cup sliced carrot
1 cup chopped celery
2 slices bacon
½ cup light cream
2 tablespoons butter *or*
    margarine

In kettle mix peas, ham bone, onion, bouillon granules, 8 cups water, ½ teaspoon salt, and ¼ teaspoon pepper. Bring to boil. Cover; reduce heat. Simmer 1½ hours; stir often. Remove ham bone; dice meat. Return meat to soup; add carrot and celery. Simmer 30 minutes. Cook bacon till crisp; drain and crumble. Stir bacon, cream, and butter into soup; heat through. Serves 8.

Cipâte

2 large chicken breasts
1½ pounds cubed boneless
    pork, veal, and/or beef
3 tablespoons cooking oil
1 13¾-ounce can chicken
    broth
1 cup chopped onion
1 cup sliced carrot
1 cup chopped celery
1 cup chopped potato

1 cup sliced fresh
    mushrooms
2 tablespoons snipped
    parsley
1 teaspoon salt
⅛ teaspoon dried savory,
    crushed
2 tablespoons all-purpose
    flour
Pastry Topper

Remove skin and bones from chicken; cube meat. In saucepan brown all meats in hot oil. Stir in broth, vegetables, parsley, salt, savory, and ⅛ teaspoon pepper. Cook, covered, till meat is tender, 1¼ to 1½ hours. Blend ⅓ cup cold water into flour. Stir into hot mixture. Cook and stir till thick and bubbly. Keep hot. Prepare Pastry Topper. Turn hot meat mixture into 2-quart casserole. Top with Pastry Topper. Cut slits. Bake at 350° till golden, 30 to 35 minutes. Serves 8 to 10.

Pastry Topper: In a bowl mix 1 cup all-purpose flour, 1½ teaspoons baking powder, and ¼ teaspoon salt. Cut in 6 tablespoons butter till size of small peas. Add ¼ cup milk; mix well. On lightly floured surface roll to fit top of 2-quart casserole.

Maple Syrup Pie

3 slightly beaten eggs
1 cup pure maple syrup
½ cup packed brown sugar
2 tablespoons butter, melted
2 tablespoons all-purpose
    flour

1 teaspoon vanilla
Dash salt
½ cup chopped pecans
1 unbaked 9-inch pastry
    shell (see recipe,
    page 351)

Mix eggs, syrup, sugar, butter, flour, vanilla, and salt. Beat smooth with rotary beater. Stir in nuts. Fill pastry shell. Bake at 350° about 40 minutes.

Sucre à la Creme

Butter sides of heavy 2-quart saucepan. In it mix 1 cup packed brown sugar, 1 cup granulated sugar, 1 cup light cream, and 1 tablespoon light corn syrup, if desired. Cook and stir over medium heat till sugars dissolve and mixture boils. Cook to soft ball stage (238°); stir only if necessary. Remove from heat; cool to lukewarm (110°). Do not stir. Add 1 tablespoon butter or margarine and 1 teaspoon vanilla. Beat vigorously till it becomes thick and starts to lose its gloss, 3 to 4 minutes. *Quickly* spread in buttered 9x5x 3-inch loaf pan. Score while candy is warm; cut when firm. Makes 1 pound.

Buche de Noel

4 egg yolks
½ cup granulated sugar
½ teaspoon vanilla
4 egg whites
½ cup granulated sugar
1 cup sifted cake flour

½ teaspoon baking powder
¼ teaspoon salt
   Powdered sugar
2 tablespoons rum
   Chocolate Filling

In mixing bowl beat egg yolks till thick and lemon-colored. Gradually add ½ cup granulated sugar, beating constantly. Stir in vanilla. Beat egg whites till soft peaks form. Gradually add ½ cup granulated sugar, beating till stiff peaks form. Fold in egg yolk mixture. Sift together cake flour, baking powder, and salt; fold into egg mixture. Pour into greased and floured 15½x10½x1½-inch baking pan. Bake at 375° till done, 10 to 12 minutes. Promptly loosen edges of cake; turn out onto a dish towel sprinkled with powdered sugar. Drizzle warm cake with rum. From the long side, roll warm cake and towel together; cool. Unroll cake; remove towel. Spread cake with *half* the Chocolate Filling. Reroll. Diagonally cut a 4-inch piece of cake from the roll.

Place the cut edge of piece against longer roll on a serving plate (see picture). Frost with remaining Chocolate Filling; mark with fork tines to resemble bark. Decorate as desired.

Chocolate Filling: In a small saucepan melt 1½ ounces unsweetened chocolate; cool. In small saucepan combine ⅔ cup granulated sugar and ⅓ cup water. Bring to boiling. Cook to soft ball stage (240°). In small mixing bowl beat 2 egg yolks till thick and lemon-colored. Very gradually add the hot syrup, beating constantly; continue beating till mixture is completely cooled. Beat in ½ cup softened butter or margarine, *1 tablespoon at a time.* Stir in melted chocolate, 1 tablespoon rum, and 1 teaspoon instant coffee crystals; beat till mixture is thick.

Among the French-Canadians, Christmastime doesn't count if it does not include *Buche de Noel*, a jelly roll cake with chocolate filling. The cake is arranged and decorated to resemble the festive Yule Log of Christmases past.

Cretons

Cretons is a pork appetizer spread that always finds a place on French-Canadian holiday tables. It is traditionally served at the Reveillon (the celebration held after midnight mass on Christmas morning) and on New Year's Day after the Benediction ceremony.

½ pound salt pork
1 pound boneless pork, cut up
1 large onion, quartered
½ teaspoon ground cinnamon

¼ teaspoon ground cloves
⅛ teaspoon ground allspice
⅛ teaspoon pepper
¼ cup fine dry bread crumbs
  Assorted crackers

Trim rind from salt pork; discard. Dice salt pork. In skillet cook salt pork till crisp and golden brown, about 15 minutes. Drain, reserving ¼ cup drippings. Using fine blade of food grinder, grind salt pork along with boneless pork and onion. Return to skillet; stir in reserved drippings, cinnamon, cloves, allspice, and pepper. Cook, covered, over medium-low heat 15 to 20 minutes, stirring occasionally. Remove from heat. Stir in fine dry bread crumbs. Turn mixture into plastic wrap-lined 1½-quart bowl, pressing gently to smooth surface. Cover and chill several hours. Invert onto serving plate and remove plastic wrap. Serve with assorted crackers. Makes about 2½ cups.

Jewish-American Delicacies

In areas where there is a large Jewish-American population the Jewish delicatessen has become an institution selling a wide variety of foods from borscht to chicken soup to chopped liver to kosher frankfurters to "Danish" pastries. The bagel, however, reigns supreme. While almost always the same ring shape, it is often dressed up with garlic, onion, salt, poppy seed, or sesame seed. Teamed with cream cheese and lox (smoked salmon) the bagel is now an American classic. But many Jewish-Americans maintain that this mainstay of the "deli" is equally good topped with smoked whitefish, sturgeon, carp, or herring.

The first Jews to set foot in America arrived in New Amsterdam in 1654. They came from Curaçao, where they had been subjected to persecution, and they numbered just twenty-three—the forerunners of eventual millions. By the end of the Revolution, between two thousand and three thousand Jews were settled in the thirteen colonies. Most of these were Sephardim (Jews who came directly or by descent from Spain or Portugal, where their ancestors had lived for many centuries). Among them were prosperous merchants, shippers, and bankers, including some—like Haym Salomon—who helped finance the young republic.

Jewish immigration in the nineteenth century came in two waves. The first followed soon after the European political upheavals in 1848, and was largely from Germany. They scattered throughout the land, often becoming peddlers or small merchants or entering some phase of banking. From them are descended some of the best-known families in America—for example, the Lehmans, the Loebs, and the Guggenheims.

Until about 1880, most of the Jews in America were from the countries of western Europe and they did not number more than about 230,000. Then, suddenly, there was a tightening of anti-Jewish laws and an intensification of anti-Jewish sentiment in the empires of Austria-Hungary and Russia. Living conditions there for Jews became intolerable. There were frequent and bloody *pogroms* that destroyed thousands. The result was a wholesale migration to the United States. Between 1880 and 1927, millions of Jews from eastern Europe and Russia made the journey. Most came in family groups. Because of the traditional Jewish respect for learning, they had a high rate of literacy, and because the governments of the countries they were leaving had made it difficult or impossible for Jews to own land, they lacked experience as farmers. Thus, many of them had some kind of mechanical training — usually in such trades as tailoring, dressmaking, and shoemaking — or were merchants, and some were moneylenders. And for these reasons, they tended to settle in cities.

After the rise of the Nazis during the 1930s, a new stream of Jewish refugees sought our shores, and among them were many who enriched our culture — from physics (Albert Einstein) to the theater (Kurt Weill).

As for Jewish cookery, any non-Jew who has lived in cities with large Jewish populations has probably become acquainted with the pleasures of chopped chicken livers, bagels, lox, blintzes, gefilte fish, and chicken soup with matzo balls. Jewish cuisine has borrowed from many cultures, yet at the same time has retained its own distinctive quality. This quality is a blend of religious tradition and culinary pragmatism. The dishes that result can truly be called Jewish-American delicacies.

Rendered Chicken Fat

½ pound chicken fat, finely chopped

¼ cup finely chopped onion

In a heavy skillet combine chicken fat and onion, mashing fat with a spoon. Cook over low heat till fat pieces are crisp and brown, about 30 minutes. Strain fat through a fine sieve; store in refrigerator. Makes about ¾ cup.

Jewish Fruit Kugel

4 ounces wide noodles
• • •
2 beaten eggs
¼ cup sugar
3 tablespoons cooking oil
⅛ teaspoon ground cinnamon

1 medium apple, peeled, cored, and diced
¼ cup dried apricots, chopped
¼ cup raisins

Cook noodles according to package directions; drain well. In a large bowl combine eggs, sugar, cooking oil, and cinnamon; beat well. Stir in apples, apricots, and raisins. Toss fruit mixture with drained noodles. Turn into a greased 1-quart casserole. Cover; bake at 350° for 30 minutes. Stir occasionally. Serve hot as a meat accompaniment or dessert. Serves 7.

Gefilte Fish

½ pound fresh *or* frozen pike fillets
½ pound fresh *or* frozen whitefish fillets
½ pound fresh *or* frozen carp fillets
6 cups water
2 medium carrots, sliced
2 medium onions, chopped
1 tablespoon salt

⅛ teaspoon pepper
• • •
2 eggs
2 tablespoons matzo meal *or* cracker meal
2 tablespoons ice water
½ teaspoon salt
Dash pepper
Prepared horseradish
Pickles

Thaw frozen fish. In large saucepan combine 6 cups water, *half* the carrots, *half* the onions, 1 tablespoon salt, and ⅛ teaspoon pepper. Bring to boiling. Simmer, covered, 30 minutes. Finely grind fish and remaining carrots and onions. Place in large bowl; add eggs, meal, ice water, ½ teaspoon salt, and dash pepper. Beat at high speed till fluffy. Shape into balls or fingers, using 3 tablespoonfuls for each. Place in broth; cover and simmer 20 minutes. Drain; serve hot or cold with prepared horseradish and pickles. Serves 6.

The cooking is influenced to a large degree by the Jewish dietary laws. These are a series of Biblical passages combined with rabbinical interpretations that have determined which foods are fit to eat, or kosher, and which foods are forbidden, or trayf. The laws dictate that only animals that are cloven-footed and chew cud are allowed. Thus, pork is eliminated because the pig does not chew its cud. The laws also state that fish must have both fins and scales, therefore lobster and shellfish are forbidden. In addition the Old Testament prohibits "seething" a kid in its mother's milk. This directive has been interpreted to mean that meat and dairy products must not be served at the same meal or even in the same china. To help in the observance of this law, a third category of foods called pareve, or neutral, can be used with either meat or dairy dishes. This group includes eggs, fish, vegetables, fruits, and grains.

Gefilte Fish *is one of the dishes typically served at the Friday night Sabbath meal. Originally this dish was prepared by gefilting or stuffing a fish skin with a filling of chopped or ground fish fillets, onion, eggs, salt, pepper, and matzo meal. The preparation has been simplified today by shaping the filling into balls, as in this recipe.*

Chicken Soup with Matzo Balls is served frequently, but particularly during the celebration of Passover when no foods with leavening are allowed. The culinary highlight of the celebration is the Seder or the Passover supper. This begins with seven foods symbolic of the story of the Passover. They are a roasted egg and a lamb shank symbolizing the ancient sacrifices for Passover, bitter herbs— such as horseradish—to indicate the bitterness of bondage, charoset—a mixture of chopped apples, nuts, and wine— to represent the mortar that went into the building of the Egyptian pyramids, leafy green vegetables to signify the hope of spring, parsley dipped in salt water to stand for the Red Sea, and matzo for the bread that was left unleavened when the Jews fled Egypt. After the religious segment of the meal, eating begins and one of the first dishes is sure to be Chicken Soup with Matzo Balls.

Chicken Soup

1 5- to 6-pound stewing
   chicken, cut up
8 sprigs parsley
3 stalks celery, cut up
2 medium carrots, cut up

2 medium onions, cut up
2 bay leaves
Matzo Balls *or*
   Kreplach (optional)
   (see recipes below)

In Dutch oven mix chicken, parsley, vegetables, bay leaves, 1 tablespoon salt, and ¼ teaspoon pepper; add 12 cups water. Simmer till chicken is tender, 2 to 2½ hours. Remove chicken.

Cool soup; skim off fat. Remove meat from bones; cut up. Strain broth; discard vegetables. Mix broth and chicken; heat through. Use to cook Matzo Balls *or* Kreplach, if desired. Serves 8.

Matzo Balls

3 egg yolks
¼ cup chicken broth
¼ cup rendered chicken fat,
   melted (see recipe,
   page 249)

1 teaspoon salt
Dash pepper
¾ cup matzo meal
3 stiffly beaten egg whites
Chicken Soup

Beat yolks well with electric mixer. Beat in broth, fat, salt, and pepper. Continue to beat, adding matzo meal ¼ cup at a time. Fold in egg whites. Cover; chill till firm, 30 minutes. For

each matzo ball, shape about 2 teaspoons dough into ball. Drop into boiling Chicken Soup; stir once or twice to prevent sticking. Simmer, covered, 40 minutes; *do not stir.* Makes 30.

Kreplach

½ pound ground beef
1 cup chopped onion
1 beaten egg

1 egg
¾ cup all-purpose flour
Chicken Soup

In skillet cook beef and onion till meat is browned and onion is tender. Remove from heat; drain off fat. Stir in beaten egg and ½ teaspoon salt. Cool. In bowl mix 1 egg, 2 tablespoons water, and ½ teaspoon salt; add enough of the flour to make a moderately stiff

dough. On floured surface roll to 14-inch square. Cut into 2-inch squares. Top each with 1 teaspoon filling. Moisten edges with water. Fold diagonally to form a triangle; seal edges. Simmer, uncovered, in chicken broth till tender, about 20 minutes. Makes 48.

Challah

In earlier days, Challah had a special significance for the opening of the weekly Sabbath. On Friday evenings, the table would be covered with a fresh cloth and set with lighted candles in brass candlesticks. The Challah at this family gathering was symbolically cut by the oldest male and from then until sunset on Saturday no other flame would be lit, no other food would be cooked, no money would be carried, and no traveling would be done except on foot.

2 packages active dry yeast
¾ cup milk
¼ cup butter *or* margarine
2 tablespoons sugar
2 teaspoons salt
   Dash ground saffron

4½ to 5 cups all-purpose
   flour
2 eggs
1 egg yolk
1 tablespoon water
1 tablespoon poppy seed

Soften yeast in ½ cup warm water (110°). Heat milk, butter, sugar, salt, and saffron till sugar dissolves; cool to lukewarm. Stir in *2 cups* flour; beat well. Add yeast and 2 eggs; beat well. Stir in enough remaining flour to make a soft dough. Knead on floured surface till smooth (8 to 10 minutes). Shape into ball. Place in greased bowl; turn once. Cover; let rise till double (about 1¼

hours). Punch down; divide in thirds. Cover; let rest 10 minutes. With hands roll each third to 18-inch-long strand; braid strands and secure ends. Place on greased baking sheet. Cover; let rise in warm place till double (about 30 minutes). Brush with egg yolk mixed with 1 tablespoon water; sprinkle with poppy seed. Bake at 375° for 45 to 50 minutes. Makes 1.

Potato Latkes

3 cups grated potatoes
½ cup shredded onion
2 beaten eggs
2 tablespoons all-purpose
    flour
1 teaspoon salt

2 to 3 tablespoons rendered
    chicken fat, melted
    (see recipe, page 249)
    or vegetable cooking oil
Dairy sour cream *or*
    applesauce

In large bowl stir together potatoes, onion, eggs, flour, and salt. Mix well. Grease a hot griddle or skillet with melted chicken fat or vegetable oil. Drop batter by tablespoonfuls onto griddle or skillet. Spread the batter slightly. Fry till browned, 2 minutes per side. Keep pancakes warm as more are fried. Serve hot with sour cream or applesauce. Makes 6 to 8 servings.

Potato Latkes are a feature of Chanukah. The temple was under seige, wrote the ancients, and there was oil enough for only one day to light it. But by a miracle it lasted for eight days. The fat used to fry the latkes is symbolic of that oil.

Cheese Blintzes *(see photo, page 253)*

¾ cup all-purpose flour
½ teaspoon salt
1 cup milk
2 eggs
1 12-ounce carton dry
    cottage cheese
    (1½ cups)

1 beaten egg
2 tablespoons sugar
½ teaspoon vanilla
    Dash ground cinnamon
2 tablespoons butter
    Canned cherry pie filling
    Dairy sour cream

In a bowl stir together flour and salt. Combine milk and the 2 eggs; gradually add to the flour mixture, beating till batter is smooth. Pour about 2 tablespoons batter into hot, lightly greased 6-inch skillet; quickly swirl skillet to spread batter evenly. Cook over medium heat till pancakes are golden on bottom, 1½ to 2 minutes. Loosen; turn out onto paper toweling. Repeat with remaining batter, making 12 pancakes. In a bowl beat together cottage cheese, 1 egg, sugar, vanilla, and cinnamon till nearly smooth. Place pancakes browned side up; spoon small amount of cheese mixture in centers. Overlap sides and ends atop cheese filling. Brown on both sides in butter. Serve hot with warmed pie filling and sour cream. Makes 6 servings.

Lighting the menorah is an important part of the celebration of Chanukah, the Jewish Feast of Lights. One candle is lit each night until all are aglow on the eighth and final night.

Pictured opposite: It has been said that the philosophy of Jewish cooking is "Eat! Eat!" and the more you eat, the happier the cook is. When *Bagels, Hamantaschen,* and *Cheese Blintzes* (see recipe, page 251) are served, it's easy to make the cook happy.

Bagels

In large bowl mix 1½ cups all-purpose flour and 2 packages active dry yeast. Combine 1½ cups warm water (110°), 3 tablespoons sugar, and 1 tablespoon salt; add to flour mixture. Beat at low speed of electric mixer for ½ minute, scraping sides of bowl. Beat 3 minutes at high speed. By hand, stir in 2¾ to 3 cups all-purpose flour to make a moderately stiff dough. Knead on lightly floured surface till smooth (8 to 10 minutes). Cover; let rest 15 minutes. Cut in 12 portions; shape into balls.

Punch a hole in centers of each. Pull gently to enlarge hole, working into uniform shape. Cover; let rise 20 minutes. (*Optional step* for glossy surface: Place raised bagels on *ungreased* baking sheet; broil 5 inches from heat 1½ to 2 minutes per side.) In kettle bring 1 gallon water and 1 tablespoon sugar to boiling. Simmer 4 bagels at a time for 7 minutes, turning once. Drain. Place on greased baking sheet. Bake at 375° for 30 to 35 minutes. (If broiled, bake bagels 25 minutes.) Makes 12.

Tsimmes has come to have a symbolic significance for several Jewish holidays. At Rosh Hashana, the Jewish New Year, a carrot and honey version of this dish is served. The round slices of carrot suggest gold coins and are a wish for prosperity and the honey represents the sweetness of life hoped for in the new year. At Succoth or the Festival of Thanksgiving, a sweet potato and fruit Tsimmes such as this one is served to suggest the bounty of the harvest.

Tsimmes

1 pound beef chuck steak, cut in 1-inch cubes
3 tablespoons all-purpose flour
2 tablespoons rendered chicken fat (see recipe, page 249) *or* pareve margarine
1 cup water
½ cup chopped onion

2 tablespoons honey
1 teaspoon salt
⅛ teaspoon ground cinnamon
3 whole cloves
1 large sweet potato, peeled and cut in 1-inch cubes
1 cup pitted dried prunes
½ cup dried apricots

Coat beef cubes with flour. In a large skillet brown beef in hot chicken fat or pareve margarine. Stir in water, onion, honey, salt, cinnamon, and cloves. Turn the mixture into 2-quart casse-

role. Bake, covered, at 350° for 30 minutes. Stir in sweet potato, prunes, and apricots. Continue baking, covered, till meat is tender, about 1 hour more. Makes 6 servings.

Purim is the Jewish feast that commemorates the triumph of Queen Esther over the enemy Haman. The triangular pastries, Hamantaschen are named after him and are traditionally served during Purim. There are several explanations of exactly what Hamantaschen symbolize. Some say they represent Haman's hat; others say his purse; and still others claim they duplicate his donkey-shaped ears.

Hamantaschen

1 package active dry yeast
¼ cup warm water (110°)
1 cup milk
¾ cup sugar
½ cup pareve margarine
1 teaspoon salt

5 to 5½ cups all-purpose flour
2 eggs
Prune *or* Lemon-Poppy Seed Filling
1 egg yolk

Soften yeast in warm water. In saucepan heat milk, sugar, margarine, and salt till sugar dissolves; cool to lukewarm. Stir in *2 cups* flour; beat well. Add softened yeast and 2 eggs; beat well. Stir in enough of the remaining flour to make a moderately stiff dough. Knead on floured surface till smooth (8 to 10 minutes). Shape into a ball. Place in greased bowl; turn once. Cover; let rise till double (1¼ to 1½ hours). Divide in half. Roll each half to 17x12-inch rectangle. Cut into 4-inch circles. Place Prune or Lemon-Poppy Seed Filling in centers. Moisten edges of dough; bring sides up and pinch together, forming a triangular base (see photo). Place on greased baking sheets;

cover and let rise till double (20 to 30 minutes). Brush tops with egg yolk mixed with 1 tablespoon water. Bake at 350° for 15 to 20 minutes. Makes 30.

Prune Filling: Rinse 2 cups unpitted dried prunes. In saucepan cover with water 1 inch above fruit. Cover pan and simmer gently 10 to 20 minutes; drain. Remove pits; chop prunes. Stir in ½ cup sugar, ½ cup chopped nuts, 1 teaspoon grated lemon peel, and 1 tablespoon lemon juice. Use about 1 tablespoon filling for each circle.

Lemon-Poppy Seed Filling: Combine one 12-ounce can poppy seed filling, 1 teaspoon grated lemon peel, and 1 tablespoon lemon juice. Use about ½ tablespoon filling for each circle.

Chopped Chicken Livers

1 pound chicken livers
¼ cup finely chopped onion
¼ cup rendered chicken fat
  (see recipe, page 249)

3 hard-cooked eggs
1 teaspoon salt
1 large lettuce leaf
Assorted crackers

Cut large chicken livers in half. In skillet combine chicken livers, onion, and chicken fat. Cook, covered, over medium heat till onion is tender but not brown, about 10 minutes. Cool. Remove livers (reserve onion and any pan juices); chop fine. Finely chop 2 *eggs* and combine with chopped livers, onion, pan juices, salt, and ¼ teaspoon pepper. Cover and chill 3 hours or overnight. To serve, mound mixture on lettuce. Sieve remaining egg yolk and chop egg white. Use as garnish. Serve with crackers. Makes 2 cups.

much food, including Chopped Chicken Livers.

One ritual important to families with sons is the Bar Mitzvah, *which in the Jewish religious community, celebrates the coming of age of a boy. After a simple religious ceremony, a party is usually held. It may be a modest party or an elaborate catered affair. Whichever it is, it will surely offer much food, including* Chopped Chicken Livers.

Food with a Mexican Flair

One gift Mexican-Americans gave the United States was tequila. The intoxicating brew originated long ago in the Toltec civilization when the women prepared a drink called Pulque, *a beer-like substance made from the juice of the agave plant. When the Spaniards arrived, they refined the process and began distilling what we know today as tequila. The name "tequila" comes from a small town in the state of Jalisco in Mexico where blue or tequilana agave is grown. The type of tequila known as* mescal *is distilled from a different species of agave and comes from the state of Oaxaca.*

Driven by political unrest or by extreme poverty, thousands of Mexican nationals have crossed the southern border of the United States since 1900, both legally and illegally, to become Mexican-Americans. Many have found work on the railroads, in mines, on ranches, and harvesting or packing fruits, vegetables, cotton, and sugar cane. They have become a large part of the labor force in southwestern states such as Texas, Arizona, and California. Mexican-American settlements of considerable size have also grown up in Chicago, Toledo, Detroit, and other northern cities. Although first attracted by the chance to earn money to send back home, many Mexican immigrants have remained in the United States to become citizens. Among their many valuable contributions to their new country, not the least has been a unique and wonderful cuisine.

Foods that originated with the Indians of what is now Mexico include corn, capsicum peppers, squashes, pumpkins, tomatoes, sweet potatoes, avocados, chocolate, and vanilla. To these tasty ingredients, the Spanish conquerors added dairy products, honey, raisins, garbanzos (chick-peas), chicken, and other European foods. The combination has created many imaginative new dishes and the United States has adopted quite a number of them: hard- and soft-shell tacos, guacamole, frijoles, and various versions of enchiladas. The most familiar enchilada recipe calls for rolling tortillas around a meat or cheese filling and baking them in a gently spiced sauce. Tortillas, made with either blue or white cornmeal, are also a Mexican specialty and are often eaten in place of bread. Another alternative is the delicious, deep-fried, pillow-shaped sopaipilla.

The history of yet another Mexican-American favorite, the tamale goes back to the Aztecs. Over the years, the recipe has been perfected to give us today's version — cornmeal mush with a chili-spiced meat filling, wrapped in cornhusks, tied, and steamed slowly over boiling water.

Mexican-Americans have also been responsible for introducing the United States to the many kinds of chili peppers, both green and red. They

are used fresh, pickled, dried, and powdered. Some are very mild, and some will take your head off. Besides chili, some other flavorings that have crossed the Rio Grande include coriander, anise, cumin, mint, black sage, and wild celery.

Oddly enough, the dish that Americans are most apt to identify as Mexican—chili con carne—isn't Mexican at all. It was invented in West Texas, though it was patterned after the stews that are sold in Mexican markets. This is just one of many dishes developed in the United States, but inspired by the cooking of Mexico. Residents of the Southwest call it Tex-Mex cooking.

In addition to being inspired by Mexican cooking, Americans are also inspired by Mexican merrymaking. Each year cities all over the Southwest hold fiestas. The atmosphere of the festival is light and happy, the air is filled with the music of mariachi bands, and people eat lots of food— all with a touch of Old Mexico.

Tamales

2 pounds boneless beef *or* pork, cubed
3 tablespoons cooking oil
¼ cup all-purpose flour
1 cup Red Chili Sauce (see recipe, page 40)
6 tablespoons finely chopped canned green chili peppers

2 cloves garlic, minced
1½ teaspoons salt
¼ teaspoon dried oregano, crushed

• • •

Cornhusks, parchment, *or* foil
Tamale Dough

In saucepan combine beef or pork cubes and enough water to cover; simmer till meat is well done, about 1½ hours. Drain, reserving 1½ cups stock. Shred meat; brown in hot oil. Stir in flour; cook and stir till flour is browned. Stir in the Red Chili Sauce, chili peppers, garlic, salt, oregano, and reserved stock. Simmer, covered, about 30 minutes. For tamale wrappers, cut cornhusks, parchment, or foil into 8x8-inch squares. (Make 12 wrappers.) Measure ½ cup tamale dough into center of each wrapper. Spread dough to 6x5-inch rectangle; spoon ⅓ cup meat mixture down center of each dough rectangle. Fold two opposite sides of wrapper toward center. Gently peel edges of dough from wrapper; seal dough edges to enclose filling. Fold wrapper edges together to seal. Tuck ends under or tie. Place tamales on rack in large steamer or electric skillet. Add water to just below rack. Cover and steam 1½ hours, adding water when necessary. Makes 12.

Tamale Dough: With electric mixer cream 1½ cups lard and 1½ teaspoons salt. Mix 4½ cups masa harina and 2⅔ cups warm water; beat into lard.

The Aztecs were making tamales long before the Spaniards arrived. They were prepared in a number of ways. One was to wrap the corn mixture (which could be anything from plain cornmeal to cornmeal with chilies, meat, or fish) in cornhusks and bury the bundles in the hot ashes of the fire. Another way was to place the bundles on a trivet in a covered pot and steam them. Where trivets were not available corncobs were used as a support. Every generation seemed to develop new variations of tamales. The Aztecs even had a sweet version.

Guacamole

4 avocados, seeded, peeled, and mashed
¼ cup finely chopped onion
2 to 4 tablespoons finely chopped canned green chili peppers
2 to 3 tablespoons lemon juice

1 teaspoon salt
1 teaspoon Worcestershire sauce
Few drops bottled hot pepper sauce
2 medium tomatoes, seeded and finely chopped
Corn chips

In a bowl stir together the mashed avocados, onion, chili peppers, lemon juice, salt, Worcestershire sauce, and hot pepper sauce. Season to taste. Stir in the tomatoes. Chill. Serve with corn chips. Makes 2⅓ cups.

April is fiesta time in San Antonio — in commemoration of the Battle of San Jacinto in which Texas won its independence from Mexico in 1836. Parades, dancing, music, and always an abundance of food mark the 10-day celebration. It's also a time to wish a special friend good luck by breaking a cascarón over his head. These richly decorated eggshells are filled with confetti.

To the people of Mexico the egg has always been a symbolic food item. In an ancient Mayan ceremony, babies were fed an egg to give them understanding. Later, the egg became a mark of prosperity. Religious pilgrims would offer them to the Virgin at the shrine of Guadalupe Hidalgo as a sign of devotion. Today eggs are still considered a valuable food. One way Mexican-Americans enjoy them is in Huevos Rancheros.

Huevos Rancheros

¼ cup cooking oil
6 Flour Tortillas (see recipe opposite) *or* frozen tortillas, thawed
½ cup chopped onion
1 small clove garlic, minced
Cooking oil
3 large tomatoes, peeled cored, and chopped

2 canned green chili peppers, drained, rinsed, seeded, and chopped (¼ cup)
¼ teaspoon salt
• • •
6 eggs
1 cup shredded Monterey Jack cheese

In a medium skillet heat the ¼ cup cooking oil. Dip the tortillas in oil for a few seconds till softened but not brown. Keep warm. In the same skillet cook the onion and garlic till tender but not brown (add more oil if necessary). Stir in the tomatoes, green chili peppers, and salt. Simmer, uncovered, 10 minutes. Slide the eggs into the hot tomato mixture, taking care not to break the egg yolks. Season the mixture with salt and pepper. Cover skillet and cook the eggs till of desired doneness. Place an egg with some of the tomato mixture on each tortilla. Top each serving with a small amount of shredded cheese. Makes 6 servings.

Sopa Ranchera

¼ cup chopped onion
1 tablespoon cooking oil
• • •
4 cups chicken broth
¼ cup regular rice

¼ cup tomato purée
¼ teaspoon salt
Dash pepper
1 cup frozen peas

In skillet cook onion in oil till tender but not brown. Stir in broth, rice, purée, salt, and pepper. Bring to boiling. Reduce heat; cover and simmer 25 minutes. Stir in peas; simmer, covered, 5 minutes more. Makes 4 servings.

Flour Tortillas

2 cups all-purpose flour
1 teaspoon salt
1 teaspoon baking powder

1 tablespoon lard
1/2 to 3/4 cup warm water
(110°)

In mixing bowl stir together flour, salt, and baking powder. Cut in lard till the mixture resembles cornmeal. Add 1/2 cup of the warm water and mix till dough can be gathered into a ball. (If needed, add additional water, 1 tablespoon at a time.) Let dough rest 15 minutes. Divide dough into 12 portions. Shape into 1-inch balls. On a lightly floured surface, roll each ball to a 7-inch circle. Trim uneven edges to make round tortillas. Cook in ungreased skillet over medium heat till lightly browned, about 1 1/2 minutes per side. Serve hot as bread with butter, if desired, or use in Huevos Rancheros or Chicken Enchiladas (see recipe, page 259). Makes 12 tortillas.

Chili Con Queso

1/2 cup finely chopped onion
2 tablespoons butter *or* margarine
• • •
2 medium tomatoes, peeled, seeded, and chopped (about 1 cup)

1 4-ounce can green chili peppers, chopped
1/2 teaspoon salt
1 3-ounce package cream cheese, cut in cubes
Corn chips

In small skillet cook finely chopped onion in butter or margarine till tender but not brown. Stir in tomatoes, chili peppers, and salt. Simmer, uncovered, 10 to 15 minutes. Add cream cheese; heat and stir till cheese is melted. Pour into small chafing dish; keep warm over candle warmer. Thin with a little milk if it thickens. Serve with corn chips. Makes 1 1/3 cups.

Frijoles

6 slices bacon
2 15-ounce cans red kidney beans

1/2 teaspoon salt
Shredded Cheddar cheese (optional)

In a 10-inch skillet cook bacon till crisp. Drain bacon, reserving 2 tablespoons drippings. Place *1 can* of the *undrained* red kidney beans in a blender container; add cooked bacon, reserved bacon drippings, and salt. Cover and blend till beans are well mashed. (When necessary, stop the blender and use a rubber spatula to scrape down the sides.) Place blended bean mixture in medium skillet. Drain and stir the remaining *1 can* red kidney beans into mixture in skillet, mashing beans slightly. Cook, uncovered, over low heat, stirring frequently, till thickened, about 10 minutes. Serve hot; garnish with shredded Cheddar cheese, if desired. Makes 6 servings.

Salsa Cruda

1 16-ounce can tomatoes, drained and finely chopped
1 4-ounce can green chili peppers, drained, seeded, and chopped

1/2 cup finely chopped onion
• • •
1 tablespoon vinegar
1 teaspoon sugar
1/8 teaspoon salt

In mixing bowl thoroughly combine finely chopped tomatoes, chopped green chili peppers, and finely chopped onion; stir in vinegar, sugar, and salt. Let mixture stand for at least 30 minutes at room temperature. Serve as sauce with Mexican dishes such as tacos and enchiladas. Makes about 1 cup.

The tortilla is an absolute basic in Mexican-American cookery. Large tortillas are fried and eaten as bread, while smaller ones are used as an ingredient in such recipes as tacos, enchiladas, and Huevos Rancheros. Both corn flour tortillas (see recipe, page 41) and wheat flour tortillas are used. Corn flour is obtained by boiling corn kernels with lime to produce a mixture called mixtamal and then grinding the mixtamal into flour. The flour tortilla is a later innovation and uses all-purpose flour. Use either of the pancakelike tortillas. They both make great eating.

Salsa Cruda is a special condiment that will almost always be found on Mexican-American tables to spice up almost any food in much the same way other Americans use mustard and catsup.

Arroz con Pollo

1 8-ounce package brown-
    and-serve sausage links
1 2½- to 3-pound ready-to-
    cook broiler-fryer
    chicken, cut up
¼ cup all-purpose flour
1¼ teaspoons salt
1 cup chopped onion

½ cup chopped celery
1 cup regular rice
1 8-ounce can tomatoes,
    cut up
1 8½-ounce can peas,
    drained
½ cup sliced pimiento-
    stuffed green olives

Brown sausages in a Dutch oven. Drain, reserving 3 tablespoons drippings; set sausages aside. Coat chicken with mixture of flour, salt, and ¼ teaspoon pepper; brown in reserved drippings. Add onion, celery, and 1¾ cups water to chicken. Cover and simmer till chicken is nearly tender, about 30 minutes. Add rice, tomatoes, and sausages. Simmer till rice is tender, about 20 minutes more. Skim off fat. Add peas; heat. Garnish with olives. Serves 4 to 6.

Chicken Molé

1 2½- to 3-pound ready-to-
    cook broiler-fryer
    chicken, cut up
¼ cup butter *or* margarine
¼ cup finely chopped onion
¼ cup finely chopped green
    pepper
1 small clove garlic,
    minced
1 7½-ounce can tomatoes,
    cut up
½ cup beef broth

2 teaspoons sugar
½ teaspoon chili powder
⅛ teaspoon ground cinnamon
⅛ teaspoon ground nutmeg
    Dash ground cloves
    Dash bottled hot pepper
    sauce
¼ of a 1-ounce square
    unsweetened chocolate
2 tablespoons cold water
1 tablespoon cornstarch

In large skillet brown chicken slowly in butter. Season lightly with salt and pepper. Set chicken aside; cover. In same skillet cook onion, green pepper, and garlic in butter remaining in pan till vegetables are tender. Add tomatoes, beef broth, sugar, chili powder, cinnamon, nutmeg, cloves, hot pepper sauce, and chocolate. Add chicken. Cover and reduce heat; cook till meat is tender, about 45 minutes. Remove chicken to a serving platter; keep warm. Slowly blend cold water into cornstarch; stir into sauce. Cook and stir till thickened and bubbly. Pour sauce over chicken. Serves 4.

Chicken Enchiladas

1 16-ounce can tomatoes
1 4-ounce can green chili
    peppers, drained and
    seeded
½ teaspoon ground coriander
½ teaspoon salt
1 cup dairy sour cream
2 cups finely chopped
    cooked chicken

1 3-ounce package cream
    cheese, softened
¼ cup finely chopped onion
    Cooking oil
12 Flour Tortillas (see
    recipe, page 257) *or*
    frozen tortillas, thawed
1 cup shredded Monterey
    Jack cheese

Place tomatoes, chili peppers, coriander, and salt in blender container. Cover; blend till smooth. Add sour cream; cover and blend just till smooth. Set aside. Mix chicken, cream cheese, onion, and ¾ teaspoon salt. In skillet heat small amount cooking oil. Dip tortillas, one at a time, into hot oil; fry just till limp, a few seconds per side. Drain. Spread chicken mixture on tortillas; roll up. Place, seam side down, in 12x7½x2-inch baking dish. Pour tomato mixture atop. Cover with foil; bake at 350° about 30 minutes. Remove foil; sprinkle with cheese. Return to oven till cheese melts. Serves 6.

Pictured opposite: Mexican main dishes often include a well-seasoned sauce as in *Chicken Molé* and *Chicken Enchiladas.* A favorite sweet is the deep-fried and then sugared, puffs of air called *Sopaipillas* (see recipe, page 260).

The national holiday dish of Mexico is molé poblano de guajolote, *a complicated recipe for turkey with a molé or sauce. It also has a legend to explain its origin. The sisters of the convent of Santa Rosa in Pueblo, Mexico, expected a visit from the archbishop. Unfortunately they had nothing elegant enough to serve such a dignitary. So they prayed and while they prayed they also put everything on hand into the sauce pot. This included tomatoes, bananas, sesame seeds, raisins, and chocolate. They also made a great sacrifice—they killed and cooked their only turkey to serve with the sauce. Was it prayers or culinary skills that made the dinner such a smashing success? Relying on the rich tradition of their past, Mexican-Americans have developed several variations of that time-honored dish, as witnessed by this recipe for* Chicken Molé.

Sopaipillas

2 cups all-purpose flour
1 tablespoon baking powder
½ teaspoon salt

1 tablespoon shortening
⅔ cup lukewarm water
Fat for frying

Stir together flour, baking powder, and salt. Cut in shortening till resembles cornmeal. Gradually add water, stirring with fork. (Dough will be crumbly.) Turn out on a floured surface; knead into smooth ball. Divide in half; let stand 10 minutes. Roll *each half* to 12½x10-inch rectangle. Cut into 2½-inch squares. (Do not reroll or patch dough.) Fry, a few at a time, in deep hot fat (400°) till golden. Drain on paper toweling. Serve hot with guacamole as a dip, *or* roll in sugar-cinnamon mixture as desired. Makes 40.

Mexican Orange Candy

3 cups sugar
¼ cup boiling water
1 cup evaporated milk
½ cup chopped pecans

1 tablespoon grated orange
  peel
1 teaspoon grated lemon
  peel

In large saucepan melt *1 cup* sugar over low heat till rich brown color. Blend in boiling water; stir to dissolve sugar. Blend in evaporated milk, remaining sugar, and ¼ teaspoon salt. Bring to a boil; cook, covered, 3 minutes. Reduce heat; cook, uncovered, over low heat, stirring occasionally, till mixture registers 236° on candy thermometer. Cool to 110° without stirring. Stir in pecans and peels. Beat till creamy. Pour into buttered 8x8x2 inch pan. Let stand 4 to 6 hours to harden. Cut candy into squares.

Hearty Russian Recipes

Although millions of immigrants from the Russian Empire came to the United States between 1880 and the First World War, most of those who carried Russian passports were not ethnic Russians. Nearly half were Jews, a large proportion were Poles, and there were also Lithuanians, Finns, Latvians, and Armenians. The ones who were considered "real" Russians included people of Ukrainian, Caucasian, Georgian, or Byelorussian heritage.

The styles of cooking practiced by the members of this second group have much in common and in America are often called by the blanket term "Russian." Prepared dishes such as tasty varenki, feathery blini, elegant beef stroganoff, and all sorts of delicious recipes made with sour cream are enjoyed by people of every nationality throughout the United States. Also typical of the cuisine is flavoring with dill, sorrel and horseradish.

Not as well-known, but nevertheless a staple of the Russian people is kasha, as common among them as pasta to Italians and potatoes among the Irish. Kasha is most often made of buckwheat, although barley, rice, wheat, or corn also are used. The whole or coarsely ground grains are browned to give them a nutty taste and then cooked in water, broth, or milk. Kasha may be eaten plain, or it may be varied with eggs or mushrooms.

Shashlik—small pieces of lamb or beef, marinated, skewered, and broiled over an open flame—was probably invented thousands of years ago by tribes on the steppes of Russia. Both the Russians and Turks claim it, and as the kabob, it spanned vast distances to become popular at our barbecues.

For Russian-Americans, baking for Christmas and Easter is an important part of the homemaker's year. For Christmas they make a very white, raised, slightly sweet bread glazed with honey, and a very special Christmas Eve doughnut enhanced with a delicious filling. At Easter, elaborately painted eggs are indispensable, as are the towering kulich and the softly molded paskha. All these foods are part of the rich legacy that Russian-Americans have given to the United States.

Ukrainian Christmas Eve Doughnuts

4½ cups all-purpose flour	3 egg yolks
2 packages active dry yeast	• • •
1 cup milk	1 12-ounce can prune cake
⅓ cup sugar	and pastry filling
¼ cup shortening	Fat for frying
1 teaspoon salt	Powdered Sugar Icing
1 teaspoon vanilla	(see recipe, page 281)
2 eggs	

In large mixing bowl mix *2 cups* flour and yeast. Heat together milk, sugar, shortening, and salt just till warm (115-120°), stirring constantly. Stir in vanilla. Add to dry mixture; add eggs and egg yolks. Beat at low speed of electric mixer ½ minute, scraping sides. Beat 3 minutes at high speed. By hand, stir in enough of the remaining flour to make a moderately stiff dough. Turn onto floured surface; knead till smooth and elastic (4 to 5 minutes). Place in lightly greased bowl; turn once to grease surface.

Cover, let rise in warm place till double (about 1¼ hours). Punch down. Cover; let rest 10 minutes. Roll dough to ⅛-inch thickness. Cut into circles with floured 2½-inch cutter. Place *1 teaspoon* of prune filling on each of *half* of circles; top with unfilled circles. Moisten edges with water; press firmly to seal. Cover; let rise till about double. Fry a few at a time in deep hot fat (375°) till golden, 1 to 1½ minutes on each side. Drain on paper toweling. Cool; frost with Powdered Sugar Icing. Makes about 24 doughnuts.

Beef Stroganoff

1 pound beef sirloin steak, cut in thin strips	2 tablespoons butter *or* margarine
1 tablespoon all-purpose flour	3 tablespoons all-purpose flour
½ teaspoon salt	1 tablespoon tomato paste
2 tablespoons butter *or* margarine	1 10½-ounce can condensed beef broth
• • •	1 cup dairy sour cream
1 3-ounce can sliced mushrooms, drained	2 tablespoons dry white wine
½ cup chopped onion	Hot buttered noodles
1 clove garlic, minced	

Coat beef strips with mixture of 1 tablespoon flour and salt. In a skillet brown beef strips quickly in 2 tablespoons butter or margarine. Add mushrooms, onion, and garlic; cook till onion is crisp-tender, 3 to 4 minutes. Remove meat and mushrooms from pan. Add 2 tablespoons butter or margarine to pan drippings; blend in 3 tablespoons flour. Add tomato paste. Stir in broth. Cook and stir over medium heat till thickened and bubbly. Return meat and mushrooms to skillet. Stir in sour cream and dry white wine; cook slowly till heated through. *(Do not boil.)* Serve over noodles. Serves 4 or 5.

While most Americans associate settlement of California with the Spanish, its early beginnings were also heavily influenced by the presence of Russian soldiers. The Russians began their first settlement at Bodega Bay, near what is now Santa Rosa, in 1809. Later they erected at Fort Ross what they hoped would be the first of a series of settlements along the coast. They planned these settlements to serve as supply bases for Russian fur trading posts in Alaska. The Spanish, however, gained control of the area and the dream faded. Ironically, the land at Fort Ross later became part of the Sutter sawmill where gold was discovered in 1848.

Russian cookery has a special approach to sour cream. It is used in many ways in many recipes, and in Beef Stroganoff *it is used to perfection. This world-renowned dish named after a leading merchant family in St. Petersburg, combines a typical Russian sour cream sauce with beef sirloin, mushrooms, and onions. The flavor has enchanted Americans for decades.*

Caucasian Eggplant Caviar *is a traditional Easter dish which was sometimes used by poor immigrants as a substitute for real caviar. It is also a favorite accompaniment for* Blini *(see recipe, page 264).*

The highlight of a Ukrainian Christmas Eve is the Holy Supper, a meatless meal comprised of at least 12 traditional dishes — one to represent each of the 12 apostles. The recipes may vary from family to family, but most of the meals will include Prosfora, *a bread that has been blessed by a priest and is used to start the meal;* Kalach, *a braided bread that is traditionally presented with a burning candle as a centerpiece; stuffed cabbage rolls called* Holubtsi; *mushroom-filled rolls; a type of dumpling filled with sauerkraut;* Kutia, *a wheat pudding popular also in Poland (see recipe, page 274); fish; and pancakes.*

Caucasian Eggplant Caviar

1 large eggplant
   (1½ to 2 pounds)
1 cup finely chopped onion
½ cup finely chopped green
   pepper
2 tablespoons cooking oil
1 6-ounce can tomato paste
1½ teaspoons salt
½ teaspoon pepper
   Assorted crackers

Cook whole eggplant in boiling water till tender, about 25 minutes. Cool; peel and finely chop. In medium skillet cook onion and green pepper in oil till tender but not brown. Add tomato paste, salt, and pepper. Simmer 5 minutes. Add chopped eggplant; simmer, uncovered, 30 minutes, stirring often. Add more oil if sticks. Chill. Serve with crackers. Makes 2½ cups.

Ukrainian Mushroom-Filled Rolls

2 cups all-purpose flour
1 package active dry yeast
2 tablespoons butter *or*
   margarine
¼ teaspoon salt
1 egg
5 ounces fresh mushrooms,
   chopped (1¼ cups)
¼ cup chopped onion
3 tablespoons butter *or*
   margarine
2 hard-cooked eggs, finely
   chopped
½ cup cooked rice
2 tablespoons snipped
   parsley
⅛ teaspoon pepper
   Milk

In small mixing bowl combine *1 cup* of the flour and the yeast. In saucepan heat the 2 tablespoons butter, ¼ teaspoon salt, and ½ cup water just till warm (115-120°); stir constantly. Add to dry mixture; add egg. Beat at low speed with electric mixer for ½ minute, scraping bowl. Beat 3 minutes at high speed. By hand, stir in enough of remaining flour to make a moderately stiff dough. Knead on lightly floured surface till smooth and elastic (5 to 8 minutes). Shape into ball. Place in greased bowl, turning once to grease top. Cover; let rise till nearly double (45 to 60 minutes). Meanwhile, cook mushrooms and onion in 3 tablespoons butter till tender. Stir in chopped eggs, cooked rice, parsley, pepper, and ¾ teaspoon salt.

On lightly floured surface roll dough to 12x12-inch square. Cut into thirty-six 2-inch squares. Place about 2 teaspoons mushroom mixture on each; fold one side of dough over filling to make rectangle. Moisten edges and seal. Place on greased baking sheet; brush with milk. Bake at 375° for 12 minutes. Serve with soup or as appetizers. Makes 36.

Haddock Rolls

6 fresh *or* frozen haddock
   or sole fillets (about
   2 pounds)
1 cup chopped onion
1 tablespoon butter
1 beaten egg
¼ cup milk
2 tablespoons snipped
   parsley
¾ teaspoon salt
¼ teaspoon dried dillweed
⅛ teaspoon pepper
3 cups dry bread cubes
1 beaten egg
¼ cup all-purpose flour
½ cup fine dry bread crumbs
   Cooking oil
   Dairy sour cream

Thaw frozen fish. Cook onion in butter till tender but not brown. Combine 1 beaten egg, milk, parsley, salt, dillweed, and pepper; add to onion mixture with bread cubes, tossing just till moistened. Sprinkle fillets with salt. Place about ½ cup stuffing mixture atop each fillet. Roll up; secure with wooden picks. Combine 1 beaten egg and 1 tablespoon water. Coat each roll lightly with flour; dip in egg mixture, then coat with bread crumbs. Fry in ¼ inch hot oil over medium heat till done, 20 to 25 minutes, turning each roll occasionally. Serve with dairy sour cream. Makes 6 servings.

Caucasian Skewered Lamb

2 pounds boneless lamb,
cut in 1-inch cubes
• • •
¾ cup dry red wine

16 small whole onions
2 medium green peppers,
cut into large pieces
Cooking oil

Sprinkle meat with 1 teaspoon salt and ¼ teaspoon pepper; place in bowl. Add wine. Cover; marinate 3 hours or overnight in refrigerator, stirring several times. Drain. Meanwhile, partially cook onions in large amount boiling salted water for 5 minutes; drain. Arrange lamb cubes, onions, and green pepper pieces alternately on long skewers. Brush with oil. Grill over *hot coals* till lamb is desired doneness, turning and basting with oil occasionally. Allow 10 to 12 minutes for medium-well. Makes 8 servings.

Its name is Spanish, but it must have Russian in its heart. San Francisco has been called the most Russian of American cities because so many immigrants, fleeing the Russian Revolution settled there. One of its most famous landmarks, Russian Hill, is named for Russian sailors who died exploring the coast and were buried on the hill top. One of the frequent recipe choices of Russian-Americans in San Francisco is Caucasian Skewered Lamb.

Chicken Kiev

4 large whole chicken
breasts, skinned and
boned
1 tablespoon chopped green
onion with tops
1 tablespoon snipped
parsley

Salt
1 ¼-pound stick butter,
chilled
1 beaten egg
All-purpose flour
½ cup fine dry bread crumbs
Fat for frying

Halve chicken breasts lengthwise. Place chicken, boned side up, between two pieces of clear plastic wrap. Pound to ¼-inch thickness. Remove wrap. Sprinkle with onion, parsley, and salt. Cut butter into 8 sticks; place a stick at end of each chicken piece. Roll up, tucking in sides; press ends to seal. Combine egg and 1 tablespoon water. Coat chicken rolls with flour; dip in egg mixture. Roll in bread crumbs. Chill at least 1 hour. Fry in deep hot fat (375°) till golden brown, about 5 minutes. Makes 4 to 8 servings.

Byelorussian Sauerkraut Soup

¼ cup chopped onion
1 clove garlic, minced
2 tablespoons butter *or*
margarine
¼ pound finely diced pork
3 cups beef broth

1 8-ounce can sauerkraut,
drained and snipped
1 tablespoon all-purpose
flour
1 tablespoon butter *or*
margarine, melted

Cook onion and garlic in 2 tablespoons butter till onion is tender. Add pork. Cover; cook over low heat 20 minutes, stirring occasionally. Add broth and sauerkraut. Cover; simmer 45 minutes. Blend flour and melted butter; add to soup. Cook and stir till thickened. Serve as appetizer. Serves 6.

Sauerkraut soup or shchi is a national dish of immigrants from a part of western Russia called Byelorussia. This soup was especially appreciated back home for carrying along when traveling. It could be frozen, stored in the sleigh, and then thawed out over the campfire at mealtime.

Ukrainian Potato Babka

3 potatoes, peeled and
halved (1 pound)
1 cup cream-style cottage
cheese
2 tablespoons butter

2 egg yolks
½ teaspoon salt
⅛ teaspoon white pepper
2 egg whites

Cook potatoes, covered, in boiling salted water till tender, about 20 minutes; drain. In mixing bowl mash hot potatoes with cottage cheese and butter. Add egg yolks, salt, and pepper; beat till fluffy. Season to taste. Beat egg whites till stiff peaks form; fold into potato mixture. Spoon into greased 1-quart casserole or soufflé dish. Bake at 375° till puffed and golden, 30 to 35 minutes. Serve immediately. Makes 6 servings.

Vareniki

2¼ cups all-purpose
    flour
½ teaspoon salt
2 egg yolks

1 pound Italian plums,
    pitted and sliced
Granulated sugar

Stir together flour and salt. Combine egg yolks and ¾ cup water; stir into flour mixture. Shape into ball, adding more water if needed. Roll out on floured surface to ⅛-inch thickness. Cut into 3-inch circles. Place a few plum slices on each; sprinkle with sugar. Fold one side of dough over plums; moisten edges and seal. Drop into large amount boiling water; cook, uncovered, 15 to 20 minutes. Remove with slotted spoon; drain. Serve hot with powdered sugar and dairy sour cream, if desired. Makes about 24.

Blini

1 tablespoon butter
1 cup buckwheat pancake mix
1 cup milk
2 egg yolks

2 stiffly beaten egg whites
Caviar, butter, *or* dairy
    sour cream

Melt butter. Combine pancake mix, milk, egg yolks, and butter; beat smooth. Fold egg whites into batter. Bake on hot greased griddle using 1 tablespoon batter for each. Serve with caviar, butter, or sour cream. Makes 36.

Paskha

1 pound dry cottage cheese
½ cup sugar
½ cup unsalted butter
1 egg yolk
½ cup dairy sour cream

¼ cup finely chopped
    almonds
½ teaspoon vanilla
White raisins
    (optional)

Push cottage cheese through a sieve. Cream sugar, butter, and egg yolk; blend in cottage cheese. Stir in sour cream, nuts, and vanilla. Press mixture into 4-cup mold. Cover; chill overnight. Unmold; garnish with raisins.

Kulich

½ cup light raisins
2 tablespoons rum
¼ teaspoon ground saffron
1 package active dry yeast
½ cup milk
⅓ cup butter *or* margarine
¼ cup sugar
3½ cups all-purpose flour

2 eggs
½ cup mixed candied fruits
    and peels
¼ cup chopped almonds
¼ teaspoon almond extract
1 egg yolk
Confectioners' Icing (see
    recipe, page 243)

Combine raisins, rum, and saffron. Soften yeast in ¼ cup warm water (110°). Mix milk, butter, sugar, and ½ teaspoon salt. Heat to dissolve sugar; cool to lukewarm. Combine milk mixture and *2 cups* flour; beat well. Add yeast and eggs; beat well. Stir in raisin mixture, candied fruits, nuts, extract, and enough remaining flour to make a soft dough. Knead on floured surface 8 to 10 minutes. Shape in ball. Place in greased bowl; turn once. Cover; let rise till double (about 1½ hours). Punch down; turn onto floured surface. Divide in half (or thirds). Cover; let rest 10 minutes. Grease bottom and sides of two 29-ounce cans (or three 16-ounce cans); place on baking sheet. Shape dough into balls; place one in each can. Cover; let rise 45 minutes. Brush with egg yolk. Bake at 350° about 40 minutes for small cans or about 50 minutes for large cans. Remove from cans; cool. Drizzle with Icing.

Berries à la Romanoff

1 pint strawberries, sliced	1 cup whipping cream
½ cup sugar	1 pint vanilla ice cream,
¼ cup orange-flavored	softened
liqueur	

Mix strawberries, sugar, and liqueur; chill 1 to 2 hours. Whip cream till soft peaks form. Fold into softened ice cream; spoon into chilled sherbet glasses. Spoon strawberry mixture atop. Serve at once. Makes 8 servings.

The Italians in the Kitchen

D uring the first half of the nineteenth century, the annual Italian immigration to the United States was measured only in hundreds and sometimes less. For example, in the year 1829 the total number was three. Many of these early arrivals were artists and stonecutters, brought here especially to work on public buildings. And one, Philip Mazzei, was a friend of Thomas Jefferson, who had invited him to experiment with the raising of grapes, olives, and silk.

Later, there were political refugees, including Garibaldi who found work in a candle factory on Staten Island. Soon there were enough Italians in New York to warrant an Italian-language newspaper. Within three weeks of the outbreak of the Civil War, six hundred New York Italians had formed the Garibaldi Volunteers and were fighting with the Union army.

After 1880 the yearly number suddenly began to increase dramatically— the citrus fruit orchards of southern Italy were suffering a depression, for now the United States had begun to supply her own needs from citrus groves in Florida and California. The new immigrants were mostly males, unskilled and illiterate. They competed with Irish and Poles for low paying jobs in the building trades, the stockyards, and the garment trade. In rural areas they started truck gardens and berry farms; in the South they grew cotton, sugar cane, and rice; and in New York State and California they contributed much to the success of American wine growing. Many Italians entered the food industry as importers, grocers, and restaurateurs. And still others became furniture craftsmen, textile designers, musicians, and decorators. After making some money, a number of these men returned to their homeland, but the majority remained and sent for their families.

Probably no other country has had its national dishes so wholeheartedly adopted by Americans. Pasta, chianti, and Italian cheeses in many varieties are as familiar to our people nowadays as apple pie, and even the smallest town is likely to have a restaurant with some type of Italian-influenced food on the menu. And why did this come about? Probably because Italian food is likely to be inexpensive, flavorful, and convenient to prepare (we won't say easy to prepare, for many Italian dishes demand just the right know-how). Benjamin Franklin wrote to a friend, "I confess that if

The love of pasta is legendary among Italians. One Italian-American tells this story about another. "Tommaso ate macaroni...every day. He bought his pasta imported from Italy in 25-pound wooden crates....Tommaso would eat two pounds of pasta at a sitting, yet he was never overweight....Tommaso... did his own cooking and he made a superb meat sauce....My mother always said that none of the Italian women...were able to duplicate Tommaso's sauce but she would add that...the reason might have something to do with the fact that Tommaso did not wash his pots as thoroughly as they washed theirs. My earliest childhood recollections of Tommaso are of the days when my two sisters and I would say, 'Let's go watch Tommaso eat.' We would stand beside him as he sat with a huge mound of pasta in front of him and watch him expertly twirl the strands on a fork and eat the pasta with great musical gusto...."[6]

I could find..., a receipt for making Parmesan cheese, it would give me more satisfaction than a transcript of any inscription from any old stone whatever."[7]

Fannie Farmer's 1896 cook book listed a number of ways to prepare macaroni and spaghetti, as well as Italian ices. Since then Americans have adopted such Italian classics as chicken cacciatore, veal parmesan, minestrone and cappuccino. As for pizza, which was first commercially made in 1905, it has been estimated that 2 billion pizzas are now consumed annually in the United States—definitely exceeding the number in Italy, where the type of pizza we know is a Neopolitan specialty.

The recipes in this section are a special invitation to investigate and enjoy the art practiced by Italians in the kitchen.

Italian Vegetable Salad

1 medium green pepper
2 cups chopped tomato
1 small red onion, thinly sliced
1 tablespoon red wine vinegar
1 tablespoon olive oil
1 teaspoon dried basil, crushed
¼ teaspoon salt
⅛ teaspoon pepper

Cut green pepper into strips 2 inches long. In a bowl mix together green pepper, tomato, and red onion. Combine wine vinegar, olive oil, basil, salt, and pepper. Pour over vegetables, tossing to coat. Makes 6 servings.

Ravioli

Basic Pasta Dough
2 tablespoons chopped onion
1 tablespoon olive oil *or* cooking oil
1 10-ounce package frozen chopped spinach
1 egg
½ cup ricotta cheese
¼ cup grated Parmesan cheese
1 cup finely diced cooked chicken
Spicy Tomato Sauce
Grated Parmesan cheese

On floured surface roll Basic Pasta Dough as thinly as possible; cover and let rest a few minutes. Repeat rolling and resting till dough measures 20x18 inches. Let rest 20 minutes. Cut into ten 18x2-inch strips.

Cook onion in oil till tender. Cook spinach according to package directions; drain, pressing out excess liquid. Measure ½ cup of spinach (use remaining elsewhere). Combine egg, ricotta, and ¼ cup Parmesan. Add the ½ cup spinach, cooked onion, and chicken; mix well. On one dough strip place spinach mixture by teaspoonfuls at 2-inch intervals beginning 1 inch from end of strip. Top with second strip of dough. Cut dough at 2-inch intervals to make squares centered with the filling. Moisten dough edges with water; seal well with fork. Repeat with remaining filling and pasta strips. Dry for 1 hour; turn once. Meanwhile, prepare Spicy Tomato Sauce. Cook ravioli in large amount rapidly boiling salted water for 8 to 10 minutes. Rinse in cold water; drain. Serve with Spicy Tomato Sauce. Pass Parmesan. Serves 6 to 8.

Basic Pasta Dough: In bowl stir together 3 cups all-purpose flour and ¼ teaspoon salt. Make a well in center and add 2 eggs. Beat well. Stir in enough of ⅓ cup water to form a very stiff dough. Turn out onto lightly floured surface. Knead till dough is smooth and elastic, about 10 minutes.

Spicy Tomato Sauce: Combine one 15-ounce can tomato sauce; one 8-ounce can tomatoes, cut up; 1 cup water; ¼ cup finely chopped onion; 2 tablespoons snipped parsley; 2 teaspoons sugar; 1 teaspoon salt; and 1 teaspoon dried oregano, crushed. Simmer 30 to 40 minutes, stirring often.

It was nice to have the store come to you. Italian-American homemakers welcomed the fruit and vegetable vendor who brought his loaded pushcart to their doorsteps. He carried all of the standard items—carrots, apples, grapes—which he carefully weighed on his hanging scale. But he also could be counted on to offer some new or different items such as plum tomatoes, broccoli, flat-leafed parsley, zucchini, fresh rosemary, oregano, and perhaps fennel. Sadly the day of the pushcart vendor is all but gone along with other symbols of a gentler way of life.

The bounty of the Italian table first came to the notice of most Americans by means of a special kind of restaurant, the "red ink joints" as they were sometimes called. Their history began when Italian women began cooking boardinghouse-type meals for the many Italian men who came to America alone. Later the pragmatic Italians discovered that non-Italians also enjoyed the array of antipasto, minestrone, spaghetti, ravioli, and veal parmesan that was offered. And on the table was the ever-present red chianti, nicknamed "red ink." During Prohibition, these little restaurants became speakeasies overnight. The chianti was served in pop bottles and cocktails came to the table in coffee cups, but business went on as usual. After Prohibition Americans found themselves "hooked" on Italian restaurants, and so they remain today.

Pictured opposite: For your next party, try planning an Italian menu. *Lasagne* or *Cheese and Mushroom Pizza* (see recipe, page 270), and a tossed salad — and your party simply has to succeed.

Thomas Jefferson is reported to have so enjoyed the pasta he tasted in Italy that he ordered the first pasta machine in the United States. He would have been happy to know that pasta in many forms is now a staple on our tables. The recipes on this page illustrate three distinctive kinds. Pasta e Fagioli (mispronounced pasta fazool) uses macaroni. Americans are most familiar with it in the elbow or shell shapes. Fettucini Verdi features thin noodles that have had spinach added to the dough to give them a distinctive color and flavor. A type of narrow flat spaghetti called linguini is the base of Linguini with Red Clam Sauce. None of these dishes includes meatballs since they were a luxury that was unknown to the Italians who migrated to America.

Fettucini Verdi

8-ounces green noodles
¼ cup butter, softened
¼ cup dairy sour cream, room temperature
2 tablespoons finely snipped fresh basil
1 clove garlic, minced
Grated Parmesan cheese

Cook noodles; drain, combine butter, sour cream, basil, garlic, ½ teaspoon salt, and ¼ teaspoon pepper. Toss with noodles; top with Parmesan. Serves 4.

Pasta e Fagioli

½ pound dry kidney *or* pinto beans (1 cup)
1 8-ounce can tomatoes, cut up
1 8-ounce can tomato sauce
1 medium carrot, chopped
¼ cup chopped onion
¼ cup chopped celery
1 clove garlic, minced
¾ teaspoon salt
⅛ teaspoon pepper
1 tablespoon olive oil
4 ounces macaroni (1 cup)
Grated Parmesan cheese

Rinse beans; combine beans and 4 cups water. Bring to boiling; simmer 2 minutes. Remove from heat; let stand 1 hour. (Or, add beans and water; soak overnight.) Cover; simmer 1 hour. Drain; reserve 1½ cups liquid. Combine reserved liquid, beans, undrained tomatoes, tomato sauce, carrot, onion, celery, garlic, salt, and pepper. Cover; simmer for 30 minutes. Stir in oil. Cook macaroni; drain. Stir into tomato mixture. Serve with Parmesan. Serves 4.

Linguini with Red Clam Sauce

2 7-ounce cans minced clams
½ cup chopped onion
1 tablespoon snipped parsley
1 clove garlic, minced
2 tablespoons olive oil
1 15-ounce can tomato sauce
1 6-ounce can tomato paste
1 teaspoon dried basil, crushed
½ teaspoon sugar
⅛ teaspoon pepper
16 ounces linguini
Grated Parmesan cheese

Drain clams, reserving liquid. Cook onion, parsley, and garlic in oil till onion is tender. Stir in tomato sauce, tomato paste, reserved clam liquid, basil, sugar, pepper, and 1½ cups water. Cover and simmer 1 hour. Add clams; heat through. Cook linguini according to package directions; drain. Pour sauce over linguini; serve with Parmesan. Makes 6 servings.

Lasagne, strictly speaking, is the wide noodle that is used in many types of Italian dishes. Americans, however, use the word to refer to a casserole made with lasagne noodles, cheese, and meat sauce. However the word is used, it means mighty fine eating. An Italian-American lady tells us her grandmother would measure her children's mouths to know how wide to make the noodles. Today most of us do it the easy way and buy them at the grocer's.

Lasagne

1 pound Italian sausage
1 16-ounce can tomatoes, cut up
2 6-ounce cans tomato paste
1 cup water
1 tablespoon dried basil, crushed
1 clove garlic, minced
10 ounces lasagne noodles
2 beaten eggs
3 cups ricotta *or* cream-style cottage cheese
½ cup grated Romano *or* Parmesan cheese
2 tablespoons dried parsley flakes
1 16-ounce package sliced mozzarella cheese

Brown sausage; drain. Add undrained tomatoes, tomato paste, water, basil, garlic, and 1½ teaspoons salt. Simmer, covered, 15 minutes; stir occasionally. Cook noodles; drain. Combine eggs, ricotta, Romano, parsley, 1 teaspoon salt, and ½ teaspoon pepper. In 13x9x 2-inch baking pan layer *half* each of the noodles, ricotta mixture, mozzarella, and meat mixture. Repeat layers. Bake at 375° for 30 minutes. Let stand 10 minutes. Serves 8 to 10.

Artichokes Parmesan

Wash 8 small artichokes. Cut off 1 inch of the top, the stem, and tips of leaves. Remove choke and any loose outer leaves. Brush cut edges with lemon juice. Cook 1 tablespoon sliced green onion with tops and 1 clove garlic, minced, in 3 tablespoons butter till tender. Combine 1½ cups soft bread crumbs, ¼ cup grated Parmesan cheese, and 2 tablespoons snipped parsley. Add onion mixture; mix lightly. Spoon into artichokes. Place in large saucepan, making sure artichokes won't tip over. Add water to saucepan to depth of 1 inch. Bring to boil; reduce heat. Cover tightly; simmer about 30 minutes. Add additional water as necessary. Makes 8 servings.

Cheese and Mushroom Pizza *(see photo, page 269)*

1 cup chopped onion
2 cloves garlic, minced
2 tablespoons cooking oil
1 15-ounce can tomato sauce
1½ teaspoons dried oregano, crushed
1 teaspoon dried thyme, crushed

1 13¾-ounce package hot roll mix
1 6-ounce can sliced mushrooms, drained
1 16-ounce package sliced mozzarella cheese
¼ cup grated Parmesan cheese

Cook onion and garlic in oil till tender. Add tomato sauce, herbs, ½ teaspoon salt, and ⅛ teaspoon pepper. Simmer till thick, about 15 minutes. Meanwhile, prepare roll mix, *using 1 cup warm water and omitting egg.* Cover; let rest 10 minutes. *(Don't let rise.)* Divide in half. On lightly floured surface roll each half to 12-inch circle. Place on greased pizza pans. Clip dough at 1-inch intervals around edge and press so edge stands up. Spread *half* of the sauce on each circle. Top with mushrooms and mozzarella. Sprinkle with Parmesan. Bake at 425° for 15 to 20 minutes. Serves 4 to 6.

A canopy of lighted arches covers the streets of Little Italy in lower Manhattan for the nine nights following September 19. It's the Feast of San Gennero, patron saint of Naples. Thousands of tourists join the crowds on the streets lined with carnival stalls and food carts.

Pizza Siciliana

4½ cups all-purpose flour
1 package active dry yeast
1½ cups *warm* water (110°)
2 tablespoons cooking oil
1 cup chopped onion
1 clove garlic, minced
2 tablespoons olive oil
1 16-ounce can tomatoes,
    cut up
1 6-ounce can tomato paste
1½ teaspoons dried basil,
    crushed

1½ teaspoons dried oregano,
    crushed
½ teaspoon sugar
½ cup chopped onion
½ cup sliced pitted ripe
    olives
1 medium green pepper,
    cut in strips
2 cups shredded mozzarella
    cheese (8 ounces)
¼ cup grated Parmesan
    cheese

Combine *2 cups* flour, yeast, and 1½ teaspoons salt. Add water and cooking oil. Beat at low speed of electric mixer for ½ minute, scraping bowl. Beat 3 minutes at high speed. By hand, stir in enough remaining flour to make moderately stiff dough. On floured surface, knead till smooth. Place in greased bowl; turn once. Cover; let rise till double (1 hour). Cook 1 cup onion and garlic in olive oil till tender. Add tomatoes, tomato paste, basil, oregano, sugar, 1 teaspoon salt, and ⅛ teaspoon pepper. Bring to boiling; cover and simmer 10 minutes. Pat dough from center to edges in greased 15½x10½x 1-inch baking pan. Cover; let rise 45 minutes. Spoon sauce over dough. Bake at 475° for 25 minutes. Sprinkle with ½ cup onion and olives. Top with pepper; sprinkle cheeses over. Bake 10 to 15 minutes. Serves 6.

Baked Veal Parmesan

⅓ cup fine dry bread crumbs
⅓ cup grated Parmesan
    cheese
¼ teaspoon salt
1 beaten egg
1 tablespoon water
4 veal cutlets, cut ¼ inch
    thick (about 1 pound)

1 8-ounce can tomato sauce
½ teaspoon dried oregano,
    crushed
½ teaspoon sugar
⅛ teaspoon onion salt
3 ounces mozzarella cheese,
    sliced

Combine crumbs, Parmesan cheese, salt, and dash pepper. Combine egg and water. Dip veal in egg mixture; coat with crumb mixture. Arrange veal in 12x7½x2-inch baking dish. Bake, uncovered, at 400° for 20 minutes. Turn meat; bake till tender, 15 to 20 minutes more. Meanwhile, combine tomato sauce, oregano, sugar, and onion salt; heat to boiling, stirring frequently. Pour sauce over meat in baking dish. Top with mozzarella cheese; return to oven to melt cheese, 1 to 2 minutes more. Makes 4 servings.

Chicken Cacciatore

1 2½- to 3-pound ready-to-
    cook broiler-fryer
    chicken, cut up
¼ cup cooking oil
2 medium onions, sliced
2 cloves garlic, minced
1 16-ounce can tomatoes

1 8-ounce can tomato sauce
1 teaspoon dried oregano *or*
    basil, crushed
½ teaspoon celery seed
1 *or* 2 bay leaves
¼ cup dry white wine

In skillet brown chicken in hot oil. Remove chicken. In same skillet cook onion and garlic till onion is tender. Return chicken to skillet. Combine undrained tomatoes, tomato sauce, oregano, celery seed, bay leaves, 1 teaspoon salt, and ¼ teaspoon pepper. Pour over chicken. Cover; simmer 30 minutes. Stir in wine. Cook chicken, uncovered, till tender, about 15 minutes more; turn often. Remove bay leaves; skim off fat. Makes 4 servings.

The first pizzeria opened in America in 1905. It specialized in Neopolitan pizza: thin crust, round shape, and delicious topping of tomatoes, cheese, olive oil, and, sometimes, meat. The restaurant served primarily Italian immigrants who lived in New York's Little Italy, plus a few adventurous non-Italians. Shortly after World War II, however, American marketing wizards went to work and the juggling pizza maker in a chef's hat was born. Today, pizza is a $1.5 billion or more industry and for the toppings you can choose among ground beef, sausage, pepperoni, Canadian-style bacon, shrimp, anchovies, mushrooms, onion, green peppers, olives, and anything else you can think of.

Sicilian pizza, on the other hand, has only just recently come to the attention of American entrepreneurs. In contrast to the round, thin Neopolitan pizza this type has a thick, soft, bread-like crust and is usually made in a rectangular shape. It has been a mainstay in many Italian-American homes for using up leftover bread dough on baking day. The toppings, too, were often leftovers, perhaps sliced cooked sausage or ground beef. Topped with anchovies or perhaps just plain sliced onion, it made a perfect meal during Lent or on traditional fast days. Today your imagination is your only limit when you make your own version of either type of pizza in your own home.

Tomato-Sauced Polenta

We got Tomato-Sauced Polenta from Italian-Americans but they got it from the ancient Romans. Originally called puls *or* pulmentum, polenta *began as a sort of mush made from millet or chick-pea flour. It was often part of the rations for the Roman soldiers. Gradually, the ingredients changed from millet to barley to wheat to corn. Today's polenta is made with cornmeal and is usually prepared in two ways. The soft version is like cornmeal mush and is eaten with milk and honey. The other kind is firmer because it has been chilled. It then can be cut into pieces and topped with a tomato sauce as in this recipe.*

½ pound ground beef
2 tablespoons chopped onion
½ clove garlic, minced
1 16-ounce can tomatoes, cut up
1 8-ounce can tomato sauce
1 3-ounce can sliced mushrooms
2 tablespoons snipped parsley
½ teaspoon dried oregano, crushed
¼ teaspoon dried thyme, crushed
1 small bay leaf
Polenta

In saucepan cook beef with onion and garlic till meat is browned. Drain off fat. Add tomatoes, tomato sauce, mushrooms, parsley, oregano, thyme, bay leaf, ⅓ cup water, and ¼ teaspoon salt. Bring to boiling; reduce heat. Simmer till thick, about 1¼ hours. Stir occasionally. Remove bay leaf. Serve over Polenta. Pass grated Parmesan cheese, if desired. Makes 6 servings.

Polenta: In saucepan bring 2½ cups water to boiling. In bowl mix 1½ cups yellow cornmeal, 1½ cups cold water, and 1½ teaspoons salt. Stir into boiling water. Cook and stir till thick. Cook, covered, over very low heat about 45 minutes; stir often. Spread in 8x8x2-inch pan. Cool well. Cut into 6 pieces. In skillet brown in ¼ cup butter till golden, 5 to 6 minutes per side.

Zucchini con Patate

1 medium onion, sliced
2 tablespoons olive oil *or* cooking oil
2 cups sliced zucchini
2 medium potatoes, peeled and diced
1 medium tomato, peeled and chopped
1 teaspoon dried oregano, crushed
½ teaspoon salt
Grated Parmesan cheese

In skillet cook onion in oil till tender but not brown. Stir in vegetables, oregano, salt, and ⅛ teaspoon pepper. Cook, covered, till potatoes are tender, about 15 minutes. Serve with grated Parmesan cheese. Serves 4.

Cappuccino

If you believe the legend, coffee was first discovered by an Ethiopian shepherd who noticed that his sheep stayed awake all night if they ate certain berries. He tried them himself and found these berries — coffee beans — had the same effect on him. Later the Arabians roasted coffee beans and from them made a dark drink called qahwah. *In 1550 coffee reached Constantinople and the first European coffeehouse was opened in Rome in 1615 and the Italians have been perfecting their ways with coffee ever since. The climax of that process of experimenting is* Cappuccino.

Whip ½ cup whipping cream till soft peaks form. Dissolve ¼ cup instant espresso coffee *or* instant coffee powder in 2 cups boiling water; pour into small cups. Top each with dollop of whipped cream; sprinkle with ground cinnamon *or* ground nutmeg. Pass sugar. Makes about 6 (3-ounce) servings.

Minestrone à la Genovese

1 cup dry navy beans
10 cups water
1 cup chopped carrots
2 cups finely shredded cabbage
1 8½-ounce can peas, drained
1 8-ounce can cut green beans, drained
1 8-ounce can tomatoes
4 ounces fine noodles
2 teaspoons salt
1 teaspoon dried basil, crushed
¼ cup light cream
3 tablespoons grated Parmesan cheese
3 tablespoons butter
3 tablespoons cooking oil
2 tablespoons snipped parsley
1 clove garlic, minced

Rinse beans. Combine beans and water; simmer 2 minutes. Remove from heat; cover and let stand 1 hour. (Or, combine beans and water; let stand overnight.) Do not drain. Add carrots; simmer, covered, 2½ to 3 hours. Add cabbage, peas, green beans, tomatoes, noodles, salt, and basil. Simmer till noodles are done, 20 to 25 minutes. Add remaining ingredients. Serves 10.

Hot Bean and Onion Salad

Cook two 9-ounce packages frozen Italian green beans according to package directions. Drain. Mix hot beans with 1 small onion, sliced and separated into rings. In screw-top jar combine 3 tablespoons olive oil; 3 tablespoons red wine vinegar; 1/2 teaspoon dried oregano, crushed; 1/4 teaspoon salt; and dash pepper. Shake well. Pour over hot bean mixture; toss. Serves 8.

Italian Fig Cookies

1 1/2 cups dried figs
3/4 cup light raisins
1/4 cup slivered almonds
1/4 cup sugar
1/4 cup hot water
1/4 teaspoon ground cinnamon
2 1/2 cups all-purpose flour
1/3 cup sugar

1/4 teaspoon baking powder
1/2 cup shortening
2 tablespoons butter *or* margarine
1/2 cup milk
1 beaten egg
Confectioners' Icing (see recipe, page 243)

Put figs, raisins, and almonds through food grinder. In mixing bowl combine 1/4 cup sugar, water, cinnamon, and dash pepper; stir into fruit mixture. Set aside. Combine flour, 1/3 cup sugar, and baking powder. Cut in shortening and butter till mixture resembles small peas. Stir in milk and egg till dry mixture is moistened. On lightly floured surface roll dough to 18x16-inch rectangle. Cut into four 18x4-inch strips. Spread *about* 1/3 *cup* fig mixture over each strip. Roll each strip up jelly-roll fashion, starting at long side. Cut each filled strip into six 3-inch lengths. Place cookies, seam side down, on ungreased cookie sheets. Curve each slightly. Snip outer edge of curve 3 times. Bake at 350° till lightly browned, 20 to 25 minutes. Remove from cookie sheets; cool on rack. Frost with Confectioners' Icing. Sprinkle with small multicolored decorative candies, if desired. Makes 24.

Biscuit Tortoni

2 cups whipping cream
6 soft coconut macaroons, finely crumbled (1 cup)
1/2 cup sifted powdered sugar
Dash salt

1/4 cup rum
1 1/2 teaspoons vanilla
1/4 cup slivered toasted almonds
6 candied cherries, halved

Combine *1 cup* of the whipping cream, the crumbled macaroons, sugar, and salt. Chill 30 minutes. Line twelve 2 1/2-inch muffin pans with paper bake cups. Whip remaining cream to soft peaks. Fold in chilled macaroon mixture, rum, and vanilla. Spoon into bake cups. Sprinkle with almonds; place a cherry half atop each. Cover; freeze till firm, 3 hours or overnight. Makes 12.

Chilled Zabaglione

6 egg yolks
2/3 cup Marsala wine
1/2 cup sugar
1/2 teaspoon vanilla
Dash ground cinnamon

Ice
1/2 cup whipping cream
8 to 10 fresh *or* canned peach halves, chilled

In the top of a double boiler beat together egg yolks and wine; blend in sugar. Place over boiling water. (Upper pan should not touch water.) Beat with electric mixer at high speed till mixture thickens and mounds, about 8 minutes. Add vanilla and cinnamon. Place over ice water; continue beating till mixture is chilled, replacing ice when necessary. Whip cream till soft peaks form; fold into wine mixture. Chill. To serve, place drained peach halves in sherbet glasses; spoon wine mixture over. Serves 8 to 10.

St. Joseph is one of the most beloved saints among Italian-Americans. As the patron of workers and the protector of the family he is honored with a feast con brio on March 19. In Italy the feast of St. Joseph used to be celebrated by entire villages, but in America the participants are usually limited to the members of a parish or the friends and relatives of one individual family. A huge table is loaded with succulent dishes prepared and brought by the guests. After the table is blessed, one person among the guests is chosen to represent each member of the Holy Family (Joseph, Mary, and the child Jesus). They must then ceremoniously sample each dish on the table. After they have finished, the rest of the guests may eat. Just one of the many sweets to be found on the St. Joseph table is cucidata or Italian Fig Cookies.

Treasured Polish Dishes

Often life was difficult for new arrivals in America. One young Polish girl describes her situation. "And now, dear auntie, I inform you that I am in the same place in service with an English master and mistress who don't know a word of Polish, and I don't know English; so we communicate with gestures and I know what to do, that's all. I know the work and therefore I don't mind much about the language. But, dear auntie, I went intentionally into an English household in order that I may learn to speak English, because it is necessary, in America, as the English language reigns. I am in good health, only I am a little ill with my feet, I don't know what it is, whether rheumatism or something else. I walk very much, because from 6 o'clock in the morning till 10 o'clock in the evening I have work and I receive $22 a month and I have 7 persons, and 16 rooms to clean and I cook; everything is on my head...."[8]

Although the majority of Polish immigrants arrived in America in the twentieth century the first handful of Polish political refugees reached our shores in colonial times. Among them were Revolutionary War soldiers, Kosciusko and Pulaski. The flow of Polish immigration was slow at first, but after 1870 unrest and persecution in their homeland plus steam travel and organized immigration agencies brought millions of Poles to the United States.

The majority of these immigrants had neither skills nor education, but they were strong and willing to work hard. Some went to the mines of Pennsylvania; some homesteaded in the West; others took over abandoned farms in New England where they eventually became prosperous farmers. The majority, however, chose city life and became factory workers—settling in places such as Chicago, which now has the second largest Polish population of all the cities in the world. These immigrants also flocked to the "Little Polands" in New York City, Buffalo, and Detroit.

Though poor in material wealth the Polish immigrants were rich in their cultural heritage—especially their food customs. Once here, they took great pains to keep the art of Polish cooking alive. Two great religious feast days when Polish cooking is at its best are Christmas and Easter. If you are lucky enough to spend Christmas Eve with a Polish family, you will eat a meatless meal at which the *Oplatek,* or the holy wafer, is broken, and rejoice in such foods as *kutia, pierogi,* borscht, and rice- and cheese-stuffed cabbage leaves. Or try to be at your Polish friends' home at Easter, when they celebrate the *Swiecone,* the midday meal which ends the Lenten season. Then you can taste the specially blessed foods—veal and ham dishes, pork sausage, decorated hard-cooked eggs, babka, and more.

Don't wait for holidays, though. Polish-American bakeries and sausage shops make the special favorites of Polish cooking available to you all year. At the Polish bakery, you'll find sugar-coated doughnuts, called *paczky* filled with candied fruits and nuts; coffee cakes, called *struklja* with every conceivable type of filling from poppy seeds to fruit; *chrust,* the deep fried, bow-shaped cookies; plus a whole assortment of breads including *buleczki,* a wheat bun; *rogi,* or butterhorns, and crescent-shaped *luky.* The choices in the sausage shop are equally varied, but most prominent would be the garlic flavored *kielbasy*—the sausage most Americans call Polish sausage. So, if you can't visit a Polish household, or you want a bit of Poland in your own home, read on.

Kutia

In Poland and parts of Russia, Kutia is a wheat pudding symbolizing a bountiful harvest. We hesitate to suggest that you test the tradition that says, "Fling a spoonful of Kutia at the ceiling. If it sticks, the bees will swarm, the harvest will be good, and the family will have good luck."

⅔ cup cracked wheat cereal	½ cup chopped walnuts
3 cups water	½ cup honey
⅓ cup poppy seed	¼ cup slivered almonds
1 cup boiling water	1 teaspoon vanilla
⅔ cup raisins	¼ cup whipping cream

Cook wheat in 3 cups water till tender, about 1 hour. Drain. Place cooked wheat, half at a time, in a blender container; cover and blend into a paste. In small saucepan cook poppy seed in 1 cup boiling water till soft, about 10 minutes. Drain. Mix together wheat paste, poppy seed, raisins, walnuts, honey, almonds, and vanilla. Chill. Stir in unwhipped cream. Makes 4 cups.

Pierogi

1 beaten egg
1 cup water
½ teaspoon salt
3 cups all-purpose flour
1½ cups cream-style cottage
    cheese, drained

1 beaten egg yolk
7 tablespoons butter *or*
    margarine
1½ teaspoons sugar
¼ teaspoon salt
1 cup chopped onion

In a bowl combine egg, water, and salt. Stir in flour to make a stiff dough. Knead till smooth. On floured surface roll till less than ⅛ inch thick. Cut into 3-inch circles. Combine cottage cheese, egg yolk, *1 tablespoon* of the butter, sugar, and salt. To make pierogi, place *1 teaspoon* cottage cheese filling off-center on each circle. Fold dough over to form half-circle; seal with tines of fork. Set aside. Cook onion in 6 tablespoons butter till lightly browned, about 20 minutes. Keep warm. Meanwhile, in large kettle bring 12 cups salted water to boiling. Add 10 to 12 pierogi; cook 8 to 10 minutes. Drain on paper toweling. Transfer to serving dish; keep warm. Repeat till all are cooked. Serve pierogi topped with cooked onion mixture. Serves 8.

Pierogi are a favorite just about any time, but especially at Christmas. On Christmas Eve, these little pouches filled with cottage cheese, potatoes, mushrooms, or sauerkraut are an important part of the Festival of the Star—a dinner to commemorate the birth of Christ. On other occasions Pierogi are served filled with a meat and egg mixture or with fruit.

Bigos

6 slices bacon, cut in
    1-inch pieces
1 large onion, chopped
½ pound boneless beef,
    cut in cubes
½ pound boneless pork,
    cut in cubes
½ pound Polish sausage,
    sliced

2 cups beef broth
1 6-ounce can sliced
    mushrooms
½ cup dry white wine
1 teaspoon paprika
½ teaspoon salt
1 bay leaf
2 16-ounce cans sauerkraut,
    drained and snipped

In a 5-quart Dutch oven cook bacon and onion till bacon is cooked and onion is tender. Drain, reserving 2 tablespoons drippings. Set onion and bacon aside. Brown beef and pork cubes in reserved drippings. Stir in bacon-onion mixture, sausage, beef broth, undrained mushrooms, wine, paprika, salt, and bay leaf. Simmer till meat is tender, about 1½ to 2 hours. Stir in sauerkraut. Cook till heated through. Remove the bay leaf. Serves 10.

Bigos, a hunter's stew, is another example of a recipe that has been altered since it was brought to the New World. In Poland it was served after bear hunts and was made with bear or other game. In America the meat has been changed to beef and pork and it is served any time that appetites are big. The sauerkraut and Polish sausage add a spiciness that is typically Polish.

Stuffed Cabbage Leaves

⅓ cup regular rice
1 large head cabbage
1 egg
¾ pound ground beef
½ cup chopped onion
½ teaspoon salt
    Dash pepper

4 slices bacon, cut in
    1-inch pieces
1 16-ounce can tomatoes
1 8-ounce can tomato sauce
1 bay leaf
    Dairy sour cream

Cook rice according to package directions. Set aside. Cut core out of cabbage; run hot water into cored area to help in removing 8 outer leaves. Set the 8 leaves aside. Chop remaining cabbage (about 6 cups) and place in a 12x7½x2-inch baking dish; sprinkle lightly with salt. Cut about 2 inches of the heavy center vein out of the reserved cabbage leaves. Boil cabbage leaves till limp, about 3 minutes; drain and set aside. Beat egg slightly with fork. Combine cooked rice, egg, ground beef, ¼ *cup* onion, ½ teaspoon salt, and pepper; mix well. Place about ¼ cup rice mixture in center of each cabbage leaf; fold in sides and roll ends over rice. Place rolls, seam side down, on top of chopped cabbage. In saucepan cook bacon and remaining onion till bacon is crisp; stir in undrained tomatoes, tomato sauce, and bay leaf. Simmer, covered, 5 minutes. Remove bay leaf. Pour over cabbage rolls. Cover; bake at 350° for 1¼ to 1½ hours. Serve with sour cream. Serves 4.

Gingerbread Layer Dessert is the American version of a Polish Christmas favorite. A rich dessert, it is a spiced layer cake, filled and frosted with sweetened whipped cream and decorated with shredded orange peel and grated chocolate. Beside it are slices of light, delicate *Poppy Seed Loaf*. A sweet filling of ground poppy seed, nuts, and honey makes this a delicious Polish specialty.

Gingerbread Layer Dessert

1 cup honey
1 teaspoon ground ginger
1 teaspoon ground cinnamon
½ teaspoon ground cloves
2¼ cups all-purpose flour
1 teaspoon baking soda
1 teaspoon baking powder
½ teaspoon salt
½ cup packed brown sugar
½ cup butter *or* margarine
1 egg

½ teaspoon grated lemon peel
1¼ cups buttermilk
1½ cups whipping cream
1 tablespoon granulated sugar
2 teaspoons shredded orange peel
1 1-ounce square semisweet chocolate, grated

In a small bowl combine the honey, ginger, cinnamon, and cloves. In a large bowl stir together the flour, baking soda, baking powder, and salt. In large mixing bowl cream the brown sugar and butter till the mixture is light and fluffy. Gradually beat honey mixture into brown sugar mixture, using high speed of electric mixer. Add the egg and lemon peel; mix well. Add the flour mixture and buttermilk alternately, stirring well after each addition. Pour batter into 2 greased and lightly floured 8x1½-inch round baking pans. Bake at 350° for 30 to 35 minutes. Cool cakes in pans 10 minutes. Turn out onto wire rack; cool completely. Whip cream with the granulated sugar till soft peaks form. Spread one layer of cake with part of the whipped cream. Sprinkle with *half* of the shredded orange peel and *half* the grated chocolate. Top with second layer of cake. Frost top and sides with remaining whipped cream; sprinkle with remaining shredded orange peel and grated chocolate. Chill at least one hour in the refrigerator.

Poppy Seed Loaf

5¼ to 5¾ cups all-purpose
    flour
2 packages active dry yeast
1½ cups milk
⅓ cup sugar
⅓ cup shortening
1 teaspoon salt

3 eggs
¾ cup poppy seed
½ cup chopped nuts
⅓ cup honey
1 teaspoon grated lemon
    peel
1 stiffly beaten egg white

Combine *2 cups* of the flour and the yeast. Heat milk, sugar, shortening, and salt just till warm (115-120°); stir constantly. Add to dry mixture. Add eggs. Beat at low speed of electric mixer for ½ minute, scraping bowl. Beat 3 minutes at high speed. By hand, stir in enough remaining flour to make a moderately stiff dough. Turn out onto lightly floured surface; knead till smooth (5 to 10 minutes). Shape into ball. Place in greased bowl; turn once. Cover; let rise in warm place till double, (about 1 hour). Meanwhile, pour 1 cup boiling water over poppy seed; let stand 30 minutes. Drain. Place in blend-er container; cover and blend till ground. (Or, put through finest blade of food grinder.) Combine poppy seed, nuts, honey, and lemon peel. Fold in egg white. Punch dough down. Divide in half. Cover; let rest 10 minutes. On lightly floured surface roll *one half* to 24x8-inch rectangle; spread with *half* the poppy seed mixture. Roll up jelly-roll style, starting with 8-inch side; seal. Place, seam side down, in greased 8½x4½x2½-inch loaf pan. Repeat with remaining dough and filling. Cover; let rise till double (30 to 45 minutes). Bake at 350° for 35 to 40 minutes. Remove from pans; cool. Makes 2.

In Poland, as in so many countries, honey is used as a sweetening agent. In ancient times Poles were always looking for ways to make the bees work harder. One way was to place magical designs on the tree trunks where the bees had their hives to charm them into producing more honey. Since magic was not always reliable, another more practical method was to stuff herbs into the hives. Honey is used in recipes such as Poppy Seed Loaf *and to make mead and a spiced liqueur called* Krupnik.

Mazurek

2 cups all-purpose flour
1½ cups sugar
½ cup butter *or* margarine
1 beaten egg

3 tablespoons milk
1 egg
3 tablespoons lemon juice
½ cup sliced almonds

Stir together flour, *1 cup* sugar, and ¼ teaspoon salt. Cut in butter till mixture resembles coarse crumbs. Mix beaten egg and milk. Add to flour mixture; stir till moistened. Pat evenly into greased 13x9x2-inch baking pan. Bake at 350° for 35 minutes. Beat 1 egg; stir in lemon juice and remaining sugar. Add almonds. Remove pastry from oven; spread with lemon mixture. Return to oven. Bake 10 to 12 minutes more. Cool. Makes 24 bars.

Mazurek is one of the rich pastries served in Polish coffee and pastry shops. Once, life was more leisurely and Poles could take time out for an afternoon break and gather at the local pastry shop or cukiernie *and nibble* Mazurek. *While Polish-Americans no longer have such pastry shops to relax in, the memory of these cakes still lingers and they are made at home using recipes such as this one.*

Cake Nalesniki with Cream Filling

2 beaten eggs
½ cup dairy sour cream
3 tablespoons granulated
    sugar
1 tablespoon all-purpose
    flour
½ teaspoon vanilla

½ teaspoon grated lemon
    peel
2 egg yolks
½ cup all-purpose flour
⅔ cup milk
2 stiffly beaten egg whites
    Powdered sugar

In top of double boiler combine eggs, sour cream, *2 tablespoons* sugar, 1 tablespoon flour, vanilla, and lemon peel. Place over boiling water. (Upper pan should not touch water.) Cook, stirring constantly, till thickened. Remove from over water. Cover surface of pudding with waxed paper; cool to room temperature. Beat egg yolks with remaining *1 tablespoon sugar* till thick and lemon-colored. Add flour and milk alternately, beating well after each addition. Fold in egg whites. Drop by tablespoonfuls onto hot, greased griddle, spreading to a 3-inch circle. Cook 1 minute on each side. Place cooked pancakes on paper toweling till all are cooked. Spoon about 1 teaspoon filling on each pancake, roll up, and place in 10x6x2-inch baking dish. Cover; bake at 350° till warmed, about 15 minutes. Sprinkle with powdered sugar. Serves 8.

Babka

4 to 4½ cups all-purpose
    flour
1 package active dry yeast
1 tablespoon grated lemon
    peel
½ teaspoon ground cinnamon

1¼ cups milk
½ cup sugar
½ cup butter *or* margarine
4 egg yolks
1 cup light raisins
¼ cup chopped almonds

Combine *2 cups* of the flour, the yeast, lemon peel, and cinnamon. Heat together milk, sugar, butter, and ¼ teaspoon salt just till warm (115-120°), stirring constantly. Add to dry mixture; add egg yolks. Beat at low speed of electric mixer for ½ minute, scraping bowl. Beat 3 minutes at high speed. By hand, stir in raisins and enough of the remaining flour to make a moderately stiff dough. Knead on floured surface till smooth (5 to 8 minutes). Shape in ball. Place in greased bowl; turn once. Cover; let rise till double (1½ to 1¾ hours). Punch down. Sprinkle almonds in well-greased 10-inch fluted tube pan. Shape dough in 8-inch ball. Make hole in center of dough, stretching it to fit over pan center. Place in pan, fitting tube through hole. Cover; let rise till double (about 1 hour). Bake at 350° for 40 to 45 minutes. Makes 1.

Borscht with Mushroom Dumplings

1 ounce *dried* mushrooms
    (¾ cup)
3½ cups boiling water
2 pounds red beets, thinly
    sliced and quartered
1 cup chopped carrot

1 cup chopped celery
½ cup chopped onion
2 bay leaves
2 tablespoons vinegar
1 teaspoon sugar
    Mushroom Dumplings

Combine mushrooms and the boiling water. Let soak at room temperature for 2 hours. Bring to boiling; simmer, uncovered, till tender, 7 to 10 minutes. Drain, reserving liquid. Use mushrooms in Mushroom Dumplings. In large saucepan combine beets, carrot, celery, onion, bay leaves, 4 cups water, and 1 teaspoon salt. Cover; cook till vegetables are tender, 40 to 45 minutes. Remove bay leaves. Stir in mushroom liquid, vinegar, sugar, 1 teaspoon salt, and ⅛ teaspoon pepper. Bring to boiling. Ladle into bowls; add Mushroom Dumplings to each serving. Makes 10 servings.

Mushroom Dumplings: Mix 1 cup all-purpose flour, 1 beaten egg, 2 to 3 tablespoons water, and ¼ teaspoon salt. Knead on floured surface till smooth and elastic. Cover; let stand 10 minutes. Cook 2 tablespoons chopped onion in 1 tablespoon butter till tender. Chop mushrooms; add to onion mixture with 1 tablespoon fine dry bread crumbs, 1 egg white, ¼ teaspoon salt, and dash pepper. Divide dough in half; roll to ⅛-inch thickness. Cut in 1½-inch squares. Place ½ teaspoon mushroom mixture on each square; fold to make triangle. Seal. Cook in large amount boiling salted water 5 minutes.

Polish Honey Kisses

1 cup sugar
½ cup butter *or* margarine
1 teaspoon grated lemon
    peel
2 teaspoons ground cinnamon
1 teaspoon ground ginger
¼ teaspoon ground cloves

¼ teaspoon ground nutmeg
1 cup honey
2 tablespoons milk
3½ cups all-purpose flour
    Powdered Sugar Icing
    (see recipe, page
    281)

Cream together sugar, butter, lemon peel and spices till light. Slowly beat in honey. Stir in milk. Stir in flour gradually. On lightly floured surface roll dough to ⅛-inch thickness. Cut into fancy shapes with cookie cutter. Place on ungreased cookie sheet. Bake at 350° till golden, 8 to 10 minutes. Remove from cookie sheet; cool. Frost with Powdered Sugar Icing. Makes 72.

Food from the Heart of Europe

Emigration from Central Europe began in force after 1880 and included a dozen or more ethnic groups who officially belonged to the Austro-Hungarian Empire. Among these groups were the Slovenes, Slovaks, Bulgarians, Czechs, Serbians, several other slavic groups, Hungarians, Montenegrins, Corats, and Dalmatians. Perhaps the most prosperous were the Bohemians and Moravians (later included in the group known as Czechs). About forty thousand came to California at the time of the Gold Rush; later, more Czechs settled in the northern Middle West, especially in Chicago and Cleveland. Still others homesteaded in the upper Mississippi Valley and in Texas, where the Czech language was taught in some public schools.

Slovaks, neighbors of the Czechs and united with them after the First World War to form the country of Czechoslovakia, came from the southern slopes of the Carpathian Mountains. Poorer than the Czechs, their immigration to America began during the 1870s, chiefly to mining and industrial towns in Pennsylvania, with a few to farms in New England and Virginia.

The plight of the Hungarians who came to the States was familiar to Americans because of Kossuth, the Magyar patriot leader, who visited America after the Hungarian Revolution of 1848 and attracted much sympathy. The Hungarians settled in San Antonio, Texas; Budapest, California; Kossuthville, Florida; and some other places. Most preferred city living and many became storekeepers and owners of small restaurants. Before long Hungarian goulash and paprika found favor with the American palate.

By the hundreds of thousands, citizens from the heart of Europe came to this country and found work as miners, factory hands, fishermen, longshoremen, and as workers in vineyards and on farms. Wherever they went, their jawbreaking names, romantic language, and their rich delicious cooking became increasingly familiar. Other Americans developed a real enthusiasm for goulash, liver dumplings, coffee cakes such as *potica,* and rich sweet rolls such as *kolache.*

Hungarians have always celebrated disznotor or the "feast of the pig's wake." In the old country the feast was held in the winter at hog-butchering time. The whole neighborhood helped with the men grinding the freshly cut meat for sausage and the women cooking. While the work was progressing, soup and roast pork were served. At the end of the day, a feast was held offering many types of pork sausage, roasts, and specialties such as pig's ears with horseradish. Hungarian-Americans still keep the tradition of the winter celebration, serving many of the same foods, but without the work involved in butchering a hog.

Chicken Paprika

2 3- to 3½-pound ready-to-cook broiler-fryer chickens, cut up
¼ cup butter *or* margarine
1 cup chopped onion
½ cup water
1 8-ounce can tomato sauce

2 tablespoons paprika
1½ teaspoons salt
¼ teaspoon pepper
1 cup dairy sour cream
¼ cup all-purpose flour
Hot cooked noodles

Season chicken with a little salt and pepper. In 12-inch skillet brown chicken pieces slowly in butter about 20 minutes; remove chicken. Cook onion in same skillet till tender. Add ¼ *cup* of the water, tomato sauce, paprika, 1½ teaspoons salt, and ¼ teaspoon pepper. Return chicken to skillet.

Cook, covered, till chicken is tender, 35 to 40 minutes. Remove chicken to serving platter. Stir together sour cream, the remaining ¼ cup water, and the flour; blend into hot mixture. Cook and stir till mixture is thickened. (Do not boil.) Serve chicken and sauce with hot cooked noodles. Serves 8.

Chicken Paprika takes its name from the red condiment made of mild capsicum peppers, dried and ground, a staple ingredient in Hungarian cooking. Europeans first learned of paprika when the capsicum peppers were brought home from South and Central America by the Spanish explorers. Later, the Turks introduced paprika peppers into Hungary. The Hungarians called the new seasoning Turkish pepper or paprika.

Hungarian Goulash

The word goulash means herdsmen's meat and the recipe for Hungarian Goulash has evolved from an old Magyar shepherd's stew. Originally the shepherds cut up what fresh meat and vegetables were available and cooked them in heavy iron kettles until no liquid remained. The stew was then dried in the sun and stored in a sack made from a sheep's stomach. To eat dinner, the men merely added water to the stew and reheated it.

2 pounds boneless beef
   chuck, cut in
   1-inch cubes
3 tablespoons cooking oil
1 14-ounce can beef broth
1 cup chopped onion
1 small green pepper, cut
   in thin strips
2 tablespoons tomato paste

2 tablespoons paprika
2 teaspoons caraway seed
   • • •
⅓ cup cold water
3 tablespoons all-purpose
   flour
   Hungarian Noodle Squares
   (see recipe below)
   Dairy sour cream

In large saucepan brown beef cubes in hot oil; add beef broth, onion, green pepper, tomato paste, paprika, caraway seed, ½ teaspoon salt, and ¼ teaspoon pepper. Blend cold water slowly into flour. Stir into beef mixture. Simmer, covered, till meat is tender, about 1½ hours; stir occasionally. Serve over Hungarian Noodle Squares. Garnish with dollops of sour cream. Serves 6.

Homemade breads are a favorite in any cuisine. *Kolache with Apricot Filling* (see recipe, page 282) and *Potica* both start with a type of yeast sweet roll dough. A fruit or nut filling is placed in the center of each *Kolache,* while the *Potica* features a rich nut filling—making it almost a cross between a coffee bread and a confection.

Hungarian Noodle Squares

2 cups all-purpose flour
½ teaspoon salt

3 beaten eggs
Water

Mix together flour and salt; stir in beaten eggs. Blend in just enough water (2 to 3 teaspoons) to make a stiff dough. Roll dough out on lightly floured surface to 20x15-inch rectangle. Cover and let rest 20 minutes. Cut into 1-inch squares. Drop into a large amount of rapidly boiling salted water; cook till noodles are tender, 15 to 18 minutes. Drain. Makes 6 servings.

Potica

4¼ to 4½ cups all-purpose
  flour
1 package active dry yeast
1 cup milk
½ cup granulated sugar

¼ cup butter *or* margarine
2 teaspoons salt
2 eggs
  Walnut Filling
  Powdered Sugar Icing

In mixing bowl combine *1½ cups* of the flour and the yeast. In saucepan heat together milk, granulated sugar, butter, and salt just till warm (115-120°), stirring constantly. Add to dry mixture in mixing bowl; add eggs. Beat at low speed of electric mixer for ½ minute, scraping bowl. Beat 3 minutes at high speed. By hand, stir in enough of the remaining flour to make moderately stiff dough. Knead on lightly floured surface till smooth and elastic (8 to 10 minutes). Place in greased bowl; turn once to grease surface. Cover; let rise till double (1 hour). Divide dough in half. Roll *each half* out on floured surface to 24x14-inch rectangle. Spread each with *half* the Walnut Filling. Beginning at long side, roll up jelly roll fashion. Pinch to seal seam and ends. Coil loosely on greased baking sheets. Cover; let rise till double (45 minutes). Bake at 350° for 20 minutes. Cover with foil; bake 15 to 20 minutes more. Cool. Frost with Powdered Sugar Icing. If desired, top with nuts. Makes 2.

Walnut Filling: Melt ¼ cup butter; stir in 1 cup granulated sugar, ¼ cup milk, ¼ cup honey, and 1 teaspoon ground cinnamon; bring to rolling boil. Stir in 12 ounces ground walnuts (3 cups). Cool slightly; stir in 2 beaten eggs and 2 teaspoons lemon juice.

Powdered Sugar Icing: Add milk (about ¼ cup) to 2 cups sifted powdered sugar to make spreading consistency. Stir in 1 teaspoon vanilla and dash salt.

The Slovenes are a central European heritage group who come from the area that is now northwestern Yugoslavia. One recipe that they particularly claim as their own is this one for Potica—a rich nut roll made with honey and topped with lots of icing and chopped nuts.

Nut Crescents

1 cup butter *or* margarine
½ cup granulated sugar
1 teaspoon vanilla

2 cups all-purpose flour
⅓ cup ground walnuts
  Sifted powdered sugar

Cream butter or margarine, granulated sugar, and vanilla. Stir in flour and walnuts. Using about 2 teaspoons dough for each, shape into crescents. Place on ungreased baking sheet. Bake at 325° for 20 minutes. While cookies are slightly warm, roll in powdered sugar. Makes 4 dozen.

Author Willa Cather once boasted that Bohemian-Americans were so enamored of their homeland pastries that they could never be corrupted by American pies. Taste their Nut Crescents *to see why. The rich butter cookies are close cousins to the cookies Americans call sandies, Mexicans call wedding cakes, and Russians call tea cakes.*

Croatian Onion Kuchen

2 cups all-purpose flour
1 package active dry yeast
¾ cup milk
3 tablespoons butter *or*
  margarine
¼ teaspoon salt

2 slices bacon
3 medium onions, cut in
  thin wedges (5 cups)
2 eggs
¼ cup dairy sour cream
¼ teaspoon salt

In mixing bowl stir together ¾ *cup* of the flour and yeast. Heat milk, butter, and ¼ teaspoon salt just till warm (115-120°), stirring constantly. Add to mixing bowl. Beat at low speed of electric mixer for ½ minute, scraping bowl. Beat 3 minutes at high speed. By hand, stir in remaining flour. Turn out on floured surface and knead till smooth and elastic (5 to 8 minutes). Place in greased bowl turning once. Cover; let rise in warm place till double (about 1 hour). Meanwhile, cook bacon till crisp; drain, reserving drippings in pan. Crumble bacon and set aside. Add onion to pan; cover and cook over low heat till onions are tender, about 10 minutes. Set aside. Punch down dough; cover; let rest 10 minutes. Roll out on floured surface to 12x8-inch rectangle. Place in greased 12x7½x2-inch baking dish. Sprinkle onions atop. Beat together eggs, sour cream, and ¼ teaspoon salt; pour over onions. Top with bacon. Let rise till double (30 minutes). Bake at 375° for 20 to 25 minutes. Serve warm. Serves 8 to 10.

Liver Dumplings

1 beaten egg
1 tablespoon butter *or* margarine, melted
1 small clove garlic, minced
½ teaspoon grated lemon peel
¼ teaspoon salt

¼ teaspoon dried marjoram, crushed
Dash ground allspice
½ pound beef liver, ground
1¼ cups fine dry bread crumbs
2 tablespoons butter *or* margarine, melted

In medium bowl stir together beaten egg, 1 tablespoon butter, garlic, lemon peel, salt, marjoram, allspice, and dash pepper. Mix in ground liver and ¾ *cup* of the crumbs. Let stand 30 minutes. Shape into 1-inch balls, using about 1 tablespoon for each. Drop into large amount of boiling salted water or broth; cook for 10 minutes. Drain. Combine remaining crumbs and 2 tablespoons butter; to serve, sprinkle on the dumplings. Makes 12 to 14.

Mushroom and Barley Casserole

½ cup *dried* mushrooms
1 cup water
½ cup pearl barley
1 clove garlic, minced
2 tablespoons finely chopped onion

2 tablespoons butter *or* margarine, melted
¼ teaspoon pepper
¼ teaspoon dried marjoram, crushed

Soak mushrooms in the water for 30 minutes. Drain, reserving liquid. Finely chop the mushrooms. Add enough cold water to mushroom liquid to make 3 cups. In saucepan combine liquid, mushrooms, barley, garlic, and 1½ teaspoons salt; bring to boiling. Cover; reduce heat and simmer till barley is tender, 45 to 60 minutes. Stir in onion, butter, pepper, and marjoram. Spoon into a 1-quart casserole. Cover and bake at 350° for 30 minutes. (Add more water during baking, if necessary.) Season to taste. Serves 6.

Kolache with Apricot Filling *(see photo, page 280)*

3½ to 4 cups all-purpose flour
1 package active dry yeast
• • •
¾ cup milk
½ cup butter *or* margarine
½ cup granulated sugar

1 teaspoon grated lemon peel
¼ teaspoon salt
2 eggs
Apricot Filling
Sifted powdered sugar

In large mixing bowl combine 1¼ *cups* of the flour and the yeast. In saucepan heat together milk, butter, granulated sugar, lemon peel, and salt just till warm (115-120°), stirring constantly. Add to dry mixture in mixing bowl; add eggs. Beat at low speed of electric mixer for ½ minute, scraping bowl constantly. Beat 3 minutes at high speed. By hand, stir in enough of the remaining flour to make a moderately soft dough. Knead on lightly floured surface till smooth and elastic (8 to 10 minutes). Shape into ball. Place in greased bowl; turn once to grease surface. Cover; let rise in warm place till double (1 to 1½ hours). Punch down; divide in half. Cover; let rest 10 minutes. Shape *each half* into 9 balls. Place balls, 3 inches apart, on greased baking sheets. With fingers, flatten each to 3½-inch circle. Cover; let rise till double (about 45 minutes). Make a depression in center of each ball. Fill depression with Apricot Filling. Bake at 375° for 10 to 12 minutes. Remove from baking sheets; cool. Dust lightly with powdered sugar. Makes 18.

Apricot Filling: Mix 1 cup snipped dried apricots and enough water to come 1 inch above apricots. Simmer for 15 to 20 minutes; drain. Stir in ¼ cup granulated sugar, 1 tablespoon butter, and ¼ teaspoon ground nutmeg.

Classics from the Greek Cuisine

Most of the more than 2 million Greek-Americans in this country have arrived since 1900. Many became textile workers in the Massachusetts mill towns. Others went to Florida and established a sponge fishing industry and, since few native-born Americans were willing to take the risks of sponge diving, the Greeks prospered. Their biggest successes, however, have been in the operation of wholesale groceries, the movie industry, and restaurants and hotels.

While most immigrant nationalities have tended to stick together and form social clubs, mutual-benefit societies, and the like, the Greek-Americans have made it a way of life. Perhaps it is because a large number of these immigrants were lonely men without families, and also because of the fact that the Greek Orthodox Church has only a few parishioners from other ethnic groups. Also an unusually large percentage of Greeks return to their homeland, even after spending most of their lifetime in America. It is rare for an American to travel in Greece without meeting someone who spent twenty years in Toledo, or who asks you, in fluent English, if you know his sister in Baltimore.

Since the Second World War, certain Greek foods have become commonplace in this country; for example *moussaka,* Greek olives, feta cheese, and *souvlak,* lamb barbecued on a vertical spit. But there are many other Hellenic favorites. One is the Greek way with fish. In the old country, the Greeks had to depend on what few fish were left in the Aegean Sea, but in the New World, they choose from a great abundance of mackerel, flounder, pompano, and red snapper. All Greek cooks pride themselves on preparing fish in their own distinctively "Greek" style. The Greek-Americans also have their own varieties of *psomi* breads, as well as their famous Greek salads. Most tempting of all Greek foods are the pastries. Leading the list is *baklava,* a flaky honey pastry. In addition, the victim of a sweet tooth can sample chocolate and nut cakes decorated with cherries and whipped cream, butter cookies dusted with sugar or sesame seeds, orange and cinnamon-flavored cookies, or an Athenian torte made with sponge cake and almond and chocolate fillings. All are classics from the Greek cuisine.

One Greek institution that is not very well known outside the Greek-American community is the coffeehouse. This all-male stronghold used to be the center of much social activity. Here the men played cards, exchanged gossip, debated politics, and, of course, sipped thick black coffee. Later wrestling and movies sent from Greece added to the fun. The most important function of the coffeehouse, however, was that it helped these immigrants preserve their identity as Greeks in a world that wanted them to become "American."

Kourabiedes

1 cup butter *or* margarine
½ cup sifted powdered sugar
• • •
1 egg yolk
½ teaspoon vanilla
¼ teaspoon ground aniseed

¼ cup finely chopped almonds
2 cups all-purpose flour
½ teaspoon baking powder
Whole cloves
Sifted powdered sugar

Cream butter and ½ cup powdered sugar. Stir in egg yolk, vanilla, and aniseed. Stir in almonds. Stir together flour and baking powder; blend into creamed mixture. Wrap and chill for 30 minutes. Form into 1-inch balls; stud each with a clove. Bake on ungreased cookie sheet at 325° till a pale sand color, about 20 minutes. Cool. Top with powdered sugar. Makes 48.

Kourabiedes are a holiday treat among Greek-Americans. Usually round, these cookies are served both at Christmas and during the celebration of the Epiphany. When they are soaked in honey, they form another confection called Melomacaroma.

Pastitsio

1½ pounds ground beef
1 cup chopped onion
1 16-ounce can tomatoes,
 cut up
1 6-ounce can tomato paste
¼ teaspoon dried thyme,
 crushed
1 7-ounce package elbow
 macaroni (2 cups)

4 slightly beaten egg
 whites
½ cup cubed feta cheese *or*
 American cheese
½ cup butter *or* margarine
½ cup all-purpose flour
¼ teaspoon ground cinnamon
4 cups milk
4 slightly beaten egg yolks

In skillet cook beef and onion till meat is browned; drain off excess fat. Add undrained tomatoes, tomato paste, thyme, and 1 teaspoon salt. Simmer, covered for 30 minutes, stirring often. Meanwhile, cook macaroni according to package directions; drain well. Stir egg whites and cheese into macaroni; stir in meat mixture. Turn into 13x9x2-inch baking pan. In large saucepan melt butter. Blend in flour, cinnamon, and 1 teaspoon salt. Add milk all at once. Cook, stirring constantly, till thickened and bubbly. Remove from heat. Gradually stir some hot sauce into egg yolks; blend well. Return yolk mixture to remaining sauce, stirring rapidly. Pour atop meat mixture. Sprinkle lightly with additional cinnamon, if desired. Bake at 375° till heated through, 35 to 40 minutes. Let stand 10 minutes before serving. Serves 12.

Pictured opposite: For a meal with the zest Greek-Americans have taught us to enjoy, try beginning with a tossed salad topped with feta cheese, anchovies, and sliced olives. Then for the main dish serve the custard-topped casserole called *Pastitsio.* Finally, for dessert set out fresh fruit, *Baklava* (see recipe, page 286), and plenty of strong black coffee.

Red Snapper with Vegetable Sauce

1 cup chopped onion
½ cup chopped celery
½ cup chopped green pepper
½ cup chopped carrot
1 clove garlic, minced
2 tablespoons cooking oil
1 28-ounce can tomatoes,
 cut up
¾ cup dry white wine

2 tablespoons finely
 snipped fresh dill
1 tablespoon finely snipped
 parsley
1 4- to 5-pound red snapper,
 dressed, head and tail
 left on
2 tablespoons lemon juice
 Cooking oil

In saucepan cook onion, celery, green pepper, carrot, and garlic in oil for 5 minutes. Add undrained tomatoes, wine, dill, parsley, and 1 teaspoon salt. Simmer, covered, 15 minutes. Meanwhile, drizzle inside of fish with lemon juice; sprinkle with salt and pepper. Place fish in a large baking pan; brush with cooking oil. Pour sauce over fish. Cover with foil. Bake at 350° for 45 minutes. Remove foil; continue baking till fish flakes easily when tested with a fork, 10 to 15 minutes more. Serve sauce over fish. Serves 6.

The Feast of the Epiphany on January 6 is a very special occasion in Tarpon Springs, Florida. For on this day the Greek Orthodox Church here officially celebrates the baptism of Christ, with the Greek Orthodox Archbishop of North and South America in attendance. After a ceremony, "the blessing of the water," young boys compete for the privilege of retrieving a cross which the archbishop tosses into the water. The boy who finds the cross receives a special blessing and a trophy. Then the less solemn festivities begin. The celebration dinner called glendi *always offers a wide assortment of Greek foods including such dishes as* Red Snapper with Vegetable Sauce.

Psomi

3¾ to 4 cups all-
 purpose flour
1 package active dry yeast
1⅓ cups milk

2 tablespoons sugar
1 tablespoon shortening
1½ teaspoons salt
 Melted butter

In large mixing bowl combine *1¼ cups* flour and the yeast. Heat milk, sugar, shortening, and salt just till warm (115-120°); stir constantly. Add to dry mixture. Beat at low speed of electric mixer for ½ minute, scraping sides of bowl constantly. Beat 3 minutes at high speed. By hand, stir in enough of the remaining flour to make moderately stiff dough. Turn dough out on lightly floured surface; knead till smooth and elastic (8 to 10 minutes). Place dough in lightly greased bowl; turn once to grease surface. Cover; let rise in warm place till double (about 1½ hours). Punch down. Divide dough in half. Shape each half into 10-inch-long loaf. Place loaves on greased baking sheets. Brush tops with melted butter. Cover; let rise till almost double (about 1 hour). Bake at 375° till golden, about 45 minutes. Makes 2 loaves.

Baklava was an invention of the Persians. They stuffed the diamond-shaped confection with nuts and perfumed it with pussy willow blossoms or jasmine. Later, Baklava was introduced to the court of Justinian I at Constantinople. The Greeks quickly caught on to the use of the special fillo pastry used for Baklava. This dessert has become a tradition for many holidays including the Feast of the Epiphany.

Baklava *(see photo, page 284)*

1 pound frozen fillo dough
   (21 16x12-inch leaves)
1 cup walnuts
½ cup blanched almonds
1 cup butter, melted

2 tablespoons sugar
1 teaspoon ground cinnamon
½ teaspoon ground nutmeg
⅛ teaspoon ground cloves
   Lemon-Honey Syrup

Thaw fillo dough at room temperature for 2 hours. Finely chop or grind nuts. Cut fillo in half crosswise. Cover with slightly damp towel. Lightly butter the bottom of 14x10x2-inch baking pan. Lay *10 of the half sheets* of fillo in pan, *brushing each sheet* with some of the melted butter. Mix walnuts, almonds, sugar, cinnamon, nutmeg, and cloves. Sprinkle *half* of the nut mixture over fillo in pan. Drizzle with some of the melted butter. Top with *another 20 of the half sheets* of fillo, *brushing each* with more of the melted butter. Repeat with another layer of the nut mixture, remaining butter, and remaining fillo. Cut *without cutting through bottom layer,* into diamond-shaped pieces or squares. Bake at 350° for 50 to 55 minutes. Finish cutting; cool thoroughly. Pour warm Lemon-Honey Syrup over. Makes about 24 diamonds.

Lemon-Honey Syrup: In a saucepan combine 1 cup sugar, 1 cup water, and ½ lemon, sliced. Boil gently for 15 minutes. Remove lemon slices. Add 2 tablespoons honey. Stir till blended. Keep the syrup warm until used.

In many Greek-American homes, New Year's Day is celebrated as St. Basil's Day. For this holiday Vaslopita or St. Basil's Bread is baked in a round shape with a coin hidden inside. When the bread is eaten, the first piece is offered to St. Basil, the second piece is saved for the poor, and the third goes to the eldest member of the family. After this brief ceremony the other family members receive a piece dipped in wine and the phrase, "This is for Father St. Basil," is repeated. The lucky person who finds the coin in his piece is supposedly assured good fortune all year.

St. Basil's Bread

4 to 4½ cups all-purpose
   flour
1 package active dry yeast
1 teaspoon grated lemon
   peel
½ teaspoon aniseed, crushed
1 cup milk

¼ cup butter *or* margarine
¼ cup sugar
¾ teaspoon salt
2 eggs
1 beaten egg yolk
   Sesame seed

In large mixing bowl combine *2 cups* flour, yeast, lemon peel, and aniseed. Heat together milk, butter, sugar, and salt just till warm (115-120°), stirring constantly. Add to dry mixture; add 2 eggs. Beat at low speed of electric mixer for ½ minute, scraping sides of bowl constantly. Beat 3 minutes at high speed. By hand, stir in enough of the remaining flour to make a moderately stiff dough. Turn out on lightly floured surface; knead till smooth and satiny (6 to 8 minutes). Shape into ball; place in lightly greased bowl, turning once to grease surface. Cover; let rise till double (1 to 1¼ hours). Punch down. Divide dough into thirds. Cover; let rest 10 minutes. Shape *one-third* of dough into flat, 8-inch round loaf. Place in greased 8x1½-inch round baking pan. Repeat with second third of dough; place in another 8x1½-inch round baking pan. Divide remaining dough in half. Shape *each half* into a strand 18 inches long. Twist each strand like rope and seal ends to form a 7-inch circle. Place one circle atop each loaf. Combine egg yolk with 1 tablespoon water; brush on loaves. Sprinkle with sesame seed. Let rise in warm place till double (30 to 45 minutes). Bake at 375° till done, 20 to 25 minutes. Remove from pans. Cool thoroughly on rack. Makes 2 round loaves.

Pilaf

1½ cups regular rice
¼ cup finely chopped onion
3 tablespoons butter *or*
   margarine

1 13¾-ounce can chicken
   broth
1 cup water
½ teaspoon salt

In 10-inch skillet cook the rice and finely chopped onion in butter or margarine till the rice is golden, stirring frequently. Stir in the chicken broth, water, and salt. Bring to boiling; reduce heat. Cover and simmer till the rice is tender, about 14 minutes. Fluff with a fork. Makes 8 servings.

Greek Moussaka

2 medium eggplants, peeled
  and cut into ½-inch
  thick slices
1 pound ground beef
1 cup chopped onion
¼ cup Burgundy
2 tablespoons snipped
  parsley
1 tablespoon tomato paste
⅔ cup soft bread crumbs
2 beaten eggs

½ cup shredded sharp
  American cheese
Dash ground cinnamon
3 tablespoons butter
3 tablespoons all-purpose
  flour
1½ cups milk
Dash ground nutmeg
1 beaten egg
Cooking oil

Sprinkle eggplant slices with a little salt and set aside. In skillet cook beef and onion till beef is browned; drain. Add Burgundy, parsley, tomato paste, ¼ cup water, 1 teaspoon salt, and dash pepper. Simmer till liquid is nearly absorbed. Cool. Stir in *half* the bread crumbs, 2 eggs, *half* the cheese, and cinnamon. In saucepan melt butter. Stir in flour. Add milk all at once; cook and stir till thick and bubbly. Stir in nutmeg, ½ teaspoon salt, and dash pepper. Add a small amount of the sauce to the one beaten egg; return to hot mixture. Cook and stir over low heat for 2 minutes.

Brown the salted eggplant slices on both sides in a little hot cooking oil. Sprinkle bottom of 12x7½x2-inch baking dish with remaining bread crumbs. Cover with *half* the eggplant slices. Spoon on meat mixture. Arrange remaining eggplant atop. Pour milk-egg sauce over all. Top with remaining cheese. Bake at 350° about 45 minutes. Makes 6 to 8 servings.

In the old country Greek Moussaka was a festival specialty because for most Greeks meat was rare—often eaten just twice a year. The two occasions were usually Easter and the feast day of the village patron saint. Here, Greek-Americans quickly took advantage of the abundance of meat to serve Moussaka often.

The Art of Asian Cooking

The exuberance of the Chinese New Year, the fragile air of Japanese maidens in their kimonos, and the exotic sound of Korean or Vietnamese speech have always intrigued Americans. The acceptance of these cultures, however, has progressed more slowly than for most other immigrant groups.

The story begins with the discovery of gold in California in 1848 which happened to coincide with a time of great political and economic hardship in China. As soon as word of it reached Shanghai, Canton, and other ports, thousands of young male Chinese began to cross the Pacific. Nearly all were very poor and totally ignorant of Western ways. Although they worked hard, obeyed the law, and aspired only to accumulate enough money to return home and support their families, they were victims of discrimination since other immigrants were competing with them for jobs. Still they continued to come and by 1880 their numbers had soared to 300,000 in California; contract labor arranged by mining and railroad companies brought many more Chinese to other parts of the country. Despite the great number who eventually returned to China, the culture and customs of those who remained had an impact on the American scene.

Most of the immigration of Japanese to the United States began after 1890 when many went to Hawaii as contract labor on sugar plantations.

Respect for food long ago led the Chinese to perfect stir-frying. Watch an adept Oriental cook arrange the sliced or cubed meat and vegetables around the large shallow pan called a wok, carefully heat the oil, quickly add the ingredients at just the right moment while stirring continually, and deftly use chopsticks to lift the finished food to serving plates. It is as enchanting and precise a procedure as a ballet. But, more important is the flavor and crisp-tenderness of the vegetables and the succulence of the meat in stir-fried dishes such as Sukiyaki (see recipe, page 291).

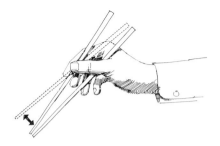

Celebrating the Chinese New Year is the high point of the year for Chinese-Americans, with feasting, visiting, parades, and fireworks. The two-week celebration is determined by the lunar calendar. It begins on the day of the first moon after the sun has left the sign of Capricorn and entered Aquarius—sometime between January 21 and February 19.

Additional thousands came to the mainland to work in lumber camps, on farms, for the railroads, and as domestics. Later Korean and Philippine immigrants came to America to find work or to live with their American soldier husbands. At present the most publicized Asian immigration involves the refugees from Vietnam. While life was difficult for all these groups, they overcame the barriers caused by discrimination and prejudice and made a priceless contribution to the American heritage.

American appreciation of the Oriental cuisine received its impetus from Chinese restaurants. In the late nineteenth century after most native Americans had recovered from their initial nervousness about sampling bamboo shoots, bean sprouts, and the like, they found that Chinese meals were not only delicious but cheap. People in the cities made meals at "the Chinamans's" a frequent habit — even though many never ordered anything but chop suey (a concoction invented in America). Gradually American tastes became more sophisticated and truly Chinese dishes such as sweet-sour pork, chow mein, egg-drop soup, and egg foo yung were being ordered.

Once Americans learned to appreciate Chinese cuisine, they began to discover other Asian foods. Many Japanese restaurants opened everywhere to serve sukiyaki, sushi and yakitori. In addition many war brides from the Philippines, Korea, and Vietnam taught their husbands and friends to enjoy the cooking treasures of their homelands.

Sesame Seed Cookies

¾ cup sugar
½ cup butter *or* margarine
1 egg
½ cup sesame seed

2 cups all-purpose flour
1 teaspoon baking powder
Toasted sesame seed
(optional)

In a large bowl cream together the sugar and butter. Beat in egg; add sesame seed. Stir together flour, baking powder, and ½ teaspoon salt. Stir into creamed mixture. Shape into 8x2x 2-inch log. Wrap dough in waxed paper and chill till firm, at least 2 hours. Cut into ¼-inch slices. Bake on ungreased cookie sheet at 350° for 12 to 15 minutes. (If desired, before baking press toasted sesame seed into the tops of cookies.) Makes about 32 cookies.

The miseries of war are responsible for the flow of Korean and Vietnamese immigrants to the United States. Although a statistical breakdown is not available, many of these immigrants were "war brides" and one of the few things they could bring from their ravaged homelands was a favorite recipe such as Korean Sesame Seed Cookies *or Vietnamese* Crab and Asparagus Soup.

Crab and Asparagus Soup

2 10½-ounce cans cut
asparagus
3 cups chicken broth
1 3-ounce can sliced
mushrooms
1 medium onion, coarsely
chopped

2 tablespoons cold water
1 tablespoon cornstarch
1 7-ounce can crab meat,
drained, flaked, and
cartilage removed
Sliced green onion with
tops

Drain asparagus, reserving liquid. Mix asparagus liquid, broth, undrained mushrooms, and onion. Cover and simmer till onion is tender, about 5 minutes. Slowly blend cold water into cornstarch. Stir into broth mixture; cook and stir till mixture thickens and bubbles. Add asparagus and crab meat. Heat through. Sprinkle each serving with sliced green onion. Serves 6.

Picadillo

½ pound ground beef
1 cup chopped onion
2 cloves garlic, minced
4 cups water
3 medium potatoes, peeled
and cubed

2 cups chopped peeled
tomato
½ cup chopped celery
1 large bay leaf
1 teaspoon sugar
¼ teaspoon pepper

In large saucepan cook beef, onion, and garlic till meat is browned. Drain fat. Add water, vegetables, bay leaf, sugar, pepper, and 1 teaspoon salt. Simmer, covered, till potatoes are tender, about 30 minutes. Serves 6.

Since the Philippine Islands were under American rule for several decades, it's not surprising that many of the dishes of the Philippines closely resemble American foods. Picadillo *is one example of familiar foods combined in a slightly different way.*

Japanese Tempura

Fresh *or* frozen shelled
shrimp
Assorted fresh vegetables
such as asparagus
spears, parsley, sweet
potatoes, mushrooms, and
green beans

Cooking oil
1 cup all-purpose flour
1 cup ice water
1 slightly beaten egg
2 tablespoons cooking oil
½ teaspoon sugar
Condiments

Thaw frozen shrimp. Wash and dry shrimp and vegetables well. Slice or cut vegetables into strips, if necessary. In skillet that is at least 3 inches deep, heat 1½ inches oil to 365°. For batter mix flour, ice water, egg, 2 tablespoons oil, sugar and ½ teaspoon salt; beat just till moistened (a few lumps should remain). Stir in one or two ice cubes. Use at once. Dip shrimp and vegetables into batter. Fry in hot oil till light brown; drain. Serve with Condiments: (1) grated fresh gingerroot; (2) equal parts grated turnip and radish, mixed; (3) ½ cup prepared mustard mixed with 3 tablespoons soy sauce.

Although credited to the Japanese, tempura actually came to Japan by way of the Portuguese. During the 16th century, Portugal carried on a flourishing trade with Japan. By the time the Japanese closed their doors to the Western world early in the 17th century, several Portuguese customs including their fondness for deep-frying seafoods had been adopted by the Japanese. Several centuries of refinement resulted in the light batter used in the tempura of today.

Yakitori

½ cup soy sauce
¼ cup sweet sake *or* dry
   sherry
1 tablespoon sugar
1 teaspoon grated fresh
   gingerroot
½ pound chicken livers,
   cut in half

1 large whole chicken
   breast, split, skinned,
   boned, and cut in
   1-inch cubes
4 scallions, cut into
   1-inch lengths
Sushi (see recipe below)

Combine soy sauce, sherry, sugar, gingerroot, and ¼ cup water. Boil 1 minute; cool. Marinate chicken livers, chicken cubes, and scallion pieces in soy mixture for 15 to 30 minutes; turn once. On short wooden skewers thread a chicken cube, a chicken liver piece, a scallion piece, another chicken liver piece, and a chicken cube. Grill over *hot* coals 4 to 5 minutes per side; brush occasionally with marinade. Serve with Sushi. Serves 4 or 5.

Sushi

Cook 1 cup regular rice according to package directions. Meanwhile, in a small saucepan combine 2 tablespoons rice vinegar *or* white vinegar, 2 tablespoons sugar, and 2 teaspoons mirin *or* sweet sake *or* dry sherry. Bring to a boil. Stir into cooked rice. Serve with Yakitori. Makes 3 cups.

Sukiyaki

2 tablespoons cooking oil
1 pound boneless beef
   tenderloin, very thinly
   sliced across the grain
2 tablespoons sugar
½ cup beef stock *or* canned
   condensed beef broth
⅓ cup soy sauce
2 cups bias-sliced green
   onions
1 cup bias-sliced celery

5 cups small spinach leaves
1 16-ounce can bean
   sprouts, drained
1 cup thinly sliced fresh
   mushrooms
1 5-ounce can water
   chestnuts, drained
   and thinly sliced
1 5-ounce can bamboo
   shoots, drained
Hot cooked rice

Preheat large skillet or wok; add oil. Add beef; cook quickly, turning meat over and over, just till browned, 1 to 2 minutes. Sprinkle with sugar. Combine stock or broth and ⅓ cup soy sauce; pour over meat. Push meat to one side. Let soy mixture bubble. Keeping in separate groups, add onions and celery. Continue cooking and toss-stirring *each group* over high heat about 1 minute; push to one side. Again keeping in separate groups, add spinach, bean sprouts, mushrooms, water chestnuts, and bamboo shoots. Cook and stir *each food* just till heated through. Serve with rice. Serves 4.

Beef Teriyaki

½ cup soy sauce
¼ cup mirin, sweet sake, *or*
   dry sherry
2 tablespoons sugar
2 teaspoons dry mustard

4 cloves garlic, minced
1½ pounds boneless beef tenderloin *or* sirloin, cut
   1 inch thick
   (partially frozen)

Combine soy sauce; mirin, sake, or sherry; sugar; mustard; and garlic. Cut partially frozen meat into thin strips. Thaw meat completely. Add to marinade and let stand 15 minutes at room temperature. Thread meat strips accordion-style on small skewers. Grill over *hot* coals to desired doneness, 5 to 7 minutes. Turn and baste with marinade frequently. Makes 18 appetizers.

Pictured opposite: To Oriental cooks, the appearance of a dish is as important as the flavor. Vegetables retain their bright colors and crisp textures because of the quick-cooking methods used. Sauces should have character and be a rich brown or clear and golden. Two main dish examples are *Sukiyaki* and *Sweet-Sour Pork* (see recipe, page 292).

The word "sukiyaki" is derived from two Japanese words — suki, meaning plow, and yaki, meaning broiled. Apparently this goes back to early times when hunters or farmers occasionally cooked their meat on a plow blade over an open fire.

The marinade for Beef Teriyaki combines two standard Japanese ingredients, sake (rice wine) and shoyu, soy sauce. Soy sauce particularly, is an essential ingredient in Oriental cooking. It is a fermented mixture of soybeans, water, and salt, and adds a distinctive flavor and color to many Oriental dishes.

Shrimp Chow Mein

The philosopher, Confucius, influenced Chinese life in many ways, even food preparation. He believed the proportion of meat in a recipe should not exceed that of vegetables. The abundance of vegetables in Shrimp Chow Mein *reflects his philosophy.*

1½ pounds fresh *or* frozen
    shelled shrimp
¼ cup cooking oil
1 medium onion, sliced
2 cups sliced fresh
    mushrooms
1 16-ounce can bean
    sprouts, drained
1 6-ounce package frozen
    pea pods, thawed and
    halved crosswise
1 cup shredded bok choy *or*
    cabbage

½ cup sliced water
    chestnuts
1 clove garlic, minced
1 13¾-ounce can chicken
    broth
¼ cup soy sauce
¼ teaspoon salt
3 tablespoons cornstarch
½ cup toasted slivered
    almonds
Hot cooked rice *or* chow
    mein noodles
Soy sauce

Thaw frozen shrimp; halve lengthwise. In large skillet cook and stir shrimp in hot oil for 1 to 2 minutes. Remove shrimp. Halve onion slices. Add onion, mushrooms, bean sprouts, pea pods, bok choy, water chestnuts, and garlic to remaining oil in skillet. Cook and stir vegetables 2 or 3 minutes. Add *1¼ cups* chicken broth, ¼ cup soy, and salt. Cover; simmer 6 to 8 minutes. Add shrimp to vegetable mixture. Blend remaining broth into cornstarch. Stir into mixture in skillet. Cook and stir till thickened and bubbly. Stir in almonds. Serve over rice or noodles. Pass soy sauce. Serves 6 to 8.

Sweet-Sour Pork *(see photo, page 290)*

Authentic Sweet-Sour Pork *depends on a two-step preparation technique. First, pork cubes are dipped in batter and deep-fried till golden and crispy. Then, the sweet-sour sauce is prepared and combined with the meat. This mixture is usually served with rice.*

1 pound boneless pork, cut
    in 1-inch cubes
1 beaten egg
¼ cup cornstarch
¼ cup all-purpose flour
¼ cup chicken broth
½ teaspoon salt
    Cooking oil
1 large green pepper, diced
½ cup chopped carrot

1 clove garlic, minced
2 tablespoons cooking oil
1 cup chicken broth
½ cup sugar
⅓ cup red wine vinegar
2 teaspoons soy sauce
¼ cup cold water
2 tablespoons cornstarch
    Hot cooked rice

Trim excess fat from pork. In a bowl combine egg, ¼ cup cornstarch, flour, ¼ cup chicken broth, and salt; beat till smooth. Dip pork cubes in batter; fry in deep hot fat (375°) till golden, 5 to 6 minutes. Drain; keep warm. In skillet cook green pepper, carrot, and garlic in 2 tablespoons oil till vegetables are tender but not brown. Stir in 1 cup broth, sugar, vinegar, and soy sauce. Bring to boiling; boil rapidly 1 minute. Slowly blend cold water into cornstarch. Stir into vegetable mixture. Cook and stir till thickened and bubbly. Stir in pork cubes. Serve with rice. Makes 4 to 6 servings.

Chinese Fried Rice

The majority of Chinese immigrants who came to the United States during the 1800s were from the southern province of Kwangtung. Chinese Fried Rice *is attributed to the Cantonese cooking of this area.*

2 beaten eggs
3 tablespoons cooking oil
½ cup finely diced fully
    cooked ham *or* raw pork
¼ cup finely chopped fresh
    mushrooms

3 tablespoons soy sauce
3 tablespoons thinly sliced
    green onion with tops
4 cups cooked rice
    Soy sauce

In a 10-inch skillet cook beaten eggs in *1 tablespoon* of the oil, without stirring, till set. Invert skillet over a baking sheet to remove cooked eggs; cut into short, narrow strips. In the same skillet cook ham or pork, mushrooms, 3 tablespoons soy sauce, and green onion in remaining oil till mushrooms and onion are tender, about 4 minutes. Stir in cooked rice and egg strips; heat through. Serve with additional soy sauce. Makes 4 to 6 servings.

Egg Drop Soup

In saucepan slowly blend two 13¾-ounce cans chicken broth into 1 tablespoon cornstarch. Cook and stir till slightly thickened. Slowly pour in 1 well-beaten egg; stir once gently. Remove from heat. Pour into soup bowls and garnish with 2 tablespoons sliced green onion with tops. Serves 4.

Egg Foo Yung

8 eggs
1 teaspoon salt
1 16-ounce can bean
    sprouts, well drained
1 cup finely chopped fully
    cooked ham
½ cup finely chopped onion
¼ cup finely chopped celery
Cooking oil

½ cup thinly sliced fresh
    mushrooms
1 tablespoon cooking oil
4 teaspoons cornstarch
1½ cups water
1 teaspoon instant beef
    bouillon granules
1½ teaspoons soy sauce
1 teaspoon catsup

Beat together eggs, salt, and ¼ teaspoon pepper. Stir in bean sprouts, ham, onion, and celery. Heat about 2 tablespoons oil till hot. Using about ¼ cup mixture for each, fry patties in hot oil till golden, about 1 minute per side. Keep warm. Repeat till all mixture is used stirring each time; add oil as needed. Cook mushrooms in 1 tablespoon cooking oil till tender. Blend in cornstarch. Add water, bouillon granules, soy sauce, and catsup. Cook and stir till thick and bubbly. Serve with Egg Foo Yung. Serves 4 or 5.

When entertaining, it's not unusual for the Chinese-Americans to serve an elaborate meal of many courses. Although there may be eight or more dishes served, care is taken to be sure that the basic flavor, color, and texture of each is different. Soups, nuts, fruits, or melon seeds are served between courses to clear the palate.

America Welcomes Alaska and Hawaii

The admission of Alaska and Hawaii as states made "official" the addition to the national food heritage of two new and totally different ways of cooking. While the Alaskans and Hawaiians were not immigrants in the sense that they physically moved from one country to another, their culture is different from that of the mainland states and has added richness.

In Alaska, frontier cooking is at its best. Here all the incomparable flavors of the wilderness—game, fish, wild birds, and wild plants—are blended with the cooking traditions of the Eskimo.

Alaskan dinners may often include caribou, venison, moose, rabbit, or bear, not to mention a great variety of game birds. The clear, icy waters of the ocean yield the famous Alaskan king crab and from the glacier-fed lakes and streams come salmon and trout unequaled anywhere.

The growing season may be short, but nature has contrived to make it produce fruits and vegetables of extraordinary size and flavor. When next you visit Alaska, be sure to go out to pick the blueberries, huckleberries, and cranberries they use for pies, sauces, jams, and cordials.

To round out a meal Alaskans serve baked goods made with sourdough starter. It is one of the culinary legacies left to them by the original mainland pioneers and gold miners called "sourdoughs."

Tropical drinks have become one of Hawaii's trademarks. Perhaps the most famous of them all is the Mai Tai (see recipe, page 298). It serves as an appropriate ambassador of the Islands because it uses pineapple juice and is often garnished with orchids and gardenias — all local products.

A number of other tropical drinks contain a liquor made from the root of the ti plant, called Okolehao. The word means "iron bottom" because this spirit was named after the distilling pots in which it was made. It seems that these pots were rounded on one side and flat on the other, and when they were used in pairs, flat sides together, the Hawaiians claim they resembled the bottom of a plump matron, thus the name.

Hawaii's combination of racial strains, plus the many foods that thrive in the rich soil and the varieties of fish that swim in its blue waters have created a unique gastronomic repertoire.

It all began with the native Hawaiians who, from time immemorial, prepared all kinds of fish, poi (pounded taro root paste), coconuts, and many tropical fruits including the pineapple, banana, breadfruit, guava, and papaya. Traditionally Hawaiian cooking was done in an *imu*, or underground oven, and the men, not the women, did most of the preparations. For special occasions, Hawaiians held a luau, which could be called the Pacific relative of the Atlantic seaboard clambake.

To the nutritious and tasty native diet, newcomers to the Islands brought additions and variations. The Japanese contributed teriyaki; various ways of preparing raw fish; soybeans and their products; and dishes made with rice — rice cakes and rice wine, among others. The Chinese added soups, noodles, vegetables such as bean sprouts, bamboo shoots, and snow peas, and dishes made with pork, fish, and duck.

Among the first Europeans on the Islands were the Portuguese. They donated dishes made with codfish, tuna, swordfish, and octopus to the Hawaiian cuisine as well as their famous Portuguese sweet bread.

Native-born Americans from the mainland added their own inventiveness. The first missionaries were accustomed to plain cooking — dishes such as chicken stew and apple pie. When they found no apples, they learned to improvise pies made with coconut and pineapple.

Together, the members of these two states have contributed many customs and a long list of delicious dishes to the catalog of American favorites. It is no wonder that the mainland heartily welcomes Alaska and Hawaii.

Sourdough Pancakes

1 cup all-purpose flour	1 beaten egg
2 tablespoons sugar	1 cup starter
1½ teaspoons baking powder	(see recipe, page 32)
½ teaspoon salt	½ cup milk
½ teaspoon baking soda	2 tablespoons cooking oil

In a bowl combine flour, sugar, baking powder, salt, and baking soda. Combine egg, the 1 cup starter, milk, and oil; stir into flour mixture till combined. Using 2 tablespoonfuls batter for each pancake, bake on hot, lightly greased griddle till golden brown; turn once. Makes about 28 pancakes.

Originally a pioneer method for leavening bread, sourdough starter began to disappear in the mainland states after the invention of commercial yeast. Miners, headed for the gold fields in Alaska, however, kept alive the technique of using sourdough because it worked well for them while they were isolated on their claims. They ate so many baked products leavened with sourdough starter that the prospector was soon being called a sourdough. Today it stands for any patriotic Alaskan. Popular with sourdoughs of all generations are Sourdough Pancakes.

Dill-Sauced Salmon

4 fresh *or* frozen salmon steaks	2 tablespoons finely chopped onion
Boiling water	2 teaspoons lemon juice
1 small onion, quartered	1 teaspoon dried dillweed
2 teaspoons salt	Lemon and lime slices (optional)
• • •	
1 cup dairy sour cream	1 fresh dillweed (optional)

Thaw frozen fish. Place on greased rack in 10-inch skillet. Add boiling water to cover. Add quartered onion and salt. Simmer, covered, till fish flakes easily when tested with a fork, 5 to 10 minutes. Carefully remove fish. Cover; chill well. In a bowl combine sour cream, chopped onion, lemon juice, and dried dillweed; chill well. Before serving, dollop sour cream mixture over chilled salmon. Garnish with lemon and lime slices and fresh dillweed, if desired before serving. Makes 4 servings.

Blueberry Pie

Prepare pastry for 2-crust 9-inch pie (see recipe, page 351). Stir together 4 cups fresh blueberries, ¾ to 1 cup sugar, 3 tablespoons all-purpose flour, ½ teaspoon grated lemon peel, ½ teaspoon ground cinnamon *or* ground nutmeg, and dash salt; pour into pastry shell. Sprinkle with 1 teaspoon lemon juice; dot with 1 tablespoon butter *or* margarine. Adjust top crust; cut slits. Seal and flute. Bake at 400° for 35 minutes. Serve warm or cooled.

In Alaska blueberries are a summertime treat and, happily, the growing season is a long one. In fact, an Alaskan saying goes, "Blueberry pie by the Fourth of July" and even in September there is still a goodly supply left. Alaska boasts several kinds of blueberries. One is the bog blueberry which grows in some mountain meadows as well as in bogs, and another is the dwarf blueberry which grows mainly in the interior of the state. Alaskans use every type of blueberry to make delicious jams, cakes, and especially, Blueberry Pie.

Crab and Cheese Sandwiches

3 tablespoons butter *or* margarine
3 tablespoons all-purpose flour
1 teaspoon chicken-flavored gravy base
¾ teaspoon dry mustard
1¾ cups milk
1 cup shredded sharp Cheddar cheese
3 English muffins, split, toasted, and buttered
12 ounces cooked crab meat *or* 2 6-ounce packages frozen crab meat, thawed

In saucepan melt butter over low heat. Stir in flour, gravy base, dry mustard, and ¼ teaspoon salt. Add milk all at once. Cook and stir till thick and bubbly; cook 2 minutes more. Remove from heat. Add cheese; stir to melt.

Arrange muffin halves on ovenproof plates or platter; top each with some of the crab meat. Top with cheese sauce. Broil 4 to 5 inches from heat just till hot and bubbly. (Do not brown.) Serve immediately. Makes 6 sandwiches.

Barbecued Venison

2 slices bacon
1 pound boneless venison, cut in 1-inch cubes
½ cup chopped onion
½ cup catsup
¼ cup red wine vinegar
2 tablespoons packed brown sugar
2 tablespoons Worcestershire sauce
1 clove garlic, minced
Hot cooked rice

Cook bacon till crisp; drain, reserving drippings. Crumble bacon; set aside. Cook meat and onion in drippings till meat is browned. Drain; set aside. In saucepan combine catsup, vinegar, sugar, Worcestershire, garlic, ½ cup water, 1 teaspoon salt, and ⅛ teaspoon pepper. Stir in venison, onion, and bacon. Cover; cook till venison is tender, 45 to 55 minutes. Serve on rice. Serves 4.

Cranberry Catsup

1 16-ounce package cranberries (4 cups)
2 cups finely chopped onion
4 cups sugar
2 cups white vinegar
1 tablespoon ground cinnamon
1 tablespoon ground allspice
1 tablespoon celery seed
2 teaspoons ground cloves
1 teaspoon freshly ground black pepper

In 3-quart Dutch oven combine cranberries, onion, and 2 cups water. Bring to boiling. Cover and simmer till berries are easily mashed, 10 minutes. Puree cranberry mixture in blender or push through sieve. In Dutch oven combine cranberry puree, sugar, vinegar, seasonings, and 1 tablespoon salt. Bring to boiling. Boil gently, uncovered, till mixture is consistency of catsup, 30 to 35 minutes, stirring occasionally. (Catsup will thicken on cooling.) Remove from heat; skim off foam. Ladle into hot canning jars, leaving ½-inch headspace. Adjust lids. Process in boiling water bath 5 minutes (start timing when water returns to boiling). Makes 2 pints.

For our northernmost citizens cranberries can and do accompany almost any meal. Two distinct types grow in the state. One is the highbush cranberry which has a red currant-like fruit and the other is the lingonberry or lowbush cranberry. Both kinds are used interchangeably in Alaskan recipes. They are used frequently in a relish that Alaskans call catsup. It mixes cranberries with onion, vinegar, cinnamon, allspice, celery seed, and cloves. Cranberry Catsup is a great accent for game of all kinds as well as beef, pork, and lamb.

Turkey Teriyaki

1 28-ounce frozen white
    meat turkey roast
½ cup packed brown sugar
½ cup soy sauce
½ cup water
¼ cup dry sherry
	2 tablespoons cooking oil
	2 teaspoons vinegar
	1 teaspoon ground ginger
	1 clove garlic, minced
	1 fresh pineapple,
	    crown removed

Partially thaw turkey roast; cut into twelve slices. Arrange in shallow dish. In a bowl mix sugar, soy sauce, water, dry sherry, oil, vinegar, ginger, and garlic; pour over turkey. Cover and chill 1 hour; drain, reserving marinade. Grill over *medium* coals till done, about 25 minutes; turn and baste often with marinade. Meanwhile, peel pineapple and remove eyes. Wash pineapple, quarter lengthwise, and remove core. Cut fruit lengthwise into spears. Grill pineapple spears till golden, about 10 minutes; turn and baste often with marinade. Serve pineapple spears with turkey slices. Makes 6 servings.

Hawaiian Curry Puffs

½ pound ground pork
½ cup finely chopped onion
¼ cup finely chopped celery
1 tablespoon cooking oil
1 4½-ounce can shrimp,
    drained and finely
    chopped
1 small apple, peeled and
    finely chopped (⅓ cup)
	1 tablespoon snipped
	    parsley
	2 teaspoons curry powder
	¼ teaspoon salt
	    Dash pepper
	½ pound won ton wrappers
	    (36 3x3-inch pieces)
	    Fat for Frying

In skillet cook pork, onion, and celery in cooking oil till meat is browned and vegetables are tender; drain well. Combine pork mixture, shrimp, apple, parsley, curry, salt, and pepper. Place about 1 tablespoon filling in center of each won ton wrapper; moisten edges of wrapper with water and fold over filling. Pinch together edges to seal. Fry in deep hot fat (375°) till puffs are golden on both sides, about 1½ minutes. Serve hot. Makes 36.

Haupia

1 3½-ounce can flaked coconut 2½ cups hot milk	¼ cup cornstarch ¼ cup sugar

Measure ¼ cup flaked coconut and set aside. In a bowl pour hot milk over remaining coconut; let stand 30 minutes. Strain through cheesecloth, squeezing out excess liquid. Discard coconut. In a saucepan combine cornstarch and sugar. Stir in the hot coconut-flavored milk. Cook, stirring constantly, till thickened and bubbly. Pour into a buttered 10x6x2-inch dish. Sprinkle with ¼ cup reserved flaked coconut. Chill till firm. Makes 10 servings.

Rumaki

9 slices bacon, halved 9 chicken livers, halved (about 5 ounces) 9 water chestnuts, halved	¼ cup soy sauce 1 tablespoon sugar ⅛ teaspoon ground ginger

Partially cook bacon. Drain on paper toweling. Combine remaining ingredients. Marinate about 20 minutes; drain. Wrap 1 liver and 1 slice water chestnut in a half-slice of bacon. Secure with a wooden pick. Place in 8x8x 2-inch baking pan. Bake at 450° till bacon is crisp, 10 to 12 minutes. Makes 18.

Lomilomi Salmon Spread

Lomi *in Hawaiian means massage
and* Lomilomi Salmon *is
salted salmon that has been worked
by hand, or "massaged," in
water to break down the fibers. In
this recipe the method has
been altered somewhat and the
"massaging" is done in
a blender to make a flavorful spread.
Originally it was served
as an appetizer or as a side dish
in the traditional luau,
to be eaten with the fingers.*

4 ounces smoked salmon,
  finely chopped
½ cup sliced green onion
  with tops

½ cup peeled chopped
  tomato
2 tablespoons chopped green
  pepper

In small bowl combine all ingredients. Mash till well blended. Cover and chill thoroughly. Stir before serving as a spread. Makes about 1⅓ cups.

Mai Tai

2 jiggers light rum
  (3 ounces)
1 jigger dark rum
  (1½ ounces)
½ jigger orange liqueur
  (¾ ounce)

½ cup pineapple juice
⅓ cup orange juice
1 tablespoon lemon juice
3 ice cubes
  Maraschino cherries *or*
    fresh pineapple spears

In blender container combine rums, liqueur, and fruit juices. Cover; blend to mix. Add ice cubes, one at a time; blend after each till chopped. Pour into glasses; garnish with cherries or pineapple. Makes 2 (6-ounce) servings.

Macadamia Nut Pie

*We think of the macadamia tree as
Hawaiian, but it actually
is native to Australia and was
planted in Hawaii less
than 100 years ago. Today, however,
all commercial growing of
macadamia nuts is done in Hawaii.
To prepare macadamia
nuts for use, their hard shells are
cracked open and the
kernels are roasted in coconut oil.*

4 beaten eggs
1 cup light corn syrup
⅔ cup sugar
¼ cup butter, melted
2 tablespoons all-purpose
  flour

1 teaspoon vanilla
1 unbaked 9-inch pastry
  shell (see recipe,
  page 351)
½ cup chopped macadamia
  nuts

Combine beaten eggs, corn syrup, sugar, melted butter, flour, vanilla, and dash salt. Beat with rotary beater till smooth. Pour egg mixture into unbaked pastry shell. Sprinkle with nuts. Bake at 350° till knife inserted off-center comes out clean, about 50 minutes. Cool before serving.

Hawaiian-Portuguese Sweet Bread

This delicious bread called Pao Doce
*was first brought to the
Islands by Portuguese settlers. Since
then it is served Christmas
morning with spiced pork cubes,
green olives, and Portuguese
wine. But you will find it is the
perfect bread to serve with
coffee or milk any time of the year.*

1 cup diced potato
2 cups boiling water
7¼ to 7½ cups all-purpose
  flour
2 packages active dry yeast
2 teaspoons grated lemon
  peel

1 cup sugar
6 tablespoons butter *or*
  margarine
2 teaspoons salt
4 eggs
1½ cups raisins
1 beaten egg

Cook potato, covered, in boiling water till tender, about 20 minutes. Drain; reserve 1⅔ cups liquid. Mash potato. In large mixing bowl combine 2½ *cups* of the flour, yeast, and lemon peel. Heat and stir sugar, butter, salt, and reserved liquid just till warm (115-120°). Add to yeast mixture with 4 eggs and the mashed potato. Beat at low speed of electric mixer for ½ minute, scraping sides of bowl constantly. Beat 3 minutes at high speed. By hand, stir in raisins and enough of the remaining flour to make moderately stiff dough. Turn out onto lightly floured surface; knead till smooth and elastic (8 to 10 minutes). Shape into ball. Place in lightly greased bowl; turn once. Cover; let rise till double (1 to 1¼ hours). Punch down. Turn out; divide into thirds. Cover; let rest 10 minutes. Shape into 3 round loaves; place on greased baking sheets. Cover; let rise till almost double (about 45 minutes). Brush tops lightly with beaten egg. Bake at 375° for 35 to 40 minutes. Cover with foil after 20 minutes to prevent overbrowning. Makes 3 loaves.

Melting Pot:
A Blending of Heritages

As the United States continued to grow, each immigrant group that arrived added some part of its heritage to the American scene. Somewhere along the line, this blending of traditions was compared to a melting pot in which all of the separate parts are fused to make a new whole. When this simile is applied to America's cooking, two trends are obvious. One is that because of the blending of cooking traditions, such anomalies as Mexican pizza and kosher Chinese food are commonplace. The other, and more important, is that immigrants who are Americanized in almost every other aspect of their lives still prepare and enjoy authentic dishes from their homelands. It is these dishes that make the American cuisine so cosmopolitan. So far in this chapter, the recipes of a number of such ethnic cuisines have been presented, but many more are still to be tasted and savored.

Besides the major national peoples that have been discussed, there are many other heritage groups whose numbers may be small, but whose influence has been significant. The Dutch, for example, in Michigan and Iowa have made their tulips, dairy products, and handmade furniture famous all over the country. The Swiss have excelled in watchmaking and dairying. The Portuguese have brought to America their knowledge of the sea, and the Armenians have contributed their skills in improving American vineyards and citrus groves. As for the Spanish, their influence dates back to the Conquistadors. They have given America names such as Florida and Colorado, as well as their architecture.

Many other people, Finnish, Belgian, Lithuanian, Puerto Rican, Cuban, Romanian, and Turkish, as well as immigrants from South America, the West Indies, and all parts of Asia have settled on American shores. All have added the genius of their cuisines to the cooking they found here. Americans are able to enjoy everything from Swiss fondue to Turkish dolmasi. The recipes on the following pages round out the many-faceted picture of the melting pot in America's kitchen.

Contributing to America's melting pot were the Russian-Germans, and they already had a mixture of heritages before they came here. Almost every aspect of their lives was a mixture of German and Russian influences—especially their marriage customs.

In the old days, the wedding invitations were given orally by two men carrying canes decorated with ribbons. Each time the invitation was accepted, a ribbon was added to the canes. The marriage celebration went on for days, beginning with the Polterabend, a party held the night before the wedding. At the feast on the wedding day, the bride's shoe was stolen and auctioned off. Gifts of money were usually pinned to the bride's gown. Dancing and both German and Russian folk songs provided the entertainment. A braided cake, Kranzkuchen, shaped in a ring was the traditional wedding cake for the event.

Dutch Letters

1 8-ounce can almond paste
1 egg
¼ cup sugar
• • •
3 cups all-purpose flour

¾ teaspoon salt
1½ cups butter *or* margarine
½ to ⅔ cup ice water
1 egg yolk

Combine almond paste, egg, and sugar; mix well and chill. Stir together flour and salt. Cut butter into flour till mixture resembles coarse crumbs. Add ice water, a tablespoon at a time, stirring till dough is well moistened. Shape into ball; cover and let stand 30 minutes. Divide dough into three parts. Roll each part on lightly floured surface to 8-inch square. Cut each square into four 8x2-inch strips. For each of the 12 strips roll about 1 tablespoon almond paste mixture into an 8-inch rope. Moisten dough edges with water. Close dough over filling; seal edges and ends. Form into S shapes. Place on ungreased cookie sheets. Combine egg yolk and 1 tablespoon water; brush on letters. Bake at 375° for 30 to 35 minutes. Cool. Makes 12.

The Dutch came to America in two distinct groups. The first group settled the New York City area in the 17th century (see chapter 2) and the second group came in the middle 1800s, settling primarily in Michigan and in Iowa. And so we now have tulip festivals in Dutch cities in both Michigan and Iowa. We also have the kaffeeklatsch or coffee hour; Edam cheese; and, of course, the popular almond pastry named Dutch Letters.

Spanish Paella

¼ cup all-purpose flour
1 teaspoon salt
Dash pepper
1 2½- to 3-pound ready-to-cook broiler-fryer chicken, cut up
¼ cup olive oil
2½ cups chicken broth
2 medium onions, quartered
2 carrots, sliced (¾ cup)
⅔ cup regular rice
½ cup chopped celery with leaves

¼ cup chopped canned pimiento
1 clove garlic, minced
½ teaspoon salt
½ teaspoon dried oregano, crushed
¼ teaspoon ground saffron
12 ounces fresh *or* frozen shelled shrimp
12 small fresh clams in shells, washed
1 9-ounce package frozen artichoke hearts

Combine flour, 1 teaspoon salt, and pepper; coat chicken with mixture. In 4-quart Dutch oven brown chicken, a few pieces at a time, in hot olive oil for 20 minutes. Drain off excess fat; return all chicken to pan. Add chicken broth, onions, carrots, rice, celery, pimiento, garlic, ½ teaspoon salt, oregano, and saffron. Simmer, covered, for 30 minutes. Add shrimp, clams, and artichokes. Simmer, covered, 15 to 20 minutes more. Makes 6 to 8 servings.

Pictured opposite: This all-embracing main dish of chicken, rice, seafood, saffron, and vegetables is a Spanish classic. It was first made in Valencia and is named *paella* after the baking pan with handles on both sides in which Spanish cooks have always prepared it. The ingredients for *Spanish Paella* vary from village to village in Spain. Here is one Spanish-American version.

Cuban Chicken with Pineapple-Rum Sauce

1 cup chopped onion
1 clove garlic, minced
2 tablespoons cooking oil
1 2½- to 3-pound ready-to-cook broiler-fryer chicken, cut up
1 8-ounce can tomatoes
2 teaspoons grated lime peel (set aside)
2 tablespoons lime juice
1 teaspoon salt

½ teaspoon dried oregano, crushed
¼ cup raisins
1 8-ounce can pineapple chunks (juice pack), drained
3 tablespoons rum
1 tablespoon all-purpose flour
Hot cooked rice *or* potatoes

Cook onion and garlic in hot oil till tender but not brown. Remove onion and garlic; set aside. Brown chicken pieces in the oil remaining in skillet. Return cooked onion and garlic. Drain tomatoes, reserving liquid; set tomatoes aside. Add reserved tomato liquid, lime juice, salt, oregano, and ⅛ teaspoon pepper to chicken. Cover and simmer 30 minutes. Cut up tomatoes and add to mixture along with raisins and lime peel. Simmer, covered, 15 minutes more. Remove chicken to platter; keep warm. Skim excess fat from tomato mixture. Stir pineapple and rum into tomato mixture. Slowly blend 2 tablespoons cold water into flour; stir into tomato mixture. Cook and stir till thickened and bubbly. Serve over rice or potatoes. Serves 4.

Cuban Chicken with Pineapple-Rum Sauce *is just one of the many culinary delights that come from the island of Cuba. The lime, pineapple, and rum that flavor this dish are all products indigenous to Cuba.*

French Chocolate Mousse

In top of double boiler combine 4 egg yolks and ¼ cup cognac; beat with electric mixer. Add ½ cup sugar, beating till thick and lemon-colored. Place over boiling water. (Upper pan should not touch water.) Cook and stir just till mixture thickens slightly, about 10 minutes. Transfer top of double boiler to pan of cold water; beat till mixture is consistency of mayonnaise, 3 to 4 minutes. Dissolve 1 teaspoon instant coffee crystals in ¼ cup hot water. Melt together one 6-ounce package semisweet chocolate pieces and ½ cup butter over low heat. Stir in coffee mixture. Remove from heat. Stir into egg yolk mixture. Beat 4 egg whites till soft peaks form. Gradually add 1 tablespoon sugar; beat to stiff peaks. Fold into chocolate mixture. Pour into 8 small soufflé dishes or sherbets. Cover and chill at least 3 hours or overnight. Serve topped with whipped cream. Makes 8 servings.

Ever since Thomas Jefferson brought a French chef to the White House, Americans have been adopting French ideas about food. In fact, restaurants here often import French chefs. Many of these experts have stayed in the United States and our cuisine is all the richer for their presence. One sample of their art is French Chocolate Mousse.

Puerto Rican Pork Pies

Although many Puerto Rican families were poor when they arrived in the United States, they quickly learned to make do and use wisely what they had. One Puerto Rican-American describes the parties of his childhood. "We entertained frequently with two standing parties a year—at Christmas and for my birthday. Parties were always large. My father would dismantle the beds and move all the furniture so that the full two rooms could be used for dancing. My mother would cook up a storm, particularly at Christmas. Pasteles, lechon asado arroz con gandules, *and a lot of* coquito *to drink (meat-stuffed plantain, roast pork, rice with pigeon peas, and coconut nog). My father always brought in a band. They played without compensation and were guests at the party. They ate and drank and danced while a Victrola covered the intermissions.... Parties always went on till daybreak, and in addition to the band, there were always volunteers to sing and declaim poetry...."*[9]*

2 cups all-purpose flour
½ teaspoon baking soda
¼ cup butter *or* margarine
2 beaten egg yolks
1 tablespoon cooking oil
½ pound ground pork
½ cup chopped onion
1 clove garlic, minced
¼ teaspoon dried oregano, crushed
¼ teaspoon dried red pepper flakes, crushed

½ of a 6-ounce can tomato paste (⅓ cup)
¼ cup raisins
1 tablespoon snipped parsley
1 tablespoon capers
2 teaspoons vinegar
1 hard-cooked egg, chopped
2 tablespoons chopped pitted ripe olives
Fat for frying (optional)

Stir together flour, baking soda, and 1 teaspoon salt. Cut in butter till the size of small peas. Combine egg yolks and ½ cup water; add to flour mixture. Stir till it clings together; form into a ball. Cover; refrigerate 1 hour. Meanwhile, heat oil in skillet. Cook pork, onion, garlic, oregano, dried red pepper, ½ teaspoon salt, and ⅛ teaspoon pepper till meat is browned and onion is tender. Stir in tomato paste, raisins, parsley, capers, vinegar, and ¼ cup water; simmer, covered, for 5 minutes.

Remove from heat. Stir in chopped hard-cooked egg and chopped ripe olives. On a lightly floured surface, roll ¼ of the dough at a time to ¹⁄₁₆-inch thickness. Cut into 3-inch circles. Place 1 teaspoon meat mixture in the center of each circle. Fold over; moisten edges and seal well, using tines of a fork. Fry a few at a time in deep hot fat (350°) till golden, about 3 minutes. (*Or,* place in a greased baking pan; bake at 425° till browned, 10 to 12 minutes.) Makes about 48 meat pies.

Armenian Lamb Meatballs

1 pound ground lamb
½ cup finely chopped onion
¼ cup finely chopped green pepper
6 tablespoons finely snipped parsley

½ teaspoon dried mint, crushed
½ cup bulgur
6 cups chicken broth
Hot cooked rice

In skillet combine ¼ *pound* of the lamb, ¼ *cup* onion, and the green pepper; cook till meat browns. Drain well. Stir in *4 tablespoons* parsley, the mint, and ⅛ teaspoon pepper. Cool. Cover bulgur with cold water; let stand 10 minutes. Drain well. Combine bulgur and remaining lamb, remaining onion, and remaining parsley; stir in ½ tea-

spoon salt and dash pepper. Divide *uncooked* lamb mixture into 16 portions. Shape each portion around about 1 teaspoon *cooked* lamb mixture to form meatballs. Heat chicken broth to boiling. Add meatballs and simmer for 10 to 12 minutes. Serve over hot cooked rice, spooning some of the broth over. Makes 5 or 6 servings.

Armenian Sesame Bread

The "Fresno sandwich" is California's version of the hoagie. It features two Armenian favorites, sesame bread and lamb meatballs. The bread, which resembles a ring with additional dough stuffed in the center, is slit and filled with sliced or whole meatballs. This unusual combination makes great eating for lunch, supper, or a late-night snack.

Combine 2½ cups all-purpose flour and 2 packages active dry yeast. Heat 2 cups milk, 3 tablespoons olive oil *or* cooking oil, 2 tablespoons sugar, and 2 teaspoons salt till warm (115-120°). Add to dry mixture. Beat at low speed of electric mixer for ½ minute, scraping bowl. Beat 3 minutes at high speed. Stir in 3 to 3¼ cups all-purpose flour to make moderately stiff dough. Knead on floured surface till smooth (5 to 8 minutes). Place in greased

bowl; turn once. Cover; let rise till double (about 1 hour). Punch down; divide in half. Cover; let rest 10 minutes. On greased baking sheet, roll one half to 8-inch circle. With a 3-inch cutter, cut one circle in center of dough (don't remove). Repeat with other half of dough. Cover; let rise 45 minutes. Mix 1 egg yolk and 1 tablespoon water; brush on loaves. Sprinkle with 2 tablespoons sesame seed. Bake at 350° for 30 minutes. Makes 2.

Portuguese Caldo Verde

4 ounces Italian sausage
  in casing
3 medium potatoes, peeled
  and sliced

½ pound spinach, chopped
  or 1 10-ounce package
  frozen chopped spinach
1 clove garlic, minced

Slice Italian sausage ¼ inch thick. In large saucepan cook sausage till browned. Drain off excess fat. Add sliced potatoes, spinach, garlic, 3 cups water, 1 teaspoon salt, and ¼ teaspoon pepper. Bring to boiling; cover and simmer till potatoes are tender, about 20 minutes. Makes 5 servings.

*Caldo verde is a favorite of many Portuguese-Americans.
This appetizer soup differs from the original served in Portugal
—spinach has been substituted for kale. Caldo verde is
usually served with a sweet bread called* broa *and much*
vinho verde, *green wine.*

Belgian Creamed Potatoes

4 cups thinly sliced
  potatoes
1 cup sliced leeks
1 teaspoon salt
1 cup whipping cream

2 tablespoons butter *or*
  margarine
1 cup shredded process
  Swiss cheese
  (4 ounces)

Mix together potatoes, leeks, and salt in a 1½-quart casserole. Add whipping cream; dot with butter. Bake, covered, at 350° till potatoes are tender, about 1 hour. Sprinkle cheese atop; bake 3 minutes more. Makes 6 servings.

Beginning in late August Belgian-Americans in Wisconsin celebrate Kermis. *This festival continues each Sunday for seven weeks and is held to give thanks for the harvest.
The elaborate meals are very much a part of the festivities and are sure to include* Belgian Creamed Potatoes.

Romanian Beef Patties

2 pounds ground beef
½ cup beef broth
2 cloves garlic, minced
1½ teaspoons salt
¾ teaspoon baking soda
¾ teaspoon ground allspice

½ teaspoon dried thyme,
  crushed
⅛ teaspoon ground nutmeg
⅛ teaspoon pepper
8 hamburger buns, split
  and toasted

Combine ground beef, beef broth, garlic, salt, baking soda, allspice, thyme, nutmeg, and pepper. Shape into 8 patties. Let stand at room temperature about 30 minutes. Broil 4 inches from heat about 8 minutes. Turn and continue broiling 4 to 7 minutes more. Serve on buns. Makes 8 servings.

Finnish Viipuri Twist

5½ to 5¾ cups all-purpose
  flour
2 packages active dry yeast
½ teaspoon ground cardamom
½ teaspoon ground nutmeg

2 cups milk
¾ cup sugar
¼ cup butter *or* margarine
1 teaspoon salt
2 eggs

Combine *2½ cups* of the flour, the yeast, cardamom, and nutmeg. Heat together milk, sugar, butter, and salt just till warm (115-120°), stirring constantly. Add to dry mixture; add *1 egg*. Beat at low speed of electric mixer for ½ minute, scraping bowl. Beat 3 minutes at high speed. By hand, stir in enough remaining flour to make a moderately stiff dough. Knead on floured surface till smooth (3 to 5 minutes). Place in greased bowl; turn once. Cover; let rise till double (1 to 1½ hours). Punch down. Divide in thirds. Cover; let rest 10 minutes. On floured surface, shape one-third of dough into rope 36 inches long. Form dough rope into circle, leaving both ends extended 6 inches at bottom. Holding ends of dough rope toward center of circle, twist together. Press ends together and tuck under center at top of circle, forming a pretzel-shaped roll. Place on greased baking sheet. Repeat with remaining dough to make 3 twists in all. Let rise till double (30 to 45 minutes). Bake at 375° till done, about 20 minutes. Beat remaining egg slightly; stir in 1 tablespoon water. Brush mixture on surfaces of the hot breads. Makes 3 twists.

Finns tell us Finnish Viipuri Twist *was first made for Christmas in a Finnish monastery, and has always been baked in the shape of a huge pretzel. The holes formed by the shaping are filled with a variety of Christmas cookies such as gingerbread men.*

Lithuanian Strawberry Torte

1¾ cups sugar
1 cup butter *or* margarine
6 egg yolks
2 cups sifted cake flour
½ teaspoon baking powder
6 egg whites

3 cups whipping cream
1 teaspoon vanilla
½ cup currant jelly
1 cup coarsely chopped
  pecans
½ cup strawberry preserves

In large mixing bowl cream together *1¼ cups* of the sugar and the butter till very light and fluffy. Add egg yolks, one at a time, beating well after each; continue beating till very fluffy, about 5 minutes. Sift together flour, baking powder, and ½ teaspoon salt; stir into creamed mixture. Beat egg whites till soft peaks form; gradually add remaining ½ cup sugar, beating to stiff peaks. Fold into creamed mixture. Pour into 3 lightly greased and floured 9x1½-inch round baking pans. Bake at 350° till done, about 20 minutes. Cool 10 minutes; remove from pans. Cool on

rack. Whip cream and vanilla just to soft peaks. Place a cake layer on serving plate. Spread with currant jelly and then with *1 cup* of the whipped cream. Sprinkle with *2 tablespoons* pecans. Spread second layer with ⅓ *cup* of the strawberry preserves, then with *1 cup* of the whipped cream; sprinkle with *2 tablespoons* pecans. Gently place atop first layer. Carefully top with third layer. Frost top and sides with remaining whipped cream; coat sides with remaining pecans. Using tip of a small spoon, dot top with remaining strawberry preserves.

Pictured opposite: There is a special knack to eating *Swiss Cheese Fondue* and learning it is half the fun of fondue. The procedure is to spear a bread cube with your fondue fork, piercing through the soft part first, and the crust last. Then swirl the cube in the cheese mixture using a figure-eight motion. This keeps the fondue moving so it won't stick. If you lose your bread cube in the cheese, you must give a kiss to your favorite friend at the table. If you get through the meal without dropping a bread cube, the crusty cheese in the bottom of the pot is yours.

Tomato Dolmasi Turkish-Style

4 large *or* 6 medium
  tomatoes
1 pound ground lamb
½ cup chopped onion
1 small clove garlic,
  minced

½ teaspoon dried marjoram,
  crushed
¼ teaspoon ground cinnamon
¼ cup regular rice
1 beaten egg

Cut off tops of tomatoes and scoop out center. Invert tomatoes to drain. Sprinkle cavities with salt. Chop tomato centers and tops. Cook lamb, onion, and garlic till meat is browned. Drain off fat. Add chopped tomato, marjoram, cinnamon, ½ teaspoon salt,

and ⅛ teaspoon pepper. Cook rice according to package directions. Combine meat mixture, cooked rice, and egg. Spoon into tomato shells. Place in 10x6x2-inch baking dish; cover loosely with foil. Bake at 350° till heated, about 30 minutes. Serves 4 to 6.

The dolma, *or stuffed vine leaf, is a trademark of Middle Eastern cooking. Usually it is made by wrapping a mixture of ground meat, rice, and seasonings in a grape leaf, but other types of "packaging" such as cabbage leaves, chard leaves, zucchini, or carrots are also used. This Turkish-American adaptation of the* dolma *fills tomato cups with a mixture of ground lamb, onion, garlic, cinnamon, marjoram, pepper, and rice.*

Swiss Cheese Fondue

3 cups shredded natural
  Swiss cheese
  (12 ounces)
1 cup shredded Gruyère
  cheese (4 ounces)
1½ teaspoons cornstarch
1 clove garlic, halved
1 cup sauterne

1 tablespoon lemon juice
Dash ground nutmeg
Dash pepper
French *or* Italian bread
  or hard rolls, cut in
  bite-size pieces, each
  with one crust

Combine cheeses and cornstarch. Rub inside of heavy saucepan with garlic; discard garlic. Pour in sauterne and lemon juice. Heat till bubbles cover surface (do not cover or boil). *Stir vigorously and constantly from now on.* Add a handful of cheese mixture, keeping heat medium. (Do not boil.) When melted, add more cheese and melt.

After all cheese is blended and bubbling, add nutmeg and pepper. Quickly transfer to fondue pot; keep warm over fondue burner. (If fondue becomes too thick, stir in a little *warmed* sauterne.) Spear bread cube with fondue fork; dip into fondue and swirl to coat. (Swirling is important to keep fondue in motion.) Serves 4 to 6.

A city in Wisconsin was founded as a project of the Swiss government. Because of crop failures in Switzerland in 1844 the government sent two agents to America to find a place where its people could settle. They chose a mountainous section of Green County, Wisconsin, and called it New Glarus after the Swiss canton. The people who settled the community were dairy farmers and they have created a thriving cheese industry. Today some of this cheese is used to make a Swiss (and now, American) favorite, fondue.

Chapter 9

Cook Books in America

The first cook book published in America was *The Compleat Housewife* in 1742. William Parks of Williamsburg edited it from an earlier English work by E. Smith. Until that time colonial women had been using recipes learned by word of mouth and by example from their mothers and neighbors. It was assumed that the housewife knew her way around the kitchen. This accounts for the sketchy directions and vague amounts in both handwritten and printed recipes of the day. Simple recipes (often called receipts), were not committed to paper even by those few women who could write.

Hand-copied recipes

The more complicated dishes were copied in a clear spidery handwriting and passed from mother to daughter on scraps of paper or in ledger books. This copy the daughter took with her when she married.

The recipe for *White Pease Soup* on page 60 is an updated version of such a recipe in the Gardiner family manuscript now in the library in Old Sturbridge Village, Massachusetts.

Many recipes had been handed down for generations and then were

---

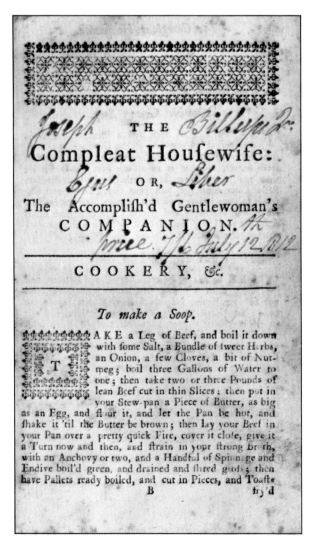

---

recopied when family members set off to the New World. The recipe, *Too Make Oat Cakes,* is from Gulielma Penn's collection of favorites. She was William Penn's first wife and although she didn't make the trip across the Atlantic, her recipes did.

Besides receipts these handwritten books often contained household hints. Some dealt with food preparation such as coloring cider while others related to mundane housekeeping tasks, making soap or whitening cloth, for instance. Interspersed with the recipes were home remedies to deal with all manner of ailments. These treatments might be as simple as rubbing crumbled sage leaves on your nose in the morning to relieve a cold in the head or as complicated as a special brew for cough or consumption. Copying cherished receipts and remedies continues even today.

It's hard to predict where, among family documents, a recipe will suddenly pop up. For example, Hester Maria, daughter of President and Mrs.

At left is the first recipe page in E. Smith's cook book, lengthily entitled *The Compleat Housewife; or, Accomplish'd Gentlewoman's Companion: being a collection of several hundred of the most approved receipts, in cookery, pastry, confectionary, preserving, pickles, cakes, creams, jellies, made wines, cordials. And also bills of fare for every month in the year. To which is added, a collection of near two hundred family receipts of medicines; viz. drinks, syrups, salves, ointments, and many other things of sovereign and approved efficacy in most distempers, pains, aches, wounds, sores, &c. never before made publick in these parts; fit either for private families, or such publick-spirited gentlewomen as would be beneficient to their poor neighbours.*

James Monroe and the first bride to be married at the White House, was an accomplished musician. However, her health was never very good and her *Music Book,* dated 1816, contained the directions for this tonic.

> *"2 oz. gentian root, 1 oz. bitter orange peal, ½ oz. Virginia snack root, ½ oz. calamus, A few camomile flowers, 1 quart brandy. Let the above ingredients stand 2 or 3 days in a bottle, then swallow 10 minutes before dinner 1/3 of a wineglass mixed with 2/3 water."*
>
> Monroe, *Music Book,* 1816

English cook books

Imported English cook books were not much help to most colonial cooks because the recipes were intended for large, noble households that had a flock of scullery servants to chop, mince, knead, pound, peel, and wash up. Also, the ingredients to complete elaborate menus were likely to be unobtainable in America. *The Compleat Housewife* promised "bills of fare for every month in the year." Here's an example from February.

> ### FEBRUARY MENU
>
> *"First Course*
> *Soop Lorain*
> *Turbot boiled with Oysters and Shrimps*
> *Grand Patty*
> *Hen Turkey with Eggs*
> *Marrow Puddings*
> *Stew'd Carps and broil'd Eels*
> *Spring Pye*
> *Chine of Mutton with Pickles*
> *Dish of Scotch Collops*
> *Dish of Salmigondin*
> Second Course
> *Fat Chickens and tame Pigeons*
> *Asparagus and Lupins*
> *Tansy and Fritters*
> *Dish of Fruit of all Sorts*
> *Dish of fried Soles*
> *Dish of Tarts, Cusstards, and Cheesecakes"*
>
> *The Compleat Housewife,* 1742

One English cook book popular on both sides of the Atlantic was Hannah Glasse's *The Art of Cookery Made Plain and Easy.* First published in 1747 it went through many editions including one in Alexandria, Virginia, in 1805.

This was the cook book of Martha Washington and other hostesses.

It is believed that Benjamin Franklin ensured his enjoyment of Paris by taking recipes from a 1760 edition with him.

Despite a penchant for involved recipes, Ms. Glasse had some sensible ideas — including cooking spinach without water and cooking cabbage quickly. "All things that are green should have a little crispness, for if they are overboiled, they neither have any sweetness or beauty."[1]

> ### YORKSHIRE CHRISTMAS PIE
>
> *"First make a good standing crust, let the wall and bottom be very thick; bone a Turkey, a Goose, a Fowl, a Partridge, and a Pigeon. Season them all very well, take half an Ounce of Mace, half an Ounce of Nutmegs, a quarter of an Ounce of Cloves, and half an Ounce of black Pepper, all beat fine together, two large Spoonfuls of Salt, and then mix them together. Open the Fowls all down the Back, and bone them; first the Pigeon, then the Partridge, cover them; then the Fowl, then the Goose, and then the Turkey, season them all well first, and lay them in the Crust, so as it will look only like a whole Turkey; then have a Hare ready cased, and wiped with a clean Cloth. Cut it to Pieces; that is joint it; season it, and lay it as close as you can on one Side; on the other Side Woodcocks, Moor Game, and what Sort of wild Fowl you can get. Season them well, and lay them close; put at least four Pounds of Butter into the Pie, then lay on your Lid, which must be a very thick one, and let it be well baked. It must have a very hot Oven, and will take at least four Hours."*
>
> Glasse, *Art of Cookery,* 1774

To Make Almond Creame

Take half a pound of Almonds a quart of Cream blanch y:e almonds & beat y:m very well with rose water y:n strain y:m through a strong canvis strainer with cream it being first boyld till all y:e ranness be out of it y:n season it with rose water & Suger boyle it again till it thicken y:n put it into your Dishes to cool & serve it up HG 1752

Another widely distributed English book was Susannah Carter's *The Frugal Housewife*. An advertisement promised, "Any person by attending to the instructions given in this book, may soon attain a complete knowledge in the art of cookery."[2]

UXBRIDGE CAKES

"Take a pound of wheat flour, seven pounds of currants, half a nutmeg, and four pounds of butter; rub your butter cold very well among the meal. Dress the currants very well in the flour, butter, and seasoning, and knead it with so much good and new yeast as will make it into a pretty high paste: usually two-penny-worth of yeast to that quantity. After it is kneaded well together, let it stand an hour to rise. You may put half a pound of paste in a cake."

Carter, *The Frugal Housewife*, 1792

TO FRICASEE A CALF'S HEAD

"Take half a calf's head that is boiled tender, cut into slices, and put it into a stew-pan with some good veal broth; season it with mace, pepper, and salt, an artichoke bottom cut in dice, some forcemeat balls first boiled, morels and truffles; let these boil together for a quarter of an hour; scum it clean; beat up the yolks of two eggs in a gill of cream, put this in, and shake it round till it is ready to boil; squeeze in a little lemon, and serve it up."

Carter, *The Frugal Housewife*, 1792

The first American edition of Maria Rundell's *A New System of Domestic Cookery* appeared in 1807. In 1844 it was in its sixty-seventh London edition. The "new system" was developed by the author to teach the principles of economy to her daughters. Ms. Rundell was said to have avoided "all excessive luxury, such as essence of ham, and that wasteful expenditure of large quantities of meat for gravy, which so greatly contributes to keep up the price, and is no less injurious to those who eat, than to those whose penury bids them abstain."[3]

The book contains many ways to make jams, pickles, and dried fruit (see *To Dry Cherries Without Sugar*, page 170), but shortcuts were not part of her system. After laborious preparatory steps for making India pickles, she says, "set [them] from the dust which must inevitably fall on them by being so long in the doing."[4]

Two more English works printed in the United States are worth noting. First came *The New Art of Cookery*, by Richard Briggs. The writer is identified as "many years cook at the Globe Tavern, Fleet-Street; the White Hart Tavern, Holborn; and now at the Temple Coffee-House, London."[5] ("Now" was 1792.) The book boasts thirty-eight chapters. Amid the "Sauces for every occasion.... Made dishes of every sort.... Baking, broiling, and frying" is a section devoted to "All sorts of aumlets and eggs."[6]

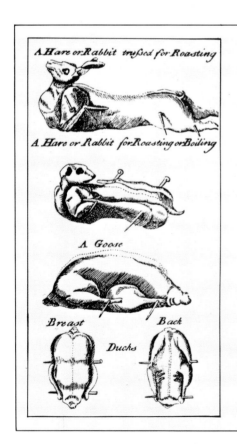

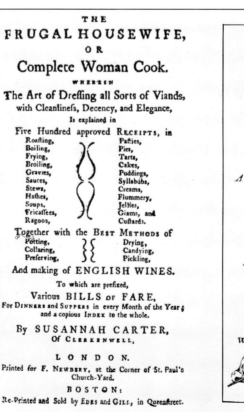

Mackenzie's Five Thousand Receipts in All the Useful and Domestic Arts, Constituting a Complete and Universal Practical Library, and Operative Cyclopaedia was printed in Philadelphia in 1825. By 1829 the medical portions of *Mackenzie's Five Thousand* were "carefully revised and adapted to the climate of the U. States." The reader who can work his way through the mass of material will also learn how to rear silkworms and how to cultivate white mulberry trees.

American cook books

In 1796 the first cook book written in this country was printed in Connecticut. Amelia Simmons, herself an orphan, wrote much of **American Cookery** for her sister orphans. But a slim volume—47 pages—it tackled a huge task: "The improvement of the rising generation of Females in America, the Lady…will not be displeased, if many hints are suggested for the more general and universal knowledge of those females in this country who, by the loss of their parents, or other unfortunate circumstances, are reduced to the necessity of going into families in the line of domestics, or taking refuge with their friends or relations, and doing those things which are really essential to the perfecting them as good wives, and useful members of society….

"It must ever remain a check upon the poor solitary orphan, that while those females who have parents, or brothers, or riches, to defend their indiscretions, that the orphan must depend solely upon character. How …important, therefore, that every action, every word, every thought, be regulated by the strictest purity, and that every movement meet the approbation of the good and wise."[7]

Ms. Simmons uses Indian meal, pumpkin, watermelon rind, barberries, cranberries, and other readily available native ingredients. She employs the word "molasses," rather than the English "treacle," and in later revisions of her book includes such patriotic treats as Independence Cake. Hers were the first known printed recipes to advise pearl ash, an American invention for leavening cakes. As earlier cooks had done, she often includes rosewater and other flowery flavors in her sweets; and among her recipes for syllabub is the famous one that requires the cow be milked directly into the mixture.

Her book is written for ordinary housewives and she gives them practical down-to-earth advice. But she had bad luck with her editors and typesetter. She even charged in print that the person she hired to prepare the recipes for publication "with a design to impose on her and injure the sale of the book."[8] Ms. Simmons had to include a page of errata. For example: "Rice pudding, No. 2: for one pound butter, read half pound—for 14 eggs read 8."[9]

All these mistakes must have been particularly distressing since the author paid to have her book published. And, although a copyright was issued on May 26, 1796, it didn't stop plagiarizers. For perhaps thirty years her recipes and advice kept appearing under somebody else's name.

The Virginia Housewife written by Mary Randolph, a relative of Thomas Jefferson, also enjoyed a wide sale and the compliment of being copied. First published in 1824, *The Virginia Housewife* went through many editions. It was still in print in 1860. Variously subtitled, "Method Is the Soul of Management" or "the Methodical Cook," the book's premise was that when running a household, "there is economy as well as comfort in a regular mode of doing business." She cautioned that, "the contents of the treasury must be known, and great care taken to keep the expenditures from being equal to the receipts." She deplored late rising, and warned that, "a late breakfast deranges the whole business of the day…which opens the door for confusion…."[10]

Although most of the dishes in *The Virginia Housewife* are Southern or English—Chicken Pudding, English Plum Pudding—the book ventures out of home territory to give

Northern dishes and some of Spanish origin. The recipe for Ollo is one of several recipes that use tomatoes. Quite a bold step in Mary Randolph's day when many people still thought tomatoes were poisonous. The author's ideas about time management come through in cooking directions that designate certain things to do at specific times of the day.

TO MAKE AN OLLO — A SPANISH DISH

"Take two pounds beef, one pound mutton, a chicken, or half a pullet, and a small piece of pork; put them into a pot with very little water, and set it on the fire at ten o'clock, to stew gently; you must sprinkle over it an onion chopped small, some pepper and salt, before you pour in the water; at half after twelve, put into the pot two or three apples or pears, peeled and cut in two, tomatos with the skin taken off, cimblins cut in pieces, a handful of mint chopped, lima beans, snaps, and any kind of vegetable you like; let them all stew together till three o'clock; some cellery tops cut small, and added at half after two, will improve it much."

Randolph, *The Virginia Housewife*, 1860

Old cook books help us trace changing tastes. For example, calf's head was once a delicacy. Handwritten directions for a calf's head hash are on the opposite page while Susannah Carter's recipe appears on page 308. *The Housekeeper's Book* of 1837 by a Lady (Frances McDougall), in her directions for carving, writes "some nice fat about the ear...a tooth in the upper jaw, called by some the sweet tooth, very full of jelly," and the eye, which "may be forced from the socket by...the point of the knife..." and divided in quarters.

"It is highly necessary that all who preside at the head of a table should be acquainted with all these particular delicacies, so that they may distribute them to their friends."[11] By the end of the century we hear no more of calf's eyes, and little of their heads.

During the period between the publication of Ms. Randolph's cook book in 1824 and the Civil War all kinds of books issued from American publishers, many of them written by women. Writing was one of the few respectable occupations for a lady — and if she could write about housekeeping, she could perform a Christian service and earn a few dollars at the same time. Four writers dominated the field. In order of publication they were Eliza Leslie, Lydia Maria Child, Catherine Beecher, and Sarah Josepha Hale.

Eliza Leslie, Philadelphian born in 1787, began to write at the age of forty in order to help support a large family of nieces and nephews. Short stories, novels, and in 1828 *Seventy-Five Receipts, for Pastry, Cakes, and Sweetmeats*. All were successful, particularly *Directions for Cookery* which went through over fifty editions. One reason for its popularity was her use of cornmeal, pumpkin, and other American products.

She knew the limitations of these ingredients, too. At the end of her

INDIAN POUND CAKE

"Sift a pint of fine yellow Indian meal, and half a pint of wheat flour, and mix them well together. Prepare a nutmeg beaten, and mixed with a table-spoonful of powdered white sugar; and half a pound of fresh butter; adding the spice, with a glass of white wine, and a glass of brandy.
Having beaten eight eggs as light as possible, stir them into the butter and sugar, a little at a time in turn with the meal. Give the whole a hard stirring at the last; put it into a well-buttered tin pan, and bake it about an hour and a half."

Leslie, *Directions for Cookery*, 1848

Indian Pound Cake recipe she cautions, "this cake (like every thing else in which Indian meal is an ingredient) should be eaten quite fresh; it is then very nice. When stale, (even a day old,) it becomes dry and rough...."[12]

Ms. Leslie was all for saving trouble where possible. She considered it safest to send large cakes to a baker and, "when practicable, to procure kisses from a confectioner's shop." In case the reader was tempted to make turtle soup, Ms. Leslie urged her to forget it. Instead, "hire a first-rate cook for the express purpose."[13] She was clearly not writing for impoverished households.

Decorating food was evidently worth the effort. After directions for "ornamenting" cold à-la-mode beef, she says, "it will at a little distance look like a large iced cake decorated with sugar flowers."[14]

A-LA-MODE BEEF TO BE EATEN COLD

"Glaze it (cooked meat) all over with beaten white of egg. Then cover it with a coat of boiled potato grated finely. Have ready some slices of cold boiled carrot, and also of beet-root. Cut them into the form of stars or flowers, and arrange them handsomely over the top of the meat by sticking them on the grated potato. In the centre place a large bunch of double parsley, interspersed with flowers cut out of raw turnips, beets, and carrots, somewhat in imitation of white and red roses, and marygolds. Fix the flowers on wooden skewers concealed with parsley."

Leslie, *Directions for Cookery*, 1848

Two New England authorities on domestic matters were Lydia Maria Child and Catherine Beecher. They brought a Puritan air of duty and rectitude to their advice. While the Philadelphian Ms. Leslie seemed to assume her readers had money, the a Calf Head Hash —   18

Take your Calf Head lay it in water wash it well & take out the Brains then parboyle one half of your head just have water to cover it when tis boyl'd take it out & put the other half into the same Liquor the other was boild in when tis boyld enough take one half slice it from the Bone then put it in a Stew pan with a good deal of the Liquor it was boild in before put into it some whole pepper a little Mace and 6 Cloves one Inch a little Nutmeg grated and a small Spoonfull of Catchop or a few Morrells stew all very well togather till tis enough then work a little peice of Butter in Flower to thicken it up the other half of the Head you must take out the Bones stuff it with Forst meat roll it up like a Roll of Bread rub it over with the yolks of eggs & grated Bread & Broil it before the Fire then take the Brains beat them in a Pot & put to them 3 yolks of eggs 2 Whites a little Nutmeg & salt some Parsley shread fine one Spoonfull of Cream beat all togather with a little grated Bread then have some Butter or nice rendered Suit boyling hot in a Frying Pan drop in your Brains in small round Cakes & fry them a fine Brown put your hash into the Dish the broild Laid upon the middle of the dish & the Cakes round it with some small thin bacon Collops broild & mix amongst the Brain Cakes you may Garnish it with Pickels puff Lemmons or Flowers

New England ladies economized. Ms. Child's *The American Frugal Housewife* was "dedicated to those who are not ashamed of economy," and included a chapter on "How to Endure Poverty." Ms. Child was a newspaper-woman, novelist, poet, abolitionist, and reformer, and the royalties from her writing were quickly used up by family and projects in which she was involved. Hers was a firsthand knowledge of the need for frugality. Her book appeared first in 1829 as *The Frugal Housewife.* The word "American" was added in 1832 to avoid confusion with the English work.

The book contained recipes, remedies, and practical information on buying, cooking, and storing everything. Ms. Child wasted nothing—not even "loaf cake slightly injured by time, or by being kept in the cellar." She told her readers to, "cut off all appearance of mould from the outside, wipe it with a clean cloth, and wet it well with strong brandy and water sweetened with sugar; then put it in your oven, and let the heat strike through it, for fifteen or twenty minutes. Unless very bad, this will restore the sweetness."[15]

Catherine Beecher had no patience with women who pleaded ignorance of household affairs as an excuse for poor management. She believed anyone could learn, particularly if she read *A Treatise on Domestic Econ-* *omy* (1841) and *Miss Beecher's Domestic Receipt Book* (1846). They contained explicit directions for handling every household task or emergency. A dinner for twelve? Very well, you will need eight dozen plates, inasmuch as you will be serving soup, fish, two meats, and three desserts, plus a saucer at each place for bones.

And what to do about wine if you happen to be a teetotaler? Ms. Beecher disapproved of wine, but recognized the right of others to serve it. The etiquette (she said) for a teetotaling lady responding to toasts was to lift the glass to her lips, meet the eye of the gentleman toasting her, and replace the glass, unsipped, upon the table. And speaking of the table, how should it be ornamented? Ms. Beecher's suggestion: a pyramid made of paper, with macaroons stuck all over it with the aid of sticky sugar. The macaroons were to be pried loose and the paper, of course, would be saved. Ms. Beecher's books were gold mines of advice on cooking, housekeeping, and kitchen planning (see page 213). Little wonder they were widely read.

Sarah Josepha Hale, another Philadelphian, was perhaps best known as the author of "Mary Had a Little Lamb," and as editor of "Godey's Lady's Book." But, her *Ladies' New Book of Cookery* in 1852 found an enthusiastic audience. Respected as an authority in all branches of domestic life, Ms. Hale laid down the latest laws of table etiquette. Whereas in previous generations the mistress of the house had done the carving, now she was to sit at the head of the table with a gentleman on either hand to assist her with this taxing assignment. A decade or two later the entire carving job passed to the host.

After mid-century there were new developments in the cook book world. Regional cook books were suddenly on the market. One, by A. M. Collins, was first printed in 1857 and for years was in great demand. Called *The Great Western Cook Book,* it reflected some of the new styles of cooking brought by immigrants. Ms. Collins included, for instance, sauerkraut, and a saddle of lamb "Russian fashion."

Another new development were cook books that attacked the alleged evils of the American diet. In *Christianity in the Kitchen* (1861) Mary Tylor (Mrs. Horace) Mann equated Christianity with simplicity of diet, and consigned to the devil a long list of popular foods, including butter, lard, and suet (she used cream as a substitute), canned and bottled fruits and vegetables, any leavening agent except eggs, and the staple so important on the frontier, pork. This book was the forerunner of many other health-minded cook books, some crackpot and some sensible, but all recognizing that the contemporary American diet needed somehow to be made lighter and more easily digestible.

Following the Civil War, many Southern women found themselves coping for the first time with the mysteries of the kitchen. To the rescue came a number of excellent books on Southern cooking. Among them were *Mrs. Hill's New Family Receipt-Book for the Kitchen* and the *Dixie Cook-Book* compiled by Estelle Woods Wilcox.

In 1871 another novelist turned cook book writer, Mary Virginia Terhune, under the name of Marion Harland, produced *Common Sense in the Household* and a series of popular books still in demand after the turn of the century. Aimed at good management of cooking and domestic responsibilities, *Common Sense* had sold 100,000 copies by 1880. With this kind of success, the author was in demand for product endorsements. Here is what she said in a booklet distributed with Agate Iron Ware in 1890, "After several years' trial and thorough satisfaction with this ware, editorial attestation to its excellence is a benefit to customer rather than to the manufacturers. It is given in hope that others may share the comfort and pleasure attendant upon its use." [16] Marion Harland also directed her efforts toward instructing readers in the *Art of Cooking by Gas* and the *Comforts of Cooking and Heating with Gas.* Her daughter, Christine Terhune Herrick collaborated on several titles and wrote cook books on her own but they never equaled her mother's cook books in readership.

Cooking schools

In spite of all these cook books and publications there remained a vast throng of perplexed young wives. Recipes were never sufficiently explicit, and it took a lot of trial and error to learn how much butter was meant by "a cup" (was it a teacup or a coffee cup?) or a "spoonful" (what size spoon?), or what was "some"?

The solution was to go to school. Catherine Beecher gave impetus to the idea with her concepts about education for women. The most famous cooking classes – in New York, Boston, and Philadelphia – were forerunners of home economics or domestic science courses in colleges.

Among the first organized classes in New York were those at the Free Training School for Women, opened in 1874. The instructor, Juliet Corson, prepared manuals and textbooks for her students, as well as publications for a broader audience. In 1877 she published *Fifteen Cent Dinners for Families of Six.* The book cost twenty-five cents. In 1888 she wrote about *Family Living on $500 a Year.*

Ms. Corson didn't limit her teaching to New York; she traveled and lectured everywhere. At the College of Agriculture in St. Paul, for instance, she spoke on the "Principles of Domestic Economy and Cookery." The lectures were printed in 1887.

In 1879 another well-known cooking authority, Maria Parloa, began to teach cooking in Boston and here, at last, recipes were explained in detail. But the best known courses were at the Boston Cooking School established about the same time by Mary Johnson Lincoln. Ms. Lincoln's textbook for students sold well in its day but was overshadowed by *The Boston Cooking-School Cook Book* (1896) compiled by a successor at the school, Fannie Merritt Farmer. An invalid since girlhood, Fannie Farmer attended class in a wheelchair. She later became the school's director. She is credited with introducing the idea of standard measuring cups and spoons and level, precise measurements, earning thereby the undying gratitude of novice cooks.

Many editions later, Ms. Farmer's book is still in print today. Each chapter begins with the composition of ingredients and how they work together for a particular dish.

Little is known about the cooking school run by a Ms. Goodfellow in Philadelphia in the early 1800s except that Eliza Leslie was a star pupil. But about a later school in that city much is known. The Philadelphia School of Domestic Science, conducted by Sarah Tyson Rorer (see also pages 154-157), opened in 1884 and continued under the founder's leadership for the next eighteen years. Sarah Rorer was a creative cook and fine teacher whose abilities translated well into more than twenty best-selling cook books. She knew the value of showmanship in presenting foods. In a footnote to a recipe for *Bird's Nest Pudding* she wrote, "Just as troublesome as it reads, but beautiful when done." [17]

RIBBON CAKE

"1 cup butter
2 cups sugar
Yolks 4 eggs
1 cup milk
3½ cups flour
5 teaspoons baking powder
Whites 4 eggs
½ teaspoon cinnamon
¼ teaspoon mace
¼ teaspoon nutmeg
⅓ cup raisins seeded and
    cut in pieces
⅓ cup figs finely chopped
1 tablespoon molasses

Mix first seven ingredients in order given. Bake two-thirds of the mixture in two layer cake pans. To the remainder add spices, fruit, and molasses, and bake in a layer cake pan. Put layers together with jelly (apple usually being preferred as it has less flavor), having the dark layer in the centre."

Farmer, *The Boston Cooking-School Cook Book,* 1896

BIRD'S NEST PUDDING

"For the nest: *Make an orange jelly. Turn a pie dish upside down in the bottom of a two-quart round tin basin, pour the jelly in the basin over the pie dish, and stand away to harden.*
For the straws: *Cut the orange peel into fine strips with the scissors. Boil one cup of sugar and half-cup of water to the crack, that is, until it hardens when dropped in cold water. Dip the straws into this syrup and place on greased papers to harden.*
For the eggs: *Put one pint of milk on to boil in a farina boiler, moisten four tablespoonfuls of corn-starch with a little cold milk, and stir into the boiling milk; stir until it thickens, then add a quarter-cup of sugar and a teaspoonful of vanilla. Have ready some egg shells that have been emptied from a small hole in the top, fill them with this mixture, stand in a pan of Indian meal or flour to prevent them from falling over, and put in a cold place to harden.*
When the jelly is hard, whip a pint of cream. Now turn the jelly out on a round glass dish, remove the pie dish carefully, put the straws around the space left by the pie dish, representing a nest, and fill the nest, inside the straws, with the whipped cream, representing feathers. Break the shells carefully off the corn-starch eggs, and put them in the centre of the nest, and it is ready to serve."

Rorer, *Philadelphia Cook Book*, 1886

PIZZA IN A BURGER

"1½ pounds ground chuck
⅓ cup grated Parmesan cheese
¼ cup finely chopped onion
¼ cup chopped pitted ripe olives
1 teaspoon dried oregano, crushed
1 6-ounce can tomato paste
4 slices mozzarella cheese, cut in strips
8 cherry tomatoes, halved
8 slices French bread, toasted

Combine first 7 ingredients, 1 teaspoon salt, and dash pepper; shape into 8 patties. Broil over medium coals 10 minutes. Turn; top each with cheese and tomatoes. Broil 5 minutes or to desired doneness. Serve on toasted French bread."

Better Homes and Gardens New Cook Book, 1968

Cook books today

In a survey of American cook books we must not forget those recipe collections privately printed by church groups or women's clubs. Sale of the cook books is to raise funds for a worthy project, but, since many of these books contain recipes gleaned from "old-timers" or charter members of the group, the books serve as perhaps the only record of a community's food history. And, if the locale has a strong ethnic character, this, too, is reflected in the recipes.

The Settlement Cook Book is one such collection that went on to become a best seller. The book, captioned in 1901 *The Way to a Man's Heart,* was a project of ladies on the board of a neighborhood house in Milwaukee. It brought together favorite recipes of the board members and the European mainstays of the women attending classes at the settlement.

Not many cook books reach the 1 million copy sales of the *Settlement Cook Book.* Even fewer sell more than 1 million copies or more. However, in the latter group you'll find *The Fannie Farmer Cook Book, Joy of Cooking, The Good Housekeeping Cook Book, The Weight Watchers Program Cook Book, McCall's Cook Book, Mastering the Art of French Cooking, Volume One,* and *Betty Crocker's Cook Book*—all topped by the *Better Homes and Gardens New Cook Book,* which has sold more than 18 million copies, making it the best selling hard cover title of all time excluding Bibles and dictionaries.

The first edition of *My Better Homes and Gardens Cook Book* in 1930 considered the homemaker as a home-business woman interested in bringing efficiency to her activities at home. Kitchen-tested recipes with clearly written directions assured her of quality.

The book has been revised and updated at intervals to keep the reader abreast of foods and equipment that will make her job easier. New features such as barbecuing have been added. The book's success has led to a series of specialized titles on breads, meats, salads, fondue, home canning, blenders, and jiffy cooking—all in the million-seller category.

With the diversity of books on the market, how long can cook books go on selling? Probably for as long as Americans like to cook and eat.

FUDGE BARS

"2 eggs
1 cupful of sugar
½ cupful of melted butter
2 squares of melted chocolate (bitter)
1 teaspoonful of vanilla
⅛ teaspoonful of salt
½ cupful of cake flour
1 cupful of broken pecan meats

Beat the eggs, add the sugar, and beat again. Add the melted butter, melted chocolate, vanilla, and salt, and beat again. Add the sifted flour and mix until smooth, then add the nutmeats. Bake in a moderate oven (350 degrees) for 25 minutes. Cool and cut into bars."

My Better Homes and Gardens Cook Book, 1930

A Nation Complete:
Changing Eating Habits

Chapter 10

A Nation Complete:
Changing Eating Habits

Dining around the turn of the century was indeed formal, and sometimes very elegant, and sometimes most unusual. For instance, long before there were carhops or drive-ins, one host provided what we might call "horsehop service." To celebrate the opening of his new stable, millionaire C. K. G. Billings invited the New York Riding Club to Louis Sherry's Grand Ballroom. The ballroom was transformed into a woodland for the occasion and a horse was provided for each guest. The guests sat atop the horses and ate from small tables attached to the saddles. Champagne was provided in the horses' saddlebags, and the guests sipped it through connecting tubes. The horses were also provided with fancy troughs and feed—so everyone at the party dined lavishly.

During the 100 years or so since 1880, America crossed an invisible borderline between a nation in the making and a nation that was complete. Of course, there was no single moment of transformation, but surely the changes in food and eating habits are among the most dramatic.

Had you been born in 1880 your early memories might include a very big kitchen, with gas lighting and a cast-iron wood-and-coal range. Well before you reached the age of sixty, the gaslight had given way to electricity. The stove had changed several times; by 1940 it would have been gas or electric. The kitchen floor had acquired a linoleum covering. Instead of the old wooden icebox there was a small, gleaming-white refrigerator, cooled by means of gas or electricity. But the most startling change was in eating habits—the meal hours, the menus, and the amounts. In 1880 most of the food brought into the kitchen was fresh, and, especially in wintertime, there was a certain monotony to it. By 1940, however, the growth of supermarkets as well as the improvements in rail shipping and the development of truck and air freight made a greater variety of foods available all year round. Some items such as strawberries, cantaloupe, and cherry tomatoes which were delicacies in 1880 were now commonplace. Advances in technology and food processing, for their part, made unheard-of products—peanut butter, flavored gelatin, cornflakes, canned cooked hams, and process cheeses—staples on American shelves.

Halfway through this period came World War I. It brought food shortages and backyard gardens; families tried to grow as much food as possible and to make do with eggless-butterless cakes and meatless-wheatless meals. In the same period novice cooks were beginning to use recipes that called for standard level measurements—a welcome change from earlier days, when experience was the chief teacher and women cooked with "some of this and a pinch of that."

Frozen foods expanded the American shopping list during the 1930s. And because of nationwide pasteurization laws, people were drinking more milk and consuming more dairy products in general. Canned goods were now on every shelf and breakfast wasn't breakfast without fresh orange juice.

With such an outpouring of new and tasty foods, one might have feared an epidemic of obesity. But by 1940 the science of nutrition had come into its own and the public was aware that calories, vitamins, and other nutrients must be given high consideration in menu planning. Americans could now enjoy a greater variety of foods as well as establish good eating habits.

Although the stove and refrigerator revolutionized our kitchens before 1940, many indeed are the changes since that date. Instead of kitchens equipped with just the basics—a gas or electric stove, a refrigerator, and perhaps a toaster or pressure cooker—a new kitchen evolved. Nowadays, millions of kitchens can boast an array of dozens of other electric appliances including frying pan, blender, mixer, popcorn popper, bun warmer, dishwasher, yogurt maker, and garbage compactor. And many families also have or are thinking of owning a microwave oven.

Our shopping habits and food preferences have also altered radically. Because of the supermarket, "one-stop shopping" has become a way of life in America, a way that is being imitated in many other countries. Chain stores, which began in the late 1800s, became firmly entrenched during the Depression because they could offer lower prices than the small, independent shopkeeper. As a result of the enormous capacity of the supermarket to display and promote myriads of different kinds of foods, products such as frozen TV dinners and pot pies, frozen pizzas, cocktail snacks, canned entrées, and brown-and-serve breads are now everyday fare.

Convenience foods are the great phenomenon of the post-World War II era. During and after the War, many women became full-time workers instead of full-time homemakers. Others found themselves busy with other kinds of away-from-home activities. As a result, they no longer had the time to devote to recipes that required lengthy preparation. They wanted foods that were fast yet delicious and easy to make. American manufacturers were quick to recognize the trend and the age of convenience was launched. New foods that helped to short-cut cooking time began appearing not only in packages, but also in canned and frozen forms as well. One of the most popular innovations of the period was mixes. Muffin, gingerbread, biscuit, pudding, pastry, and pancake mixes were available in 1944 and by 1949, butter cake, corn bread, brownie, hot roll, and angel food cake mixes had been added to the list. Now cooks could not claim they were too busy to make their own baked goods.

Next time you walk your supermarket aisles, try counting the products that have appeared since 1950 — dried soups, frozen entrées, canned soda pop, and freeze-dried coffee. In the fish department find breaded fish, either ready-to-fry or prefried, frozen fillets, Rocky Mountain trout, Alaskan crab, and South African lobster tails. A new variety of shrimp, discovered only in the 1940s, are the very large ones from the Gulf of Mexico. In fancy markets, one can buy Dover sole from England, Nova Scotia salmon, and herring from Scandinavia.

In the dairy case, there are new additions almost every week — cheese spreads, prepared dips, cottage cheese with pineapple or chives, flavored yogurts, chocolate milk, and ice cream in all forms — plain, in cones, as bars, and even combined with chocolate cake.

In the meat department, instead of the old-time butcher who carefully cut the meat and poultry to meet each customer's order, there is a vast array of steaks, chops, roasts, and ground meats — all precut, preweighed, and plastic wrapped. Neatly displayed are Rock Cornish game hens, packaged and frozen; dozens of kinds of prepackaged luncheon meats; sausages, bacon, and frankfurters; and one of the newest additions, the ground-beef-textured vegetable-protein mixtures which are ground beef extended with soy protein.

Remember when your mother sent you to the grocery for bread and there were only one or two kinds? Now one can choose from a dozen or more enriched breads from white to darkest pumpernickel, frozen bread doughs, hamburger and frankfurter buns, English muffins, packages of sweet rolls, as well as the ever-growing list of snack cakes.

Just like the old-fashioned general store, the modern supermarket carries a great many things besides food. Paper supplies, cleaning equipment, stockings, utensils, potted plants, toys, magazines. In short, the concept of the old-fashioned country store has been reincarnated. Alas, gone are the cracker barrel, the rocking chairs around the stove, and the

The concept of the self-service store or supermarket, which we now take for granted, was in the beginning considered a hair-brained notion. "Any system that involved the customer doing any work was a shoddy way of doing business," thought most storekeepers in the 1920s. Even the Atlantic and Pacific Tea Company felt self-service stores had no future and promptly rejected such an idea from one of their district managers. The determined district manager, Patrick Cullen, went out on his own and converted a large garage in Jamaica, New York, into the first large self-service food store. In 1931 three merchants from Syracuse followed his example and ever so gradually the self-service supermarket became an American institution.

Traveling by train in the 1930s and 1940s was often a gourmet treat. From the Baltimore and Ohio in the East to the Union Pacific in the West, trains specialized in hearty and lavish eating. The Northern Pacific, for example, featured two-pound potatoes on its line, and the Great Northern, which traveled through Washington apple country, specialized in baked Rome Beauty apples. The Santa Fe Super Chiefs were famous for their Harvey Girls who served delicious chicken pies concocted by Fred Harvey. At the same time, the Baltimore and Ohio had its "Flagman's Signal Dinner," the Panama Limited took pride in its Gulf shrimp, and the Burlington Zephyr featured trout.

With the increase in kinds of restaurants in the 1950s and 1960s, a stop at any one of them became an adventure. For example, at a pancake house, no one ordered just pancakes and maple syrup. The diner chose from among silver-dollar-sized buckwheats, buttermilk flapjacks, fruit-filled Swedish pancakes, strawberry and whipped-cream-topped dessert pancakes, as well as waffles, French toast, and omelets. Equally impressive were the variety of syrups—from boysenberry to crème de menthe.

chatty storekeeper. In their place are busy, efficient stores, where the modern shopper can find foods from almost anywhere in the world.

Dining out, too, "ain't what it used to be." In 1880 ladies didn't dine out at all unless they either were accompanied by their husbands or were traveling. In the latter case, young girls were supposed to be accompanied by a chaperone. Standards of public eating had risen considerably since the early years of the nineteenth century. One could now eat well at most hotels, as well as aboard the palatial new dining cars on trains. Not only was the food good, the quantity would amaze the customer and stagger the owner of today's restaurant. For example, in the late 1800s at the Fifth Avenue Hotel in New York, a fascinated foreign visitor counted fifty-two items on the breakfast menu, and watched a gentleman put away twenty-six "farinaceous preparations . . . merely the garniture of his matutinal board."[1]

Sixty years later, there was an entirely new world of dining out. Menus had become much simpler, with dinners down to four or five courses except on ocean liners and at the grandest hotels; and there was a wide choice of inexpensive restaurants serving good meals. There were chain restaurants, like Schraffts and Childs; cafeterias; New York's "Automat"; and truck stops and diners where the food was plain, hearty, and often very good. Immigrants with a flair for cooking their native dishes had made native-born Americans more adventurous about eating. Chinese, Italians, French, Germans, and middle Europeans seem to have been especially successful as restaurateurs. And in every town or small city there was likely to be a favorite tearoom, where women liked to meet their friends for lunch. Dining out was no longer a pleasure reserved for the rich.

After World War II the world of restaurant eating was again set awhirl. Suddenly there were restaurants that advertised "all you can eat" for a fixed price. Steak houses proliferated and dinner theaters, where patrons could enjoy both dinner and a show at the same table, sprang up across the country in the 1960s. But the most far-reaching innovation of all was the rise of the fast-food restaurants. Now hamburgers, French fries, hot dogs, fried chicken, and malts could all be ordered and eaten within minutes. Another part of the restaurant revolution was the opening of single-specialty restaurants. Some of these featured pizza, tacos, pancakes, or delicatessen-type sandwiches. The survival of such a variety of restaurants is proof enough that Americans enjoy eating out.

Nor did the revolution stop with America's shopping habits and restaurant eating; the way we now eat at home would have caused utter confusion in a nineteenth-century household. Informality has become the watchword. Because the demands of modern life make it difficult for families to eat three meals together every day, Americans are adapting to simple meals that each family member can prepare for himself. The trend has become to eat breakfast and lunch on the run and to take dinner at a more leisurely pace whenever possible. Barbecuing is a national mania that strikes the populace almost any weekend when the weather is warm. Meals cooked outdoors are especially fun because the whole family can get into the act. Dad takes care of the grilling of the hamburgers or steaks, Mom fixes the vegetables and the youngsters toss the salad or churn the ice cream.

Not all Americans, however, are trapped into eating meals in a hurry. More and more creative cooks are taking time out to try some of the recipes their grandparents enjoyed; more and more people are making breads and cakes from scratch and perfecting the art of home canning.

Since American family meals are becoming more casual, it isn't surprising that American entertaining is also less formal and more spontaneous. Dinner parties are often spur-of-the-moment get-togethers. Late-evening suppers are as frequent as sit-down dinners. Sunday brunches have replaced bridge luncheons, and the coffee klatch has become a great way to get to know the neighbors. Participation dinners, with guests actively preparing their own food, have made fondue pots and hibachi grills standard equipment for many, while progressive dinners where the whole party moves from one participant's house to another for each successive course are also popular. All in all the impromptu party is America's relaxation entertainment, and the food served may range from the most elegant gourmet dish to carry-out food from a local restaurant.

Where is America headed with all these changes in technology and attitudes toward food? No doubt our future holds such things as new and different convenience foods, home-computer systems that will order items from the grocery store and plan balanced menus, packages or wrappings that will self-destruct as the food is cooked, and metric weights and measures. The years ahead are going to be fast paced, exciting ones — and Americans are sure to make the most of them.

This "transition" store exhibits the beginnings of today's self-service supermarket. Individually packaged boxes of cereals, crackers, and dog foods, plus canned fruit juices and other canned items share the shelf space with old-time cookie bins. Other evidences of the past are the bushel baskets of fresh produce and the meat counter where one can imagine the butcher standing ready to cut and wrap your order.

The improved techniques used on farms have increased the variety and quality of foods Americans eat.

From the Farm to the Table

In the last hundred years the eating habits of our country have changed dramatically. We have gone from a nation that built its meals from what fresh foods were available at home or at the local general store to one that creates menus from the worldwide selection of fresh, canned, frozen, dried, and packaged foods displayed at the supermarket. Many factors have made this transformation possible. Among these are new seed varieties, better farming methods, and a transportation system that includes everything from refrigerated railcars and trucks to airplanes. In addition the food processing industry has created a variety of convenience and synthetic foods our great grandparents would never have dreamed possible. The tremendous scope of these foods has made the American cuisine the richest in the world.

Improved transportation gets fruits and vegetables to the supermarket faster.

Self-service supermarkets present Americans with a great array of new foods and convenience products.

Food processing methods such as canning and freezing allow Americans to eat seasonal foods all year.

Americans use foods made possible by improved farming, transportation, and processing at every meal.

Shortly after the beginning of World War I, Mrs. Wilson called a meeting of the wives of cabinet members who pledged "to reduce living to its simplest form and deny ourselves luxuries in order to free those who produce them for the cultivation of necessities. We have decided to omit the usual entertaining and to eliminate largely our social activities to enable us to give more time and money to constructive preparedness and relief work. In the management of our domestic economy, we pledge ourselves to buy simple clothing and food and not demand out-of-season delicacies. We make an appeal to all the women of America to do everything in their power along these lines not only as individuals but organizations to hasten the end of the struggle and win the war."² Some of the simple recipes Americans used to save resources during this time include Parsonage-Style Lentils, Salmon Kedgeree, and Cheesy Spoon Bread.

Parsonage-Style Lentils

1 28-ounce can tomatoes,
   cut up
1 cup dry lentils
½ cup finely chopped onion

½ teaspoon curry powder
⅛ teaspoon ground mace
1 bay leaf
1 cup regular rice

In heavy saucepan combine tomatoes, lentils, onion, curry powder, mace, bay leaf, 2 cups water, 1 teaspoon salt, and ⅛ teaspoon pepper. Bring to boiling. Simmer, covered, till lentils are tender, about 40 minutes. Meanwhile, combine rice, 2 cups water, and ½ tea- spoon salt in another saucepan; cover. Bring to boiling, reduce heat and con- tinue cooking for 14 minutes (do not lift lid). Remove from heat; let stand, covered, for 10 minutes. To serve, spoon lentil mixture atop rice in bowls. Makes 4 or 5 servings.

Salmon Kedgeree

¾ cup regular rice
1 16-ounce can salmon,
   drained, boned, and
   coarsely flaked
1¼ cups milk
4 hard-cooked eggs, chopped

¼ cup snipped parsley
2 tablespoons butter *or*
   margarine
½ teaspoon salt
Dash pepper

Cook rice according to package direc- tions. In saucepan combine rice, salmon, milk, eggs, parsley, butter, salt, and pepper. Cover and cook, stirring carefully once or twice, till heated through. Makes 4 servings.

Cheesy Spoon Bread

1½ cups water
1 cup yellow cornmeal
1 cup milk
½ cup grated Parmesan
   cheese
2 tablespoons butter

2 teaspoons sugar
2 teaspoons baking powder
½ teaspoon salt
3 beaten egg yolks
3 stiffly beaten egg whites

In saucepan combine water and corn- meal; cook till the consistency of mush. Remove from heat. Stir in milk, cheese, butter, sugar, baking powder, and salt. Stir in egg yolks; fold in egg whites. (Batter will be thin.) Bake in greased 2-quart casserole at 325° for 55 to 60 minutes. Spoon into warm dishes; top each serving with a pat of butter, if desired. Makes 6 to 8 servings.

Rationing during World War I necessitated many substitutions or omissions in cooking. Using mar- garine in place of butter, and honey, corn syrup or molasses in place of sugar were common techniques. Ingenious cooks worked out recipes like Eggless-Butterless Cake and Eggless, Milkless, and Butterless Cake. These cakes may have been short on ingredients, but they were never short on flavor.

Eggless-Butterless Cake

2 cups all-purpose flour
1 cup sugar
¼ cup unsweetened cocoa
   powder
1 teaspoon baking powder
½ teaspoon baking soda

1 cup mayonnaise *or*
   salad dressing
1 cup cold water
1 teaspoon vanilla
Chocolate Icing

Stir together flour, sugar, cocoa, bak- ing powder, and soda. Combine may- onnaise, water, and vanilla. Stir may- onnaise mixture into dry ingredients; beat till blended, about 2 minutes. Pour batter into greased and floured 9x9x2-inch baking pan. Bake at 350° till done, about 30 minutes. Cool thoroughly. Frost with Chocolate Icing.

Chocolate Icing: In small saucepan combine one 1-ounce square unsweet- ened chocolate and 1 tablespoon short- ening. Melt chocolate and shortening over low heat, stirring constantly. Re- move from heat; stir in 1 cup sifted powdered sugar and ½ teaspoon va- nilla. Blend in enough boiling water to make of spreading consistency.

Eggless, Milkless, and Butterless Cake

¾ cup raisins
1 cup packed brown sugar
½ cup shortening
2¼ cups all-purpose flour
2 teaspoons baking powder
¾ teaspoon ground allspice

½ teaspoon salt
½ teaspoon ground cloves
½ teaspoon ground cinnamon
¼ teaspoon baking soda
½ cup chopped walnuts
  Cider Sauce

Combine raisins and 1½ cups hot water; let stand 15 to 20 minutes. Using electric mixer, thoroughly cream together brown sugar and shortening, about 5 minutes. Stir together flour, baking powder, allspice, salt, cloves, cinnamon, and soda. Add dry ingredients to creamed mixture alternately with raisin mixture, beating after each addition. Fold in nuts. Pour into greased and floured 9x9x2-inch baking pan. Bake at 350° till done, 40 to 45 minutes. Serve with warm Cider Sauce.

Cider Sauce: In saucepan combine 2 tablespoons cornstarch, 2 tablespoons packed brown sugar, ¼ teaspoon ground cinnamon, dash ground cloves, and dash salt. Gradually blend 1⅓ cups apple cider *or* apple juice into mixture; cook and stir till thickened and bubbly.

Barley-Whole Wheat Muffins

1½ cups whole wheat flour
1 cup barley flour
¼ cup sugar
1½ teaspoons baking powder
¾ teaspoon salt

½ teaspoon baking soda
1⅔ cups buttermilk
2 well-beaten eggs
¼ cup cooking oil

In mixing bowl stir together the whole wheat flour, barley flour, sugar, baking powder, salt, and baking soda. Combine buttermilk, eggs, and cooking oil. Add all at once to dry mixture, stirring just till moistened. Fill greased muffin pans ⅔ full. Bake at 400° for 20 to 25 minutes. Makes 12 muffins.

During World War I, it was Herbert Hoover's task as administrator of the Lever Act to ask the public's help in conserving food by instituting meatless and wheatless days. Recipes such as Barley-Whole Wheat Muffins helped conserve wheat by replacing part of the wheat flour with barley flour.

Mock Champagne Punch

3 cups water
1 6-ounce can frozen orange
  juice concentrate,
  thawed
1 6-ounce can frozen
  lemonade concentrate,
  thawed

2 cups cranberry juice
  cocktail
½ cup sugar
2 25-ounce bottles
  sparkling pink catawba
  juice, chilled

In large bowl combine water and the concentrates. Add cranberry juice and sugar; stir till sugar dissolves. Chill thoroughly. Before serving, very slowly add sparkling catawba juice; stir gently. Makes 24 (4-ounce) servings.

Under the Prohibition Law, manufacturers were allowed to make imitation alcohol flavors and cooking wines to be used in place of the real spirits for cooking. The law went to great lengths to ensure that these products could not be used in cocktails. The brandy and rum flavorings were concentrated much the same as vanilla or lemon extracts. Although cooking wines were real wines, salt and sugar were added so they did not taste good alone, but still could be used in recipes. Two beverages from this era that used alcohol substitutes are Mock Champagne Punch and Eggnog.

Eggnog

⅓ cup sugar
2 egg yolks
4 cups milk
2 egg whites
3 tablespoons sugar

1 teaspoon vanilla
  Brandy *or* rum flavoring
½ cup whipping cream
  Ground nutmeg

Beat the ⅓ cup sugar into egg yolks. Add ¼ teaspoon salt; stir into milk. Cook and stir over medium heat till mixture coats a metal spoon; cool. Beat egg whites till foamy. Gradually add the 3 tablespoons sugar, beating to soft peaks. Add to egg mixture and mix well. Add vanilla and flavoring to taste. Chill. Whip cream to soft peaks. Pour egg mixture into punch bowl; top with whipped cream and sprinkle with nutmeg. Makes 8 (4-ounce) servings.

Baked Bean Sandwiches

Mash 2 cups chilled baked beans (see recipe, page 30); stir in 2 tablespoons chopped onion, 1 tablespoon prepared mustard, and enough mayonnaise *or* salad dressing to make of spreading consistency. Butter 8 slices sourdough *or* whole wheat bread; set aside. Spread 8 more slices bread with bean mixture; top with lettuce. Cover with the buttered bread. Makes 8 sandwiches.

Zani Zaza Cocktail

1⅓ jiggers brandy (2 ounces)
⅔ jigger gin (1 ounce)
2 egg whites

1 tablespoon grenadine
syrup
2 ice cubes

In blender container combine brandy, gin, egg whites, grenadine, and *1* ice cube. Cover; blend 15 seconds. Add the second ice cube; cover and blend 15 seconds. Strain into 2 chilled cocktail glasses. Garnish with twists of lemon peel, if desired. (Drinks separate slightly upon standing.) Serves 2.

Goldfish Cocktail

1 jigger Goldwasser *or*
orange liqueur
(1½ ounces)

1 jigger gin (1½ ounces)
½ jigger sweet vermouth
(¾ ounce)

In a chilled cocktail glass, combine the Goldwasser or orange liqueur, gin, and sweet vermouth. Add ice cubes to serve, if desired. Makes 1 serving.

One result of national Prohibition was the growth of the speakeasies. These colorful institutions strove to create unusual, highly flavored cocktails (often to cover up the poor quality of the alcohol). At Zani's speakeasy in New York, the biggest seller was the Zani Zaza Cocktail. Another New York speakeasy, the Park Avenue, featured a bar that was a huge goldfish tank. Their Goldfish Cocktail was named not for the bar but because it was prepared with Goldwasser (an orange liqueur containing flecks of edible gold).

Age of Opulence

When high society sat down to dine during the late nineteenth century, they sat a long time. Dinners of twelve courses were normal and eighteen courses were not unusual, though generally considered a trifle showy. The guests were expected to arrive fifteen minutes before the dinner hour. No cocktails were served; that development came in the early 1900s when each guest received a thimble-sized glass and no refills. Each gentleman took a lady on his arm and then, led by the host with the lady who was to sit at his right, all paraded into the dining room — and remained for three hours or more. The first course might be oysters, followed by consommé. These courses were purposely light to leave room for what was to follow: a fish course, a dish of sweetbreads, a beefsteak, pâté de foie gras, a patty shell filled with creamed chicken, lamb chops, sherbet, roast larks, salad, cheese, and a spectacular dessert such as spun-sugar birds' nests containing molded ice cream in the shape of birds. Each course was accompanied by a different wine. That made twelve glasses of wine, which the ladies were expected merely to sip, even as the gentlemen quaffed. The ladies then retired to the drawing room for coffee or tea and little cakes, while the gentlemen lingered at the table over port and walnuts.

A show like this could not be put on without a corps of servants, and middle-class party-givers had to simplify. A book called *Housekeeping and Dinner Giving in Kansas City* (1887) told them how to do it with the help of one or two maids, plus hired waiters. Oysters and clear soup were suggested as a start—even as in the most exalted households. After that, poached salmon and boiled potatoes; chicken croquettes with asparagus; broiled plovers on toast; fillet of beef with mushrooms; wine jelly with whipped cream; Neapolitan ice cream; two kinds of cake; fruits; and coffee. Having given all these directions, the author suggested that an early evening party might be easier on all concerned, including the men guests, who could thus hope to get to bed earlier and be ready for work in the morning.

As far back as the 1790s, wealthy families had adopted the habit of repairing in summer to Saratoga Springs, Newport, White Sulphur Springs, Cape May, and many other resorts. The original excuse was that their health required they drink the waters or get a change of air. But by the end of the nineteenth century the resorts had become quite elaborate and the reasons for visiting them purely hedonistic. California acquired its own posh hotels—at Monterey and Santa Barbara, for instance—and easterners were willing to make the seven-day transcontinental train trip to stay at them, rubbing elbows with the elite from San Francisco. California menus offered exotic dishes yet unknown in the East, such as Chinese duck, chili dishes, and tiny succulent Olympia oysters; not to mention avocados, olives, and tree-ripened citrus fruits.

The advent of the income tax (1911) and the First World War put a crimp in the grand style. However, the Roaring Twenties brought a return to extravagant living. Easterners paid large sums for the privilege of "roughing it" at dude ranches. Winter vacations became popular, particularly in Florida, California, the Gulf Coast, and the islands of Georgia; in summer, the ocean liners were packed with rich Americans, as were the grand hotels of Europe.

After the stock market crash of 1929, bankruptcies were frequent among the big resorts, and the great liners put to sea with empty cabins in first class. They kept their long, elaborate menus—in fact, ocean liners were the last refuge of those who craved twelve-course dinners—but the age of opulence had ended and grandeur would never again be quite the same.

Many middle-class but fairly affluent families also enjoyed spending the warm weather at the beach or country inns. Father might stay a week or two and then leave his family at the resort while he returned to spend the rest of the summer in town earning (it was hoped) more money. The inns served plentiful meals of honest country cooking. Patrons dined at white-clothed tables adorned with a gladiola or two in a bud vase and perhaps listened to a lady pianist in the dining room, playing The Merry Widow Waltz *or* To a Wild Rose.

Fillet of Sole Americaine

Brown Sauce
1½ pounds fresh *or* frozen
   sole fillets
Boiling water
1 small onion, quartered
½ cup sliced leeks
½ cup chopped peeled tomato

¼ cup shredded carrot
3 tablespoons butter *or*
   margarine
1 5-ounce can lobster,
   drained, broken in
   large pieces, and
   cartilage removed

Prepare Brown Sauce; set aside. Thaw frozen fish. Cut into 6 serving-size pieces. Place in greased 12-inch skillet. Add boiling water to cover. Add onion and 1½ teaspoons salt. Simmer, covered, till fish flakes when tested with fork, about 10 minutes. Carefully remove fish with slotted spatula. Keep warm; discard liquid. Cook leeks, tomato, and carrot in butter till carrot is tender, about 5 minutes. Stir in lobster and Brown Sauce; cook and stir till lobster is hot, about 5 minutes. Serve sauce over fillets. Serves 6.

Brown Sauce: In saucepan melt 2 tablespoons butter; blend in 2 tablespoons all-purpose flour. Cook and stir over low heat till lightly browned. Stir in 1¼ cups beef broth. Bring to boiling; boil till reduced to 1 cup.

After the First World War, the Emerson Fleet Corporation inaugurated a luxury transatlantic steamship service. Its fleet was headed by the liner S. S. Leviathan, which was the most elegant commercial passenger ship afloat. Its menu was extensive and delectable. Included among its specialties was Fillet of Sole Americaine.

Cherries Jubilee

1 16-ounce can pitted dark
    sweet cherries
¼ cup sugar
2 tablespoons cornstarch

¼ cup brandy, kirsch, *or*
    cherry brandy
Vanilla ice cream

Drain cherries; reserve syrup. Add cold water to make 1 cup liquid. In saucepan mix sugar and cornstarch; slowly blend in reserved syrup. Cook and stir till thickened. Remove from heat; stir in cherries. Turn into blazer

pan of chafing dish. Set pan over hot water (bain-marie). Heat brandy in small saucepan. (If desired, pour heated brandy into large ladle.) Ignite and pour over cherry mixture; blend into sauce. Serve over ice cream. Serves 6 to 8.

Pictured opposite: Typical of the elegant desserts of the 1890s is *Cherries Jubilee.* Flamed and served at the table, it makes the dessert course an entertaining performance. Supposedly it was created by a French chef on the occasion of his fiftieth anniversary.

Eggs Benedict

6 eggs
6 slices Canadian-style
    bacon (6 ounces)
4 egg yolks
2 tablespoons lemon juice

Dash white pepper
½ cup butter *or* margarine
6 rusks *or* 3 English
    muffins, split,
    toasted, and buttered

In 10-inch skillet heat 1 inch of water to boiling. Break egg into small dish; slide egg into water, tipping dish toward edge of pan. Repeat with remaining eggs. Reduce heat; cover and simmer till eggs are just soft-cooked, about 3 minutes. Remove with slotted spoon; place in pan of warm water to keep warm. In 12-inch skillet brown bacon over medium heat for 3 minutes on each side. Cover; keep warm.

In top of double boiler beat the 4 egg yolks slightly; stir in lemon juice. Place over boiling water (upper pan should not touch water). Add pepper and ⅛ teaspoon salt. Add butter, a little at a time, stirring constantly with wooden spoon till mixture thickens. Top each rusk or English muffin half with bacon slice and an egg; spoon on sauce. Sprinkle with paprika, if desired. Makes 6 servings.

Over the years "breakfast at Brennan's" has become a special treat for visitors to New Orleans. The tradition began when Owen Brennan took over the Vieux Carré Restaurant and began serving authentic French and Creole dishes. Brennan decided to specialize in breakfasts since there was less competition from other restaurants in the morning than at dinner time. The dishes he presented were to be distinctive to Brennan's alone. Collaborating with Lucius Beebe, he came up with exotic breakfast menus that included everything from grilled grapefruit to flambéed bananas. The game cock he chose as his symbol (the crowing cock symbolizing morning and breakfast), and this symbol has become synonymous in New Orleans with Brennan's. Since the restaurant first opened many Brennan favorites have become popular. Two of the most widely known are Eggs Benedict and Bananas Foster.

Bananas Foster

4 small ripe bananas
Lemon juice
⅔ cup packed brown sugar
6 tablespoons butter *or*
    margarine

Ground cinnamon
3 tablespoons banana
    liqueur
3 tablespoons light rum
Vanilla ice cream

Peel bananas and cut in half crosswise and lengthwise; brush with lemon juice. In blazer pan of chafing dish cook sugar and butter over direct heat till melted. Add bananas; cook 3

to 4 minutes, turning once. Sprinkle lightly with cinnamon. Drizzle liqueur over all. In small saucepan heat rum just till warm; ignite and pour over bananas. Serve over ice cream. Serves 6.

Cardinal Punch

1 tea bag
1 cup sugar
1 cup orange juice

½ cup lemon juice
¼ cup brandy
¼ cup orange liqueur

Pour ½ cup boiling water over tea bag; let stand 5 minutes. Remove and discard tea bag. Meanwhile, in saucepan combine the sugar and 3 cups water; bring to boiling and stir till sugar dissolves. Remove from heat. Add orange juice, lemon juice, and the pre-

pared tea. Stir in brandy and orange liqueur. Transfer to two 3-cup refrigerator trays. Cover and freeze till firm. With fork, break into pieces; stir till slushy. Serve immediately. Serve ¼ cup as meat accompaniment or ½ cup as dessert. Makes 6 cups.

William McKinley could be called the last of our Victorian presidents. His administration entertained with an elegance that was the ultimate of the Victorian style. During his first year in office he presided over a 71 course meal. Part of that meal was a slush called Cardinal Punch — the usual McKinley accompaniment to turkey or chicken.

Lobster Newburg

The wealthy father of a colonial bride was sure to give his daughter at least one chafing dish. They were used in America as early as 1720, but reached the peak of their popularity in the 1890s. One of the most famous chafing dish foods is Lobster Newburg. The chef who created it named it after the American tycoon, Wenburg — but reversed the first part of the name.

1 5-ounce can lobster, drained
6 tablespoons butter *or* margarine
2 tablespoons all-purpose flour
1½ cups light cream

3 beaten egg yolks
3 tablespoons dry white wine
2 teaspoons lemon juice
Paprika
Toast Cups (see recipe below)

Break lobster into chunks, removing cartilage. Set aside. In blazer pan of chafing dish melt butter over direct heat; blend in flour. Add cream all at once. Cook and stir till thickened and bubbly. Place over hot water (bain-marie). Stir a moderate amount of hot mixture into beaten egg yolks; return to hot mixture. Cook, stirring constantly, till thickened. Add lobster; heat through. Stir in wine, lemon juice, and ¼ teaspoon salt. Sprinkle with paprika. Serve in Toast Cups. Makes 4 or 5 servings.

Toast Cups

Entertaining on a grand scale was the only way to meet the accepted standards of Victorian society. Multi-course dinners and elaborate decorations were the rule as each hostess tried to outdo the last.

¼ cup butter *or* margarine

4 or 5 slices white bread

Soften the butter. Trim crusts from the bread slices; spread bread with butter. Press into ungreased muffin pans. Place in oven. Toast at 350° till lightly browned, about 15 minutes. Serve warm. Makes 4 or 5 cups.

Cold Filet of Beef Waldorf

1 2-pound whole beef
    tenderloin
2 large carrots
½ teaspoon salt
6 tablespoons liver pâté
    or liverwurst spread

2 packages unflavored
    gelatin
2 teaspoons instant beef
    bouillon granules
2 cups water
1½ cups rosé wine

With a sharp knife, cut a deep slit horizontally in meat. Cut off narrow ends of carrots. (The carrots should be equal in diameter, and together as long as the roast.) Insert carrots into slit. Rub meat with the salt and ⅛ teaspoon pepper; place on rack in roasting pan. Insert meat thermometer. Roast at 425° till thermometer registers 140°, about 50 minutes. Cool 30 minutes. Remove and discard carrots; stuff the opening with liver pâté or liverwurst spread. Cover and chill meat. Soften gelatin and beef bouillon granules in the water; dissolve over low heat. Add wine; chill till slightly thickened. Place meat in shallow pan. Carefully spoon ¼ *of the gelatin mixture* over meat; chill meat till gelatin coating is nearly set (keep remaining gelatin mixture at room temperature). Repeat 3 times. Cover loosely; chill 5 hours or overnight. Cut roast into ½-inch slices; arrange on platter. Dice excess gelatin from bottom of pan; arrange around meat. Serves 10 to 12.

The Waldorf-Astoria long ago became the model of hotel high-life. Since 1893, its management has sought to provide the most elegant in dining and entertaining. One celebrity of the hotel, maitre d' Oscar Tschirky, known as Oscar of the Waldorf, was responsible for many highly lauded recipes on the menu, especially the well-known Waldorf Salad (see recipe, page 374). He also created Cold Filet of Beef Waldorf *and* Oscar's Planked Chopped Steak.

Oscar's Planked Chopped Steak

1½ pounds ground beef
    sirloin
½ teaspoon salt
⅛ teaspoon pepper
    Fluffy Potatoes

8 small carrots, cooked
    and buttered
2 cups peas, cooked and
    buttered
    Snipped parsley

Shape ground sirloin into 4 oval patties about 1 inch thick. In skillet cook patties till rare, about 5 minutes per side. Place *each* on a well-buttered seasoned steak plank; sprinkle with salt and pepper. Place Fluffy Potatoes in pastry bag; pipe onto plank to form border 1 inch larger than patty. Place 2 planks under broiler, 4 inches from heat; broil till potatoes brown lightly, about 4 minutes. Repeat with remaining planks. Arrange carrots and peas within potato border; sprinkle with snipped parsley. Makes 4 servings.

Fluffy Potatoes: Peel and quarter 1½ pounds potatoes. Place in saucepan with 2 cups water and 1 teaspoon salt. Cover; cook till tender, about 25 minutes. Drain well. Combine potatoes with 2 tablespoons butter, 2 slightly beaten eggs, and salt and pepper to taste; beat till fluffy.

One of the most important steps in preparing planked steak is choosing the proper plank. Select those of unfinished hardwood. Planks made from oak, maple, or hickory are best. Before preparing steaks, season the planks by brushing them with cooking oil and heating them in a 300° oven for about 1 hour.

Parker House Rolls

4½ to 5 cups all-purpose
    flour
2 packages active dry yeast
1 cup milk

½ cup sugar
½ cup shortening
3 eggs
    Melted butter

In mixing bowl combine *2 cups* flour and the yeast. Heat together milk, sugar, shortening, and 2 teaspoons salt till warm (115-120°), stirring constantly. Add to dry mixture; add eggs. Beat at low speed of electric mixer for ½ minute, scraping bowl. Beat 3 minutes at high speed. By hand, stir in enough remaining flour to make a moderately stiff dough. Knead on floured surface till smooth (5 to 8 minutes). Shape in ball. Place in greased bowl; turn once. Cover; let rise till double (1 to 1½ hours). Punch down; turn out on floured surface. Cover; let rest 10 minutes. Divide in half. Roll each half ¼ inch thick. Cut with floured 2½-inch round cutter. Brush with butter. Make an off-center crease in each round. Fold large half over small half. place 2 to 3 inches apart on greased baking sheet. Cover; let rise till double (30 to 45 minutes). Bake at 400° for 10 to 12 minutes. Makes 36.

The Parker House, founded in 1855 by Harvey D. Parker, is one of Boston's most renowned eating places. It is also the home of Parker House Rolls. *These yeast rolls, which are made by folding a round of dough in half, are also called pocketbook rolls because they look like small purses.*

Vichyssoise

Vichyssoise was created by chef Louis Diat to celebrate the opening of the roof garden at the Ritz-Carlton Hotel in 1910. Chef Diat took the traditional leek and potato soup his mother had made and added cool milk. He named this delicious appetizer soup after the fashionable French resort, Vichy.

4 leeks, sliced (no tops)
1 medium onion, sliced
¼ cup butter *or* margarine
5 medium potatoes, peeled and thinly sliced

4 cups chicken broth
2 cups milk
2 cups light cream
1 cup whipping cream
Snipped chives

In saucepan cook leeks and onion in butter till tender but not brown; add potatoes, broth, and 1 tablespoon salt. Cook for 35 to 40 minutes. Rub through fine sieve. Return to heat; add milk and light cream. Season to taste. Bring to boiling. Cool; rub through very fine sieve. Stir in whipping cream. Chill thoroughly before serving. Garnish with chives. Makes 8 servings.

Elegant Chicken à la King

Chef George Greenwald of Brighton Beach Hotel outside New York City created a new dish that combined a creamy sauce with chicken and mushrooms. He served it over toast points. His dish drew such approbation from Charles E. King II that he named it after the famous hotelier.

1 cup sliced fresh mushrooms
¼ cup chopped green pepper
2 tablespoons butter
2 tablespoons all-purpose flour
2 cups light cream
3 cups cubed cooked chicken

¼ cup butter, softened
3 egg yolks
½ teaspoon paprika
2 tablespoons dry sherry
1 tablespoon lemon juice
1 teaspoon onion juice
2 tablespoons chopped canned pimiento
Toast points

In saucepan cook mushrooms and green pepper in 2 tablespoons butter till tender but not brown; push vegetables to one side. Blend flour and ¾ teaspoon salt into butter in saucepan. Stir in light cream; cook and stir till thickened and bubbly. Add chicken; heat, stirring occasionally. Meanwhile, in small bowl blend together ¼ cup butter, egg yolks, and paprika; set aside. Stir the sherry, lemon juice, and onion juice into chicken mixture; bring to boiling. Add yolk mixture, stirring till blended. Remove from heat. Stir in chopped pimiento. Serve over toast points. Makes 6 to 8 servings.

Baked Alaska

Baked Alaska is a specialty of the famed Delmonico's restaurant in New York City. Delmonico's, however, was not the first to serve it. Benjamin Thompson, an American scientist who was later known as Count Rumford, claimed to have created his "omelette surprise" while studying the resistance of stiffly beaten egg whites to heat. When the dessert first became popular, it was called Alaska-Florida; later the name became Baked Alaska.

1 1-inch thick piece sponge *or* layer cake
1 quart *or* 2 pints brick-style ice cream*

5 egg whites
1 teaspoon vanilla
½ teaspoon cream of tartar
⅔ cup sugar

Trim cake 1 inch larger on all sides than ice cream; place cake on plate. center ice cream on cake (place pints side by side). Cover; freeze firm. At serving time, beat egg whites with vanilla and cream of tartar till soft peaks form. Gradually add sugar, beating till stiff peaks form. Transfer cake with ice cream to baking sheet; spread with egg white mixture, sealing to edges of cake all around. Swirl to make peaks. Bake at 500° till golden, about 3 minutes. Slice; serve immediately. Makes 8 servings.
*Note: If using half of ½ gallon ice cream, cut in half lengthwise.

Nun's Sigh

Stir together ½ cup all-purpose flour, 1 teaspoon granulated sugar, and dash salt. In small saucepan combine ½ cup water and 3 tablespoons butter *or* margarine; bring to boiling. Add flour mixture all at once; cook and stir vigorously till mixture forms a ball. Remove from heat. By hand, beat in 2 eggs, one at a time, beating well after each. Beat in ½ teaspoon vanilla. Using *half a tablespoon* dough for each, carefully drop dough into deep hot fat (375°). Fry till puffed and golden brown, 5 to 7 minutes. Drain on paper toweling. Sprinkle with powdered sugar; serve warm. Makes 24.

Pompano en Papillote

6 fresh *or* frozen pompano
    fillets *or* other fish
    fillets
2 lemon slices
1 bay leaf
1/8 teaspoon dried thyme,
    crushed
    Parchment *or* brown paper
1/2 cup finely chopped onion
1 clove garlic, minced
2 tablespoons butter *or*
    margarine

3 tablespoons all-purpose
    flour
2 beaten egg yolks
2 tablespoons dry white
    wine (optional)
1 7½-ounce can crab meat,
    drained, flaked, and
    cartilage removed
4 ounces shelled shrimp,
    cooked and chopped
1 3-ounce can sliced
    mushrooms, drained

Thaw frozen fish. In saucepan combine lemon, bay leaf, thyme, 3 cups water, and 1 teaspoon salt; bring to boiling. Add fish and poach till fish flakes easily when tested with a fork, about 15 minutes. Remove fish, reserving stock. Cut 6 pieces parchment or brown paper into 12x9-inch heart shapes. Place *one fillet* on half of *each* heart. Strain stock, reserving 1½ cups. Cook onion and garlic in butter till onion is tender. Blend in flour and ¼ teaspoon salt. Add reserved stock. Cook and stir till thickened and bubbly. Gradually stir moderate amount of hot mixture into

egg yolks; return to hot mixture. Cook and stir over low heat till bubbly. Stir in wine, if desired. Stir in crab, shrimp, and mushrooms; heat through. Spoon about ½ cup sauce over each fillet. Fold other half of each heart over fillet to form an individual case. Seal, starting at top of heart, by turning edges up and folding; twist tip of heart to hold closed. Place cases in shallow baking pans. Bake at 400° for 10 to 15 minutes. Cut open with large X on top; fold back each segment. Transfer paper cases to dinner plates. Makes 6 servings.

M. Antoine Alciatore opened his restaurant in New Orleans in 1899. Before long dining at Antoine's was a must. Two seafood dishes invented at Antoine's were Oysters Rockefeller and *Pompano en Papillote*. The pompano dish was developed to celebrate the visit of a renowned balloonist. The paper bag, while sealing in all the flavor, also symbolizes an inflated balloon.

Saratoga Chips

Scrub and peel 3 medium baking potatoes. Using a waffle slicer, knife, or the thinnest slicer on hand grater, cut potatoes into *very thin* slices. Rinse well in cold water and pat dry with paper toweling. In deep saucepan heat 1 quart cooking oil to 360°. Fry potatoes in oil till golden, 3 to 5 minutes. Stir potatoes while frying to keep from sticking together. Drain on paper toweling. Season to taste with salt. Makes about 4½ cups chips.

Fillet of Sole Marguery à la Diamond Jim

1 pound fresh *or* frozen
    sole fillets
1 pound frozen haddock *or*
    other white fish
½ pound fresh *or* frozen
    shelled shrimp
• • •
2 cups water
½ cup sliced carrots
½ cup chopped leeks *or*
    onion
10 whole black peppercorns

3 sprigs parsley
1 bay leaf
½ teaspoon dried thyme,
    crushed
½ teaspoon salt
1 cup shucked fresh
    oysters, drained
• • •
½ cup butter *or* margarine
¼ cup dry white wine
4 slightly beaten egg yolks

Thaw frozen fish and seafood. Keep sole and shrimp refrigerated. In saucepan combine water, carrots, leeks, peppercorns, parsley, bay leaf, and thyme; bring to boiling. Add haddock. Reduce heat; cover and cook 6 to 8 minutes. Strain, reserving stock and haddock* (discard vegetables and seasonings). Add salt to stock. Arrange sole fillets in buttered 11x7½x1½-inch baking pan; top with *1 cup* of the fish stock. Arrange shrimp and oysters atop fish. Cover; bake at 325° till fish flakes easily when tested with a fork, 15 to 20 minutes. Carefully lift fillets, oysters, and shrimp to a hot oven-proof serving platter. Reserve pan juices.* Keep fish and seafood hot. Meanwhile, boil *1 cup* of the reserved stock till reduced to ¼ cup; place in top of double boiler. Add butter and wine. Place over hot water; cook and stir just till butter melts. Add egg yolks; cook and stir till thickened. Pour over fish, oysters, and shrimp; broil 4 inches from heat till lightly browned, 2 to 3 minutes. Serves 6.

Note: Use 2 cups fish stock as directed in this recipe. Save remaining stock, pan juices, and haddock for your favorite chowder or for Fish à la Reine (see recipe, page 96).

Fairs and Expositions

C hurch fairs, school fairs, county fairs, state fairs, expositions, and world fairs—for more than 150 years fairs have been high points of local and national history. Although they have had a multiplicity of themes and star attractions, a very important common denominator has been the chance for good cooks to show off their skills and for food lovers to indulge in their favorite activity—eating.

    Fairs date back into the mists of history. Credit for making them so successful in America is given to Elkanah Watson, an enterprising farmer and leading citizen of Berkshire County, Massachusetts. In the summer of 1810, Watson decided to organize a cattle show. Everyone came from miles around, not only cattle owners, but farmers eager to look at new machinery and crop breeds and many, many others who wanted just to look in on the excitement. Lonely farm wives welcomed a chance to get together with neighbors to exchange news and recipes and perhaps show off a new baby, a new quilt, or the sampler little Mary made. And, of course, everyone had to eat, so the women turned out their best baking, pickling, and preserving. They were always glad for a little social life, and the fair was more relaxing than a cornhusking — and more cheerful than a funeral.

In short, Elkanah Watson's Berkshire County Fair was such a success that it was repeated year after year and the idea was widely copied.

The first state fairs were held in New Jersey and New York, both in the year 1841, and the first national fair held in the United States was the Crystal Palace Exhibition in New York in 1853. There were also regional fairs, and, in 1876, the first international fair held in America was the Philadelphia Centennial Exposition. Every state was represented and so were many foreign countries. They exhibited, in five main buildings and a number of smaller ones, "the gamut of human endeavor."

Philadelphia's great success was bound to be topped — especially in that highly competitive age. And the "gamut of human endeavor" was run again and again in even more elaborate ways — at the Chicago Columbian Exposition (1893), the St. Louis World's fair (1904), Chicago again in 1933, and both New York and San Francisco in 1939. It is said that the popcorn snack Cracker Jack was first introduced at the Chicago 1893 event, and that the ice cream cone made its debut at the St. Louis fair. World War II interrupted the growth of world fairs for a while, but they came back strong with the Century 21 Exposition in Seattle in 1962, another New York World's Fair in 1964 and 1965, and Expo 74 in Spokane, Washington.

Meantime, the old-time local fairs continued — still continue. The 4-H Clubs, founded in 1915, added the entries of boys and girls. There are always numerous carnival attractions, as well as contests for every conceivable "best," from the most glorious flower arrangement to the bouncingest baby. As for food, Phil Stong, the author of the novel *State Fair,* once put it like this, describing the Iowa State Fair:

> By half past five ... with nothing to stick to one's ribs
> since lunch but seven hot dogs, four hamburgers, a cubic
> foot of cotton candy, three sacks of popcorn, and assorted pops,
> colas, and ades, one is beginning to look forward to the big
> plates of baked ham or fried chicken, mashed potatoes, and
> pie à la mode that even now are being served in the dining
> halls and tents dotted about the fairgrounds.[3]

Every fair has its special events typical of the region. One small town in Louisiana has an annual crawfish-peeling contest (and those peeled crawfish aren't allowed to go to waste). In the southwest, the best recipe for chili is a source of never-ending argument — but a pleasant one while the debaters taste here and sample there. In Oregon there are contests for delicious apple dishes, and Vermont is bound to come up with a new triumph using maple syrup.

But in any of the fifty states, you can be sure that the best cooking at the fair will be found among the dishes entered in contests. And what better fair job than to be one of the judges tasting all those pies, cakes, pickles, jams, and jellies. You can judge the best of the country's fairs right in your own kitchen with the recipes on the next few pages.

A new food innovation to come out of the Columbian Exposition in Chicago in 1893 was Cracker Jack. The molasses-covered popcorn and peanut snack was sold by German immigrants, Fred and Louis Rueckheim. The tidbit got its name when one pleased customer exclaimed "That's really a crackerjack!"

In many countries waffles are commonly associated with festivals and holidays. In Sweden, March 25 is designated Waffle Day, and heart-shaped waffles are customarily offered. Shrove Tuesday is Belgium's waffle day, and they are served with fresh strawberries and a whipped cream topping. In America, too, waffles have long been popular, but Belgian Waffles became a favorite only after they were featured at the New York World's Fair in 1963.

If any food is a symbol of Americana, it is the hot dog and it was born at—where else?—a ball game. According to legend, Harry Stevens, the owner of the refreshment concession at the New York Polo Grounds needed a warm food to serve to the cold fans. Sausages, he decided, were the most practical. His salesmen sold the frankfurters in the stands by yelling, "Get your red hot dachshund sausages." Sportswriter Tad Dorgan, hearing the cry at one of the games, was inspired to create a talking sausage as a cartoon character. He named his creation "hot dog" because he couldn't spell dachshund. The cartoon character has faded, but the name has stuck.

Belgian Waffles

1 quart fresh strawberries
⅓ cup sugar
1 cup whipping cream
1 cup vanilla ice cream
1 cup dairy sour cream
½ cup milk
3 tablespoons butter *or* margarine, melted
1 egg yolk
1 cup all-purpose flour
2 teaspoons sugar
1 teaspoon baking powder
½ teaspoon salt
¼ teaspoon baking soda
1 stiffly beaten egg white

In a bowl crush *1 cup* strawberries with ⅓ cup sugar. Slice remaining strawberries; stir into crushed berry mixture. Set aside. In small mixing bowl beat whipping cream till it thickens but does not hold its shape. Add vanilla ice cream by spoonfuls, beating just till smooth. Refrigerate ice cream mixture while making waffles. In a bowl combine sour cream, milk, melted butter, and egg yolk. Stir together flour, 2 teaspoons sugar, baking powder, salt, and baking soda. Stir dry mixture into sour cream mixture; beat till smooth. Fold in stiffly beaten egg white, leaving a few fluffs *(do not overmix)*. Bake in preheated waffle baker. *To serve,* spoon strawberries over waffles; top with a dollop of ice cream mixture. Makes two 9-inch waffles.

Cornmeal-Coated Franks

1 cup all-purpose flour
⅔ cup yellow cornmeal
2 tablespoons sugar
1½ teaspoons baking powder
1 teaspoon salt
2 tablespoons shortening
1 beaten egg
¾ cup milk
1 pound frankfurters
Cooking oil
Catsup
Prepared mustard

In a bowl mix flour, cornmeal, sugar, baking powder, and salt. Cut in shortening till mixture resembles fine crumbs. Mix egg and milk. Add to dry mixture; mix well. Insert wooden skewer in end of frankfurters. Pour oil into skillet to depth of 1 inch; heat to 375°. Coat franks with batter. Brown in hot oil 3 to 4 minutes. Serve with catsup and mustard. Serves 4 or 5.

Hot Dogs Delicious

½ cup chopped onion
1 tablespoon shortening
1 14-ounce bottle hot-style catsup (1¼ cups)
2 tablespoons sweet pickle relish
1 tablespoon sugar
1 tablespoon vinegar
¼ teaspoon salt
Dash pepper
1 pound frankfurters (8 to 10)
8 to 10 frankfurter buns, split and toasted

In skillet cook chopped onion in the hot shortening till tender but not brown. Stir in the hot-style catsup, sweet pickle relish, sugar, vinegar, salt, and pepper. Score the frankfurters and add to catsup mixture in skillet. Simmer till frankfurters are heated through, about 10 minutes. Serve franks and sauce in hot toasted frankfurter buns. Serves 8 to 10.

Dill Pickles

Scrub 3- or 4-inch cucumbers. Pack loosely into hot quart jars, leaving ½-inch headspace. *To each quart* add 3 or 4 heads fresh dill and 1 teaspoon mustard seed. *For each quart* combine 2 cups water, 1 cup vinegar, and 1 tablespoon pickling salt. Bring to boiling. Slowly pour hot brine over cucumbers, leaving ½-inch headspace. Adjust lids. Process in boiling water bath for 20 minutes (start timing as soon as jars are placed in water).

Entry day at the fair brings bushel baskets full of garden-grown vegetables and fresh-cut flowers along with high hopes for a top-prize ribbon and an impatience for the fun to begin.

No fair is complete without prizewinning and taste-tempting homemade breads, cakes, cookies, and pies—and visitors who wish they could taste and judge, rather than "look, but don't touch."

Bushels of corn decorate the world's only Corn Palace in Mitchell, South Dakota. Each ear is carefully cut in half lengthwise, then nailed in place to form colorful murals. Various other grains and grasses, also indigenous to the area, are used as trim.

Symbolic of fair time is the unbreakable affinity between kids and hot dogs. Find one and you'll probably find the other—especially when the distinctive foot-long is available.

A top-prize ribbon on your glass of shimmering homemade jelly, jam, or preserves helps dim the memory of all the work involved in peeling, cooking, and straining the fruit.

When fair time rolls around each year, almost everyone looks forward to the food judging contests. The entries for pickles, jams, jellies, and all types of home-canned foods are the best of the area. One time-honored fair favorite is Tomato Conserve.

The Mississippi-Alabama Fair and Dairy Show is one of the best-attended events in the South. Food categories featured at this fair include Southern preferences such as recipes using the muscadine grape and okra.

The Governor's Cookie Jar Contest is a special feature of the Oklahoma State Fair. According to the rules, each contestant must bake nine different kinds of cookies and pack them in a hand-decorated jar. The winning jar is presented to the governor of Oklahoma. Following custom, during the governor's next press conference, the winning jar is opened and the cookies are passed around to the lucky members of the press.

Tomato Conserve

1 medium orange
2½ pounds fresh tomatoes, peeled, cored, and diced (6 cups)
½ cup chopped mixed candied fruits and peels

3 cups sugar
¼ teaspoon salt
¼ teaspoon ground allspice
¼ teaspoon ground nutmeg
¼ teaspoon ground ginger

Remove peel from orange; scrape off excess white. Section and chop orange. Cut peel into very thin strips. In 4-quart Dutch oven, cook chopped orange, orange peel, tomatoes, and candied fruits and peels till orange peel is tender, about 20 minutes. Add sugar, salt, and spices; bring to a full rolling boil. Boil mixture till thick enough to sheet from a metal spoon, 8 to 10 minutes. Skim off foam with metal spoon. Pour immediately into hot sterilized jars to within ½ inch of top. Wipe jar rims. Seal with metal lids and screw bands. Invert jars; turn upright and cool. Makes 5 half-pints.

Garlic Okra Pickles

3 pounds uncut fresh okra
1 cup white vinegar

¼ cup pickling salt
2 cloves garlic, minced

Wash okra well. Drain thoroughly; pack into hot pint jars. Combine vinegar, pickling salt, garlic, and 3 cups water. Bring to boiling; slowly pour into jars to within ½ inch of top. Adjust lids. Process in boiling water bath for 5 minutes (start timing when water returns to boiling). Makes 4 pints.

Muscadine Grape Jelly

Wash and stem 3½ pounds Muscadine *or* Concord grapes. (Should have about 10 cups stemmed grapes.) Crush grapes; measure 6½ cups. In Dutch oven combine grapes and ½ cup water; bring to boiling. Reduce heat; cover and simmer till grapes are very soft, 10 to 15 minutes. Strain cooked grapes and liquid through jelly bag; *do not squeeze.* (Press very gently, if necessary.) Let juice stand overnight in refrigerator. Strain juice again to remove crystals. Measure juice; add water, if necessary, to make 4 cups. In 10-quart kettle or Dutch oven, stir together grape juice and 3 cups sugar. Bring mixture to a full rolling boil. Boil hard, uncovered, till syrup sheets off metal spoon, 8 to 9 minutes. Remove from heat; quickly skim off foam with metal spoon. Pour at once into hot sterilized jars to within ½ inch of top. Wipe rims. Seal with metal lids and screw bands. Invert jars; turn upright and cool. (Or, seal with ⅛-inch layer paraffin. Do not invert jars.) Makes 4 half-pints.

Jam-Filled Cookies

1 cup shortening
1 cup granulated sugar
1 cup packed brown sugar
2 eggs
¼ cup buttermilk
1 teaspoon vanilla

3½ cups all-purpose flour
1 teaspoon baking powder
1 teaspoon baking soda
1 teaspoon ground nutmeg
Strawberry preserves

In bowl cream together shortening, granulated sugar, and brown sugar. Add eggs, buttermilk, and vanilla; mix till smooth. Stir together flour, baking powder, soda, nutmeg, and 1 teaspoon salt; stir into creamed mixture till well blended. Cover and chill. On floured surface, roll dough to ⅛-inch thickness. Cut into 1½-inch rounds with cookie cutter. Place *1 teaspoon* preserves in center of *half* of the rounds; top with remaining rounds. Lightly seal edges with a fork. With knife, cut a crisscross slit in top of each cookie. Bake at 350° till golden, 10 to 15 minutes. Makes 60 cookies.

Orange Layer Cake

1½ cups sugar
½ cup butter *or* margarine
1 tablespoon grated orange
  peel
2¼ cups all-purpose flour
2 teaspoons baking powder
¼ teaspoon baking soda

¾ cup cold water
¼ cup orange juice
4 stiffly beaten egg whites
  Orange Filling
  Orange Buttercream
    Frosting (see below)

In large mixing bowl cream together sugar and butter till light and fluffy. Add orange peel. Stir together flour, baking powder, soda, and ½ teaspoon salt. Combine water and orange juice; add to creamed mixture alternately with dry ingredients, beating well after each addition. Fold in egg whites. Pour into 2 greased and floured 8x1½-inch round baking pans. Bake at 375° till done, about 30 minutes. Cool 5 minutes; remove from pans. When cool, spread Orange Filling on one layer; top with remaining layer. Frost with Orange Buttercream Frosting.

Orange Filling: In saucepan combine ½ cup sugar, 2 tablespoons cornstarch, 1½ teaspoons grated orange peel, and ¼ teaspoon salt. Gradually blend in ¾ cup orange juice, ¼ cup water, and 2 slightly beaten egg yolks. Cook and stir over medium heat till thickened and bubbly. Remove from heat; stir in 2 tablespoons butter till melted. Cool.

Orange Buttercream Frosting

6 tablespoons butter *or*
  margarine, softened
1 16-ounce package powdered
  sugar, sifted (4½ cups)

1 tablespoon grated orange
  peel
4 to 6 tablespoons orange
  juice

Cream butter; blend in powdered sugar, orange peel, and dash salt. Add enough orange juice to make of spreading consistency. Beat till smooth.

The Iowa State Fair is constant motion and a barrage of scheduled activities and displays. Standing apart from the rest of the fairgrounds is the food judging area. It is tense and quiet. The judges and their helpers, all dressed in white, make their selections in a glassed-in room. Outside, the entrants wait — the suspense may last for hours — for the announcement of winners. High on the list of popular food categories is the baked goods division where favorites such as Apricot-Topped Daisy Coffee Bread *(see recipe, page 338) and* Orange Layer Cake *are top-prize winners.*

Before the days of mass communication, fairs and expositions became the showplace for new inventions and ideas. They also provided a judging stage on which farmers of the area could compare their grains and vegetables.

Apricot-Topped Daisy Coffee Bread

3 to 3½ cups all-purpose flour	2 tablespoons honey
1 package active dry yeast	2 eggs
¾ cup milk	½ cup apricot preserves
¼ cup butter *or* margarine	2 tablespoons chopped nuts
1 tablespoon sugar	Confectioners' Icing (see recipe, page 243)

In large mixing bowl combine 1½ *cups* of the flour and the yeast. In saucepan heat together milk, butter, sugar, *1 tablespoon* honey, and 1 teaspoon salt just till warm (115-120°); stir constantly. Add to dry mixture in bowl; add eggs. Beat at low speed of electric mixer for ½ minute, scraping sides of bowl constantly. Beat 3 minutes at high speed. By hand, stir in enough remaining flour to make a moderately stiff dough. Turn out on lightly floured surface; knead till smooth. Place in greased bowl; turn once to grease surface. Cover; let rise in warm place till double (about 1¼ hours). Punch down; cover and let rest 10 minutes. Roll dough to 14-inch circle. Place a beverage tumbler in center. Make 4 cuts in dough, at equal intervals, from outside of circle to glass. Cut each section into 5 strips in same manner, making 20 strips in all. Twist two strips together; continue around circle making 10 twists in all. Remove and reserve one twist. Coil remaining twists toward center to form daisy design. Remove tumbler; coil reserved twist in center. Let rise till double (about 45 minutes). Bake at 375° till golden brown, about 25 minutes. Blend together preserves, nuts, and remaining honey; spoon over hot bread. Glaze with Confectioners' Icing.

Maple-Frosted Golden Cake

2 cups all-purpose flour	½ cup shortening
1¼ cups sugar	2 eggs
2½ teaspoons baking powder	1 teaspoon vanilla
1 teaspoon salt	Maple Frosting
1 cup milk	

In mixing bowl stir together flour, sugar, baking powder, and salt. Add ¾ *cup* of the milk and the shortening. Beat 2 minutes on medium speed of electric mixer. Add remaining milk, eggs, and vanilla. Beat 2 minutes more. Pour batter into 2 greased and floured 8x1½-inch round baking pans. Bake at 350° for 35 to 40 minutes. Cool 5 minutes; remove from pans. When cool, fill and frost with Maple Frosting.

Maple Frosting: In saucepan cook 1¼ cups pure maple syrup to soft ball stage (238°). Gradually add the hot maple syrup to 2 stiffly beaten egg whites, beating constantly with electric mixer. Stir in ¼ cup sifted powdered sugar and beat till well blended.

Julekake

In large mixing bowl combine 2½ cups all-purpose flour, 2 packages active dry yeast, and ¾ teaspoon ground cardamom. In saucepan heat 1¼ cups milk, ½ cup butter *or* margarine, ½ cup sugar, and 1 teaspoon salt just till warm (115-120°); stir constantly. Add to dry mixture in mixing bowl; add 1 egg. Beat at low speed of electric mixer for ½ minute, scraping sides of bowl constantly. Beat 3 minutes at high speed. By hand, stir in 1 cup mixed candied fruits and 1 cup light raisins. Stir in enough of 2 to 2½ cups all-purpose flour to make a soft dough. Turn out on lightly floured surface; knead till smooth (8 to 10 minutes). Place in greased bowl; turn once. Cover; let rise till double (1¼ to 1½ hours). Punch down; divide in half. Cover and let rest 10 minutes. Shape into 2 loaves. Place in two 9x5x3-inch loaf pans. Cover; let rise till double (about 45 minutes). Combine 1 beaten egg yolk and 2 tablespoons water; brush over loaves. Bake at 350° for 35 to 40 minutes. Remove from pans; cool. Drizzle with Confectioners' Icing (see recipe, page 243). Trim with almonds and candied cherries. Makes 2.

While fresh fruits and vegetables, homemade quilts, and the finest livestock abound at the Champlain Valley Exposition in Essex Junction, Vermont, the fair also features a special competition for the best quart of maple syrup in the county. In addition, the usual pies, cakes, cookies, rolls, and breads are also judged. Two past prizewinners in the baked goods category are Maple-Frosted Golden Cake *and* Julekake.

Blueberry-Orange Nut Bread

3 cups all-purpose flour
¾ cup sugar
1 tablespoon baking powder
1 teaspoon salt
¼ teaspoon baking soda
3 eggs
½ cup butter *or* margarine, melted
½ cup milk

1 tablespoon grated orange peel
⅔ cup orange juice
• • •
1 cup fresh, frozen, *or* drained canned blueberries
½ cup chopped walnuts

In mixing bowl stir together the all-purpose flour, sugar, baking powder, salt, and baking soda. Beat together the eggs, melted butter or margarine, milk, grated orange peel, and orange juice. Stir the butter mixture into the flour mixture, stirring just till dry ingredients are moistened. Fold in the blueberries and walnuts.

Pour batter into a greased 9x5x3-inch loaf pan. Bake at 350° till golden brown, 60 to 70 minutes. Remove from pan; cool. Wrap in foil and store overnight before slicing.

There's no better place to find marvelous homemade foods than at the Oregon State Fair. Think of the amount of flour, sugar, and butter — not to mention the time and care — that goes into perfecting entries such as Blueberry-Orange Nut Bread.

Focus on Nutrition

Most of us tend to think of nutrition as a modern topic, but the truth is that Americans have been interested in diet and nutrition for a long time. As far back as 1846, Dr. William Alcott begged his readers to eat whole grains and a wide variety of fruits and green vegetables. Another popular physician, Dr. Russell Trall, advised a diet of whole grains, fruits, and vegetables, cooked and eaten, he cautioned, without sugar, butter, milk, or anything else added. Still another specialist, in a booklet published in 1909 for the guidance of poor families in New York, recommended that cooked vegetables be eaten no oftener than three times a week, and applesauce once. The booklet also advised against using eggs in the diet and fish more than once or twice a week. In addition, the daily midday dinner was to consist of meat, potatoes, bread, and a pudding made of rice or cornmeal.

All through the nineteenth century and into ours, there were many self-appointed health experts and they attracted large followings. The trouble was, they were working in the dark and when they happened to be right they didn't know why. Until well after 1900, the average doctor believed that protein, carbohydrates, fats, and certain inorganic salts were all the human body needed. That dietary deficiencies had any relationship with beriberi, scurvy, rickets, goiter, and some anemia was not established until the period between 1910 and 1940.

The big breakthrough in the science of nutrition came in 1913, when vitamin A was discovered by Dr. Elmer McCollum and his laboratory assistant, Marguerite Davis. Between that date and 1948, the thirteen essential vitamins were identified. In 1941 the "Recommended Dietary Allowances" were officially established — that is, the daily amounts of calories, protein, calcium, iron, vitamin A, thiamine, riboflavin, niacin, and ascorbic acid needed by adults and children in order to maintain good health. Anyone

Another significant milestone in America's nutritional story was the discovery of the relationship between intake of calories and body weight. As soon as the general public heard about calories, there was a clamor among the overweight to be told what to eat and what to avoid. Overnight everyone wanted to be slim and trim. It sounded simple: Eat fewer calories than you burn up and, voilà, you lose weight. However, as we all know, countless citizens are still overweight, and still spend millions of dollars to support a whole industry of diet books and special treatments.

addicted to reading the small type on cereal boxes is well aware of these things. Also, some of these nutrients are now, by law, added to white bread, to replace the loss incurred in the milling of white flour. Vitamin D is added to milk, and iodine to salt. And every schoolchild now learns about the Basic Four Food Groups: dairy products, the meat group, vegetables and fruits, and breads and cereals.

A s Americans learned more about the nutritional value of the foods they were eating, they also became more concerned about the purity of these foods. A law against the adulteration of tea was passed in 1883, and in various states it was forbidden to add chalk, water, or anything else to milk. But not until 1907 was there a really effective federal law to control the adulteration of a wide variety of common products. This was the Pure Food and Drug Act. But there was still a long way to go. In 1931, an amendment to that Act set up more rigid standards and established the Food and Drug Administration as a national watchdog. In 1938 the Food, Drug, and Cosmetic Act dealt with misbranding, adulteration, and the indiscriminate use of chemical preservatives. And in 1966 Congress passed the Fair Packaging and Labeling Act. With these laws and a broadened nutritional awareness, consumers no longer had to buy a pig in a poke.

Pictured opposite: Use the Basic Four Food Groups like a jigsaw puzzle. Fit the proper variety of foods in each group into your daily diet and you'll be practicing good nutrition. Remember that *dairy products* are your primary source of calcium. *Fruits and vegetables* provide vitamins A and C plus other nutrients. Protein and iron are provided by *meat, fish, poultry, eggs, dried beans, and nuts.* Whole grain, enriched, or restored *breads and cereals* are rich sources of vitamins and other important nutrients.

Cinnamon-Graham Crackers

2 cups whole wheat flour
1 cup all-purpose flour
1 teaspoon baking powder
½ teaspoon baking soda
¾ cup packed brown sugar
½ cup shortening

⅓ cup honey
1 teaspoon vanilla
½ cup milk
3 tablespoons granulated sugar
1 teaspoon ground cinnamon

Stir together whole wheat flour, all-purpose flour, baking powder, baking soda, and ¼ teaspoon salt. Cream together brown sugar and shortening till light. Beat in honey and vanilla till fluffy. Add flour mixture alternately with milk to creamed mixture, beating well after each addition. Chill dough several hours or overnight. Divide chilled mixture into quarters. On well-floured surface roll each quarter to 15x5-inch rectangle. Cut rectangle crosswise into 6 small rectangles measuring 5x2½ inches. Place on ungreased baking sheet. Mark a line crosswise across center of each small rectangle with tines of fork; score a pattern of holes on squares with fork tines. Combine granulated sugar and cinnamon; sprinkle over crackers. Bake at 350° for 13 to 15 minutes. Remove from sheet at once. Makes 24.

In the early 1800s the Reverend Sylvester Graham was a temperance lecturer and a nutritional "expert." He encouraged the use of coarse cereals which later led to breakfast cereals. He also urged the use of more fruits and vegetables in the American diet. Yet, for all his work, he is known to history as something of a crank, barely tolerating the use of milk, eggs, honey, salt, shellfish, or pork. In 1835 specialized shops featuring Graham-approved foods were started. The graham cracker, however, is perhaps his most well-known legacy to America.

Steamed Cranberry Pudding *(122 calories/serving)*

1 cup all-purpose flour
1 teaspoon baking soda
¼ teaspoon ground cinnamon
¼ teaspoon ground cloves
¼ teaspoon ground nutmeg
⅓ cup hot water

⅓ cup light molasses
¼ cup packed brown sugar
1 cup halved fresh cranberries
½ cup whipped low-calorie dessert topping

Stir together flour, soda, and spices. Combine hot water, molasses, and sugar; stir into flour mixture with cranberries. Pour into greased 1-quart mold (not ring mold). Cover with greased foil; tie securely with string. Place on rack in deep kettle; add boiling water to kettle to depth of 1 inch. Cover; steam for 2½ hours, adding more boiling water, if needed. Cool 10 minutes; unmold. Serve warm with whipped topping. Makes 8 servings.

Because Americans are both weight conscious and love sweets, they have improvised many, many low-calorie desserts such as Steamed Cranberry Pudding or Fruit Melange (see recipe, page 342). When next you crave something sweet but your waistline says it's time to count calories, try serving either of these desserts.

Pictured opposite: If watching calories is a problem for you but you still enjoy entertaining, try serving this low-calorie (547 calories) menu (see below). Serve it buffet-style, so non-dieters can take a little more, if they wish. If you don't tell, your guests will never suspect it's a low-calorie meal.

Menu

Hot Tomato Refresher
Shrimp Elegante
Hot Cooked Rice
Spinach-Artichoke Salad
French Bread   Butter
Fruit Melange
Coffee or Tea

Hot Tomato Refresher *(35 calories/serving)*

2 24-ounce cans vegetable
  juice cocktail
2 tablespoons lemon juice

2 teaspoons Worcestershire
  sauce
½ teaspoon ground allspice

In large saucepan combine vegetable juice cocktail, lemon juice, Worcestershire sauce, and ground allspice. Heat through. Just before serving, pour into small mugs or heat-proof glasses. Float a thin lemon slice atop each serving, if desired. Makes 12 (4-ounce) servings.

Shrimp Elegante *(152 calories/serving)*

3 pounds fresh *or* frozen
  shrimp in shells
  (50 large shrimp)
Boiling water
2 6-ounce packages frozen
  pea pods
3 chicken bouillon cubes
2½ cups boiling water

½ cup sliced green onion
  with tops
3 tablespoons soy sauce
1 teaspoon salt
¼ cup cold water
¼ cup cornstarch
4 medium tomatoes, cut into
  eighths

Thaw frozen shrimp. Peel and devein shrimp; set aside. Pour a little boiling water over pea pods and carefully break apart with fork; drain immediately and set aside. In large saucepan or Dutch oven dissolve bouillon cubes in the 2½ cups boiling water; add shrimp, green onion, soy sauce, and salt. Return to boiling; cook for 3 minutes, stirring occasionally. Slowly blend cold water into cornstarch; stir into shrimp mixture. Cook, stirring constantly, till mixture is thick and bubbly. Add tomatoes and pea pods. Cook till tomatoes are heated through, about 3 minutes longer. Serves 12.

Spinach-Artichoke Salad *(78 calories/serving)*

4 7-ounce cans artichoke
  hearts, drained
1 cup low-calorie Italian
  salad dressing

3 hard-cooked eggs
Salt
6 cups torn fresh spinach
6 cups torn lettuce

Halve artichoke hearts; marinate in dressing for 1 hour in refrigerator. Drain hearts; reserve dressing. Dice 2 of the eggs; sprinkle with salt. In large bowl toss spinach, lettuce, artichokes, and diced eggs lightly with reserved dressing. Slice remaining egg; arrange atop salad. Serves 12.

Fruit Melange *(87 calories/serving)*

1 16-ounce can pitted dark
  sweet cherries (water
  pack), drained
1 pint fresh strawberries,
  sliced
1 medium cantaloupe, cut
  into balls (2½ cups)
1 15¼-ounce can pineapple
  chunks (juice pack),
  drained

½ cup low-calorie orange
  marmalade
¼ cup hot water
1 teaspoon finely chopped
  candied ginger
1 medium banana, sliced
  (1 cup)
  • • •
Fresh mint (optional)

Halve cherries. Chill fruits; layer cherries, strawberries, melon, and pineapple in compote or large glass bowl. Combine marmalade, hot water, and candied ginger. Drizzle over fruit. Chill. Arrange banana atop fruit. (To keep banana from darkening dip in ascorbic acid color keeper or lemon juice mixed with a little water.) Garnish with fresh mint, if desired. Makes 12 servings.

In school most of us are taught the Basic Four Plan for good nutrition. This plan depends on combinations of four groups — meat, dairy products, vegetables and fruits, and breads and cereals — to provide all the nutrients a person normally needs. Critics of the plan often complain that it is difficult to follow and still remain within recommended calorie levels. The menu for the three meals given below has been designed to fullfill the Basic Four requirements within reasonable calorie limits.

Menu

Breakfast
448 calories/serving

Orange Juice
Hot Oatmeal   Milk
Peach Omelet

Lunch
710 calories/serving

Barbecued Pork Sandwich
Tossed Salad
with
Cheddar Cheese Strips
Apple
Coffee or Tea

Dinner
893 calories/serving

Saucy Pot Roast
or
Mexican-Style Liver*
with
Hot Cooked Rice*
Broccoli Spears
Molded Melon Salad
Hard Rolls   Butter
Vanilla Pudding
Coffee or Tea

*with Mexican-Style Liver and Rice, *851 calories/serving for this meal*

Peach Omelet

1 8¾-ounce can peach slices
9 eggs
¼ cup milk
½ teaspoon salt

1 tablespoon cooking oil
Ground cinnamon
Ground allspice

Dice peaches; drain well. With a fork, beat together the eggs, milk, and salt. Heat *1 teaspoon* of the oil in an 8-inch skillet or omelet pan. Pour in *⅓ of the egg mixture;* cook over medium-high heat till egg is set but still shiny. Top with *⅓ of the peaches;* sprinkle with cinnamon and allspice. Run spatula around edge of omelet; fold one side over peaches. Tilt pan and roll omelet onto hot plate. Keep warm in 250° oven. Repeat to make 3 omelets in all. Warm last filled omelet before serving. Serves 6.

Molded Melon Salad

Drain one 8-ounce can pineapple slices (juice pack); reserve juice. Dice fruit. Add enough water to juice to make 1 cup liquid; heat to boiling. Add one 3-ounce package lime-flavored gelatin, 2 teaspoons sugar, and dash salt; stir till dissolved. Stir in ¾ cup cold water. Beat in 1 cup plain yogurt; chill till partially set. Fold in pineapple and 2 cups diced cantaloupe. Pour into 5-cup mold; chill till firm. Serves 6 to 8.

Barbecued Pork Sandwich

1 pound ground pork
¾ cup chopped onion
2 cloves garlic, minced
1 8-ounce can tomato sauce
1 tablespoon vinegar
2 teaspoons Worcestershire sauce

¾ teaspoon salt
¼ teaspoon fennel seed
Few dashes bottled hot pepper sauce
6 hamburger buns, split and toasted

In medium skillet cook pork, onion, and garlic till pork is cooked thoroughly and onion is tender. Drain well. Stir in tomato sauce, vinegar, Worcestershire, salt, fennel seed, and hot pepper sauce. Simmer for 7 to 8 minutes, stirring once or twice. Serve on toasted buns. Makes 6 servings.

Saucy Pot Roast

1 2½-pound beef chuck pot roast
2 cups tomato juice
¼ cup wine vinegar
1 clove garlic, minced
2 teaspoons Worcestershire sauce
1½ teaspoons salt
1 teaspoon sugar

½ teaspoon dried basil, crushed
½ teaspoon dried thyme, crushed
12 small potatoes, peeled
6 small onions
6 carrots, halved crosswise
3 tablespoons all-purpose flour

Trim excess fat from roast. Place meat in plastic bag; set in deep bowl. Mix tomato juice, wine vinegar, garlic, Worcestershire, salt, sugar, basil, thyme, and ¼ teaspoon pepper. Pour over meat; close bag. Marinate overnight in refrigerator, turning bag occasionally. Transfer roast from bag to Dutch oven. Add marinade. Cover; simmer for 1 hour. Add vegetables. Cover and simmer till meat and vegetables are tender, 45 to 60 minutes more. Remove meat and vegetables to serving platter; keep warm. Skim fat from pan juices; reserve 2 cups juices. Slowly blend ½ cup cold water into flour; add to reserved juices. Cook and stir till thickened and bubbly. Serve with sliced meat and vegetables. Makes 6 servings.

Mexican-Style Liver

6 slices bacon
¾ cup chopped onion
1 clove garlic, minced
¼ cup all-purpose flour
1½ teaspoons chili powder
1 teaspoon salt

1½ pounds beef liver
1 16-ounce can tomatoes,
    cut up
1 12-ounce can whole kernel
    corn, drained
Hot cooked rice

In large skillet cook bacon till crisp. Reserve 3 tablespoons drippings in skillet; crumble bacon and set aside. Cook onion and garlic in drippings till onion is tender but not brown, about 5 minutes. Combine flour, chili powder, and salt. Cut liver into thin strips; toss in flour mixture to coat. Add liver to onion in skillet; brown quickly on all sides. Stir in crumbled bacon, undrained tomatoes, and whole kernel corn. Simmer, covered, till mixture is heated through. Serve over hot cooked rice. Makes 6 servings.

Fortified Breakfast Drink

Combine 2¼ cups instant nonfat dry milk powder and 1 cup Ovaltine. Stir mixture till blended thoroughly. Store in a covered container at room temperature until needed.

For each serving: In large serving glass combine ¾ *cup plus 1 tablespoon* of the dry mixture and 1 cup cold water. Stir till well blended. Makes enough for 4 servings.

It is not always possible to take time out to enjoy a big breakfast each morning. Fortified Breakfast Drink *will provide a good start to a busy day.*

Canning, Freezing, and Drying

Four completely innovative methods of food processing — commercial canning, pasteurization, freezing, and freeze-drying — changed America's food habits more thoroughly than any other factors since 1800.

By 1880 commercial canning was firmly established in America, but the struggle to establish and maintain quality continued for the next thirty years. To begin with, quality of canned goods was variable. Some canners tried to improve the appearance of the food with questionable dyes and preservatives. Also, the canning process itself needed improvement and standardization. But after the success of Van Camp's canned baked beans in tomato sauce, the public became more receptive to the whole concept of canned food as a time- and effort-saver. In the late 1890s an important milestone was the introduction of Campbell's condensed soups. And the famous red-and-white can became one of the most familiar sights on any canned-goods shelf (not to mention in the Pop Art galleries).

Corned beef was successfully canned in the 1870s. Used first by the armed forces, it gradually became a kitchen standby. Since 1930 hams have been cooked in cans during heat processing. Spam and other processed meats helped feed our World War II soldiers.

The canning industry really came of age during the first decade of this century with the invention of new machinery that turned out sealed cans much faster than before and in a more sanitary process. Cans were now

The principles of canning were first discovered by Nicolas Appert. The Frenchman was awarded a prize for developing a way to get food to the French army. Appert canned by heating food in sealed containers. Though his method proved successful, Appert wrongly attributed his achievement to the airtight container. In reality the food did not spoil because the bacteria in it were destroyed by the heat. However, in 1819, ten years after Appert's work, commercial canning began in America.

In the late 1800s two of the most famous names in coffee, Chase and Sanborn and Maxwell House, helped make us a nation of coffee drinkers. In 1878 James Sanborn and Caleb Chase, owners of coffee businesses in New England, joined forces and produced the first coffee in sealed cans. The name of their coffee has been a household word ever since general stores began selling their one- and two-pound cans of coffee.

Maxwell House Coffee, on the other hand, resulted from the experiments of Joel Cheek in Nashville, Tennessee. It took almost two years of full-time work to develop a blend of coffee that suited his taste. Maxwell House, a well-known hotel in Nashville, agreed to serve his coffee, and the guests agreed the coffee was the best they had ever tasted. Later, Theodore Roosevelt was served Maxwell House Coffee. When asked if he would like another cup, he replied, "Delighted! It's good to the last drop." And thus was a slogan born.

made of steel with a tin coating and lined with enamel.

The pasteurization of milk ranks with the great discoveries of all time. After Pasteur's magnificent discovery, additional improvements leading to today's high milk standards were the cream separator (1880), sterilized milk bottles (1889), and milking machines (invented in 1902 but not common in this country until after World War II). Tuberculin and brucellosis tests were introduced in the early 1900s. Mechanical refrigeration, widely developed in the 1880s, was of prime importance to the dairy industry and to all industries that dealt in perishable products. And it made possible the frozen-food industry.

Quick-freezing was not a new discovery since people in cold climates had been freezing food for centuries. The idea of commercial quick-freezing was new, the credit belonging to Clarence Birdseye.

As a young geologist in Labrador in 1912, Birdseye noted that at very low winter temperatures, a fresh-caught fish would freeze solid almost as soon as it was out of the water. When defrosted and cooked, it would taste as good as fresh. Some years after World War I, Birdseye went into business for himself, trying to perfect a method of quick-freezing fish. After a number of false starts he finally found a way to quick-freeze and package not only fish but other perishable foods.

Unfortunately, that didn't solve his problems. Frozen foods had to be reasonable in price; the always conservative public had to be introduced to this radically different form of food; grocers had to have suitable freezers and display cabinets; and housewives had to have freezing compartments in their refrigerators. And all this in the early 1930s, at the beginning of the worst depression in history. Lack of funds forced Clarence Birdseye to sell out to the Postum Company (later to change its name to General Foods). By 1940, and after some $5 million had been spent to get started, frozen foods became a way of life in America.

As for freeze-drying, the armed forces spearheaded the development of this fourth new process, which quick-freezes food first and then evaporates the water from the food. Homemakers may not realize it, but they often freeze-dry laundry. Clothes hung out to dry in below-freezing weather freeze first, but eventually they dry. The armed forces used freeze-drying to produce large quantities of freeze-dried orange juice for the soldiers in World War II. After the war, commercial producers took over where the service left off. The new products developed had the advantage of better quality than conventionally dried foods, in addition to being stable for up to a year without refrigeration.

Festive Cheese Ball

Pasteurized process cheese was the brainchild of James L. Kraft. In 1920 he devised a rindless five-pound cheese that was an immediate success. Since then manufacturers have been selling process cheeses in many forms, of many kinds, including spreads, slices, and dips. Because of its smooth texture, process cheese is particularly good in recipes such as Festive Cheese Ball.

2 5-ounce jars cheese
   spread with hickory
   smoke flavor
1 5-ounce jar sharp
   American cheese spread
2 3-ounce packages cream
   cheese, softened

2 teaspoons grated onion
½ teaspoon Worcestershire
   sauce
½ cup snipped parsley
• • •
Assorted crackers

In small mixing bowl combine cheese spreads, cream cheese, grated onion, and Worcestershire sauce; beat with electric mixer till smooth and well blended. Shape cheese mixture into a ball. Roll the ball in snipped parsley. Cover and refrigerate up to 24 hours. Serve with assorted crackers.

Cheese-Sauced Striped Bass

2 pounds fresh *or* frozen
    striped bass fillets *or*
    other fish fillets *or*
    fish steaks
1/4 cup butter *or* margarine
1/4 cup all-purpose flour
1/4 teaspoon garlic salt

Dash pepper
1 1/2 cups milk
1/2 cup dry white wine
3 tablespoons grated
    Parmesan cheese
Dash paprika

Thaw frozen fish. Cut fish into 6 serving-size pieces. Arrange fish pieces in shallow baking dish. In saucepan melt butter or margarine. Blend in flour, garlic salt, and pepper. Add milk and dry white wine. Cook, stirring constantly, till thickened and bubbly. Stir in *1 tablespoon* grated Parmesan cheese. Pour sauce over fish. Bake at 350° till fish flakes easily when tested with a fork, 20 to 25 minutes. Sprinkle remaining Parmesan cheese and paprika over top. Place under broiler just till cheese is browned and sauce is slightly bubbly, about 1 minute. Trim with parsley, if desired. Serves 6.

Since Clarence Birdseye first used his quick-freezing process on fish, a wide variety of frozen fish products have come on the market. One of them, frozen fish fillets, is used to make Cheese-Sauced Striped Bass.

Banana-Strawberry Freeze

1 10-ounce package frozen
    strawberries, partially
    thawed and broken up
1/4 cup lemon juice

2/3 cup sugar
1 fully-ripe banana,
    quartered
1 cup whipping cream

Put strawberries into blender container. Add lemon juice. Cover and blend till smooth. Add sugar and banana; blend till smooth. Pour into mixing bowl. Whip cream till soft peaks form; fold into strawberry mixture. Pour into 4-cup refrigerator tray. Freeze till firm. Makes about 1 quart.

The needs of the armed forces in World War II boosted the growth of the business of freezing fruit juices, fruits, and vegetables. During the war years, these types of foods were rationed, but in 1945 producers began in earnest to make them for the general public. Their quality and year-round convenience made them an instant success. It's hard to remember they were not "always there." Now homemakers use them almost daily in recipes such as Pineapple-Wine Pitcher Punch and Banana-Strawberry Freeze.

Pineapple-Wine Pitcher Punch

2 6-ounce cans frozen
    pineapple-orange juice
    concentrate
    • • •
1 4/5-quart bottle dry white
    wine, chilled

1/4 cup sugar
1/4 cup lemon juice
1 28-ounce bottle ginger
    ale, chilled
Ice cubes

In large pitcher prepare pineapple-orange juice concentrate according to label directions. Add chilled wine, sugar, and lemon juice; stir till sugar is dissolved. Slowly pour in ginger ale, stirring with an up-and-down motion. Pour over ice in glasses. Makes about 15 (6-ounce) servings.

Turkey Jambalaya

3/4 cup uncooked regular rice
1/2 cup chopped celery
1/4 cup chopped green pepper
1/4 cup chopped onion
1/4 cup butter *or* margarine
1 16-ounce can tomatoes,
    cut up

1/4 teaspoon dried thyme,
    crushed
Dash cayenne
    • • •
1 28-ounce package frozen
    sliced turkey and
    giblet gravy

In large skillet cook rice, celery, green pepper, and onion in butter till vegetables are tender and rice is browned; stir occasionally. Meanwhile, combine tomatoes, thyme, and cayenne; stir into rice mixture. Place frozen block of sliced turkey atop rice mixture. Cover and simmer till turkey is heated through and rice is tender, about 30 minutes; stir occasionally. Remove from heat; let stand 5 minutes before serving. Makes 5 or 6 servings.

In the 1960s frozen food manufacturers began expanding their lines to include more and more frozen food entrées. Frozen macaroni and cheese, potpies, sliced turkey, and other products were designed to be eaten as packaged, but inventive cooks soon realized they could be made even better by using them in recipes such as Turkey Jambalaya.

Pictured opposite: Two tempting desserts that will round out almost any meal are *Peach-Caramel Cobbler* (see recipe, page 356) and *Choco-Mo Ice Cream. Choco-Mo Ice Cream* is made in the refrigerator and uses evaporated milk to give it a rich creaminess. Evaporated milk was invented by Gail Borden in 1856 and was first used by the troops in the Civil War in place of fresh milk. Today we're more apt to use evaporated milk as a cooking ingredient.

Sweetened condensed milk was the invention of Gail Borden. In fact it was the first item sold by the Borden Company. The product begins as fresh whole milk. Then sugar is added and water is removed. Its special flavor and smooth consistency make it ideal for use in desserts, sauces, and cookies such as Toffee Bars.

Canned ham has really "attained its majority" during this century. At first hams were not canned at all, but were merely cured and then smoked in the smokehouse. These hams were then cooked in the same way as raw meat. Even when manufacturers began putting hams in cans, they were only partially cooked, so the homemaker still had to do most of the cooking. Today canned hams are fully-cooked and all they require is heating through.

Choco-Mo Ice Cream

2/3 cup cold water
1 tablespoon cornstarch
1 13-ounce can evaporated
   milk
3 beaten egg yolks
1/4 cup light molasses

Dash salt
3 egg whites
1/4 cup sugar
1/2 cup semisweet chocolate
   pieces, finely chopped

In saucepan slowly blend cold water into cornstarch. Stir in evaporated milk. Cook, stirring constantly, till mixture boils. Stir a moderate amount hot mixture into beaten egg yolks. Return to remaining hot mixture in saucepan. Cook, stirring constantly, till mixture is *almost boiling.* Stir in molasses and salt; chill thoroughly. Beat egg whites till soft peaks form. Gradually add sugar, beating till stiff peaks form. Fold into molasses mixture. Turn into 11x7 1/2x1 1/2-inch pan. Freeze till firm. Break into chunks and place in chilled bowl; beat till smooth with electric mixer. Fold in chopped chocolate pieces. Return to cold pan. Freeze till firm. Makes 8 to 10 servings.

Toffee Bars

1/2 cup butter *or* margarine,
   softened
1/2 cup sugar
1/2 teaspoon salt
1 cup all-purpose flour
1 14-ounce can *sweetened
   condensed* milk

2 tablespoons butter *or*
   margarine
1/4 teaspoon salt
2 teaspoons vanilla
• • •
Fudge Frosting

Cream 1/2 cup butter, sugar, and 1/2 teaspoon salt; stir in flour. Pat into ungreased 13x9x2-inch baking pan. Bake at 350° till lightly browned, about 15 minutes. In heavy saucepan cook and stir sweetened condensed milk, 2 tablespoons butter, and 1/4 teaspoon salt over low heat till butter melts. Cook and stir for 5 minutes over medium heat. (Mixture will thicken and become smooth.) Stir in vanilla. Spread over baked layer. Bake at 350° till golden, 12 to 15 minutes. Spread warm cookies with Fudge Frosting. While warm, cut into bars and remove from pan. Makes 48.

Fudge Frosting: In saucepan melt 2 tablespoons butter and one 1-ounce square unsweetened chocolate over low heat; stir constantly. Remove from heat; stir in 1 1/2 cups sifted powdered sugar and 1 teaspoon vanilla. Blend in hot water (about 2 tablespoons) till *almost* pourable consistency.

Ham en Croustade

1 5-pound canned ham
   (unglazed)
• • •
1 1/2 cups all-purpose flour
2 teaspoons baking powder
1/2 teaspoon rubbed sage
1/4 teaspoon dry mustard

3 tablespoons shortening
1/2 cup milk
1 teaspoon caraway seed
1 tablespoon prepared
   mustard
2 tablespoons milk

Place ham on rack in shallow baking pan; bake at 325° till meat thermometer registers 135°, 1 1/2 to 2 hours.

Meanwhile, stir together flour, baking powder, sage, and dry mustard. Cut in shortening till size of coarse crumbs. Add 1/2 cup milk and caraway seed; stir till dough follows fork around bowl. Turn out on floured surface. Knead gently 12 strokes. Roll into a 12-inch square. Remove ham from oven; increase oven temperature to 450°. Remove rack; discard drippings. Brush top and sides of ham with prepared mustard. Drape pastry over ham; mold to surface. Trim pastry to fit. Make slits in top. Make cutouts from pastry trimmings; arrange on loaf. Brush with 2 tablespoons milk. Bake at 450° till browned, about 10 minutes. Serves 12.

Herbed Potato Fluff

Packaged instant mashed
  potatoes (enough for
  4 servings)
1 cup small curd cream-
  style cottage cheese
½ cup dairy sour cream
3 egg yolks

2 tablespoons snipped
  chives
½ teaspoon celery salt
3 egg whites
2 tablespoons finely
  snipped parsley
2 tablespoons butter

Prepare potatoes according to package directions. Beat in cheese, sour cream, yolks, chives, and celery salt. Beat whites till stiff peaks form; fold whites and parsley into potatoes. Turn into a 2-quart casserole; dot with butter. Bake at 350° till lightly browned, about 1 hour. Makes 6 to 8 servings.

Easy Chicken Divan

2 10-ounce packages frozen
  broccoli spears
2 packages hollandaise
  sauce mix (*each* enough
  for ¾ cup sauce)
½ cup dairy sour cream

¼ cup dry sherry
¼ teaspoon ground nutmeg
3 cups cubed cooked chicken
¼ cup grated Parmesan
  cheese
Butter *or* margarine

Cook broccoli according to package directions. Meanwhile, prepare sauce mixes according to package directions. Stir in sour cream, sherry, and nutmeg. Stir in chicken; heat through. Drain broccoli; arrange on oven-proof platter. Top with chicken mixture. Sprinkle with cheese; dot with butter. Broil 4 inches from heat till bubbly, about 3 minutes. Makes 6 servings.

Chilled Eggnog Soufflé

1 envelope unflavored
  gelatin
½ cup nonfat dry milk
  powder
⅓ cup sugar

¼ teaspoon salt
4 beaten egg yolks
1 teaspoon rum flavoring
4 egg whites
Ground nutmeg

In saucepan mix gelatin, milk powder, sugar, and salt; stir in 1½ cups cold water. Blend in yolks. Cook and stir over low heat till it just coats metal spoon. Remove from heat; stir in flavoring. Chill till partially set; stir occasionally. Beat whites to stiff peaks; fold into gelatin. Turn into a 4-cup soufflé dish with foil collar; top with nutmeg. Chill till firm. Serves 8.

Pumpkin Rice Pudding

1 16-ounce can pumpkin
¾ cup sugar
1 teaspoon ground cinnamon
½ teaspoon salt
½ teaspoon ground ginger
¼ teaspoon ground cloves

2 slightly beaten eggs
1 13-ounce can evaporated
  milk
⅔ cup uncooked quick-
  cooking rice
½ cup raisins

Combine pumpkin, sugar, cinnamon, salt, ginger, and cloves. Add eggs. Stir in milk. Stir in rice and raisins. Pour into a 1½-quart casserole. Place in shallow pan on oven rack; pour hot water around casserole into pan to depth of 1 inch. Bake at 350° for 15 minutes; stir till well combined. Bake till knife inserted just off-center comes out clean, 50 to 60 minutes more. (Or, spoon into six to eight 5-ounce custard cups; place in pan. Fill pan with hot water to depth of 1 inch. Bake at 350° till knife inserted just off-center comes out clean, 25 to 30 minutes.) Makes 6 to 8 servings.

Plain Pastry

For an 8-, 9-, or 10-inch 2-crust or lattice-top pie, or 6 to 8 tart shells:

 2 cups all-purpose flour
 1 teaspoon salt
 ⅔ cup shortening
 5 to 7 tablespoons cold
     water

For one 8-, 9-, or 10-inch pastry shell, or 4 to 6 tart shells:

 1½ cups all-purpose flour
 ½ teaspoon salt
 ½ cup shortening
 4 to 5 tablespoons cold
     water

Stir flour and salt together; cut in shortening with pastry blender till pieces are the size of small peas. Sprinkle *1 tablespoon* water over part of mixture. Gently toss with fork; push to side of bowl. Repeat till all is moistened. Form into a ball. (For 2-crust and lattice-top pies, divide dough for lower and upper crust and form into balls.) Flatten on lightly floured surface by pressing with edge of hand 3 times across in both directions. Roll from center to edge till ⅛ inch thick.

For lattice-top pie: Trim lower crust ½ inch beyond edge of pie plate. Roll remaining dough ⅛ inch thick. Cut strips of pastry ½ to ¾ inch wide with pastry wheel or knife. Lay strips on filled pie at 1-inch intervals. Fold back alternate strips as you weave cross strips. Trim lattice even with outer rim of pie plate; fold lower crust over strips. Seal; flute edge.

For 2-crust pie: Trim lower crust even with rim of pie plate. Cut slits in top crust. Lift pastry by rolling it over rolling pin, then unroll loosely over well-filled pie. Trim ½ inch beyond edge. Tuck top crust under edge of lower crust. Flute edge as desired.

To bake single-crust pie shells: Fit pastry into pie plate; trim ½ to 1 inch beyond edge; fold under and flute edge. Prick bottom and sides well with fork. (If filling and crust are baked together, *do not prick.*) Bake at 450° till golden, 10 to 12 minutes.

Sorting is one of the first steps in the processing of vegetables for canning or freezing. Leaves and stems as well as damaged vegetables are discarded.

Coffee Punch

¼ cup sugar
2 tablespoons instant
coffee crystals
1 teaspoon vanilla
6 cups milk

¼ cup crème de cacao *or*
orange liqueur
½ cup whipping cream
1 quart vanilla ice cream
Ground nutmeg

Combine the sugar, instant coffee crystals, vanilla, and dash salt; add the milk and crème de cacao or orange liqueur. Stir till the sugar dissolves. Chill. Whip the cream to soft peaks.

Spoon the ice cream into a punch bowl. Pour the coffee mixture over ice cream. Top with the whipped cream and sprinkle with nutmeg. Makes about 12 (6-ounce) servings.

Freeze-drying is a process wherein the foods are first quick-frozen, then heat is used to vaporize the ice. Although freeze-drying is expensive, foods retain their shape, color, and structure better than with regular dehydration. The most popular freeze-dried foods today are coffee crystals and some types of camping provisions.

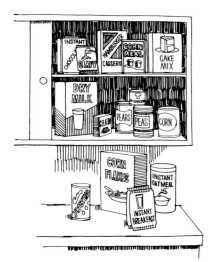

The Changing Pantry: New Food Staples

The foods stocked on our pantry shelves today are far different from those in our forefathers' cupboards. In colonial days foods were mostly fresh or home-preserved; but soon even nature's offerings were changed as men began to experiment with grafting, hybridization, and genetics. In the last century hundreds of new foods have been created by man's ingenuity.

Perhaps the earliest changes occurred in the variations of fruits and vegetables. The naturalist, Luther Burbank, led the way by introducing the Idaho russet potato to the nation in 1873. Then came stringless green beans, navel oranges, iceberg lettuce, commercially grown olives, pimientos, and mushrooms, and Golden Delicious apples.

Nor were the changes limited to the naturally grown foods. More and more commercially preserved or manufactured edibles began to appear as factories produced new food items. An early, and certainly a most important, item was baking powder. Though available in the late 1860s as yeast powder, it took a couple of decades for homemakers to recognize that their muffins and cakes were more likely to succeed with baking powder.

Another early product was gelatin. Unflavored gelatin was available first, but by 1900 the flavored kind had become popular particularly because its usefulness had been expanded by putting it into molded fruit salads as well as desserts. Such combinations as carrot and pineapple encased in orange-flavored gelatin was a new and strictly American idea.

Movie audiences agitated by *The Perils of Pauline* sought solace with penny candy and peanuts. (Early in the 1900s, an Italian immigrant storekeeper in Wilkes-Barre, Pennsylvania, had begun selling the nibbler's delight [or downfall, for some], shelled, roasted, and salted peanuts.) Popcorn, which had always been known in American kitchens, found a new generation of munchers when the theaters installed electric cornpoppers and began selling the treat in bags. Still later, moviegoers added potato chips, pretzels, and many other snack foods to the list of munchables.

The first soda pop to be advertised and distributed nationally was Hires Root Beer. Later, Coca-Cola was invented and Pepsi-Cola followed in 1903. Consumption increased steadily until Americans now drink over 200 cans or bottles of soda pop per capita annually.

The first dry cereal started quite a revolution. W. K. Kellogg began it all by inventing cornflakes. It was a long shot since the notion of eating dry cereal and milk for breakfast (and not much more) was unheard of in a nation addicted to six-course breakfasts. But Kellogg, having decided that his product was good for everybody, not just for health food fans, put on a national advertising campaign in 1906. Its success was spectacular. Although there were soon other producers of dry cereals, cornflakes retains an enthusiastic following.

The first packaged baking mix was Bisquick, which appeared on the market in 1931. Cake mixes followed in the 1940s. Soon there were also soup mixes, instant rice, instant mashed potatoes, and instant puddings on the grocer's shelves. Every modern shopper knows that this list of new foods could go on endlessly. What is perhaps not so evident, until you compare today's recipes with those of one-hundred years ago, is the gradual change in the foods Americans call staples.

The creator of Root Beer was a Philadelphia druggist who got the recipe from the owner of the boardinghouse where he lived. The drink was a combination of wintergreen, hops, juniper, spikenard, and a dozen other roots and berries. After testing it in his drugstore, Hires made a dry compound of all these elements, packaged it, and launched it at the Philadelphia Exposition of 1876 under the name Root Beer. The buyer had to add water, sugar, and yeast. Later, Hires advertised it nationally, and in 1893 started bottling it ready to drink.

Golden Fruit Punch

2 6-ounce cans frozen orange juice concentrate, thawed
1 6-ounce can frozen pineapple juice concentrate, thawed

1 pint light rum (2 cups)*
2 cups water
1 28-ounce bottle ginger ale, chilled
1 quart lemon *or* pineapple sherbet

Combine juice concentrates, rum, and water. Cover and chill. Pour into punch bowl. Slowly pour ginger ale down side of bowl; stir gently. Scoop sherbet atop. Makes 24 (4-ounce) servings.
*Or, substitute 2 cups water for rum.

For most Americans fresh orange juice may be but a childhood memory or an occasional luxury. Far more common on American breakfast tables is reconstituted frozen orange juice concentrate. Unlike fresh orange juice, the concentrate is a blend of several orange varieties selected to produce a juice with just the right flavor, color, consistency, and vitamin C content. Americans enjoy it in sundry ways including recipes such as Golden Fruit Punch.

Goldilocks Potatoes

4 or 5 medium potatoes, peeled and quartered
¼ cup hot milk

½ cup whipping cream
½ cup shredded process cheese spread

Cook potatoes in large amount of boiling, salted water till tender, 20 to 25 minutes. Drain well. Shake over low heat till thoroughly dry. Mash; measure 2½ cups. Beat in enough hot milk to make potatoes fluffy. Salt and pepper to taste. Spoon into six 6-ounce custard cups. Whip cream; fold in cheese. Spoon atop potatoes. Bake at 350° till golden, about 15 minutes. Serves 6.

Cheese-Sauced Baked Potatoes

1 cup shredded sharp American cheese
½ cup dairy sour cream
¼ cup butter *or* margarine, softened

2 tablespoons chopped green onion with tops
• • •
6 baking potatoes

Have cheese, sour cream, butter, and onion at room temperature. Bake potatoes at 425° till done, 45 to 60 minutes. Meanwhile, in small bowl combine cheese, sour cream, butter, and onion; beat till fluffy. To serve, roll potatoes gently under hand. Immediately criss-cross tops with fork; press ends, pushing up to fluff. Top with cheese mixture. Makes 6 servings.

Luther Burbank worked with many types of living plants including plums, prunes, peaches, walnuts, tomatoes, and squash. His biggest success, however, was the Idaho russet potato. This potato once called the "Rolls-Royce" of potatoes" has made Idaho the largest producer of potatoes in the country.

Cranberry-Orange Spread

In bowl stir together ¾ cup cranberry-orange relish, ¼ cup soft-spread margarine, 1 tablespoon sugar, and ¼ teaspoon ground cinnamon. Makes 1 cup.

Layered Gelatin Parfaits

1 3-ounce package lemon-flavored gelatin
Dash salt
1 cup boiling water

1 10-ounce package frozen mixed fruit
½ cup lemon yogurt
2 teaspoons sugar

Dissolve gelatin and salt in boiling water; stir in ¾ cup cold water. Set aside ½ cup mixture. Add fruit to remaining gelatin; stir carefully to separate fruits. Chill till partially set, 10 to 12 minutes; spoon into 6 parfait glasses. Chill till almost set. Meanwhile, chill reserved ½ cup gelatin till partially set. Beat with rotary or electric beater till fluffy, 1 to 2 minutes. Mix yogurt and sugar; fold into whipped gelatin. Spoon whipped mixture atop gelatin in glasses. Chill till set. Makes 6 servings.

Italian Salad Mold

2 3-ounce packages lemon-flavored gelatin
½ envelope Italian salad dressing mix
¼ cup vinegar
1 cup chopped lettuce

1 cup quartered and thinly sliced zucchini
½ cup shredded carrot
¼ cup sliced radishes
Lettuce
Mayonnaise (optional)

In bowl combine lemon gelatin and salad dressing mix. Add 1½ cups boiling water; stir to dissolve gelatin. Stir in vinegar and 2 cups cold water. Chill till partially set. Fold in chopped lettuce, zucchini, carrot, and radishes. Pour into 5½-cup mold. Chill till firm. Unmold salad on a lettuce-lined plate. Serve with mayonnaise, if desired. Makes 6 to 8 servings.

Turkey in Aspic

6 *or* 12 slices cooked turkey white meat cut ¼ inch thick (about 2 ounces each)
4 hard-cooked eggs, sliced
1 pound fresh asparagus spears, cooked and drained
6 canned pimiento strips
2 envelopes unflavored gelatin

2 13¾-ounce cans chicken broth
½ cup water
• • •
1 tablespoon snipped parsley
1 tablespoon chopped onion
1 tablespoon lemon juice
1 teaspoon prepared horseradish

Trim turkey slices to uniform shapes; arrange in 13x9x2-inch baking pan. (If using 12 slices, make 6 stacks.) Top each portion with 4 egg slices, 3 or 4 asparagus spears, and a pimiento strip. In saucepan soften gelatin in chicken broth and water. Stir in remaining ingredients. Bring to boiling, stirring constantly. Remove from heat; strain through cheesecloth. Chill till *slightly* thickened. Spoon a little gelatin mixture over each turkey stack in pan. Chill till almost set; keep remaining gelatin mixture at room temperature and stir occasionally. Repeat spooning room-temperature gelatin mixture over turkey slices and chilling till a thin glaze of gelatin forms. Pour remaining gelatin mixture around turkey in pan. Chill till set. To serve, trim around each turkey stack; transfer to serving plates. Break up remaining gelatin in pan with a fork; arrange around salads on serving plates. Serves 6.

Corned Beef Chowder

3 cups milk
1 10½-ounce can condensed
    cream of potato soup
Dash pepper

1 10-ounce package frozen
    Brussels sprouts, thawed
1 12-ounce can corned beef,
    broken into pieces

In large saucepan blend *1⅓ cups* of the milk, potato soup, and pepper. Cut up Brussels sprouts; stir into soup. Bring to boiling, stirring occasionally.

Reduce heat; simmer till Brussels sprouts are tender, about 15 minutes. Add remaining milk and corned beef. Heat through. Makes 4 or 5 servings.

Although canned corned beef was first introduced in 1872, it wasn't until the First World War that quality corned beef came into general use; along with canned salmon it became standard rations for the American soldiers. The doughboys, not fully appreciative, scornfully called them Goldfish and Corned Willie. Never mind the scorn—American homemakers have found dozens of delicious ways to use corned beef.

Sweet Potato-Turkey Pie

3 tablespoons butter
⅛ teaspoon ground nutmeg
⅛ teaspoon ground allspice
1 17-ounce can sweet
    potatoes, drained and
    mashed
½ cup chopped onion
2 cups diced cooked turkey

1 10¾-ounce can condensed
    cream of mushroom soup
1 8¾-ounce can whole kernel
    corn, drained
1 8½-ounce can peas, drained
1 small tomato, peeled and
    diced

Melt *2 tablespoons* butter; beat melted butter, nutmeg, allspice, and ¼ teaspoon salt into mashed sweet potatoes. Line a 9-inch pie plate with potato mixture, building up edges ½ inch high.

Cook onion in remaining butter till almost tender. Stir in turkey, soup, vegetables, and ¼ teaspoon salt. Spoon into potato shell. Bake at 350° for 35 minutes. Makes 6 servings.

Shrimp and Tuna Bake

⅔ cup regular rice
1 9-ounce package frozen
    cut green beans
1 10½-ounce can condensed
    cream of celery soup
½ cup milk
2 tablespoons chopped
    canned pimiento
¼ teaspoon dried thyme,
    crushed

Dash cayenne
1 6½- or 7-ounce can tuna,
    drained and broken into
    chunks
1 4½-ounce can shrimp,
    drained
½ of a 3½-ounce can French-
    fried onions (about 1
    cup)

Cook rice according to package directions. Cook beans according to package directions; drain and set aside. Mix soup, milk, pimiento, thyme, and cayenne till smooth. Stir *half* of soup mixture into rice; fold in tuna. Turn into a

1½-quart casserole. Spread beans over rice; top with shrimp. Pour remaining soup mixture over all. Bake, covered, at 325° for 25 to 30 minutes. Sprinkle onions atop; bake, uncovered, till crisp, about 5 minutes. Serves 6.

One staple of American kitchens that most of us take for granted is canned soup. When first marketed, it was considered just a short-cut way of making soup, but soon inspired cooks began using it in all kinds of recipes such as Sweet Potato-Turkey Pie and Shrimp and Tuna Bake.

Toll House Chocolate Chip Cookies

1 cup shortening
¾ cup granulated sugar
¾ cup packed brown sugar
2 eggs
1 teaspoon vanilla

2¼ cups all-purpose flour
1 teaspoon baking soda
2 6-ounce packages semi-
    sweet chocolate pieces
1 cup chopped walnuts

Cream together shortening, sugars, eggs, and vanilla till light. Stir together flour, soda, and 1 teaspoon salt; add to creamed mixture. Beat well. Stir in

chocolate, nuts, and 1 teaspoon hot water. Drop by teaspoonfuls onto *ungreased* cookie sheet. Bake at 350° for 10 to 12 minutes. Makes about 72.

In 1940 the owner of New England's Toll House Inn, Ruth Wakefield, folded chopped chocolate into cookie dough and the Toll House Cookie "burst upon the scene." Almost immediately these tasty cookies were being baked in home kitchens. They really took hold when a machine was invented to mold chocolate into chips.

Peanut Butter Logs

1 cup chunk-style peanut butter
2 tablespoons butter *or* margarine, softened
1¼ cups sifted powdered sugar
3 cups crisp rice cereal
Chopped peanuts

Combine peanut butter and softened butter; stir in powdered sugar thoroughly. Add cereal; mix well, crushing cereal slightly. Shape mixture into three 7x1¼-inch logs. Cover with peanuts. Wrap in plastic wrap or waxed paper; chill till firm. Carefully slice ½ inch thick. Makes about 1 pound candy.

Blintz Bubble Ring

2 3-ounce packages cream cheese
2 packages refrigerated biscuits (20 biscuits)
½ cup sugar
1 teaspoon ground cinnamon
3 tablespoons butter *or* margarine, melted
⅓ cup chopped pecans

Cut cream cheese into 20 pieces; shape each piece into a ball. Roll each refrigerated biscuit to about 3 inches in diameter. Combine sugar and cinnamon. Place *one* cheese ball and *1 teaspoon* cinnamon mixture on *each* biscuit; bring up edges of dough and pinch to seal. Pour melted butter or margarine into bottom of 5-cup ring mold. Sprinkle *half* the chopped pecans and *half* the remaining cinnamon mixture into mold. Place *half* the filled biscuits atop mixture, seam side up; repeat layers. Bake at 375° till golden, about 20 minutes. Cool 5 minutes in pan; invert onto plate. Makes 1 coffee cake.

Raspberry Coffee Cake

1 3-ounce package cream cheese
¼ cup butter *or* margarine
2 cups packaged biscuit mix
⅓ cup milk
½ cup raspberry preserves
Confectioners' Icing (see recipe, page 243)

In mixing bowl cut cream cheese and butter or margarine into biscuit mix till mixture is crumbly; blend in milk. Turn biscuit dough out onto lightly floured surface and knead 8 to 10 strokes. On waxed paper roll dough to form a 12x8-inch rectangle. Carefully turn onto greased baking sheet; remove waxed paper. Spread raspberry preserves evenly down center of dough. Make 2½-inch long slits at 1-inch intervals on long sides of rectangle. Fold each strip over raspberry filling. Bake coffee cake at 425° for 12 to 15 minutes. Drizzle warm coffee cake with Confectioners' Icing. Makes 1.

Peach-Caramel Cobbler *(see photo, page 349)*

1 29-ounce can peach halves
1 package refrigerated caramel Danish rolls with nuts (8 rolls)
• • •
¼ cup all-purpose flour
½ teaspoon grated lemon peel
¼ teaspoon salt
1 7-ounce bottle ginger ale
1 tablespoon butter *or* margarine

Drain peaches, reserving 1 cup syrup. Cut up peaches and set aside. Crumble sugar-nut mixture from refrigerated caramel rolls into saucepan; add flour, lemon peel, and salt. Stir in ginger ale and reserved peach syrup; mix well. Cook, stirring constantly, over medium heat till thickened; stir in butter or margarine. Add peaches; bring to boiling. Pour hot peach mixture into 8x8x2-inch baking dish. Immediately separate caramel rolls; arrange atop the hot mixture. Bake at 400° till done, 25 to 30 minutes. Makes 8 servings.

Butterscotch Bombe

Mix 1 cup finely crushed gingersnaps and 3 tablespoons melted butter. Press mixture firmly into 5-cup mold; freeze. Soften 1 quart vanilla ice cream; stir in two 1⅛-ounce chocolate-coated English toffee bars, crushed. Spoon into mold; smooth top. Cover; freeze firm. To serve, uncover and invert on chilled plate. Rub mold with warm, damp towel to loosen; remove mold. Pass warm Praline Sauce. Serves 10.

Praline Sauce: Mix ½ cup packed brown sugar, ½ cup light cream, and ¼ cup butter. Bring to boiling; stir constantly. Stir in ¼ cup chopped toasted almonds and 1 teaspoon vanilla.

The development of the ice cream freezer in 1846 opened the way for commercial production of ice cream. The industry proved so successful that there are now plants in all of the states. Butterscotch Bombe *uses commercial ice cream to make a tempting dessert.*

Fruited Cheese Salad

- 1 quart frozen whipped dessert topping, thawed
- 3 cups cream-style cottage cheese
- 2 3-ounce packages orange-pineapple-flavored gelatin
- 1 13¼-ounce can pineapple tidbits, drained
- 1 11-ounce can mandarin orange sections, drained
- Endive (optional)

In bowl blend topping and cheese thoroughly. Stir in dry gelatin. Fold in pineapple and oranges. Press into 7- or 8-cup mold. Chill several hours. Unmold onto serving plate; garnish with endive, if desired. Serves 12.

Convenient mixes have simplified home baking so that it's easy to prepare a fancy bread such as *Raspberry Coffee Cake.*

Bean Pot Soybeans

2½ cups dry soybeans
   (16 ounces)
4 ounces salt pork, sliced
1 cup chopped onion

½ cup packed brown sugar
⅓ cup molasses
2 teaspoons salt
1 teaspoon dry mustard

Wash soybeans; cover with cold water and soak overnight. Drain. In 6- to 8-quart pressure saucepan combine soybeans, salt pork, and 6 cups water. Close cover of pressure saucepan securely. Put pressure regulator in place. Cook for 40 minutes with pressure regulator rocking gently (15 pounds pressure). Let saucepan cool for 5 minutes, then reduce pressure under cold running water. Remove cover. Drain beans; reserve 1 cup liquid. Combine remaining ingredients and reserved liquid. Stir into beans. Bake in 2-quart casserole at 350° for 1½ hours. Stir after 1 hour. Makes 6 to 8 servings.

Saucy Beef Meatballs

1 beaten egg
2 tablespoons milk
1 cup soft bread crumbs
½ teaspoon salt
   Dash pepper
1½ pounds ground beef-
   textured vegetable
   protein mixture
2 tablespoons all-purpose
   flour
2 tablespoons cooking oil

1 15-ounce can tomato sauce
1 3-ounce can chopped
   mushrooms
¼ cup dry white wine
1 tablespoon snipped
   parsley
½ teaspoon dried oregano,
   crushed
   Hot cooked noodles
   Grated Parmesan cheese

Combine beaten egg, milk, bread crumbs, salt, and pepper. Add ground beef-textured vegetable protein mixture; mix well. Shape into 24 meatballs. Coat lightly with flour. Brown the meatballs in hot oil in skillet. Drain off fat. Combine tomato sauce, undrained mushrooms, dry white wine, snipped parsley, and oregano; pour mixture over meat. Cover; simmer 20 to 25 minutes. Serve over noodles; sprinkle with Parmesan cheese. Serves 8.

Pineapple Jubilee

½ cup orange marmalade
2 tablespoons packed brown
   sugar
2 tablespoons light corn
   syrup

1 13¼-ounce can pineapple
   tidbits, drained
¼ cup orange liqueur
   Vanilla ice cream

Combine orange marmalade, brown sugar, and corn syrup. Add pineapple tidbits. Cook and stir till heated through. Heat orange liqueur; ignite and pour over fruit mixture. Spoon over vanilla ice cream. Serves 6.

Cran-Citrus Salad

1 16-ounce can orange and
   grapefruit sections,
   chilled and drained
1 16-ounce can jellied
   cranberry sauce,
   chilled and cut into 6
   slices

   Lettuce
     • • •
½ cup mayonnaise *or* salad
   dressing
¼ cup honey
1 tablespoon vinegar

Arrange fruit and cranberry sauce slices on lettuce-lined plates. Combine remaining ingredients thoroughly; serve as a dressing. Makes 6 servings.

Frosty Lime Fizz

1 12-ounce can pineapple
   juice, chilled
   (1½ cups)
½ cup lime juice
½ cup sugar

1 quart lime sherbet
1 28-ounce bottle lemon-
   lime carbonated
   beverage, chilled

Put pineapple juice, lime juice, and sugar into blender container; spoon *half* of the lime sherbet into blender container. Cover and blend till mixture is smooth. Pour ½ *cup* of the pineapple-lime mixture into *each* of six 12-ounce glasses. Add an additional scoop of lime sherbet to each glass. Fill each glass with chilled lemon-lime beverage. Makes 6 servings.

Our national appetite for carbonated beverages began when Elias Durand and Joseph Hawkins started bottling carbonated water in 1835. They capped their bottles by holding them between their knees and pounding the cork in. When the cork was removed, it popped out taking some of the water with it. So customers began calling the beverage pop.

Peanut Brittle

2 cups sugar
1 cup light corn syrup
1 cup water
• • •
2 cups raw Spanish peanuts

½ teaspoon salt
1 tablespoon butter *or*
   margarine
1 teaspoon baking soda

In heavy 3-quart saucepan combine sugar, light corn syrup, and water. Cook and stir till sugar dissolves. Cook over medium heat to soft ball stage (234°). Stir in raw Spanish peanuts and salt. Cook to hard crack stage (305°), stirring frequently. Stir in butter or margarine and baking soda. (Mixture will bubble.) Pour at once onto 2 well-buttered cookie sheets, spreading with spatula. If desired, cool *slightly* and pull with forks to make thinner. Break into pieces when cooled. Makes about 1½ pounds candy.

Peanuts were the special province of horticulturist George Washington Carver. He advocated planting peanuts as a diversifying crop for soil exhausted by cotton growing. In order to assure farmers that growing the goober was profitable, he researched nearly three hundred ways to use them.

Double Peanut Cookies

1 cup shortening
1 cup peanut butter
1 cup granulated sugar
1 cup packed brown sugar
2 eggs
1 teaspoon vanilla

2¼ cups all-purpose flour
2 teaspoons baking soda
¼ teaspoon salt
1 cup coarsely chopped
   salted peanuts

In mixing bowl cream together shortening, peanut butter, granulated sugar, and brown sugar; beat in eggs and vanilla. Stir together all-purpose flour, baking soda, and salt; blend into creamed mixture. Stir in chopped peanuts. Form into 1-inch balls. Place on ungreased cookie sheet; flatten slightly with fingers. Bake at 350° about 10 minutes. Makes 72 cookies.

Although South Americans have been eating a mixture of ground peanuts and honey for centuries, peanut butter in the United States was the invention of a St. Louis doctor. He found that it was the perfect food for his patients who needed an easily digested, high-protein diet. The new creation caught on quickly and by the 1920s peanut butter was a national staple.

Lemon Pudding Pound Cake

4 eggs
1 package 2-layer-size
   yellow cake mix
1 3⅝- *or* 3¾-ounce package
   instant lemon pudding
   mix

¾ cup water
⅓ cup cooking oil
2 cups sifted powdered
   sugar
⅓ cup lemon juice

Beat eggs till thick and lemon-colored. Add dry cake mix, pudding mix, water, and oil; beat 10 minutes at medium speed of electric mixer, scraping bowl occasionally. Pour into *ungreased* 10-inch tube pan with removable bottom. Bake at 350° till done, about 50 minutes. Meanwhile, combine powdered sugar and lemon juice; heat to boiling. *Leaving cake on pan bottom*, remove sides of pan from hot cake. Using 2-tined fork, prick holes in top of cake. Brush hot lemon mixture over entire cake. Cool. Remove pan bottom.

When researchers began work on commercial cake mixes, they created a machine to simulate the motion of a fast-moving train. They tested their cake mix packages on this machine to prove their durability during shipping. As a result of these and other tests, cake mixes began appearing in greater and greater numbers and flavors. Today it is easy to create a tasty cake mix variation as, for instance, Lemon Pudding Pound Cake.

The American Cuisine

Chapter 11

The American Cuisine

Throughout our history, great plenty has always been the American boast and blessing In 1631 John Winthrop, writing of a great feast, expressed his wonder at the "great store of provisions, fat hogs, kids, venison, poultry, geese, partridges, etc....

It was a great marvel, that so much people and such store of provisions could be gathered together at so few hours' warning."[1]

If John Winthrop could come back and visit us today, he would undoubtedly be overawed at the variety and abundance of food available today.

In the eyes of historians, American cookery is a newcomer — only 350 years old. In this short time, we have established a cuisine of which we can be proud. From the start it was innovative — it had to be. We have borrowed from everywhere — recipes from the classic cuisines of European cultures and from the comic-strip world of the Dagwood sandwich. All have been tested, the best improved upon, and the unworkable left by the wayside. And ours is now a rich and fascinating food heritage somewhere between tradition and modern technology, and incorporating the best of both.

The history of American cuisine starts with the modest food of the Indians who taught the hard-pressed Europeans where to find and how to grow the native foods and how to capture wild game. The colonists added their European culinary arts, imported foods, a touch of imagination, and a willingness to accept the new. The recipes they created form the rudiments of our great food heritage.

Once the joys and ruggedness of the wilderness had been experienced and conquered, many Americans found it preferable to life in any other environment. So, as the Eastern seaboard became more populated, the restless pioneers pierced the wilderness, moving into Pennsylvania, Ohio, Kentucky, and eventually on to the fertile Great Plains. In Lancaster County, Pennsylvania, a settlement of practical Pennsylvania Dutch worked to create a type of country-style cooking — rich in everything from shoofly pie to tasty pickles and relishes. The Southern plantation homes specialized in elegant dishes. Growing frontier settlements added to America's food heritage with simple, but distinctive cooking.

Moving still farther westward into the Indian buffalo hunting grounds, the pioneers found a land fraught with hardship and peril. They hewed away at the wilderness and with the largess of the forests — venison, game birds, wild fruits, and berries — built a legacy of new resourceful recipes. As they widened the belt of settlement, their cooking discoveries and ingenuity broadened the scope of our cuisine.

Later, immigrants from every corner of the world brought to this country many more significant culinary changes. They had much to contribute to their newly adopted nation. And we have taken to our hearts (or, rather our palates) the scores of new foods, ethnic, recipes, and cooking methods that were introduced by these immigrants.

Eager to establish themselves in their new home, the newcomers adapted as best they could to the American way. They learned to substitute and use American foodstuffs, creating new dishes with a traditional cooking style. Americans were also quick to learn the special seasonings of other lands and dishes such as tamale pie or goulash made with ground beef began to appear. These tasty improvisations, though hardly authentic, grew very popular. What used to be ethnic foods — zucchini, eggplant, pea pods, broccoli — were now a cherished part of this country's pantry.

Food habits and eating styles changed rapidly as Americans became more mobile. People traveled across the U.S.A. pursuing new careers, relocating on job transfers, or vacationing. As the opportunity increased to taste new flavor combinations and different dishes, the distribution nationwide of what had previously been called regional food naturally followed.

Now families in Chicago enjoy Texas-style chili. Boston baked beans are just as popular in Seattle as Boston. And, New Yorkers fix hush puppies and Creole jambalaya.

Travel by jets enables Americans to sample the cuisines of the most distant lands. And this foreign exposure also influenced eating habits and heightened appreciation of the genuine indigenous dishes. Nontravelers, too, shared the adventure as they found themselves inundated in a ceaseless flow of magazines, cook books, television programs, and culinary experts urging more daring cooking exploits; and gourmet clubs proved contagious. With typical Yankee enthusiasm, the nation pursued the new sophistication in cooking.

The native foods that kept the first settlers alive—corn, squash, pumpkins, sweet potatoes, various berries, and the Thanksgiving turkey—are still very much a part of our larder, and no doubt will remain so. But the quantity, quality, and variety of our present foodstuffs would be mind-boggling to those early settlers. In just the past few decades, improved production methods and ingenious marketing techniques have revolutionized the competence and sophistication of our cuisine. Cattle, hogs, and poultry mature faster and are larger. The dairies produce excellent milk and cheese. Experiments have created new strains of fruits and vegetables. The fishing industry brings an increased variety of fish. And our wines now rival or surpass those of Europe. Modern transportation, supermarkets, and scientific agriculture have placed at America's fingertips fresh foods from every corner of the world.

The uniqueness of the American cuisine would have pleased our forefathers who strove to make this a "new and different" country. Americans are always looking for something new and the tremendous array of convenience foods, is proof of the success of that quest. Although detractors put down convenience foods, citing cost, quality, or authenticity, the truth is Americans will accept only those products that are practical and useful—the poor ones are voted down in the marketplace. American cooks have proved their ability to combine the classics from the past with the best from the present and come up with whatever the heart desires.

The recipes in this chapter bring us up to date on the way we cook and feature dishes that have become American classics—strawberry shortcake, fried chicken, potato salad, and apple pie, to name a few. Added to the classics throughout the book, these recipes complete our sampling of America's flavorful dishes. They prove without a doubt that America does have a cuisine—bountiful, distinctive, dynamic.

As this book's story of America's food heritage has shown, many recipes have long histories. Perhaps one of the best examples is Green Corn Pudding (see recipe, page 27) now called scalloped corn. Basically, the recipe is the same as it was in colonial days, except saltine crackers have been added, giving it a fluffier texture. It's quite probable, however, that today's version tastes better because our corn is juicer and our dairy products are a better quality than those available to the colonists.

Meat-Vegetable Kabobs

2½ pounds boneless lamb *or* beef
½ cup soy sauce
¼ cup cooking oil
1 tablespoon dark corn syrup
2 cloves garlic, minced
1 teaspoon dry mustard
1 teaspoon ground ginger
3 green peppers
5 small firm tomatoes, quartered

Cut meat in 1½-inch cubes. In large bowl mix soy, oil, syrup, garlic, mustard, and ginger. Add meat; refrigerate several hours or overnight. Drain, reserving marinade. Cut peppers in 1-inch squares. Alternate meat, pepper, and tomato on skewers. Grill over *medium-hot* coals till desired doneness. (Allow 15 minutes for rare.) Baste often with marinade. Serves 8.

Although the original Near Eastern recipes for kabobs featured lamb cubes skewered on a stick, modern recipes use a wide variety of other meats, seafood, and vegetables. This tasty kabob recipe blends the marinated lamb cubes with green pepper and tomatoes.

Menu

Roast Turkey
Herb Stuffing
Mallowed Sweet Potatoes
Scalloped Corn Supreme
Cherry-Cran Salad
Hot Rolls   Butter
Pumpkin Pie
or
Mincemeat Pie
Beverage

*This dinner comprises dishes much
the same as the first Thanksgiving meals. The early settlers'
feast included wild turkey or
other game, cooked squash, pumpkin,
corn, fresh cranberries, and
baked beans. There is an important
difference, however, in
the preparation of the meal. Modern
cooking equipment and time-
saving appliances have replaced the
heavy iron pots and kettles
used in the fireplace. The convenience
of canned and packaged foods
saves today's homemaker much of the
time and work of the early settlers.*

Mallowed Sweet Potatoes

6 medium sweet potatoes,
cooked and peeled
¾ cup packed brown sugar

1 teaspoon salt
¼ cup butter *or* margarine
½ cup tiny marshmallows

Cut sweet potatoes into ½-inch thick slices; place in buttered 1½-quart casserole. Sprinkle with sugar and salt; dot with butter. Bake, uncovered, at 375° till glazed, about 25 minutes. Top with marshmallows; bake till marshmallows are lightly browned, about 5 minutes more. Makes 6 servings.

Scalloped Corn Supreme

1 17-ounce can cream-style
corn
1 cup milk
1 well-beaten egg
1 cup coarsely crumbled
saltine crackers
¼ cup finely chopped onion

3 tablespoons chopped
canned pimiento
¾ teaspoon salt
Dash pepper
½ cup coarsely crumbled
saltine crackers
1 tablespoon butter, melted

In saucepan combine corn and milk; heat through. Gradually stir in egg. Add 1 cup crumbs, onion, pimiento, salt, and pepper. Mix well. Pour into greased 8x1½-inch round baking dish. Combine ½ cup crumbs and butter. Sprinkle over corn. Bake at 350° for 20 minutes. Makes 6 servings.

Herb Stuffing

12 cups slightly dry bread
cubes
⅓ cup snipped parsley
⅓ cup finely chopped onion
1½ teaspoons salt
1 teaspoon ground sage

1 teaspoon dried thyme,
crushed
1 teaspoon dried rosemary,
crushed
1 cup chicken broth
6 tablespoons butter, melted

Combine bread, parsley, onion, salt, sage, thyme, and rosemary. Add broth and butter; toss lightly to mix. Use to stuff a 12-pound turkey or bake, covered, in 2-quart casserole at 325° till heated through, about 1 hour.

Cherry-Cran Salad

1 20-ounce can frozen
pitted tart red
cherries, thawed
1 3-ounce package cherry-
flavored gelatin
1 8-ounce can jellied
cranberry sauce
1 3-ounce package lemon-
flavored gelatin
1 cup boiling water

1 3-ounce package cream
cheese, softened
⅓ cup mayonnaise
1 8¼-ounce can crushed
pineapple
½ cup whipping cream
1 cup tiny marshmallows
2 tablespoons chopped
walnuts

Drain cherries; reserve syrup. If needed, add water to syrup to make 1 cup liquid; bring liquid to boiling. Remove from heat. Add cherry-flavored gelatin; stir to dissolve. With fork, break up cranberry sauce; stir into cherry gelatin till smooth. Stir in drained cherries. Turn into 9x9x2-inch dish; chill till mixture is *almost* firm.

Dissolve lemon-flavored gelatin in the boiling water. Beat cream cheese with mayonnaise; gradually add lemon gelatin. Stir in undrained pineapple; chill till partially set. Whip cream; fold into lemon mixture with marshmallows. Spread atop *almost* set cherry layer; sprinkle with nuts. Cover; chill till firm. Makes 12 servings.

Wine-Glazed Cornish Hens

1/4 cup chopped onion
2 tablespoons slivered
  almonds
2 tablespoons butter
4 cups dry bread cubes
2 medium oranges, peeled
  and diced

1/4 cup light raisins
1/2 teaspoon salt
6 1-pound ready-to-cook
  Rock Cornish game hens
  Salad oil
• • •
Wine Glaze

Cook and stir onion and almonds in butter about 5 minutes. Toss with dry bread cubes, oranges, raisins, and the salt. Rinse hens; pat dry with paper toweling. Season with salt and pepper. Lightly stuff birds with bread mixture. Skewer shut. Tie legs together; tie legs to tail. Place hens, breast up, on rack in shallow roasting pan. Brush

with salad oil; cover loosely. Roast at 375° for 30 minutes. Uncover; baste with Wine Glaze. Roast till done, about 1 hour more, basting frequently with the glaze. (When done, drumstick can be twisted easily.) Makes 6 servings.
Wine Glaze: Mix 1/2 cup Burgundy; 1/4 cup butter or margarine, melted; and 2 tablespoons orange juice.

Fortunately for America, their wine-making knowledge was among the traditions European immigrants brought with them. Attempts to grow their grapevine cuttings on the East Coast failed, but, the cuttings thrived in California. During the late 1800s, United States wineries began producing wine commercially.

Raisin-Coconut Bars

3/4 cup butter *or* margarine,
  softened
1/2 cup granulated sugar
2 cups all-purpose flour
3 eggs
1 teaspoon vanilla
1 cup packed brown sugar

3 tablespoons all-purpose
  flour
1 cup raisins
1/2 cup shredded coconut
1 cup sifted powdered sugar
1/2 teaspoon vanilla
  Milk

Cream together butter, granulated sugar, and 1/2 teaspoon salt. Stir in 2 cups flour. Pat onto bottom of 13x9x2-inch baking pan. Bake at 350° till lightly browned, about 20 minutes. Beat eggs slightly with fork; add 1 teaspoon vanilla. Gradually add brown sugar, beating just till blended. Add 3

tablespoons flour and 1/2 teaspoon salt. Stir in raisins and coconut. Spread over baked layer. Bake at 350° till golden brown, 20 to 25 minutes. Combine powdered sugar, 1/2 teaspoon vanilla, and enough milk to make a glaze consistency. Drizzle over warm cookies. Cool. Cut into bars. Makes 36 bars.

In 1873 the summer was so hot and dry that grapes dried on the vines in California's San Joaquin Valley. One enterprising grower, refusing to see a year's work wasted, shipped the dried grapes to a grocer friend in San Francisco. The grocer, just as enterprising, marketed them as "Peruvian delicacies" for no better reason than that a Peruvian ship was in port. The promotion was such a success that it inspired the beginnings of the raisin industry in the San Joaquin Valley.

Orange-Ginger Ham Grill

1/4 cup frozen orange juice
  concentrate, thawed
1/4 cup dry white wine
1 teaspoon dry mustard
1/4 teaspoon ground ginger

1 11/2- to 2-pound fully
  cooked ham slice, cut
  1 inch thick
6 canned pineapple slices

Combine orange juice concentrate, wine, mustard, and ginger; brush over ham. Grill over *medium* coals for 20 to 30 minutes, turning once and brushing with sauce occasionally. Grill pine-

apple slices alongside the ham, brushing frequently with sauce. Place pineapple atop ham during last 5 to 10 minutes of grilling. Garnish with orange slices, if desired. Serves 6.

Cooking every meal over an open fire is no longer necessary, thank heavens. However, the popularity of barbecuing illustrates that occasionally cooking this way can be fun. Perhaps our enjoyment of the special smoky flavor of grilled foods is an "inherited" taste.

Speedy Creamed Potatoes

In 4-quart pressure saucepan combine 4 cups cubed peeled potatoes, 1/3 cup chopped onion, 1/3 cup water, and 11/2 teaspoons salt. Close cover securely; cook 2 minutes with pressure regulator rocking gently (15 pounds

pressure). Immediately remove from heat; reduce pressure quickly by placing under cold running water. Add 1/2 cup light cream and 2 tablespoons snipped parsley. Heat through, uncovered, stirring gently. Makes 6 servings.

Food cooks in a pressure saucepan in a third of the time required otherwise. As the pressure increases in the pan so does the temperature; the combination cooks the food quickly.

Favorite Fried Chicken

Cut up one 2½- to 3-pound ready-to-cook chicken. In paper or plastic bag combine ⅓ cup all-purpose flour, 1 teaspoon salt, 1 teaspoon paprika, and ¼ teaspoon pepper. Add 2 or 3 pieces chicken at a time; shake well to coat pieces evenly. Dry on rack. Pour cooking oil into 12-inch skillet to depth of ¼ inch. Brown the chicken slowly, turning with tongs. Reduce heat. Cover tightly; cook till tender, 30 to 40 minutes. Uncover last 10 minutes. Serves 4.

Batter-Fried Chicken

Simmer one 2- to 2½-pound ready-to-cook broiler-fryer chicken, cut up, in salted water for 20 minutes; drain. Combine 1 cup pancake mix and ½ teaspoon salt; stir in ¾ cup water. Beat 2 minutes. Dip chicken in batter; drain on rack over waxed paper. In heavy skillet at least 3 inches deep, pour cooking oil to depth of 1¼ inches; heat to 350°. Regulate heat so chicken fries at 325°. Fry a few pieces at a time till golden, about 5 minutes. Drain. Serves 4.

Oven Chicken Romano

Question: *"What is the all-American picnic favorite?"* Answer: *"fried chicken." Various parts of the country have their own traditional methods of preparing fried chicken, perhaps simmering in milk or deep-fat frying. No matter how it's fixed—oven-baked, skillet-fried, or batter-coated —it is an excellent choice to serve indoors or out.*

Looking for an easy version of fried chicken? Then, try *Oven Chicken Romano.* Simply dip the chicken pieces into melted butter, coat with a superbly cheese-seasoned crumb mixture, and bake. The chicken browns beautifully in the oven and has a tasty, crunchy coating.

2 2½- to 3-pound ready-to-cook broiler-fryer chickens, cut up
1 cup butter, melted

1⅓ cups seasoned fine dry bread crumbs
⅔ cup grated Romano cheese
½ cup snipped parsley

Dip chicken into butter; roll in a mixture of bread crumbs, cheese, and parsley. Place pieces, skin side up, not touching in two greased large shallow baking pans. Top with remaining butter and crumb mixture. Bake at 375° till done, about 1 hour. Garnish with parsley, if desired. Makes 8 servings.

Pheasant with Wild Rice

Cook ½ cup chopped onion in ¼ cup butter till tender. Add 2 cups water; ⅔ cup wild rice, rinsed; and 1 teaspoon salt. Cover; cook till rice is tender, 35 to 40 minutes. Stir in one 6-ounce can sliced mushrooms, drained and ½ teaspoon ground sage. Season cavities of two 1½- to 3-pound ready-to-cook pheasants with salt; stuff with rice mixture. Tie legs together, then tie to tail. Place 6 to 8 slices bacon over pheasant breasts. Roast at 350° till done, 1 to 2½ hours depending on size of birds. Makes 6 to 8 servings.

Fondued Flank Steak

1 1-pound beef flank steak
½ cup cooking oil
½ cup red wine
2 tablespoons snipped candied ginger
2 tablespoons catsup
2 tablespoons molasses
1 clove garlic, minced
½ teaspoon curry powder
Cooking oil

Bias-cut steak in very thin 3x1-inch strips. Combine ½ cup oil, wine, snipped ginger, catsup, molasses, garlic, curry powder, ½ teaspoon salt, and ½ teaspoon pepper. Pour oil mixture over steak. Cover; marinate 2 hours at room temperature. Drain well; pat dry with paper toweling. Thread on bamboo skewers accordion style. Pour cooking oil into metal fondue cooker to no more than ½ capacity or to depth of 2 inches. Heat oil in fondue cooker over range to 425°. Add 1 teaspoon salt. Transfer cooker to fondue burner. Have skewered meat strips at room temperature on serving plate. Fry in hot oil till desired doneness, 1 to 2 minutes. Makes 4 servings.

Sweet Pickle Meat Loaf

2 beaten eggs
1 cup soft bread crumbs
¼ cup catsup
¼ cup finely chopped onion
2 tablespoons sweet pickle relish
1 tablespoon prepared mustard
1 teaspoon prepared horseradish
1½ pounds ground beef
¼ cup catsup

Mix eggs, bread crumbs, ¼ cup catsup, onion, pickle relish, mustard, horseradish, and 1 teaspoon salt. Add ground beef and mix well. Shape mixture into a 9x4-inch loaf; place in 10x6x2-inch baking dish. Bake at 350° for 1 hour. Spread with ¼ cup catsup. Bake 15 minutes more. Makes 6 to 8 servings.

Tamale Pie

1 pound ground beef
1 cup chopped onion
1 cup chopped green pepper
2 8-ounce cans tomato sauce
1 12-ounce can whole kernel corn, drained
½ cup chopped pitted ripe olives
1 clove garlic, minced
1 tablespoon sugar
2 to 3 teaspoons chili powder
1½ cups shredded sharp American cheese (6 ounces)
¾ cup yellow cornmeal
2 cups cold water
1 tablespoon butter

In large skillet cook beef, onion, and green pepper till meat is lightly browned and vegetables are tender. Drain off fat. Stir in tomato sauce, corn, olives, garlic, sugar, chili powder, 1 teaspoon salt, and dash pepper. Simmer till thick, 20 to 25 minutes. Add cheese; stir till melted. Turn into a well-greased 9x9x2-inch baking dish. For topping, stir cornmeal and ½ teaspoon salt into cold water. Cook and stir till thick. Stir in butter. Spoon over hot meat mixture. Bake at 375° about 40 minutes. Serves 6.

Cioppino

¼ cup chopped green pepper
2 tablespoons finely
   chopped onion
1 clove garlic, minced
1 tablespoon cooking oil
1 16-ounce can tomatoes,
   cut up
1 8-ounce can tomato sauce
½ cup dry red wine
3 tablespoons snipped
   parsley
½ teaspoon salt

¼ teaspoon dried oregano,
   crushed
¼ teaspoon dried basil,
   crushed
   Dash pepper
      • • •
1 pound frozen perch
   fillets, thawed
1 7½-ounce can minced clams
1 4½-ounce can shrimp,
   drained

In large saucepan cook green pepper, onion, and garlic in oil till tender but not brown. Add undrained tomatoes, tomato sauce, wine, parsley, salt, oregano, basil, and pepper. Bring to boiling. Reduce heat; cover and simmer 20 minutes. Skin perch fillets. Cut fillets into pieces, removing any bones. Add fish to tomato mixture; simmer, covered, 5 minutes. Add undrained clams and shrimp; simmer, covered, about 3 minutes more. Makes 6 servings.

Pictured opposite: A delectable fish stew with an Italian name and ingredients, *Cioppino* supposedly originated on the Monterey peninsula and was popularized at Fisherman's Wharf in San Francisco. Although many variations exist, this easy version is made with frozen fish, canned shrimp, and clams. The seafood simmers in a richly seasoned tomato, herb, and red wine broth. Delight your guests by ladling up generous servings of this soup.

Chicken Chop Suey

1 pound chicken breasts,
   skinned and boned
¼ cup cooking oil
2 cups sliced onions
2 cups sliced fresh
   mushrooms
½ cup sliced water
   chestnuts
⅓ cup chopped green pepper

¼ cup chopped canned
   pimiento
1 16-ounce can chop suey
   vegetables, drained
1 13¾-ounce can chicken
   broth
⅓ cup soy sauce
2 tablespoons cornstarch
   Hot cooked rice

Cut skinned and boned chicken breasts into 2x½-inch strips. In large heavy skillet or wok, cook chicken strips quickly in hot oil, about 2 minutes, stirring constantly. Add sliced onions, sliced fresh mushrooms, water chestnuts, green pepper, and pimiento. Cook and stir 2 minutes more. Add chop suey vegetables, chicken broth, and soy sauce. Bring the mixture to boiling; cover and cook for 2 to 3 minutes over low heat. Slowly blend ¼ cup cold water into the cornstarch. Stir cornstarch mixture into vegetable mixture. Cook, stirring constantly, till mixture is thickened and bubbly. Serve over hot cooked rice. Pass additional soy sauce, if desired. Makes 6 servings.

Because early California Chinese restaurants catered to the occidental tastes of their non-Chinese customers, a special category of cooking called American-Chinese was developed. Most popular of the American-Chinese dishes is chop suey, a flavorful stew served with rice and soy sauce. Even after World War II when Americans learned to appreciate genuine Chinese food, this dish retained its place on restaurant and home menus.

Five-Spice Chicken

1 teaspoon ground cinnamon
1 teaspoon crushed aniseed
½ teaspoon salt
¼ teaspoon ground allspice
⅛ teaspoon ground cloves
⅛ teaspoon freshly ground
   pepper
4 whole chicken breasts

2 tablespoons peanut oil *or*
   cooking oil
1 clove garlic, minced
¾ cup unsweetened pineapple
   juice
      • • •
   Parsley

Combine ground cinnamon, crushed aniseed, salt, ground allspice, cloves, and pepper. Rub the chicken breasts with *1 teaspoon* of the spice mixture. (Save remainder of mixture for another day.) Heat peanut or cooking oil and garlic in skillet. Add the chicken breasts to the hot oil; brown on both sides. Reduce heat. Add unsweetened pineapple juice; simmer, covered, till chicken is tender, about 35 minutes. Transfer chicken breasts to platter; spoon sauce over chicken. Garnish with parsley. Makes 4 servings.

Macaroni and Cheese

1½ cups elbow macaroni
3 tablespoons butter
2 tablespoons all-purpose
    flour
2 cups milk

2 cups cubed sharp
    American cheese
¼ cup finely chopped onion
    (optional)
1 tomato, sliced

Cook macaroni in boiling salted water till tender; drain. In saucepan melt butter; blend in flour, ½ teaspoon salt, and dash pepper. Add milk; cook and stir till thickened and bubbly. Add cheese and onion, if desired; cook and stir till cheese melts. Mix cheese sauce with macaroni. Turn into 1½-quart casserole. Sprinkle tomato slices with salt; arrange atop macaroni. Bake at 350° till heated through, 35 to 40 minutes. Makes 6 servings.

Ham Cups with Curried Peas

1 beaten egg
2 tablespoons milk
¾ cup soft bread crumbs
3 tablespoons finely
    chopped onion

½ teaspoon dry mustard
½ pound ground fully cooked
    ham
Curried Peas

In mixing bowl combine egg, milk, soft bread crumbs, onion, and mustard; add ground ham and mix well. Shape ham mixture into two 4-inch patties; fit each into a 6-ounce custard cup to form a shell. Cook, uncovered, in countertop microwave oven till meat shells are cooked, about 4 minutes. Remove from oven; keep warm. Prepare Curried Peas. Lift meat shells from custard cups to serving plate; fill with Curried Peas. Makes 2 servings.

Curried Peas: In 2-cup glass measuring cup heat 1 tablespoon butter or margarine and ½ teaspoon curry powder in microwave oven till butter melts, about 20 seconds. Stir in 1 tablespoon all-purpose flour, ⅛ teaspoon salt, and dash pepper. Stir in ⅔ cup milk. Cook in microwave oven till thickened, about 2 minutes; stir every 30 seconds. Fold in one 8½-ounce can peas, drained. Cook in microwave oven till hot, about 30 seconds.

Macroburger

½ cup dry soybeans, rinsed
¼ cup millet
2 tablespoons soy sauce
1 tablespoon cooking oil
½ teaspoon dried thyme,
    crushed
¼ teaspoon dried dillweed,
    crushed
¼ teaspoon chili powder
⅛ teaspoon ground cumin
    Dash cayenne
1 clove garlic, minced
½ cup finely chopped onion

½ cup fine dry bread crumbs
¼ cup finely chopped celery
¼ cup grated carrot
1 tablespoon finely
    chopped green pepper
    Cooking oil
8 slices Monterey Jack
    cheese
16 slices whole wheat bread,
    toasted
    Lettuce leaves
    Tomato slices

Combine soybeans and 1¾ cups water. Soak overnight. Cover and cook till tender, about 3 hours. Drain. Meanwhile, combine millet and 1 cup water in saucepan. Bring to a boil; reduce heat. Cover and cook, stirring often, till tender, 40 to 45 minutes. In blender container combine soybeans, soy sauce, 1 tablespoon oil, herbs and spices, garlic, and 3 tablespoons water.

Cover; blend thoroughly, stopping occasionally to push mixture down. Remove from blender. Mix in millet, onion, crumbs, celery, carrot, and green pepper. Shape into patties, using ⅓ cup mixture for each. Brown in hot oil, about 3 minutes on each side. Top with a cheese slice when browning second side. Serve between bread slices with lettuce and tomato. Makes 8.

Grilled Reubens

12 slices pumpernickel *or*
    rye bread
    • • •
½ cup Thousand Island salad
    dressing
6 slices Swiss cheese

¾ cup well-drained
    sauerkraut
    Thinly sliced cooked *or*
    canned corned beef
    Butter *or* margarine,
    softened

Spread *half* the pumpernickel or rye bread with Thousand Island dressing; top each with *1 slice* Swiss cheese, *2 tablespoons* well-drained sauerkraut, a few slices cooked or canned corned beef, and a second bread slice. Spread tops and bottoms of sandwiches with softened butter. Grill on both sides till hot and cheese melts. Serve hot. Makes 6 sandwiches.

A restaurant cook from Omaha, Nebraska, won the National Sandwich Idea Contest in 1956 with his version of "The Reuben." Always on the lookout for a good thing, the whole country soon adopted this flavorful grilled cheese, corned beef, and sauerkraut combination.

Submarine Sandwich

Bake one giant brown-and-serve French roll (about 8 inches long) according to package directions. Split French roll lengthwise. Scoop out some of the center. Spread roll generously with prepared mustard, garlic butter, *or* mayonnaise or salad dressing mixed with curry powder. Line the bottom of roll with leaf lettuce. Pile on slices of cooked corned beef, boiled ham, bologna, salami, pickled tongue, cooked chicken, tuna, and herring as desired. Add slices of American and Swiss cheese, onion, green and ripe olives, and dill pickle. Replace top of roll; anchor with wooden picks. Serves 1.

The Submarine Sandwich originated in a sandwich shop nestled among the wharves of New Orleans where it's called a Poor Boy. Benny and Clovis Martin can take credit for providing us with this substantial sandwich. To serve their regular customers — hardworking banana carriers and longshoremen — during the depression, they came up with a specially baked French bread on which they could pile some roast beef or ham. It was inexpensive, filling, and nutritious. With their usual ingenuity, Americans soon expanded the single layer of meat into layers of meats, cheese, relish, and whatever is left over in the refrigerator, as popularized by the comic strip character, Dagwood Bumstead.

Skilletburgers

1 pound ground beef
1 cup chopped onion
1 cup chopped celery
    • • •
1 10¾-ounce can condensed
    tomato soup
1 8-ounce can tomato sauce

¾ teaspoon salt
¼ teaspoon chili powder
    Dash bottled hot pepper
    sauce
    Hamburger buns, split and
    toasted

In skillet brown ground beef, breaking up meat. Add chopped onion and chopped celery; cook till vegetables are tender but not brown. Drain off excess fat. Add condensed tomato soup, tomato sauce, salt, chili powder, and hot pepper sauce; stir till blended. Simmer meat mixture, uncovered, about 30 minutes. Spoon ground beef mixture into toasted buns. Serves 8 to 10.

Super Dagwood

2 12-inch loaves unsliced
    dark rye *or* white bread
½ cup butter *or* margarine,
    softened
16 slices fully cooked ham
12 slices Provolone cheese
    (12 ounces)

1 cup Thousand Island salad
    dressing
    Leaf lettuce
2 tomatoes, thinly sliced
14 *or* 16 slices cooked
    turkey
16 to 20 slices salami

Cut *each* loaf of dark rye or white bread *lengthwise* into four slices; spread evenly with butter or margarine. For *each loaf*, place bottom slice on platter or board; top with *half* the sliced ham and cheese. Spread with some of the salad dressing. Place second slice of bread atop cheese and ham; top with lettuce, *half* the tomato slices, and more salad dressing. Add third slice bread; top with *half* the sliced turkey and salami and more salad dressing. Add top slice bread. Skewer loaves from top to bottom; cut into serving-size slices. Makes 14 servings.

(Sandwich may be made ahead, covered with clear plastic wrap or foil, and chilled, if desired.)

Blender Mayonnaise

1 large egg
1 tablespoon vinegar
½ teaspoon salt
¼ teaspoon dry mustard

⅛ teaspoon paprika
Dash cayenne
1 cup salad oil
1 tablespoon lemon juice

Put egg, vinegar, salt, dry mustard, paprika, and cayenne in blender container; cover and blend till mixed very thoroughly. With blender running slowly, *gradually pour half* of the salad oil into blender container. (When necessary, stop blender and use rubber spatula to scrape sides.) Add lemon juice to mixture in blender container; slowly pour remaining salad oil into blender container with the blender running slowly. Makes about 1¼ cups.

Salad Burgers

¼ cup vinegar
¼ cup water
2 tablespoons sugar
1 teaspoon salt
⅛ teaspoon pepper
1 cup chopped onion
1 large tomato, diced

½ medium cucumber, thinly
   sliced
2 pounds ground beef
1½ teaspoons salt
⅛ teaspoon pepper
8 hamburger buns, split and
   toasted

Mix vinegar, water, sugar, 1 teaspoon salt, and ⅛ teaspoon pepper. Add vegetables. Cover; chill thoroughly. Mix beef, 1½ teaspoons salt, and ⅛ teaspoon pepper; shape into 16 patties. Broil beef patties 3 inches from heat till done, about 8 minutes, turning once. Place *half* the beef patties on bottom of buns. Drain vegetable mixture; spoon some onto patties. Top with remaining beef patties and more vegetables. Add bun tops. Serves 8.

The hamburger on a bun has long been regarded as a classic American sandwich. *Salad Burgers* expands on this popular sandwich idea and offers you a deliciously different version.

Perfect White Bread

In large mixing bowl combine 2½ cups all-purpose flour and 1 package active dry yeast. Heat together 2¼ cups milk, 2 tablespoons sugar, 1 tablespoon shortening, and 2 teaspoons salt just till warm (115-120°), stirring constantly. Add to dry mixture. Beat at low speed of electric mixer for ½ minute, scraping sides. Beat 3 minutes at high speed. By hand, stir in enough of 3¼ to 3¾ cups all-purpose flour to make a moderately stiff dough. Turn out onto lightly floured surface; knead till smooth and elastic, 8 to 10 minutes. Shape into ball. Place in greased bowl, turning once. Cover; let rise in warm place until double (1¼ hours). Punch down; turn out on lightly floured surface. Divide in half. Cover; let rest 10 minutes. Shape into two loaves; place in two greased 8½x4½x2½-inch loaf pans. Cover and let rise till double (45 to 60 minutes). Bake at 375° about 45 minutes. If tops brown too fast, cover with foil last 15 minutes. Remove from pans; cool. Makes 2 loaves.

Legend has it that bread wasn't leavened until an ancient Egyptian baker set some dough aside and discovered much later that it had expanded and soured from wild yeast plants in the air. He baked it anyway and created the first leavened bread. Breadmaking has come a long way since then — and even since colonial bakers depended on home-made "starters." Today's homemaker can take advantage of packaged active dry yeast to make plump loaves of fine-textured breads such as Perfect White Bread.

Caramel-Pecan Rolls

3½ to 4 cups all-purpose
   flour
1 package active dry yeast
1 cup milk
¾ cup granulated sugar
¼ cup shortening
1 teaspoon salt
2 eggs

3 tablespoons butter,
   melted
1 teaspoon ground cinnamon
⅔ cup packed brown sugar
¼ cup butter *or* margarine
2 tablespoons light corn
   syrup
½ cup chopped pecans

In large mixing bowl combine *2 cups* flour and yeast. Heat and stir milk, ¼ *cup* granulated sugar, shortening, and salt just till warm (115-120°). Add to dry mixture in bowl; add eggs. Beat at low speed of electric mixer for ½ minute, scraping bowl. Beat 3 minutes at high speed. By hand, stir in enough of remaining flour to make a moderately stiff dough. Knead on floured surface till smooth, 8 to 10 minutes. Shape into ball. Place in greased bowl; turn once. Cover; let rise till double, 45 to 60 minutes.

Punch down; divide in half. Cover; let rest 10 minutes. Roll *each half* to 12x8-inch rectangle. Brush with the melted butter. Combine remaining ½ cup granulated sugar and cinnamon; sprinkle over dough. Roll each up jelly-roll style, starting with long side; seal seams. Slice each roll into 12 pieces. In saucepan mix brown sugar, ¼ cup butter, and corn syrup; cook and stir till butter melts. Distribute mixture evenly in two 9x1½-inch round baking pans. Top with nuts. Place 12 rolls, cut side down, in each prepared pan. Cover; let rise till double (about 30 minutes). Bake at 375° for 18 to 20 minutes. Cool 30 seconds; invert on rack and remove pans. Makes 24 rolls.

Best Tomato Catsup

1½ inches stick cinnamon
1 cup white vinegar
1½ teaspoons whole cloves
1 teaspoon celery seed

8 pounds tomatoes
1 medium onion, chopped
¼ teaspoon cayenne
1 cup sugar

Break cinnamon. In saucepan combine cinnamon, vinegar, cloves, and celery seed. Cover; bring to a boil. Remove from heat; let stand. Wash and core tomatoes; quarter into large kettle. Add onion and cayenne. Bring to boil; cook 15 minutes, stirring often. Put tomatoes through food mill or coarse sieve. Add sugar to tomatoes. *Simmer* briskly till mixture is reduced to half (measure depth with wooden ruler at beginning and end), 1½ to 2 hours. Strain vinegar mixture into tomato mixture; discard spices. Stir in 4 teaspoons salt. Simmer till of desired consistency, about 30 minutes; stir often. Fill hot pint jars with hot tomato mixture to within ½ inch of top; wipe jar rims and adjust lids. Process in boiling water bath 5 minutes (start counting time when water covering jars returns to boiling). Makes 2 pints.

Families concerned about their rising food budgets are discovering that home food canning is an economical way to use the fresh produce of the rapidly multiplying backyard garden. Other homemakers do home canning chiefly for the convenience of having the prepared foods on hand and ready to use. Whatever their reason for learning this skill, canners derive a sense of personal satisfaction and accomplishment from completing a rewarding task.

Natural limestone caves provide ideal conditions for producing blue-veined cheeses. The most famous such caves are in Roquefort, France, but near Fairbault, Minnesota, sandstone caves are used to ripen an excellent domestic blue cheese.

Blue Cheese-Onion Dip

1½ cups dairy sour cream
2 tablespoons onion
    soup mix
½ cup crumbled blue cheese

Sliced pimiento-stuffed
    green olives (optional)
Vegetable dippers

In mixing bowl combine dairy sour cream and onion soup mix. Mix until ingredients are thoroughly blended. Stir in crumbled blue cheese. Chill until ready to serve. Garnish with sliced pimiento-stuffed green olives, if desired. Serve dip with assorted vegetable dippers. Makes 2 cups.

Potlucks and casual social gatherings such as church suppers, company picnics, family reunions, and neighborhood block parties are truly an American tradition. The affairs are a delightful blend of lively conversation, warm-hearted laughter, and lots of good eating. A tasty vegetable dish to take to a potluck dinner is Carrot-Cheddar Casserole.

Carrot-Cheddar Casserole

1 pound carrots, cut up
2 tablespoons butter *or*
    margarine
• • •
1½ cups milk

1 cup shredded Cheddar
    cheese (4 ounces)
¾ cup coarsely crushed
    saltine crackers
2 well-beaten eggs

Cook carrots, covered, in small amount of boiling salted water for 15 to 20 minutes. Drain thoroughly. Stir butter or margarine into the carrots and mash coarsely with a fork. Combine the mashed carrots, milk, cheese, cracker crumbs, beaten eggs, and 1 teaspoon salt; mix well. Turn the carrot mixture into an 8x8x2-inch baking dish. Bake at 325° till a knife inserted just off-center comes out clean, 35 to 40 minutes. Makes 6 servings.

Waldorf Salad

3 cups diced apples
½ cup chopped celery
½ cup red grapes, halved
    and seeded
½ cup chopped walnuts

½ cup mayonnaise *or* salad
    dressing
1 tablespoon sugar
½ teaspoon lemon juice
½ cup whipping cream

Combine apples, celery, grapes, and walnuts. Combine mayonnaise, sugar, and lemon juice. Whip cream till soft peaks form; fold into mayonnaise mixture. Fold all into fruit mixture. Chill. Makes 6 servings.

In the fifties we were becoming more weight conscious. And with the trend toward lighter eating, the small side-dish salads grew into whole meals atop crisp lettuce. Soon, Americans began creating all types of main-dish salads, from molded ones with tuna to the the tossed lettuce ones with ham.

Chef's Salad Bowl

1 clove garlic, halved
1 medium head lettuce, torn
    in bite-size pieces
1 cup chopped cucumber
2 tomatoes, cut in wedges
3 hard-cooked eggs
3 small carrots, cut in
    strips (1 cup)
1 cup fully cooked ham cut
    in strips (5 ounces)
1 cup cooked chicken cut
    in strips
Salt

Freshly ground pepper
• • •
½ cup salad oil
3 tablespoons vinegar
1 tablespoon prepared
    horseradish
½ teaspoon Worcestershire
    sauce
½ teaspoon salt
½ teaspoon pepper
2 drops bottled hot pepper
    sauce

Rub large salad bowl with cut clove of garlic. In bowl combine lettuce, cucumber, and tomato. Quarter eggs. Arrange eggs, carrot strips, ham strips, and chicken strips on top of the salad. Sprinkle with salt and freshly ground pepper. In screw-top jar combine oil, vinegar, horseradish, Worcestershire, the ½ teaspoon salt, pepper, and hot pepper sauce. Shake till well mixed. Pour over salad and toss lightly till well coated. Makes 8 servings.

Calico Potato Salad

7 medium potatoes, cooked, peeled, and diced	2 hard-cooked eggs
½ cup diced cucumber	⅓ cup mayonnaise
½ cup chopped onion	3 tablespoons vinegar
¼ cup chopped green pepper	2 tablespoons sugar
3 tablespoons chopped canned pimiento	1 tablespoon prepared mustard
¾ teaspoon celery seed	½ cup whipping cream
	Lettuce

Combine potatoes, cucumber, onion, green pepper, pimiento, celery seed, 1½ teaspoons salt, and ¼ teaspoon pepper. Coarsely chop eggs. Add to potato mixture; chill. Combine mayonnaise, vinegar, sugar, and mustard; whip cream and fold into mayonnaise mixture. A ½-hour before serving, toss with potato mixture. To serve, spoon into lettuce-lined bowl. Serves 6 to 8.

Perfect Apple Pie

6 to 8 tart apples, peeled, cored, and thinly sliced (6 cups)*	Dash ground nutmeg
	Dash salt
¾ to 1 cup sugar	Pastry for 2-crust 9-inch pie (see recipe, page 351)
2 tablespoons all-purpose flour	2 tablespoons butter *or* margarine
½ to 1 teaspoon ground cinnamon	Sugar

(If apples lack tartness, sprinkle with about 1 tablespoon lemon juice.) Combine ¾ to 1 cup sugar, flour, ground cinnamon, ground nutmeg, and salt; mix with thinly sliced apples. Line 9-inch pie plate with pastry. Fill with apple mixture; dot with butter. Adjust top crust, cutting slits for escape of steam; seal and flute. Sprinkle with sugar. Bake at 400° till done, about 50 minutes. (If necessary, cover edge with foil to prevent overbrowning.)

Or, use two 20-ounce cans pie-sliced apples, drained (about 5 cups).

Lemon Meringue Pie

3 egg yolks	½ teaspoon grated lemon peel
1½ cups sugar	⅓ cup lemon juice
3 tablespoons cornstarch	1 *baked* 9-inch pastry shell, cooled (see recipe, page 351)
3 tablespoons all-purpose flour	Meringue
2 tablespoons butter *or* margarine	

Beat egg yolks slightly with fork; set aside. In medium saucepan thoroughly combine sugar, cornstarch, all-purpose flour, and dash salt. Gradually add 1½ cups hot water to the mixture, stirring constantly. Cook and stir over high heat till the mixture comes to boiling. Reduce the heat; cook 2 minutes more, stirring constantly.

Stir a moderate amount of hot mixture into egg yolks, then immediately return to remaining hot mixture in saucepan. Bring to boiling and cook 2 minutes, stirring constantly. Remove from heat. Add butter or margarine and grated lemon peel. Slowly add lemon juice while stirring constantly. Pour hot filling into cooled pastry shell. Spread Meringue atop hot filling. Bake the pie at 350° till peaks are golden brown, 12 to 15 minutes. Cool.

Meringue: In a mixing bowl combine 3 egg whites, ½ teaspoon vanilla, and ¼ teaspoon cream of tartar. Beat with electric mixer till soft peaks form. Gradually add 6 tablespoons sugar, beating the meringue till stiff and glossy peaks form and all the sugar is dissolved. Spread the meringue over the hot lemon pie filling; carefully seal all around the edge of the pastry so there will be no shrinking.

This spectacular Lemon Meringue Pie *is an all-time dessert classic. Fluffy meringue is piled high on a pleasantly tart, creamy lemon filling and baked to a golden perfection. Can you think of a better use for fresh lemons from the Florida and California groves?*

Pictured opposite: Elegant *Straw-berry Shortcake* tastes as delicious as it looks. Luscious, sweetened fresh strawberries and whipped cream fill a tender, flaky shortcake and grace the top.

Strawberry Shortcake

4 cups all-purpose flour
1/4 cup sugar
2 tablespoons baking powder
1 cup butter *or* margarine
2 beaten eggs

1 1/3 cups light cream
1 cup whipping cream
Butter *or* margarine
3 to 4 cups sliced fresh strawberries, sweetened

Stir together dry ingredients and 1 tea-spoon salt; cut in 1 cup butter to form coarse crumbs. Mix eggs and light cream; stir into dry ingredients. Spread into two greased 8x1½-inch round bak-ing pans; build up edges. Bake at 450° about 15 minutes. Remove from pans; cool 5 minutes. Whip cream. Spread one layer with butter. Layer berries and cream in middle and atop. Serves 8.

Red Devil's Food Cake

1¾ cups sugar
½ cup shortening
3 egg yolks
1 teaspoon vanilla
2½ cups sifted cake flour

½ cup unsweetened cocoa powder
1½ teaspoons baking soda
1⅓ cups cold water
3 egg whites

Cream *1 cup* sugar and shortening till light. Add egg yolks, one at a time, and vanilla; beat well after each addition. Sift together cake flour, cocoa, soda, and 1 teaspoon salt; add to creamed mixture alternately with the cold wa-ter, beating well after each addition. Beat egg whites to soft peaks; gradu-ally add remaining sugar, beating till stiff peaks form. Fold into batter; blend well. Turn mixture into two greased and lightly floured 9x1½-inch round baking pans. Bake at 350° till cake tests done, 30 to 35 minutes.

Pineapple Chiffon Cake

Chiffon cake was invented by a professional baker and introduced in May, 1948. Made with cooking oil instead of solid shortening and beaten—not creamed—this light cake was the first new cake to have been developed in one hundred years of baking.

2¼ cups sifted cake flour
1½ cups sugar
1 tablespoon baking powder
½ cup cooking oil
5 egg yolks

¾ cup unsweetened pineapple juice
1 cup egg whites (8)
½ teaspoon cream of tartar
Pineapple Topping

Sift together flour, sugar, baking pow-der, and 1 teaspoon salt. Make well in center and add in order: oil, yolks, and juice. Beat smooth. In large mixing bowl beat egg whites and cream of tar-tar to form *very stiff peaks.* Pour batter in thin stream over all egg white sur-face; fold in gently. Bake in *ungreased* 10-inch tube pan at 350° for 60 min-utes. Invert; cool. Split into 2 layers. Fill and frost with Pineapple Topping. *Pineapple Topping:* Whip 2 cups whipping cream; fold in one 20-ounce can crushed pineapple, well drained.

Nutty Brownies

Brownie lovers come in all sizes and ages. The rich, moist, all-American chocolate brownie can be one of two types—the chewy, fudgy kind like Nutty Brownies *or a cake-like bar with a fluffier texture.*

1 cup sugar
1/3 cup shortening
2 eggs
2 1-ounce squares unsweetened chocolate, melted and cooled

1 teaspoon vanilla
2/3 cup all-purpose flour
½ teaspoon baking powder
¼ teaspoon salt
½ cup chopped walnuts
Chocolate Frosting

Cream sugar, shortening, and eggs. Stir in chocolate and vanilla. Mix dry ingre-dients; stir into sugar mixture. Stir in nuts. Bake in greased 9x9x2-inch bak-ing pan at 350° for 25 to 30 minutes. Cool; frost with Chocolate Frosting. *Chocolate Frosting:* Heat one 1-ounce square unsweetened chocolate and 1 tablespoon butter till melted; stir con-stantly. Add 1 cup sifted powdered sugar, 2 tablespoons water, and ½ teaspoon vanilla. Beat till spreadable.

Very Best Fruitcake

8 ounces pitted dates 　chopped (1½ cups)	2 cups all-purpose flour
8 ounces candied pineapple, 　chopped (1 cup)	1 cup shortening
8 ounces candied cherries, 　quartered (1 cup)	½ cup sugar
8 ounces raisins (1 cup)	½ cup honey
4 ounces candied lemon 　peel, chopped (½ cup)	5 eggs
4 ounces candied orange 　peel, chopped (½ cup)	1 teaspoon salt
1 cup broken walnuts	1 teaspoon baking powder
1 cup broken pecans	1 teaspoon ground allspice
	½ teaspoon ground nutmeg
	½ teaspoon ground cloves
	⅓ cup orange *or* grape juice
	¼ cup wine, brandy, *or* 　fruit juice

Combine dates, pineapple, cherries, raisins, lemon peel, orange peel, walnuts, and pecans. Toss with ¼ *cup* of the flour. Cream shortening and sugar. Stir in honey. Add eggs, one at a time, beating well after each. Combine remaining flour, salt, baking powder, and spices. Add to creamed mixture alternately with ⅓ cup orange or grape juice; beat well. Pour batter over floured fruits; mix well. Pour into two greased and floured 11x4x3-inch loaf pans. Bake at 275° till done, about 2 hours. Cool. Soak cheesecloth in wine, brandy, or fruit juice. Wrap fruitcakes in cheesecloth, then in foil. Store in cool place 1 to 2 weeks. Brush fruitcakes with corn syrup and decorate with candied fruits before serving, if desired. Makes 2 loaves.

Homemade Custard Ice Cream

When the mechanical refrigerator replaced the icebox in the thirties, homemade ice cream became an even greater part of the American way of life. Now it could be made effortlessly in freezer trays instead of by the old muscle-building, hand-cranking method.

2 cups milk	2 teaspoons vanilla
¾ cup sugar	2 stiffly beaten egg whites
2 beaten egg yolks	1 cup whipping cream

In a heavy saucepan combine milk, sugar, egg yolks, and ¼ teaspoon salt. Cook the mixture over medium-low heat, stirring constantly, till mixture coats a metal spoon. Stir in vanilla. Cool. Fold custard mixture into the stiffly beaten egg whites. Chill thoroughly. Whip the cream till thick and custard-like. Fold cream into the chilled custard mixture. Pour into two 3-cup refrigerator trays. Place in freezer; stir every 30 minutes for the first 1½ hours. Freeze till firm. Makes 5½ cups.

Chocolate-Macaroon Ice Cream: Prepare Ice Cream as above, *except* fold 1 cup crumbled chocolate wafers and 1 cup crumbled soft coconut macaroons along with whipped cream into custard.

Date-Nut Ice Cream: Prepare Ice Cream as above, *except* fold 1 cup chopped walnuts and ½ cup chopped dates with whipped cream into custard.

Orange Marmalade Ice Cream: Prepare Ice Cream as above, *except* fold ⅓ cup orange marmalade along with the whipped cream into the custard.

Fresh Fruit Ice Cream: Prepare Ice Cream as above, *except* fold 1 cup mashed fresh fruit along with whipped cream into the chilled custard mixture.

Marshmallow Ice Cream

Ice cream is the great American dessert and who can resist it if it's homemade ice cream. One of the most delicious home-made versions you could make is Marshmallow Ice Cream. This fluffy treat is very much like soft-serve ice cream.

2 eggs	3 cups milk
¾ cup sugar	1 cup whipping cream
1 7-, 9-, or 10-ounce jar 　marshmallow creme	1½ teaspoons vanilla

In large mixing bowl beat eggs till light; gradually beat in sugar till mixture is thick. Blend in marshmallow creme, then the milk, whipping cream, and vanilla. Mix thoroughly. Turn into 1-gallon ice cream freezer container; freeze according to manufacturer's directions. Makes 2 quarts.

Cheesecake Supreme

1 cup all-purpose flour
¼ cup sugar
1 teaspoon grated lemon
    peel
½ cup butter *or* margarine
1 beaten egg yolk
¼ teaspoon vanilla
5 8-ounce packages cream
    cheese, softened
¾ teaspoon grated lemon
    peel

¼ teaspoon vanilla
1¾ cups sugar
3 tablespoons all-purpose
    flour
¼ teaspoon salt
4 large eggs
2 egg yolks
¼ cup whipping cream
• • •
Cherry Sauce *or*
Strawberry Glaze

For crust, combine 1 cup flour, ¼ cup sugar, and 1 teaspoon grated lemon peel. Cut in butter till crumbly. Add 1 beaten egg yolk and ¼ teaspoon vanilla; mix well. Pat *one-third* of the dough on bottom of a 9-inch springform pan (sides removed). Bake at 400° about 8 minutes. Cool. Butter sides of springform pan; attach to the bottom. Pat remaining dough on sides of pan to a height of 1¾ inches.

For filling, beat cream cheese till creamy; add ¾ teaspoon grated lemon peel and ¼ teaspoon vanilla. Combine 1¾ cups sugar, 3 tablespoons flour, and ¼ teaspoon salt; gradually blend into cheese mixture. Add eggs and 2 egg yolks, one at a time, beating after each addition just to blend. Gently stir in whipping cream. Turn into crust-lined pan. Bake at 450° for 12 minutes. Reduce heat to 300°; bake till knife inserted off-center comes out clean, about 55 minutes longer. Remove from oven; cool 30 minutes. (Cheesecake will dip slightly.) Loosen sides of cheesecake from pan with spatula. Cool 30 minutes more; remove sides of pan. Cool 2 hours. Meanwhile, prepare Cherry Sauce or Strawberry Glaze; top cheesecake. Serves 12.

Cherry Sauce: In a saucepan combine ½ cup sugar, 2 tablespoons cornstarch, and dash salt. Add one 20-ounce can frozen pitted tart red cherries, thawed. Cook, stirring constantly, till the mixture is thickened and bubbly. Simmer 10 minutes. Chill thoroughly.

Strawberry Glaze: Crush 1 cup fresh strawberries; add ¾ cup water. Cook 2 minutes; sieve. In saucepan combine ½ cup sugar and 2 tablespoons cornstarch; gradually stir in the hot strawberry mixture. Bring to boiling, stirring constantly. Cook and stir till thickened and clear. (Add red food coloring, if needed.) Cool to room temperature. Place 3 cups halved fresh strawberries on cheesecake. Pour glaze over strawberries. Chill cheesecake 2 hours.

The most sensational of all dessert creations is Cheesecake Supreme. *This rich, creamy dessert won its initial glory at New York's old Lindy's Restaurant. For many years Broadway people enjoyed this exquisite cheesecake dessert after theater performances. Its fame soon reached all the way to the West Coast — and, who knows, beyond.*

Key Lime Pie

1 envelope unflavored
    gelatin
½ cup sugar
¼ teaspoon salt
4 egg yolks
1 teaspoon grated lime peel
    (set aside)
½ cup lime juice
¼ cup water

Green food coloring
    (about 2 drops)
• • •
4 egg whites
½ cup sugar
1 cup whipping cream
1 *baked* 9-inch pastry
    shell, cooled (see
    recipe, page 351)

In saucepan combine unflavored gelatin, ½ cup sugar, and salt. Beat egg yolks, lime juice, and water till blended; stir into gelatin. Cook over medium heat, stirring constantly, just till mixture comes to boiling. Remove saucepan from heat; add grated lime peel. Add enough drops of green food coloring to give pale green color; mix thoroughly. Chill, stirring occasionally, till mixture mounds when spooned.

In bowl beat egg whites till soft peaks form. Gradually add ½ cup sugar; beat till stiff peaks form. Fold chilled lime gelatin mixture into stiffly beaten egg whites. Whip cream till soft peaks form; fold into gelatin-egg white mixture. Pile filling into cooled baked pastry shell. Chill till firm. Garnish with additional whipped cream, lime peel, chopped pistachio nuts, and lime wedges, if desired.

A variety of lime referred to as Key lime, because it was once grown extensively on the Florida Keys, is harvested and marketed when yellow. The lime is very popular in Florida and many trees are cultivated in home gardens. The commercial production of Key limes is not for the fresh fruit marketing, but goes instead into frozen juice for Key Lime Pie.

Remarkable Fudge

Fudge making is sometimes rather frustrating because the candy fails to set up or else gets stiff too quickly. The addition of marshmallow creme has eliminated the problems and given Remarkable Fudge *a smooth creamy texture as well as a delicious flavor.*

Butter sides of heavy 3-quart saucepan. Add 4 cups sugar, one 13-ounce can evaporated milk, and 1 cup butter *or* margarine. Cook over medium heat to soft-ball stage (234°), stirring frequently. Remove from heat. Add one 12-ounce package semisweet chocolate pieces (not imitation chocolate); stir till chocolate is almost melted. Stir in one 7-, 9-, or 10-ounce jar marshmallow creme, 1 cup broken walnuts, and 1 teaspoon vanilla. Beat till chocolate melts completely. Immediately pour fudge into buttered 13x9x2-inch pan. Score fudge while warm; cut into pieces when cool and firm.

Marshmallow Popcorn Balls

12 cups popped corn
6 tablespoons butter *or*
   margarine
3 cups tiny marshmallows

½ of a 3-ounce package
   raspberry-flavored
   gelatin (3 tablespoons)

Keep popped corn warm in 225° oven. In saucepan melt butter or margarine over medium heat. Add marshmallows; stir till melted. Blend in raspberry-flavored gelatin. Pour over popped corn, mixing well. With buttered hands, form into balls. Makes 12 medium (3-inch) or 18 small (2-inch) balls.

Old-Fashioned Lemonade

2½ cups water
2 cups sugar
   • • •
3 oranges
6 lemons

¼ cup lightly packed fresh
   mint leaves (optional)
Water
Ice cubes

Heat the 2½ cups water and sugar till sugar dissolves. Cool. Grate 2 tablespoons of peel from oranges. Squeeze juice from oranges and lemons (should be 1½ cups each). Add juices and peel to cooled syrup; pour over mint leaves, if used. Cover and steep 1 hour. Strain into jars; cover and refrigerate. *To serve,* mix equal parts fruit syrup and water. Serve over ice. Garnish with fruit slices and mint leaves, if desired. Makes 6 cups concentrate.

Breakfast Cocoa

Early Spanish explorers greatly improved the bitter flavor of chocolate when they added sugar, and made it into a hot beverage. Although today's hot chocolate uses basically the same ingredients, some people add the extra filling of a marshmallow in each cup.

⅓ cup unsweetened cocoa
   powder
⅓ cup sugar
Dash salt

½ cup water
3½ cups milk
½ teaspoon vanilla
Marshmallows

In a saucepan mix unsweetened cocoa powder, sugar, and salt; stir in water. Bring to boiling, stirring constantly. Boil 1 minute. Stir in milk; heat almost to boiling *(do not boil)*. Add vanilla; beat with rotary beater just before serving. Float marshmallows atop hot beverage. Makes 4 cups.

Strawberry-Eggnog Shake

1 quart strawberry ice
   cream, softened
1 cup fresh strawberries,
   mashed

2 cups canned eggnog,
   chilled
Ground nutmeg
Whole fresh strawberries

In chilled, large mixing bowl combine ice cream and mashed strawberries; blend with electric mixer. Stir in eggnog. Serve in chilled glasses with a sprinkle of nutmeg. Garnish with whole strawberries, if desired. Serves 4.

Acknowledgments

Notes for Chapter 1
1. Harold E. Driver and Wilhelmine Driver, *Indian Farmers of Northern America*, p. 6. Reprinted by permission of Rand-McNally and Co., 1967.
2. Ibid., p. 9.
3. Ibid., p. 14.

Notes for Chapter 2
1. Michael Drayton, *Minor Poems of Michael Drayton.*
2. Anonymous.
3. Alice Morse Earle, *Customs and Fashions of Old New England.*
4. Alice Morse Earle, *Colonial Days in Old New York.*
5. John Josselyn, *New England's Rarities Discovered.*
6. Ibid.
7. *Benjamin Franklin: The Art of Eating,* p. 19. Reprinted by permission of author, 1958.
8. Ibid.
9. C. S. Adams, ed., *The Words of John Adams,* Volume 10, p. 345.
10. Hunter D. Farish, *The Journal and Letters of Philip Vickers Fithian.* Reprinted by permission of Univ. Press of Virginia, 1957.
11. Peter Kalm, *Travels in North America.*
12. Rose Gouverneur Hoes, *Septimia Jefferson Randolph Meikelham Family Cook Book.*
13. Frederick W. Hodge, *Spanish Explorers of the Southern United States.*
14. *Garfield Woman's Club Cook Book,* p. 17.
15. John Smith, *Works.*
16. David Hawke, *The Colonial Experience.* Reprinted by permission of Bobbs-Merrill, 1966.
17. Farish, *The Journal and Letters of Philip Vickers Fithian.*
18. Ibid.
19. James Wharton, *The Bounty of The Chesapeake: Fishing in Colonial Virginia,* pp. 1,2. Reprinted by permission of University Press of Virginia, 1957.
20. Mary Randolph, *The Virginia Housewife,* p. 95.
21. Eugene Walter, *American Cooking: Southern Style,* p. 68.
22. Alice Cooke Brown, *Early American Herb Recipes.* Reprinted by permission of Charles E. Tuttle Co., 1966.
23. Alistair Cooke, *Alistair Cooke's America,* pp. 104-105. Reprint permission granted with Random House, 1973.
24. Edward Johnson, *Wonder Working Providence of Sions Saviour in New England: A History of New England from the English Planting Yeere 1628, until the Yeere 1652.*
25. Imogene Wolcott, *The New England Yankee Cook Book,* p. 99.
26. Ibid., p. 330.
27. Kalm, *Travels.*
28. *A Description of the New Netherlands.* Adriaen Van Der Donck; Thomas F. O'Donnell, editor (Syracuse University Press, 1968.)
29. Earle, *Colonial Days,* p. 141.
30. Washington Irving, *The Legend of Sleepy Hollow.* Used by permission of Franklin Watts, Inc., 1966.
31. James Truslow Adams, *Provincial Society: 1690-1763.* Used by permission of Franklin Watts, Inc., 1971.
32. Ruth Hutchinson, *Pennsylvania Dutch Cook Book.* Reprinted by permission of Harper and Row Publishers, 1948.
33. John Hull Brown, *Early American Beverages,* p. 22. Reprinted by permission of Charles E. Tuttle Co., 1966.

34. Hawke, *The Colonial Experience,* p. 492. Reprinted by permission of Bobbs-Merrill Co., 1966.
35. *Favorite Recipes of Lower Cape Fear,* p. 112. Reprinted by permission of the Ministering Circle, 1964.
36. *Charleston Receipts,* compiled and edited by the Junior League of Charleston, Inc., South Carolina, 1950.
37. Duc de la Rochefoucauld-Liancourt, *Travels.*
38. Catherine Drinker Bowen, *John Adams and the American Revolution.* Reprinted by permission of Little, Brown & Co., 1950.
39. Ibid.
40. Carl Van Doren, *Benjamin Franklin: A Biography.* Reprinted by permission of Viking Press, Inc., 1956.
41. Thomas Paine, *Writings.*
42. Edwin Morris Betts, annot., *Thomas Jefferson's Garden Book 1766-1824: With Relevant Extracts from His Other Writings.* Reprinted by permission of American Philosophical Society, 1944.
43. Reprinted by permission from *American Heritage Cookbook and Illustrated History of American Eating & Drinking, The,* p. 135. American Heritage Publishing, 1964.
44. *Better Homes and Gardens Encyclopedia of Cooking,* 17:2327.
45. Stewart Mitchell, ed., *New Letters, 1788-1801, of Abigail Adams.* Reprinted by permission of Houghton Mifflin Co., 1947.

Notes for Chapter 4
1. From *The Paths of Inland Commerce* by Hulbert, Volume 21 in the Yale Chronicles of America Series. Copyright United States Publishers Association, Inc., 1920.
2. John A. Krout and Dixon Ryan Fox, *The Completion of Independence: 1790-1830.* Used by permission of Franklin Watts, 1944.
3. Daniel J. Boorstin, *The Americans: The National Experience,* p. 141. Reprint permission granted with Random House, 1965.
4. John Hull Brown, *Early American Beverages,* pp. 137-138. Reprinted by permission of Charles E. Tuttle Co., 1966.
5. Margaret B. Klapthor, *The First Ladies Cook Book: Favorite Recipes of All the Presidents of the United States,* p. 30. Reprinted by permission of Parents' Magazine Press, 1969.
6. Margaret Bayard Smith, *The First Forty Years of Washington Society.*
7. Esther Singleton, *The Story of the White House.*
8. Jessie B. Fremont, *Souvenirs Of My Time.*
9. Charles Ogle, *Speech on the Regal Splendor of the President's Palace, Delivered in the House of Representatives April 14, 1840.*
10. Klapthor, *The First Ladies Cook Book,* p. 92, 93.
11. Jefferson Williamson, *The American Hotel.* Reprint permission granted with Random House, 1930.
12. B. Zincke, *Last Winter in the United States.*
13. Charles Dickens, *American Notes.*
14. American Association of University Women, *Bethlehem Recipes.*
15. Dickens, *American Notes.*
16. Frederick Law Olmstead, *A Journey Through Texas: Or A Saddle Trip on the Southwestern Frontier.* Reprinted by Lenox Hill Publishing and Distributing Corp., 1969.
17. Taken from *The Shaker Cookbook* by Caroline B. Piercy. © 1953 by Caroline B. Piercy. Used by permission of Crown Publishers, Inc.
18. Ibid.
19. Reprinted with permission of Macmillan Publishing Co., Inc. from *The Best of Shaker Cooking* by Amy Bess Miller and Persis Fuller, pp. 7-8. © 1970 by Shaker Community, Inc.

20. Ibid., p. 9.
21. Thomas Nelson Page, *The Old South.*
22. *Confederate Receipt Book,* p. 16. Reprinted by permission of Univ. of Georgia Press, 1960.
23. Bell Irvin Wiley, *The Life of Johnny Reb.* Reprinted by permission of the author, 1943.
24. Ibid.
25. John D. Billings, *Hard Tack and Coffee.* Reprinted by permission of Corner House Publishers, 1973.
26. Mary Cable, *The Avenue of the Presidents.* Reprinted by permission of Houghton Mifflin Co., 1969.
27. Ward McAllister, *Society As I Have Found It.*
28. *Maryland's Way,* p. 347. Reprinted by permission of Hammond-Harwood House Assn., 1963.
29. Ibid., p. 340.
30. Margaret Godley and Lillian C. Bragg, *Savannah Anecodotes,* pp. 10, 11. Reprinted by permission of the authors, 1963.

Notes for Chapter 5.
1. William Byrd, *Histories of the Dividing Line, and Other Tracts.*
2. [Maria] Child, *The American Frugal Housewife,* p. 40.

Notes for Chapter 6
1. Bernard DeVoto, *The Journals of Lewis and Clark.* Reprinted by permission of Houghton Mifflin Co., 1953.
2. Josiah Gregg, *Commerce of the Prairies.* Reprinted by permission of University of Oklahoma Press, 1954.
3. D. Griffiths, Jr., *Two Years in the New Settlements of Ohio.*
4. *"Mormon Panorama, A."* Reprinted by permission from American Heritage, p. 101. American Heritage Publishing, Feb., 1963.
5. Ralph K. Andrist, *"Gold!"* Reprinted by permission from American Heritage, p. 10. American Heritage Publishing, 1962.
6. Charles Hanna, *The Scotch-Irish,* pp. 84-85.

Notes for Chapter 7
1. Margaret Bayard Smith, *The First Forty Years of Washington Society.*
2. Siegfried Giedion, *Mechanization Takes Command,* p. 538.
3. Ibid., p. 616, footnoted to *Architectural Record.* Reprinted by permission of McGraw-Hill Publishing Co., March, 1930.
4. Laurence A. Johnson, *Over the Counter and On the Shelf: Country Storekeeping in America 1620-1920,* p. 46. Reprinted by permission of Charles E. Tuttle Co., 1961.
5. Ronald Pearsall, *Collecting Mechanical Antiques,* p. 163. Reprinted by permission of Arco Publishing Co., 1973.

Notes for Chapter 8
1. Marcus L. Hansen, *The Immigrant in American History,* pp. 36-37. Reprinted by permission of Harvard University Press, 1940.
2. David B. Greenberg, *Land That Our Fathers Plowed: The Settlement of Our Country as Told by the Pioneers Themselves and Their Contemporaries.* Reprinted by permission of University of Oklahoma Press, 1969.
3. Arthur Mann, *Immigrants in American Life,* p. 45.
4. Greenberg, *Land That Our Fathers Plowed.*
5. Theodore C. Blegen, *Land of Their Choice: Immigrants Write Home,* pp. 398-399. Reprinted by permission of Norwegian-American Historical Assn., 1955.
6. Edward Giobbi, *Italian Family's Cookbook,* pp. 35-36. Reprint permission granted with Random House, 1971.
7. Reprinted by permission from *American Heritage Cookbook and Illustrated History of American Eating & Drinking, The,* p. 26. American Heritage Publishing Co., 1964.
8. Mann, *Immigrants In American Life,* p. 77.

(Acknowledgments continued)

9. Excerpts from *The Immigrant Experience: The Anguish of Becoming American.* Edited by Thomas C. Wheeler. Copyright © 1971 by The Dial Press. Used with the permission of The Dial Press.

Notes for Chapter 9
1. *Benjamin Franklin: The Art of Eating.* Reprinted by permission of the author, 1958.
2. Susannah Carter, *The Frugal Housewife.*
3. Maria Eliza Rundell, *A New System of Domestic Cookery: And Adapted to the Use of Private Families.*
4. Ibid.
5. Richard Briggs, *The New Art of Cookery.*
6. Ibid.

7. Amelia Simmons, *American Cookery.*
8. Ibid.
9. Ibid.
10. Mary Randolph, *The Virginia Housewife.*
11. [Francis McDougall], By a Lady, *The Housekeeper's Book.* Reprinted with permission of New Hampshire Publishing Company, 1972.
12. Eliza Leslie, *Directions for Cookery In Its Various Branches.* Reprinted by Arno Press, Inc., 1973.
13. Ibid.
14. Ibid.
15. [Maria] Child, *The American Frugal Housewife.*
16. *Agate Cook Book, The,* Manufacturers of

Agate Iron Ware.
17. S[arah] T. Rorer, *Philadelphia Cook Book: A Manual of Home Economics.*

Notes for Chapter 10
1. B. Zincke, ed., *Last Winter in the United States.*
2. *Woodrow Wilson House Cook Book.* Quote from *Recollections of a Cabinet Minister's Wife, 1913-1921* by Mrs. J. Daniels. Reprinted by permission of *Saturday Evening Post.*
3. Phil Stong, "State Fair," *Holiday,* August 1948, p. 113.

Notes for Chapter 11
1. *Winthrop Papers,* Reprinted by permission of the Massachusetts Historical Society.

Bibliography

Adams, C. S., ed. *The Words of John Adams.* Boston: Little, Brown, 1856.

Adams, James Truslow. *Provincial Society 1690-1763.* Edited by Arthur M. Schlesinger and Dixon R. Fox. N.Y.: Watts, Franklin, Inc., 1971.

Adams, Ramon F. *Come An' Get It: The Story of the Old Cowboy Cook,* Norman: University of Oklahoma Press, 1972.

Agate Cook Book, The. Manufacturers of Agate Iron Ware, 1890

Alaskan Camp Cook, The. Anchorage: Alaska Northwest Publishing Co., 1973.

Amana Colony Recipes. Homestead, Ia.: Homestead Welfare Club, 1948.

American Heritage Cookbook and Illustrated History of American Eating & Drinking, The. N.Y.: American Heritage Publishing Co., 1964.

American Philosophical Society. *Benjamin Franklin: The Art of Eating.* Princeton: Princeton Univ. Press (paperbound), 1958.

Andrist, Ralph K. "Gold!" *American Heritage,* Volume XIV, No. 1, N.Y.: American Heritage Publishing Co., December, 1962.

Arnow, Harriette S. *Flowering of the Cumberland.* Riverside, N.J.: MacMillan, 1963.

Arnow, Harriette S. *Seedtime on the Cumberland.* Riverside, N.J.: Macmillan, 1960.

Asselin, E. Donald. *A French-Canadian Cookbook.* Rutland, Vt.: Charles E. Tuttle, 1973.

Barnes, Cass G. *The Sod House.* Lincoln: University of Nebraska Press, 1970.

Benson, Evelyn Abraham, ed. *Penn Family Recipes: Cooking Recipes of Wm. Penn's Wife, Gulielma.* York, Pa.: George Shumway, 1966.

Bethlehem Recipes. Bethlehem, Pa.: American Association of University Women, 1972.

My Better Homes and Gardens Cook Book. Des Moines: Meredith Publishing Co., 1930.

Better Homes and Gardens Encyclopedia of Cooking. Vols. No. 1 thru 18. Des Moines: Meredith Corp., 1971.

Better Homes and Gardens New Cook Book. Des Moines. Meredith Corp., 1968.

Betts, Edwin Morris, annot. *Thomas Jefferson's Garden Book 1766-1824: With Relevant Extracts from his Other Writings.* Philadelphia: American Philosophical Society, 1944.

Billings, John D. *Hard Tack and Coffee.* 1888. Reprint. Chicago: Corner House, 1960.

Billington, Ray Allen, with Hedges, James Blaine. *Westward Expansion: A History of the American Frontier,* 4th ed. N.Y.: Macmillan, 1974.

Bitting, Katherine G. *Gastronomic Bibliography.* Ann Arbor, Mich.: Gryphon Books, 1971.

Blegen, Theodore C., ed. *Land of Their Choice: Immigrants Write Home.* Minneapolis: University of Minnesota Press, 1955.

Boorstin, Daniel J. *The Americans: The Colonial Experience,* N.Y.: Random House, 1958.

Boorstin, Daniel J. *The Americans: The Democratic Experience.* N.Y.: Random House, 1973.

Boorstin, Daniel J. *The Americans: The National Experience.* N.Y.: Random House, 1973.

Bowen, Catherine D. *John Adams and The American Revolution.* Boston: Little, Brown, 1950.

Briggs, Richard. *The New Art of Cookery.* Philadelphia, 1792.

Brown, Alice Cooke. *Early American Herb Recipes.* Rutland, Vt.: Charles E. Tuttle, 1966.

Brown, Dale. *American Cooking.* Foods of the World (series). N.Y.: Time-Life Books, 1968.

Brown, Dale. *American Cooking: The Northwest.* Foods of the World (series). N.Y.: Time-Life Books, 1970.

Brown, John Hull. *Early American Beverages.* Rutland, Vt.: Charles E. Tuttle, 1966.

Bullock, Helen. *The Williamsburg Art of Cookery.* Williamsburg: Colonial Williamsburg, 1966.

Byrd, Thomas. *Pioneer from Missouri.* Philadelphia: Dorrance, 1972.

Byrd, William. *Histories of the Dividing Line, and Other Tracts.* Richmond, Va., 1866.

Cable, Mary. *The Avenue of the Presidents.* Boston: Houghton Mifflin, 1969.

Carter, Susannah. *The Frugal Housewife.* Boston, 1772.

Child, [Maria]. *The American Frugal Housewife.* Boston: Carter, Hendee, and Co., 1832.

Cleveland, Bess A. *California Mission Recipes.* Rutland, Vt.: Charles E. Tuttle, 1965.

Congressional Club Cook Book, The. Washington, D.C.: The Congressional Club, 1927.

Cooke, Alistair. *Alistair Cooke's America.* New York: Alfred A. Knopf, 1973.

Corbett, John M. *Aztec Ruins.* National Park Service Historical Handbook Series No. 36. Wash., D.C.: U.S. Gov. Printing Office, 1962.

Coulter, Ellis M. ed. *Confederate Receipt Book: A Compilation of Over One Hundred Receipts, Adapted to the Times.* Athens: University of Georgia Press, 1960.

Crosby, Alfred W., Jr. *The Columbian Exchange: Biological and Cultural Consequences of 1942.* Contributions in American Studies Number 2. Westport, Conn.: Greenwood Press, 1973.

Cullen, Joseph P. "Saratoga." *American History Illustrated,* Vol. X, No. 1. April, 1975.

DeVoto, Bernard, ed. *The Journals of Lewis and Clark.* Boston: Houghton Mifflin, 1953.

Dick, Everett. *Tales of the Frontier: From Lewis and Clark to the Last Roundup.* Lincoln: University of Nebraska Press, 1964.

Dickens, Charles. *American Notes.* Edited by Arnold Goldman and John Whitley. N.Y.: Penguin Books, 1972.

Drayton, Michael. *Minor Poems of Michael Drayton.* Edited by Cyril Brett. Oxford: Clarendon Press, 1907.

Driver, Harold E. and Driver, Wilhelmine. *Indian Farmers of North America.* Chicago: Rand-McNally, 1967.

Earle, Alice M. *Colonial Days in Old New York.* 1896. Detroit: Singing Tree Press, 1968.

Earle, Alice M. *Customs and Fashions of Old New England.* N.Y.: 1893.

Farnish, Hunter Dickinson, ed. *The Journal and Letters of Philip Vickers, Fithian.* Williamsburg: Colonial Williamsburg, 1957.

Farmer, Fannie Merritt. *The Boston Cooking-School Cook Book.* Boston, 1896.

Favorite Recipes of Lower Cape Fear. Wilmington, N.C.: The Ministering Circle, 1964.

Feibleman, Peter S. *American Cooking: Creole and Acadian.* Foods of the World (series). N.Y.: Time-Life Books, 1971.

Forbis, William A. *The Cowboys.* The Old West (series). N.Y.: Time-Life Books, 1973.

Fremont, Jessie Benton. *Souvenirs of My Time.* Boston: Lothrop, Lee & Shepherd Co., 1887.

Garfield Woman's Club Cook Book, The. Garfield, Ut: 1916. Reprint. Southwestern Cookery. N.Y.: Arno Press, 1973.

Georgakas, Dan. *The Broken Hoop.* Garden City, N.Y.: Doubleday (Zenith Books), 1973.

Giedion, Siegfried. *Mechanization Takes Command.* N.Y.: Oxford University Press, 1948.

Giobbi, Edward. *Italian Family's Cookbook.* N.Y.: Random House, 1971.

Godley, Margaret, and Bragg, Lillian C. *Savannah Anecdotes.* Savannah, 1963.

Gray, Sarah V. "A History of the Publication of Cookbooks in the United States, 1796-1896." Master's thesis, Univ. of N. Carolina, 1964.

Greenberg, David B., ed. *Land That Our Fathers Plowed: The Settlement of our Country as Told by the Pioneers Themselves and Their Contemporaries.* Norman: University of Oklahoma Press, 1969.

Gregg, Josiah. *Commerce of the Prairies.* Norman: University of Oklahoma Press, 1954.

Griffiths, D., Jr. *Two Years in the New Settlements of Ohio.* Ann Arbor, Mich.: University Microfilms, 1966.

Hansen, Marcus L. *The Immigrant in American History.* Edited by Arthur M. Schlesinger. N.Y.: Harvard University Press, 1940.

Hanna, Charles A. *The Scotch-Irish.* N.Y.: G. P. Putnam's Sons, 1902.

Hawke, David. *The Colonial Experience.* Indianapolis: Bobbs-Merrill, 1966.

Hays, Wilma, and Hays, R. Vernon. *Foods the Indians Gave Us.* N.Y.: Ives Washburn, 1974.

Hesse, Zora G. *Southwestern Indian Recipe Book.* Palmer Lake, Co.: Filter Press, 1973.

Higham, John, ed. *The Reconstruction of American History.* N.Y.: Harper and Row, Harper Torchbooks, the Academy Library, 1962.

Hodge, Frederick, W., ed. *Spanish Explorers of the Southern United States, 1528-1543.* New York: Scribner's Sons, 1907.

Hoes, Rose Gouverneur. "Septimia Jefferson Randolph Meikelham Family Cook Book." Handwritten copy at James Monroe Museum and Memorial Library, Fredericksburg, Va.

Hughes, Phyllis. *Pueblo Indian Cook Book.* Santa Fe: Museum of New Mexico Press, 1972.

Huguenin, Mary V. and Stoney, Anne M., ed. *Charleston Receipts.* Junior League of Charleston. Charleston, 1950.

Hulbert, Archer B. *The Paths of Inland Commerce.* New Haven: Yale Univ. Press, 1920.

Hutchison, Ruth. *Pennsylvania Dutch Cook Book.* N.Y.: Harper and Brothers, 1948.

Irving, Washington. *The Legend of Sleepy Hollow.* N.Y.: Watts, Franklin, 1966.

Jardine, Winnifred C. *Famous Mormon Recipes.* Salt Lake City: Liddle Enterprises, 1967.

Johnson, Edward. *Wonder Working Providence of Sions Saviour in New England: A History of New England from the English Planting Yeere 1628, until the Yeere 1652.* 1654. Reprint. N.Y.: 1910.

Johnson, Laurence A. *Over the Counter and On the Shelf: Country Storekeeping in America 1620-1920.* Edited by Maria Ray. Rutland, Vt.: Charles E. Tuttle, 1961.

Jones, Maldwyn Allen. *American Immigration.* Chicago History of American Civilization, edited by Daniel J. Boorstin. Chicago: University of Chicago Press, 1970.

Josephy, Alvin N., Jr. *The Indian Heritage of America.* N.Y.: Bantam Books, 1969.

Josselyn, John. *New England's Rarities Discovered.* London: 1672.

Kalm, Peter. *Travels in North America.* Translations 1770, 1812, 1892. Warrington, Eng.: Imprint Society.

Kimball, Yeffe, and Anderson, Jean. *The Art of American Indian Cooking.* Garden City, N.Y.: Doubleday, 1965.

Klapthor, Margaret Brown, ed. *The First Ladies Cook Book: Favorite Recipes of All Presidents of the United States.* N.Y.: Parent's Magazine Press, 1969.

Koehler, Margaret H. *Recipes from the Russians of San Francisco.* Riverside, Conn.: The Chatham Press, Inc., 1974.

Krout, John Allan and Fox, Dixon Ryan. *The Completion of Independence: 1790-1830.* Edited by Arthur M. Schlesinger. N.Y.: Franklin, Watts, 1944.

Langer, William L., ed. *An Encyclopedia of World History.* 5th rev. ed. Boston: Houghton Mifflin, 1972.

Lantz, Louise K. *Old American Kitchenware 1725-1925.* N.Y.: Thomas Nelson jointly with Hanover, Penn.: Everybody's Press, 1970.

Leonard, Jonathan Norton. *American Cooking: New England.* Foods of the World (series). N.Y.: Time-Life Books, 1970.

Leonard, Jonathan Norton. *American Cooking: The Great West.* Foods of the World (series). N.Y.: Time-Life Books, 1971.

Leslie, Eliza. *Directions for Cookery in its Various Branches.* 1848. Reprint. N.Y.: Arno Press, 1973.

Longstreet, Stephen and Longstreet, Ethel. *A Salute To American Cooking.* N.Y.: Hawthorn Books, 1968.

Lowenstein, Eleanor. *Bibliography of American Cookery Books 1742-1860.* Worcester, Mass.: American Antiquarian Society, 1972.

Mackenzie, Colin, *Five Thousand Receipts.* 4th Amer. ed. Philadelphia: Kay, 1829.

McAllister, Ward. *Society As I Have Found It.* N.Y.: Cassell Publishing Co., 1890.

[McDougall, Frances.] By a Lady. *The Housekeeper's Book.* 1837. Reprint. Somersworth: New Hampshire Publishing Co., 1972.

Mann, Arthur. *Immigrants in American Life.* Life in America Services. Boston: Houghton Mifflin, 1968.

Maryland's Way: Hammond-Harwood House Cook Book. Annapolis: Hammond-Harwood House Association, 1963.

Meyers, Marvin; Kern, Alexander; Cawelti, John G. *Sources of the American Republic.* Vol. 1. Chicago: Scott, Foresman, 1960.

Miller, Amy Bess, and Fuller, Persis. *The Best of Shaker Cooking.* N.Y.: Macmillan, 1970.

Mitchell, Stewart, ed. *New Letters, 1788-1801, of Abigail Adams.* Boston: Houghton, 1947.

Moore, D. *Shoot Me a Biscuit: Some Chuckwagon Cooks I Have Known.* Tucson: Univ. Arizona, 1974.

"Mormon Panorama, A." *American Heritage,* Vol. XIV, No. 2. American Heritage Publishing, Feb., 1963.

Morris, Richard B., ed. *Encyclopedia of American History.* Chief Consultant Editor, Henry Steele Commager. N.Y.: Harper and Row, 1970.

Niethammer, Carolyn. *American Indian Food and Lore.* Riverside, N.J.: Macmillan, 1974.

Olge, Charles. *Speech on the Regal Splendor of the President's Palace, Delivered in the House of Representatives, April 14, 1840.*

Olesky, Walter. *The Old Country Cookbook.* Chicago: Nelson-Hall, 1974.

Olmstead, Frederick Law. *A Journey Through Texas.* Boston, 1859.

Orton, Vrest. *The American Cider Book.* N.Y.: Noonday Press, 1973.

Page, Thomas N. *The Old South.* N.Y.: 1892.

Paine, Thomas. *Writings.* Edited by M. D. Conway. New York: G. P. Putnam, 1894.

Parloa, Maria. *Miss Parloa's Kitchen Companion.* Boston: Dana Estes and Co., 1887.

Pearsall, Ronald. *Collecting Mechanical Antiques.* N.Y.: Arco Publishing Co., 1973.

Phipps, Frances. *Colonial Kitchens, Their Furnishings and Their Gardens.* N.Y.: Hawthorn Books, Inc., 1972.

Piercy, Caroline B. *The Shaker Cook Book.* N.Y.: Crown Publishers, Inc., 1953.

Pioneer Cook Book. Decorah, Ia.: Volunteers of the Norwegian-American Museum, 1969.

Randolph, Mary. *The Virginia Housewife.* Philadelphia: E. H. Butler & Co., 1860.

Receipt Book of Mrs. Ann Blencowe A.D. 1694, The. 1925. Reprint. Cottonport, La.: Polyanthos, Inc., 1972.

Rochefoucauld-Liancourt, Duc de la. *Travels.* London, 1799.

Root, Waverley. *The Cooking of Italy.* Foods of the World (series). N.Y.: Time-Life Books, 1968.

Rorer, S[arah] T. *Philadelphia Cook Book: A Manual of Home Economics.* Philadelphia: Arnold and Co., 1886.

Rundell, Maria Eliza. *A New System of Domestic Cookery: And Adapted to the Use of Private Families.* Boston: William Andrews, 1807.

Saver, Carl O. *Seeds, Spades, Hearths, and Herds: The Domestication of Animals and Foodstuffs,* 2nd ed. Cambridge: Massachusetts Institute of Technology, 1969.

Scherer, Joanna C. *Indian Images: Photographs of North American Indians 1847-1928.* Wash., D.C.: Smithsonian Institution Press, 1970.

Schlebecker, John T. *Bibliography of Books and Pamphlets on the History of Agriculture in the United States 1607-1967.* Santa Barbara: A B C-Clio Inc. (paperbound), 1969.

Schlebecker, John T. *A History of American Dairying.* Chicago: Rand-McNally, 1967.

Settlement Cook Book. Edited by Settlement Cook Book Board. N.Y.: Simon and Schuster, 1965.

Shenton, James P.; Pellegrini, Angelo M.; Brown, Dale; Shenker, Israel; and Wood, Peter. *American Cooking: The Melting Pot.* Foods of the World (series). N.Y.: Time-Life Books, 1971.

Simmons, Amelia. *American Cookery.* Hartford: Hudson and Goodwin, 1796.

Singleton, Esther. *The Story of the White House.* N.Y.: Blom, Benjamin Inc., 1907.

Smith, John. *Works 1608-1631.* Edited by Edward Arber. Scribner and Welford, 1884.

Smith, Margaret B. *The First Forty Years of Washington Society.* N.Y.: Scribner and Sons, 1906.

Sokolowski, Marie, and Jasinski, Irene, eds. *Treasured Polish Recipes for Americans.* Minneapolis: Polanie Publishing Co., 1948.

Steinberg, Rafael. *Pacific and Southeast Asian Cooking.* Foods of the World (series). N.Y.: Time-Life Books, 1970.

Stong, Phil. "State Fair." *Holiday.* August, 1948,

Sutter, Ruth. *The Next Place You Come To: A Historical Introduction to Communities in North America.* Englewood Cliffs, N.J.: Prentice-Hall, 1973.

Toupin, Elizabeth A. Introduction to *Hawaii: Cookbook and Backyard Luau,* by James A. Michener. N.Y.: Bantam Books, 1967.

Tunis, Edwin. *Colonial Living.* Cleveland: World Publishing Co., 1957.

Tunis, Edwin. *Frontier Living.* Cleveland: World Publishing Co., 1961.

VanCronkhite, Mary, ed. *The Ethnic Epicure.* Wauwatosa Junior Woman's Club with State Historical Society of Wisconsin, 1973.

Van der Donck, Adriaen. *A Description of the New Netherlands, 1653.* Syracuse: Syracuse University Press, 1968.

Van Doren, Carl. *Benjamin Franklin: A Biography.* N.Y.: Viking Press, Inc., 1956.

Walter, Eugene. *American Cooking: Southern Style.* Foods of the World (series). N.Y.: Time-Life Books, 1971.

Washington, D.C. Smithsonian Institution. Music Book of Hester Maria Monroe.

Wayman, Norbury L. *Life on the River.* N.Y.: Crown Publishers, 1971.

Weslager, C. D. *Log Cabin in America: From Pioneer Days to the Present.* New Brunswick, N.J.: Rutgers Univ. Press, 1969.

Wharton, James. *The Bounty of the Chesapeake: Fishing in Colonial Virginia.* Williamsburg: University Press of Virginia, Virginia 350th Anniversary Celebration (paperbound), 1957.

Wheeler, Thomas C., Introduction. *The Immigrant Experience: The Anguish of Becoming American.* N.Y.: Dial Press, 1971.

Wilder, Laura Ingalls, *Little House in the Big Woods.* 1932. Reprint. N.Y.: Harper and Row, 1973.

Wilder, Laura Ingalls. *Little House on the Prairie.* Reprint. N.Y.: Harper and Row, 1973.

Wiley, Bell Irvin. *The Life of Johnny Reb.* Indianapolis: Bobbs-Merrill, 1943.

Williamson, Jefferson. *The American Hotel.* N.Y.: Alfred A. Knopf, 1930.

Wilson, José. *American Cooking: The Eastern Heartland.* Foods of the World (series). N.Y.: Time-Life Books, 1971.

Winthrop Papers. Boston: Massachusetts Historical Society, 1929-1947.

Wittke, Carl. *We Who Built America: The Saga of the Immigrant.* 2nd rev. ed. The Press of Case Western Reserve University, 1967.

Woodrow Wilson House Cook Book. Wash., D.C., National Trust for Historic Preservation, 1974.

Wolcott, Imogene. *The New England Yankee Cook Book.* N.Y.: Coward, McCann, 1939.

Wright, Louis B. *Life in Colonial America.* New York: Capricorn Books, 1965.

Wyman, Walker D. *Lumberjack Frontier: The Life of a Logger in the Early Days on the Chippeway, Retold from Recollections of Louie Blanchard.* Lincoln: Univ. of Nebraska Press, 1969.

Yeffee, Kimball and Anderson, Jean. *The Art of American Indian Cooking.* Garden City, N.Y.: Doubleday, 1965.

Zincke, F. Barham, ed. *Last Winter in the United States.* London, 1868.

Picture Credits

George Ratkai: Cover
George de Gennaro: pp. 2, 6, 43, 51, 80, 91, 122, 127, 139, 146, 159, 189, 194, 201, 205, 224, 229, 235, 253, 258, 265, 269, 280, 290, 297, 300, 304, 326, 331, 360, 368.
James Jerome Hill Reference Library: p. 8.
Library of Congress: pp. 12 (top and bottom), 13 (bottom), 22 (top and bottom), 23 (top and bottom), 25 (top), 40, 46, 57, 61, 75, 94 (bottom), 114, 116 (bottom), 117 (top and bottom), 118, 124, 132, 157, 171, 172, 173, 180 (center and bottom left), 191, 199, 202 (Erwin E. Smith Collection of Range Photographs), 212 (top), 220 (bottom), 221 (top, bottom left, and bottom right), 288, 307, 311, 319, 328, 337.
Smithsonian Institution: p. 12 (center).
Minnesota Historical Society: p. 13 (top).
Royal Ontario Museum: p. 13 (center).
National Geographic Society (map redrawn): p. 17.

Pennsylvania Academy of Fine Arts: p. 18.
Society for the Preservation of New England Antiquities: p. 20 (top).
National Archives: p. 20 (bottom).
Businessmen's Assurance Co. of America: p. 23 (center).
John Nelson (drawings): pp. 25 (bottom), 27, 41, 74, 79, 92, 96, 102, 103, 104, 105, 106, 107, 108, 109, 129, 141, 170, 178, 187, 207, 208, 215, 232, 244, 254, 262, 271, 275, 283, 288, 295, 303, 324, 338, 352, 371.
William Helms: pp. 29, 34, 37, 64, 72, 99, 102, 166, 335 (top left and bottom left).
Alingh, Wuerker, and Associates, Inc. (maps): pp. 39, 47, 56, 69, 75, 85, 151, 196.
National Park Service: p. 48.
Museum of City of New York: p. 70.
Albert Gommi: pp. 55, 247.
Prints Division, The New York City Public Library: pp. 83 (Astor, Lenox, and Tilden Foundation), 94 (top).
Mariner's Museum, Newport News, Va.: pp. 86, 148.
Yale University: p. 100.
New York Historical Society: p. 110.
Louisiana State Museum: p. 116 (top).
Albany Institute of History and Art: p. 117 (center).
Tulane University: p. 130.

Vince Lisanti: p. 135.
McIlhenny Co., Mfgrs. of Tabasco products: p. 143.
New York State Historical Assoc.: p. 163.
Nelson Gallery – Atkins Museum: p. 174.
Walters Art Gallery: p. 180 (top).
Oklahoma Historical Society: p. 180 (bottom right).
Scotts Bluff National Monument: p. 181 (top).
Denver Public Library: p. 181 (bottom).
Fred Lyon: pp. 184, 335 (top right).
Collections of Henry Ford Museum, Dearborn, Mi.: pp. 208, 209, 210 (bottom), 211 (top and bottom), 212 (center and bottom).
Old American Kitchenware 1725-1925 by Louise K. Lantz: p. 210 (top).
Mechanization Takes Command by Siegfried Giedion: p. 213 (top left and right).
L-W Promotions: p. 214 (top).
Agate Cook Book, The, Mfgrs. of Agate Iron Ware: p. 214 (bottom).
Collecting Mechanical Antiques by Ronald Pearsall: p. 215.
Courtesy of Mr. August A. Busch, Jr.: p. 216.
U.S. Department of Agriculture: p. 220 (top).
Decorah, Iowa, Nordic Fest: p. 239.

Banner and Burns: p. 242.
Bradley Olman: p. 251.
Texas Highway Dept.: p. 256.
"New York News": p. 270.
Allen Snook: pp. 276, 284, 304, 377.
American Antiquarian Society: pp. 306, 308.
Tom Wesselmann (Collection of the Museum of Modern Art): p. 314.
Farm Bureau: p. 320 (top).
William Hopkins: p. 320 (bottom).
Del Monte Corp.: p. 320 (center).
Safeway Stores, Inc.: p. 321 (top).
Cereal Institute: p. 321 (bottom).
Clyde Goin: p. 335 (left center).
"Wallaces Farmer": p. 335 (bottom right).
Vincent Maselli: pp. 340, 349, 357, 372.
William Sladcik: p. 343.
General Foods: p. 351.
Special Locations
Old Sturbridge Village, Mass.: pp. 29, 34, 37, 64, 102, 166.
Casa Adobe of Museum of the Southwest, Los Angeles, Ca.: p. 43.
Super Valu, Inc. warehouse, Des Moines, Ia.: p. 320 (bottom).
Special Photography Props
Early Pennsylvania Dutch redware and graffiti reproductions by Barbara Jean and Lester Breininger, Jr., Robesonia, Pa.: p. 80.
Easter eggs courtesy of Mrs. Nicholas Boldereff, Los Angeles, Ca.: p. 265.

Historical Index

A-B

385

Bisquick, 353, 356
Blackbirds in pioneer diet, 179
Black pepper, importance of, 167
Black pot colonial cookery, 65, 104
Blacks: cuisine, 138, 228-231; immigration of, 218; of Louisiana, 137; running Southern plantations, 145; "soul food," 145, 228, 229
Blini, 260, 264
Bohemians, 279; food heritage of, 281; immigration of, 219
Boiled dinner, New England, 58
Boone, Daniel, 182
Borden, Gail, 131, 151, 348
Boston: first covered market in, 154; Irish immigrants of, 219; Parker House, 329; Tremont House, 129
Boston Cooking School, 154, 209, 312
Boston Cooking-School Cook Book, The, 312
Boston Tea Party, 24, 57
Bourne, Reverend Richard, 67
Box socials, 188
Bradford, Governor James, 11
Brady, "Diamond Jim," 332
Bread (*See also* Biscuits): Central European, 280; city commercial bakers, 154-155; for Civil War soldiers, 150, 151; colonial, 24, 32, 35, 57, 62, 65, 71, 89, 90, 107; French pain perdu, 140; German, 236, 237; Greek, 283, 286; Hawaiian pao doce, 298; Irish soda bread, 226; Jewish, 248, 249, 250; leavenings for, 35, 107, 169, 352, 373; Mexican, 254, 260; New England, 57; Norwegian lefse, 240, 243; packaged mixes for, 353, 357, pioneer, 179, 185, 195; Polish, 274, 278; Russian, 261, 264; sourdough, 32, 71, 107, 293, 294; Southern, 90; Swedish limpa, 240, 242
Brennan's of New Orleans, 327
Briggs, Richard, 308, 309
Britannia ware for cooking, 214
British Isles (*See* English; Irish; Scotch; Scotch-Irish; Welsh)
Brunches, origin of, 160
Buchanan, James, as host, 119, 124
Buche de Noel, 245, 247
Buffalo hunting, 12, 17, 176
Bulgarians, 279
Burbank, Luther, 352, 353
Burgoo, 196
Burnett, Joseph, 168
Butter churning, 83, 199
Butterfield, John, 197
Bynner, E. L., 115
Byrd, William II, 47, 170

C

Cabbage, use of, 71, 73
Cactus, for salads, 44
Cafeterias, 318
Cajuns of New Orleans, 137
Cakes: cheesecake, 379; chiffon, 376; Civil War shortages and, 152; colonial, 38, 54, 65, 73, 76, 97; Dutch, 73; French-Canadian, 247; leavening for, 107, 169, 352; New Orleans, 138; pioneer, 185, 194; Polish, 276; prepared mixes for, 353, 359; Russian-German wedding cake, 299; Shaker, 133, 134; World War I rationing and, 322
California, 302 (*See also* San Francisco): Chinese in, 287; Czechs in, 279; foundation for Spanish occupation of, 46; Gold Rush, 177, 178, 261, 279, 287; Hungarians in, 279; Italians in, 266; Mexicans in, 254; origin of citrus industry, 45; resort

California *(continued)*
hotels of, 325; Russians in, 261; seed gathering Indians of, 11, 16; Spain and history and traditions of, 39, 42, 46, 261; wine-making in, 365
Calories: body weight and, 339, 341; low calorie menus and recipes, 341, 342; recommended daily requirements, 339
Campbell's soups, 345
Canada: French-Canadian heritage, 245-248; Ukrainian immigrants in, 260
Canal building, 113
Candy: first chocolate for making, 165; fudge making, 380; sold in general stores, 162, 163, 165; nougat, 129; origin of machine-made, 163
Canning: discovery of principles of, 345; establishment of commercial, 345; expansion of industry, 345-346; first canned food, 169, 345; home, 173, 318, 373; increase in commercial, 169; tin can development of, 214
Carré, Ferdinand, 212
Carson, Kit, 176
Carter, Robert, 47
Carter, Susannah, 308, 310
Carteret, Sir George, 75-76
Carver, George Washington, 359
Carving, etiquette of, 311
Cather, Willa, 281
Cattle barons, 179
Cattle drives, era of, 202-207
Chafing dish, 328
Chain restaurants, 318
Challah (Jewish bread), 250
Champlain, Samuel de, 14, 30
Chanukah, 251
Chapman, John, 195
Charles I of England, 47
Charles II of England, 47, 75
Chase, Caleb, 346
Chase and Sanborn Coffee, 346
Chastelleux, Marquis de, 126
Cheek, Joel, 346
Cheese: at Andrew Jackson's public reception, 124; caves for ripening, 374; cheesemaking at home, 170, 172; Dutch, 299; Italian, 266; nutritive value of, 370; sold at general stores, 168; Swiss fondue, 305
Cheesecake, 379
Chianti, 266, 267
Chicago, 115; immigrants settling in, 219, 274, 279; world's fairs at, 211, 333
Chicken: molé, 259; popularity of fried, 366; use by colonists, 35, 48, 81, 82, 107
Chiffon cake, 376
Child, Lydia Maria, 103, 171, 173, 310, 311
Chili con carne, 255
Chili peppers, 15; chili sauce with, 41; introduction of, 39, 254; vitamins in, 39
Chinese: customs and rituals of, 287, 288, 293; food heritage of, 219, 287, 288, 292; of Hawaii, 294; immigration of, 218, 219, 287, 292; restaurants, 288, 369; settlement in California, 219
Chitterlings, 36, 228, 229
Chocolate: for candy bars, 165; first American, 162; hot chocolate drink, 380; introduction of, 39, 41, 254
Chop suey, 288, 369
Chow mein, 219, 292
Christianity in the Kitchen, 312

Christmas: celebration by slaves, 150; Dutch celebration, 69; French-Canadian celebration, 245, 247, 248; German celebration, 232, 237; Norwegian celebration, 243; trees, 232; Ukrainian celebration, 262
Chuck wagons: cooking, 203, 204, 206, 207; design of, 203; eating practices at, 206; importance of cooks, 202, 203; supplies of, 203
Church socials, 188, 193, 374
Cider, 195; making of, 170, 172
Cinnamon, 106
Cipâte, 245, 246
Cities (*See* Urbanization and specific city)
Civil War, 115, 266; army food in, 117, 150-151; cooking in, 150-151; food shortages in, 151, 152, 153, 167
Clam chowder, 60
Clambakes, 59
Clark, George, 176
Clark, William, 137
Clergy, 193, 195
Cloves, 106
Coca-Cola, 352
Cock-a-leekie soup, 227
Cocktails: before dinner, 324; of New Orleans, 138; origin of, 76, 138; of speakeasies, 324
Cocoa, introduction of, 21, 165
Coffee: adulteration of packaged, 163; Chase and Sanborn, 346; Civil War and popularity of, 151; colonial use of, 21, 104; freeze-dried, 352; Greek coffeehouses, 283; history of, 272, 346; Italian Cappuccino, 272; Maxwell House, 346; New Orleans French, 138; percolator, 209; pioneer substitutes for, 179; substitutes in Civil War, 151
Cold storage of foods, 170, 171
Coleslaw, 71, 73
Collins, A. M., 312
Colonial America, 20-109 (*See also* specific topic); American Revolution, 24, 25, 57; chafing dish use in, 328; conditions luring Europeans to, 20; cook books of, 306-310; cooking with flowers in, 108; corn stealing from Indians in, 10-11; dining equipment in, 109; Dutch influence in, 69-75; eating habits in, 109, 155; fireplace cooking in, 103; food staples of, 106-108; foods brought to, 20; gardens of, 108; housewife's work in, 107; Jews in, 248, life of Indians in, 10-17; mealtimes and menus, 109; "mess it forth," 109; new foods available in, 20-21, 24; Poles in, 274; pots and equipment in, 65, 102, 103, 104, 105; river commerce in, 113, store trading in, 162
Colorado, 181; Denver, 115, 130; homesteading in, 179; Indians of, 15
Columbus, Christopher, 10, 11
Comforts of Cooking and Heating with Gas, 312
Commerce: advances in, 114, 115; of American Indians, 10, 11
Common Sense in the Household, 312
Communal settlements, 112, 192
Compleat Housewife, The, 306, 307
Conestoga wagons, 112, 182
"Confederate cush," 151
Confucius, 292
Connecticut: 'lection cake, 65; settlement of, 57
Consumers, laws protecting, 341
Continental Congress, 94, 95
Convenience foods: baked beans as first, 169, 345; canned meat and fish, 345, 355; canned soups, 345,

Convenience foods *(continued)*
355; commercial canning and, 169, 316, 345-346; dry cereals, 353, 356; frozen foods, 316, 345, 346, 347; importance after World War II, 317; packaged mixes, 353, 356, 357, 359; process cheeses, 346; soup as colonial, 31
Cook books, 306-313; best-selling, 313; colonial, 306-310; history of American, 309-313; imported from England, 307-308; privately printed, 313; regional, 312
Cookies, Bohemian, 281; brownies, 376; colonial, 36, 37, 66, 69, 84; Dutch, 69, 299; German, 237, 238; Greek, 283; Norwegian, 240, 243; Polish, 274; Swedish, 240
Cooking schools, 209; development of, 154, 155, 312; industrial cooking institutes, 213
Cookstoves, 208-209
Cookware: advances in, 214, 365; for colonial fireplaces, 102, 103, 104
Cooper, Peter, 354
Corats, 279
Corn: chewed kernels as sweetener, 15; colonial use of, 20, 24, 27, 28, 42, 58, 59, 76, 81, 82, 363; cultivation and use by American Indians, 10-11, 12, 14, 15, 17; dried, 82; early canning of, 169; as generic term, 10; Green Corn Ceremony, 14; hybrids, 10; introduction of, 20, 254; New England use of, 58, 59; parched, 14; Pennsylvania Dutch use of, 76, 81, 82; in pioneer diet, 179, 182, 186; problem of growing on prairie, 188; soil debilitation and planting, 27; Southern use of, 145; Southwestern use of, 42; stealing from Indians, 11
Corn husking, 188
Corn bread, Indian, 14
Corned beef, 171; canned, 345, 355
Cornflakes, invention of, 353, 356
Corning in meat preservation, 171
Cornish pasty, 224
Cornmeal: colonial use of, 20, 28, 87, 89, 106; Indian corn bread, 14; introduction of, 20; Italian polenta, 272; Southern use of, 87, 89, 150
Cornstarch, use in desserts, 168
Coronado, Francisco Vasquez de, 15, 23
Corson, Juliet, 154, 312
Cortez, Hernando, 41
Cowboys: cattle drivers, 202-207; cooks and, 202, 203
Crab cakes, 77
Cracker barrels of general stores, 162
Cracker Jack, 333
Crackers, history of, 162
Cranberries: Alaskan use of, 295; legend of Cape Cod's bogs, 67; origin of name, 78; separator for, 77
Creoles: cuisine, 138, 141, 142, 143, 144, 327; Acadian cuisine vs., 142; food heritage of, 138, 141, 142, 143, 144, 327; of New Orleans, 137
Crullers, 74
Crum, George, 332
Crumpets, 225
Cubans, 299, 301
Cullen, Patrick, 317
Cumberland Road, 113
Czechs: food heritage of, 282; immigration of, 218, 219, 279

D-I

Dairy products (*See also* Cheese): churning butter, 83, 199; colonial, 84, 107; Dutch, 69, 70, 73; improvements in 363; modern diver-

Recipe Index
A-B

K-O

Q-R

S

T-Z